PREFACE.

'THE author arrived in the East as a Missionary towards the end of 1839, and was stationed at Malacca for between three and four years. Before leaving England, he had enjoyed the benefit of a few months' instruction in Chinese from the late Professor Kidd at University College, London, and was able in the beginning of 1840 to commence the study of the first of the Works in the present publication. It seemed to him then—and the experience of one and twenty years gives its sanction to the correctness of the judgment— that he should not be able to consider himself qualified for the duties of his position, until he had thoroughly mastered the Classical Books of the Chinese, and had investigated for himself the whole field of thought through which the sages of China had ranged, and in which were to be found the foundations of the moral, social, and political life of the people. Under this conviction he addressed himself eagerly to the reading of the Confucian Analects, and proceeded from them to the other Works. Circumstances occurred in the Mission at Malacca to throw various engagements upon him which left him little time to spend at his books, and he consequently sought about for all the assistance which he could find from the labours of men who had gone before.

'In this respect he was favourably situated, the charge of the Anglo-Chinese College having devolved upon him, so that he had free access to all the treasures in its Library. He had translations and dictionaries in abundance, and they facilitated his progress. Yet he desiderated some Work upon the Classics, more critical, more full and exact, than any which he had the opportunity of consulting, and he sketched to himself the plan of its execution. This was distinctly before him in 1841, and for several years he hoped to hear that some experienced Chinese scholar was preparing to give to the public something of the kind. As time went on, and he began to feel assured as to his own progress in the language, it occurred to him that he might venture on such an undertaking himself. He studied, wrote out translations, and made notes, with the project in his mind.

He hopes he can say that it did not divert him from the usual active labours of a Missionary in preaching and teaching, but it did not allow him to rest satisfied in any operations of the time then being.

'In 1856 he first talked with some of his friends about his purpose, and among them was the Rev. Josiah Cox, of the Wesleyan Missionary Society. The question of the expense of publication came up. The author's idea was that by-and-by he would be able to digest his materials in readiness for the press, and that then he would be likely, on application, to meet with such encouragement from the British and other foreign merchants in China, as would enable him to go forward with his plan. Mr. Cox, soon after, without the slightest intimation of his intention, mentioned the whole matter to his friend, Mr. Joseph Jardine. In consequence of what he reported of Mr. Jardine's sentiments, the author had an interview with that gentleman, when he very generously undertook to bear the expense of carrying the Work through the press. His lamented death leaves the author at liberty to speak more freely on this point than he would otherwise have done. Mr. Jardine expressed himself favourably of the plan, and said, "I know the liberality of the merchants in China, and that many of them would readily give their help to such an undertaking, but you need not have the trouble of canvassing the community. If you are prepared for the toil of the publication, I will bear the expense of it. We make our money in China, and we should be glad to assist in whatever promises to be of benefit to it."

'The author could not but be grateful to Mr. Jardine for his proffer, nor did he hesitate to accept it. The interruption of missionary labours, consequent on the breaking out of hostilities in the end of 1856, was favourable to retired and literary work, and he immediately set about preparing some of his materials for the press. A necessary visit to England in 1857, which kept him absent from the colony for eighteen months, proved a serious interruption, but the first-fruits of his labours are now in a state to be presented to the public.'

The preface to the former edition of this volume, when it was published at Hongkong in 1861, commenced with the preceding paragraphs. The author has thought it desirable to reproduce them, as giving an account of the first conception in his mind of his labour on the Chinese Classics, and of the circumstances under which his earlier volumes were published.

Though Mr. Joseph Jardine died before the publication of the first volume, the assistance given by him was continued with equal generosity by his brother, now Sir Robert Jardine, Baronet, until the second and third volumes had been published, and also during the preparation of the fourth and fifth volumes.

Soon after the publication of the fifth volume, which contained, besides the translation of the Confucian Text, a version of all the notes and additions to it in the voluminous Work of Tso Ch'iû-ming, the author was obliged to return to this country in 1873; but since he was appointed to his present position in the University here, translations of the Hsiâo-ching, the Yi-ching, and the Lî Chî, have been contributed by him to the series of 'The Sacred Books of the East,' which has been issued from the Clarendon Press since 1879. He has thus done for the Confucian Classics more than he contemplated in 1861. He then undertook to produce versions of what are called 'The Four Books' and 'The Five King (Ching),' and added that 'if life and health were spared' he would like to give a supplementary volume or two, so as to embrace all the Books in the collection of 'The Thirteen Ching,' which began to appear under the T'ang dynasty in our seventh century. He has translated ten of those Books, including the extensive Work of Tso Ch'iû-ming mentioned above. Other scholars have also done their part. M. Edouard Biot, the younger, indeed, had published at Paris in 1851 his translation of 'Le Cheou Lî,' the Rites, or the Official Book, of the dynasty of Châu, under which Confucius lived; and in the present year Professor C. de Harlez, of Louvaine, has given to the world a version of the other great Ritual work, the Î Lî.

Thus all the 'Thirteen Ching' of China have been made accessible to scholars of the West, excepting the Urh (R) Yâ, which has been named 'The Literary Expositor,' a lexical work, the precursor of the dictionaries which Chinese literature possesses in abundance.

To return to the volume of which a revised edition is now submitted to the public, the author would state that 1200 copies of it were printed in 1861. These were exhausted several years ago, and many calls for a new edition have come to him from China, to which only other engagements have prevented his responding sooner. So far as typographical execution is concerned, this edition ought to excel the former very much. Other improvements will also be discovered. The author has carefully gone over

the text of the translation and notes.   He is glad to have found
occasion but rarely for correction and alteration of the former.   He
thought indeed at one time of recasting the whole version in a
terser and more pretentious style.   He determined, however, on
reflection to let it stand as it first occurred to him, his object
having always been faithfulness to the original Chinese rather than
grace of composition.   Not that he is indifferent to the value of an
elegant and idiomatic rendering in the language of the translation,
and he hopes that he was able to combine in a considerable degree
correctness of interpretation and acceptableness of style.   He has
to thank many friends whose Chinese scholarship is widely acknowledged for assuring him of this.

He has seen it objected to his translations that they were
modelled on the views of the great critic and philosopher of the
Sung dynasty, the well-known Chû Hsî.   He can only say that he
commenced and has carried on his labours with the endeavour to
search out the meaning for himself, independent of all commentators.   He soon became aware, however, of the beauty and strength
of Chû's style, the correctness of his analysis, and the comprehension and depth of his thought.   That his own views of passages
generally coincide with those of 'The Old Man of the Cloudy Valley'
should be accepted, he submits, as complimentary to him rather
than the reverse.

While this volume now reappears with few alterations of translation, it will be found that the alterations in the representation of
proper names and names of Chinese characters generally are very
many.   The method adopted in it for the transliteration of their
sounds may be considered as a compromise between that proposed
by Sir Thomas F. Wade in his Hsin Ching Lû and that with
which the author has become familiar through his work in connexion with 'The Sacred Books of the East.'   The principal
differences in the two transliterations are ă for ê, âu for ou, z for j,
ze for zŭ, r for urh, and w for u.   He has also given up attempting
to reproduce in the notes and in the seventh Appendix the names
and tones of the Southern Mandarin dialect, and has endeavoured
to confine himself to the tones as given in the Hsin Ching Lû.

J. L.

CONTENTS.

THE PROLEGOMENA.

CHAPTER I.

OF THE CHINESE CLASSICS GENERALLY.

CHAPTER II.

OF THE CONFUCIAN ANALECTS.

CHAPTER III.

OF THE GREAT LEARNING.

CHAPTER IV.

THE DOCTRINE OF THE MEAN.

CHAPTER V.

CONFUCIUS AND HIS IMMEDIATE DISCIPLES.

CHAPTER VI.

LIST OF THE PRINCIPAL WORKS WHICH HAVE BEEN CONSULTED IN THE PREPARATION OF THIS VOLUME.

THE BODY OF THE VOLUME.

INDEXES.

PROLEGOMENA.

CHAPTER I.

OF THE CHINESE CLASSICS GENERALLY.

SECTION I.

BOOKS INCLUDED UNDER THE NAME OF THE CHINESE CLASSICS.

1. The Books now recognised as of highest authority in China are comprehended under the denominations of 'The five *Ching*[1]' and 'The four *Shû*[2].' The term *Ching* is of textile origin, and signifies the warp threads of a web, and their adjustment. An easy application of it is to denote what is regular and insures regularity. As used with reference to books, it indicates their authority on the subjects of which they treat. 'The five *Ching*' are the five *canonical* Works, containing the truth upon the highest subjects from the sages of China, and which should be received as law by all generations. The term *Shû* simply means *Writings* or *Books*, = the *Pencil Speaking;* it may be used of a single character, or of books containing thousands of characters.

2. 'The five Ching' are: the *Yî*[3], or, as it has been styled, 'The Book of Changes;' the *Shû*[4], or 'The Book of History;' the *Shih*[5], or 'The Book of Poetry;' the *Lî Chî*[6], or 'Record of Rites;' and the *Ch'un Ch'iû*[7], or 'Spring and Autumn,' a chronicle of events, extending from 722 to 481 B.C. The authorship, or compilation rather, of all these Works is loosely attributed to Confucius. But much of the Lî Chî is from later hands. Of the Yî, the Shû, and the Shih, it is only in the first that we find additions attributed to the philosopher himself, in the shape of appendixes. The Ch'un Ch'iû is the only one of the five Ching which can, with an approximation to correctness, be described as of his own 'making.'

[1] 五經. [2] 四書. [3] 易經. [4] 書經. [5] 詩經. [6] 禮記. [7] 春秋.

'The Four Books' is an abbreviation for 'The Books of the Four
Philosophers [1].' The first is the Lun Yü [2], or 'Digested Conversations,' being occupied chiefly with the sayings of Confucius. He
is the philosopher to whom it belongs. It appears in this Work
under the title of 'Confucian Analects.' The second is the Tâ
Hsio [3], or 'Great Learning,' now commonly attributed to Tsăng
Shăn [4], a disciple of the sage. He is the philosopher of it. The
third is the Chung Yung [5], or 'Doctrine of the Mean,' as the name
has often been translated, though it would be better to render it,
as in the present edition, by 'The State of Equilibrium and Harmony.' Its composition is ascribed to K'ung Chî [6], the grandson of
Confucius. He is the philosopher of it. The fourth contains the
works of Mencius.

3. This arrangement of the Classical Books, which is commonly
supposed to have originated with the scholars of the Sung dynasty,
is defective. The *Great Learning* and the *Doctrine of the Mean*
are both found in the Record of Rites, being the thirty-ninth and
twenty-eighth Books respectively of that compilation, according
to the best arrangement of it.

4. The oldest enumerations of the Classical Books specify only
the *five Ching*. The Yo Chî, or 'Record of Music [7],' the remains of
which now form one of the Books in the Lî Chî, was sometimes
added to those, making with them the *six Ching*. A division was
also made into *nine Ching*, consisting of the Yî, the Shih, the Shû,
the Châu Lî [8], or 'Ritual of Châu,' the Î Lî [9], or certain 'Ceremonial Usages,' the Lî Chî, and the three annotated editions of the
Ch'un Ch'iû [10], by Tso Ch'iû-ming [11], Kung-yang Kâo [12], and Kû-
liang Ch'ih [13]. In the famous compilation of the Classical Books,
undertaken by order of T'âi-tsung, the second emperor of the
T'ang dynasty (A. D. 627–649), and which appeared in the reign
of his successor, there are *thirteen Ching*, viz. the Yî, the Shih,
the Shû, the three editions of the Ch'un Ch'iû, the Lî Chî, the
Châu Lî, the Î Lî, the Confucian Analects, the *R* Yâ [14], a sort
of ancient dictionary, the Hsiâo Ching [15], or 'Classic of Filial Piety,'
and the works of Mencius.

5. A distinction, however, was made among the Works thus

---

[1] 四子之書. [2] 論語. [3] 大學. [4] 曾參. [5] 中庸.
[6] 孔伋. [7] 樂記. [8] 周禮. [9] 儀禮. [10] 春秋三傳.
[11] 左丘明. [12] 公羊高. [13] 穀梁赤. [14] 爾雅. [15] 孝經.

comprehended under the same common name; and Mencius, the
Lun Yü, the Tâ Hsio, the Chung Yung, and the Hsiâo Ching were
spoken of as the Hsiâo Ching, or 'Smaller Classics.' It thus appears,
contrary to the ordinary opinion on the subject, that the Tâ Hsio
and Chung Yung had been published as separate treatises before
the Sung dynasty, and that Four Books, as distinguished from the
greater Ching, had also previously found a place in the literature
of China [1].

SECTION II.

THE AUTHORITY OF THE CHINESE CLASSICS.

1. This subject will be discussed in connexion with each separate
Work, and it is only designed here to exhibit generally the evidence
on which the Chinese Classics claim to be received as genuine productions of the time to which they are referred.

2. In the memoirs of the Former Han dynasty (B.C. 202–
A.D. 24), we have one chapter which we may call the History of
Literature [2]. It commences thus : 'After the death of Confucius [3],
there was an end of his exquisite words; and when his seventy
disciples had passed away, violence began to be done to their
meaning. It came about that there were five different editions of
the Ch'un Ch'iû, four of the Shih, and several of the Yî. Amid
the disorder and collisions of the warring States (B.C. 481–220),
truth and falsehood were still more in a state of warfare, and a sad
confusion marked the words of the various scholars. Then came the
calamity inflicted under the Ch'in dynasty (B.C. 220–205), when
the literary monuments were destroyed by fire, in order to keep
the people in ignorance. But, by and by, there arose the Han
dynasty, which set itself to remedy the evil wrought by the Ch'in.
Great efforts were made to collect slips and tablets [4], and the way
was thrown wide open for the bringing in of Books. In the time
of the emperor Hsiâo-wû [5] (B.C. 140–85), portions of Books being
wanting and tablets lost, so that ceremonies and music were

---

[1] For the statements in the two last paragraphs, see 西河合集, 大學證文,
卷一.   [2] 前漢書, 本志, 第十卷, 藝文志.   [3] 仲尼.
[4] 篇籍,—slips and tablets of bamboo, which supplied in those days the place of paper.
[5] 世宗孝武皇帝.

suffering great damage, he was moved to sorrow, and said, "I am
very sad for this." He therefore formed the plan of Repositories,
in which the Books might be stored, and appointed officers to
transcribe Books on an extensive scale, embracing the works of the
various scholars, that they might all be placed in the Repositories.
The emperor Ch'ăng[1] (B. C. 32–5), finding that a portion of the
Books still continued dispersed or missing, commissioned Ch'ăn
Năng, the Superintendent of Guests[2], to search for undiscovered
Books throughout the empire, and by special edict ordered the
chief of the Banqueting House, Liû Hsiang[3], to examine the Classical
Works, along with the commentaries on them, the writings of the
scholars, and all poetical productions; the Master-controller of
Infantry, Zăn Hwang[4], to examine the Books on the art of war;
the Grand Historiographer, Yin Hsien[5], to examine the Books
treating of the art of numbers (i. e. divination); and the imperial
Physician, Lî Chû-kwo[6], to examine the Books on medicine. Whenever any book was done with, Hsiang forthwith arranged it,
indexed it, and made a digest of it, which was presented to the
emperor. While this work was in progress, Hsiang died, and the
emperor Âi (B.C. 6–A. D. 1) appointed his son, Hsin[7], a Master of
the imperial carriages, to complete his father's work. On this, Hsin
collected all the Books, and presented a report of them, under
seven divisions.'

The first of these divisions seems to have been a general catalogue[8] containing perhaps only the titles of the works included in
the other six. The second embraced the Classical Works[9]. From
the abstract of it, which is preserved in the chapter referred to, we
find that there were 294 collections of the Yî-ching from thirteen
different individuals or editors[10]; 412 collections of the Shû-ching,
from nine different individuals; 416 volumes of the Shih-ching,
from six different individuals[11]; of the Books of Rites, 555 collec-

---

[1] 孝成皇帝.   [2] 謁者陳農.   [3] 光祿大夫劉向.
[4] 步兵校尉任宏. [5] 太史令尹咸. [6] 侍醫李柱國.
[7] 侍中奉車都尉歆. [8] 輯略. [9] 六藝略. [10] 凡易,
十三家, 二百九十四篇. How much of the whole work was contained
in each 篇, it is impossible for us to ascertain. P. Regis says: 'Pien, quemadmodum Gallice
dicimus "des pieces d'éloquence, de poésie."'   [11] 詩, 六家, 四百一十六卷.
The collections of the Shih-ching are mentioned under the name of chüan, 'sections,' 'portions.'
Had p'ien been used, it might have been understood of individual odes. This change of terms
shows that by p'ien in the other summaries, we are not to understand single blocks or chapters.

tions, from thirteen different individuals ; of the Books on Music, 165 collections, from six different editors ; 948 collections of History, under the heading of the Ch'un Ch'iû, from twenty-three different individuals ; 229 collections of the Lun Yü, including the Analects and kindred fragments, from twelve different individuals ; of the Hsiâo-ching, embracing also the R Yâ, and some other portions of the ancient literature, 59 collections, from eleven different individuals ; and finally of the lesser Learning, being works on the form of the characters, 45 collections, from eleven different individuals.   The works of Mencius were included in the second division [1], among the writings of what were deemed orthodox scholars [2], of which there were 836 collections, from fifty-three different individuals.

3. The above important document is sufficient to show how the emperors of the Han dynasty, as soon as they had made good their possession of the empire, turned their attention to recover the ancient literature of the nation, the Classical Books engaging their first care, and how earnestly and effectively the scholars of the time responded to the wishes of their rulers.   In addition to the facts specified in the preface to it, I may relate that the ordinance of the Ch'in dynasty against possessing the Classical Books (with the exception, as it will appear in its proper place, of the Yî-ching) was repealed by the second sovereign of the Han, the emperor Hsiâo Hûi [3], in the fourth year of his reign, B.C. 191, and that a large portion of the Shû-ching was recovered in the time of the third emperor, B.C. 179–157, while in the year B.C. 136 a special Board was constituted, consisting of literati, who were put in charge of the five *Ching* [4].

4. The collections reported on by Liû Hsin suffered damage in the troubles which began A.D. 8, and continued till the rise of the second or eastern Han dynasty in the year 25.   The founder of it (A.D. 25–57) zealously promoted the undertaking of his predecessors, and additional repositories were required for the Books which were collected.   His successors, the emperors Hsiâo-ming [5] (58–75), Hsiâo-chang [6] (76–88), and Hsiâo-hwo [7] (89–105), took a part themselves in the studies and discussions of the literary tribunal, and

---

[1] 諸子略.　[2] 儒家者流.　[3] 孝惠皇帝.　[4] 武帝建元五年,初置五經博士.　[5] 顯宗孝明皇帝.　[6] 肅宗孝章皇帝.　[7] 孝和皇帝.

the emperor Hsiâo-ling[1], between the years 172–178, had the text of the five *Ching*, as it had been fixed, cut in slabs of stone, and set up in the capital outside the gate of the Grand College. Some old accounts say that the characters were in three different forms, but they were only in one form;—see the 287th book of Chû Î-tsun's great Work.

5. Since the Han, the successive dynasties have considered the literary monuments of the country to be an object of their special care. Many of them have issued editions of the Classics, embodying the commentaries of preceding generations. No dynasty has distinguished itself more in this line than the present Manchâu possessors of the empire. In fine, the evidence is complete that the Classical Books of China have come down from at least a century before our Christian era, substantially the same as we have them at present.

6. But it still remains to inquire in what condition we may suppose the Books were, when the scholars of the Han dynasty commenced their labours upon them. They acknowledge that the tablets—we cannot here speak of *manuscripts*—were mutilated and in disorder. Was the injury which they had received of such an extent that all the care and study put forth on the small remains would be of little use ? This question can be answered satisfactorily, only by an examination of the evidence which is adduced for the text of each particular Classic ; but it can be made apparent that there is nothing, in the nature of the case, to interfere with our believing that the materials were sufficient to enable the scholars to execute the work intrusted to them.

7. The burning of the ancient Books by order of the founder of the Ch'in dynasty is always referred to as the greatest disaster which they sustained, and with this is coupled the slaughter of many of the Literati by the same monarch.

The account which we have of these transactions in the Historical Records is the following[2] :

' In his 34th year [the 34th year, that is, after he had ascended the throne of Ch'in. It was only the 9th after he had been acknowledged Sovereign of the empire, coinciding with B. C. 213], the emperor, returning from a visit to the south, which had extended

---

[1] 孝靈皇帝.   [2] I have thought it well to endeavour to translate the whole of the passages. Father de Mailla merely constructs from them a narrative of his own ; see *L'Histoire Générale de La Chine*, tome ii. pp. 399–402. The 通 鑑 綱 目 avoids the difficulties of the original by giving an abridgment of it.

as far as Yüeh, gave a feast in his palace at Hsien-yang, when the
Great Scholars, amounting to seventy men, appeared and wished
him long life [1].   One of the principal ministers, Chău Ch'ing-ch'ăn [2],
came forward and said, "Formerly, the State of Ch'in was only
1000 lî in extent, but Your Majesty, by your spirit-like efficacy
and intelligent wisdom, has tranquillised and settled the whole
empire, and driven away all barbarous tribes, so that, wherever
the sun and moon shine, all rulers appear before you as guests
acknowledging subjection.   You have formed the states of the
various princes into provinces and districts, where the people enjoy
a happy tranquillity, suffering no more from the calamities of war
and contention.   This condition of things will be transmitted for
10,000 generations.   From the highest antiquity there has been
no one in awful virtue like Your Majesty."

'The emperor was pleased with this flattery, when Shun-yü
Yüeh [3], one of the Great Scholars, a native of Ch'î, advanced and
said, "The sovereigns of Yin and Châu, for more than a thousand
years, invested their sons and younger brothers, and meritorious
ministers, with domains and rule, and could thus depend upon
them for support and aid;—that I have heard.   But now Your
Majesty is in possession of all within the seas, and your sons and
younger brothers are nothing but private individuals.   The issue
will be that some one will arise to play the part of T'ien Ch'ang [4],
or of the six nobles of Tsin.   Without the support *of your own
family*, where will you find the aid which you may require ?   That
a state of things not modelled from the lessons of antiquity can
long continue;—that is what I have not heard.   Ch'ing is now
showing himself to be a flatterer, who increases the errors of Your
Majesty, and not a loyal minister."

'The emperor requested the opinions of others on this representation, and the premier, Lî Sze [5], said, "The five emperors were
not one the double of the other, nor did the three dynasties accept
one another's ways.   Each had a peculiar system of government,
not for the sake of the contrariety, but as being required by the
changed times.   Now, Your Majesty has laid the foundations of

[1] 博士七十人前爲壽. The 博士 were not only 'great scholars,'
but had an official rank. There was what we may call a college of them, consisting of seventy
members.   [2] 僕射, 周青臣.   [3] 淳于越.   [4] 田常, 一常
should probably be 恆, as it is given in the T'ung Chien. See Analects XIV. xxii. T'ien
Hăng was the same as Ch'ăn Ch'ăng of that chapter.   [5] 丞相李斯.

imperial sway, so that it will last for 10,000 generations. This is indeed beyond what a stupid scholar can understand. And, moreover, Yüeh only talks of things belonging to the Three Dynasties, which are not fit to be models to you. At other times, when the princes were all striving together, they endeavoured to gather the wandering scholars about them; but now, the empire is in a stable condition, and laws and ordinances issue from one *supreme authority*. Let those of the people who abide in their homes give their strength to the toils of husbandry, while those who become scholars should study the various laws and prohibitions. Instead of doing this, however, the scholars do not learn what belongs to the present day, but study antiquity. They go on to condemn the present time, leading the masses of the people astray, and to disorder.

' "At the risk of my life, I, the prime minister, say: Formerly, when the nation was disunited and disturbed, there was no one who could give unity to it. The princes therefore stood up together; constant references were made to antiquity to the injury of the present state; baseless statements were dressed up to confound what was real, and men made a boast of their own peculiar learning to condemn what their rulers appointed. And now, when Your Majesty has consolidated the empire, and, distinguishing black from white, has constituted it a stable unity, they still honour their peculiar learning, and combine together; they teach men what is contrary to your laws. When they hear that an ordinance has been issued, every one sets to discussing it with his learning. In the court, they are dissatisfied in heart; out of it, they keep talking in the streets. While they make a pretence of vaunting their Master, they consider it fine to have extraordinary views of their own. And so they lead on the people to be guilty of murmuring and evil speaking. If these things are not prohibited, Your Majesty's authority will decline, and parties will be formed. The best way is to prohibit them. I pray that all the Records in charge of the Historiographers be burned, excepting those of Ch'in; that, with the exception of those officers belonging to the Board of Great Scholars, all throughout the empire who presume to keep copies of the Shih-ching, or of the Shû-ching, or of the books of the Hundred Schools, be required to go with them to the officers in charge of the several districts, and burn them[1]; that all who may dare to speak

----

[1] 悉詣守尉雜燒之.

together about the Shih and the Shû be put to death, and their
bodies exposed in the market-place; that those who make mention
of the past, so as to blame the present, be put to death along with
their relatives; that officers who shall know of the violation of
those rules and not inform against the offenders, be held equally
guilty with them; and that whoever shall not have burned their
Books within thirty days after the issuing of the ordinance, be
branded and sent to labour on the wall for four years. The only
Books which should be spared are those on medicine, divination,
and husbandry. Whoever wants to learn the laws may go to the
magistrates and learn of them."

'The imperial decision was—" Approved."'

The destruction of the scholars is related more briefly. In the
year after the burning of the Books, the resentment of the emperor
was excited by the remarks and flight of two scholars who had been
favourites with him, and he determined to institute a strict inquiry
about all of their class in Hsien-yang, to find out whether they had
been making ominous speeches about him, and disturbing the minds
of the people. The investigation was committed to the Censors [1],
and it being discovered that upwards of 460 scholars had violated
the prohibitions, they were all buried alive in pits [2], for a warning
to the empire, while degradation and banishment were employed
more strictly than before against all who fell under suspicion. The
emperor's eldest son, Fû-sû, remonstrated with him, saying that
such measures against those who repeated the words of Confucius
and sought to imitate him, would alienate all the people from their
infant dynasty, but his interference offended his father so much
that he was sent off from court, to be with the general who was
superintending the building of the great wall.

8. No attempts have been made by Chinese critics and historians
to discredit the record of these events, though some have questioned
the extent of the injury inflicted by them on the monuments of
their ancient literature [3]. It is important to observe that the
edict against the Books did not extend to the Yî-ching, which was

---

[1] 御 史 悉 案 間 諸 生, 諸 生 傳 相 告 引.   [2] 自 除 犯
禁 者, 四 百 六 十 餘 人, 皆 阬 之 咸 陽. The meaning of this passage
as a whole is sufficiently plain, but I am unable to make out the force of the phrase 自 除.
[3] See the remarks of Chăng Chiă-tsî (夾 際 鄭 氏), of the Sung dynasty, on the subject,
in the 文 獻 通 考, Bk. clxxiv. p. 5.

exempted as being a work on divination, nor did it extend to the
other classics which were in charge of the Board of Great Scholars.
There ought to have been no difficulty in finding copies when the
Han dynasty superseded that of Ch'in, and probably there would
have been none but for the sack of the capital in B.C. 206 by
Hsiang Yü, the formidable opponent of the founder of the House
of Han.   Then, we are told, the fires blazed for three months
among the palaces and public buildings, and must have proved
as destructive to the copies of the Great Scholars as the edict of
the tyrant had been to the copies among the people.

It is to be noted also that the life of Shih Hwang Tî lasted only
three years after the promulgation of his edict.   He died in B.C.
210, and the reign of his second son who succeeded him lasted only
other three years.   A brief period of disorder and struggling for
the supreme authority between different chiefs ensued ; but the
reign of the founder of the Han dynasty dates from B.C. 202.
Thus, eleven years were all which intervened between the order
for the burning of the Books and the rise of that family, which
signalized itself by the care which it bestowed for their recovery ;
and from the edict of the tyrant of Ch'in against private individuals
having copies in their keeping, to its express abrogation by the
emperor Hsiâo Hûi, there were only twenty-two years.   We may
believe, indeed, that vigorous efforts to carry the edict into effect
would not be continued longer than the life of its author,—that is,
not for more than about three years.   The calamity inflicted on
the ancient Books of China by the House of Ch'in could not have
approached to anything like a complete destruction of them.   There
would be no occasion for the scholars of the Han dynasty, in regard
to the bulk of their ancient literature, to undertake more than the
work of recension and editing.

9. The idea of forgery by them on a large scale is out of the
question.   The catalogues of Liang Hsin enumerated more than
13,000 volumes of a larger or smaller size, the productions of
nearly 600 different writers, and arranged in thirty-eight subdivisions of subjects[1].   In the third catalogue, the first subdivision
contained the orthodox writers[2], to the number of fifty-three, with
836 Works or portions of their Works.   Between Mencius and

[1] 凡書六略, 三十八種, 五百九十六家, 萬三千
二百六十九卷.   [2] 儒家者流.

K'ung Chî, the grandson of Confucius, eight different authors have place. The second subdivision contained the Works of the Tâoist school [1], amounting to 993 collections, from thirty-seven different authors. The sixth subdivision contained the Mohist writers [2], to the number of six, with their productions in 86 collections. I specify these two subdivisions, because they embrace the Works of schools or sects antagonistic to that of Confucius, and some of them still hold a place in Chinese literature, and contain many references to the five Classics, and to Confucius and his disciples.

10. The inquiry pursued in the above paragraphs conducts us to the conclusion that the materials from which the Classics, as they have come down to us, were compiled and edited in the two centuries preceding our Christian era, were genuine remains, going back to a still more remote period. The injury which they sustained from the dynasty of Ch'in was, I believe, the same in character as that to which they were exposed during all the time of 'the Warring States.' It may have been more intense in degree, but the constant warfare which prevailed for some centuries among the different states which composed the kingdom was eminently unfavourable to the cultivation of literature. Mencius tells us how the princes had made away with many of the records of antiquity, from which their own usurpations and innovations might have been condemned [3]. Still the times were not unfruitful, either in scholars or statesmen, to whom the ways and monuments of antiquity were dear, and the space from the rise of the Ch'in dynasty to the death of Confucius was not very great. It only amounted to 258 years. Between these two periods Mencius stands as a connecting link. Born probably in the year B.C. 371, he reached, by the intervention of Kung Chî, back to the sage himself, and as his death happened B.C. 288, we are brought down to within nearly half a century of the Ch'in dynasty. From all these considerations we may proceed with confidence to consider each separate Work, believing that we have in these Classics and Books what the great sage of China and his disciples gave to their country more than 2000 years ago.

[1] 道家者流.   [2] 墨家者流.   [3] See Mencius, V. Pt. II. ii. 2.

CHAPTER II.

OF THE CONFUCIAN ANALECTS.

SECTION I.

FORMATION OF THE TEXT OF THE ANALECTS BY THE SCHOLARS OF THE
HAN DYNASTY.

1. When the work of collecting and editing the remains of the
Classical Books was undertaken by the scholars of Han, there
appeared two different copies of the Analects, one from Lû, the
native State of Confucius, and the other from Ch'î, the State
adjoining. Between these there were considerable differences. The
former consisted of twenty Books or Chapters, the same as those
into which the Classic is now divided. The latter contained two
Books in addition, and in the twenty Books, which they had in
common, the chapters and sentences were somewhat more numerous
than in the Lû exemplar.

2. The names of several individuals are given, who devoted
themselves to the study of those two copies of the Classic. Among
the patrons of the Lû copy are mentioned the names of Hsiâ-hâu
Shăng, grand-tutor of the heir-apparent, who died at the age of
90, and in the reign of the emperor Hsüan (B.C. 73–49)[1]; Hsiâo
Wang-chih[2], a general-officer, who died in the reign of the emperor
Yüan (B.C. 48–33); Wei Hsien, who was premier of the empire
from B.C. 70–66; and his son Hsüan-ch'ăng[3]. As patrons of the Ch'î
copy, we have Wang Ch'ing, who was a censor in the year B.C. 99[4];
Yung Shăng[5]; and Wang Chî[6], a statesman who died in the
beginning of the reign of the emperor Yüan.

3. But a third copy of the Analects was discovered about
B.C. 150. One of the sons of the emperor Ching was appointed
king of Lû[7] in the year B.C. 154, and some time after, wishing to
enlarge his palace, he proceeded to pull down the house of the
K'ung family, known as that where Confucius himself had lived.

[1] 太子大傅夏侯勝.   [2] 前將軍, 蕭望之.   [3] 丞相,
韋賢, 及子, 玄成.   [4] 王卿.   [5] 庸生.   [6] 中尉王吉.
[7] 魯王共 (or 恭).

While doing so, there were found in the wall copies of the Shû-ching, the Ch'un Ch'iû, the Hsiâo-ching, and the Lun Yü or Analects, which had been deposited there, when the edict for the burning of the Books was issued. They were all written, how-ever, in the most ancient form of the Chinese character [1], which had fallen into disuse, and the king returned them to the K'ung family, the head of which, K'ung Ân-kwo [2], gave himself to the study of them, and finally, in obedience to an imperial order, published a Work called 'The Lun Yü, with Explanations of the Characters, and Exhibition of the Meaning [3].'

4. The recovery of this copy will be seen to be a most important circumstance in the history of the text of the Analects. It is referred to by Chinese writers, as 'The old Lun Yü.' In the historical narrative which we have of the affair, a circumstance is added which may appear to some minds to throw suspicion on the whole account. The king was finally arrested, we are told, in his purpose to destroy the house, by hearing the sounds of bells, musical stones, lutes, and cithern, as he was ascending the steps that led to the ancestral hall or temple. This incident was contrived, we may suppose, by the K'ung family, to preserve the house, or it may have been devised by the historian to glorify the sage, but we may not, on account of it, discredit the finding of the ancient copies of the Books. We have K'ung Ân-kwo's own account of their being committed to him, and of the ways which he took to decipher them. The work upon the Analects, mentioned above, has not indeed come down to us, but his labours on the Shû-ching still remain.

5. It has been already stated, that the Lun Yü of Ch'î contained two Books more than that of Lû. In this respect, the old Lun Yü agreed with the Lû exemplar. Those two books were wanting in it as well. The last book of the Lû Lun was divided in it, however, into two, the chapter beginning, 'Yâo said,' forming a whole Book by itself, and the remaining two chapters formed another Book beginning 'Tsze-chang.' With this trifling difference, the old and the Lû copies appear to have agreed together.

6. Chang Yü, prince of Ân-ch'ang [4], who died B.C. 4, after having

---

[1] 科斗文子,—lit. 'tadpole characters.' They were, it is said, the original forms devised by Ts'ang-chieh, with large heads and fine tails, like the creature from which they were named. See the notes to the preface to the Shû-ching in 'The Thirteen Classics.'

[2] 孔安國. 　[3] 論語訓解. See the preface to the Lun Yü in 'The Thirteen Ching.' It has been my principal authority in this section. 　[4] 安昌侯, 張禹.

sustained several of the highest offices of the empire, instituted a comparison between the exemplars of Lû and Ch'î, with a view to determine the true text. The result of his labours appeared in twenty-one Books, which are mentioned in Liû Hsin's catalogue. They were known as the Lun of prince Chang[1], and commanded general approbation. To Chang Yü is commonly ascribed the ejecting from the Classic the two additional books which the Ch'î exemplar contained, but Mâ Twan-lin prefers to rest that circumstance on the authority of the old Lun, which we have seen was without them[2]. If we had the two Books, we might find sufficient reason from their contents to discredit them. That may have been sufficient for Chang Yü to condemn them as he did, but we can hardly suppose that he did not have before him the old Lun, which had come to light about a century before he published his Work.

7. In the course of the second century, a new edition of the Analects, with a commentary, was published by one of the greatest scholars which China has ever produced, Chăng Hsüan, known also as Chăng K'ang-ch'ăng[3]. He died in the reign of the emperor Hsien (A.D. 190–220)[4] at the age of 74, and the amount of his labours on the ancient classical literature is almost incredible. While he adopted the Lû Lun as the received text of his time, he compared it minutely with those of Ch'î and the old exemplar. In the last section of this chapter will be found a list of the readings in his commentary different from those which are now acknowledged in deference to the authority of Chû Hsî, of the Sung dynasty. They are not many, and their importance is but trifling.

8. On the whole, the above statements will satisfy the reader of the care with which the text of the Lun Yü was fixed during the dynasty of Han.

SECTION II.

AT WHAT TIME, AND BY WHOM, THE ANALECTS WERE WRITTEN; THEIR PLAN;
AND AUTHENTICITY.

1. At the commencement of the notes upon the first Book, under the heading, 'The Title of the Work,' I have given the received account of its authorship, which precedes the catalogue

---

[1] 張侯論.   [2] 文獻通考, Bk. clxxxiv. p. 3.   [3] 鄭玄, 字康成.
[4] 孝獻皇帝.

of Liû Hsin. According to that, the Analects were compiled by
the disciples of Confucius coming together after his death, and
digesting the memorials of his discourses and conversations which
they had severally preserved. But this cannot be true. We may
believe, indeed, that many of the disciples put on record conversations which they had had with their master, and notes about his
manners and incidents of his life, and that these have been incorporated with the Work which we have, but that Work must have
taken its present form at a period somewhat later.

In Book VIII, chapters iii and iv, we have some notices of the
last days of Tsăng Shăn, and are told that he was visited on his
death-bed by the officer Măng Ching. Now *Ching* was the posthumous title of Chung-sun Chîeh [1], and we find him alive (Lî Chî, II.
Pt. ii. 2) after the death of duke Tâo of Lû [2], which took place
B.C. 431, about fifty years after the death of Confucius.

Again, Book XIX is all occupied with the sayings of the
disciples. Confucius personally does not appear in it. Parts of
it, as chapters iii, xii, and xviii, carry us down to a time when
the disciples had schools and followers of their own, and were
accustomed to sustain their teachings by referring to the lessons
which they had heard from the sage.

Thirdly, there is the second chapter of Book XI, the second
paragraph of which is evidently a note by the compilers of the
Work, enumerating ten of the principal disciples, and classifying
them according to their distinguishing characteristics. We can
hardly suppose it to have been written while any of the ten were
alive. But there is among them the name of Tsze-hsiâ, who lived
to the age of about a hundred. We find him, B.C. 407, three-
quarters of a century after the death of Confucius, at the court
of Wei, to the prince of which he is reported to have presented
some of the Classical Books [3].

2. We cannot therefore accept the above account of the origin
of the Analects,—that they were compiled by the disciples of
Confucius. Much more likely is the view that we owe the work
to their disciples. In the note on I. ii. 1, a peculiarity is pointed
out in the use of the surnames of Yew Zo and Tsăng Shăn, which

----

[1] See Chû Hsî's commentary, *in loc.*—孟敬子, 魯大夫, 仲孫氏, 名捷.
[2] 悼公.   [3] 晉魏斯受經於卜子夏; see the 歷代統紀表,
Bk. i. p. 77.

has made some Chinese critics attribute the compilation to their followers. But this conclusion does not stand investigation. Others have assigned different portions to different schools. Thus, Book V is given to the disciples of Tsze-kung; Book XI, to those of Min Tsze-ch'îen; Book XIV, to Yüan Hsien; and Book XVI has been supposed to be interpolated from the Analects of Ch'î. Even if we were to acquiesce in these decisions, we should have accounted only for a small part of the Work. It is best to rest in the general conclusion, that it was compiled by the disciples of the disciples of the sage, making free use of the written memorials concerning him which they had received, and the oral statements which they had heard, from their several masters. And we shall not be far wrong, if we determine its date as about the end of the fourth, or the beginning of the fifth century before Christ.

3. In the critical work on the Four Books, called 'Record of Remarks in the village of Yung[1],' it is observed, 'The Analects, in my opinion, were made by the disciples, just like this record of remarks. There they were recorded, and afterwards came a first-rate hand, who gave them the beautiful literary finish which we now witness, so that there is not a character which does not have its own indispensable place[2].' We have seen that the first of these statements contains only a small amount of truth with regard to the materials of the Analects, nor can we receive the second. If one hand or one mind had digested the materials provided by many, the arrangement and style of the work would have been different. We should not have had the same remark appearing in several Books, with little variation, and sometimes with none at all. Nor can we account on this supposition for such fragments as the last chapters of the ninth, tenth, and sixteenth Books, and many others. No definite plan has been kept in view throughout. A degree of unity appears to belong to some Books more than others, and in general to the first ten more than to those which follow, but there is no progress of thought or illustration of subject from Book to Book. And even in those where the chapters have

---

[1] 榕村語錄,－榕村, 'the village of Yung,' is, I conceive, the writer's *nom de plume*. [2] 論語想是門弟子, 如語錄一般, 記在那裏, 後來有一高手, 鍊成文理這樣少, 下字無一不渾.

a common subject, they are thrown together at random more than on any plan.

4. We cannot tell when the Work was first called the Lun Yü[1]. The evidence in the preceding section is sufficient to prove that when the Han scholars were engaged in collecting the ancient Books, it came before them, not in broken tablets, but complete, and arranged in Books or Sections, as we now have it. The Old copy was found deposited in the wall of the house which Confucius had occupied, and must have been placed there not later than B.C. 211, distant from the date which I have assigned to the compilation, not much more than a century and a half. That copy, written in the most ancient characters, was, possibly, the autograph of the compilers.

We have the Writings, or portions of the Writings, of several authors of the third and fourth centuries before Christ. Of these, in addition to 'The Great Learning,' 'The Doctrine of the Mean,' and 'The Works of Mencius,' I have looked over the Works of Hsün Ch'ing[2] of the orthodox school, of the philosophers Chwang and Lieh of the Tâoist school[3], and of the heresiarch Mo[4].

In the Great Learning, Commentary, chapter iv, we have the words of Ana. XII. xiii. In the Doctrine of the Mean, ch. iii, we have Ana. VI. xxvii; and in ch. xxviii. 5, we have substantially Ana. III. ix. In Mencius, II. Pt. I. ii. 19, we have Ana. VII. xxxiii, and in vii. 2, Ana. IV. i; in III. Pt. I. iv. 11, Ana. VIII. xviii, xix; in IV. Pt. I. xiv. 1, Ana. XI. xvi. 2; in V. Pt. II. vii. 9, Ana. X. xiii. 4; and in VII. Pt. II. xxxvii. 1, 2, 8, Ana. V. xxi, XIII. xxi, and XVII. xiii. These quotations, however, are introduced by 'The Master said,' or 'Confucius said,' no mention being made of any book called 'The Lun Yü,' or Analects. In the Great Learning, Commentary, x. 15, we have the words of Ana. IV. iii, and in

---

[1] In the continuation of the 'General Examination of Records and Scholars (續文獻通考),' Bk. cxcviii. p. 17, it is said, indeed, on the authority of Wang Ch'ung (王充), a scholar of our first century, that when the Work came out of the wall it was named a Chwan or Record (傳), and that it was when K'ung Ân-kwo instructed a native of Tsin, named Fû-ch'ing, in it, that it first got the name of Lun Yü :—武帝得論語于孔壁中, 皆名曰傳, 孔安國以古論教晉人扶卿, 始曰論語. If it were so, it is strange the circumstance is not mentioned in Ho Yen's preface. [2] 荀卿. [3] 莊子, 列子. [4] 墨子.

Mencius, III. Pt. II. vii. 3, those of Ana. XVII. i, but without any notice of quotation.

In the Writings of Hsün Ch'ing, Book I. page 2, we find something like the words of Ana. XV. xxx; and on p. 6, part of XIV. xxv. But in these instances there is no mark of quotation.

In the Writings of Chwang, I have noted only one passage where the words of the Analects are reproduced. Ana. XVIII. v is found, but with large additions, and no reference of quotation, in his treatise on 'Man in the World, associated with other Men[1].' In all those Works, as well as in those of Lieh and Mo, the references to Confucius and his disciples, and to many circumstances of his life, are numerous[2]. The quotations of sayings of his not found in the Analects are likewise many, especially in the Doctrine of the Mean, in Mencius, and in the Works of Chwang. Those in the latter are mostly burlesques, but those by the orthodox writers have more or less of classical authority. Some of them may be found in the Chiâ Yü[3], or 'Narratives of the School,' and in parts of the Lî Chî, while others are only known to us by their occurrence in these Writings. Altogether, they do not supply the evidence, for which I am in quest, of the existence of the Analects as a distinct Work, bearing the name of the Lun Yü, prior to the Ch'in dynasty. They leave the presumption, however, in favour of those conclusions, which arises from the facts stated in the first section, undisturbed. They confirm it rather. They show that there was abundance of materials at hand to the scholars of Han, to compile a much larger Work with the same title, if they had felt it their duty to do the business of compilation, and not that of editing.

SECTION III.

OF COMMENTARIES UPON THE ANALECTS.

1. It would be a vast and unprofitable labour to attempt to give a list of the Commentaries which have been published on this Work. My object is merely to point out how zealously the business of interpretation was undertaken, as soon as the text had been

---

[1] 人間世.   [2] In Mo's chapter against the Literati, he mentions some of the characteristics of Confucius in the very words of the Tenth Book of the Analects.
[3] 家語.

recovered by the scholars of the Han dynasty, and with what industry it has been persevered in down to the present time.

2. Mention has been made, in Section I. 6, of the Lun of prince Chang, published in the half century before our era. Pâo Hsien[1], a distinguished scholar and officer, of the reign of Kwang-wû[2], the first emperor of the Eastern Han dynasty, A.D. 25–57, and another scholar of the surname Châu[3], less known but of the same time, published Works, containing arrangements of this in chapters and sentences, with explanatory notes. The critical work of K'ung Ân-kwo on the old Lun Yü has been referred to. That was lost in consequence of suspicions under which Ân-kwo fell towards the close of the reign of the emperor Wû, but in the time of the emperor Shun, A.D. 126–144, another scholar, Mâ Yung[4], undertook the exposition of the characters in the old Lun, giving at the same time his views of the general meaning. The labours of Chăng Hsüan in the second century have been mentioned. Not long after his death, there ensued a period of anarchy, when the empire was divided into three governments, well known from the celebrated historical romance, called ' The Three Kingdoms.' The strongest of them, the House of Wei, patronized literature, and three of its high officers and scholars, Ch'ăn Ch'ün, Wang Sû, and Châu Shăng-lieh[5], in the first half, and probably the second quarter, of the third century, all gave to the world their notes on the Analects.

Very shortly after, five of the great ministers of the Government of Wei, Sun Yung, Chăng Ch'ung, Tsâo Hsî, Hsün K'aî, and Ho Yen[6], united in the production of one great Work, entitled, 'A Collection of Explanations of the Lun Yü[7].' It embodied the labours of all the writers which have been mentioned, and, having been frequently reprinted by succeeding dynasties, it still remains. The preface of the five compilers, in the form of a memorial to the emperor, so called, of the House of Wei, is published with it, and has been of much assistance to me in writing these sections. Ho

[1]包咸. 　[2]光武. 　[3]周氏. 　[4]至順帝時, 南郡太守, 馬融, 亦爲之訓說. 　[5]司農, 陳羣; 太常, 王肅; 博士, 周生列. 　[6]光祿大夫, 關內侯, 孫邕; 光祿大夫, 鄭沖; 散騎常侍, 中領軍, 安鄉亭侯, 曹羲; 侍中, 荀顗; 尚書, 駙馬都尉, 關內侯, 何晏. 　[7]論語集解. I possess a copy of this work, printed about the middle of our fourteenth century.

Yen was the leader among them, and the work is commonly quoted as if it were the production of him alone.

3. From Ho Yen downwards, there has hardly been a dynasty which has not contributed its labourers to the illustration of the Analects. In the Liang, which occupied the throne a good part of the sixth century, there appeared the 'Comments of Hwang K'an[1],' who to the seven authorities cited by Ho Yen added other thirteen, being scholars who had deserved well of the Classic during the intermediate time. Passing over other dynasties, we come to the Sung, A.D. 960-1279. An edition of the Classics was published by imperial authority, about the beginning of the eleventh century, with the title of 'The Correct Meaning.' The principal scholar engaged in the undertaking was Hsing P'ing[2]. The portion of it on the Analects[3] is commonly reprinted in 'The Thirteen Classics,' after Ho Yen's explanations. But the names of the Sung dynasty are all thrown into the shade by that of Chû Hsî, than whom China has not produced a greater scholar. He composed, or his disciples compiled, in the twelfth century, three Works on the Analects :—the first called 'Collected Meanings[4];' the second, 'Collected Comments[5];' and the third, 'Queries[6].' Nothing could exceed the grace and clearness of his style, and the influence which he has exerted on the literature of China has been almost despotic.

The scholars of the present dynasty, however, seem inclined to question the correctness of his views and interpretations of the Classics, and the chief place among them is due to Mâo Ch'î-ling[7], known by the local name of Hsî-ho[8]. His writings, under the name of 'The collected Works of Hsî-ho[9],' have been published in eighty volumes, containing between three and four hundred books or sections. He has nine treatises on the Four Books, or parts of them, and deserves to take rank with Chăng Hsüan and Chû Hsî at the head of Chinese scholars, though he is a vehement opponent of the latter. Most of his writings are to be found also in the great Work called 'A Collection of Works on the Classics, under the Imperial dynasty of Ch'ing[10],' which contains 1400 sections, and is a noble contribution by the scholars of the present dynasty to the illustration of its ancient literature.

¹ 皇侃論語疏.   ² 邢昺.   ³ 論語正義.   ⁴ 論語集義.   ⁵ 論語集註.   ⁶ 論語或問   ⁷ 毛奇齡.   ⁸ 西河.   ⁹ 西河全集.   ¹⁰ 皇清經解.

SECTION IV.

OF VARIOUS READINGS.

In 'The Collection of Supplementary Observations on the Four Books [1],' the second chapter contains a general view of commentaries on the Analects, and from it I extract the following list of various readings of the text found in the comments of Chăng Hsüan, and referred to in the first section of this chapter.

Book II. i, 拱 for 共; viii, 餕 for 饌; xix, 措 for 錯; xxiii. 1, 十世可知, without 也, for 十世可知也. Book III. vii, in the clause 必也射乎, he makes a full stop at 也; xxi. 1, 主 for 社. Book IV. x, 敵 for 適, and 慕 for 莫. Book V. xxi, he puts a full stop at 子. Book VI. vii, he has not the characters 則吾. Book VII. iv, 晏 for 燕; xxxiv, 子疾 simply, for 子疾病. Book IX. ix, 弁 for 冕. Book XI. xxv. 7, 僎 for 撰, and 饋 for 歸. Book XIII. iii. 3, 于往 for 迂; xviii. 1, 弓 for 躬. Book XIV. xxxi, 謗 for 方; xxxiv. 1, 何是栖栖者與 for 何爲是栖栖者與. Book XV. i. 2, 粻 for 糧. Book XVI. i. 13, 封 for 那. Book XVII. i, 饋 for 歸; xxiv. 2, 絞 for 徼. Book XVIII. iv, 饋 for 歸; viii. 1, 侏 for 朱.

These various readings are exceedingly few, and in themselves insignificant. The student who wishes to pursue this subject at length, is provided with the means in the Work of Tî Chiâo-shâu [2], expressly devoted to it. It forms sections 449–473 of the Works on the Classics, mentioned at the close of the preceding section. A still more comprehensive work of the same kind is, 'The Examination of the Text of the Classics and of Commentaries on them,' published under the superintendence of Yüan Yüan, forming chapters 818 to 1054 of the same Collection. Chapters 1016 to 1030 are occupied with the Lun Yü; see the reference to Yüan Yüan farther on, on p. 132.

[1] 四書拓餘說. Published in 1798. The author was a Tsâo Yin-kû—曹寅谷. [2] 翟教授, 四書考異.

CHAPTER III.

OF THE GREAT LEARNING.

SECTION I.

1. It has already been mentioned that 'The Great Learning' forms one of the Books of the Lî Chî, or 'Record of Rites,' the formation of the text of which will be treated of in its proper place. I will only say here, that the Records of Rites had suffered much more, after the death of Confucius, than the other ancient Classics which were supposed to have been collected and digested by him. They were in a more dilapidated condition at the time of the revival of the ancient literature under the Han dynasty, and were then published in three collections, only one of which—the Record of Rites—retains its place among the five Ching.

The Record of Rites consists, according to the ordinary arrangement, of forty-nine Chapters or Books. Liû Hsiang (see ch. I. sect. II. 2) took the lead in its formation, and was followed by the two famous scholars, Tâi Teh [1], and his relative, Tâi Shăng [2]. The first of these reduced upwards of 200 chapters, collected by Hsiang, to eighty-nine, and Shăng reduced these again to forty-six. The three other Books were added in the second century of our era, the Great Learning being one of them, by Mâ Yung, mentioned in the last chapter, section III. 2. Since his time, the Work has not received any further additions.

2. In his note appended to what he calls the chapter of 'Classical Text,' Chû Hsî says that the tablets of the 'old copies' of the rest of the Great Learning were considerably out of order. By those old copies, he intends the Work of Chăng Hsüan, who published his commentary on the Classic, soon after it was completed by the additions of Mâ Yung; and it is possible that the tablets were in confusion, and had not been arranged with sufficient care; but such a thing does not appear to have been suspected until the

---

[1] 戴德.   [2] 戴聖. Shăng was a second cousin of Teh.

twelfth century, nor can any evidence from ancient monuments be adduced in its support.

I have related how the ancient Classics were cut on slabs of stone by imperial order, A.D. 175, the text being that which the various literati had determined, and which had been adopted by Chăng Hsüan. The same work was performed about seventy years later, under the so-called dynasty of Wei, between the years 240 and 248, and the two sets of slabs were set up together. The only difference between them was, that whereas the Classics had been cut in the first instance only in one form, the characters in the slabs of Wei were in three different forms. Amid the changes of dynasties, the slabs both of Han and Wei had perished, or nearly so, before the rise of the T'ang dynasty, A.D. 624; but under one of its emperors, in the year 836, a copy of the Classics was again cut on stone, though only in one form of the character. These slabs we can trace down through the Sung dynasty, when they were known as the tablets of Shen [1]. They were in exact conformity with the text of the Classics adopted by Chăng Hsüan in his commentaries ; and they exist at the present day at the city of Hsî-an, Shen-hsî, still called by the same name.

The Sung dynasty did not accomplish a similar work itself, nor did either of the two which followed it think it necessary to engrave in stone in this way the ancient Classics. About the middle of the sixteenth century, however, the literary world in China was startled by a report that the slabs of Wei which contained the Great Learning had been discovered. But this was nothing more than the result of an impudent attempt at an imposition, for which it is difficult to a foreigner to assign any adequate cause. The treatise, as printed from these slabs, has some trifling additions, and many alterations in the order of the text, but differing from the arrangements proposed by Chû Hsî, and by other scholars. There seems to be now no difference of opinion among Chinese critics that the whole affair was a forgery. The text of the Great Learning, as it appears in the Record of Rites with the commentary of Chăng Hsüan, and was thrice engraved on stone, in three different dynasties, is, no doubt, that which was edited in the Han dynasty by Mâ Yung.

3. I have said, that it is possible that the tablets containing the

---

[1] 陝 碑.

text were not arranged with sufficient care by him; and indeed, any one who studies the treatise attentively, will probably come to the conclusion that the part of it forming the first six chapters of commentary in the present Work is but a fragment. It would not be a difficult task to propose an arrangement of the text different from any which I have yet seen; but such an undertaking would not be interesting out of China. My object here is simply to mention the Chinese scholars who have rendered themselves famous or notorious in their own country by what they have done in this way. The first was Ch'ăng Hâo, a native of Lo-yang in Ho-nan province, in the eleventh century[1]. His designation was Po-shun, but since his death he has been known chiefly by the style of Ming-tâo[2], which we may render the Wise-in-doctrine. The eulogies heaped on him by Chû Hsî and others are extravagant, and he is placed immediately after Mencius in the list of great scholars. Doubtless he was a man of vast literary acquirements. The greatest change which he introduced into the Great Learning, was to read *sin*[3] for *ch'in*[4], at the commencement, making the second object proposed in the treatise to be the *renovation* of the people, instead of *loving* them. This alteration and his various transpositions of the text are found in Mâo Hsî-ho's treatise on 'The Attested Text of the Great Learning[5].'

Hardly less illustrious than Ch'ăng Hâo was his younger brother Ch'ăng Î, known by the style of Chăng-shû[6], and since his death by that of Î-chwan[7]. He followed Hâo in the adoption of the reading '*to renovate*,' instead of '*to love*.' But he transposed the text differently, more akin to the arrangement afterwards made by Chû Hsî, suggesting also that there were some superfluous sentences in the old text which might conveniently be erased. The Work, as proposed to be read by him, will be found in the volume of Mâo just referred to.

We come to the name of Chû Hsî who entered into the labours of the brothers Ch'ăng, the younger of whom he styles his Master, in his introductory note to the Great Learning. His arrangement of the text is that now current in all the editions of the Four Books, and it had nearly displaced the ancient text

[1] 程子顥, 字伯淳, 河南, 洛陽人. [2] 明道. [3] 新. [4] 親. [5] 大學證文. [6] 程子頤, 字正叔, 明道之弟. [7] 伊川.

altogether. The sanction of Imperial approval was given to it during the Yüăn and Ming dynasties. In the editions of the Five *Ching* published by them, only the names of the Doctrine of the Mean and the Great Learning were preserved. No text of these Books was given, and Hsî-ho tells us that in the reign of Chiâ-ching[1], the most flourishing period of the Ming dynasty (A.D. 1522–1566), when Wang Wăn-ch'ăng[2] published a copy of the Great Learning, taken from the T'ang edition of the Thirteen *Ching*, all the officers and scholars looked at one another in astonishment, and were inclined to suppose that the Work was a forgery. Besides adopting the reading of *sin* for *ch'in* from the Ch'ăng, and modifying their arrangements of the text, Chû Hsî made other innovations. He first divided the whole into one chapter of Classical text, which he assigned to Confucius, and ten chapters of Commentary, which he assigned to the disciple Tsăng. Previous to him, the whole had been published, indeed, without any specification of chapters and paragraphs. He undertook, more-over, to supply one whole chapter, which he supposed, after his master Ch'ăng, to be missing.

Since the time of Chû Hsî, many scholars have exercised their wit on the Great Learning. The work of Mâo Hsî-ho contains four arrangements of the text, proposed respectively by the scholars Wang Lû-châi[3], Chî P'ăng-shan[4], Kâo Ching-yî[5], and Ko Ch'î-chan[6]. The curious student may examine them there.

Under the present dynasty, the tendency has been to depreciate the labours of Chû Hsî. The integrity of the text of Chăng Hsüan is zealously maintained, and the simpler method of interpretation employed by him is advocated in preference to the more refined and ingenious schemes of the Sung scholars. I have referred several times in the notes to a Work published a few years ago, under the title of 'The Old Text of the sacred *Ching*, with Commentary and Discussions, by Lo Chung-fan of Nan-hâi[7].' I knew the man many years ago. He was a fine scholar, and had taken the second degree, or that of Chü-zân. He applied to me in 1843 for Christian baptism, and, offended by my hesitancy, went and enrolled himself among the disciples of another missionary. He soon, however,

[1] 嘉靖.　　[2] 王文成.　　[3] 王魯齋.　　[4] 季彭山.
[5] 高景逸.　　[6] 葛屺瞻.　　[7] 聖經古本, 南海羅仲
藩註辨.

withdrew into seclusion, and spent the last years of his life in literary studies. His family have published the Work on the Great Learning, and one or two others. He most vehemently impugns nearly every judgment of Chû Hsî; but in his own exhibitions of the meaning he blends many ideas of the Supreme Being and of the condition of human nature, which he had learned from the Christian Scriptures.

SECTION II.

OF THE AUTHORSHIP, AND DISTINCTION OF THE TEXT INTO CLASSICAL TEXT AND COMMENTARY.

1. The authorship of the Great Learning is a very doubtful point, and one on which it does not appear possible to come to a decided conclusion. Chû Hsî, as I have stated in the last section, determined that so much of it was *Ching*, or Classic, being the very words of Confucius, and that all the rest was *Chwan*, or Commentary, being the views of Tsăng Shăn upon the sage's words, recorded by *his* disciples. Thus, he does not expressly attribute the composition of the Treatise to Tsăng, as he is generally supposed to do. What he says, however, as it is destitute of external support, is contrary also to the internal evidence. The fourth chapter of commentary commences with 'The Master said.' Surely, if there were anything more, directly from Confucius, there would be an intimation of it in the same way. Or, if we may allow that short sayings of Confucius might be interwoven with the Work, as in the fifteenth paragraph of the tenth chapter, without referring them expressly to him, it is too much to ask us to receive the long chapter at the beginning as being from him. With regard to the Work having come from the disciples of Tsăng Shăn, recording their master's views, the paragraph in chapter sixth, commencing with 'The disciple Tsăng said,' seems to be conclusive against such an hypothesis. So much we may be sure is Tsăng's, and no more. Both of Chû Hsî's judgments must be set aside. We cannot admit either the distinction of the contents into Classical text and Commentary, or that the Work was the production of Tsăng's disciples.

2. Who then was the author? An ancient tradition attributes it to K'ung Chî, the grandson of Confucius. In a notice published, at the time of their preparation, about the stone slabs of Wei, the

following statement by Chiâ K'wei, a noted scholar of the first century, is found :— 'When K'ung Chî was living, and in straits, in Sung, being afraid lest the lessons of the former sages should become obscure, and the principles of the ancient sovereigns and kings fall to the ground, he therefore made the Great Learning as the warp of them, and the Doctrine of the Mean as the woof[1].' This would seem, therefore, to have been the opinion of that early time, and I may say the only difficulty in admitting it is that no mention is made of it by Chăng Hsüan.   There certainly is that agreement between the two treatises, which makes their common authorship not at all unlikely.

3. Though we cannot positively assign the authorship of the Great Learning, there can be no hesitation in receiving it as a genuine monument of the Confucian school.   There are not many words in it from the sage himself, but it is a faithful reflection of his teachings, written by some of his followers, not far removed from him by lapse of time.   It must synchronize pretty nearly with the Analects, and may be safely referred to the fifth century before our era.

SECTION III.

ITS SCOPE AND VALUE.

1. The worth of the Great Learning has been celebrated in most extravagant terms by Chinese writers, and there have been foreigners who have not yielded to them in their estimation of it. Pauthier, in the 'Argument Philosophique,' prefixed to his translation of the Work, says :— 'It is evident that the aim of the Chinese philosopher is to exhibit the duties of political government as those of the perfecting of self, and of the practice of virtue by all men.   He felt that he had a higher mission than that with which the greater part of ancient and modern philosophers have contented themselves ; and his immense love for the happiness of humanity, which dominated over all his other sentiments, has made of his

---

[1] 唐氏奏疏有曰, 虞松校刻石經于魏表, 引漢 賈逵之言, 曰, 孔伋窮居于宋, 懼先聖之學不明, 而帝王之道墜, 故作大學以經之, 中庸以緯之; see the 大學證文, 一, p. 5.

philosophy a system of social perfectionating, which, we venture to say, has never been equalled.'

Very different is the judgment passed upon the treatise by a writer in the Chinese Repository: 'The *Tâ Hsio* is a short politico-moral discourse. *Tâ Hsio*, or "Superior Learning," is at the same time both the name and the subject of the discourse; it is the *summum bonum* of the Chinese. In opening this Book, compiled by a disciple of Confucius, and containing his doctrines, we might expect to find a Work like Cicero's *De Officiis;* but we find a very different production, consisting of a few commonplace rules for the maintenance of a good government[1].'

My readers will perhaps think, after reading the present section, that the truth lies between these two representations.

2. I believe that the Book should be styled *T'âi Hsio*[2], and not *Tâ Hsio*, and that it was so named as setting forth the higher and more extensive principles of moral science, which come into use and manifestation in the conduct of government. When Chû Hsî endeavours to make the title mean—'The principles of Learning, which were taught in the higher schools of antiquity,' and tells us how at the age of fifteen, all the sons of the sovereign, with the legitimate sons of the nobles, and high officers, down to the more promising scions of the common people, all entered these seminaries, and were taught the difficult lessons here inculcated, we pity the ancient youth of China. Such 'strong meat' is not adapted for the nourishment of youthful minds. But the evidence adduced for the existence of such educational institutions in ancient times is unsatisfactory, and from the older interpretation of the title we advance more easily to contemplate the object and method of the Work.

3. The *object* is stated definitely enough in the opening paragraph: 'What the Great Learning teaches, is—to illustrate illustrious virtue; to love the people; and to rest in the highest excellence.' The political aim of the writer is here at once evident. He has before him on one side, *the people*, the masses of the empire, and over against them are those whose work and duty, delegated by Heaven, is to govern them, culminating, as a class, in 'the son of Heaven[3],' 'the One man[4],' the sovereign. From the fourth and

---

[1] Chinese Repository, vol. iii. p. 98.   [2] 太學, not 大學. See the note on the title of the Work below.   [3] 天子, Cl. classical) Text, par. 6, 2.   [4] 一人, Comm. ix. 3.

fifth paragraphs, we see that if the lessons of the treatise be learned and carried into practice, the result will be that ' illustrious virtue will be illustrated throughout the nation,' which will be brought, through all its length and breadth, to a condition of happy tranquillity. This object is certainly both grand and good ; and if a reasonable and likely method to secure it were proposed in the Work, language would hardly supply terms adequate to express its value.

4. But the above account of the object of the Great Learning leads us to the conclusion that the student of it should be a sovereign. What interest can an ordinary man have in it ? It is high up in the clouds, far beyond his reach. This is a serious objection to it, and quite unfits it for a place in schools, such as Chû Hsî contends it once had. Intelligent Chinese, whose minds were somewhat quickened by Christianity, have spoken to me of this defect, and complained of the difficulty they felt in making the book a practical directory for their conduct. ' It is so vague and vast,' was the observation of one man. The writer, however, has made some provision for the general application of his instructions. He tells us that, from the sovereign down to the mass of the people, all must consider the cultivation of the person to be the root, that is, the first thing to be attended to[1]. As in his method, moreover, he reaches from the cultivation of the person to the tranquillization of the kingdom, through the intermediate steps of the regulation of the family, and the government of the State[2], there is room for setting forth principles that parents and rulers generally may find adapted for their guidance.

5. The method which is laid down for the attainment of the great object proposed, consists of seven steps :—the investigation of things ; the completion of knowledge ; the sincerity of the thoughts ; the rectifying of the heart ; the cultivation of the person ; the regulation of the family ; and the government of the State. These form the steps of a climax, the end of which is the kingdom tranquillized. Pauthier calls the paragraphs where they occur instances of the sorites, or abridged syllogism. But they belong to *rhetoric*, and not to *logic*.

6. In offering some observations on these steps, and the writer's treatment of them, it will be well to separate them into those preceding the cultivation of the person, and those following it ; and to

---

[1] Cl. Text, par. 6.   [2] Cl. Text, pars. 4, 5.

deal with the latter first.—Let us suppose that the cultivation of
the person is fully attained, every discordant mental element having
been subdued and removed. It is assumed that the regulation of
the family will necessarily flow from this. Two short paragraphs
are all that are given to the illustration of the point, and they are
vague generalities on the subject of men's being led astray by their
feelings and affections.

The family being regulated, there will result from it the government of the State. First, the virtues taught in the family have
their correspondencies in the wider sphere. Filial piety will appear
as loyalty. Fraternal submission will be seen in respect and
obedience to elders and superiors. Kindness is capable of universal
application. Second, ' From the loving example of one family, a
whole State becomes loving, and from its courtesies the whole State
becomes courteous[1].' Seven paragraphs suffice to illustrate these
statements, and short as they are, the writer goes back to the topic
of self-cultivation, returning from the family to the individual.

The State being governed, the whole empire will become peaceful and happy. There is even less of connexion, however, in the
treatment of this theme, between the premiss and the conclusion,
than in the two previous chapters. Nothing is said about the
relation between the whole kingdom, and its component States, or
any one of them. It is said at once, ' What is meant by " The
making the whole kingdom peaceful and happy depends on the
government of the State," is this:—When the sovereign behaves to
his aged, as the aged should be behaved to, the people become filial ;
when the sovereign behaves to his elders, as elders should be
behaved to, the people learn brotherly submission ; when the
sovereign treats compassionately the young and helpless, the people
do the same[2].' This is nothing but a repetition of the preceding
chapter, instead of that chapter's being made a step from which to
go on to the splendid consummation of the good government of the
whole kingdom.

The words which I have quoted are followed by a very striking
enunciation of the golden rule in its negative form, and under the
name of *the measuring square,* and all the lessons of the chapter are
connected more or less closely with that. The application of this
principle by a ruler, whose heart is in the first place in loving
sympathy with the people, will guide him in all the exactions which

---

[1] See Comm. ix. 3.   [2] See Comm. x. i.

he lays upon them, and in his selection of ministers, in such a way that he will secure the affections of his subjects, and his throne will be established, for 'by gaining the people, the kingdom is gained, and, by losing the people, the kingdom is lost[1].' There are in this part of the treatise many valuable sentiments, and counsels for all in authority over others. The objection to it is, that, as the last step of the climax, it does not rise upon all the others with the accumulated force of their conclusions, but introduces us to new principles of action, and a new line of argument. Cut off the commencement of the first paragraph which connects it with the preceding chapters, and it would form a brief but admirable treatise by itself on the art of government.

This brief review of the writer's treatment of the concluding steps of his method will satisfy the reader that the execution is not equal to the design ; and, moreover, underneath all the reasoning, and more especially apparent in the eighth and ninth chapters of commentary (according to the ordinary arrangement of the work), there lies the assumption that example is all but omnipotent. We find this principle pervading all the Confucian philosophy. And doubtless it is a truth, most important in education and government, that the influence of example is very great. I believe, and will insist upon it hereafter in these prolegomena, that we have come to overlook this element in our conduct of administration. It will be well if the study of the Chinese Classics should call attention to it. Yet in them the subject is pushed to an extreme, and represented in an extravagant manner. Proceeding from the view of human nature that it is entirely good, and led astray only by influences from without, the sage of China and his followers attribute to personal example and to instruction a power which we do not find that they actually possess.

7. The steps which precede the cultivation of the person are more briefly dealt with than those which we have just considered. 'The cultivation of the person results from the rectifying of the heart or mind[2].' True, but in the Great Learning very inadequately set forth.

'The rectifying of the mind is realised when the thoughts are made sincere[3].' And the thoughts are sincere, when no self-deception is allowed, and we move without effort to what is right and wrong, 'as we love what is beautiful, and as we dislike a bad

---

[1] Comm. x. 5.　　　　　[2] Comm. vii. 1.　　　　　[3] Comm. Ch. vi.

smell[1].' How are we to attain to this state ?   Here the Chinese
moralist fails us.   According to Chû Hsî's arrangement of the
Treatise, there is only one sentence from which we can frame a
reply to the above question.   'Therefore,' it is said, 'the superior
man must be watchful over himself when he is alone[2].'   Following
Chû's sixth chapter of commentary, and forming, we may say, part
of it, we have in the old arrangement of the Great Learning all
the passages which he has distributed so as to form the previous
five chapters.   But even from the examination of them, we do not
obtain the information which we desire on this momentous inquiry.

8. Indeed, the more I study the Work, the more satisfied I
become, that from the conclusion of what is now called the chapter
of classical text to the sixth chapter of commentary, we have only
a few fragments, which it is of no use trying to arrange, so as
fairly to exhibit the plan of the author.   According to his method,
the chapter on the connexion between making the thoughts sincere
and so rectifying the mental nature, should be preceded by one on
the completion of knowledge as the means of making the thoughts
sincere, and that again by one on the completion of knowledge by
the investigation of things, or whatever else the phrase *ko wû*
may mean.   I am less concerned for the loss and injury which this
part of the Work has suffered, because the subject of the connexion
between intelligence and virtue is very fully exhibited in the
Doctrine of the Mean, and will come under our notice in the review
of that Treatise.   The manner in which Chû Hsî has endeavoured
to supply the blank about the perfecting of knowledge by the
investigation of things is too extravagant.   'The Learning for
Adults,' he says, 'at the outset of its lessons, instructs the learner,
in regard to all things in the world, to proceed from what knowledge he has of their principles, and pursue his investigation of
them, till he reaches the extreme point.   After exerting himself
for a long time, he will suddenly find himself possessed of a wide
and far-reaching penetration.   Then, the qualities of all things,
whether external or internal, the subtle or the coarse, will be
apprehended, and the mind, in its entire substance and its relations
to things, will be perfectly intelligent.   This is called the investigation of things.   This is called the perfection of knowledge[3].'
And knowledge must be thus perfected before we can achieve
the sincerity of our thoughts, and the rectifying of our hearts!

[1] Comm. vi. 1.   [2] Comm. vi. 2.   [3] Suppl. to Comm. Ch. v.

Verily this would be learning not for adults only, but even Methuselahs would not be able to compass it. Yet for centuries this has been accepted as the orthodox exposition of the Classic. Lo Chung-fan does not express himself too strongly when he says that such language is altogether incoherent. The author would only be 'imposing on himself and others.'

9. The orthodox doctrine of China concerning the connexion between intelligence and virtue is most seriously erroneous, but I will not lay to the charge of the author of the Great Learning the wild representations of the commentator of our twelfth century, nor need I make here any remarks on what the doctrine really is. After the exhibition which I have given, my readers will probably conclude that the Work before us is far from developing, as Pauthier asserts, 'a system of social perfectionating which has never been equalled.'

10. The Treatise has undoubtedly great merits, but they are not to be sought in the severity of its logical processes, or the large-minded prosecution of any course of thought. We shall find them in the announcement of certain seminal principles, which, if recognised in government and the regulation of conduct, would conduce greatly to the happiness and virtue of mankind. I will conclude these observations by specifying four such principles.

First. The writer conceives nobly of the object of government, that it is to make its subjects happy and good. This may not be a sufficient account of that object, but it is much to have it so clearly laid down to 'all kings and governors,' that they are to love the people, ruling not for their own gratification but for the good of those over whom they are exalted by Heaven. Very important also is the statement that rulers have no divine right but what springs from the discharge of their duty. 'The decree does not always rest on them. Goodness obtains it, and the want of goodness loses it[1].'

Second. The insisting on personal excellence in all who have authority in the family, the state, and the kingdom, is a great moral and social principle. The influence of such personal excellence may be overstated, but by the requirement of its cultivation the writer deserved well of his country.

Third. Still more important than the requirement of such excellence, is the principle that it must be rooted in the state of

---

[1] Comm. x. 11.

the heart, and be the natural outgrowth of internal sincerity.   'As a man thinketh in his heart, so is he.'   This is the teaching alike of Solomon and the author of the Great Learning.

Fourth.   I mention last the striking exhibition which we have of the golden rule, though only in its negative form :—' What a man dislikes in his superiors, let him not display in the treatment of his inferiors; what he dislikes in inferiors, let him not display in his service of his superiors; what he dislikes in those who are before him, let him not therewith precede those who are behind him ; what he dislikes in those who are behind him, let him not therewith follow those who are before him ; what he dislikes to receive on the right, let him not bestow on the left; what he dislikes to receive on the left, let him not bestow on the right. This is what is called the principle with which, as with a measuring square, to regulate one's conduct[1].'

The Work which contains those principles cannot be thought meanly of.   They are 'commonplace,' as the writer in the Chinese Repository calls them, but they are at the same time eternal verities.

[1] Comm. x. 2.

CHAPTER IV.

THE DOCTRINE OF THE MEAN.

SECTION I.

ITS PLACE IN THE LÎ CHÎ, AND ITS PUBLICATION SEPARATELY.

1. The Doctrine of the Mean was one of the treatises which came to light in connexion with the labours of Liû Hsiang, and its place as the thirty-first Book in the Lî Chî was finally determined by Mâ Yung and Chăng Hsüan. In the translation of the Lî Chî in 'The Sacred Books of the East' it is the twenty-eighth Treatise.

2. But while it was thus made to form a part of the great collection of Treatises on Ceremonies, it maintained a separate footing of its own. In Liû Hsin's Catalogue of the Classical Works, we find 'Two *p'ien* of Observations on the Chung Yung[1].' In the Records of the dynasty of Sûi (A.D. 589–618), in the chapter on the History of Literature[2], there are mentioned three Works on the Chung Yung;—the first called 'The Record of the Chung Yung,' in two *chüan*, attributed to Tâi Yung, a scholar who flourished about the middle of the fifth century; the second, 'A Paraphrase and Commentary on the Chung Yung,' attributed to the emperor Wû (A.D. 502–549) of the Liang dynasty, in one *chüan*; and the third, 'A Private Record, Determining the Meaning of the Chung Yung,' in five *chüan*, the author, or supposed author, of which is not mentioned[3].

It thus appears, that the Chung Yung had been published and commented on separately, long before the time of the Sung dynasty. The scholars of that, however, devoted special attention to it, the way being led by the famous Châu Lien-ch'î[4]. He was followed by the two brothers Ch'ăng, but neither of them published upon it. At last came Chû Hsî, who produced his Work called

[1] 中庸說二篇. [2] 隋書, 卷三十二, 志第二十七, 經籍, 一, p. 12. [3] 禮記中庸傳, 二卷, 宋散騎常侍戴顒撰; 中庸講疏, 一卷, 梁武帝撰; 私記制旨中庸義, 五卷. [4] 周濂溪.

'The Chung Yung, in Chapters and Sentences[1],' which was made the text book of the Classic at the literary examinations, by the fourth emperor of the Yüan dynasty (A.D. 1312–1320), and from that time the name merely of the Treatise was retained in editions of the Lî Chî. Neither text nor ancient commentary was given.

Under the present dynasty it is not so. In the superb edition of 'The Three Lî Ching,' edited by numerous committees of scholars towards the middle of the Ch'ien-lung reign, the Chung Yung is published in two parts, the ancient commentaries from 'The Thirteen Ching' being given side by side with those of Chû Hsî.

SECTION II.

ITS AUTHOR; AND SOME ACCOUNT OF HIM.

1. The composition of the Chung Yung is attributed to K'ung Chî, the grandson of Confucius[2]. Chinese inquirers and critics are agreed on this point, and apparently on sufficient grounds. There is indeed no internal evidence in the Work to lead us to such a conclusion. Among the many quotations of Confucius's words and references to him, we might have expected to find some indication that the sage was the grandfather of the author, but nothing of the kind is given. The external evidence, however, or that from the testimony of authorities, is very strong. In Sze-mâ Ch'ien's Historical Records, published about B.C. 100, it is expressly said that 'Tsze-sze made the Chung Yung.' And we have a still stronger proof, a century earlier, from Tsze-sze's own descendant, K'ung Fû, whose words are, 'Tsze-sze compiled the Chung Yung in forty-nine p'ien[3].' We may, therefore, accept the received account without hesitation.

2. As Chî, spoken of chiefly by his designation of Tsze-sze, thus occupies a distinguished place in the classical literature of China, it

---

[1] 中庸章句.   [2] 子思作中庸; see the 史記, 四十七, 孔子世家.   [3] This K'ung Fû (孔鮒) was that descendant of Confucius, who hid several books in the wall of his house, on the issuing of the imperial edict for their burning. He was a writer himself, and his Works are referred to under the title of 孔叢子. I have not seen them, but the statement given above is found in the 四書拓餘說; — art. 中庸. — 孔叢子云, 子思撰中庸之書, 四十九篇.

may not be out of place to bring together here a few notices of him gathered from reliable sources.

He was the son of Lî, whose death took place B.C. 483, four years before that of the sage, his father. I have not found it recorded in what year he was born. Sze-mâ Ch'ien says he died at the age of 62. But this is evidently wrong, for we learn from Mencius that he was high in favour with the duke Mû of Lû[1], whose accession to that principality dates in B.C. 409, seventy years after the death of Confucius. In the 'Plates and Notices of the Worthies, sacrificed to in the Sage's Temples[2],' it is supposed that the sixty-two in the Historical Records should be eighty-two[3]. It is maintained by others that Tsze-sze's life was protracted beyond 100 years[4]. This variety of opinions simply shows that the point cannot be positively determined. To me it seems that the conjecture in the Sacrificial Canon must be pretty near the truth[5].

During the years of his boyhood, then, Tsze-sze must have been with his grandfather, and received his instructions. It is related, that one day, when he was alone with the sage, and heard him sighing, he went up to him, and, bowing twice, inquired the reason of his grief. 'Is it,' said he, 'because you think that your descendants, through not cultivating themselves, will be unworthy of you? Or is it that, in your admiration of the ways of Yâo and Shun, you are vexed that you fall short of them?' 'Child,' replied Confucius, 'how is it that you know my thoughts?' 'I have often,' said Tsze-sze, 'heard from you the lesson, that when the father has gathered and prepared the firewood, if the son cannot carry the bundle, he is to be pronounced degenerate and unworthy. The remark comes frequently into my thoughts, and fills me with great apprehensions.' The sage was delighted. He

---

[1] 魯穆 (or 繆) 公.   [2] 聖廟祀典圖考.   [3] 或以六十二似八十二之誤. Eighty-two and sixty-two may more easily be confounded, as written in Chinese, than with the Roman figures.   [4] See the 四書集證, on the preface to the Chung Yung,—年百餘歲卒.   [5] Lî himself was born in Confucius's twenty-first year, and if Tsze-sze had been born in Lî's twenty-first year, he must have been 103 at the time of duke Mû's accession. But the tradition is, that Tsze-sze was a pupil of Tsăng Shăn who was born B.C. 504. We must place his birth therefore considerably later, and suppose him to have been quite young when his father died. I was talking once about the question with a Chinese friend, who observed:—'Lî was fifty when he died, and his wife married again into a family of Wei. We can hardly think, therefore, that she was anything like that age. Lî could not have married so soon as his father did. Perhaps he was about forty when Chî was born.'

smiled and said, 'Now, indeed, shall I be without anxiety! My undertakings will not come to nought. They will be carried on and flourish[1].'

After the death of Confucius, Chî became a pupil, it is said, of the philosopher Tsăng. But he received his instructions with discrimination, and in one instance which is recorded in the Lî Chî, the pupil suddenly took the place of the master. We there read:— 'Tsăng said to Tsze-sze, "Chî, when I was engaged in mourning for my parents, neither congee nor water entered my mouth for seven days." Tsze-sze answered, "In ordering their rules of propriety, it was the design of the ancient kings that those who would go beyond them should stoop and keep by them, and that those who could hardly reach them should stand on tiptoe to do so. Thus it is that the superior man, in mourning for his parents, when he has been three days without water or congee, takes a staff to enable himself to rise[2]."'

While he thus condemned the severe discipline of Tsăng, Tsze-sze appears, in various incidents which are related of him, to have been himself more than sufficiently ascetic. As he was living in great poverty, a friend supplied him with grain, which he readily received. Another friend was emboldened by this to send him a bottle of spirits, but he declined to receive it. 'You receive your corn from other people,' urged the donor, 'and why should you decline my gift, which is of less value? You can assign no ground in reason for it, and if you wish to show your independence, you should do so completely.' 'I am so poor,' was the reply, 'as to be in want, and being afraid lest I should die and the sacrifices not be offered to my ancestors, I accept the grain as an alms. But the spirits and the dried flesh which you offer to me are the appliances of a feast. For a poor man to be feasting is certainly unreasonable. This is the ground of my refusing your gift. I have no thought of asserting my independence[3].'

To the same effect is the account of Tsze-sze, which we have from Liû Hsiang. That scholar relates:— 'When Chî was living in Wei, he wore a tattered coat, without any lining, and in thirty days had only nine meals. T'ien Tsze-fang having heard of his

---

[1] See the 四書集證, in the place just quoted from. For the incident we are indebted to K'ung Fû; see note 3, p. 36.   [2] Lî Chî, II. Sect. I. ii. 7.   [3] See the 四書集證, as above.

distress, sent a messenger to him with a coat of fox-fur, and being afraid that he might not receive it, he added the message,—"When I borrow from a man, I forget it; when I give a thing, I part with it freely as if I threw it away." Tsze-sze declined the gift thus offered, and when Tsze-fang said, "I have, and you have not; why will you not take it?" he replied, "You give away as rashly as if you were casting your things into a ditch. Poor as I am, I cannot think of my body as a ditch, and do not presume to accept your gift[1]."'

Tsze-sze's mother married again, after Lî's death, into a family of Wei. But this circumstance, which is not at all creditable in Chinese estimation, did not alienate his affections from her. He was in Lû when he heard of her death, and proceeded to weep in the temple of his family. A disciple came to him and said, 'Your mother married again into the family of the Shû, and do you weep for her in the temple of the K'ung?' 'I am wrong,' said Tsze-sze, 'I am wrong;' and with these words he went to weep elsewhere[2].

In his own married relation he does not seem to have been happy, and for some cause, which has not been transmitted to us, he divorced his wife, following in this, it has been wrongly said, the example of Confucius. On her death, her son, Tsze-shang[3], did not undertake any mourning for her. Tsze-sze's disciples were surprised and questioned him. 'Did your predecessor, a superior man,' they asked, 'mourn for his mother who had been divorced?' 'Yes,' was the reply. 'Then why do you not cause Pâi[4] to mourn for his mother?' Tsze-sze answered, 'My progenitor, a superior man, failed in nothing to pursue the proper path. His observances increased or decreased as the case required. But I cannot attain to this. While she was my wife, she was Pâi's mother; when she ceased to be my wife, she ceased to be Pâi's mother.' The custom of the K'ung family not to mourn for a mother who had been divorced, took its rise from Tsze-sze[5].

These few notices of K'ung Chî in his more private relations bring him before us as a man of strong feeling and strong will, independent, and with a tendency to asceticism in his habits.

---

[1] See the 四 書 集 證, as above.   [2] See the Lî Chî, II. Sect. II. iii. 15.
庶 氏 之 母 死 must be understood as I have done above, and not with Chăng Hsüan,
—'Your mother was born a Miss Shû.'   [3] 子 上,—this was the designation of Tsze-
sze's son.   [4] 白,—this was Tsze-shang's name.   [5] See the Lî Chî, II. Sect. I. i. 4.

As a public character, we find him at the ducal courts of Wei, Sung, Lû, and Pî, and at each of them held in high esteem by the rulers. To Wei he was carried probably by the fact of his mother having married into that State. We are told that the prince of Wei received him with great distinction and lodged him honourably. On one occasion he said to him, 'An officer of the State of Lû, you have not despised this small and narrow Wei, but have bent your steps hither to comfort and preserve it;—vouchsafe to confer your benefits upon me.' Tsze-sze replied, 'If I should wish to requite your princely favour with money and silks, your treasuries are already full of them, and I am poor. If I should wish to requite it with good words, I am afraid that what I should say would not suit your ideas, so that I should speak in vain and not be listened to. The only way in which I can requite it, is by recommending to your notice men of worth.' The duke said, 'Men of worth are exactly what I desire.' 'Nay,' said Chî, 'you are not able to appreciate them.' 'Nevertheless,' was the reply, 'I should like to hear whom you consider deserving that name.' Tsze-sze replied, 'Do you wish to select your officers for the name they may have or for their reality?' 'For their reality, certainly,' said the duke. His guest then said, 'In the eastern borders of your State, there is one Lî Yin, who is a man of real worth.' 'What were his grandfather and father?' asked the duke. 'They were husbandmen,' was the reply, on which the duke broke into a loud laugh, saying, 'I do not like husbandry. The son of a husbandman cannot be fit for me to employ. I do not put into office all the cadets of those families even in which office is hereditary.' Tsze-sze observed, 'I mention Lî Yin because of his abilities; what has the fact of his forefathers being husbandmen to do with the case? And moreover, the duke of Châu was a great sage, and K'ang-shû was a great worthy. Yet if you examine their beginnings, you will find that from the business of husbandry they came forth to found their States. I did certainly have my doubts that in the selection of your officers you did not have regard to their real character and capacity.' With this the conversation ended. The duke was silent[1].

Tsze-sze was naturally led to Sung, as the K'ung family originally sprang from that principality. One account, quoted in 'The

[1] See the 氏姓譜, 卷一百二, 孔氏, 孔伋.

Four Books, Text and Commentary, with Proofs and Illustrations[1],'
says that he went thither in his sixteenth year, and having foiled
an officer of the State, named Yo So, in a conversation on the Shû
Ching, his opponent was so irritated at the disgrace put on him by
a youth, that he listened to the advice of evil counsellors, and made
an attack on him to put him to death.   The duke of Sung, hearing
the tumult, hurried to the rescue, and when Chî found himself in
safety, he said, 'When king Wăn was imprisoned in Yû-lî, he made
the Yî of Châu.   My grandfather made the Ch'un Ch'iû after he
had been in danger in Ch'ăn and Ts'âi.   Shall I not make something when rescued from such a risk in Sung?'   Upon this he
made the Chung Yung in forty-nine p'ien.

According to this account, the Chung Yung was the work of
Tsze-sze's early manhood, and the tradition has obtained a wonderful prevalence.   The notice in 'The Sacrificial Canon' says, on the
contrary, that it was the work of his old age, when he had finally
settled in Lû, which is much more likely[2].

Of Tsze-sze in Pî, which could hardly be said to be out of Lû, we
have only one short notice,—in Mencius, V. Pt. II. iii. 3, where the
duke Hûi of Pî is introduced as saying, 'I treat Tsze-sze as my
master.'

We have fuller accounts of him in Lû, where he spent all the
latter years of his life, instructing his disciples to the number of
several hundred[3], and held in great reverence by the duke Mû.
The duke indeed wanted to raise him to the highest office, but he
declined this, and would only occupy the position of a 'guide,
philosopher, and friend.'   Of the attention which he demanded,
however, instances will be found in Mencius, II. Pt. II. xi. 3; V. Pt.
II. vi. 4, and vii. 4.   In his intercourse with the duke he spoke the
truth to him fearlessly.   In the 'Cyclopædia of Surnames[4],' I find
the following conversations, but I cannot tell from what source
they are extracted into that Work.— 'One day, the duke said to
Tsze-sze, "The officer Hsien told me that you do good without

---

[1] This is the Work so often referred to as the 四書集證, the full title being
四書經註集證. The passage here translated from it will be found in the place
several times referred to in this section.   [2] The author of the 四書拓餘說
adopts the view that the Work was composed in Sung. Some have advocated this from ch.
xxviii. 5, compared with Ana. III. ix, 'it being proper,' they say, 'that Tsze-sze, writing in
Sung, should not depreciate it as Confucius had done out of it!'   [3] See in the 'Sacrificial Canon,' on Tsze-sze.   [4] This is the Work referred to in note 1, p. 40.

wishing for any praise from men;—is it so?" Tsze-sze replied, "No, that is not my feeling. When I cultivate what is good, I wish men to know it, for when they know it and praise me, I feel encouraged to be more zealous in the cultivation. This is what I desire, and am not able to obtain. If I cultivate what is good, and men do not know it, it is likely that in their ignorance they will speak evil of me. So by my good-doing I only come to be evil spoken of. This is what I do not desire, but am not able to avoid. In the case of a man, who gets up at cock-crowing to practise what is good and continues sedulous in the endeavour till midnight, and says at the same time that he does not wish men to know it, lest they should praise him, I must say of such a man, that, if he be not deceitful, he is stupid."'

Another day, the duke asked Tsze-sze, saying, 'Can my state be made to flourish?' 'It may,' was the reply. 'And how?' Tsze-sze said, 'O prince, if you and your ministers will only strive to realise the government of the duke of Châu and of Po-ch'in; practising their transforming principles, sending forth wide the favours of your ducal house, and not letting advantages flow in private channels;—if you will thus conciliate the affections of the people, and at the same time cultivate friendly relations with neighbouring states, your state will soon begin to flourish.'

On one occasion, the duke asked whether it had been the custom of old for ministers to go into mourning for a prince whose service and state they had left. Tsze-sze replied to him, 'Of old, princes advanced their ministers to office according to propriety, and dismissed them in the same way, and hence there was that rule. But now-a-days, princes bring their ministers forward as if they were going to take them on their knees, and send them away as if they would cast them into an abyss. If they do not treat them as their greatest enemies, it is well.—How can you expect the ancient practice to be observed in such circumstances[1]?'

These instances may suffice to illustrate the character of Tsze-sze, as it was displayed in his intercourse with the princes of his time. We see the same independence which he affected in private life, and a dignity not unbecoming the grandson of Confucius. But we miss the reach of thought and capacity for administration which belonged to the Sage. It is with him, how-

---

[1] This conversation is given in the Li Chî, II. Sect. II. Pt. ii. 1.

ever, as a thinker and writer that we have to do, and his rank in that capacity will appear from the examination of the Chung Yung in the section iv below. His place in the temples of the Sage has been that of one of his four assessors, since the year 1267. He ranks with Yen Hûi, Tsăng Shăn, and Mencius, and bears the title of 'The Philosopher Tsze-sze, Transmitter of the Sage[1].'

SECTION III.

ITS INTEGRITY.

In the testimony of K'ung Fû, which has been adduced to prove the authorship of the Chung Yung, it is said that the Work consisted originally of forty-nine *p'ien*. From this statement it is argued by some, that the arrangement of it in thirty-three chapters, which originated with Chû Hsî, is wrong[2]; but this does not affect the question of integrity, and the character *p'ien* is so vague and indefinite, that we cannot affirm that K'ung Fû meant to tell us by it that Tsze-sze himself divided his Treatise into so many paragraphs or chapters.

It is on the entry in Liû Hsin's Catalogue, quoted section i,— 'Two *p'ien* of Observations on the Chung Yung,' that the integrity of the present Work is called in question. Yen Sze-kû, of the T'ang dynasty, has a note on that entry to the effect :—'There is now the Chung Yung in the Lî Chî in one *p'ien*. But that is not the original Treatise here mentioned, but only a branch from it[3].' Wang Wei, a writer of the Ming dynasty, says :—'Anciently, the Chung Yung consisted of two *p'ien*, as appears from the History of Literature of the Han dynasty, but in the Lî Chî we have only one *p'ien*, which Chû Hsî, when he made his "Chapters and Sentences," divided into thirty-three chapters. The old Work in two *p'ien* is not to be met with now[4].'

These views are based on a misinterpretation of the entry in the

---

[1] 述聖子思子.   [2] See the 四書拓餘說, art. 中庸.   [3] 顏師古曰,今禮記有中庸一篇,亦非本禮經,蓋此之流.   [4] 王氏緯曰,中庸古有二篇,見漢藝文志,而在禮記中者,一篇而已,朱子爲章句,因其一篇者,分爲三十三章,而古所謂二篇者不可見矣.

Catalogue. It does not speak of two *p'ien* of the Chung Yung, but of *two p'ien of Observations* thereon. The Great Learning carries on its front the evidence of being incomplete, but the student will not easily believe that the Doctrine of the Mean is so. I see no reason for calling its integrity in question, and no necessity therefore to recur to the ingenious device employed in the edition of the five *ching* published by the imperial authority of K'ang Hsî, to get over the difficulty which Wang Wei supposes. It there appears in two *p'ien*, of which we have the following account from the author of 'Supplemental Remarks upon the Four Books:'—'The proper course now is to consider the first twenty chapters in Chû Hsî's arrangement as making up the first *p'ien*, and the remaining thirteen as forming the second. In this way we retain the old form of the Treatise, and do not come into collision with the views of Chû. For this suggestion we are indebted to Lû Wang-châi' (an author of the Sung dynasty)[1].

SECTION IV.

ITS SCOPE AND VALUE.

1. The Doctrine of the Mean is a work not easy to understand. 'It first,' says the philosopher Ch'ăng, 'speaks of one principle; it next spreads this out and embraces all things; finally, it returns and gathers them up under the one principle. Unroll it, and it fills the universe; roll it up, and it retires and lies hid in secrecy[2].' There is this advantage, however, to the student of it, that, more than most other Chinese Treatises, it has a beginning, a middle, and an end. The first chapter stands to all that follows in the character of a text, containing several propositions of which we have the expansion or development. If that development were satisfactory, we should be able to bring our own minds *en rapport* with that of the author. Unfortunately it is not so. As a writer he belongs to the intuitional school more than to the logical. This is well put in the 'Continuation of the General Examination of Literary Monuments and Learned Men,'—'The philosopher Tsăng reached his conclusions by following in the train of things, watch-

---

[1] See the 四 書 拓 餘 說, art. 中 庸.   [2] See the Introductory note of Chû Hsî.

ing and examining; whereas Tsze-sze proceeds directly and reaches
to Heavenly virtue. His was a mysterious power of discernment,
approaching to that of Yen Hûi[1].' We must take the Book and
the author, however, as we have them, and get to their meaning, if
we can, by assiduous examination and reflection.

2. 'Man has received his *nature* from *Heaven*. Conduct in
accordance with that nature constitutes what is right and true,—
is a pursuing of the proper *Path*. The cultivation or regulation of
that path is what is called *Instruction*.' It is with these axioms
that the Treatise commences, and from such an introduction we
might expect that the writer would go on to unfold the various
principles of duty, derived from an analysis of man's moral constitution.

Confining himself, however, to the second axiom, he proceeds to
say that 'the path may not for an instant be left, and that the
superior man is cautious and careful in reference to what he does
not see, and fearful and apprehensive in reference to what he does
not hear. There is nothing more visible than what is secret, and
nothing more manifest than what is minute, and therefore the
superior man is watchful over his *aloneness*.' This is not all very
plain. Comparing it with the sixth chapter of Commentary in the
Great Learning, it seems to inculcate what is there called 'making
the thoughts sincere.' The passage contains an admonition about
equivalent to that of Solomon,—'Keep thy heart with all diligence,
for out of it are the issues of life.'

The next paragraph seems to speak of *the nature* and *the path*
under other names. 'While there are no movements of pleasure,
anger, sorrow, or joy, we have what may be called the state of
equilibrium. When those feelings have been moved, and they all
act in the due degree, we have what may be called the state of
harmony. This equilibrium is the great root of the world, and
this harmony is its universal path.' What is here called 'the state
of equilibrium,' is the same as the nature given by Heaven,
considered absolutely in itself, without deflection or inclination.
This nature acted on from without, and responding with the
various emotions, so as always 'to hit[2]' the mark with entire

---

[1] See the 續文獻通考, Bk. cxcix, art. 子思,-曾子得之于隨
事省察, 而子思之學, 則直達天德; 庶幾顏氏之
妙悟.   [2] 中節.

correctness, produces the state of harmony, and such harmonious response is the path along which all human activities should proceed.

Finally. 'Let the states of equilibrium and harmony exist in perfection, and a happy order will prevail throughout heaven and earth, and all things will be nourished and flourish.' Here we pass into the sphere of mystery and mysticism. The language, according to Chû Hsî, 'describes the meritorious achievements and transforming influence of sage and spiritual men in their highest extent.' From the path of duty, where we tread on solid ground, the writer suddenly raises us aloft on wings of air, and will carry us we know not where, and to we know not what.

3. The paragraphs thus presented, and which constitute Chû Hsî's first chapter, contain the sum of the whole Work. This is acknowledged by all;—by the critics who disown Chû Hsî's interpretations of it, as freely as by him[1]. Revolving them in my own mind often and long, I collect from them the following as the ideas of the author:—Firstly, Man has received from Heaven a moral nature by which he is constituted a law to himself; secondly, Over this nature man requires to exercise a jealous watchfulness; and thirdly, As he possesses it, absolutely and relatively, in perfection, or attains to such possession of it, he becomes invested with the highest dignity and power, and may say to himself— 'I am a god; yea, I sit in the seat of God.' I will not say here that there is impiety in the last of these ideas; but do we not have in them the same combination which we found in the Great Learning,—a combination of the ordinary and the extraordinary, the plain and the vague, which is very perplexing to the mind, and renders the Book unfit for the purposes of mental and moral discipline?

And here I may inquire whether we do right in calling the Treatise by any of the names which foreigners have hitherto used for it? In the note on the title, I have entered a little into this question. The Work is not at all what a reader must expect to find in what he supposes to be a treatise on 'The Golden Medium,' 'The Invariable Mean,' or 'The Doctrine of the Mean.' Those

---

[1] Compare Chû Hsî's language in his concluding note to the first chapter:—楊 氏 所 謂 一 篇 之 體 要, and Mâo Hsî-ho's, in his 中 庸 說, 卷 一, p. 11:— 此 中 庸 一 書 之 領 要 也.

names are descriptive only of a portion of it. Where the phrase
Chung Yung occurs in the quotations from Confucius, in nearly
every chapter from the second to the eleventh, we do well to translate it by 'the course of the Mean,' or some similar terms; but the
conception of it in Tsze-sze's mind was of a different kind, as the
preceding analysis of the first chapter sufficiently shows[1].

4. I may return to this point of the proper title for the Work
again, but in the meantime we must proceed with the analysis of
it.—The ten chapters from the second to the eleventh constitute
the second part, and in them Tsze-sze quotes the words of
Confucius, 'for the purpose,' according to Chû Hsî, 'of illustrating
the meaning of the first chapter.' Yet, as I have just intimated,
they do not to my mind do this. Confucius bewails the rarity of
the practice of the Mean, and graphically sets forth the difficulty of
it. 'The empire, with its component States and families, may be
ruled; dignities and emoluments may be declined; naked weapons
may be trampled under foot; but the course of the Mean can not
be attained to[2].' 'The knowing go beyond it, and the stupid do
not come up to it[3].' Yet some have attained to it. Shun did so,
humble and ever learning from people far inferior to himself[4]; and
Yen Hûi did so, holding fast whatever good he got hold of, and
never letting it go[5]. Tsze-lû thought the Mean could be taken by
storm, but Confucius taught him better[6]. And in fine, it is only
the sage who can fully exemplify the Mean[7].

All these citations do not throw any light on the ideas presented
in the first chapter. On the contrary, they interrupt the train of
thought. Instead of showing us how virtue, or the path of duty is
in accordance with our Heaven-given nature, they lead us to think
of it as a mean between two extremes. Each extreme may be a
violation of the law of our nature, but that is not made to appear.
Confucius's sayings would be in place in illustrating the doctrine of
the Peripatetics, 'which placed all virtue in a medium between
opposite vices[8].' Here in the Chung Yung of Tsze-sze I have
always felt them to be out of place.

5. In the twelfth chapter Tsze-sze speaks again himself, and
we seem at once to know the voice. He begins by saying that
'the way of the superior man reaches far and wide, and yet is

---

[1] In the version in 'The Sacred Books of the East,' I call the Treatise 'The State of
Equilibrium and Harmony.'   [2] Ch. ix.   [3] Ch. iv.   [4] Ch. vi.   [5] Ch. viii.
[6] Ch. x.   [7] Ch. xi.   [8] Encyclopædia Britannica, Preliminary Dissertations, p. 318,
eighth edition.

secret,' by which he means to tell us that the path of duty is to be pursued everywhere and at all times, while yet the secret spring and rule of it is near at hand, in the Heaven-conferred nature, the individual consciousness, with which no stranger can intermeddle. Chû Hsî, as will be seen in the notes, gives a different interpretation of the utterance. But the view which I have adopted is maintained convincingly by Mâo Hsî-ho in the second part of his 'Observations on the Chung Yung.' With this chapter commences the third part of the Work, which embraces also the eight chapters which follow. 'It is designed,' says Chû Hsî, 'to illustrate what is said in the first chapter that "the path may not be left."' But more than that one sentence finds its illustration here. Tsze-sze had reference in it also to what he had said—'The superior man does not wait till he sees things to be cautious, nor till he hears things to be apprehensive. There is nothing more visible than what is secret, and nothing more manifest than what is minute. Therefore, the superior man is watchful over himself when he is alone.'

It is in this portion of the Chung Yung that we find a good deal of moral instruction which is really valuable. Most of it consists of sayings of Confucius, but the sentiments of Tsze-sze himself in his own language are interspersed with them. The sage of China has no higher utterances than those which are given in the thirteenth chapter.—'The path is not far from man. When men try to pursue a course which is far from the common indications of consciousness, this course cannot be considered *the path*. In the Book of Poetry it is said—

> "In hewing an axe-handle, in hewing an axe-handle,
>   The pattern is not far off."

We grasp one axe-handle to hew the other, and yet if we look askance from the one to the other, we may consider them as apart. Therefore, the superior man governs men according to their nature, with what is proper to them; and as soon as they change what is wrong, he stops. When one cultivates to the utmost the moral principles of his nature, and exercises them on the principle of reciprocity, he is not far from the path. What you do not like when done to yourself, do not do to others.'

'In the way of the superior man there are four things, to none of which have I as yet attained.—To serve my father as I would require my son to serve me: to this I have not attained; to serve my elder brother as I would require my younger brother to serve me: to this I have not attained; to serve my ruler as I would require my minister to serve me: to this I have not attained; to set the example in behaving to a friend as I would require him to behave to me: to this I have not attained.   Earnest in practising the ordinary virtues, and careful in speaking about them; if in his practice he has anything defective, the superior man dares not but exert himself; and if in his words he has any excess, he dares not allow himself such license.   Thus his words have respect to his actions, and his actions have respect to his words;—is it not just an entire sincerity which marks the superior man?'

We have here the golden rule in its negative form expressly propounded:—'What you do not like when done to yourself, do not do to others.'   But in the paragraph which follows we have the rule virtually in its positive form.   Confucius recognises the duty of taking the initiative,—of behaving himself to others in the first instance as he would that they should behave to him.   There is a certain narrowness, indeed, in that the sphere of its operations seems to be confined to the relations of society, which are spoken of more at large in the twentieth chapter, but let us not grudge the tribute of our warm approbation to the sentiments.

This chapter is followed by two from Tsze-sze, to the effect that the superior man does what is proper in every change of his situation, always finding his rule in himself; and that in his practice there is an orderly advance from step to step,—from what is near to what is remote.   Then follow five chapters from Confucius:—the first, on the operation and influence of spiritual beings, to show 'the manifestness of what is minute, and the irrepressibleness of sincerity;' the second, on the filial piety of Shun, and how it was rewarded by Heaven with the throne, with enduring fame, and with long life; the third and fourth, on the kings Wăn and Wû, and the duke of Châu, celebrating them for their filial piety and other associate virtues; and the fifth, on the subject of government.   These chapters are interesting enough in themselves, but when I go back from them, and examine whether I have from them any better understanding of the paragraphs in the first chapter which they are said to illustrate, I do not find that I have.   Three of them, the seventeenth, eighteenth, and nineteenth, would be more in place in the Classic of Filial Piety than here in the Chung Yung.   The meaning of the

sixteenth is shadowy and undefined. After all the study which
I have directed to it, there are some points in reference to which I
have still doubts and difficulties.

The twentieth chapter, which concludes the third portion of the
Work, contains a full exposition of Confucius's views on government,
though professedly descriptive only of that of the kings Wăn and
Wû. Along with lessons proper for a ruler there are many also of
universal application, but the mingling of them perplexes the mind.
It tells us of ' the five duties of universal application,'— those between sovereign and minister, husband and wife, father and son, elder
and younger brother, and friends; of ' the three virtues by which
those duties are carried into effect,' namely, knowledge, benevolence,
and energy; and of ' the one thing, by which those virtues are
practised,' which is singleness or sincerity [1]. It sets forth in detail
the ' nine standard rules for the administration of government,' which
are 'the cultivation by the ruler of his own character; the honouring
men of virtue and talents; affection to his relatives; respect towards
the great ministers; kind and considerate treatment of the whole
body of officers; cherishing the mass of the people as children;
encouraging all classes of artizans; indulgent treatment of men
from a distance; and the kindly cherishing of the princes of the
States [2].' There are these and other equally interesting topics in this
chapter; but, as they are in the Work, they distract the mind,
instead of making the author's great object more clear to it, and
I will not say more upon them here.

6. Doubtless it was the mention of ' singleness,' or ' sincerity,' in
the twentieth chapter, which made Tsze-sze introduce it into this
Treatise, for from those terms he is able to go on to develope what
he intended in saying that 'if the states of Equilibrium and
Harmony exist in perfection, a happy order will prevail throughout
heaven and earth, and all things will be nourished and flourish.'
It is here, that now we are astonished at the audacity of the
writer's assertions, and now lost in vain endeavours to ascertain
his meaning. I have quoted the words of Confucius that it is
'singleness' by which the three virtues of knowledge, benevolence,
and energy are able to carry into practice the duties of universal
obligation. He says also that it is this same ' singleness' by which
' the nine standard rules of government' can be effectively carried
out [3]. This 'singleness' is merely a name for 'the states of Equilibrium

[1] Par. 8.   [2] Par. 12.   [3] Par. 15.

and Harmony existing in perfection.' It denotes a character absolutely and relatively good, wanting nothing in itself, and correct in all its outgoings. 'Sincerity' is another term for the same thing, and in speaking about it, Confucius makes a distinction between sincerity absolute and sincerity acquired. The former is born with some, and practised by them without any effort; the latter is attained by study, and practised by strong endeavour[1]. The former is 'the way of Heaven;' the latter is 'the way of men[2].' 'He who possesses sincerity,'—absolutely, that is,—'is he who without effort hits what is right, and apprehends without the exercise of thought; he is the sage who naturally and easily embodies the right way. He who attains to sincerity, is he who chooses what is good and firmly holds it fast. And to this attainment there are requisite the extensive study of what is good, accurate inquiry about it, careful reflection on it, the clear discrimination of it, and the earnest practice of it[3].' In these passages Confucius unhesitatingly enunciates his belief that there are some men who are absolutely perfect, who come into the world as we might conceive the first man was, when he was created by God 'in His own image,' full of knowledge and righteousness, and who grow up as we know that Christ did, 'increasing in wisdom and in stature.' He disclaimed being considered to be such an one himself[4], but the sages of China were such. And moreover, others who are not so naturally may make themselves to become so. Some will have to put forth more effort and to contend with greater struggles, but the end will be the possession of the knowledge and the achievement of the practice.

I need not say that these sentiments are contrary to the views of human nature which are presented in the Bible. The testimony of Revelation is that 'there is not a just man upon earth that doeth good and sinneth not.' 'If we say that we have no sin,' and in writing this term, I am thinking here not of sin against God, but, if we can conceive of it apart from that, of failures in regard to what ought to be in our regulation of ourselves, and in our behaviour to others;—'if we say that we have no sin, we deceive ourselves, and the truth is not in us.' This language is appropriate in the lips of the learned as well as in those of the ignorant, to the highest sage as to the lowest child of the soil. Neither the scriptures of God nor the experience of man know of individuals

[1] Par. 9.   [2] Par. 18.   [3] Pars. 18, 19.   [4] Ana. VII. xix.

absolutely perfect. The other sentiment that men can make themselves perfect is equally wide of the truth. Intelligence and goodness by no means stand to each other in the relation of cause and
effect. The sayings of Ovid, '*Video meliora proboque, deteriora
sequor,*' '*Nitimur in vetitum semper, cupimusque negata,*' are a
more correct expression of the facts of human consciousness and
conduct than the high-flown praises of Confucius.

7. But Tsze-sze adopts the dicta of his grandfather without
questioning them, and gives them forth in his own style at the
commencement of the fourth part of his Treatise. 'When we have
intelligence resulting from sincerity, this condition is to be ascribed
to nature; when we have sincerity resulting from intelligence,
this condition is to be ascribed to instruction. But given the
sincerity, and there shall be the intelligence; given the intelligence,
and there shall be the sincerity [1].'

Tsze-sze does more than adopt the dicta of Confucius. He applies
them in a way which the Sage never did, and which he would
probably have shrunk from doing. The sincere, or perfect man of
Confucius, is he who satisfies completely all the requirements of duty
in the various relations of society, and in the exercise of government; but the sincere man of Tsze-sze is a potency in the universe.
'Able to give its full development to his own nature, he can do the
same to the nature of other men. Able to give its full development to the nature of other men, he can give their full development
to the natures of animals and things. Able to give their full
development to the natures of creatures and things, he can assist
the transforming and nourishing powers of Heaven and Earth.
Able to assist the transforming and nourishing powers of Heaven
and Earth, he may with Heaven and Earth form a ternion [2].'
Such are the results of sincerity natural. The case below this—of
sincerity acquired, is as follows,—'The individual cultivates its
shoots. From these he can attain to the possession of sincerity.
This sincerity becomes apparent. From being apparent, it becomes
manifest. From being manifest, it becomes brilliant. Brilliant, it
affects others. Affecting others, they are changed by it. Changed
by it, they are transformed. It is only he who is possessed of
the most complete sincerity that can exist under heaven, who
can transform [3].' It may safely be affirmed, that when he thus
expressed himself, Tsze-sze understood neither what he said nor

[1] Ch. xxi.   [2] Ch. xxii.   [3] Ch. xxiii.

whereof he affirmed.   Mâo Hsî-ho and some other modern writers
explain away many of his predicates of sincerity, so that in their
hands they become nothing but extravagant hyperboles, but the
author himself would, I believe, have protested against such a
mode of dealing with his words.   True, his structures are castles
in the air, but he had no idea himself that they were so.

In the twenty-fourth chapter there is a ridiculous descent from
the sublimity of the two preceding.   We are told that the possessor
of entire sincerity is like a spirit and can foreknow, but the foreknowledge is only a judging by the milfoil and tortoise and other
auguries!   But the author recovers himself, and resumes his theme
about sincerity as conducting to self-completion and the completion
of other men and things, describing it also as possessing all the
qualities which can be predicated of Heaven and Earth.   Gradually
the subject is made to converge to the person of Confucius, who is
the ideal of the sage, as the sage is the ideal of humanity at large.
An old account of the object of Tsze-sze in the Chung Yung is that
he wrote it to celebrate the virtue of his grandfather[1].   He certainly
contrives to do this in the course of it.   The thirtieth, thirty-first,
and thirty-second chapters contain his eulogium, and never has any
other mortal been exalted in such terms.   'He may be compared to
heaven and earth in their supporting and containing, their overshadowing and curtaining all things; he may be compared to the
four seasons in their alternating progress, and to the sun and moon
in their successive shining.'   'Quick in apprehension, clear in
discernment, of far-reaching intelligence, and all-embracing knowledge, he was fitted to exercise rule; magnanimous, generous,
benign, and mild, he was fitted to exercise forbearance; impulsive,
energetic, strong, and enduring, he was fitted to maintain a firm
hold; self-adjusted, grave, never swerving from the Mean, and
correct, he was fitted to command reverence; accomplished, distinctive, concentrative, and searching, he was fitted to exercise
discrimination.'   'All-embracing and vast, he was like heaven;
deep and active as a fountain, he was like the abyss.'   'Therefore
his fame overspreads the Middle Kingdom, and extends to all
barbarous tribes.   Wherever ships and carriages reach; wherever
the strength of man penetrates; wherever the heavens overshadow

[1] 唐 陸 德 明 釋 文 謂 孔 子 之 孫, 子 思, 作 此 以 昭
明 祖 德; see the 中 庸 唐 說 一, p. 1.

and the earth sustains; wherever the sun and moon shine; wherever frosts and dews fall;—all who have blood and breath unfeignedly honour and love him. Hence it is said,—He is the equal of Heaven!' 'Who can know him but he who is indeed quick in apprehension, clear in discernment, of far-reaching intelligence, and all-embracing knowledge, possessing all heavenly virtue?'

8. We have arrived at the concluding chapter of the Work, in which the author, according to Chû Hsî, 'having carried his descriptions to the highest point in the preceding chapters, turns back and examines the source of his subject; and then again from the work of the learner, free from all selfishness and watchful over himself when he is alone, he carries out his description, till by easy steps he brings it to the consummation of the whole world tranquillized by simple and sincere reverentialness. He moreover eulogizes its mysteriousness, till he speaks of it at last as without sound or smell[1].' Between the first and last chapters there is a correspondency, and each of them may be considered as a summary of the whole treatise. The difference between them is, that in the first a commencement is made with the mention of Heaven as the conferrer of man's nature, while in this the progress of man in virtue is traced, step by step, till at last it is equal to that of High Heaven.

9. I have thus in the preceding paragraphs given a general and somewhat copious review of this Work. My object has been to seize, if I could, the train of thought and to hold it up to the reader. Minor objections to it, arising from the confused use of terms and singular applications of passages from the older Classics, are noticed in the notes subjoined to the translation. I wished here that its scope should be seen, and the means be afforded of judging how far it is worthy of the high character attributed to it. 'The relish of it,' says the younger Ch'ăng, 'is inexhaustible. The whole of it is solid learning. When the skilful reader has explored it with delight till he has apprehended it, he may carry it into practice all his life, and will find that it cannot be exhausted[2].'

My own opinion of it is less favourable. The names by which it has been called in translations of it have led to misconceptions of its character. Were it styled 'The states of Equilibrium and Harmony,' we should be prepared to expect something strange and probably extravagant. Assuredly we should expect nothing more

---

[1] See the concluding note by Chû Hsî.   [2] See the Introductory note below.

strange or extravagant than what we have. It begins sufficiently well, but the author has hardly enunciated his preliminary apophthegms, when he conducts into an obscurity where we can hardly grope our way, and when we emerge from that, it is to be bewildered by his gorgeous but unsubstantial pictures of sagely perfection. He has eminently contributed to nourish the pride of his countrymen. He has exalted their sages above all that is called God or is worshipped, and taught the masses of the people that with them they have need of nothing from without. In the meantime it is antagonistic to Christianity. By-and-by, when Christianity has prevailed in China, men will refer to it as a striking proof how their fathers by their wisdom knew neither God nor themselves.

CHAPTER V.

CONFUCIUS AND HIS IMMEDIATE DISCIPLES.

SECTION I.

LIFE OF CONFUCIUS.

1. 'And have you foreigners surnames as well?' This question has often been put to me by Chinese. It marks the ignorance His ancestry. which belongs to the people of all that is external to themselves, and the pride of antiquity which enters largely as an element into their character. If such a pride could in any case be justified, we might allow it to the family of the K'ung, the descendants of Confucius. In the reign of K'ang-hsî, twenty-one centuries and a half after the death of the sage, they amounted to eleven thousand males. But their ancestry is carried back through a period of equal extent, and genealogical tables are common, in which the descent of Confucius is traced down from Hwang-tî, in whose reign the cycle was invented, B.C. 2637 [1].

The more moderate writers, however, content themselves with exhibiting his ancestry back to the commencement of the Châu dynasty, B.C. 1121. Among the relatives of the tyrant Châu, the last emperor of the Yin dynasty, was an elder brother, by a concubine, named Ch'î [2], who is celebrated by Confucius, Ana. XVIII. i, under the title of the viscount of Wei. Foreseeing the impending ruin of their family, Ch'î withdrew from the court; and subsequently he was invested by the emperor Ch'ăng, the second of the house of Châu, with the principality of Sung, which embraced the eastern portion of the present province of Ho-nan, that he might there continue the sacrifices to the sovereigns of Yin. Ch'î was followed as duke of Sung by a younger brother, in whose line the succession continued. His great-grandson, the duke Min [3], was

---

[1] See Mémoires concernant les Chinois, Tome XII, p. 447 *et seq.* Father Amiot states, p. 501, that he had seen the representative of the family, who succeeded to the dignity of 衍聖公 in the ninth year of Ch'ien-lung, A. D. 1744. The last duke, not the present, was visited in our own time by the late Dr. Williamson and Mr. Consul Markham. It is hardly necessary that I should say here, that the name Confucius is merely the Chinese characters 孔夫子 (K'ung Fû-tsze, 'The master K'ung') Latinized.   [2] 啟.   [3] 愍公.

followed, B.C. 908, by a younger brother, leaving, however, two sons, Fû-fû Ho[1] and Fang-sze[2]. Fû Ho[3] resigned his right to the dukedom in favour of Fang-sze, who put his uncle to death in B.C. 893, and became master of the State. He is known as the duke Lî[4], and to his elder brother belongs the honour of having the sage among his descendants.

Three descents from Fû Ho, we find Chăng K'âo-fû[5], who was a distinguished officer under the dukes Tâi, Wû, and Hsüan[6] (B.C. 799–728). He is still celebrated for his humility, and for his literary tastes. We have accounts of him as being in communication with the Grand-historiographer of the kingdom, and engaged in researches about its ancient poetry, thus setting an example of one of the works to which Confucius gave himself[7]. K'âo gave birth to K'ung-fû Chiâ[8], from whom the surname of K'ung took its rise. Five generations had now elapsed since the dukedom was held in the direct line of his ancestry, and it was according to the rule in such cases that the branch should cease its connexion with the ducal stem, and merge among the people under a new surname. K'ung Chiâ was Master of the Horse in Sung, and an officer of well-known loyalty and probity. Unfortunately for himself, he had a wife of surpassing beauty, of whom the chief minister of the State, by name Hwâ Tû[9], happened on one occasion to get a glimpse. Determined to possess her, he commenced a series of intrigues, which ended, B.C. 710, in the murder of Chiâ and of the ruling duke Shang[10]. At the same time, Tû secured the person of the lady, and hastened to his palace with the prize, but on the way she had strangled herself with her girdle.

An enmity was thus commenced between the two families of K'ung and Hwâ which the lapse of time did not obliterate, and the latter being the more powerful of the two, Chiâ's great-grandson withdrew into the State of Lû to avoid their persecution. There he was appointed commandant of the city of Fang[11], and is known

---

[1] 弗父何.　　　[2] 鮒 (al. 方) 祀.　　　[3] I drop here the 父 (second tone), which seems to have been used in those times in a manner equivalent to our Mr.

[4] 厲公.　　　[5] 正考甫; 甫 is used in the same way as 父; see note 3.

[6] 戴, 武, 宣, 三公.　　　[7] See the 魯語, and 商頌詩序; quoted in Chiang Yung's (工 永) Life of Confucius, which forms a part of the 鄉黨圖考.

[8] 孔父嘉.　　　[9] 華督.　　　[10] 殤公.　　　[11] 防.

in history by the name of Fang-shû[1]. Fang-shû gave birth to Po-hsiâ[2], and from him came Shû-liang Hêh[3], the father of Confucius. Hêh appears in the history of the times as a soldier of great prowess and daring bravery. In the year B.C. 562, when serving at the siege of a place called Pêh-yang[4], a party of the assailants made their way in at a gate which had purposely been left open, and no sooner were they inside than the portcullis was dropped. Hêh was just entering; and catching the massive structure with both his hands, he gradually by dint of main strength raised it and held it up, till his friends had made their escape.

Thus much on the ancestry of the sage. Doubtless he could trace his descent in the way which has been indicated up to the imperial house of Yin, nor was there one among his ancestors during the rule of Châu to whom he could not refer with satisfaction. They had been ministers and soldiers of Sung and Lû, all men of worth, and in Chăng K'âo, both for his humility and literary researches, Confucius might have special complacency.

2. Confucius was the child of Shû-liang Hêh's old age. The soldier had married in early life, but his wife brought him only daughters,—to the number of nine, and no son. By a concubine he had a son, named Măng-p'î, and also Po-nî[5], who proved a cripple, so that, when he was over seventy years, Hêh sought a second wife in the Yen family[6], from which came subsequently Yen Hui, the favourite disciple of his son. There were three daughters in the family, the youngest being named Chăng-tsâi[7]. Their father said to them, 'Here is the commandant of Tsâu. His father and grandfather were only scholars, but his ancestors before them were descendants of the sage sovereigns. He is a man ten feet high[8], and of extraordinary prowess, and I am very desirous of his alliance. Though he is old and austere, you need have no misgivings about him. Which of you three will be his wife?' The two elder daughters were silent, but Chăng-tsâi said, 'Why do you ask us, father? It is for you to determine.' 'Very well,' said her father in reply, 'you will do.' Chăng-tsâi, accordingly, became Hêh's wife, and in due time gave

From his birth to his first public employments.

B.C. 551–531.

---

[1] 防 叔.   [2] 伯 夏.   [3] 叔 梁 紇.   [4] 偪 陽.   [5] 孟 皮,
一 字 伯 尼.   [6] 顏 氏.   [7] 徵 在.   [8] 其 人, 身 長 十 尺.
See, on the length of the ancient foot, Ana. VIII. vi, but the point needs a more sifting investigation than it has yet received.

birth to Confucius, who received the name of Ch'iû, and was subsequently styled Chung-nî[1]. The event happened on the twenty-first day of the tenth month of the twenty-first year of the duke Hsiang, of Lû, being the twentieth year of the emperor Ling, B.C. 552 [2]. The birth-place was in the district of Tsâu [3], of which Hêh was the governor. It was somewhere within the limits of the present department of Yen-châu in Shan-tung, but the honour of being the exact spot is claimed for two places in two different districts of the department.

The notices which we have of Confucius's early years are very scanty. When he was in his third year his father died. It is related of him, that as a boy he used to play at the arrangement of

[1] 名邱, 字仲尼. The legends say that Chăng-tsâi, fearing lest she should not have a son, in consequence of her husband's age, privately ascended the Nî-ch'iû hill to pray for the boon, and that when she had obtained it, she commemorated the fact in the names—Ch'iû and Chung-nî. But the cripple, Măng-p'î, had previously been styled Po-nî. There was some reason, previous to Confucius's birth, for using the term *nî* in the family. As might be expected, the birth of the sage is surrounded with many prodigious occurrences. One account is, that the husband and wife prayed together for a son in a dell of mount Nî. As Chăng-tsâi went up the hill, the leaves of the trees and plants all erected themselves, and bent downwards on her return. That night she dreamt the black *Tî* appeared, and said to her, 'You shall have a son, a sage, and you must bring him forth in a hollow mulberry tree.' One day during her pregnancy, she fell into a dreamy state, and saw five old men in the hall, who called themselves the essences of the five planets, and led an animal which looked like a small cow with one horn, and was covered with scales like a dragon. This creature knelt before Chăng-tsâi, and cast forth from its mouth a slip of jade, on which was the inscription,—'The son of the essence of water shall succeed to the decaying Châu, and be a throneless king.' Chăng-tsâi tied a piece of embroidered ribbon about its horn, and the vision disappeared. When Hêh was told of it, he said, 'The creature must be the Ch'î-lin.' As her time drew near, Chăng-tsâi asked her husband if there was any place in the neighbourhood called 'the hollow mulberry tree.' He told her there was a dry cave in the south hill, which went by that name. Then she said, 'I will go and be confined there.' Her husband was surprised, but when made acquainted with her former dream, he made the necessary arrangements. On the night when the child was born, two dragons came and kept watch on the left and right of the hill, and two spirit-ladies appeared in the air, pouring out fragrant odours, as if to bathe Chăng-tsâi ; and as soon as the birth took place, a spring of clear warm water bubbled up from the floor of the cave, which dried up again when the child had been washed in it. The child was of an extraordinary appearance ; with a mouth like the sea, ox lips, a dragon's back, &c. &c. On the top of his head was a remarkable formation, in consequence of which he was named Ch'iû, &c. See the 列國志, Bk. lxxviii.—Sze-mâ Ch'ien seems to make Confucius to have been illegitimate, saying that Hêh and Miss Yen cohabited in the wilderness (野合). Chiang Yung says that the phrase has reference simply to the disparity of their ages.

[2] Sze-mâ Ch'ien says that Confucius was born in the twenty-second year of duke Hsiang, B.C. 550. He is followed by Chû Hsî in the short sketch of Confucius's life prefixed to the Lun Yü, and by 'The Annals of the Empire' (歷代統紀表), published with imperial sanction in the reign of Chiâ-ch'ing. (To this latter work I have generally referred for my dates.) The year assigned in the text above rests on the authority of Kû-liang and Kung-yang, the two commentators on the Ch'un-Ch'iû. With regard to the month, however, the tenth is that assigned by Kû-liang, while Kung-yang names the eleventh.

[3] Tsâu is written 耶, 鄹, 陬, and 鄒.

sacrificial vessels, and at postures of ceremony. Of his schooling we have no reliable account. There is a legend, indeed, that at seven he went to school to Yen P'ing-chung[1], but it must be rejected as P'ing-chung belonged to the State of Ch'î. He tells us himself that at fifteen he bent his mind to learning[2]; but the condition of the family was one of poverty. At a subsequent period, when people were astonished at the variety of his knowledge, he explained it by saying, 'When I was young, my condition was low, and therefore I acquired my ability in many things; but they were mean matters[3].'

When he was nineteen, he married a lady from the State of Sung, of the Chien-kwan family[4], and in the following year his son Lî was born. On the occasion of this event, the duke Châo sent him a present of a couple of carp. It was to signify his sense of his prince's favour, that he called his son Lî (The Carp), and afterwards gave him the designation of Po-yü[5] (Fish Primus). No mention is made of the birth of any other children, though we know, from Ana. V. i, that he had at least one daughter. We know also, from an inscription on her grave, that he had one other daughter, who died when she was quite young. The fact of the duke of Lû's sending him a gift on the occasion of Lî's birth, shows that he was not unknown, but was already commanding public attention and the respect of the great.

It was about this time, probably in the year after his marriage, that Confucius took his first public employment, as keeper of the stores of grain[6], and in the following year he was put in charge of the public fields and lands[7]. Mencius adduces these employments in illustration of his doctrine that the superior man may at times take office on account of his poverty, but must confine himself in such a case to places of small emolument, and aim at nothing but the discharge of their humble duties. According to him, Confucius, as keeper of stores, said, 'My calculations must all be right:—that is all I have to care about;' and when in charge of the public fields, he said, 'The oxen and sheep must be fat and strong and

---

[1] 晏平仲.   [2] Ana. II. iv.   [3] Ana. IX. vi.   [4] 娶宋之开官氏.
[5] 名曰鯉，而字伯魚.   [6] 爲委吏. This is Mencius's account.
Sze-mâ Ch'ien says 嘗爲季氏吏, but his subsequent words 料量平 show
that the office was the same.   [7] Mencius calls this office 乘田, while Sze-mâ Ch'ien
says 爲司職吏.

superior :—that is all I have to care about[1].' It does not appear whether these offices were held by Confucius in the direct employ-ment of the State, or as a dependent of the Chî family in whose jurisdiction he lived. The present of the carp from the duke may incline us to suppose the former.

3. In his twenty-second year, Confucius commenced his labours as a public teacher, and his house became a resort for young and inquiring spirits, who wished to learn the doctrines of antiquity.

Commencement of his labours as a teacher. The death of his mother.
B. C. 531–527.

However small the fee his pupils were able to afford, he never refused his instructions[2]. All that he re-quired, was an ardent desire for improvement, and some degree of capacity. 'I do not open up the truth,' he said, 'to one who is not eager to get knowledge, nor help out any one who is not anxious to explain himself. When I have presented one corner of a subject to any one, and he cannot from it learn the other three, I do not repeat my lesson[3].'

His mother died in the year B.C. 527, and he resolved that her body should lie in the same grave with that of his father, and that their common resting-place should be in Fang, the first home of the K'ung in Lû. But here a difficulty presented itself. His father's coffin had been for twenty years where it had first been deposited, off the road of *The Five Fathers*, in the vicinity of Tsâu :—would it be right in him to move it ? He was relieved from this perplexity by an old woman of the neighbourhood, who told him that the coffin had only just been put into the ground, as a temporary arrangement, and not regularly buried. On learning this, he carried his purpose into execution. Both coffins were conveyed to Fang, and put in the ground together, with no intervening space between them, as was the custom in some States. And now came a new perplexity. He said to himself, 'In old times, they had graves, but raised no tumulus over them. But I am a man, who belongs equally to the north and the south, the east and the west. I must have something by which I can remember the place.' Accordingly he raised a mound, four feet high, over the grave, and returned home, leaving a party of his disciples to see everything properly completed. In the meantime there came on a heavy storm of rain, and it was a considerable time before the disciples joined him. 'What makes you so late ?' he asked. 'The grave in Fang fell down,' they said. He made no reply, and they repeated their

---

[1] Mencius, V. Pt. II. v. 4.　　　[2] Ana. VII. vii.　　　[3] Ana. VII. viii.

answer three times, when he burst into tears, and said, 'Ah! they did not make their graves so in antiquity[1].'

Confucius mourned for his mother the regular period of three years,—three years nominally, but in fact only twenty-seven months. Five days after the mourning was expired, he played on his lute, but could not sing. It required other five days before he could accompany an instrument with his voice[2].

Some writers have represented Confucius as teaching his disciples important lessons from the manner in which he buried his mother, and having a design to correct irregularities in the ordinary funeral ceremonies of the time. These things are altogether 'without book.' We simply have a dutiful son paying the last tribute of affection to a good parent. In one point he departs from the ancient practice, raising a mound over the grave, and when the fresh earth gives way from a sudden rain, he is moved to tears, and seems to regret his innovation. This sets Confucius vividly before us,—a man of the past as much as of the present, whose own natural feelings were liable to be hampered in their development by the traditions of antiquity which he considered sacred. It is important, however, to observe the reason which he gave for rearing the mound. He had in it a presentiment of much of his future course. He was 'a man of the north, the south, the east, and the west.' He might not confine himself to any one State. He would travel, and his way might be directed to some 'wise ruler,' whom his counsels would conduct to a benevolent sway that would break forth on every side till it transformed the empire.

4. When the mourning for his mother was over, Confucius remained in Lû, but in what special capacity we do not know.

He learns music; visits the court of Châu; and returns to Lû.
B. C. 526–517.

Probably he continued to encourage the resort of inquirers to whom he communicated instruction, and pursued his own researches into the history, literature, and institutions of the empire. In the year B. C. 525, the chief of the small State of T'an[3], made his appearance at the court of Lû, and discoursed in a wonderful manner, at a feast given to him by the duke, about the names which the most ancient sovereigns, from Hwang-tî downwards, gave to their

[1] Lî Chî, II. Sect. I. i. 10; Sect. II. iii. 30; Pt. I. i. 6. See also the discussion of those passages in Chiang Yung's 'Life of Confucius.'   [2] Lî Chî, II. Sect. I. i. 23.   [3] See the Ch'un Ch'iû, under the seventh year of duke Châo,—秋, 郯 子 來 朝.

ministers.   The sacrifices to the emperor Shâo-hâo, the next in
descent from Hwang-tî, were maintained in T'an, so that the chief
fancied that he knew all about the abstruse subject on which
he discoursed.   Confucius, hearing about the matter, waited on
the visitor, and learned from him all that he had to communicate [1].

To the year B.C. 525, when Confucius was twenty-nine years old,
is referred his studying music under a famous master of the name
of Hsiang [2].   He was approaching his thirtieth year when, as he
tells us, 'he stood [3]' firm, that is, in his convictions on the subjects
of learning to which he had bent his mind fifteen years before.   Five
years more, however, were still to pass by, before the anticipation
mentioned in the conclusion of the last paragraph began to receive
its fulfilment [4], though we may conclude from the way in which it
was brought about that he was growing all the time in the
estimation of the thinking minds in his native State.

In the twenty-fourth year of duke Châo, B.C. 518, one of the
principal ministers of Lû, known by the name of Măng Hsî, died.
Seventeen years before, he had painfully felt his ignorance of
ceremonial observances, and had made it his subsequent business to
make himself acquainted with them.   On his deathbed, he addressed
his chief officer, saying, 'A knowledge of propriety is the stem
of a man.   Without it he has no means of standing firm.   I have
heard that there is one K'ung Ch'iû, who is thoroughly versed in it.
He is a descendant of sages, and though the line of his family was
extinguished in Sung, among his ancestors there were Fû-fû Ho,
who resigned the State to his brother, and Chang K'âo-fû, who was
distinguished for his humility.   Tsang Hêh has observed that if
sage men of intelligent virtue do not attain to eminence, distinguished men are sure to appear among their posterity.   His words are
now to be verified, I think, in K'ung Ch'iû.   After my death, you must

---

[1] This rests on the respectable authority of Tso Ch'iû-ming's annotations on the Ch'un
Ch'iû, but I must consider it apocryphal.   The legend-writers have fashioned a journey to
T'an.   The slightest historical intimation becomes a text with them, on which they enlarge to
the glory of the sage.   Amiot has reproduced and expanded their romancings, and others,
such as Pauthier (Chine, pp. 121-183) and Thornton (History of China, vol. i. pp. 151-215),
have followed in his wake.   [2] 師襄. See the 'Narratives of the School,' 卷三,
art. 辯樂解; but the account there given is not more credible than the chief of
T'an's expositions.   [3] Ana. II. iv.   [4] The journey to Châu is placed by Sze-mâ Ch'ien
before Confucius's holding of his first official employments, and Chû Hsî and most other
writers follow him.   It is a great error, and arisen from a misunderstanding of the passage
from the 左氏傳 upon the subject.

tell Ho-chî to go and study proprieties under him[1].' In consequence
of this charge, Ho-chî[2], Măng Hsî's son, who appears in the Analects
under the name of Măng Î[3], and a brother, or perhaps only a
near relative, named Nan-kung Chăng-shû[4], became disciples of
Confucius. Their wealth and standing in the State gave him a
position which he had not had before, and he told Chăng-shû of a wish
which he had to visit the court of Châu, and especially to confer on
the subject of ceremonies and music with Lâo Tan. Chăng-shû
represented the matter to the duke Ch'âo, who put a carriage and
a pair of horses at Confucius's disposal for the expedition[5].

At this time the court of Châu was in the city of Lo[6], in the
present department of Ho-nan of the province of the same name.
The reigning sovereign is known by the title of Chăng[7], but the
sovereignty was little more than nominal. The state of China was
then analogous to that of one of the European kingdoms during the
prevalence of the feudal system. At the commencement of the
dynasty, the various states of the kingdom had been assigned to
the relatives and adherents of the reigning family. There were
thirteen principalities of greater note, and a large number of
smaller dependencies. During the vigorous youth of the dynasty,
the sovereign or lord paramount exercised an effective control over
the various chiefs, but with the lapse of time there came weakness
and decay. The chiefs—corresponding somewhat to the European
dukes, earls, marquises, barons, &c.—quarrelled and warred among
themselves, and the stronger among them barely acknowledged
their subjection to the sovereign. A similar condition of things
prevailed in each particular State. There there were hereditary
ministerial families, who were continually encroaching on the
authority of their rulers, and the heads of those families again were
frequently hard pressed by their inferior officers. Such was the
state of China in Confucius's time. The reader must have it clearly
before him, if he would understand the position of the sage, and
the reforms which, we shall find, it was subsequently his object to
introduce.

Arrived at Châu, he had no intercourse with the court or any of

---

[1] See 左氏傳, 昭公七年.   [2] 何忌.   [3] 孟懿子.
[4] 南宮敬叔.   [5] The 家語 makes Chăng-shû accompany Confucius to Châu. It
is difficult to understand this, if Chăng-shû were really a son of Măng Hsî who had died that
year.   [6] 洛.   [7] 敬王 (B.C. 519-475).

the principal ministers. He was there not as a politician, but as an inquirer about the ceremonies and maxims of the founders of the existing dynasty. Lâo Tan [1], whom he had wished to see, generally acknowledged as the founder of the Tâoists, or Rationalistic sect (so called), which has maintained its ground in opposition to the followers of Confucius, was then a curator of the royal library. They met and freely interchanged their views, but no reliable account of their conversations has been preserved. In the fifth Book of the Lî Chî, which is headed 'The philosopher Tsăng asked,' Confucius refers four times to the views of Lâo-tsze on certain points of funeral ceremonies, and in the 'Narratives of the School,' Book XXIV, he tells Chî K'ang what he had heard from him about 'The Five Tîs,' but we may hope their conversation turned also on more important subjects. Sze-mâ Ch'ien, favourable to Lâo-tsze, makes him lecture his visitor in the following style :—'Those whom you talk about are dead, and their bones are mouldered to dust ; only their words remain. When the superior man gets his time, he mounts aloft ; but when the time is against him, he moves as if his feet were entangled. I have heard that a good merchant, though he has rich treasures deeply stored, appears as if he were poor, and that the superior man whose virtue is complete, is yet to outward seeming stupid. Put away your proud air and many desires, your insinuating habit and wild will [2]. These are of no advantage to you. This is all which I have to tell you.' On the other hand, Confucius is made to say to his disciples, ' I know how birds can fly, how fishes can swim, and how animals can run. But the runner may be snared, the swimmer may be hooked, and the flyer may be shot by the arrow. But there is the dragon. I cannot tell how he mounts on the wind through the clouds, and rises to heaven. To-day I have seen Lâo-tsze, and can only compare him to the dragon [3].'

While at Lo, Confucius walked over the grounds set apart for the great sacrifices to Heaven and Earth ; inspected the pattern of the Hall of Light, built to give audience in to the princes of the kingdom; and examined all the arrangements of the ancestral temple and the court. From the whole he received a profound

---

[1] According to Sze-mâ Ch'ien, Tan was the posthumous epithet of this individual, whose surname was Lî (李), name R (耳), and designation Po-yang (伯陽).   [2] 逸態 與淫志.   [3] See the 史記, 列傳第三, and compare the remarks attributed to Lâo-tsze in the account of the K'ung family near the beginning.

impression.   'Now,' said he with a sigh, 'I know the sage wisdom
of the duke of Châu, and how the House of Châu attained to the
royal sway[1].'   On the walls of the Hall of Light were paintings
of the ancient sovereigns from Yâo and Shun downwards, their
characters appearing in the representations of them, and words of
praise or warning being appended.   There was also a picture of the
duke of Châu sitting with his infant nephew, the king Ch'ăng,
upon his knees, to give audience to all the princes.   Confucius surveyed the scene with silent delight, and then said to his followers,
'Here you see how Châu became so great.   As we use a glass to
examine the forms of things, so must we study antiquity in order
to understand the present time[2].'   In the hall of the ancestral
temple, there was a metal statue of a man with three clasps upon
his mouth, and his back covered over with an enjoyable homily on
the duty of keeping a watch upon the lips.   Confucius turned to
his disciples and said, 'Observe it, my children.   These words are
true, and commend themselves to our feelings[3].'

About music he made inquiries at Ch'ang Hung, to whom the
following remarks are attributed :—'I have observed about Chung-
nî many marks of a sage.   He has river eyes and a dragon forehead,
—the very characteristics of Hwang-tî.   His arms are long, his
back is like a tortoise, and he is nine feet six inches in height,—the
very semblance of T'ang the Completer.   When he speaks, he praises
the ancient kings.   He moves along the path of humility and
courtesy.   He has heard of every subject, and retains with a strong
memory.   His knowledge of things seems inexhaustible.—Have we
not in him the rising of a sage[4]?'

I have given these notices of Confucius at the court of Châu,
more as being the only ones I could find, than because I put much
faith in them.   He did not remain there long, but returned the
same year to Lû, and continued his work of teaching.   His fame
was greatly increased; disciples came to him from different parts,
till their number amounted to three thousand.   Several of those
who have come down to us as the most distinguished among his
followers, however, were yet unborn, and the statement just given
may be considered as an exaggeration.   We are not to conceive of
the disciples as forming a community, and living together.   Parties

---

[1] [2] [3] See the 家語, 卷二, art. 觀周.   [4] Quoted by Chiang Yung from
the 'Narratives of the School.'

of them may have done so. We shall find Confucius hereafter always moving amid a company of admiring pupils; but the greater number must have had their proper avocations and ways of living, and would only resort to the Master, when they wished specially to ask his counsel or to learn of him.

5. In the year succeeding the return to Lû, that State fell into great confusion. There were three Families in it, all connected irregularly with the ducal House, which had long kept the rulers in a condition of dependency. They appear frequently

He withdraws to Chî, and returns to Lû the following year.
B.C. 515, 516.

in the Analects as the Chî clan, the Shû, and the Măng; and while Confucius freely spoke of their usurpations [1], he was a sort of dependent of the Chî family, and appears in frequent communication with members of all the three. In the year B.C. 517, the duke Châo came to open hostilities with them, and being worsted, fled into Ch'î, the State adjoining Lû on the north. Thither Confucius also repaired, that he might avoid the prevailing disorder of his native State. Ch'î was then under the government of a ruler (in rank a marquis, but historically called duke), afterwards styled Ching [2], who 'had a thousand teams, each of four horses, but on the day of his death the people did not praise him for a single virtue [3].' His chief minister, however, was Yen Ying [4], a man of considerable ability and worth. At his court the music of the ancient sage-emperor, Shun, originally brought to Ch'î from the State of Ch'ăn [5], was still preserved.

According to the 'Narratives of the School,' an incident occurred on the way to Ch'î, which I may transfer to these pages as a good specimen of the way in which Confucius turned occurring matters to account, in his intercourse with his disciples. As he was passing by the side of the Tâi mountain, there was a woman weeping and wailing by a grave. Confucius bent forward in his carriage, and after listening to her for some time, sent Tsze-lû to ask the cause of her grief. 'You weep, as if you had experienced sorrow upon sorrow,' said Tsze-lû. The woman replied, 'It is so. My husband's father was killed here by a tiger, and my husband also; and now my son has met the same fate.' Confucius asked her why she did not remove from the place, and on her answering, 'There is here no oppressive government,' he turned to his disciples, and said, 'My

---

[1] See Analects, III. i. ii, *et al.*　[2] 景公.　[3] Ana. XVI. xii.　[4] 晏嬰. This is the same who was afterwards styled 晏平仲.　[5] 陳.

children, remember this. Oppressive government is fiercer than a tiger[1].'

As soon as he crossed the border from Lû, we are told he discovered from the gait and manners of a boy, whom he saw carrying a pitcher, the influence of the sages' music, and told the driver of his carriage to hurry on to the capital[2]. Arrived there, he heard the strain, and was so ravished with it, that for three months he did not know the taste of flesh. 'I did not think,' he said, 'that music could have been made so excellent as this[3].' The duke Ching was pleased with the conferences which he had with him[4], and proposed to assign to him the town of Lin-ch'iû, from the revenues of which he might derive a sufficient support; but Confucius refused the gift, and said to his disciples, 'A superior man will only receive reward for services which he has done. I have given advice to the duke Ching, but he has not yet obeyed it, and now he would endow me with this place! Very far is he from understanding me[5]!'

On one occasion the duke asked about government, and received the characteristic reply, 'There is government when the ruler is ruler, and the minister is minister; when the father is father, and the son is son[6].' I say that the reply is characteristic. Once, when Tsze-lû asked him what he would consider the first thing to be done if entrusted with the government of a State, Confucius answered, 'What is necessary is to rectify names[7].' The disciple thought the reply wide of the mark, but it was substantially the same with what he said to the marquis Ching. There is a sufficient foundation in nature for government in the several relations of society, and if those be maintained and developed according to their relative significancy, it is sure to obtain. This was a first principle in the political ethics of Confucius.

Another day the duke got to a similar inquiry the reply that the art of government lay in an economical use of the revenues; and being pleased, he resumed his purpose of retaining the philosopher in his State, and proposed to assign to him the fields of Nî-ch'î. His

---

[1] See the 家語, 卷四, art. 正論解. I have translated, however, from the Lî Chî, II. Sect. II. iii. 10, where the same incident is given, with some variations, and without saying when or where it occurred.   [2] See the 說苑, 卷十九, p. 13.   [3] Ana. VII. xiii.   [4] Some of these are related in the 'Narratives of the School;'—about the burning of the ancestral shrine of the sovereign 釐, and a one-footed bird which appeared hopping and flapping its wings in Ch'î. They are plainly fabulous, though quoted in proof of Confucius's sage wisdom. This reference to them is more than enough.   [5] 家語, 卷二, 六本.
[6] Ana. XII. xi.   [7] Ana. XIII. iii.

chief minister Yen Ying dissuaded him from the purpose, saying, 'Those scholars are impracticable, and cannot be imitated. They are haughty and conceited of their own views, so that they will not be content in inferior positions. They set a high value on all funeral ceremonies, give way to their grief, and will waste their property on great burials, so that they would only be injurious to the common manners. This Mr. K'ung has a thousand peculiarities. It would take generations to exhaust all that he knows about the ceremonies of going up and going down. This is not the time to examine into his rules of propriety. If you, prince, wish to employ him to change the customs of Ch'î, you will not be making the people your primary consideration [1].'

I had rather believe that these were not the words of Yen Ying, but they must represent pretty correctly the sentiments of many of the statesmen of the time about Confucius. The duke of Ch'î got tired ere long of having such a monitor about him, and observed, 'I cannot treat him as I would the chief of the Chî family. I will treat him in a way between that accorded to the chief of the Chî, and that given to the chief of the Măng family.' Finally he said, 'I am old; I cannot use his doctrines [2].' These observations were made directly to Confucius, or came to his hearing [3]. It was not consistent with his self-respect to remain longer in Ch'î, and he returned to Lû [4].

6. Returned to Lû, he remained for the long period of about fifteen years without being engaged in any official employment. It was a time, indeed, of great disorder. The duke Châo continued a refugee in Ch'î, the government being in the hands of the great Families, up to his death in B.C. 510, on which event the rightful heir was set aside, and another member of the ducal House, known to us by the title of Ting [5], substituted in his place. The ruling authority of the principality became thus still more enfeebled than it had been before, and, on the other hand, the chiefs of the Chî, the Shû, and the Măng, could hardly keep their ground against their own officers. Of those latter, the two most conspicuous were Yang Hû [6], called also Yang Ho [7], and

He remains without office in Lû, B.C. 516–501.

---

[1] See the 史 記, 孔 子 世 家, p. 2.   [2] Ana. XVIII. iii.   [3] Sze-mâ Ch'ien makes the first observation to have been addressed directly to Confucius.   [4] According to the above account Confucius was only once, and for a portion of two years, in Ch'î. For the refutation of contrary accounts, see Chiang Yung's Life of the Sage.   [5] 定 公.

[6] 陽 虎.   [7] 陽 貨.

Kung-shan Fû-zâo [1]. At one time Chî Hwan, the most powerful of the chiefs, was kept a prisoner by Yang Hû, and was obliged to make terms with him in order to obtain his liberation. Confucius would give his countenance to none, as he disapproved of all, and he studiously kept aloof from them. Of how he comported himself among them we have a specimen in the incident related in the Analects, XVII. i.—'Yang Ho wished to see Confucius, but Confucius would not go to see him. On this, he sent a present of a pig to Confucius, who, having chosen a time when Ho was not at home, went to pay his respects for the gift. He met him, however, on the way. "Come, let me speak with you," said the officer. "Can he be called benevolent, who keeps his jewel in his bosom, and leaves his country to confusion?" Confucius replied, "No." "Can he be called wise, who is anxious to be engaged in public employment, and yet is constantly losing the opportunity of being so?" Confucius again said, "No." The other added, "The days and months are passing away; the years do not wait for us." Confucius said, "Right; I will go into office."' Chinese writers are eloquent in their praises of the sage for the combination of propriety, complaisance and firmness, which they see in his behaviour in this matter. To myself there seems nothing remarkable in it but a somewhat questionable dexterity. But it was well for the fame of Confucius that his time was not occupied during those years with official services. He turned them to better account, prosecuting his researches into the poetry, history, ceremonies, and music of the nation. Many disciples continued to resort to him, and the legendary writers tell us how he employed their services in digesting the results of his studies. I must repeat, however, that several of them, whose names are most famous, such as Tsǎng Shǎn, were as yet children, and Min Sun [2] was not born till B. C. 500.

To this period we must refer the almost single instance which we have of the manner of Confucius's intercourse with his son Lî. 'Have you heard any lessons from your father different from what we have all heard?' asked one of the disciples once of Lî. 'No,' said Lî. 'He was standing alone once, when I was passing through the court below with hasty steps, and said to me, "Have you learned the Odes?" On my replying, "Not yet," he added, "If you do not learn the Odes, you will not be fit to converse with." Another day, in the same place and the same way, he said to me, " Have you read the rules of Propriety ?"   On my replying, " Not yet," he added, " If you do not learn the rules of Propriety, your character cannot be established."   I have heard only these two things from him.' The disciple was delighted and observed, ' I asked one thing, and I have got three things.   I have heard about the Odes.   I have heard about the rules of Propriety.   I have also heard that the superior man maintains a distant reserve towards his son [1].'

I can easily believe that this distant reserve was the rule which Confucius followed generally in his treatment of his son.   A stern dignity is the quality which a father has to maintain upon his system.   It is not to be without the element of kindness, but that must never go beyond the line of propriety.   There is too little room left for the play and development of natural affection.

The divorce of his wife must also have taken place during these years, if it ever took place at all, which is a disputed point.   The curious reader will find the question discussed in the notes on the second Book of the Lî Chî.   The evidence inclines, I think, against the supposition that Confucius did put his wife away.   When she died, at a period subsequent to the present, Lî kept on weeping aloud for her after the period for such a demonstration of grief had expired, when Confucius sent a message to him that his sorrow must be subdued, and the obedient son dried his tears [2].   We are glad to know that on one occasion—the death of his favourite disciple, Yen Hûi—the tears of Confucius himself would flow over and above the measure of propriety [3].

7. We come to the short period of Confucius's official life.   In the

He holds office.   year B. C. 501, things had come to a head between the
B. C. 500–496.   chiefs of the three Families and their ministers, and
had resulted in the defeat of the latter.   In that year the resources of Yang Hû were exhausted, and he fled into Ch'î, so that the State was delivered from its greatest troubler, and the way was made more clear for Confucius to go into office, should an opportunity occur.   It soon presented itself.   Towards the end of that year he was made chief magistrate of the town of Chung-tû [4].

---

[1] Ana. XVI. xiii.   [2] See the Lî Chî, II. Pt. I. i. 27.   [3] Ana. XI. ix.   [4] 中 都 宰.
Amiot says this was ' la ville même où le Souverain tenoit sa Cour' (Vie de Confucius, p. 147). He is followed of course by Thornton and Pauthier.   My reading has not shown me that such was the case.   In the notes to K'ang-hsî's edition of the ' Five Ching,' Lî Chî, II. Sect. I. iii. 4, it is simply said—' Chung-tû,—the name of a town of Lû.   It afterwards belonged to Ch'î when it was called P'ing-lû (平 陸).'

Just before he received this appointment, a circumstance occurred of which we do not well know what to make. When Yang-hû fled into Ch'î, Kung-shan Fû-zâo, who had been confederate with him, continued to maintain an attitude of rebellion, and held the city of Pî against the Chî family. Thence he sent a message to Confucius inviting him to join him, and the Sage seemed so inclined to go that his disciple Tsze-lû remonstrated with him, saying, 'Indeed you cannot go! why must you think of going to see Kung-shan?' Confucius replied, 'Can it be without some reason that he has invited me? If any one employ me, may I not make an eastern Châu [1]?' The upshot, however, was that he did not go, and I cannot suppose that he had ever any serious intention of doing so. Amid the general gravity of his intercourse with his followers, there gleam out a few instances of quiet pleasantry, when he amused himself by playing with their notions about him. This was probably one of them.

As magistrate of Chung-tû he produced a marvellous reformation of the manners of the people in a short time. According to the 'Narratives of the School,' he enacted rules for the nourishing of the living and all observances to the dead. Different food was assigned to the old and the young, and different burdens to the strong and the weak. Males and females kept apart from each other in the streets. A thing dropped on the road was not picked up. There was no fraudulent carving of vessels. Inner coffins were made four inches thick, and the outer ones five. Graves were made on the high grounds, no mounds being raised over them, and no trees planted about them. Within twelve months, the princes of the other States all wished to imitate his style of administration [2].

The duke Ting, surprised at what he saw, asked whether his rules could be employed to govern a whole State, and Confucius told him that they might be applied to the whole kingdom. On this the duke appointed him assistant-superintendent of Works [3], in which capacity he surveyed the lands of the State, and made many improvements in agriculture. From this he was quickly made minister of Crime [4], and the appointment was enough to put an end to crime. There was no necessity to put the penal laws in execution. No offenders showed themselves [5].

---

[1] Ana. XVII. v.   [2] 家語, Bk. I.   [3] 司空. This office, however, was held by the chief of the Măng family. We must understand that Confucius was only an assistant to him, or perhaps acted for him.   [4] 大司寇.   [5] 家語, Bk. I.

These indiscriminating eulogies are of little value. One incident, related in the annotations of Tso-shih on the Ch'un-Ch'iû [1], commends itself at once to our belief, as in harmony with Confucius's character. The chief of the Chî, pursuing with his enmity the duke Châo, even after his death, had placed his grave apart from the graves of his predecessors; and Confucius surrounded the ducal cemetery with a ditch so as to include the solitary resting-place, boldly telling the chief that he did it to hide his disloyalty [2]. But he signalised himself most of all in B. C. 500, by his behaviour at an interview between the dukes of Lû and Ch'î, at a place called Shih-ch'î [3], and Chiâ-kû [4], in the present district of Lâi-wû, in the department of T'âi-an [5]. Confucius was present as master of ceremonies on the part of Lû, and the meeting was professedly pacific. The two princes were to form a covenant of alliance. The principal officer on the part of Ch'î, however, despising Confucius as 'a man of ceremonies, without courage,' had advised his sovereign to make the duke of Lû a prisoner, and for this purpose a band of the half-savage original inhabitants of the place advanced with weapons to the stage where the two dukes were met. Confucius understood the scheme, and said to the opposite party, 'Our two princes are met for a pacific object. For you to bring a band of savage vassals to disturb the meeting with their weapons, is not the way in which Ch'î can expect to give law to the princes of the kingdom. These barbarians have nothing to do with our Great Flowery land. Such vassals may not interfere with our covenant. Weapons are out of place at such a meeting. As before the spirits, such conduct is unpropitious. In point of virtue, it is contrary to right. As between man and man, it is not polite.' The duke of Ch'î ordered the disturbers off, but Confucius withdrew, carrying the duke of Lû with him. The business proceeded, notwithstanding, and when the words of the alliance were being read on the part of Ch'î,—'So be it to Lû, if it contribute not 300 chariots of war to the help of Ch'î, when its army goes across its borders,' a messenger from Confucius added,—'And so be it to us, if we obey your orders, unless you return to us the fields on the south of the Wăn.' At the conclusion of the ceremonies, the prince of Ch'î wanted to give a grand entertainment, but Confucius demonstrated that such a thing would be

[1] 左傳, 定公元年.　　[2] 家語, Bk. I.　　[3] 實其.　　[4] 夾谷.
[5] 泰安府, 萊蕪縣.

contrary to the established rules of propriety, his real object being to keep his sovereign out of danger. In this way the two parties separated, they of Ch'î filled with shame at being foiled and disgraced by 'the man of ceremonies;' and the result was that the lands of Lû which had been appropriated by Ch'î were restored [1].

For two years more Confucius held the office of minister of Crime. Some have supposed that he was further raised to the dignity of chief minister of the State [2], but that was not the case. One instance of the manner in which he executed his functions is worth recording. When any matter came before him, he took the opinion of different individuals upon it, and in giving judgment would say, 'I decide according to the view of so and so.' There was an approach to our jury system in the plan, Confucius's object being to enlist general sympathy, and carry the public judgment with him in his administration of justice. A father having brought some charge against his son, Confucius kept them both in prison for three months, without making any difference in favour of the father, and then wished to dismiss them both. The head of the Chî was dissatisfied, and said, 'You are playing with me, Sir minister of Crime. Formerly you told me that in a State or a family filial duty was the first thing to be insisted on. What hinders you now from putting to death this unfilial son as an example to all the people?' Confucius with a sigh replied, 'When superiors fail in their duty, and yet go to put their inferiors to death, it is not right. This father has not taught his son to be filial;—to listen to his charge would be to slay the guiltless. The manners of the age have been long in a sad condition; we cannot expect the people not to be transgressing the laws [3].'

At this time two of his disciples, Tsze-lû and Tsze-yû, entered the employment of the Chî family, and lent their influence, the former especially, to forward the plans of their master. One great cause of disorder in the State was the fortified cities held by the three chiefs, in which they could defy the supreme authority, and were in turn defied themselves by their officers. Those cities were like the castles of the barons of England in the time of the Norman

---

[1] This meeting at Chiâ-kû is related in Sze-mâ Ch'ien, the 'Narratives of the School,' and Kû-liang, with many exaggerations. I have followed 左 氏 傳, 定 公 十 年.

[2] The 家 語 says, Bk. II, 孔 子 爲 魯 司 寇, 攝 相 事. But he was a 相 only in the sense of an assistant of ceremonies, as at the meeting in Chiâ-kû, described above.

[3] See the 家 語, Bk. II.

kings. Confucius had their destruction very much at heart, and partly by the influence of persuasion, and partly by the assisting counsels of Tsze-lû, he accomplished his object in regard to Pî [1], the chief city of the Chî, and Hâu [2], the chief city of the Shû.

It does not appear that he succeeded in the same way in dismantling Ch'ăng [3], the chief city of the Măng [4]; but his authority in the State greatly increased. 'He strengthened the ducal House and weakened the private Families. He exalted the sovereign, and depressed the ministers. A transforming government went abroad. Dishonesty and dissoluteness were ashamed and hid their heads. Loyalty and good faith became the characteristics of the men, and chastity and docility those of the women. Strangers came in crowds from other States [5].' Confucius became the idol of the people, and flew in songs through their mouths [6].

But this sky of bright promise was soon overcast. As the fame of the reformations in Lû went abroad, the neighbouring princes began to be afraid. The duke of Ch'î said, 'With Confucius at the head of its government, Lû will become supreme among the States, and Ch'î which is nearest to it will be the first swallowed up. Let us propitiate it by a surrender of territory.' One of his ministers proposed that they should first try to separate between the sage and his sovereign, and to effect this, they hit upon the following scheme. Eighty beautiful girls, with musical and dancing accomplishments, and a hundred and twenty of the finest horses that could be found, were selected, and sent as a present to duke Ting. They were put up at first outside the city, and Chî Hwan having gone in disguise to see them, forgot the lessons of Confucius, and took the duke to look at the bait. They were both captivated. The women were received, and the sage was neglected. For three days the duke gave no audience to his ministers. 'Master,' said Tsze-lû to Confucius, 'it is time for you to be going.' But Confucius was very unwilling to leave. The spring was coming on, when the sacrifice to Heaven would be offered, and he determined to wait and see whether the

---

[1] 費.　　[2] 郈.　　[3] 成.　　[4] In connexion with these events, the 'Narratives of the School' and Sze-mâ Ch'ien mention the summary punishment inflicted by Confucius on an able but unscrupulous and insidious officer, the Shaou-chăng, Maou (少正卯). His judgment and death occupy a conspicuous place in the legendary accounts. But the Analects, Tsze-sze, Mencius, and Tso Ch'iû-ming are all silent about it, and Chiang Yung rightly rejects it as one of the many narratives invented to exalt the sage.　　[5] See the 家語, Bk. II.　　[6] See 孔叢子, quoted by Chiang Yung.

solemnization of that would bring the duke back to his right mind. No such result followed. The ceremony was hurried through, and portions of the offerings were not sent round to the various ministers, according to the established custom. Confucius regretfully took his departure, going away slowly and by easy stages [1]. He would have welcomed a message of recall. But the duke continued in his abandonment, and the sage went forth to thirteen weary years of homeless wandering.

8. On leaving Lû, Confucius first bent his steps westward to the State of Wei, situate about where the present provinces of Chih-lî and Ho-nan adjoin. He was now in his fifty-sixth year, and felt depressed and melancholy. As he went along, he gave expression to his feelings in verse :—

He wanders
from State to
State.
B.C. 497–484.

'Fain would I still look towards Lû,
But this Kwei hill cuts off my view.
With an axe, I'd hew the thickets through :—
Vain thought! 'gainst the hill I nought can do ;'

and again,—

'Through the valley howls the blast,
Drizzling rain falls thick and fast.
Homeward goes the youthful bride,
O'er the wild, crowds by her side.
How is it, O azure Heaven,
From my home I thus am driven,
Through the land my way to trace,
With no certain dwelling-place?
Dark, dark, the minds of men!
Worth in vain comes to their ken.
Hastens on my term of years ;
Old age, desolate, appears [2].'

A number of his disciples accompanied him, and his sadness infected them. When they arrived at the borders of Wei, at a place called Î, the warden sought an interview, and on coming out from the sage, he tried to comfort the disciples, saying, ' My friends, why are you distressed at your master's loss of office? The world has been long without the principles of truth and right ; Heaven is going to use your master as a bell with its wooden tongue [3].' Such was the thought of this friendly stranger. The bell did indeed sound, but few had ears to hear.

---

[1] 史記, 孔子世家, p. 5.   See also Mencius, V. Pt. II. i. 4 ; *et al.*   [2] See Chiang Yung's Life of Confucius, 去魯周遊考.   [3] Ana. III. xxiv.

Confucius's fame, however, had gone before him, and he was in little danger of having to suffer from want. On arriving at the capital of Wei, he lodged at first with a worthy officer, named Yen Ch'âu-yû [1]. The reigning duke, known to us by the epithet of Ling [2], was a worthless, dissipated man, but he could not neglect a visitor of such eminence, and soon assigned to Confucius a revenue of 60,000 measures of grain [3]. Here he remained for ten months, and then for some reason left it to go to Ch'ăn [4]. On the way he had to pass by K'wang [5], a place probably in the present department of K'âi-fung in Ho-nan, which had formerly suffered from Yang-hû. It so happened that Confucius resembled Hû, and the attention of the people being called to him by the movements of his carriage-driver, they thought it was their old enemy, and made an attack upon him. His followers were alarmed, but he was calm, and tried to assure them by declaring his belief that he had a divine mission. He said to them, 'After the death of king Wăn, was not the cause of truth lodged here in me? If Heaven had wished to let this cause of truth perish, then I, a future mortal, should not have got such a relation to that cause. While Heaven does not let the cause of truth perish, what can the people of K'wang do to me [6]?' Having escaped from the hands of his assailants, he does not seem to have carried out his purpose of going to Ch'ăn, but returned to Wei.

On the way, he passed a house where he had formerly lodged, and finding that the master was dead, and the funeral ceremonies going on, he went in to condole and weep. When he came out, he told Tsze-kung to take the outside horses from his carriage, and give them as a contribution to the expenses of the occasion. 'You never did such a thing,' Tsze-kung remonstrated, 'at the funeral of any of your disciples; is it not too great a gift on this occasion of the death of an old host?' 'When I went in,' replied Confucius, 'my presence brought a burst of grief from the chief mourner, and I joined him with my tears. I dislike the thought of my tears not being followed by anything. Do it, my child [7].'

On reaching Wei, he lodged with Chü Po-yü, an officer of whom

---

[1] 顏讐由. See Mencius, V. Pt. I. viii. 2.　　[2] 靈公.　　[3] See the 史記, 孔子世家, p. 5.　　[4] 陳國.　　[5] 匡.　　[6] Ana. IX. v. In Ana. XI. xxii, there is another reference to this time, in which Yen Hûi is made to appear.　　[7] See the Lî Chî, II. Sect. I. ii. 16.

honourable mention is made in the Analects [1]. But this time he
did not remain long in the State. The duke was
married to a lady of the house of Sung, known by the
name of Nan-tsze, notorious for her intrigues and wickedness. She
sought an interview with the sage, which he was obliged unwillingly
to accord [2]. No doubt he was innocent of thought or act of evil,
but it gave great dissatisfaction to Tsze-lû that his master should
have been in company with such a woman, and Confucius, to assure
him, swore an oath, saying, ‘ Wherein I have done improperly, may
Heaven reject me! May Heaven reject me [3]!’ He could not well
abide, however, about such a court. One day the duke rode out
through the streets of his capital in the same carriage with Nan-tsze,
and made Confucius follow them in another. Perhaps he intended
to honour the philosopher, but the people saw the incongruity, and
cried out, ‘ Lust in the front; virtue behind!’ Confucius was
ashamed, and made the observation, ‘ I have not seen one who loves
virtue as he loves beauty [4].’ Wei was no place for him. He left it,
and took his way towards Ch‘ăn.

B.C. 495.

Ch‘ăn, which formed part of the present province of Ho-nan, lay
south from Wei. After passing the small State of Ts‘âo [5], he
approached the borders of Sung, occupying the present prefecture
of Kwei-teh, and had some intentions of entering it, when an incident
occurred, which it is not easy to understand from the meagre style
in which it is related, but which gave occasion to a remarkable
saying. Confucius was practising ceremonies with his disciples, we
are told, under the shade of a large tree. Hwan T‘ûi, an ill-minded
officer of Sung, heard of it, and sent a band of men to pull down
the tree, and kill the philosopher, if they could get hold of him.
The disciples were much alarmed, but Confucius observed, ‘ Heaven
has produced the virtue that is in me;—what can Hwan T‘ûi do to
me [6]?’ They all made their escape, but seem to have been driven
westwards to the State of Chăng [7], on arriving at the gate conducting into which from the east, Confucius found himself separated
from his followers. Tsze-kung had arrived before him, and was told
by a native of Chăng that there was a man standing by the east gate,
with a forehead like Yâo, a neck like Kâo-yâo, his shoulders on a
level with those of Tsze-ch‘an, but wanting, below the waist, three

---

[1] Ana. XIV. xxvi; XV. vi.   [2] See the account in the 史 記, 孔 子 世 家,
p. 6.   [3] Ana. VI. xxvi.   [4] Ana. IX. xvii.   [5] 曹.   [6] Ana. IX. xxii.   [7] 鄭.

inches of the height of Yü, and altogether having the disconsolate appearance of a stray dog.' Tsze-kung knew it was the master, hastened to him, and repeated to his great amusement the description which the man had given. 'The bodily appearance,' said Confucius, 'is but a small matter, but to say I was like a stray dog, —capital! capital [1]!' The stay they made at Chăng was short, and by the end of B. C. 495, Confucius was in Ch'ăn.

All the next year he remained there, lodging with the warder of the city wall, an officer of worth, of the name of Chăng [2], and we have no accounts of him which deserve to be related here [3].

In B. C. 494, Ch'ăn was much disturbed by attacks from Wû [4], a large State, the capital of which was in the present department of Sû-châu, and Confucius determined to retrace his steps to Wei. On the way he was laid hold of at a place called P'ŭ [5], which was held by a rebellious officer against Wei, and before he could get away, he was obliged to engage that he would not proceed thither. Thither, notwithstanding, he continued his route, and when Tsze-kung asked him whether it was right to violate the oath he had taken, he replied, 'It was a forced oath. The spirits do not hear such [6].' The duke Ling received him with distinction, but paid no more attention to his lessons than before, and Confucius is said then to have uttered his complaint, 'If there were any of the princes who would employ me, in the course of twelve months I should have done something considerable. In three years the government would be perfected [7].'

A circumstance occurred to direct his attention to the State of Tsin [8], which occupied the southern part of the present Shan-hsî, and extended over the Yellow river into Ho-nan. An invitation came to Confucius, like that which he had formerly received from Kung-shan Fû-zǎo. Pî Hsî, an officer of Tsin, who was holding the town of Chung-mâu against his chief, invited him to visit him, and Confucius was inclined to go. Tsze-lû was always the mentor on such occasions. He said to him, 'Master, I have heard you say,

---

[1] See the 史 記, 孔 子 世 家, p. 6.   [2] 司 城 貞 子. See Mencius, V. Pt. I. viii. 3.   [3] Chiang Yung digests in this place two foolish stories,—about a large bone found in the State of Yüeh, and a bird which appeared in Ch'iă and died, shot through with a remarkable arrow. Confucius knew all about them.   [4] 吳.   [5] 蒲.   [6] This is related by Sze-mâ Ch'ien 孔 子 世 家, p. 7, and also in the 'Narratives of the School.' I would fain believe it is not true. The wonder is, that no Chinese critic should have set about disproving it.   [7] Ana. XII. x.   [8] 晉.

that when a man in his own person is guilty of doing evil, a superior man will not associate with him. Pî Hsî is in rebellion; if you go to him, what shall be said?' Confucius replied, 'Yes, I did use those words. But is it not said that if a thing be really hard, it may be ground without being made thin; and if it be really white, it may be steeped in a dark fluid without being made black? Am I a bitter gourd? Am I to be hung up out of the way of being eaten [1]?'

These sentiments sound strangely from his lips. After all, he did not go to Pî Hsî; and having travelled as far as the Yellow river that he might see one of the principal ministers of Tsin, he heard of the violent death of two men of worth, and returned to Wei, lamenting the fate which prevented him from crossing the stream, and trying to solace himself with poetry as he had done on leaving Lû. Again did he communicate with the duke, but as ineffectually, and disgusted at being questioned by him about military tactics, he left and went back to Ch'ăn.

He resided in Ch'ăn all the next year, B. C. 491, without anything occurring there which is worthy of note[2]. Events had transpired in Lû, however, which were to issue in his return to his native State. The duke Ting had deceased B. C. 494, and Chî Hwan, the chief of the Chî family, died in this year. On his death-bed, he felt remorse for his conduct to Confucius, and charged his successor, known to us in the Analects as Chî K'ang, to recall the sage; but the charge was not immediately fulfilled. Chî K'ang, by the advice of one of his officers, sent to Ch'ăn for the disciple Yen Ch'iû instead. Confucius willingly sent him off, and would gladly have accompanied him. 'Let me return!' he said, 'Let me return[3]!' But that was not to be for several years yet.

In B. C. 490, accompanied, as usual, by several of his disciples, he went from Ch'ăn to Ts'âi, a small dependency of the great fief of Ch'û, which occupied a large part of the present provinces of Hû-nan and Hû-pei. On the way, between Ch'ăn and Ts'âi, their provisions became exhausted, and they were cut off somehow from obtaining a fresh supply. The disciples were quite overcome with want, and Tsze-lû said to the master, 'Has the superior man indeed to endure in this way?' Confucius answered him, 'The superior man may indeed have to endure want; but the mean man,

[1] Ana. XVII. vii.   [2] Tso Ch'iû-ming, indeed, relates a story of Confucius, on the report of a fire in Lû, telling whose ancestral temple had been destroyed by it.   [3] Ana. V. xxi.

when he is in want, gives way to unbridled license[1].'　According to the 'Narratives of the School,' the distress continued seven days, during which time Confucius retained his equanimity, and was even cheerful, playing on his lute and singing[2].　He retained, however, a strong impression of the perils of the season, and we find him afterwards recurring to it, and lamenting that of the friends that were with him in Ch'ăn and Ts'âi, there were none remaining to enter his door[3].

Escaped from this strait, he remained in Ts'âi over B. C. 489, and in the following year we find him in Sheh, another district of Ch'û, the chief of which had taken the title of duke, according to the usurping policy of that State.　Puzzled about his visitor, he asked Tsze-lû what he should think of him, but the disciple did not venture a reply.　When Confucius heard of it, he said to Tsze-lû, 'Why did you not say to him:—He is simply a man who in his eager pursuit of knowledge forgets his food, who in the joy of its attainment forgets his sorrows, and who does not perceive that old age is coming on[4]?'　Subsequently, the duke, in conversation with Confucius, asked him about government, and got the reply, dictated by some circumstances of which we are ignorant, 'Good government obtains, when those who are near are made happy, and those who are far off are attracted[5].'

After a short stay in Sheh, according to Sze-mâ Ch'ien, he returned to Ts'âi, and having to cross a river, he sent Tsze-lû to inquire for the ford of two men who were at work in a neighbouring field.　They were recluses,—men who had withdrawn from public life in disgust at the waywardness of the times.　One of them was called Ch'ang-tsü, and instead of giving Tsze-lû the information he wanted, he asked him, 'Who is it that holds the reins in the carriage there?'　'It is K'ung Ch'iû.'　'K'ung Ch'iû of Lû?'　'Yes,' was the reply, and then the man rejoined, '*He* knows the ford.'

Tsze-lû applied to the other, who was called Chieh-nî, but got for answer the question, 'Who are you, Sir?'　He replied, 'I am Chung Yû.'　'Chung Yû, who is the disciple of K'ung Ch'iû of Lû?'　'Yes,' again replied Tsze-lû, and Chieh-nî said to him, 'Disorder, like a swelling flood, spreads over the whole kingdom,

---

[1] Ana. XV. i. 2, 3.　　[2] 家語, 卷二, 在危, 二十篇.　　[3] Ana. XI. ii.
[4] Ana. VII. xviii.　　[5] Ana. XIII. xvi.

and who is he that will change it for you? Than follow one who merely withdraws from this one and that one, had you not better follow those who withdraw from the world altogether?' With this he fell to covering up the seed, and gave no more heed to the stranger. Tsze-lû went back and reported what they had said, when Confucius vindicated his own course, saying, 'It is impossible to associate with birds and beasts as if they were the same with us. If I associate not with these people,—with mankind,—with whom shall I associate? If right principles prevailed through the kingdom, there would be no need for me to change its state[1].'

About the same time he had an encounter with another recluse, who was known as 'The madman of Ch'û.' He passed by the carriage of Confucius, singing out, 'O phœnix, O phœnix, how is your virtue degenerated! As to the past, reproof is useless, but the future may be provided against. Give up, give up your vain pursuit.' Confucius alighted and wished to enter into conversation with him, but the man hastened away[2].

But now the attention of the ruler of Ch'û—king, as he styled himself—was directed to the illustrious stranger who was in his dominions, and he met Confucius and conducted him to his capital, which was in the present district of Î-ch'âng, in the department of Hsiang-yang[3], in Hû-pei. After a time, he proposed endowing the philosopher with a considerable territory, but was dissuaded by his prime minister, who said to him, 'Has your majesty any officer who could discharge the duties of an ambassador like Tsze-kung? or any one so qualified for a premier as Yen Hûi? or any one to compare as a general with Tsze-lû? The kings Wăn and Wû, from their hereditary dominions of a hundred *li*, rose to the sovereignty of the kingdom. If K'ung Ch'iû, with such disciples to be his ministers, get the possession of any territory, it will not be to the prosperity of Ch'û[4]? On this remonstrance the king gave up his purpose; and, when he died in the same year, Confucius left the State, and went back again to Wei.

The duke Ling had died four years before, soon after Confucius had last parted from him, and the reigning duke, known to us by the title of Ch'û[5], was his grandson, and was holding the principality against his own father. The relations

B.C. 489.

---

[1] Ana. XVIII. vi.　　[2] Ana. XVII. v.　　[3] 襄陽府宜城縣.　　[4] See the 史記, 孔子世家, p. 10.　　[5] 出公.

between them were rather complicated. The father had been driven out in consequence of an attempt which he had instigated on the life of his step-mother, the notorious Nan-tsze, and the succession was given to his son. . Subsequently, the father wanted to reclaim what he deemed his right, and an unseemly struggle ensued. The duke Ch'û was conscious how much his cause would be strengthened by the support of Confucius, and hence when he got to Wei, Tsze-lû could say to him, ' The prince of Wei has been waiting for you, in order with you to administer the government;— what will you consider the first thing to be done [1] ? ' The opinion of the philosopher, however, was against the propriety of the duke's course [2], and he declined taking office with him, though he remained in Wei for between five and six years. During all that time there is a blank in his history. In the very year of his return, according to the 'Annals of the Empire,' his most beloved disciple, Yen Hûi, died, on which occasion he exclaimed, ' Alas ! Heaven is destroying me ! Heaven is destroying me [3] !' The death of his wife is assigned to B.C. 484, but nothing else is related which we can connect with this long period.

9. His return to Lû was brought about by the disciple Yen Yû, who, we have seen, went into the service of Chî K'ang, in B.C. 491.

From his return to Lû to his death.
B. C. 484–478.
In the year B.C. 483, Yû had the conduct of some military operations against Ch'î, and being successful, Chî K'ang asked him how he had obtained his military skill;—was it from nature, or by learning ? He replied that he had learned it from Confucius, and entered into a glowing eulogy of the philosopher. The chief declared that he would bring Confucius home again to Lû. ' If you do so,' said the disciple, ' see that you do not let mean men come between you and him.' On this K'ang sent three officers with appropriate presents to Wei, to invite the wanderer home, and he returned with them accordingly [4].

This event took place in the eleventh year of the duke Âi [5], who succeeded to Ting, and according to K'ung Fû, Confucius's descendant, the invitation proceeded from him [6]. We may suppose that

---

[1] Ana. XIII. iii. In the notes on this passage, I have given Chû Hsî's opinion as to the time when Tsze-lû made this remark. It seems more correct, however, to refer it to Confucius's return to Wei from Ch'û, as is done by Chiang Yung.   [2] Ana. VII. xiv.
[3] Ana. XI. viii. In the notes on Ana. XI. vii, I have adverted to the chronological difficulty connected with the dates assigned respectively to the deaths of Yen Hûi and Confucius's own son, Lî.   Chiang Yung assigns Hûi's death to B.C. 481.   [4] See the 史 記, 孔 子 世 家.   [5] 哀 公.   [6] See Chiang Yung's memoir, in loc.

while Chî K'ang was the mover and director of the proceeding, it
was with the authority and approval of the duke. It is represented
in the chronicle of Tso Ch'iû-ming as having occurred at a very
opportune time. The philosopher had been consulted a little before
by K'ung Wăn [1], an officer of Wei, about how he should conduct a
feud with another officer, and disgusted at being referred to on
such a subject, had ordered his carriage and prepared to leave the
State, exclaiming, 'The bird chooses its tree. The tree does not
choose the bird.' K'ung Wăn endeavoured to excuse himself, and
to prevail on Confucius to remain in Wei, and just at this juncture
the messengers from Lû arrived [2].

Confucius was now in his sixty-ninth year. The world had not
dealt kindly with him. In every State which he had visited he had
met with disappointment and sorrow. Only five more years remained to him, nor were they of a brighter character than the past.
He had, indeed, attained to that state, he tells us, in which ' he
could follow what his heart desired without transgressing what was
right [3],' but other people were not more inclined than they had
been to abide by his counsels. The duke Âi and Chî K'ang often
conversed with him, but he no longer had weight in the guidance
of state affairs, and wisely addressed himself to the completion of
his literary labours. He wrote a preface, according to Sze-mâ
Ch'ien, to the Shû-ching; carefully digested the rites and ceremonies determined by the wisdom of the more ancient sages and
kings; collected and arranged the ancient poetry; and undertook
the reform of music [4]. He has told us himself, 'I returned from
Wei to Lû, and then the music was reformed, and the pieces in the
Songs of the Kingdom and Praise Songs found all their proper
place [5].' To the Yî-ching he devoted much study, and Sze-mâ
Ch'ien says that the leather thongs by which the tablets of his
copy were bound together were thrice worn out. 'If some years
were added to my life,' he said, 'I would give fifty to the study of
the Yî, and then I might come to be without great faults [6].' During
this time also, we may suppose that he supplied Tsăng Shăn with
the materials of the classic of Filial Piety. The same year that he
returned, Chî K'ang sent Yen Yû to ask his opinion about an

---

[1] 孔文子, the same who is mentioned in the Analects, V. xiv.   [2] See the
左傳, 哀公十一年.   [3] Ana. II. iv. 6.   [4] See the 史記, 孔子
世家, p. 12.   [5] Ana. IX. xiv.   [6] Ana. VII. xvi.

additional impost which he wished to lay upon the people, but Confucius refused to give any reply, telling the disciple privately his disapproval of the proposed measure. It was carried out, however, in the following year, by the agency of Yen, on which occasion, I suppose, it was that Confucius said to the other disciples, 'He is no disciple of mine; my little children, beat the drum and assail him[1].' The year B.C. 483 was marked by the death of his son Lî, which he seems to have borne with more equanimity than he did that of his disciple Yen Hûi, which some writers assign to the following year, though I have already mentioned it under the year B.C. 489.

In the spring of B.C. 481, a servant of Chî K'ang caught a Ch'î-lin on a hunting excursion of the duke in the present district of Chiâ-hsiang[2]. No person could tell what strange animal it was, and Confucius was called to look at it. He at once knew it to be a *lin*, and the legend-writers say that it bore on one of its horns the piece of ribbon, which his mother had attached to the one that appeared to her before his birth. According to the chronicle of Kung-yang, he was profoundly affected. He cried out, 'For whom have you come? For whom have you come?' His tears flowed freely, and he added, 'The course of my doctrines is run[3].'

Notwithstanding the appearance of the *lin*, the life of Confucius was still protracted for two years longer, though he took occasion to terminate with that event his history of the Ch'un Ch'iû. This Work, according to Sze-mâ Ch'ien, was altogether the production of this year, but we need not suppose that it was so. In it, from the standpoint of Lû, he briefly indicates the principal events occurring throughout the country, every term being expressive, it is said, of the true character of the actors and events described. Confucius said himself, 'It is the Spring and Autumn which will make men know me, and it is the Spring and Autumn which will make men condemn me[4].' Mencius makes the composition of it to have been an achievement as great as Yû's regulation of the waters of the deluge :—'Confucius completed the Spring and Autumn, and rebellious ministers and villainous sons were struck with terror[5].'

Towards the end of this year, word came to Lû that the duke

---

[1] Ana. XI. xvi.　　[2] 兗州府嘉祥縣.　　[3] 公羊傳, 哀公十四年. According to Kung-yang, however, the *lin* was found by some wood-gatherers.
[4] Mencius III. Pt. II. ix. 8.　　[5] Mencius III. Pt. II. ix. 11.

of Ch'î had been murdered by one of his officers. Confucius was moved with indignation. Such an outrage, he felt, called for his solemn interference. He bathed, went to court, and represented the matter to the duke, saying, 'Ch'ăn Hăng has slain his sovereign, I beg that you will undertake to punish him.' The duke pleaded his incapacity, urging that Lû was weak compared with Ch'î, but Confucius replied, 'One half the people of Ch'î are not consenting to the deed. If you add to the people of Lû one half the people of Ch'î, you are sure to overcome.' But he could not infuse his spirit into the duke, who told him to go and lay the matter before the chiefs of the three Families. Sorely against his sense of propriety, he did so, but they would not act, and he withdrew with the remark, 'Following in the rear of the great officers, I did not dare not to represent such a matter [1].'

In the year B.C. 479, Confucius had to mourn the death of another of his disciples, one of those who had been longest with him,—the well-known Tsze-lû. He stands out a sort of Peter in the Confucian school, a man of impulse, prompt to speak and prompt to act. He gets many a check from the master, but there is evidently a strong sympathy between them. Tsze-lû uses a freedom with him on which none of the other disciples dares to venture, and there is not one among them all, for whom, if I may speak from my own feeling, the foreign student comes to form such a liking. A pleasant picture is presented to us in one passage of the Analects. It is said, 'The disciple Min was standing by his side, looking bland and precise; Tsze-lû (named Yû), looking bold and soldierly; Yen Yû and Tsze-kung, with a free and straight-forward manner. The master was pleased, but he observed, "Yû there!—he will not die a natural death [2]."'

This prediction was verified. When Confucius returned to Lû from Wei, he left Tsze-lû and Tsze-kâo [3] engaged there in official service. Troubles arose. News came to Lû, B.C. 479, that a revolution was in progress in Wei, and when Confucius heard it, he said, 'Ch'âi will come here, but Yû will die [4].' So it turned out. When Tsze-kâo saw that matters were desperate he made his escape, but Tsze-lû would not forsake the chief who had treated

---

[1] See the 左傳, 哀公十四年 and Analects XIV. xxii.   [2] Ana. XI. xii.

[3] 子羔, by surname Kâo (高), and name Ch'âi (柴).   [4] See the 左傳, 哀公十五年.

him well. He threw himself into the melée, and was slain. Confucius wept sore for him, but his own death was not far off. It took place on the eleventh day of the fourth month in the same year, B.C. 479 [1].

Early one morning, we are told, he got up, and with his hands behind his back, dragging his staff, he moved about by his door, crooning over,—

> 'The great mountain must crumble ;
> The strong beam must break ;
> And the wise man wither away like a plant.'

After a little, he entered the house and sat down opposite the door. Tsze-kung had heard his words, and said to himself, ' If the great mountain crumble, to what shall I look up ? If the strong beam break, and the wise man wither away, on whom shall I lean? The master, I fear, is going to be ill.' With this he hastened into the house. Confucius said to him, ' Ts'ze, what makes you so late ? According to the statutes of Hsiâ, the corpse was dressed and coffined at the top of the eastern steps, treating the dead as if he were still the host. Under the Yin, the ceremony was performed between the two pillars, as if the dead were both host and guest. The rule of Châu is to perform it at the top of the western steps, treating the dead as if he were a guest. I am a man of Yin, and last night I dreamt that I was sitting with offerings before me between the two pillars. No intelligent monarch arises ; there is not one in the kingdom that will make me his master. My time has come to die.' So it was. He went to his couch, and after seven days expired [2].

Such is the account which we have of the last hours of the great philosopher of China. His end was not unimpressive, but it was melancholy. He sank behind a cloud. Disappointed hopes made his soul bitter. The great ones of the kingdom had not received his teachings. No wife nor child was by to do the kindly offices of affection for him. Nor were the expectations of another life present with him as he passed through the dark valley. He uttered no prayer, and he betrayed no apprehensions. Deep-treasured in his own heart may have been the thought that he had endeavoured to serve his generation by the will of God, but he gave no sign. ' The mountain falling came to nought, and the rock was removed

---

[1] See the 左傳, 哀公十六年, and Chiang Yung's Life of Confucius, *in loc.*
[2] See the Lî Chî, II. Sect. I. ii. 20.

out of his place.   So death prevailed against him and he passed; his countenance was changed, and he was sent away.'

10. I flatter myself that the preceding paragraphs contain a more correct narrative of the principal incidents in the life of Confucius than has yet been given in any European language.   They might easily have been expanded into a volume, but I did not wish to exhaust the subject, but only to furnish a sketch, which, while it might satisfy the general reader, would be of special assistance to the careful student of the classical Books.   I had taken many notes of the manifest errors in regard to chronology and other matters in the 'Narratives of the School,' and the chapter of Sze-mâ Ch'ien on the K'ung family, when the digest of Chiang Yung, to which I have made frequent reference, attracted my attention.   Conclusions to which I had come were confirmed, and a clue was furnished to difficulties which I was seeking to disentangle.   I take the opportunity to acknowledge here my obligations to it.   With a few notices of Confucius's habits and manners, I shall conclude this section.

Very little can be gathered from reliable sources on the personal appearance of the sage.   The height of his father is stated, as I have noted, to have been ten feet, and though Confucius came short of this by four inches, he was often called 'the tall man.'   It is allowed that the ancient foot or cubit was shorter than the modern, but it must be reduced more than any scholar I have consulted has yet done, to bring this statement within the range of credibility. The legends assign to his figure 'nine-and-forty remarkable peculiarities[1],' a tenth part of which would have made him more a monster than a man.   Dr. Morrison says that the images of him, which he had seen in the northern parts of China, represent him as of a dark, swarthy colour[2].   It is not so with those common in the south.   He was, no doubt, in size and complexion much the same as many of his descendants in the present day.   Dr. Edkins and myself enjoyed the services of two of those descendants, who acted as 'wheelers' in the wheelbarrows which conveyed us from Ch'ü-fâu to a town on the Grand Canal more than 250 miles off.   They were strong, capable men, both physically and mentally superior to their companions.

---

[1] 四十九表.   [2] Chinese and English Dictionary, char. 孔.   Sir John Davis also mentions seeing a figure of Confucius, in a temple near the Po-yang lake, of which the complexion was 'quite black' (The Chinese, vol. ii. p. 66).

But if his disciples had nothing to chronicle of his personal appearance, they have gone very minutely into an account of many of his habits.   The tenth Book of the Analects is all occupied with his deportment, his eating, and his dress.   In public, whether in the village, the temple, or the court, he was the man of rule and ceremony, but 'at home he was not formal.'   Yet if not formal, he was particular.   In bed even he did not forget himself;—'he did not lie like a corpse,' and 'he did not speak.'   'He required his sleeping dress to be half as long again as his body.'   'If he happened to be sick, and the prince came to visit him, he had his face set to the east, made his court robes be put over him, and drew his girdle across them.'

He was nice in his diet,—'not disliking to have his rice dressed fine, nor to have his minced meat cut small.'   'Anything at all gone he would not touch.'   'He must have his meat cut properly, and to every kind its proper sauce ; but he was not a great eater.' 'It was only in drink that he laid down no limit to himself, but he did not allow himself to be confused by it.'   'When the villagers were drinking together, on those who carried staffs going out, he went out immediately after.'   There must always be ginger at the table, and 'when eating, he did not converse.'   'Although his food might be coarse rice and poor soup, he would offer a little of it in sacrifice, with a grave, respectful air.'

'On occasion of a sudden clap of thunder, or a violent wind, he would change countenance.   He would do the same, and rise up moreover, when he found himself a guest at a loaded board.'   'At the sight of a person in mourning, he would also change countenance, and if he happened to be in his carriage, he would bend forward with a respectful salutation.'   'His general way in his carriage was not to turn his head round, nor talk hastily, nor point with his hands.'   He was charitable.   'When any of his friends died, if there were no relations who could be depended on for the necessary offices, he would say, "I will bury him."'

The disciples were so careful to record these and other characteristics of their master, it is said, because every act, of movement or of rest, was closely associated with the great principles which it was his object to inculcate.   The detail of so many small matters, however, hardly impresses a foreigner so favourably.   There rather seems to be a want of freedom about the philosopher.

SECTION II.

HIS INFLUENCE AND OPINIONS.

1. Confucius died, we have seen, complaining that of all the princes of the kingdom there was not one who would adopt his principles and obey his lessons. He had hardly passed from the stage of life, when his merit began to be acknowledged. When the duke Âi heard of his death, he pronounced his eulogy in the words, 'Heaven has not left to me the aged man. There is none now to assist me on the throne. Woe is me! Alas! O venerable Nî [1]!' Tsze-kung complained of the inconsistency of this lamentation from one who could not use the master when he was alive, but the prince was probably sincere in his grief. He caused a temple to be erected, and ordered that sacrifice should be offered to the sage, at the four seasons of the year [2].

Homage rendered to Confucius by the sovereigns of China.

The sovereigns of the tottering dynasty of Châu had not the intelligence, nor were they in a position, to do honour to the departed philosopher, but the facts detailed in the first chapter of these prolegomena, in connexion with the attempt of the founder of the Ch'in dynasty to destroy the literary monuments of antiquity, show how the authority of Confucius had come by that time to prevail through the nation. The founder of the Han dynasty, in passing through Lû, B.C. 195, visited his tomb and offered the three victims in sacrifice to him. Other sovereigns since then have often made pilgrimages to the spot. The most famous temple in the empire now rises near the place of the grave. The second and greatest of the rulers of the present dynasty, in the twenty-third year of his reign, the K'ang-hsî period, there set the example of kneeling thrice, and each time laying his forehead thrice in the dust, before the image of the sage.

In the year of our Lord 1, began the practice of conferring honorary designations on Confucius by imperial authority. The emperor P'ing [3] then styled him—'The duke Nî, all-complete and

---

[1] Li Chî, II. Sect. I. iii. 43. This eulogy is found at greater length in the 左傳, immediately after the notice of the sage's death.   [2] See the 聖廟祀典圖考, 卷一, art. on Confucius. I am indebted to this for most of the notices in this paragraph.   [3] 平帝.

illustrious [1].' This was changed, in A.D. 492, to—'The venerable Nî, the accomplished Sage [2].' Other titles have supplanted this. Shun-chih [3], the first of the Man-châu dynasty, adopted, in his second year, A.D. 1645, the style,—'K'ung, the ancient Teacher, accomplished and illustrious, all-complete, the perfect Sage [4];' but twelve years later, a shorter title was introduced,—'K'ung, the ancient Teacher, the perfect Sage [5].' Since that year no further alteration has been made.

At first, the worship of Confucius was confined to the country of Lû, but in A.D. 57 it was enacted that sacrifices should be offered to him in the imperial college, and in all the colleges of the principal territorial divisions throughout the empire. In those sacrifices he was for some centuries associated with the duke of Châu, the legislator to whom Confucius made frequent reference, but in A.D. 609 separate temples were assigned to them, and in 628 our sage displaced the older worthy altogether. About the same time began the custom, which continues to the present day, of erecting temples to him,—separate structures, in connexion with all the colleges, or examination-halls, of the country.

The sage is not alone in those temples. In a hall behind the principal one occupied by himself are the tablets—in some cases, the images—of several of his ancestors, and other worthies; while associated with himself are his principal disciples, and many who in subsequent times have signalized themselves as expounders and exemplifiers of his doctrines. On the first day of every month, offerings of fruits and vegetables are set forth, and on the fifteenth there is a solemn burning of incense. But twice a year, in the middle months of spring and autumn, when the first *ting* day [6] of the month comes round, the worship of Confucius is performed with peculiar solemnity. At the imperial college the emperor himself is required to attend in state, and is in fact the principal performer. After all the preliminary arrangements have been made, and the emperor has twice knelt and six times bowed his head to the earth, the presence of Confucius's spirit is invoked in the words, 'Great art thou, O perfect sage! Thy virtue is full; thy doctrine is complete. Among mortal men there has not been thine equal. All kings honour thee. Thy statutes and laws have come gloriously

[1] 成宣尼公.　　[2] 文聖尼父.　　[3] 順治.　　[4] 大成至聖, 文宣先師, 孔子.　　[5] 至聖先師孔子.　　[6] 上丁日.

down. Thou art the pattern in this imperial school. Reverently have the sacrificial vessels been set out. Full of awe, we sound our drums and bells [1].'

The spirit is supposed now to be present, and the service proceeds through various offerings, when the first of which has been set forth, an officer reads the following [2], which is the prayer on the occasion:—' On this ... month of this ... year, I, *A.B.*, the emperor, offer a sacrifice to the philosopher K'ung, the ancient Teacher, the perfect Sage, and say,—O Teacher, in virtue equal to Heaven and Earth, whose doctrines embrace the past time and the present, thou didst digest and transmit the six classics, and didst hand down lessons for all generations! Now in this second month of spring (or autumn), in reverent observance of the old statutes, with victims, silks, spirits, and fruits, I carefully offer sacrifice to thee. With thee are associated the philosopher Yen, Continuator of thee; the philosopher Tsăng, Exhibiter of thy fundamental principles; the philosopher Tsze-sze, Transmitter of thee; and the philosopher Măng, Second to thee. May'st thou enjoy the offerings!'

I need not go on to enlarge on the homage which the emperors of China render to Confucius. It could not be more complete. He was unreasonably neglected when alive. He is now unreasonably venerated when dead.

2. The rulers of China are not singular in this matter, but in entire sympathy with the mass of their people. It is the distinction of this empire that education has been highly prized in it from the earliest times. It was so before the era of Confucius, and we may be sure that the system met with his approbation. One of his remarkable sayings was,— 'To lead an uninstructed people to war is to throw them away [3].' When he pronounced this judgment, he was not thinking of military training, but of education in the duties of life and citizenship. A people so taught, he thought, would be morally fitted to fight for their government. Mencius, when lecturing to the ruler of T'ăng on the proper way of governing a kingdom, told him that he must provide the means of education for all, the poor as well as the rich. 'Establish,' said he, ' *hsiang, hsü, hsio,* and *hsiâo,*—all those educational institutions,—for the instruction of the people [4].'

General appreciation of Confucius.

---

[1] [2] See the 大清通禮卷十二. [3] Ana. XIII. xxx. [4] Mencius III. Pt. I. iii. 10.

At the present day, education is widely diffused throughout China. In few other countries is the schoolmaster more abroad, and in all schools it is Confucius who is taught. The plan of competitive examinations, and the selection for civil offices only from those who have been successful candidates,—good so far as the competition is concerned, but injurious from the restricted range of subjects with which an acquaintance is required,—have obtained for more than twelve centuries. The classical works are the text books. It is from them almost exclusively that the themes proposed to determine the knowledge and ability of the students are chosen. The whole of the magistracy of China is thus versed in all that is recorded of the sage, and in the ancient literature which he preserved. His thoughts are familiar to every man in authority, and his character is more or less reproduced in him.

The official civilians of China, numerous as they are, are but a fraction of its students, and the students, or those who make literature a profession, are again but a fraction of those who attend school for a shorter or longer period. Yet so far as the studies have gone, they have been occupied with the Confucian writings. In the schoolrooms there is a tablet or inscription on the wall, sacred to the sage, and every pupil is required, on coming to school on the morning of the first and fifteenth of every month, to bow before it, the first thing, as an act of reverence[1]. Thus all in China who receive the slightest tincture of learning do so at the fountain of Confucius. They learn of him and do homage to him at once. I have repeatedly quoted the statement that during his life-time he had three thousand disciples. Hundreds of millions are his disciples now. It is hardly necessary to make any allowance in this statement for the followers of Tâoism and Buddhism, for, as Sir John Davis has observed, 'whatever the other opinions or faith of a Chinese may be, he takes good care to treat Confucius with respect[2].' For two thousand years he has reigned supreme, the undisputed teacher of this most populous land.

3. This position and influence of Confucius are to be ascribed, I conceive, chiefly to two causes:—his being the preserver, namely of

---

[1] During the present dynasty, the tablet of 文昌帝君, the god of literature, has to a considerable extent displaced that of Confucius in schools. Yet the worship of him does not clash with that of the other. He is 'the father' of composition only.

[2] The Chinese, vol. ii. p. 45.

the monuments of antiquity, and the exemplifier and expounder of
The causes of   the maxims of the golden age of China; and the devo-
his influence.   tion to him of his immediate disciples and their early
followers.   The national and the personal are thus blended in him,
each in its highest degree of excellence.   He was a Chinese of the
Chinese; he is also represented as, and all now believe him to have
been, the *beau ideal* of humanity in its best and noblest estate.

4. It may be well to bring forward here Confucius's own estimate
of himself and of his doctrines.   It will serve to illustrate the
His own esti-   statements just made.   The following are some of
mate of himself   his sayings:—'The sage and the man of perfect
and of his doc-
trines.   virtue;—how dare I rank myself with them?   It
may simply be said of me, that I strive to become such without
satiety, and teach others without weariness.'   'In letters I am
perhaps equal to other men; but the character of the superior
man, carrying out in his conduct what he professes, is what I have
not yet attained to.'   'The leaving virtue without proper cultivation; the not thoroughly discussing what is learned; not being
able to move towards righteousness of which a knowledge is gained;
and not being able to change what is not good;—these are the
things which occasion me solicitude.'   'I am not one who was born
in the possession of knowledge; I am one who is fond of antiquity
and earnest in seeking it there.'   'A transmitter and not a maker,
believing in and loving the ancients, I venture to compare myself
with our old P'ăng [1].'

Confucius cannot be thought to speak of himself in these
declarations more highly than he ought to do.   Rather we may
recognise in them the expressions of a genuine humility.   He was
conscious that personally he came short in many things, but he
toiled after the character, which he saw, or fancied that he saw,
in the ancient sages whom he acknowledged; and the lessons of
government and morals which he laboured to diffuse were those
which had already been inculcated and exhibited by them.
Emphatically he was 'a transmitter and not a maker.'   It is not
to be understood that he was not fully satisfied of the truth of the
principles which he had learned.   He held them with the full
approval and consent of his own understanding.   He believed that
if they were acted on, they would remedy the evils of his time.

---

[1] All these passages are taken from the seventh Book of the Analects.   See chapters
xxxiii, xxxii, iii, xix, and i.

There was nothing to prevent rulers like Yâo and Shun and the great Yü from again arising, and a condition of happy tranquillity being realised throughout the kingdom under their sway.

If in anything he thought himself 'superior and alone,' having attributes which others could not claim, it was in his possessing a divine commission as the conservator of ancient truth and rules. He does not speak very definitely on this point. It is noted that 'the appointments of Heaven was one of the subjects on which he rarely touched[1].' His most remarkable utterance was that which I have already given in the sketch of his Life :—'When he was put in fear in K'wang, he said, "After the death of king Wăn, was not the cause of truth lodged here in me ? If Heaven had wished to let this cause of truth perish, then I, a future mortal, should not have got such a relation to that cause. While Heaven does not let the cause of truth perish, what can the people of K'wang do to me[2] ? " ' Confucius, then, did feel that he was in the world for a special purpose. But it was not to announce any new truths, or to initiate any new economy. It was to prevent what had previously been known from being lost. He followed in the wake of Yâo and Shun, of T'ang, and king Wăn. Distant from the last by a long interval of time, he would have said that he was distant from him also by a great inferiority of character, but still he had learned the principles on which they all happily governed the country, and in their name he would lift up a standard against the prevailing lawlessness of his age.

5. The language employed with reference to Confucius by his disciples and their early followers presents a striking contrast with

Estimate of him by his disciples and their early followers.

his own. I have already, in writing of the scope and value of 'The Doctrine of the Mean,' called attention to the extravagant eulogies of his grandson Tsze-sze. He only followed the example which had been set by those among whom the philosopher went in and out. We have the language of Yen Yüan, his favourite, which is comparatively moderate, and simply expresses the genuine admiration of a devoted pupil[3]. Tsze-kung on several occasions spoke in a different style. Having heard that one of the chiefs of Lû had said that he himself— Tsze-kung—was superior to Confucius, he observed, ' Let me use the comparison of a house and its encompassing wall. My wall

---

[1] Ana. IX. i.   [2] Ana. IX. iii.   [3] Ana. IX. x.

only reaches to the shoulders. One may peep over it, and see whatever is valuable in the apartments. The wall of my master is several fathoms high. If one do not find the door and enter by it, he cannot see the rich ancestral temple with its beauties, nor all the officers in their rich array. But I may assume that they are few who find the door. The remark of the chief was only what might have been expected [1].'

Another time, the same individual having spoken revilingly of Confucius, Tsze-kung said, 'It is of no use doing so. Chung-nî cannot be reviled. The talents and virtue of other men are hillocks and mounds which may be stepped over. Chung-nî is the sun or moon, which it is not possible to step over. Although a man may wish to cut himself off from the sage, what harm can he do to the sun and moon? He only shows that he does not know his own capacity [2].'

In conversation with a fellow-disciple, Tsze-kung took a still higher flight. Being charged by Tsze-ch'in with being too modest, for that Confucius was not really superior to him, he replied, 'For one word a man is often deemed to be wise, and for one word he is often deemed to be foolish. We ought to be careful indeed in what we say. Our master cannot be attained to, just in the same way as the heavens cannot be gone up to by the steps of a stair. Were our master in the position of the prince of a State, or the chief of a Family, we should find verified the description which has been given of a sage's rule :—He would plant the people, and forthwith they would be established; he would lead them on, and forthwith they would follow him; he would make them happy, and forthwith multitudes would resort to his dominions; he would stimulate them, and forthwith they would be harmonious. While he lived, he would be glorious. When he died, he would be bitterly lamented. How is it possible for him to be attained to [3]?'

From these representations of Tsze-kung, it was not a difficult step for Tsze-sze to take in exalting Confucius not only to the level of the ancient sages, but as 'the equal of Heaven.' And Mencius took up the theme. Being questioned by Kung-sun Ch'âu, one of his disciples, about two acknowledged sages, Po-î and Î Yin, whether they were to be placed in the same rank with Confucius, he replied, 'No. Since there were living men until now, there never was another Confucius;' and then he proceeded to fortify his

---

[1] Ana. XIX. xxiii.　　　[2] Ana. XIX. xxiv.　　　[3] Ana. XIX. xxv.

opinion by the concurring testimony of Tsâi Wo, Tsze-kung, and
Yû Zo, who all had wisdom, he thought, sufficient to know their
master. Tsâi Wo's opinion was, 'According to my view of our
master, he is far superior to Yâo and Shun.' Tsze-kung said, 'By
viewing the ceremonial ordinances of a prince, we know the
character of his government. By hearing his music, we know the
character of his virtue. From the distance of a hundred ages after,
I can arrange, according to their merits, the kings of those hundred
ages;—not one of them can escape me. From the birth of mankind
till now, there has never been another like our master.' Yû Zo
said, 'Is it only among men that it is so? There is the ch'î-lin
among quadrupeds; the fung-hwang among birds; the T'âi mountain among mounds and ant-hills; and rivers and seas among rain-
pools. Though different in degree, they are the same in kind. So
the sages among mankind are also the same in kind. But they
stand out from their fellows, and rise above the level; and from
the birth of mankind till now, there never has been one so complete
as Confucius[1].' I will not indulge in farther illustration. The
judgment of the sage's disciples, of Tsze-sze, and of Mencius, has
been unchallenged by the mass of the scholars of China. Doubtless
it pleases them to bow down at the shrine of the Sage, for their
profession of literature is thereby glorified. A reflection of the
honour done to him falls upon themselves. And the powers that
be, and the multitudes of the people, fall in with the judgment.
Confucius is thus, in the empire of China, the one man by whom
all possible personal excellence was exemplified, and by whom all
possible lessons of social virtue and political wisdom are taught.

6. The reader will be prepared by the preceding account not
to expect to find any light thrown by Confucius on the great prob-

Subjects on
which Confucius
did not treat.—
That he was un-
religious, unspi-
ritual, and open
to the charge of
insincerity.

lems of the human condition and destiny. He did
not speculate on the creation of things or the end of
them. He was not troubled to account for the origin
of man, nor did he seek to know about his hereafter.
He meddled neither with physics nor metaphysics[2].
The testimony of the Analects about the subjects of his teaching is
the following:—'His frequent themes of discourse were the Book

---

[1] Mencius, II. Pt. I. ii. 23–28.

[2] 'The contents of the Yî-ching, and Confucius's labours upon it, may be objected in opposition to this statement, and I must be understood to make it with some reservation. Six
years ago, I spent all my leisure time for twelve months in the study of that Work, and wrote
out a translation of it, but at the close I was only groping my way in darkness to lay hold of

of Poetry, the Book of History, and the maintenance of the rules of Propriety.' 'He taught letters, ethics, devotion of soul, and truth-fulness.' 'Extraordinary things; feats of strength; states of dis-order; and spiritual beings, he did not like to talk about[1].'

Confucius is not to be blamed for his silence on the subjects here indicated. His ignorance of them was to a great extent his misfortune. He had not learned them. No report of them had come to him by the ear; no vision of them by the eye. And to his practical mind the toiling of thought amid uncertainties seemed worse than useless.

The question has, indeed, been raised, whether he did not make changes in the ancient creed of China[2], but I cannot believe that he did so consciously and designedly. Had his idiosyncrasy been dif-ferent, we might have had expositions of the ancient views on some points, the effect of which would have been more beneficial than the indefiniteness in which they are now left, and it may be doubted so far, whether Confucius was not unfaithful to his guides. But that he suppressed or added, in order to bring in articles of belief originating with himself, is a thing not to be charged against him.

I will mention two important subjects in regard to which there is a conviction in my mind that he came short of the faith of the older sages. The first is the doctrine of God. This name is common in the Shih-ching and Shû-ching. *Tî* or *Shang-Tî* appears there as a personal being, ruling in heaven and on earth, the author of man's moral nature, the governor among the nations, by whom kings reign and princes decree justice, the rewarder of the good, and the punisher of the bad. Confucius preferred to speak of Heaven. Instances have already been given of this. Two others may be cited :—' He who offends against Heaven has none to whom he can pray[3]?' 'Alas!' said he, 'there is no one that knows me.' Tsze-kung said, 'What do you mean by thus saying that no one knows you?' He replied, 'I do not murmur against Heaven. I do

its scope and meaning, and up to this time I have not been able to master it so as to speak positively about it. It will come in due time, in its place, in the present Publication, and I do not think that what I here say of Confucius will require much, if any, modification.' So I wrote in 1861; and I at last accomplished a translation of the Yî, which was published in 1882, as the sixteenth volume of 'The Sacred Books of the East.' I should like to bring out a revision of that version, with the Chinese text, so as to make it uniform with the volumes of the Classics previously published. But as Yang Ho said to Confucius, 'The years do not wait for us.'

[1] Ana. VII. xvii; xxiv; xx.   [2] See Hardwick's 'Christ and other Masters,' Part iii. pp. 18, 19, with his reference in a note to a passage from Meadows's 'The Chinese and their Rebellions.'   [3] Ana. III. xiii.

not grumble against men. My studies lie low, and my penetration rises high. But there is Heaven;—THAT knows me [1]!' Not once throughout the Analects does he use the personal name. I would say that he was unreligious rather than irreligious; yet by the coldness of his temperament and intellect in this matter, his influence is unfavourable to the development of ardent religious feeling among the Chinese people generally; and he prepared the way for the speculations of the literati of mediæval and modern times, which have exposed them to the charge of atheism.

Secondly, Along with the worship of God there existed in China, from the earliest historical times, the worship of other spiritual beings,—especially, and to every individual, the worship of departed ancestors. Confucius recognised this as an institution to be devoutly observed. 'He sacrificed to the dead as if they were present; he sacrificed to the spirits as if the spirits were present. He said, "I consider my not being present at the sacrifice as if I did not sacrifice [2]."' The custom must have originated from a belief in the continued existence of the dead. We cannot suppose that they who instituted it thought that with the cessation of this life on earth there was a cessation also of all conscious being. But Confucius never spoke explicitly on this subject. He tried to evade it. 'Chî Lû asked about serving the spirits of the dead, and the master said, "While you are not able to serve men, how can you serve their spirits?" The disciple added, "I venture to ask about death," and he was answered, "While you do not know life, how can you know about death [3]."' Still more striking is a conversation with another disciple, recorded in the 'Narratives of the School.' Tsze-kung asked him, saying, 'Do the dead have knowledge (of our services, that is), or are they without knowledge?' The master replied, 'If I were to say that the dead have such knowledge, I am afraid that filial sons and dutiful grandsons would injure their substance in paying the last offices to the departed; and if I were to say that the dead have not such knowledge, I am afraid lest unfilial sons should leave their parents unburied. You need not wish, Ts'ze, to know whether the dead have knowledge or not. There is no present urgency about the point. Hereafter you will know it for yourself [4].' Surely this was not the teaching proper to a sage.

---

[1] Ana. XIV. xxxvii.   [2] Ana. III. xii.   [3] Ana. XI. xi.   [4] 家語, 卷二, art. 致思, towards the end.

He said on one occasion that he had no concealments from his disciples[1]. Why did he not candidly tell his real thoughts on so interesting a subject? I incline to think that he doubted more than he believed. If the case were not so, it would be difficult to account for the answer which he returned to a question as to what constituted wisdom:—'To give one's self earnestly,' said he, 'to the duties due to men, and, while respecting spiritual beings, to keep aloof from them, may be called wisdom[2].' At any rate, as by his frequent references to Heaven, instead of following the phraseology of the older sages, he gave occasion to many of his professed followers to identify God with a principle of reason and the course of nature; so, in the point now in hand, he has led them to deny, like the Sadducees of old, the existence of any spirit at all, and to tell us that their sacrifices to the dead are but an outward form, the mode of expression which the principle of filial piety requires them to adopt when its objects have departed this life.

It will not be supposed that I wish to advocate or to defend the practice of sacrificing to the dead. My object has been to point out how Confucius recognised it, without acknowledging the faith from which it must have originated, and how he enforced it as a matter of form or ceremony. It thus connects itself with the most serious charge that can be brought against him,—the charge of insincerity. Among the four things which it is said he taught, 'truthfulness' is specified[3], and many sayings might be quoted from him, in which 'sincerity' is celebrated as highly and demanded as stringently as ever it has been by any Christian moralist; yet he was not altogether the truthful and true man to whom we accord our highest approbation. There was the case of Măng Chih-fan, who boldly brought up the rear of the defeated troops of Lû, and attributed his occupying the place of honour to the backwardness of his horse. The action was gallant, but the apology for it was weak and unnecessary. And yet Confucius saw nothing in the whole but matter for praise[4]. He could excuse himself from seeing an unwelcome visitor on the ground that he was sick, when there was nothing the matter with him[5]. These were small matters, but what shall we say to the incident which I have given in the sketch of his Life, p. 79,—his deliberately breaking the oath which he had sworn, simply on the ground that it had been forced from him?

---

[1] Ana. VII. xxiii.   [2] Ana. VI. xx.   [3] See above, near the beginning of this paragraph.   [4] Ana. VI. xiii.   [5] Ana. XVII. xx.

I should be glad if I could find evidence on which to deny the truth of that occurrence. But it rests on the same authority as most other statements about him, and it is accepted as a fact by the people and scholars of China. It must have had, and it must still have, a very injurious influence upon them. Foreigners charge a habit of deceitfulness upon the nation and its government ;—on the justice or injustice of this charge I say nothing. For every word of falsehood and every act of insincerity, the guilty party must bear his own burden, but we cannot but regret the example of Confucius in this particular. It is with the Chinese and their sage, as it was with the Jews of old and their teachers. He that leads them has caused them to err, and destroyed the way of their paths[1].

But was not insincerity a natural result of the un-religion of Confucius ? There are certain virtues which demand a true piety in order to their flourishing in the heart of man. Natural affection, the feeling of loyalty, and enlightened policy, may do much to build up and preserve a family and a state, but it requires more to maintain the love of truth, and make a lie, spoken or acted, to be shrunk from with shame. It requires in fact the living recognition of a God of truth, and all the sanctions of revealed religion. Unfortunately the Chinese have not had these, and the example of him to whom they bow down as the best and wisest of men, does not set them against dissimulation.

7. I go on to a brief discussion of Confucius's views on government, or what we may call his principles of political science. It

His views on government.

could not be in his long intercourse with his disciples but that he should enunciate many maxims bearing on character and morals generally, but he never rested in the improvement of the individual. 'The kingdom, the world, brought to a state of happy tranquillity[2],' was the grand object which he delighted to think of ; that it might be brought about as easily as 'one can look upon the palm of his hand,' was the dream which it pleased him to indulge[3]. He held that there was in men an adaptation and readiness to be governed, which only needed to be taken advantage of in the proper way. There must be the right administrators, but given those, and 'the growth of government would be rapid, just as vegetation is rapid in the earth ; yea, their

---

[1] Isaiah iii. 12.   [2] 天下平. See the 大學, 經, pars. 4, 5 ; &c.

[3] Ana. III. xi ; et al.

government would display itself like an easily-growing rush[1].' The same sentiment was common from the lips of Mencius. Enforcing it one day, when conversing with one of the petty rulers of his time, he said in his peculiar style, 'Does your Majesty understand the way of the growing grain? During the seventh and eighth months, when drought prevails, the plants become dry. Then the clouds collect densely in the heavens; they send down torrents of rain, and the grain erects itself as if by a shoot. When it does so, who can keep it back[2]?' Such, he contended, would be the response of the mass of the people to any true 'shepherd of men.' It may be deemed unnecessary that I should specify this point, for it is a truth applicable to the people of all nations. Speaking generally, government is by no device or cunning craftiness; human nature demands it. But in no other family of mankind is the characteristic so largely developed as in the Chinese. The love of order and quiet, and a willingness to submit to 'the powers that be,' eminently distinguish them. Foreign writers have often taken notice of this, and have attributed it to the influence of Confucius's doctrines as inculcating subordination; but it existed previous to his time. The character of the people moulded his system, more than it was moulded by it.

This readiness to be governed arose, according to Confucius, from 'the duties of universal obligation, or those between sovereign and minister, between father and son, between husband and wife, between elder brother and younger, and those belonging to the intercourse of friends[3].' Men as they are born into the world, and grow up in it, find themselves existing in those relations. They are the appointment of Heaven. And each relation has its reciprocal obligations, the recognition of which is proper to the Heaven-conferred nature. It only needs that the sacredness of the relations be maintained, and the duties belonging to them faithfully discharged, and the 'happy tranquillity' will prevail all under heaven. As to the institutions of government, the laws and arrangements by which, as through a thousand channels, it should go forth to carry plenty and prosperity through the length and breadth of the country, it did not belong to Confucius, 'the throneless king,' to set them forth minutely. And indeed they were existing in the records of 'the ancient sovereigns.' Nothing new was needed. It was only

---

[1] 中 庸, xx. 3.   [2] Mencius, I. Pt. I. vi. 6.   [3] 中 庸, xx. 8.

requisite to pursue the old paths, and raise up the old standards. 'The government of Wăn and Wû,' he said, 'is displayed in the records,—the tablets of wood and bamboo. Let there be the men, and the government will flourish; but without the men, the government decays and ceases[1].' To the same effect was the reply which he gave to Yen Hûi when asked by him how the government of a State should be administered. It seems very wide of the mark, until we read it in the light of the sage's veneration for ancient ordinances, and his opinion of their sufficiency. 'Follow,' he said, 'the seasons of Hsiâ. Ride in the state-carriages of Yin. Wear the ceremonial cap of Châu. Let the music be the Shâo with its pantomimes. Banish the songs of Chăng, and keep far from specious talkers[2].'

Confucius's idea then of a happy, well-governed State did not go beyond the flourishing of the five relations of society which have been mentioned; and we have not any condensed exhibition from him of their nature, or of the duties belonging to the several parties in them. Of the two first he spoke frequently, but all that he has said on the others would go into small compass. Mencius has said that 'between father and son there should be affection; between sovereign and minister righteousness; between husband and wife attention to their separate functions; between old and young, a proper order; and between friends, fidelity[3].' Confucius, I apprehend, would hardly have accepted this account. It does not bring out sufficiently the authority which he claimed for the father and the sovereign, and the obedience which he exacted from the child and the minister. With regard to the relation of husband and wife, he was in no respect superior to the preceding sages who had enunciated their views of 'propriety' on the subject. We have a somewhat detailed exposition of his opinions in the 'Narratives of the School.'—'Man,' said he, 'is the representative of Heaven, and is supreme over all things. Woman yields obedience to the instructions of man, and helps to carry out his principles[4]. On this account she can determine nothing of herself, and is subject to the rule of the three obediences. When young, she must obey her father and elder brother; when married, she must obey her husband;

---

[1] 中庸, xx. 2.   [2] Ana. XV. x.   [3] Mencius, III. Pt. I. iv. 8.   [4] 男子者, 任 天 道 而 長 萬 物 者 也; 女 子 者, 順 男 子 之 道, 而 長 其 理 者 也.

when her husband is dead, she must obey her son. She may not think of marrying a second time. No instructions or orders must issue from the harem. Woman's business is simply the preparation and supplying of drink and food. Beyond the threshold of her apartments she should not be known for evil or for good. She may not cross the boundaries of the State to attend a funeral. She may take no step on her own motion, and may come to no conclusion on her own deliberation. There are five women who are not to be taken in marriage :—the daughter of a rebellious house ; the daughter of a disorderly house ; the daughter of a house which has produced criminals for more than one generation ; the daughter of a leprous house ; and the daughter who has lost her father and elder brother. A wife may be divorced for seven reasons, which, however, may be overruled by three considerations. The grounds for divorce are disobedience to her husband's parents ; not giving birth to a son ; dissolute conduct ; jealousy—(of her husband's attentions, that is, to the other inmates of his harem) ; talkativeness ; and thieving. The three considerations which may overrule these grounds are—first, if, while she was taken from a home, she has now no home to return to ; second, if she have passed with her husband through the three years' mourning for his parents ; third, if the husband have become rich from being poor. All these regulations were adopted by the sages in harmony with the natures of man and woman, and to give importance to the ordinance of marriage[1].'

With these ideas of the relations of society, Confucius dwelt much on the necessity of personal correctness of character on the part of those in authority, in order to secure the right fulfilment of the duties implied in them. This is one grand peculiarity of his teaching. I have adverted to it in the review of ' The Great Learning,' but it deserves some further exhibition, and there are three conversations with the chief Chî K'ang in which it is very expressly set forth. ' Chî K'ang asked about government, and Confucius replied, " To govern means to rectify. If you lead on the people with correctness, who will dare not to be correct ?"' ' Chî K'ang, distressed about the number of thieves in the State, inquired of Confucius about how to do away with them. Confucius said, " If you, sir, were not covetous, though you should reward them to do it, they would not steal."' ' Chî K'ang asked about government,

---

[1] 家語卷三, 本命解.

saying, "What do you say to killing the unprincipled for the good of the principled?" Confucius replied, "Sir, in carrying on your government, why should you use killing at all? Let your evinced desires be for what is good, and the people will be good. The relation between superiors and inferiors is like that between the wind and the grass. The grass must bend, when the wind blows across it[1].'"

Example is not so powerful as Confucius in these and many other passages represented it, but its influence is very great. Its virtue is recognised in the family, and it is demanded in the church of Christ. 'A bishop'—and I quote the term with the simple meaning of overseer—'must be blameless.' It seems to me, however, that in the progress of society in the West we have come to think less of the power of example in many departments of state than we ought to do. It is thought of too little in the army and the navy. We laugh at the 'self-denying ordinance,' and the 'new model' of 1644, but there lay beneath them the principle which Confucius so broadly propounded,—the importance of personal virtue in all who are in authority. Now that Great Britain is the governing power over the masses of India, and that we are coming more and more into contact with tens of thousands of the Chinese, this maxim of our sage is deserving of serious consideration from all who bear rule, and especially from those on whom devolves the conduct of affairs. His words on the susceptibility of the people to be acted on by those above them ought not to prove as water spilt on the ground.

But to return to Confucius.—As he thus lays it down that the mainspring of the well-being of society is the personal character of the ruler, we look anxiously for what directions he has given for the cultivation of that. But here he is very defective. 'Self-adjustment and purification,' he said, 'with careful regulation of his dress, and the not making a movement contrary to the rules of propriety;—this is the way for the ruler to cultivate his person[2].' This is laying too much stress on what is external; but even to attain to this is beyond unassisted human strength. Confucius, however, never recognised a disturbance of the moral elements in the constitution of man. The people would move, according to him, to the virtue of their ruler as the grass bends to the wind, and that virtue

---

[1] Ana. XII. xvii; xviii; xix.　　　　　[2] 中庸, xx. 14.

would come to the ruler at his call.   Many were the lamentations which he uttered over the degeneracy of his times; frequent were the confessions which he made of his own shortcomings. It seems strange that it never came distinctly before him, that there is a power of evil in the prince and the peasant, which no efforts of their own and no instructions of sages are effectual to subdue.

The government which Confucius taught was a despotism, but of a modified character.   He allowed no '*jus divinum*,' independent of personal virtue and a benevolent rule.   He has not explicitly stated, indeed, wherein lies the ground of the great relation of the governor and the governed, but his views on the subject were, we may assume, in accordance with the language of the Shû-ching :—'Heaven and Earth are the parents of all things, and of all things men are the most intelligent.   The man among them most distinguished for intelligence becomes chief ruler, and ought to prove himself the parent of the people[1].'   And again, ' Heaven, protecting the inferior people, has constituted for them rulers and teachers, who should be able to be assisting to God, extending favour and producing tranquillity throughout all parts of the kingdom[2].'   The moment the ruler ceases to be a minister of God for good, and does not administer a government that is beneficial to the people, he forfeits the title by which he holds the throne, and perseverance in oppression will surely lead to his overthrow.   Mencius inculcated this principle with a frequency and boldness which are remarkable. It was one of the things about which Confucius did not like to talk. Still he held it.   It is conspicuous in the last chapter of ' The Great Learning.'   Its tendency has been to check the violence of oppression, and maintain the self-respect of the people, all along the course of Chinese history.

I must bring these observations on Confucius's views of government to a close, and I do so with two remarks.   First, they are adapted to a primitive, unsophisticated state of society.   He is a good counsellor for the father of a family, the chief of a clan, and even the head of a small principality.   But his views want the comprehension which would make them of much service in a great dominion.   Within three centuries after his death, the government of China passed into a new phase.   The founder of the Ch'in dynasty conceived the grand idea of abolishing all its feudal kingdoms, and centralizing their administration in himself.   He effected the revo-

[1] [2] See the Shû-ching, V. i. Sect. I. 2, 7.

lution, and succeeding dynasties adopted his system, and gradually moulded it into the forms and proportions which are now existing. There has been a tendency to advance, and Confucius has all along been trying to carry the nation back. Principles have been needed, and not 'proprieties.' The consequence is that China has increased beyond its ancient dimensions, while there has been no corresponding development of thought. Its body politic has the size of a giant, while it still retains the mind of a child. Its hoary age is in danger of becoming but senility.

Second, Confucius makes no provision for the intercourse of his country with other and independent nations. He knew indeed of none such. China was to him 'The Middle Kingdom[1],' 'The multitude of Great States[2],' 'All under heaven[3].' Beyond it were only rude and barbarous tribes. He does not speak of them bitterly, as many Chinese have done since his time. In one place he contrasts their condition favourably with the prevailing anarchy of the kingdom, saying 'The rude tribes of the east and north have their princes, and are not like the States of our great land which are without them[4].' Another time, disgusted with the want of appreciation which he experienced, he was expressing his intention to go and live among the nine wild tribes of the east. Some one said, 'They are rude. How can you do such a thing?' His reply was, 'If a superior man dwelt among them, what rudeness would there be[5]?' But had he been a ruler-sage, he would not only have influenced them by his instructions, but brought them to acknowledge and submit to his sway, as the great Yü did[6]. The only passage of Confucius's teachings from which any rule can be gathered for dealing with foreigners, is that in the 'Doctrine of the Mean,' where 'indulgent treatment of men from a distance' is laid down as one of the nine standard rules for the government of the country[7]. But 'the men from a distance' are understood to be *pin* and *lü*[8] simply,—'guests,' that is, or officers of one State seeking employment in another, or at the royal court; and 'visitors,' or travelling merchants. Of independent nations the ancient classics have not any knowledge, nor has Confucius. So long as merchants from Europe and other parts of the world could have been content to appear in China as suppliants, seeking the privilege of trade, so

[1] 中國.　　[2] 諸 夏; Ana. III. v.　　[3] 天 下; *passim*.　　[4] Ana. III. v.

[5] Ana. IX. xiii.　　[6] 書 經, III. ii. 10; *et al.*　　[7] 柔 遠 人.　　[8] 賓 旅.

long the government would have ranked them with the barbarous hordes of antiquity, and given them the benefit of the maxim about 'indulgent treatment,' according to its own understanding of it. But when their governments interfered, and claimed to treat with that of China on terms of equality, and that their subjects should be spoken to and of as being of the same clay with the Chinese themselves, an outrage was committed on tradition and prejudice, which it was necessary to resent with vehemence.

I do not charge the contemptuous arrogance of the Chinese government and people upon Confucius; what I deplore, is that he left no principles on record to check the development of such a spirit. His simple views of society and government were in a measure sufficient for the people while they dwelt apart from the rest of mankind. His practical lessons were better than if they had been left, which but for him they probably would have been, to fall a prey to the influences of Tâoism and Buddhism, but they could only subsist while they were left alone. Of the earth earthy, China was sure to go to pieces when it came into collision with a Christianly-civilized power. Its sage had left it no preservative or restorative elements against such a case.

It is a rude awakening from its complacency of centuries which China has now received. Its ancient landmarks are swept away. Opinions will differ as to the justice or injustice of the grounds on which it has been assailed, and I do not feel called to judge or to pronounce here concerning them. In the progress of events, it could hardly be but that the collision should come ; and when it did come it could not be but that China should be broken and scattered. Disorganization will go on to destroy it more and more, and yet there is hope for the people, with their veneration for the relations of society, with their devotion to learning, and with their habits of industry and sobriety ;—there is hope for them, if they will look away from all their ancient sages, and turn to Him, who sends them, along with the dissolution of their ancient state, the knowledge of Himself, the only living and true God, and of Jesus Christ whom He hath sent.

8. I have little more to add on the opinions of Confucius. Many of his sayings are pithy, and display much knowledge of character ; but as they are contained in the body of the Work, I will not occupy the space here with a selection of those which have struck myself as most worthy of notice. The fourth Book of the Analects,

which is on the subject of zăn, or perfect virtue, has several utterances which are remarkable.

Thornton observes:—'It may excite surprise, and probably incredulity, to state that the golden rule of our Saviour, 'Do unto others as you would that they should do unto you,' which Mr. Locke designates as ' the most unshaken rule of morality, and foundation of all social virtue,' had been inculcated by Confucius, almost in the same words, four centuries before[1].' I have taken notice of this fact in reviewing both ' The Great Learning ' and ' The Doctrine of the Mean.' I would be far from grudging a tribute of admiration to Confucius for it. The maxim occurs also twice in the Analects. In Book XV. xxiii, Tsze-kung asks if there be one word which may serve as a rule of practice for all one's life, and is answered, ' Is not reciprocity such a word ? What you do not want done to yourself do not do to others.' The same disciple appears in Book V. xi, telling Confucius that he was practising the lesson. He says, 'What I do not wish men to do to me, I also wish not to do to men ; ' but the master tells him, ' Ts'ze, you have not attained to that.' It would appear from this reply, that he was aware of the difficulty of obeying the precept ; and it is not found, in its condensed expression at least, in the older classics. The merit of it is Confucius's own.

When a comparison, however, is drawn between it and the rule laid down by Christ, it is proper to call attention to the positive form of the latter,—'All things whatsoever ye would that men should do unto you, do ye even so to them.' The lesson of the gospel commands men to do what they feel to be right and good. It requires them to commence a course of such conduct, without regard to the conduct of others to themselves. The lesson of Confucius only forbids men to do what they feel to be wrong and hurtful. So far as the point of priority is concerned, moreover, Christ adds, 'This is the law and the prophets.' The maxim was to be found substantially in the earlier revelations of God. Still it must be allowed that Confucius was well aware of the importance of taking the initiative in discharging all the relations of society. See his words as quoted from ' The Doctrine of the Mean ' on pages 48, 49 above.

But the worth of the two maxims depends on the intention of the enunciators in regard to their application. Confucius, it seems to me, did not think of the reciprocity coming into action beyond the circle of his five relations of society. Possibly, he might have

---

[1] History of China, vol. i. p. 209.

required its observance in dealings even with the rude tribes, which were the only specimens of mankind besides his own countrymen of which he knew anything, for on one occasion, when asked about perfect virtue, he replied, ' It is, in retirement, to be sedately grave ; in the management of business, to be reverently attentive; in intercourse with others, to be strictly sincere. Though a man go among the rude uncultivated tribes, these qualities may not be neglected[1].' Still, Confucius delivered his rule to his countrymen only, and only for their guidance in their relations of which I have had so much occasion to speak. The rule of Christ is for man as man, having to do with other men, all with himself on the same platform, as the children and subjects of the one God and Father in heaven.

How far short Confucius came of the standard of Christian benevolence, may be seen from his remarks when asked what was to be thought of the principle that injury should be recompensed with kindness. He replied, ' With what then will you recompense kindness ? Recompense injury with justice, and recompense kindness with kindness[2].' The same deliverance is given in one of the Books of the Lî Chî, where he adds that ' he who recompenses injury with kindness is a man who is careful of his person[3].' Chăng Hsüan, the commentator of the second century, says that such a course would be 'incorrect in point of propriety[4].' This 'propriety' was a great stumbling-block in the way of Confucius. His morality was the result of the balancings of his intellect, fettered by the decisions of men of old, and not the gushings of a loving heart, responsive to the promptings of Heaven, and in sympathy with erring and feeble humanity.

This subject leads me on to the last of the opinions of Confucius which I shall make the subject of remark in this place. A commentator observes, with reference to the inquiry about recompensing injury with kindness, that the questioner was asking only about trivial matters, which might be dealt with in the way he mentioned, while great offences, such as those against a sovereign or a father, could not be dealt with by such an inversion of the principles of justice[5]. In the second Book of the Lî Chî there is the following passage :—' With the slayer of his father, a man may not live under the same heaven ; against the slayer of his brother, a man must never have to go home to fetch a weapon ; with the slayer of

---

[1] Ana. XIII. xix.   [2] Ana. XIV. xxxvi.   [3] 禮 記, 表 記, par. 12.

'非 禮 之 正.'   [5] See notes *in loc.*, p. 288.

his friend, a man may not live in the same State[1].' The *lex talionis*
is here laid down in its fullest extent.   The Châu Lî tells us of a
provision made against the evil consequences of the principle, by the
appointment of a minister called 'The Reconciler[2].'   The provision
is very inferior to the cities of refuge which were set apart by Moses
for the manslayer to flee to from the fury of the avenger.   Such
as it was, however, it existed, and it is remarkable that Confucius,
when consulted on the subject, took no notice of it, but affirmed the
duty of blood-revenge in the strongest and most unrestricted terms.
His disciple Tsze-hsiâ asked him, 'What course is to be pursued in
the case of the murder of a father or mother?'   He replied, 'The
son must sleep upon a matting of grass, with his shield for his
pillow; he must decline to take office; he must not live under the
same heaven with the slayer.   When he meets him in the market-
place or the court, he must have his weapon ready to strike him.'
'And what is the course on the murder of a brother?'   'The surviving brother must not take office in the same State with the
slayer; yet if he go on his prince's service to the State where the
slayer is, though he meet him, he must not fight with him.'   'And
what is the course on the murder of an uncle or a cousin?'   'In this
case the nephew or cousin is not the principal.   If the principal on
whom the revenge devolves can take it, he has only to stand behind
with his weapon in his hand, and support him[3].'

Sir John Davis has rightly called attention to this as one of the
objectionable principles of Confucius[4].   The bad effects of it are
evident even in the present day.   Revenge is sweet to the Chinese.
I have spoken of their readiness to submit to government, and wish to
live in peace, yet they do not like to resign even to government the
'inquisition for blood.'   Where the ruling authority is feeble, as it is
at present, individuals and clans take the law into their own hands,
and whole districts are kept in a state of constant feud and warfare.

But I must now leave the sage.   I hope I have not done him
injustice; the more I have studied his character and opinions, the
more highly have I come to regard him.   He was a very great man,
and his influence has been on the whole a great benefit to the
Chinese, while his teachings suggest important lessons to ourselves
who profess to belong to the school of Christ.

---

[1] 禮記, I. Sect. I. Pt. v. 10.   [2] 周禮, 卷之十四, pp. 14-18.   [3] 禮記,
II. Sect. I. Pt. ii. 24. See also the 家語, 卷四, 子貢問.   [4] The Chinese, vol. ii. p. 41.

SECTION III.

HIS IMMEDIATE DISCIPLES.

Sze-mâ Ch'ien makes Confucius say :—' The disciples who received my instructions, and could themselves comprehend them, were seventy-seven individuals. They were all scholars of extraordinary ability[1]. The common saying is, that the disciples of the sage were three thousand, while among them there were seventy-two worthies. I propose to give here a list of all those whose names have come down to us, as being his followers. Of the greater number it will be seen that we know nothing more than their names and surnames. My principal authorities will be the 'Historical Records,' the 'Narratives of the School,' 'The Sacrificial Canon for the Sage's Temple, with Plates,' and the chapter on ' The Disciples of Confucius ' prefixed to the 'Four Books, Text and Commentary, with Proofs and Illustrations.' In giving a few notices of the better-known individuals, I will endeavour to avoid what may be gathered from the Analects.

1. Yen Hûi, by designation Tsze-yüan (顏 回, 字 子 淵). He was a native of Lû, the favourite of his master, whose junior he was by thirty years, and whose disciple he became when he was quite a youth. 'After I got Hûi,' Confucius remarked, 'the disciples came closer to me.' We are told that once, when he found himself on the Năng hill with Hûi, Tsze-lû, and Tsze-kung, Confucius asked them to tell him their different aims, and he would choose between them. Tsze-lû began, and when he had done, the master said, 'It marks your bravery.' Tsze-kung followed, on whose words the judgment was, ' They show your discriminating eloquence.' At last came Yen Yüan, who said, ' I should like to find an intelligent king and sage ruler whom I might assist. I would diffuse among the people instructions on the five great points, and lead them on by the rules of propriety and music, so that they should not care to fortify their cities by walls and moats, but would fuse their swords and spears into implements of agriculture. They should send forth their flocks without fear into the plains and forests. There should be no sunderings of families, no widows or widowers. For a thousand

[1] 孔子曰, 受業身通者, 七十有七人, 皆異能之士也.

years there would be no calamity of war. Yû would have no opportunity to display his bravery, or Ts'ze to display his oratory.' The master pronounced, 'How admirable is this virtue!'

When Hûi was twenty-nine, his hair was all white, and in three years more he died. He was sacrificed to, along with Confucius, by the first emperor of the Han dynasty. The title which he now has in the sacrificial Canon,—'Continuator of the Sage,' was conferred in the ninth year of the emperor, or, to speak more correctly, of the period, Chiâ-ching, A. D. 1530. Almost all the present sacrificial titles of the worthies in the temple were fixed at that time. Hûi's place is the first of the four Assessors, on the east of the sage[1].

2. Min Sun, styled Tsze-ch'ien (閔損, 字子騫). He was a native of Lû, fifteen years younger than Confucius, according to Sze-mâ Ch'ien, but fifty years younger, according to the 'Narratives of the School,' which latter authority is followed in 'The Annals of the Empire.' When he first came to Confucius, we are told, he had a starved look[2], which was by-and-by exchanged for one of fulness and satisfaction[3]. Tsze-kung asked him how the change had come about. He replied, 'I came from the midst of my reeds and sedges into the school of the master. He trained my mind to filial piety, and set before me the examples of the ancient kings. I felt a pleasure in his instructions; but when I went abroad, and saw the people in authority, with their umbrellas and banners, and all the pomp and circumstance of their trains, I also felt pleasure in that show. These two things assaulted each other in

---

[1] I have referred briefly, at p. 91, to the temples of Confucius. The principal hall, called 大成殿, or 'Hall of the Great and Complete One,' is that in which is his own statue or the tablet of his spirit, having on each side of it, within a screen, the statues, or tablets, of his 'four Assessors.' On the east and west, along the walls of the same apartment, are the two 序, the places of the 十二哲, or 'twelve Wise Ones,' those of his disciples, who, next to the 'Assessors,' are counted worthy of honour. Outside this apartment, and running in a line with the two 序, but along the external wall of the sacred inclosure, are the two 廡, or side-galleries, which I have sometimes called the ranges of the outer court. In each there are sixty-four tablets of the disciples and other worthies, having the same title as the Wise Ones, that of 先賢, or 'Ancient Worthy,' or the inferior title of 先儒, 'Ancient Scholar.' Behind the principal hall is the 崇聖祠殿, sacred to Confucius's ancestors, whose tablets are in the centre, fronting the south, like that of Confucius. On each side are likewise the tablets of certain 'ancient Worthies,' and 'ancient Scholars.'

[2] 菜色.   [3] 芻豢之色.

my breast. I could not determine which to prefer, and so I wore that look of distress. But now the lessons of our master have penetrated deeply into my mind. My progress also has been helped by the example of you my fellow-disciples. I now know what I should follow and what I should avoid, and all the pomp of power is no more to me than the dust of the ground. It is on this account that I have that look of fulness and satisfaction.' Tsze-ch'ien was high in Confucius's esteem. He was distinguished for his purity and filial affection. His place in the temple is the first, east, among 'The Wise Ones,' immediately after the four assessors. He was first sacrificed to along with Confucius, as is to be understood of the other 'Wise Ones,' excepting in the case of Yû Zo, in the eighth year of the style K'aî-yüan of the sixth emperor of the T'ang dynasty, A.D. 720. His title, the same as that of all but the Assessors, is—'The ancient Worthy, the philosopher Min.'

3. Zan Kǎng, styled Po-niû (冉耕, 字白 [*al.* 百] 牛). He was a native of Lû, and Confucius's junior only by seven years. When Confucius became minister of Crime, he appointed Po-niû to the office, which he had himself formerly held, of commandant of Chung-tû. His tablet is now fourth among 'The Wise Ones,' on the west.

4. Zan Yung, styled Chung-kung (冉雍, 字仲弓). He was of the same clan as Zan Kǎng, and twenty-nine years younger than Confucius. He had a bad father, but the master declared that was not to be counted to him, to detract from his admitted excellence. His place is among 'The Wise Ones,' the second, east.

5. Zan Ch'iû, styled Tsze-yû (冉求, 字子有). He was related to the two former, and of the same age as Chung-kung. He was noted among the disciples for his versatile ability and many acquirements. Tsze-kung said of him, 'Respectful to the old, and kind to the young; attentive to guests and visitors; fond of learning and skilled in many arts; diligent in his examination of things:—these are what belong to Zan Ch'iû.' It has been noted in the life of Confucius that it was by the influence of Tsze-yû that he was finally restored to Lû. He occupies the third place, west, among 'The Wise Ones.'

6. Chung Yû, styled Tsze-lû and Chî-lû (仲由, 字子路, 又字季路). He was a native of P'ien (卞) in Lû, and only

nine years younger than Confucius. At their first interview, the master asked him what he was fond of, and he replied, 'My long sword.' Confucius said, 'If to your present ability there were added the results of learning, you would be a very superior man.' 'Of what advantage would learning be to me?' asked Tsze-lû. 'There is a bamboo on the southern hill, which is straight itself without being bent. If you cut it down and use it, you can send it through a rhinoceros's hide;—what is the use of learning?' 'Yes,' said the master; 'but if you feather it and point it with steel, will it not penetrate more deeply?' Tsze-lû bowed twice, and said, 'I will reverently receive your instructions.' Confucius was wont to say, 'From the time that I got Yû, bad words no more came to my ears.' For some time Tsze-lû was chief magistrate of the district of P'û (蒲), where his administration commanded the warm commendations of the master. He died finally in Wei, as has been related above, pp. 86, 87. His tablet is now the fourth, east, from those of the Assessors.

7. Tsâi Yü, styled Tsze-wo (宰 予, 字 子 我). He was a native of Lû, but nothing is mentioned of his age. He had 'a sharp mouth,' according to Sze-mâ Ch'ien. Once, when he was at the court of Ch'û on some commission, the king Châo offered him an easy carriage adorned with ivory for his master. Yü replied, 'My master is a man who would rejoice in a government where right principles were carried out, and can find his joy in himself when that is not the case. Now right principles and virtue are as it were in a state of slumber. His wish is to rouse and put them in motion. Could he find a prince really anxious to rule according to them, he would walk on foot to his court, and be glad to do so. Why need he receive such a valuable gift as this from so great a distance?' Confucius commended this reply; but where he is mentioned in the Analects, Tsze-wo does not appear to great advantage. He took service in the State of Ch'î, and was chief magistrate of Lin-tsze, where he joined with T'ien Ch'ang in some disorderly movement[1], which led to the destruction of his kindred, and made Confucius ashamed of him. His tablet is now the second, west, among 'The Wise Ones.'

8. Twan-mû Ts'ze, styled Tsze-kung (端 木 賜, 字 子 貢 [al. 子 贛]), whose place is now third, east, from the Assessors. He

---

[1] 與 田 常 作 亂. See Sze-mâ Ch'ien's Biographies, chap. 7, though some have doubted the genuineness of this part of the notice of Tsze-wo.

was a native of Wei (衞), and thirty-one years younger than
Confucius. He had great quickness of natural ability, and appears
in the Analects as one of the most forward talkers among the
disciples. Confucius used to say, 'From the time that I got Ts'ze,
scholars from a distance came daily resorting to me.' Several
instances of the language which he used to express his admiration
of the master have been given in the last section. Here is another :
—The duke Ching of Ch'î asked Tsze-kung how Chung-nî was to
be ranked as a sage. 'I do not know,' was the reply. 'I have all
my life had the heaven over my head, but I do not know its height,
and the earth under my feet, but I do not know its thickness. In
my serving of Confucius, I am like a thirsty man who goes with
his pitcher to the river, and there he drinks his fill, without
knowing the river's depth.' He took leave of Confucius to become
commandant of Hsin-yang (信 陽 宰), when the master said to
him, 'In dealing with your subordinates, there is nothing like
impartiality ; and when wealth comes in your way, there is nothing
like moderation. Hold fast these two things, and do not swerve
from them. To conceal men's excellence is to obscure the worthy ;
and to proclaim people's wickedness is the part of a mean man.
To speak evil of those whom you have not sought the opportunity
to instruct is not the way of friendship and harmony.' Subsequently Tsze-kung was high in office both in Lû and Wei, and
finally died in Ch'î. We saw how he was in attendance on Confucius at the time of the sage's death. Many of the disciples built
huts near the master's grave, and mourned for him three years, but
Tsze-kung remained sorrowing alone for three years more.

9. Yen Yen, styled Tsze-yû (言 偃, 字 子 游), now the fourth
in the western range of 'The Wise Ones.' He was a native of Wû
(吳), forty-five years younger than Confucius, and distinguished
for his literary acquirements. Being made commandant of Wû-ch'ăng,
he transformed the character of the people by 'proprieties' and
music, and was praised by the master. After the death of Confucius, Chî K'ang asked Yen how that event had made no sensation
like that which was made by the death of Tsze-ch'an, when the
men laid aside their bowstring rings and girdle ornaments, and
the women laid aside their pearls and ear-rings, and the voice of
weeping was heard in the lanes for three months. Yen replied,
'The influences of Tsze-ch'an and my master might be compared

to those of overflowing water and the fattening rain. Wherever the water in its overflow reaches, men take knowledge of it, while the fattening rain falls unobserved.'

10. Pû Shang, styled Tsze-hsiâ (卜 商, 字 子 夏). It is not certain to what State he belonged, his birth being assigned to Wei (衞), to Wei (魏), and to Wăn (温). He was forty-five years younger than Confucius, and lived to a great age, for we find him, B. C. 406, at the court of the prince Wăn of Wei (魏), to whom he gave copies of some of the classical Books. He is represented as a scholar extensively read and exact, but without great comprehension of mind. What is called Mâo's Shih-ching (毛 詩) is said to contain the views of Tsze-hsiâ. Kung-yang Kâo and Kû-liang Ch'ih are also said to have studied the Ch'un Ch'iû with him. On the occasion of the death of his son he wept himself blind. His place is the fifth, east, among 'The Wise Ones.'

11. Chwan-sun Shih, styled Tsze-chang (顓 孫 師, 字 子 張), has his tablet, corresponding to that of the preceding, on the west. He was a native of Ch'ăn (陳), and forty-eight years younger than Confucius. Tsze-kung said, 'Not to boast of his admirable merit; not to signify joy on account of noble station; neither insolent nor indolent; showing no pride to the dependent:—these are the characteristics of Chwan-sun Shih.' When he was sick, he called (his son) Shăn-hsiang to him, and said, 'We speak of his *end* in the case of a superior man, and of his *death* in the case of a mean man. May I think that it is going to be the former with me to-day?'

12. Tsăng Shăn [or Ts'an], styled Tsze-yü (曾 參, 字 子 輿 [*al.* 子 與]). He was a native of south Wû-ch'ăng, and forty-six years younger than Confucius. In his sixteenth year he was sent by his father into Ch'û, where Confucius then was, to learn under the sage. Excepting perhaps Yen Hûi, there is not a name of greater note in the Confucian school. Tsze-kung said of him, 'There is no subject which he has not studied. His appearance is respectful. His virtue is solid. His words command credence. Before great men he draws himself up in the pride of self-respect. His eyebrows are those of longevity.' He was noted for his filial piety, and after the death of his parents, he could not read the rites of mourning without being led to think of them, and moved to tears. He was a voluminous writer. Ten Books of his composition are said to be contained in the 'Rites of the elder Tâi'

(大戴禮). The Classic of Filial Piety he is said to have made under the eye of Confucius. On his connexion with 'The Great Learning,' see above, Ch. III. Sect. II. He was first associated with the sacrifices to Confucius in A.D. 668, but in 1267 he was advanced to be one of the sage's four Assessors. His title—'Exhibitor of the Fundamental Principles of the Sage,' dates from the period of Chiâ-ching, as mentioned in speaking of Yen Hûi.

13. Tan-t'âi Mieh-ming, styled Tsze-yü (澹臺滅明, 字子羽). He was a native of Wû-ch'ăng, thirty-nine years younger than Confucius, according to the 'Historical Records,' but forty-nine, according to the 'Narratives of the School.' He was excessively ugly, and Confucius thought meanly of his talents in consequence, on his first application to him. After completing his studies, he travelled to the south as far as the Yang-tsze. Traces of his presence in that part of the country are still pointed out in the department of Sû-châu. He was followed by about three hundred disciples, to whom he laid down rules for their guidance in their intercourse with the princes. When Confucius heard of his success, he confessed how he had been led by his bad looks to misjudge him. He, with nearly all the disciples whose names follow, first had a place assigned to him in the sacrifices to Confucius in A.D. 739. The place of his tablet is the second, east, in the outer court, beyond that of the 'Assessors' and 'Wise Ones.'

14. Corresponding to the preceding, on the west, is the tablet of Fû Pû-ch'î, styled Tsze-tsien (宓 [al. 密 and 虙, all＝伏] 不齊, 字子賤). He was a native of Lû, and, according to different accounts, thirty, forty, and forty-nine years younger than Confucius. He was commandant of Tan-fû (單父宰), and hardly needed to put forth any personal effort. Wû-mâ Ch'î had been in the same office, and had succeeded by dint of the greatest industry and toil. He asked Pû-ch'î how he managed so easily for himself, and was answered, 'I employ men; you employ men's strength.' People pronounced Fû to be a superior man. He was also a writer, and his works are mentioned in Liû Hsin's Catalogue.

15. Next to that of Mieh-ming is the tablet of Yüan Hsien, styled Tsze-sze (原憲, 字子思), a native of Sung, or, according to Chăng Hsüan, of Lû, and younger than Confucius by thirty-six years. He was noted for his purity and modesty, and for his

happiness in the principles of the master amid deep poverty. After the death of Confucius, he lived in obscurity in Wei. In the notes to Ana. VI. iii, I have referred to an interview which he had with Tsze-kung.

16. Kung-yê Ch'ang [*al.* Chih], styled Tsze-ch'ang [*al.* Tsze-chih], (公冶長 [*al.* 芝], 字子長 [*al.* 子之]), has his tablet next to that of Pû-ch'î. He was son-in-law to Confucius. His nativity is assigned both to Lû and to Ch'î.

17. Nan-kung Kwo, styled Tsze-yung (南宮括 [*al.* 适 and, in the 'Narratives of the School,' 縚 (T'âo)], 字子容), has the place at the east next to Yüan Hsien. It is a question much debated whether he was the same with Nan-kung Chǎng-shû, who accompanied Confucius to the court of Châu, or not. On occasion of a fire breaking out in the palace of duke Âi, while others were intent on securing the contents of the Treasury, Nan-kung directed his efforts to save the Library, and to him was owing the preservation of the copy of the Châu Lî which was in Lû, and other ancient monuments.

18. Kung-hsî Âi, styled Chî-ts'ze [*al.* Chî-ch'ǎn] (公皙哀, 字季次 [*al.* 季沉]). His tablet follows that of Kung-yê. He was a native of Lû, or of Ch'î. Confucius commended him for refusing to take office with any of the Families which were encroaching on the authority of the princes of the States, and for choosing to endure the severest poverty rather than sacrifice a tittle of his principles.

19. Tsǎng Tien, styled Hsî (曾蒧 [*al.* 點], 字皙). He was the father of Tsǎng Shǎn. His place in the temples is the hall to Confucius's ancestors, where his tablet is the first, west.

20. Yen Wû-yâo, styled Lû (顏無繇, 字路). He was the father of Yen Hûi, younger than Confucius by six years. His sacrificial place is the first, east, in the same hall as the last.

21. Following the tablet of Nan-kung Kwo is that of Shang Chü, styled Tsze-mû (商瞿, 字子木). To him, it is said, we are indebted for the preservation of the Yî-ching, which he received from Confucius. Its transmission step by step, from Chü down to the Han dynasty, is minutely set forth.

22. Next to Kung-hsî Âi is the place of Kâo Ch'âi, styled Tsze-kâo and Chî-kâo (高柴, 字子羔 [*al.* 季羔; for 羔 moreover, we find 皋, and 翠]), a native of Ch'î, according to the 'Narratives

of the School,' but of Wei, according to Sze-mâ Ch'ien and Chăng
Hsüan.   He was thirty (some say forty) years younger than Confucius, dwarfish and ugly, but of great worth and ability.   At one
time he was criminal judge of Wei, and in the execution of his
office condemned a prisoner to lose his feet.   Afterwards that same
man saved his life, when he was flying from the State.   Confucius
praised Ch'âi for being able to administer stern justice with such a
spirit of benevolence as to disarm resentment.

23. Shang Chü is followed by Ch'î-tiâo K'âi [prop. Ch'î], styled
Tsze-k'âi, Tsze-zo, and Tsze-hsiû (漆 雕 開 [pr. 啟], 字 子 開,
子 若, and 子 脩), a native of Ts'âi (蔡), or, according to Chăng
Hsüan, of Lû.   We only know him as a reader of the Shû-ching,
and refusing to go into office.

24. Kung-po Liâo, styled Tsze-châu (公 伯 僚, 字 子 周).
He appears in the Analects, XIV. xxxiii, slandering Tsze-lû.   It is
doubtful whether he should have a place among the disciples.

25. Sze-mâ Kăng, styled Tsze-niû (司 馬 耕, 字 子 牛),
follows Ch'î-tiâo K'âi ; also styled 黎 耕.   He was a great talker,
a native of Sung, and a brother of Hwan T'ûi, to escape from whom
seems to have been the labour of his life.

26. The place next Kâo Ch'âi is occupied by Fan Hsü, styled
Tsze-ch'ih (樊 須, 字 子 遲), a native of Ch'î, or, according to
others, of Lû, and whose age is given as thirty-six and forty-six
years younger than Confucius.   When young, he distinguished himself in a military command under the Chî family.

27. Yû Zo, styled Tsze-zo (有 若, 字 子 若).   He was a
native of Lû, and his age is stated very variously.   He was noted
among the disciples for his great memory and fondness for antiquity.
After the death of Confucius, the rest of the disciples, because of
some likeness in Zo's speech to the Master, wished to render the
same observances to him which they had done to Confucius, but on
Tsăng Shăn's demurring to the thing, they abandoned the purpose.
The tablet of Tsze-zo is now the sixth, east, among 'The Wise
Ones,' to which place it was promoted in the third year of Ch'ien-
lung of the present dynasty.   This was done in compliance with a
memorial from the president of one of the Boards, who said he was
moved by a dream to make the request.   We may suppose that his
real motives were—a wish to do justice to the merits of Tsze-zo,
and to restore the symmetry of the tablets in the 'Hall of the

Great and Complete One,' which had been disturbed by the introduction of the tablet of Chû Hsî in the preceding reign.

28. Kung-hsî Ch'ih, styled Tsze-hwâ (公西赤, 字子華), a native of Lû, younger than Confucius by forty-two years, whose place is the fourth, west, in the outer court. He was noted for his knowledge of ceremonies, and the other disciples devolved on him all the arrangements about the funeral of the Master.

29. Wû-mâ Shih [or Ch'î], styled Tsze-Ch'î (巫馬施 [al. 期], 字子期 [al. 子旗]), a native of Ch'ǎn, or, according to Chǎng Hsüan, of Lû, thirty years younger than Confucius. His tablet is on the east, next to that of Sze-mâ Kǎng. It is related that on one occasion, when Confucius was about to set out with a company of the disciples on a walk or journey, he told them to take umbrellas. They met with a heavy shower, and Wû-mâ asked him, saying, 'There were no clouds in the morning; but after the sun had risen, you told us to take umbrellas. How did you know that it would rain?' Confucius said, 'The moon last evening was in the constellation Pî, and is it not said in the Shih-ching, "When the moon is in Pî, there will be heavy rain?" It was thus I knew it.'

30. Liang Chan [al. Lî], styled Shû-yü (梁鱣 [al. 鯉] 字叔魚), occupies the eighth place, west, among the tablets of the outer court. He was a man of Ch'î, and his age is stated as twenty-nine and thirty-nine years younger than Confucius. The following story is told in connexion with him.—When he was thirty, being disappointed that he had no son, he was minded to put away his wife. 'Do not do so,' said Shang Chü to him. 'I was thirty-eight before I had a son, and my mother was then about to take another wife for me, when the Master proposed sending me to Ch'î. My mother was unwilling that I should go, but Confucius said, 'Don't be anxious. Chü will have five sons after he is forty.' It has turned out so, and I apprehend it is your fault, and not your wife's, that you have no son yet.' Chan took this advice, and in the second year after, he had a son.

31. Yen Hsing [al. Hsin, Liû, and Wei], styled Tsze-liû (顏幸 [al. 辛, 柳, and 韋], 字子柳), occupies the place, east, after Wûmâ Shih. He was a native of Lû, and forty-six years younger than Confucius.

32. Liang Chan is followed on the west by Zan Zǔ, styled Tsze-lû [al. Tsze-tsǎng and Tsze-yü] (冉孺 [al. 儒] 字子魯 [al. 子曾

and 子魚]), a native of Lû, and fifty years younger than Confucius.

33. Yen Hsing is followed on the east by Ts'âo Hsü, styled Tsze-hsün (曹卹, 字子循), a native of Ts'âi, fifty years younger than Confucius.

34. Next on the west is Po Ch'ien, styled Tsze-hsî, or, in the current copies of the 'Narratives of the School,' Tsze-ch'iâi (伯虔, 字子皙 [al. 子析] or 子楷), a native of Lû, fifty years younger than Confucius.

35. Following Tsze-hsün is Kung-sun Lung [al. Ch'ung], styled Tsze-shih (公孫龍 [al. 寵], 字子石), whose birth is assigned by different writers to Wei, Ch'û, and Châo (趙). He was fifty-three years younger than Confucius. We have the following account:—'Tsze-kung asked Tsze-shih, saying, "Have you not learned the Book of Poetry?" Tsze-shih replied, "What leisure have I to do so? My parents require me to be filial; my brothers require me to be submissive; and my friends require me to be sincere. What leisure have I for anything else?" "Come to my Master," said Tsze-kung, "and learn of him."'

Sze-mâ Ch'ien here observes:—'Of the thirty-five disciples which precede, we have some details. Their age and other particulars are found in the Books and Records. It is not so, however, in regard to the fifty-two which follow.'

36. Zan Chî, styled Tsze-ch'an [al. Chî-ch'an and Tsze-tâ] (冉季, 字子產 [al. 季產 and 子達]), a native of Lû, whose place is the 11th, west, next to Po Ch'ien.

37. Kung-tsû Kâu-tsze or simply Tsze, styled Tsze-chih (公祖勾茲 [or simply 茲], 字子之), a native of Lû. His tablet is the 23rd, east, in the outer court.

38. Ch'in Tsû, styled Tsze-nan (秦祖, 字子南), a native of Ch'in. His tablet precedes that of the last, two places.

39. Ch'î-tiâo Ch'ih, styled Tsze-lien (漆雕哆 [al. 侈], 字子歛), a native of Lû. His tablet is the 13th, west.

40. Yen Kâo, styled Tsze-chiâo (顏高字子驕). According to the 'Narratives of the School,' he was the same as Yen K'o (刻, or 尅), who drove the carriage when Confucius rode in Wei after the duke and Nan-tsze. But this seems doubtful. Other

authorities make his name Ch'an (產), and style him Tsze-tsing (子精). His tablet is the 13th, east.

41. Ch'î-tiâo T'ǔ-fû [al. Ts'ung], styled Tsze-yû, Tsze-ch'î, and Tsze-wǎn (漆 雕 徒 父 [al. 從], 字 子 有 or 子 友 [al. 子 期 and 子 文]), a native of Lû, whose tablet precedes that of Ch'î-tiâo Ch'ih.

42. Zang Sze-ch'ih, styled Tsze-t'û, or Tsze-ts'ung (壤 [al. 穰] 駟 赤, 字 子 徒 [al. 子 從]), a native of Ch'in. Some consider Zang-sze (壤 駟) to be a double surname. His tablet comes after that of No. 40.

43. Shang Châi, styled Tsze-chî and Tsze-hsiû (商 澤, 字 子 季 [al. 子 秀]), a native of Lû. His tablet is immediately after that of Fan Hsü, No. 26.

44. Shih Tso [al. Chih and Tsze]-shû, styled Tsze-ming (石 作 [al. 之 and 子], 蜀, 字 子 明). Some take Shih-tso (石 作) as a double surname. His tablet follows that of No. 42.

45. Zǎn Pû-ch'î, styled Hsüan (任 不 齊, 字 選), a native of Ch'û, whose tablet is next to that of No. 28.

46. Kung-liang Zǔ, styled Tsze-chǎng (公 艮 孺 [al. 儒], 字 子 正), a native of Ch'in, follows the preceding in the temples. The 'Sacrificial Canon' says :—'Tsze-chǎng was a man of worth and bravery. When Confucius was surrounded and stopped in P'û, Tsze-chǎng fought so desperately, that the people of P'û were afraid, and let the Master go, on his swearing that he would not proceed to Wei.'

47. Hâu [al. Shih] Ch'û [al. Ch'ien], styled Tsze-lî [al. Lî-chih] (后 [al. 石] 處 [al. 虔], 字 子 里 [al. 里 之]), a native of Ch'î, having his tablet the 17th, east.

48. Ch'in Zan, styled K'âi (秦 冉, 字 開), a native of Ts'âi. He is not given in the list of the 'Narratives of the School,' and on this account his tablet was put out of the temples in the ninth year of Chiâ-tsing. It was restored, however, in the second year of Yung-chǎng, A.D. 1724, and is the 33rd, east, in the outer court.

49. Kung-hsiâ Shâu, styled Shǎng [and Tsze-shǎng] (公 夏 首 [al. 守], 字 乘 [and 子 乘]), a native of Lû, whose tablet is next to that of No. 44.

50. Hsî Yung-tien [or simply Tien], styled Tsze-hsî [al. Tsze-

chieh and Tsze-ch'ieh] (系容葳 [or 黕], 字子晳 [al. 子偕 and 子楷]), a native of Wei, having his tablet the 18th, east.

51. Kung Chien-ting [al. Kung Yŭ], styled Tsze-chung (公肩 [al. 堅] 定 [al. 公有], 字子仲 [al. 中 and 忠]). His nativity is assigned to Lû, to Wei, and to Tsin (晉). He follows No. 46.

52. Yen Tsŭ [al. Hsiang], styled Hsiang and Tsze-hsiang (顏祖 [al. 相], 字襄, and 子襄), a native of Lû, with his tablet following that of No. 50.

53. Chiâo Tan [al. Wû], styled Tsze-këa (鄡單 [al. 鄝], 字子家), a native of Lû. His place is next to that of No. 51.

54. Chü [al. Kâu] Tsing-ch'iang [and simply Tsing], styled Tsze-ch'iang [al. Tsze-chieh and Tsze-măng] (句 [al. 勾 and 鉤] 井疆 [and simply 井], 字子疆 [al. 子界 and 子孟]), a native of Wei, following No. 52.

55. Han [al. Tsâi]-fû Hêi, styled Tsze-hêi [al. Tsze-so and Tsze-sŭ] (罕 [al. 宰] 父黑, 字子黑 [al. 子索 and 子素]), a native of Lû, whose tablet is next to that of No. 53.

56. Ch'in Shang, styled Tsze-p'ei [al. P'ei-tsze and Pû-tsze] (秦商, 字子丕 [al. 丕茲 and 不茲]), a native of Lû, or, according to Chăng Hsüan, of Ch'û. He was forty years younger than Confucius. One authority, however, says he was only four years younger, and that his father and Confucius's father were both celebrated for their strength. His tablet is the 12th, east.

57. Shin Tang, styled Châu (申黨字周). In the 'Narratives of the School' there is a Shin Chî, styled Tsze-châu (申續, 字子周). The name is given by others as T'ang (堂 and 儻) and Tsŭ (續), with the designation Tsze-tsŭ (子續). These are probably the same person mentioned in the Analects as Shin Ch'ang (申棖). Prior to the Ming dynasty they were sacrificed to as two, but in A.D. 1530, the name Tang was expunged from the sacrificial list, and only that of Ch'ang left. His tablet is the 31st, east.

58. Yen Chih-p'o, styled Tsze-shû [or simply Shû] (顏之僕, 字子叔 [or simply 叔]), a native of Lû, who occupies the 29th place, east.

59. Yung Ch'î, styled Tsze-ch'î [al. Tsze-yen] (榮旂 [or 祈], 字子旗 or 子祺 [al. 子顏]), a native of Lû, whose tablet is the 20th, west.

60. Hsien Ch'ăng, styled Tsze-ch'î [al. Tsze-hung] (縣成, 字子祺 [al. 子橫]), a native of Lû. His place is the 22nd, east.

61. Tso Zăn-ying [or simply Ying], styled Hsing and Tsze-hsing (左人郢 [or simply 郢], 字行 and 子行), a native of Lû. His tablet follows that of No. 59.

62. Yen Chî, styled An [al. Tsze-sze] (燕伋 [or 級], 字恩 [al. 子思]), a native of Ch'in. His tablet is the 24th, east.

63. Chăng Kwo, styled Tsze-t'û (鄭國, 字子徒), a native of Lû. This is understood to be the same with the Hsieh Pang, styled Tsze-ts'ung (薛邦, 字子從), of the 'Narratives of the School.' His tablet follows No. 61.

64. Ch'in Fei, styled Tsze-chih (秦非, 字子之), a native of Lû, having his tablet the 31st, west.

65. Shih Chih-ch'ang, styled Tsze-hăng [al. ch'ang] (施之常, 字子恆 [al. 常]), a native of Lû. His tablet is the 30th, east.

66. Yen K'wâi, styled Tsze-shăng (顏噲, 字子聲), a native of Lû. His tablet is the next to that of No. 64.

67. Pû Shû-shăng, styled Tsze-ch'ê (步叔乘 [in the 'Narratives of the School' we have an old form of 乘], 字子車), a native of Ch'î. Sometimes for Pû (步) we find Shâo (少). His tablet is the 30th, west.

68. Yüan K'ang, styled Tsze-chî (原亢, 字子籍), a native of Lû. Sze-mâ Ch'ien calls him Yüan K'ang-chî, not mentioning any designation. The 'Narratives of the School' makes him Yüan K'ang (抗), styled Chî. His tablet is the 23rd, west.

69. Yo K'o [al. Hsin], styled Tsze-shăng (樂欬 [al. 欣], 字子聲), a native of Lû. His tablet is the 25th, east.

70. Lien Chieh, styled Yung and Tsze-yung [al. Tsze-ts'âo] (廉潔, 字庸 and 子庸 [al. 子曹]), a native of Wei, or of Ch'î. His tablet is next to that of No. 68.

71. Shû-chung Hûi [al. K'wâi], styled Tsze-ch'î (叔仲會 [al. 噲], 字子期), a native of Lû, or, according to Chăng Hsüan, of Tsin. He was younger than Confucius by fifty-four years. It is said that he and another youth, called K'ung Hsüan (孔璇), attended by turns with their pencils, and acted as amanuenses to the sage, and when Măng Wû-po expressed a doubt of their competency, Confucius declared his satisfaction with them. He follows Lien Chieh in the temples.

72. Yen Ho, styled Zan (顏何, 字冉), a native of Lû. The present copies of the 'Narratives of the School' do not contain this name, and in A.D. 1588 Zan was displaced from his place in the temples. His tablet, however, has been restored during the present ·dynasty. It is the 33rd, west.

73. Tî Hêi, styled Chê [al. Tsze-chê and Chê-chih] (狄黑, 字晳 [al. 子晳 and 晳之]), a native of Wei, or of Lû. His tablet is the 26th, east.

74. Kwei [al. Pang] Sun, styled Tsze-lien [al. Tsze-yin] (邽 [al. 邧] 巽, 字子斂 [al. 子歛]), a native of Lû. His tablet is the 27th, west.

75. K'ung Chung, styled Tsze-mieh (孔忠, 字子蔑). This was the son, it is said, of Confucius's elder brother, the cripple Măng-p'î. His tablet is next to that of No. 73. His sacrificial title is 'The ancient Worthy, the philosopher Mieh.'

76. Kung-hsî Yü-zû [al. Yü], styled Tsze-shang (公西輿如 [al. 輿], 字子上), a native of Lû. His place is the 26th, west.

77. Kung-hsî Tien, styled Tsze-shang (公西蒧 [or 點], 字子上 [al. 子尚]), a native of Lû. His tablet is the 28th, east.

78. Ch'in Chang [al. Lâo], styled Tsze-k'âi (琴張 [al. 牢], 字子開), a native of Wei. His tablet is the 29th, west.

79. Ch'ăn K'ang, styled Tsze-k'ang [al. Tsze-ch'in] (陳亢, 字子亢 [al. 子禽]), a native of Ch'ăn. See notes on Ana. I. x.

80. Hsien Tan [al. Tan-fû and Făng], styled Tsze-hsiang (縣亶 [al. 亶父 and 豐], 字子象), a native of Lû. Some suppose that this is the same as No. 53. The advisers of the present dynasty in such matters, however, have considered them to be different, and in 1724, a tablet was assigned to Hsien Tan, the 34th, west.

The three preceding names are given in the 'Narratives of the School.'

The research of scholars has added about twenty others.

81. Lin Fang, styled Tsze-ch'iû (林放, 字子邱), a native of Lû. The only thing known of him is from the Ana. III. iv. His tablet was displaced under the Ming, but has been restored by the present dynasty. It is the first, west.

82. Chü Yüan, styled Po-yü (蘧瑗, 字伯玉), an officer of Wei, and, as appears from the Analects and Mencius, an intimate

friend of Confucius. Still his tablet has shared the same changes as that of Lin Fang. It is now the first, east.

83 and 84. Shăn Ch'ang (申 棖) and Shăn T'ang (申 堂). See No. 57.

85. Mû P'î (牧 皮), mentioned by Mencius, VII. Pt. II. xxxvii. 4. His entrance into the temple has been under the present dynasty. His tablet is the 34th, east.

86. Tso Ch'iû-ming or Tso-ch'iû Ming (左 丘 明) has the 32nd place, east. His title was fixed in A.D. 1530 to be—'The Ancient Scholar,' but in 1642 it was raised to that of 'Ancient Worthy.' To him we owe the most distinguished of the annotated editions of the Ch'un Ch'iû. But whether he really was a disciple of Confucius, and in personal communication with him, is much debated.

The above are the only names and surnames of those of the disciples who now share in the sacrifices to the sage. Those who wish to exhaust the subject, mention in addition, on the authority of Tso Ch'iû-ming, Chung-sun Ho-chî (仲 孫 何 忌), a son of Măng Hsî (see p. 63), and Chung-sun Shwo (仲 孫 說), also a son of Măng Hsî, supposed by many to be the same with No. 17; Zû Pei, (孺 悲), mentioned in the Analects, XVII. xx, and in the Lî Chî, XVIII. Sect. II. ii. 22; Kung-wang Chih-ch'iû (公 罔 之 裘) and Hsü Tien (序 點), mentioned in the Lî Chî, XLIII. 7; Pin-mâu Chiâ (賓 牟 賈), mentioned in the Lî Chî, XVII. iii. 16; K'ung Hsüan (孔 璇) and Hûi Shû-lan (惠 叔 蘭), on the authority of the 'Narratives of the School;' Ch'ang Chî (常 季), mentioned by Chwang-tsze; Chü Yü (鞠 語), mentioned by Yen-tsze (晏 子); Lien Yü (廉 瑀) and Lû Chün (魯 峻), on the authority of 文 翁 石 室; and finally Tsze-fû Ho (子 服 何), the Tsze-fû Ching-po (子 服 景 伯) of the Analects, XIV. xxxviii.

CHAPTER VI.

LIST OF THE PRINCIPAL WORKS WHICH HAVE BEEN CONSULTED IN THE PREPARATION OF THIS VOLUME.

SECTION I.

CHINESE WORKS, WITH BRIEF NOTICES.

十三經註疏, 'The Thirteen Ching, with Commentary and Explanations.' This is the great repertory of ancient lore upon the Classics. On the Analects, it contains the 'Collection of Explanations of the Lun Yü,' by Ho Yen and others (see p. 19), and 'The Correct Meaning,' or Paraphrase of Hsing Ping (see p. 20). On the Great Learning and the Doctrine of the Mean, it contains the comments and glosses of Chăng Hsüan, and of K'ung Ying-tâ (孔穎達) of the T'ang dynasty.

新刻批點四書讀本, 'A new edition of the Four Books, Punctuated and Annotated, for Reading.' This work was published in the seventh year of Tâo-kwang (1827) by a Kâo Lin (高琳). It is the finest edition of the Four Books which I have seen, in point of typographical execution. It is indeed a volume for reading. It contains the ordinary 'Collected Comments' of Chû Hsî on the Analects, and his 'Chapters and Sentences' of the Great Learning and Doctrine of the Mean. The editor's own notes are at the top and bottom of the page, in rubric.

四書朱子本義匯參, 'The Proper Meaning of the Four Books as determined by Chû Hsî, Compared with, and Illustrated from, other Commentators.' This is a most voluminous work, published in the tenth year of Ch'ien-lung, A.D. 1745, by Wang Pû-ch'ing (王步青), a member of the Han-lin College. On the Great Learning and the Doctrine of the Mean, the 'Queries' (或問) addressed to Chû Hsî and his replies are given in the same text as the standard commentary.

四書經註集證, 'The Four Books, Text and Commentary, with Proofs and Illustrations.' The copy of this Work which I have was edited by a Wang T'ing-chî (汪廷機), in the third

year of Chiâ-ch'ing, A. D. 1798. It may be called a commentary
on the commentary. The research in all matters of Geography,
History, Biography, Natural History, &c., is immense.

四書諸儒輯要, 'A Collection of the most important Comments of Scholars on the Four Books.' By Lî P'ei-lin (李沛霖);
published in the fifty-seventh K'ang-hsî year, A. D. 1718. This
Work is about as voluminous as the 匯參, but on a different plan.
Every chapter is preceded by a critical discussion of its general
meaning, and the logical connexion of its several paragraphs. This
is followed by the text, and Chû Hsî's standard commentary. We
have then a paraphrase, full and generally perspicuous. Next,
there is a selection of approved comments, from a great variety of
authors ; and finally, the reader finds a number of critical remarks
and ingenious views, differing often from the common interpretation,
which are submitted for his examination.

四書翼註論文, 'A Supplemental Commentary, and Literary
Discussions, on the Four Books.' By Chang Chăn-t'âo [al. T'î-
an] (張甄陶 [al. 惕菴]), a member of the Han-lin college, in
the early part, apparently, of the reign of Ch'ien-lung. The work
is on a peculiar plan. The reader is supposed to be acquainted
with Chû Hsî's commentary, which is not given ; but the author
generally supports his views, and defends them against the criticisms
of some of the early scholars of this dynasty. His own exercita-
tions are of the nature of essays more than of commentary. It is a
book for the student who is somewhat advanced, rather than for the
learner. I have often perused it with interest and advantage.

四書遵註合講, 'The Four Books, according to the Commentary, with Paraphrase.' Published in the eighth year of Yung
Chăng, A. D. 1730, by Wăng Fû [al. K'eh-fû] (翁復 [al. 克夫]).
Every page is divided into two parts. Below, we have the text
and Chû Hsî's commentary. Above, we have an analysis of every
chapter, followed by a paraphrase of the several paragraphs. To
the paraphrase of each paragraph are subjoined critical notes,
digested from a great variety of scholars, but without the mention
of their names. A list of 116 is given who are thus laid under
contribution. In addition, there are maps and illustrative figures
at the commencement; and to each Book there are prefixed biographical notices, explanations of peculiar allusions, &c.

新增四書補註附考備旨, 'The Four Books, with a

Complete Digest of Supplements to the Commentary, and additional Suggestions. A new edition, with Additions.' By Tû Ting-chî (杜 定 基). Published A. D. 1779. The original of this Work was by Tǎng Lin (鄧 林), a scholar of the Ming dynasty. It is perhaps the best of all editions of the Four Books for a learner. Each page is divided into three parts. Below, is the text divided into sentences and members of sentences, which are followed by short glosses. The text is followed by the usual commentary, and that by a paraphrase, to which are subjoined the Supplements and Suggestions. The middle division contains a critical analysis of the chapters and paragraphs; and above, there are the necessary biographical and other notes.

四 書 味 根 錄, 'The Four Books, with the Relish of the Radical Meaning.' This is a new Work, published in 1852. It is the production of Chin Ch'ǎng, styled Chi'û-t'an (金 澂, 字 秋 潭), an officer and scholar, who, returning, apparently to Canton province, from the North in 1836, occupied his retirement with reviewing his literary studies of former years, and employed his sons to tránscribe his notes. The writer is fully up in all the commentaries on the Classics, and pays particular attention to the labours of the scholars of the present dynasty. To the Analects, for instance, there is prefixed Chiang Yung's History of Confucius, with criticisms on it by the author himself. Each chapter is preceded by a critical analysis. Then follows the text with the standard commentary, carefully divided into sentences, often with glosses, original and selected, between them. To the commentary there succeeds a paraphrase, which is not copied by the author from those of his predecessors. After the paraphrase we have Explanations (解). The book is beautifully printed, and in small type, so that it is really a *multum in parvo*, with considerable freshness.

日 講 四 書 義 解, 'A Paraphrase for Daily Lessons, Explaining the Meaning of the Four Books.' This work was produced in 1677, by a department of the members of the Han-lin college, in obedience to an imperial rescript. The paraphrase is full, perspicuous, and elegant.

御 製 周 易 折 中; 書 經 傳 說 彙 纂; 詩 經 傳 說 彙 纂; 禮 記 義 疏; 春 秋 傳 說 彙 纂. These works form together a superb edition of the Five Ching, published by imperial authority in the K'ang-hsî and Yung-chăng reigns. They contain the standard views (傳); various opinions (說); critical decisions of the editors (晏); prolegomena; plates or cuts; and other apparatus for the student.

毛西河先生全集, 'The Collected Writings of Mâo Hsî-ho.' See prolegomena, p. 20. The voluminousness of his Writings is understated there. Of 經集, or Writings on the Classics, there are 236 sections, while his 文集, or other literary compositions, amount to 257 sections. His treatises on the Great Learning and the Doctrine of the Mean have been especially helpful to me. He is a great opponent of Chû Hsî, and would be a much more effective one, if he possessed the same graces of style as that 'prince of literature.'

四書拓餘說, 'A Collection of Supplemental Observations on the Four Books.' The preface of the author, Ts'âo Chih-shăng (曹之升), is dated in 1795, the last year of the reign of Ch'ien-lung. The work contains what we may call prolegomena on each of the Four Books, and then excursus on the most difficult and disputed passages. The tone is moderate, and the learning displayed extensive and solid. The views of Chû Hsî are frequently well defended from the assaults of Mâo Hsî-ho. I have found the Work very instructive.

鄕黨圖考, 'On the Tenth Book of the Analects, with Plates.' This Work was published by the author, Chiang Yung (江永), in the twenty-first Ch'ien-lung year, A. D. 1761, when he was seventy-six years old. It is devoted to the illustration of the above portion of the Analects, and is divided into ten sections, the first of which consists of woodcuts and tables. The second contains the Life of Confucius, of which I have largely availed myself in the preceding chapter. The whole is a remarkable specimen of the minute care with which Chinese scholars have illustrated the Classical Books.

四書釋地; 四書釋地續; 四書釋地又續; 四書釋地三續. We may call these volumes—'The Topography of the Four Books; with three Supplements.' The Author's name is Yen Zo-ch'ü (閻若璩). The first volume was published in 1698, and the second in 1700. I have not been able to find the dates of publication of the other two, in which there is more biographical and general matter than topographical. The author apologizes for the inappropriateness of their titles by saying that he could not help calling them Supplements to the Topography, which was his 'first love.'

皇 清 經 解, 'Explanations of the Classics, under the Imperial Ts'ing Dynasty.' See above, p. 20. The Work, however, was not published, as I have there supposed, by imperial authority, but under the superintendence, and at the expense (aided by other officers), of Yüan Yüan (阮 元), Governor-general of Kwang-tung and Kwang-hsî, in the ninth year of the last reign, 1829. The publication of so extensive a Work shows a public spirit and zeal for literature among the high officers of China, which should keep foreigners from thinking meanly of them.

孔 子 家 語, 'Sayings of the Confucian Family.' Family is to be taken in the sense of Sect or School. In Liû Hsin's Catalogue, in the subdivision devoted to the Lun Yü, we find the entry:—'Sayings of the Confucian Family, twenty-seven Books,' with a note by Yen Sze-kû of the T'ang dynasty,—'Not the existing Work called the Family Sayings.' The original Work was among the treasures found in the wall of Confucius's old house, and was deciphered and edited by K'ung An-kwo. The present Work is by Wang Sû of the Wei (魏) dynasty, grounded professedly on the older one, the blocks of which had suffered great dilapidation during the intervening centuries. It is allowed also, that, since Sû's time, the Work has suffered more than any of the acknowledged Classics. Yet it is a very valuable fragment of antiquity, and it would be worth while to incorporate it with the Analects. My copy is the edition of Lî Yung (李 容), published in 1780. I have generally called the Work 'Narratives of the School.'

聖 廟 祀 典 圖 考, 'Sacrificial Canon of the Sage's Temples, with Plates.' This Work, published in 1826, by Kû Yüan, styled Hsiang-châu (顧 沅, 字 湘 舟), is a very painstaking account of all the Names sacrificed to in the temples of Confucius, the dates of their attaining to that honour, &c. There are appended to it Memoirs of Confucius and Mencius, which are not of so much value.

十 子 全 書, 'The Complete Works of the Ten *Tsze*.' See Morrison's Dictionary, under the character 子. I have only had occasion, in connexion with this Work, to refer to the writings of Chwang-tsze (莊 子) and Lieh-tsze (列 子). My copy is an edition of 1804.

歷代名賢列女氏姓譜, 'A Cyclopædia of Surnames, or Biographical Dictionary, of the Famous Men and Virtuous Women of the Successive Dynasties.' This is a very notable work of its class; published in 1793, by 蕭智漢, and extending through 157 chapters or Books.

文獻通考, 'General Examination of Records and Scholars.' This astonishing Work, which cost its author, Mâ Twan-lin (馬端臨), twenty years' labour, was first published in 1321. Rémusat says—'This excellent Work is a library in itself, and if Chinese literature possessed no other, the language would be worth learning for the sake of reading this alone.' It does indeed display all but incredible research into every subject connected with the Government, History, Literature, Religion, &c., of the empire of China. The author's researches are digested in 348 Books. I have had occasion to consult principally those on the Literary Monuments, embraced in seventy-six Books, from the 174th to the 249th.

朱彝尊經義考, 'An Examination of the Commentaries on the Classics,' by Chû Î-tsun. The author was a member of the Han-lin college, and the work was first published with an imperial preface by the Ch'ien-lung emperor. It is an exhaustive work on the literature of the Classics, in 300 chapters or Books.

續文獻通考, 'A Continuation of the General Examination of Records and Scholars.' This Work, which is in 254 Books, and nearly as extensive as the former, was the production of Wang Ch'î (王圻), who dates his preface in 1586, the fourteenth year of Wan-lî, the style of the reign of the fourteenth emperor of the Ming dynasty. Wang Ch'î brings down the Work of his predecessor to his own times. He also frequently goes over the same ground, and puts things in a clearer light. I have found this to be the case in the chapters on the classical and other Books.

二十四史, 'The Twenty-four Histories.' These are the imperially-authorized records of the empire, commencing with the 'Historical Records,' the work of Sze-mâ Ch'ien, and ending with the History of the Ming dynasty, which appeared in 1742, the result of the joint labours of 145 officers and scholars of the present dynasty. The extent of the collection may be understood from this, that my copy, bound in English fashion, makes sixty-three volumes, each one larger than this. No nation has a history so thoroughly digested; and on the whole it is trustworthy. In preparing this volume, my necessities have been confined mostly to the Works of Sze-mâ Ch'ien, and his successor, Pan Kû (班 固), the Historian of the first Han dynasty.

歷 代 統 記 表, 'The Annals of the Nation.' Published by imperial authority in 1803, the eighth year of Ch'iâ-ch'ing. This Work is invaluable to a student, being, indeed, a collection of chronological tables, where every year, from the rise of the Châu dynasty, B.C. 1121, has a distinct column to itself, in which, in different compartments, the most important events are noted. Beyond that date, it ascends to nearly the commencement of the cycles in the sixty-first year of Hwang-tî, giving—not every year, but the years of which anything has been mentioned in history. From Hwang-tî also, it ascends through the dateless ages up to P'an-kû, the first of mortal sovereigns.

歷 代 疆 域 表, 'The Boundaries of the Nation in the successive Dynasties.' This Work by the same author, and published in 1817, does for the boundaries of the empire the same service which the preceding renders to its chronology.

歷 代 沿 革 表, 'The Topography of the Nation in the successive Dynasties.' Another Work by the same author, and of the same date as the preceding.

The Dictionaries chiefly consulted have been:—

The well-known Shwo Wăn (說文解字), by Hsü Shăn, styled Shû-chung (許 慎, 字 叔 重), published in A.D. 100; with the supplement (繫 傳) by Hsü Ch'ieh (徐 鍇), of the southern T'ang dynasty. The characters are arranged in the Shwo Wăn under 540 keys or radicals, as they are unfortunately termed.

The Liû Shû Kû (六 書 故), by Tâi T'ung, styled Chung-tâ (戴 侗, 字 仲 達), of our thirteenth century. The characters are arranged in it, somewhat after the fashion of the *R* Yâ (p. 2), under six general divisions, which again are subdivided, according to the affinity of subjects, into various categories.

The Tsze Hûi (字 彙), which appeared in the Wan-lî (萬 歷) reign of the Ming dynasty (1573–1619). The 540 radicals of the Shwo Wăn were reduced in this to 214, at which number they have since continued.

The K'ang-hsî Tsze Tien (康 熙 字 典), or K'ang-hsî Dictionary, prepared by order of the great K'ang-hsî emperor in 1716. This is the most common and complete of all Chinese dictionaries for common use.

The Î Wăn Pî Lan (藝文備覽), 'A Complete Exhibition of all the Authorized Characters,' published in 1787; 'furnishing,' says Dr. Williams, 'good definitions of all the common characters, whose ancient forms are explained.'

The Pei Wăn Yun Fû (佩文韻府), generally known among foreigners as 'The K'ang-hsî Thesaurus.' It was undertaken by an imperial order, and published in 1711, being probably, as Wylie says, 'the most extensive work of a lexicographical character ever produced.' It does for the phraseology of Chinese literature all, and more than all, that the K'ang-hsî dictionary does for the individual characters. The arrangement of the characters is according to their tones and final sounds. My copy of it, with a supplement published about ten years later, is in forty-five large volumes, with much more letter-press in it than the edition of the Dynastic Histories mentioned on p. 133.

The Ching Tsî Tswan Kû, ping Pû Wei (經籍纂詁幷補遺), 'A Digest of the Meanings in the Classical and other Books, with Supplement,' by, or rather under the superintendence of, Yüan Yüan (p. 132). This has often been found useful. It is arranged according to the tones and rhymes like the characters in the Thesaurus.

SECTION II.

TRANSLATIONS AND OTHER WORKS.

CONFUCIUS SINARUM PHILOSOPHUS ; sive Scientia Sinensis Latine Exposita. Studio et opera Prosperi Intorcetta, Christiani Herdritch, Francisci Rougemont, Philippi Couplet, Patrum Societatis JESU. Jussu Ludovici Magni. Parisiis, 1837.

THE WORKS OF CONFUCIUS ; containing the Original Text, with a Translation. Vol. I. By J. Marshman. Serampore, 1809. This is only a fragment of ' The Works of Confucius.'

THE FOUR BOOKS ; Translated into English, by Rev. David Collie, of the London Missionary Society. Malacca, 1828.

L'INVARIABLE MILIEU ; Ouvrage Moral de Tseu-sse, en Chinois et en Mandchou, avec une Version littérale Latine, une Traduction Françoise, &c. &c. Par M. Abel-Rémusat. A Paris, 1817.

LE TA HIO, OU LA GRANDE ÉTUDE ; Traduit en François, avec une Version Latine, &c. Par G. Pauthier. Paris, 1837.

Y-King; Antiquissimus Sinarum Liber, quem ex Latina Interpretatione P. Regis, aliorumque ex Soc. Jesu PP. edidit Julius Mohl. Stuttgartiæ et Tubingæ, 1839.

Mémoires concernant L'Histoire, Les Sciences, Les Arts, Les Mœurs, Les Usages, &c., des Chinois. Par les Missionaires de Pêkin. A Paris, 1776–1814.

Histoire Générale de La Chine ; ou Annales de cet Empire. Traduites du Tong-Kien-Kang-Mou. Par le feu Père Joseph-Annie-Marie de Moyriac de Mailla, Jesuite François, Missionaire à Pekin. A Paris, 1776–1785.

Notitia Linguæ Sinicæ. Auctore P. Prémare. Malaccæ, cura Academiæ Anglo-Sinensis, 1831.

The Chinese Repository. Canton, China, 20 vols., 1832–1851.

Dictionnaire des Noms, Anciens et Modernes, des Villes et Arrondissements de Premier, Deuxième, et Troisième ordre, compris dans L'Empire Chinois, &c. Par Édouard Biot, Membre du Conseil de la Société Asiatique. Paris, 1842.

The Chinese. By John Francis Davis, Esq., F.R.S., &c. In two volumes. London, 1836.

China : its State and Prospects. By W. H. Medhurst, D.D., of the London Missionary Society. London, 1838.

L'Univers : Histoire et Déscription des tous les Peuples. Chine. Par M. G. Pauthier. Paris, 1838.

History of China, from the earliest Records to the Treaty with Great Britain in 1842. By Thomas Thornton, Esq., Member of the Royal Asiatic Society. In two volumes. London, 1844.

The Middle Kingdom : A Survey of the Geography, Government, Education, Social Life, Arts, Religion, &c., of the Chinese Empire. By S. Wells Williams, LL.D. In two volumes. New York and London, 1848. The Second Edition, Revised, 1883.

The Religious Condition of the Chinese. By Rev. Joseph Edkins, B.A., of the London Missionary Society. London, 1859.

Christ and other Masters. By Charles Hardwick, M.A., Christian Advocate in the University of Cambridge. Part III. Religions of China, America, and Oceanica. Cambridge, 1858.

Introduction to the Study of Chinese Characters. By J. Edkins, D.D. London, 1876.

The Structure of Chinese Characters, under 300 Primary Forms. By John Chalmers, M.A., LL.D. Aberdeen, 1882.

CONFUCIAN ANALECTS.

BOOK I. HSIO *R*.

CHAPTER I. 1. The Master said, 'Is it not pleasant to learn with a constant perseverance and application?

2. 'Is it not delightful to have friends coming from distant quarters?

3. 'Is he not a man of complete virtue, who feels no discomposure though men may take no note of him?'

TITLE OF THE WORK.—論語, 'Discourses and Dialogues;' that is, the discourses or discussions of Confucius with his disciples and others on various topics, and his replies to their inquiries. Many chapters, however, and one whole book, are the sayings, not of the sage himself, but of some of his disciples. The characters may also be rendered 'Digested Conversations,' and this appears to be the more ancient signification attached to them, the account being that, after the death of Confucius, his disciples collected together and compared the memoranda of his conversations which they had severally preserved, digesting them into the twenty books which compose the work. Hence the title—論語, 'Discussed Sayings,' or 'Digested Conversations.' See 論語註疏解經序. I have styled the work 'Confucian Analects,' as being more descriptive of its character than any other name I could think of.

HEADING OF THIS BOOK.—學而第一. The two first characters in the book, after the introductory—'The Master said,' are adopted as its heading. This is similar to the custom of the Jews, who name many books in the Bible from the first word in them. 第一, 'The first;' that is, of the twenty books composing the whole work. In some of the books we find a unity or analogy of subjects, which evidently guided the compilers in grouping the chapters together. Others seem devoid of any such principle of combination. The sixteen chapters

of this book are occupied, it is said, with the fundamental subjects which ought to engage the attention of the learner, and the great matters of human practice. The word 學, 'learn,' rightly occupies the forefront in the studies of a nation, of which its educational system has so long been the distinction and glory.

1. THE WHOLE WORK AND ACHIEVEMENT OF THE LEARNER, FIRST PERFECTING HIS KNOWLEDGE, THEN ATTRACTING BY HIS FAME LIKE-MINDED INDIVIDUALS, AND FINALLY COMPLETE IN HIMSELF. I. 子, at the commencement, indicates Confucius. 子, 'a son,' is also the common designation of males,—especially of virtuous men. We find it, in conversations, used in the same way as our 'Sir.' When it *follows* the surname, it is equivalent to our 'Mr.,' or may be rendered 'the philosopher,' 'the scholar,' 'the officer,' &c. Often, however, it is better to leave it untranslated. When it *precedes* the surname, it indicates that the person spoken of was the master of the writer, as 子沈子, 'my master, the philosopher 沈.' Standing single and alone, as in the text, it denotes Confucius, *the philosopher*, or, rather, *the master*. If we render the term by Confucius, as all preceding translators have done, we miss the indication which it gives of the handiwork of his disciples, and the reverence which it bespeaks for him. 學, in the old commentators, is explained by 誦, 'to read chantingly,' 'to discuss.' Chû Hsî

CHAP. II. 1. The philosopher Yû said, 'They are few who, being filial and fraternal, are fond of offending against their superiors. There have been none, who, not liking to offend against their superiors, have been fond of stirring up confusion.

2. 'The superior man bends his attention to what is radical.

interprets it by 效, 'to imitate,' and makes its results to be 明善而復初, 'the understanding of all excellence, and the bringing back original goodness.' Subsequent scholars profess, for the most part, great admiration of this explanation. It is an illustration, to my mind, of the way in which Chû Hsî and his followers are continually being wise above what is written in the classical books. 習 is the rapid and frequent motion of the wings of a bird in flying, used for 'to repeat,' 'to practise.' 之 is the obj. of the third pers. pronoun, and its antecedent is to be found in the pregnant meaning of 學. 不亦 ... 乎 is explained by 豈不, 'is it not?' See 四書補註備旨. To bring out the force of 'also' in 亦, some say thus :—'The occasions for pleasure are many, *is this not also one?*' But it is better to consider 亦 as merely redundant ; —see Wang Yin-chih's masterly Treatise on the particles, chap. iii ; it forms chaps. 1208 to 1217 of the 皇清經解. 說, read *yuě*, as always when it has the entering tone marked, stands for 悅. What is learned becomes by practice and application one's own, and hence arises complacent pleasure in the mastering mind. 悅, as distinguished from 樂, (*lŏh*), in the next paragraph, is the internal, individual feeling of pleasure, and the other, its external manifestation, implying also companionship. 2. 朋, properly 'fellow-students ;' but, generally, individuals of the same class and character, like-minded. 3. 君子 I translate here—'a man of complete virtue.' Literally, it is—'a princely man.' See on 子, above. It is a technical term in Chinese moral writers, for which there is no exact correspondency in English, and which cannot be rendered always in the same way. See Morrison's Dictionary,

character 子. Its opposite is 小人, 'a small, mean man.' 人不知, 'Men do not know him,' but anciently some explained —'men do not know,' that is, are stupid under his teaching. The interpretation in the text is, doubtless, the correct one.

2. FILIAL PIETY AND FRATERNAL SUBMISSION ARE THE FOUNDATION OF ALL VIRTUOUS PRACTICE.

1. Yû, named 若, and styled 子有, and 子若, a native of 魯, was famed among the other disciples of Confucius for his strong memory, and love for the doctrines of antiquity. In something about him he resembled the sage. See Mencius, III. Pt. I. iv. 13. 有子 is 'Yû, the philosopher,' and he and Tsăng Shăn are the only two of Confucius's disciples who are mentioned in this style in the *Lun Yü*. This has led to an opinion on the part of some, that the work was compiled by their disciples. This may not be sufficiently supported, but I have not found the peculiarity pointed out satisfactorily explained. The tablet of Yû's spirit is now in the same apartment of the sage's temples as that of the sage himself, occupying the 6th place in the eastern range of 'the wise ones.' To this position it was promoted in the 3rd year of Ch'ien-lung of the present dynasty. A degree of activity enters into the meaning of 為 in 為人, = 'playing the man,' 'as men, showing themselves filial,' &c. 弟, here = 悌, 'to be submissive as a younger brother,' is in the 4th tone. With its proper signification, it was anciently in the 3rd tone. 而 = 'and yet,' different from its simple conjunctive use = 'and,' in the preceding chapter. 好, a verb, 'to love,' in the 4th tone, differs from the same character in the 3rd tone, an adjective, = 'good.' ᵒ鮮, 3rd tone, = 'few.' On the idiom 未之有, see Prémare's Grammar, p. 156. 2. 君子 has

That being established, all practical courses naturally grow up. Filial piety and fraternal submission!—are they not the root of all benevolent actions?'

CHAP. III. The Master said, 'Fine words and an insinuating appearance are seldom associated with true virtue.'

CHAP. IV. The philosopher Tsăng said, 'I daily examine myself on three points:—whether, in transacting business for others, I may have been not faithful;—whether, in intercourse with friends, I may have been not sincere;—whether I may have not mastered and practised the instructions of my teacher.'

a less intense signification here than in the last chapter. I translate—'The superior man,' for want of a better term. 本, 'the root,' 'what is radical,' is here said of filial and fraternal duties, and 道, 'ways' or 'courses,' of all that is intended by 爲(=行)仁, below. The particles 也 者 resume the discourse about 孝 弟, and introduce some further description of them. See Prémare, p. 158. 與, in the 2nd tone, is half interrogative, an answer in the affirmative being implied. 仁 is explained here as 'the principle of love,' 'the virtue of the heart.' Mencius says 一仁也者人也, '仁 is man,' in accordance with which, Julien translates it by *humanitas*. *Benevolence* often comes near it, but, as has been said before of 君子, we cannot give a uniform rendering of the term.

3. FAIR APPEARANCES ARE SUSPICIOUS. 巧 言令色,—see Shû-ching, II. iii. 2. 巧, 'skill in workmanship;' then, 'skill,' 'cleverness,' generally, and sometimes with a bad meaning, as here, = 'artful,' 'hypocritical.' 令, 'a law,' 'an order,' also 'good,' and here like 巧, with a bad meaning, = 'pretending to be good.' 色, 'the manifestation of the feelings made in the colour of the countenance,' is here used for the appearance generally.

4. HOW THE PHILOSOPHER TSĂNG DAILY EXAMINED HIMSELF, TO GUARD AGAINST HIS BEING GUILTY OF ANY IMPOSITION. *Tsăng*, whose name was 參 (*Shăn*), and his designation 子輿, was one of the principal disciples of Confucius. A follower of the sage from his 16th year, though inferior in natural ability to some others, by his filial piety and other moral qualities, he entirely won the Master's esteem, and by persevering attention mastered his doctrines. Confucius, it is said, employed him in the composition of the 孝 經, or 'Classic of Filial Piety.' The authorship of the 大 學, 'The Great Learning,' is also ascribed to him, though incorrectly, as we shall see. Portions, moreover, of his composition are preserved in the Lî Chî. His spirit tablet among the sage's four assessors, occupying the first place on the west, has precedence of that of Mencius. 省, read *hsing*, 'to examine.' 三省 is naturally understood of 'three times,' but the context and consent of commentators make us assent to the interpretation—'on three points.' 身, 'the body,' 'one's personality;' 吾身 = *myself*. 爲 is in the 4th tone, = 'for.' So, frequently, below. 忠 from 中, 'middle,' 'the centre,' and 心, 'the heart,' = loyalty, faithfulness, action with and from the heart. 朋, see chap. i. 友, 'two hands joined,' denoting union. 朋友, =

CHAP. V. The Master said, 'To rule a country of a thousand chariots, there must be reverent attention to business, and sincerity; economy in expenditure, and love for men; and the employment of the people at the proper seasons.'

CHAP. VI. The Master said, 'A youth, when at home, should be filial, and, abroad, respectful to his elders. He should be earnest and truthful. He should overflow in love to all, and cultivate the friendship of the good. When he has time and opportunity, after the performance of these things, he should employ them in polite studies.'

CHAP. VII. Tsze-hsiâ said, 'If a man withdraws his mind from the love of beauty, and applies it as sincerely to the love of the virtuous; if, in serving his parents, he can exert his utmost strength;

when together, 'friends.' 傳不習 is very enigmatical. The translation follows Chû Hsî. 何晏 explained quite differently: 'whether I have given instruction in what I had not studied and practised?' It does seem more correct to take 傳 actively, 'to give instruction,' rather than passively, 'to receive instruction.' See Mâo Hsî-ho's 四書改錯, XV. article 17.

5. FUNDAMENTAL PRINCIPLES FOR THE GOVERNMENT OF A LARGE STATE. 道 is used for 導, 'to rule,' 'to lead,' and is marked in the 4th tone, to distinguish it from 道, the noun, which was anciently read with the 3rd tone. It is different from 治, which refers to the actual business of government, while 導 is the duty and purpose thereof, apprehended by the prince. The standpoint of the principles is the prince's mind. 乘, in 4th tone, 'a chariot,' different from its meaning in the 2nd tone, 'to ride.' A country of 1000 chariots was one of the largest fiefs of the empire, which could bring such an armament into the field. The last principle,—使民

以時, means that the people should not be called from their husbandry at improper seasons, to do service on military expeditions and public works.

6. RULES FOR THE TRAINING OF THE YOUNG:— DUTY FIRST AND THEN ACCOMPLISHMENTS. 弟子, 'younger brothers and sons,' taken together, = youths, a youth. The 2nd 弟 is for 悌, as in chap. ii. 入出, 'coming in, going out,'= at home, abroad. 汎 is explained by Chû Hsî by 廣, 'wide,' 'widely;' its proper meaning is 'the rush or overflow of water.' 力, 'strength,' here embracing the idea of leisure. 學文, not literary studies merely, but all the accomplishments of a gentleman also:—ceremonies, music, archery, horsemanship, writing, and numbers.

7. TSZE-HSIÂ'S VIEWS OF THE SUBSTANCE OF LEARNING. Tsze-hsiâ was the designation of 卜商, another of the sage's distinguished disciples, and now placed 5th in the eastern range of 'the wise ones.' He was greatly famed for his learning, and his views on the Shih-ching and the Ch'un Ch'iû are said to be preserved in the com-

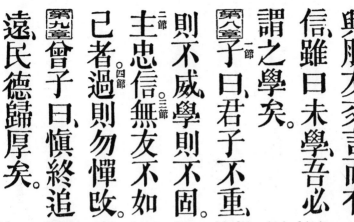

遠民德歸厚矣。 第九章 曾子曰慎終追 己者過則勿憚改。 主忠信無友不如 則不威學則不固。 第八章 子曰君子不重， 謂之學矣。 信雖曰未學吾必 與朋友交言而有

if, in serving his prince, he can devote his life; if, in his intercourse with his friends, his words are sincere:—although men say that he has not learned, I will certainly say that he has.'

Chap. VIII. 1. The Master said, 'If the scholar be not grave, he will not call forth any veneration, and his learning will not be solid.

2. 'Hold faithfulness and sincerity as first principles.

3. 'Have no friends not equal to yourself.

4. 'When you have faults, do not fear to abandon them.'

Chap. IX. The philosopher Tsǎng said, 'Let there be a careful attention *to perform the funeral rites* to parents, and let them be followed when long gone *with the ceremonies of sacrifice;*—then the virtue of the people will resume its proper excellence.'

mentaries of 毛, and of 公羊高 and 穀梁赤. He wept himself blind on the death of his son, but lived to a great age, and was much esteemed by the people and princes of the time. With regard to the scope of this chapter, there is some truth in what the commentator Wû, 吳, says,—that Tsze-hsiâ's words may be wrested to depreciate learning, while those of the Master in the preceding chapter hit exactly the due medium. The 2nd 賢 is a concrete noun. Written in full, it is composed of the characters for a *minister, loyal,* and *a precious shell.* It conveys the ideas of *talents* and *worth* in the concrete, but it is not easy to render it uniformly by any one term of another language. The 1st 賢 is a verb, = 'to treat as a *hsien.*' 色 has a different meaning from that in the 3rd chapter. Here it means 'sensual pleasure.' Literally rendered, the first sentence would be, 'esteeming properly the virtuous, and changing the love of woman,' and great fault is found by some, as in 四書改錯, XIII. i, with Chû Hsî's interpretation which I have followed; but there is force in what his adherents say, that the passage is not to be understood as if the individual spoken of had ever been given

to pleasure, but simply signifies the sincerity of his love for the virtuous. 致 here = 委, 'to give to,' 'to devote.'

8. Principles of self-cultivation. 1. 君子 has here its lightest meaning, = *a student,* one who wishes to be a *Chün-tsze.* 孔安國, of the Han dynasty, in the 2nd century B.C., took 固, in the sense of 'obscured,' 'dulled,' and interprets—'Let him learn, and he will not fall into error.' The received interpretation, as in the transl. is better. 2. 主, as a verb, 'to hold to be chief.' It is often used thus. 3. The object of friendship, with Chinese moralists, is to improve one's knowledge and virtue;—hence, this seemingly, but not really, selfish maxim.

9. The good effect of attention on the part of superiors to the offices to the dead:—an admonition of Tsâng Shǎn. 終, 'the end,' = death, and 遠, 'distant,' have both the force of adjectives, = 'the dead' and 'the departed,' or 'the long gone.' 慎 and 追 mean, 'to be careful of,' 'to follow,' but their application is

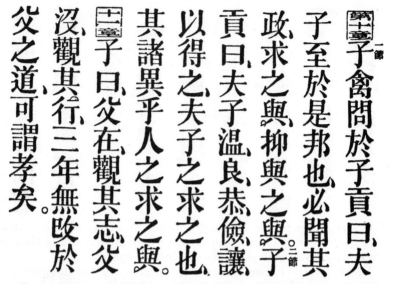

CHAP. X. 1. Tsze-ch'in asked Tsze-kung, saying, 'When our master comes to any country, he does not fail to learn all about its government. Does he ask his information? or is it given to him?'

2. Tsze-kung said, 'Our master is benign, upright, courteous, temperate, and complaisant, and thus he gets his information. The master's mode of asking information!—is it not different from that of other men?'

CHAP. XI. The Master said, 'While a man's father is alive, look at the bent of his will; when his father is dead, look at his conduct. If for three years he does not alter from the way of his father, he may be called filial.'

as in the translation. 厚, 'thick,' in opposition to 薄, 'thin;' metaphorically, = *good, excellent*. The force of 歸, 'to return,' is to show that this virtue is naturally proper to the people.

10. CHARACTERISTICS OF CONFUCIUS, AND THEIR INFLUENCE ON THE PRINCES OF THE TIME. 1. Tsze-ch'in and Tsze-k'ang (亢) are designations of 陳亢, one of the minor disciples of Confucius. His tablet occupies the 28th place, on the west, in the outer part of the temples. On the death of his brother, his wife and major-domo wished to bury some living persons with him, to serve him in the regions below. Tsze-ch'in proposed that the wife and steward should themselves submit to the immolation, which made them stop the matter. Tsze-kung, with the double surname 端木, and named 賜, occupies a higher place in the Confucian ranks. He is conspicuous in this work for his readiness and smartness in reply, and

displayed on several occasions practical and political ability. 夫, 'a general designation for males,' = a man. 夫子,—a common designation for a teacher or master. 是邦, 'this country' = *any* country. 必, 'must,' = *does not fail to*. The antecedent to both the 之 is the whole clause 聞其政. 與, with no tone marked = 'to give to,' 'with,' 'to'; 與, as in chap. ii. 2. The force of 其諸 is well enough expressed by the dash in English, the previous 也 indicating a pause in the discourse, which the 其, 'it,' resumes. See Wang Yin-chih's Treatise, chap. ix.

11. ON FILIAL DUTY. 行 is, in the 4th tone, explained by 行迹, 'traces of walking,' = *conduct*. It is to be understood that the way of the father had not been very bad. An

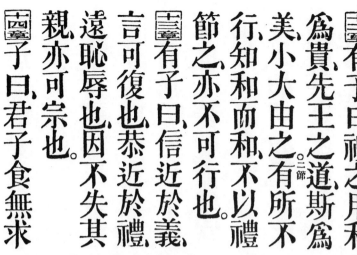

CHAP. XII. 1. The philosopher Yû said, 'In practising the rules of propriety, a natural ease is to be prized. In the ways prescribed by the ancient kings, this is the excellent quality, and in things small and great we follow them.

2. 'Yet it is not to be observed in all cases. If one, knowing *how* such ease *should be prized*, manifests it, without regulating it by the rules of propriety, this likewise is not to be done.'

CHAP. XIII. The philosopher Yû said, 'When agreements are made according to what is right, what is spoken can be made good. When respect is shown according to what is proper, one keeps far from shame and disgrace. When the parties upon whom a man leans are proper persons to be intimate with, he can make them his guides and masters.'

CHAP. XIV. The Master said, 'He who aims to be a man of complete virtue in his food does not seek to gratify his appetite, nor

old interpretation, that the three years are to be understood of the three years of mourning for the father, is now rightly rejected. The meaning should not be confined to that period.

12. IN CEREMONIES A NATURAL EASE IS TO BE PRIZED, AND YET TO BE SUBORDINATE TO THE END OF CEREMONIES,—THE REVERENTIAL OBSERVANCE OF PROPRIETY. 1. 禮 is not easily rendered in another language. There underlies it the idea of *what is proper*. It is 事之宜, 'the fitness of things,' what reason calls for in the performance of duties towards superior beings, and between man and man. Our term 'ceremonies' comes near its meaning here. 道 is here a name for 禮, as indicating the *courses* or *ways* to be trodden by men. In 小大由之, the antecedent to 之 is not 和, but 禮 or 道. 2. Observe the force of the 亦, 'also,' in

the last clause, and how it affirms the general principle enunciated in the first paragraph.

13. TO SAVE FROM FUTURE REPENTANCE, WE MUST BE CAREFUL IN OUR FIRST STEPS. A different view of the scope of this chapter is taken by Ho Yen. It illustrates, according to him, the difference between being sincere and righteousness, between being respectful and propriety, and how a man's conduct may be venerated. The later view commends itself, the only difficulty being with 近於, 'near to,' which we must accept as a *meiosis* for 合乎, 'agreeing with.' 信=信約, 'a covenant,' 'agreement.' 遠, 4th tone, 'to keep away from.' The force of the 亦 = 'he can *go on* to make them his masters,' 宗 being taken as an active verb.

14. WITH WHAT MIND ONE AIMING TO BE A CHÜN-TSZE PURSUES HIS LEARNING. He may be well, even luxuriously, fed and lodged, but,

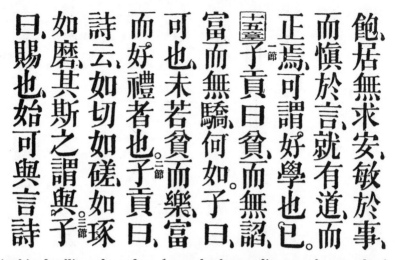

曰賜也始可與言詩
如磨其斯之謂與。子〔三節〕
詩云如切如磋如琢
而好禮者也。〔二節〕子貢曰
可也未若貧而樂富
富而無驕何如。子曰
正焉可謂好學也已。〔一節〕子貢曰貧而無諂
而慎於言就有道而
飽居無求安敏於事

in his dwelling-place does he seek the appliances of ease; he is earnest in what he is doing, and careful in his speech; he frequents the company of men of principle that he may be rectified:—such a person may be said indeed to love to learn.'

CHAP. XV. 1. Tsze-kung said, 'What do you pronounce concerning the poor man who yet does not flatter, and the rich man who is not proud?' The Master replied, 'They will do; but they are not equal to him, who, though poor, is yet cheerful, and to him, who, though rich, loves the rules of propriety.'

2. Tsze-kung replied, 'It is said in the Book of Poetry, "As you cut and then file, as you carve and then polish."—The meaning is the same, I apprehend, as that which you have just expressed.'

3. The Master said, 'With one like Ts'ze, I can begin to talk

with his higher aim, these things are not his seeking,—無求. A nominative to 可謂 must be supposed,—*all this*, or *such a person.* The closing particles, 也 已, give emphasis to the preceding sentence, = *yes, indeed.*

15. AN ILLUSTRATION OF THE SUCCESSIVE STEPS IN SELF-CULTIVATION. 1. Tsze-kung had been poor, and then did not cringe. He became rich and was not proud. He asked Confucius about the style of character to which he had attained. Confucius allowed its worth, but sent him to higher attainments. 而, here, = 'and yet.'

何如, 'what as?' = 'what do you say—what is to be thought—of this?' Observe the force of the 未, 'not yet.' 2. The ode quoted is the first of the songs of Wei (衛), praising the prince Wû, who had dealt with himself as an ivory-worker who first cuts the bone, and then files it smooth, or a lapidary whose hammer and chisel are followed by all the appliances for

smoothing and polishing. See the Shih-ching, I. v. Ode I. st. 2. In 其斯之謂, the antecedent to 其 is the passage of the ode, and that to 斯 is the reply of Confucius. 之謂, see Prémare, p. 156. The clause might be translated—'Is not that passage the saying of this?' Or, 'Does not that mean this?' 3. Intorcetta and his co-adjutors translate here as if 賜 were in the 2nd pers. But the Chinese comm. put it in the 3rd, and correctly. Prémare, on the character 也, says, '*Fere semper adjungitur nominibus propriis. Sic in libro Lun Yu, Confucius loquens de suis discipulis, Yeou, Keou, Hoei, vel ipsos alloquens, dicit* 由也, 求也, 回也,' It is not to be denied that the name before 也 is sometimes in the 2nd pers., but generally it is in the 3rd, and the force of the 也 = *quoad.* 賜也, *quoad Ts'ze.* 已矣, nearly = 也

CH. XVI.] CONFUCIAN ANALECTS. **145**

about the odes. I told him one point, and he knew its proper sequence.'

CHAP. XVI. The Master said, 'I will not be afflicted at men's not knowing me ; I will be afflicted that I do not know men.'

已, (or 已 without marking the tone), in chap. xiv. The last clause may be given—'Tell him the past, and he knows the future ;' but the connexion determines the meaning as in the translation. 諸, as in chap. x, is a particle, a mere 語助, as it is called, 'a helping or supporting word.'

16. PERSONAL ATTAINMENT SHOULD BE OUR CHIEF AIM. Comp. chap. i. 3. After the negative 不, as in chapter ii. 1, observe the transposition in 已 知, which is more elegant than 知 已 would be. 已, 'self,' the person depending on the context. We cannot translate 'do not be afflicted,' because 不 is not used imperatively, like 勿. A nominative to 患 has to be assumed,—我, 'I,' or 君子, 'the superior man.'

BOOK II. WEI CHĂNG.

CHAPTER I. The Master said, 'He who exercises government by means of his virtue may be compared to the north polar star, which keeps its place and all the stars turn towards it.'

HEADING OF THIS BOOK.—為政第二. This second Book contains twenty-four chapters, and is named 為政, 'The practice of government.' That is the object to which learning, treated of in the last Book, should lead, and here we have the qualities which constitute, and the character of the men who administer, good government.

1. THE INFLUENCE OF VIRTUE IN A RULER. 德 is explained by 得, and the old commentators say 物得以生謂之德, 'what creatures get at their birth is called their virtue ;' but this is a mere play on the common sound of different words. Chû Hsî makes it =

行道而有得於心, 'the practice of truth and acquisition thereof in the heart.' His view of the comparison is that it sets forth the illimitable influence which virtue in a ruler exercises without his using any effort. This is extravagant. His opponents say that virtue is the polar star, and the various departments of government the other stars. This is far-fetched. We must be content to accept the vague utterance without minutely determining its meaning. 北辰 is, no doubt, 'the north polar star,' anciently believed to coincide exactly with the place of the real pole. 共 in the 3rd tone, used for 拱, 'to fold the hands in saluting,' here = 'to turn respectfully towards.'

CHAP. II. The Master said, 'In the Book of Poetry are three hundred pieces, but the design of them all may be embraced in one sentence—"Having no depraved thoughts."'

CHAP. III. 1. The Master said, 'If the people be led by laws, and uniformity sought to be given them by punishments, they will try to avoid *the punishment*, but have no sense of shame.

2. 'If they be led by virtue, and uniformity sought to be given them by the rules of propriety, they will have the sense of shame, and moreover will become good.'

CHAP. IV. 1. The Master said, 'At fifteen, I had my mind bent on learning.

2. 'At thirty, I stood firm.

3. 'At forty, I had no doubts.

4. 'At fifty, I knew the decrees of Heaven.

2. THE PURE DESIGN OF THE BOOK OF POETRY. The number of compositions in the Shih-ching is rather more than the round number here given. 一言＝一句, 'one sentence.' 蔽 ＝蓋, 'to cover,' 'to embrace.' 思無邪, see Shih-ching, IV. ii. 1. st. 4. The sentence there is indicative, and in praise of the duke Hsî, who had no depraved thoughts. The sage would seem to have been intending the design in compiling the *Shih*. A few individual pieces are calculated to have a different effect.

3. HOW RULERS SHOULD PREFER MORAL APPLIANCES. 1. 道, as in I. v. 之, 'them,' refers to 民, below. 政, as opposed to 德, ＝laws and prohibitions. 齊 ＝ 'corn earing evenly;' hence, what is level, equal, adjusted, and here with the corresponding verbal force. 民免, 'The people will avoid,' that is, avoid breaking the laws through fear of the punishment. 2. 格 has the signification of 'to come to,' and 'to correct,' from either of which the text may

be explained,—'will come to good,' or 'will correct themselves.' Observe the different application of 且 and 而 in pars. 1 and 2. i. 而 ＝ 'but;' 且 ＝ 'moreover.'

4. CONFUCIUS'S OWN ACCOUNT OF HIS GRADUAL PROGRESS AND ATTAINMENTS. Commentators are perplexed with this chapter. Holding of Confucius that 生而知之, 安而行之, 'he was born with knowledge, and did what was right with entire ease,' they say that he here conceals his sagehood, and puts himself on the level of common men, to set before them a stimulating example. We may believe that the compilers of the Analects, the sage's immediate disciples, did not think of him so extravagantly as later men have done. It is to be wished, however, that he had been more definite and diffuse in his account of himself. 1. 有, in 4th tone, ＝ 'and.' The 'learning,' to which, at 15, Confucius gave himself, is to be understood of the subjects of the 'Superior Learning.' See Chû Hsî's preliminary essay to the Tâ Hsio.

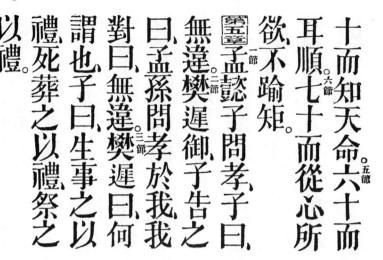

5. 'At sixty, my ear was an obedient organ *for the reception of truth.*

6. 'At seventy, I could follow what my heart desired, without transgressing what was right.'

CHAP. V. 1. Măng Î asked what filial piety was. The Master said, 'It is not being disobedient.'

2. *Soon after,* as Fan Ch'ih was driving him, the Master told him, saying, 'Măng-sun asked me what filial piety was, and I answered him,—"not being disobedient."'

3. Fan Ch'ih said, 'What did you mean?' The Master replied, 'That parents, when alive, should be served according to propriety; that, when dead, they should be buried according to propriety; and that they should be sacrificed to according to propriety.'

2. The 'standing firm' probably indicates that he no more needed to bend his will. 3. The 'no doubts' may have been concerning what was proper in all circumstances and events. 4. 'The decrees of Heaven,' = the things decreed by Heaven, the constitution of things making what was proper to be so. 5. 'The ear obedient' is the mind receiving as by intuition the truth from the ear. 6. 矩, 'an instrument for determining the square.' 不踰矩, 'without transgressing the square.' The expressions describing the progress of Confucius at the different periods of his age are often employed as numerical designations of age.

5. FILIAL PIETY MUST BE SHOWN ACCORDING TO THE RULES OF PROPRIETY. I. Măng Î was a great officer of the State of Lû, by name Ho-chî (何 忌), and the chief of one of the three great families by which in the time of Confucius the authority of that State was grasped. Those families were descended from three brothers, the sons by a concubine of the duke Hwan (B.C. 711-694), who were distinguished at first by the prenomens of 仲, 叔, and 季. To these was subsequently added the character 孫, 'grandson,' to indicate their princely descent, and 仲孫, 叔孫, and 季孫 became the respective surnames of the families. 仲孫 was changed into 孟孫 by the father of Măng Î, on a principle of humility, as he thereby only claimed to be the eldest of the inferior sons or their representatives, and avoided the presumption of seeming to be a younger full brother of the reigning duke. 懿, 'mild and virtuous,' was the posthumous honorary title given to Ho-chî. On 子, see I. i. I. 2. Fan, by name 須, and designated 子遲, was a minor disciple of the sage. Confucius repeated his remark to Fan, that he might report the explanation of it to his friend Măng Î, or Măng-sun Î, and thus prevent him from supposing that all the sage intended was disobedience to parents. Comp. the whole of Confucius's explanation with I. ix.

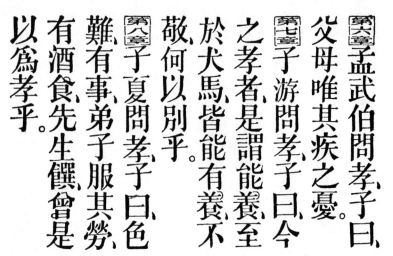

CHAP. VI. Măng Wŭ asked what filial piety was. The Master said, 'Parents are anxious lest their children should be sick.'

CHAP. VII. Tsze-yû asked what filial piety was. The Master said, 'The filial piety of now-a-days means the support of one's parents. But dogs and horses likewise are able to do something in the way of support;—without reverence, what is there to distinguish the one support given from the other?'

CHAP. VIII. Tsze-hsiâ asked what filial piety was. The Master said, 'The difficulty is with the countenance. If, when *their elders* have any *troublesome* affairs, the young take the toil of them, and if, when *the young* have wine and food, they set them before their elders, is THIS to be considered filial piety?'

6. THE ANXIETY OF PARENTS ABOUT THEIR CHILDREN AN ARGUMENT FOR FILIAL PIETY. This enigmatical sentence has been interpreted in two ways. Chû Hsî takes 唯(=惟) not in the sense of 'only,' but of 'thinking anxiously.'—'Parents have the sorrow of thinking anxiously about their—i. e. their children's—being unwell. Therefore children should take care of their persons.' The old commentators again take 唯 in the sense of 'only.'—'Let parents have only the sorrow of their children's illness. Let them have no other occasion for sorrow. This will be filial piety.' Măng Wû (the honorary epithet,='Bold and of straightforward principle') was the son of Măng Î, and by name 彘 (Chih). 伯 merely indicates that he was the eldest son.

7. HOW THERE MUST BE REVERENCE IN FILIAL DUTY. Tsze-yû was the designation of 言偃, a native of 吳, and distinguished among the disciples of Confucius for his learning. He is now 4th on the west among 'the wise ones.' 養 is in the 4th tone,='to minister support to,'

the act of an inferior to a superior. Chû Hsî gives a different turn to the sentiment.—'But dogs and horses likewise manage to get their support.' The other and older interpretation is better. 至 於, 'Coming to,'=as to, *quoad*. 別='to discriminate,' 'distinguish.'

8. THE DUTIES OF FILIAL PIETY MUST BE PERFORMED WITH A CHEERFUL COUNTENANCE. 事 followed by 勞=the 'troublesome affairs' in the translation. The use of 弟子 in the phrase here extends filial duty to elders generally,—to the 父兄 as well as to the 父母. We have in translating to supply their respective nominatives to the two 有. 食, read *tsze*, 'rice,' and then, food generally. 先生 饌=與先生饌之, 'They give them to their elders to eat.' 先生=elders. The phrase, here meaning parents, uncles, and elders generally, is applied by foreign students to their teachers. 曾, aspirated, = 則, 'then,'

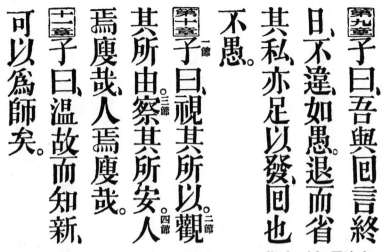

CHAP. IX. The Master said, 'I have talked with Hûi for a whole day, and he has not made any objection *to anything I said;* —as if he were stupid. He has retired, and I have examined his conduct when away from me, and found him able to illustrate *my teachings.* Hûi!—He is not stupid.'

CHAP. X. 1. The Master said, 'See what a man does.

2. 'Mark his motives.

3. 'Examine in what things he rests.

4. 'How can a man conceal his character?

5. 'How can a man conceal his character?'

CHAP. XI. The Master said, 'If a man keeps cherishing his old knowledge, so as continually to be acquiring new, he may be a teacher of others.'

a transition particle. To these different interrogatories, the sage, we are told, made answer according to the character of the questioner, as each one needed instruction.

9. THE QUIET RECEPTIVITY OF THE DISCIPLE Hûi. Yen Hûi (顏回), styled 子淵, was Confucius's favourite disciple, and is now honoured with the first place east among his four assessors in his temples, and with the title of 復聖顏子, 'The second sage, the philosopher Yen.' At 29 his hair was entirely white, and at 33 he died, to the excessive grief of the sage. The subject of 退 is 囘, and that of 省 (as in I. iv) is 吾. 其私, 'his privacy,' meaning only his way when not with the master. 亦, 'also,' takes up 如愚,—He was so, and also thus. 囘也, see I. xv. 3.

10. HOW TO DETERMINE THE CHARACTERS OF MEN. 1. 以 is explained as = 行, or 行用, 'does.' The same, though not its common meaning,

is the first given to it in the dict. For the noun to which the three 其 refer, we must go down to 人 in the 4th par. There is a climax in 所以, 所由 ('what from'), and 所安, and a corresponding one in the verbs 視, 觀, and 察. 4. 焉, generally a final particle, in 2nd tone, is here in the 1st, an interrogative, = how? Its interrogative force blends with the exclamatory of 哉 at the end.

11. TO BE ABLE TO TEACH OTHERS ONE MUST FROM HIS OLD STORES BE CONTINUALLY DEVELOPING THINGS NEW. 溫 is expressed in the dictionary by 燖, and, with reference to this very passage, it is said, 'one's old learning being thoroughly mastered, again constantly to practise it, is called 溫.' Modern commentators say that the 'new learning is in the old.' The idea probably is that of assimilating old acquisitions and new. Compare 中庸, XXVII. vi.

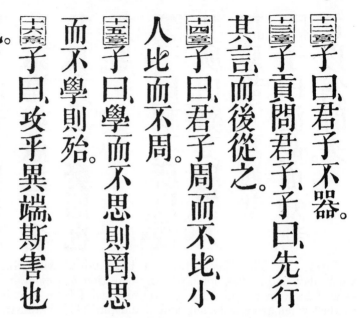

子曰攻乎異端斯害也已。

而不學則殆。

子曰學而不思則罔思

人比而不周。

子曰君子周而不比小

其言而後從之。

子貢問君子子曰先行

子曰君子不器。

CHAP. XII. The Master said, 'The accomplished scholar is not a utensil.'

CHAP. XIII. Tsze-kung asked what constituted the superior man. The Master said, 'He acts before he speaks, and afterwards speaks according to his actions.'

CHAP. XIV. The Master said, 'The superior man is catholic and no partizan. The mean man is a partizan and not catholic.'

CHAP. XV. The Master said, 'Learning without thought is labour lost; thought without learning is perilous.'

CHAP. XVI. The Master said, 'The study of strange doctrines is injurious indeed!'

12. THE GENERAL APTITUDE OF THE CHÜN-TSZE. This is not like our English saying, that 'such a man is a machine,'—a blind instrument. A utensil has its particular use. It answers for that and no other. Not so with the superior man, who is *ad omnia paratus*.

13. HOW WITH THE SUPERIOR MAN WORDS FOLLOW ACTIONS. The reply is literally—'He first acts his words and afterwards follows them.' A translator's difficulty is with the latter clause. What is the antecedent to 之? It would seem to be 其言, but in that case there is no room for words at all. Nor is there according to the old commentators. In the interpretation I have given, Chû Hsî follows the famous Châu Lien-ch'î (周濂溪).

14. THE DIFFERENCE BETWEEN THE CHÜN-TSZE AND THE SMALL MAN. 比, here in 4th tone, =

'partial,' 'partizanly.' The sentiment is this: — 'With the Chün-tsze, it is principles not men; with the small man, the reverse'

15. IN LEARNING, READING AND THOUGHT MUST BE COMBINED. 罔, 'a net,' used also in the sense of 'not,' as an adverb, and here as an adjective. The old commentators make 殆, 'perilous,' simply = 'wearisome to the body.'

16. STRANGE DOCTRINES ARE NOT TO BE STUDIED. 攻, often 'to attack,' as an enemy, here = 'to apply one's self to,' 'to study.' 端, 'correct;' then, 'beginnings,' 'first principles;' here = 'doctrines.' 也已, as in I. xiv. In Confucius's time Buddhism was not in China, and we can hardly suppose him to intend Tâoism. Indeed, we are ignorant to what doctrines he referred, but his maxim is of general application.

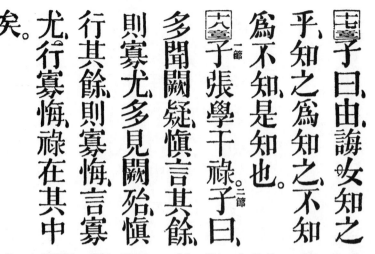

CHAP. XVII. The Master said, 'Yû, shall I teach you what knowledge is? When you know a thing, to hold that you know it; and when you do not know a thing, to allow that you do not know it;—this is knowledge.'

CHAP. XVIII. 1. Tsze-chang was learning with a view to official emolument.

2. The Master said, 'Hear much and put aside the points of which you stand in doubt, while you speak cautiously at the same time of the others:—then you will afford few occasions for blame. See much and put aside the things which seem perilous, while you are cautious at the same time in carrying the others into practice:—then you will have few occasions for repentance. When one gives few occasions for blame in his words, and few occasions for repentance in his conduct, he is in the way to get emolument.'

17. THERE SHOULD BE NO PRETENCE IN THE PROFESSION OF KNOWLEDGE, OR THE DENIAL OF IGNORANCE. 由, by surname 仲, and generally known by his designation of *Tsze-lû* (子路), was one of the most famous disciples of Confucius, and now occupies in the temples the 4th place east in the sage's own hall. He was noted for his courage and forwardness, a man of impulse rather than reflection. Confucius foretold that he would come to an untimely end. He was killed through his own rashness in a revolution in the State of Wei. The tassel of his cap being cut off when he received his death-wound, he quoted a saying—'The superior man must not die without his cap,' tied on the tassel, adjusted the cap, and expired. This action—結纓禮全—is much lauded. Of the six 知, the 1st and 6th are knowledge subjective, the other four are knowledge objective. 爲＝以爲, 'to take to be,' 'to con-

sider,' 'to allow.' 女, thus marked with a tone, is used for 汝, 'you.'

18. THE END IN LEARNING SHOULD BE ONE'S OWN IMPROVEMENT, AND NOT EMOLUMENT. 1. Tsze-chang, named 師, with the double surname 顓孫, a native of Ch'än (陳), was not undistinguished in the Confucian school. Tsze-kung praised him as a man of merit without boasting, humble in a high position, and not arrogant to the helpless. From this chapter, however, it would appear that inferior motives sometimes ruled him. 學 = 'was learning,' i. e. at some particular time. 干 = 求, 'to seek for.' 2. 闕 is explained by 姑舍置, but this meaning of it is not given clearly in the dictionary. Compare its use in XIII. iii. 4. 祿在其中, 'Emolument is herein,' i. e. it will come without seeking; the individual

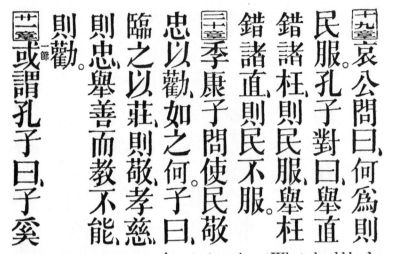

CHAP. XIX. The duke Âi asked, saying, 'What should be done in order to secure the submission of the people?' Confucius replied, 'Advance the upright and set aside the crooked, then the people will submit. Advance the crooked and set aside the upright, then the people will not submit.'

CHAP. XX. Chî K'ang asked how to cause the people to reverence *their ruler*, to be faithful to him, and to go on to nerve themselves to virtue. The Master said, 'Let him preside over them with gravity; —then they will reverence him. Let him be filial and kind to all;— then they will be faithful to him. Let him advance the good and teach the incompetent;—then they will eagerly seek to be virtuous.'

CHAP. XXI. 1. Some one addressed Confucius, saying, 'Sir, why are you not engaged in the government?'

is on the way to it. The lesson is that we are to do what is right, and not be anxious about temporal concerns.

19. How A PRINCE BY THE RIGHT EMPLOYMENT OF HIS OFFICERS MAY SECURE THE REAL SUBMISSION OF HIS SUBJECTS. Âi was the honorary epithet of 蔣, duke of Lû (B.C. 494–468);—Confucius died in his 16th year. According to the laws for posthumous titles, 哀 denotes 'the respectful and benevolent, early cut off.' 哀公 = 'The to-be-lamented duke.' 錯, 4th tone, = 置, 'to set aside.' 諸 is partly euphonious, but also indicates the plural. 孔子對曰, 'The philosopher K'ung replied.' Here, for the first time, the sage is called by his surname, and 對 is used, as indicating the reply of an inferior to a superior.

20. EXAMPLE IN SUPERIORS IS MORE POWERFUL THAN FORCE. K'ang, 'easy and pleasant, people-

soother,' was the honorary epithet of Chî-sun Fei (肥), the head of one of the three great families of Lû; see chap. v. His idea is seen in 使, 'to cause,' the power of force; that of Confucius appears in 則, 'then,' the power of influence. In 以勸, 以 is said to = 與, 'together with,' 'mutually.' 勸, 'to advise,' 'to teach,' has also in the dictionary the meaning—'to rejoice to follow,' which is its force here, 爲善, 'the practice of goodness,' being understood. Wang Yin-chih (on the Particles) says that in this (and similar passages) 以 unites the meanings of 與 and 而; and this is the view which I have myself long held.

21. CONFUCIUS'S EXPLANATION OF HIS NOT BEING IN ANY OFFICE. 1. 或謂孔子,—the surname indicates that the questioner was not a disciple. Confucius had his reason for not being in office at the time, but it was not ex-

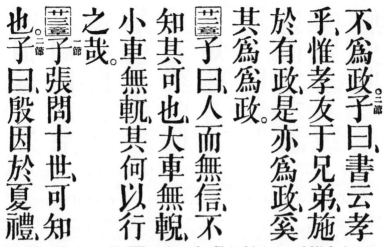

2. The Master said, 'What does the Shû-ching say of filial piety?—
"You are filial, you discharge your brotherly duties. These qualities
are displayed in government." This then also constitutes the exercise
of government. Why must there be THAT—making one be in the
government?'

CHAP. XXII. The Master said, 'I do not know how a man without truthfulness is to get on. How can a large carriage be made to go
without the cross-bar for yoking the oxen to, or a small carriage
without the arrangement for yoking the horses?'

CHAP. XXIII. 1. Tsze-chang asked whether *the affairs of* ten
ages *after* could be known.

2. Confucius said, 'The Yin dynasty followed the regulations of the
Hsiâ: wherein it took from or added to them may be known. The
Châu dynasty has followed the regulations of the Yin: wherein it
took from or added to them may be known. Some other may follow
the Châu, but though it should be at the distance of a hundred ages,
its affairs may be known.'

pedient to tell it. He replied therefore, as in
par. 2. 2. See the Shû-ching, V. xxi. 1. But
the text is neither correctly applied nor exactly
quoted. The old interpreters read in one sentence 孝乎惟孝, 'O filial piety! nothing
but filial piety!' Chû Hsî, however, pauses at
乎, and commences the quotation with 惟
孝. 奚其爲爲政, the 1st 爲 =
以爲, and 其 refers to the thought in the
question, that *office* was necessary to one's being
in government.

22. THE NECESSITY TO A MAN OF BEING TRUTH-
FUL AND SINCERE. 輗 and 軏 are explained
in the dictionary in the same way—'the cross-
bar at the end of the carriage-pole.' Chû Hsî
says, 'In the light carriage the end of the pole

curved upwards, and the cross-bar was suspended from a hook.' This would give it
more elasticity.

23. THE GREAT PRINCIPLES GOVERNING SOCIETY
ARE UNCHANGEABLE. 1. 世 may be taken as an
age = our 'century,' or as a generation = thirty
years, which is its radical meaning, being
formed from *three tens* and *one* (卅 and 一).
Confucius made no pretension to supernatural
powers, and all commentators are agreed that
the things here asked about were not what
we call contingent or indifferent events.
He merely says that the great principles of
morality and relations of society had continued
the same and would ever do so. 也 = 乎.
2. The Hsiâ, Yin, and Châu are now spoken
of as the 三代, 'The three changes,' i. e. the

無勇也。
也、見義不爲、
鬼而祭之、諂
子曰、非其
可知也。
周者、雖百世、
知也、其或繼
禮、所損益、可
也、周因於殷
所損益、可知

二節

CHAP. XXIV. 1. The Master said, 'For a man to sacrifice to a spirit which does not belong to him is flattery.

2. 'To see what is right and not to do it is want of courage.'

three great dynasties. The first sovereign of the Hsià was 'The great Yü,' B.C. 2205 ; of the Yin, T'ang, B.C. 1766 ; and of Châu, Wû, B.C. 1122.

24. NEITHER IN SACRIFICE NOR IN ANY OTHER PRACTICE MAY A MAN DO ANYTHING BUT WHAT IS RIGHT. 1. 人神曰鬼, 'The spirit of man (i.e. of the dead) is called 鬼.' The 鬼 of which a man may say that they are his, are those only of his ancestors, and to them only he may sacrifice. The ritual of China provides for sacrifices to three classes of objects—天神, 地示, 人鬼, 'spirits of heaven, of the earth, of men.' This chapter is not to be extended to all the three. It has reference only to the manes of departed men.

BOOK III. PÂ YIH.

忍也。
孰不可
可忍也、
於庭、是
八佾舞
謂季氏、
孔子
第三
八佾

第一章

CHAPTER I. Confucius said of the head of the Chî family, who had eight rows of pantomimes in his area, 'If he can bear to do this, what may he not bear to do?'

HEADING OF THIS BOOK.—八佾第三. The last Book treated of the practice of government, and therein no things, according to Chinese ideas, are more important than ceremonial rites and music. With those topics, therefore, the twenty-six chapters of this Book are occupied, and 'eight rows,' the principal words in the first chapter, are adopted as its heading.

1. CONFUCIUS'S INDIGNATION AT THE USURPATION OF ROYAL RITES. 季氏, by contraction for 季孫氏; see on II. v. 氏 and 姓 are now used without distinction, meaning 'surname,' only that the 氏 of a woman is always spoken of, and not her 姓. Originally the 氏 appears to have been used to denote the branch families of one surname. 季氏, 'The Chî family,' with special reference to its head, 'The Chî,' as we should say. 佾, 'a row of dancers,' or pantomimes rather, who kept time in the temple services, in the 庭, the front space before the raised portion in the principal hall, moving or brandishing feathers, flags, or other articles. In his ancestral temple, the king had eight rows, each row consisting of eight men, a duke or prince had six, and a great officer only four. For the Chî, therefore,

CHAP. II.　The three families used the YUNG ode, while the vessels were being removed, *at the conclusion of the sacrifice.*　The Master said, ' " Assisting are the princes ;—the son of heaven looks profound and grave :"—what application can these words have in the hall of the three families ? '

CHAP. III.　The Master said, 'If a man be without the virtues proper to humanity, what has he to do with the rites of propriety ? If a man be without the virtues proper to humanity, what has he to do with music ? '

CHAP. IV.　1. Lin Fang asked what was the first thing to be attended to in ceremonies.

2. The Master said, 'A great question indeed !

3. 'In *festive* ceremonies, it is better to be sparing than extravagant.

to use eight rows was a usurpation, for though it may be argued, that to the ducal family of Lû royal rites were conceded, and that the offshoots of it (II. v) might use the same, still great officers were confined to the ordinances proper to their rank. 謂 is used here, as frequently, in the sense—'to speak of.' Confucius's remark may also be translated, 'If this be endured, what may not be endured ?' For there is force in the observations of the author of the 四書翼註, that this par. and the following must be assigned to the sage during the short time that he held high office in Lû.

2. AGAIN AGAINST USURPED RIGHTS. 三家者. '*Those* belonging to the three families.' They assembled together, as being the descendants of duke Hwan (II. v), in one temple. To this belonged the 庭 in the last chapter, which is called 季氏庭, circumstances having concurred to make the Chî the chief of the three families; see 四書改錯, VIII. vii. For the Yung ode, see Shih-ching, IV. i. sec. ii. Ode VII. It was, properly, sung in the royal temples of the Châu dynasty, at the 徹, 'the clearing away,' of the sacrificial apparatus, and contains the lines quoted

by Confucius, quite inappropriate to the circumstances of the three families. 辟,—without an aspirate. 相,—4th tone, 'assistant,' 'assisting.'

3. CEREMONIES AND MUSIC VAIN WITHOUT VIRTUE. 仁, see I. ii. I don't know how to render it here, otherwise than in the translation. Commentators define it—心之全德, 'the entire virtue of the heart.' As referred to 禮, it indicates the feeling of reverence ; as referred to 樂 (*yŏ*), it indicates harmoniousness.

4. THE OBJECT OF CEREMONIES SHOULD REGULATE THEM :—AGAINST FORMALISM. 1. Lin Fang, styled 子邱, was a man of Lû, whose tablet is now placed first, on the west, in the outer court of the temples. He is known only by the question in this chapter. According to Chû Hsî, 本 here is not 根本, 'the radical idea,' 'the essence ;' but = 初, 'the beginning' (opposed to 末), 'the first thing to be attended to.' 3. 禮, as opposed to 喪 (1st

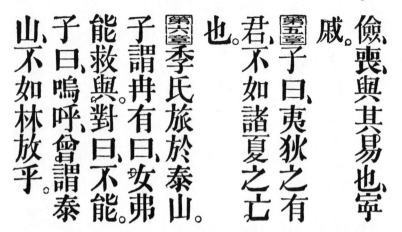

儉、喪、與其易也寧戚。

第五章 子曰、夷狄之有君、不如諸夏之亡也。

第六章 季氏旅於泰山。子謂冉有曰、女弗能救與。對曰、不能。子曰、嗚呼曾謂泰山、不如林放乎。

In the ceremonies of mourning, it is better that there be deep sorrow than a minute attention to observances.'

CHAP. V. The Master said, 'The rude tribes of the east and north have their princes, and are not like the States of our great land which are without them.'

CHAP. VI. The chief of the Chî family was about to sacrifice to the T'âi mountain. The Master said to Zan Yû, 'Can you not save him from this?' He answered, 'I cannot.' Confucius said, 'Alas! will you say that the T'âi mountain is not so discerning as Lin Fang?'

tone), must indicate the festive or fortunate (吉) ceremonies, — capping, marriage, and sacrifices. 易, read î, 4th tone. Chû Hsî explains it by 治, as in Mencius—易其田疇, 'to cleanse and dress the fields,' and interprets as in the translation. The old commentators take the meaning—和易, 'harmony and ease,' i.e. not being overmuch troubled.

5. THE ANARCHY OF CONFUCIUS'S TIME. The 夷 were the barbarous tribes on the east of China, and 狄, those on the north. See 禮記王制, III. xiv. The two are here used for the barbarous tribes about China generally. 諸夏 is a name for China because of the multitude of its regions (諸), and its greatness (夏). 華夏, 'The Flowery and Great,' is still a common designation of it. Chû Hsî takes 如 as simply = 似, and hence the sentiment in the translation. Ho Yen's commentary is to this effect :—'The rude tribes with their princes are still not equal to China with its anarchy.' 亡, read as, and = 無.

6. ON THE FOLLY OF USURPED SACRIFICES. 旅 is said to be the name appropriate to sacrifices to mountains, but we find it applied also to sacrifices to God. The T'âi mountain is the first of the 'five mountains' (五嶽), which are celebrated in Chinese literature and have always received religious honours. It was in Lû, or rather on the borders between Lû and Ch'î, about two miles north of the present department city of T'âi-an (泰安), in Shantung. According to the ritual of China, sacrifice could only be offered to those mountains by the sovereign, and by the princes in whose States any of them happened to be. For the chief of the Chî family, therefore, to sacrifice to the T'âi mountain was a great usurpation. 女 as in II. vii = 汝, and 曾 as in II. viii = 則, or we may take it as = 經, 'Have you said,' &c.? 泰山 = 泰山之神, 'The spirit of the T'âi mountain.' Lin Fang,—see chap. iv, from which the reason of this reference to him may be understood. Zan Yû, named (求), and by designation 子有, was one of the disciples of Confucius, and is now third, in the hall, on the west. He entered the service of the Chî family, and was a man of ability and resource.

CHAP. VII.   The Master said, 'The student of virtue has no contentions. If it be said he cannot avoid them, shall this be in archery? *But* he bows complaisantly *to his competitors;* thus he ascends *the hall*, descends, and exacts the forfeit of drinking. In his contention, he is still the Chün-tsze.'

CHAP. VIII.   1. Tsze-hsiâ asked, saying, 'What is the meaning of the passage—" The pretty dimples of her artful smile! The well-defined black and white of her eye! The plain ground for the colours?"'

2. The Master said, 'The business of laying on the colours follows (the preparation of) the plain ground.'

3. 'Ceremonies then are a subsequent thing?' The Master said, 'It is Shang who can bring out my meaning. Now I can begin to talk about the odes with him.'

7. THE SUPERIOR MAN AVOIDS ALL CONTENTIOUS STRIVING. Here 君子 = 尚德之人, 'the man who prefers virtue.' 必也射乎, literally, 'if he must, shall it be in archery?' 揖讓, according to Chû Hsî, extend over all the verbs, 升, 下, 飲. 下 is marked in the 4th tone, anciently appropriate to it as a verb. 飲, 4th tone, 'to give to drink,' here = to exact from the vanquished the forfeit cup. In Confucius's time there were three principal exercises of archery:—the great archery, under the eye of the sovereign; the guests' archery, which might be at the royal court or at the visits of the princes among themselves; and the festive archery, for amusement. The regulations for the archers were substantially the same in them all, and served to prove their virtue, instead of giving occasion to quarrelling. There is no end to the controversies among commentators on minor points.

8. CEREMONIES ARE SECONDARY AND MERELY ORNAMENTAL.   1. The sentences quoted by Tsze-hsiâ are, it is supposed, from a 逸詩, one of the poems which Confucius did not admit into the Shih-ching. The two first lines, however, are found in it, I. v; III. ii. The disciple's inquiry turns on the meaning of 以爲 in the last line, which he took to mean—'The plain ground is to be regarded as the colouring.'   2. Confucius, in his reply, makes 後 a verb, governing 素, = 'comes after the plain ground.'   3. 禮後乎;—Tsze-hsiâ's remark is an exclamation rather than a question. 起予者, 'He who stirs me up,' = 'He who brings out my meaning.' On the last sentence, see I. xv.—The above interpretation, especially as to the meaning of 繪事後素, after Chû Hsî, is quite the opposite of that of the old interpreters. Their view is of course strongly supported by the author of 四書改錯, VIII. iii.

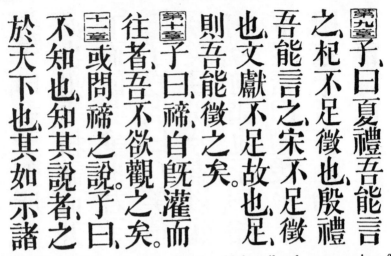

於天下也其如示諸
不知也知其說者之
十一章 或問禘之說子曰
往者吾不欲觀之矣。
第十章 子曰禘自既灌而
則吾能徵之矣。
也文獻不足故也足
吾能言之宋不足徵
之杞不足徵也殷禮
第九章 子曰夏禮吾能言

CHAP. IX. The Master said, 'I could describe the ceremonies of the Hsiâ dynasty, but Chî cannot sufficiently attest my words. I could describe the ceremonies of the Yin dynasty, but Sung cannot sufficiently attest my words. (*They cannot do so*) because of the insufficiency of their records and wise men. If those were sufficient, I could adduce them in support of my words.'

CHAP. X. The Master said, 'At the great sacrifice, after the pouring out of the libation, I have no wish to look on.'

CHAP. XI. Some one asked the meaning of the great sacrifice. The Master said, 'I do not know. He who knew its meaning would

9. THE DECAY OF THE MONUMENTS OF ANTIQUITY. Of Hsiâ and Yin, see II. xxiii. In the small State of Chî (originally what is now the district of the same name in K'âi-fung department in Ho-nan, but in Confucius's time a part of Shantung), the sacrifices to the emperors of the Hsiâ dynasty were maintained by their descendants. So with the Yin dynasty and Sung, a part also of Ho-nan. But the 文, 'literary monuments' of those countries, and their 獻 (= 賢, so in the Shû-ching, V. vii. 5, *et al.*), 'wise men,' had become few. Had Confucius therefore delivered all his knowledge about the two dynasties, he would have exposed his truthfulness to suspicion. 徵, in the sense of 證, 'to witness,' and, at the end, 'to appeal to for evidence.' The old commentators, however, interpret the whole differently.—Already in the time of Confucius many of the records of antiquity had perished.

10. THE SAGE'S DISSATISFACTION AT THE WANT OF PROPRIETY IN CEREMONIES. 禘 is the name belonging to different sacrifices, but here indicates the 大祭, 'great sacrifice,' which could properly be celebrated only by the sovereign. The individual sacrificed to in it was the remotest ancestor from whom the founder of the reigning dynasty traced his descent. As to who were his assessors in the sacrifice and how often it was offered;—these are disputed points. See K'ang-hsî's dict., char. 禘. Compare also 四書改錯, VII. viii, and 四書拓餘說, I. xiii. A royal rite, its use in Lû was wrong (see next chap.), but there was something in the service after the early act of libation inviting the descent of the spirits, which more particularly moved the anger of Confucius. 而往 = 以後, different from 往 in I. xv.

11. THE PROFOUND MEANING OF THE GREAT SACRIFICE. This chapter is akin to II. xxi. Confucius evades replying to his questioner, it being contrary to Chinese propriety to speak in a country of the faults of its government or rulers. 說, 'explanation,' = *meaning*. The antecedent to the second 其 is the whole of the preceding clause:—'The relation to the kingdom of him who knew its meaning;—*that* would be as to look on this.' 乎, interjective, more than interrogative. 示 = 視, 'to see.' 天下, 'under heaven,' an ambitious designation for the Chinese empire, as ἡ οἰκουμένη and *orbis terræ* were used by the Greeks and Romans.

find it as easy to govern the kingdom as to look on this;'—pointing to his palm.

CHAP. XII. 1. He sacrificed *to the dead,* as if they were present. He sacrificed to the spirits, as if the spirits were present.

2. The Master said, 'I consider my not being present at the sacrifice, as if I did not sacrifice.'

CHAP. XIII. 1. Wang-sun Chiâ asked, saying, 'What is the meaning of the saying, "It is better to pay court to the furnace than to the south-west corner?"'

2. The Master said, 'Not so. He who offends against Heaven has none to whom he can pray.'

12. CONFUCIUS'S OWN SINCERITY IN SACRIFIC-ING. 1. 祭 here is historical and not to be translated in the imperative. We have to supply an objective to the first 祭, viz. 先祖, *the dead,* his forefathers, as contrasted with 神 in the next clause, = all the 'spirits' to which in his official capacity he would have to sacrifice. 2. Observe 與 in the 4th tone, 'to be present at,' 'to take part in.'

13. THAT THERE IS NO RESOURCE AGAINST THE CONSEQUENCES OF VIOLATING THE RIGHT. 1. Chiâ was a great officer of Wei (衛), and having the power of the State in his hands insinuated to Confucius that it would be for his advantage to pay court to him. The 奧, or south-west corner, was from the structure of ancient houses the cosiest nook, and the place of honour. Chû Hsî explains the proverb by reference to the customs of sacrifice. The furnace was comparatively a mean place, but when the spirit of the furnace was sacrificed to, then the rank of the two places was changed for the time, and the proverb quoted was in vogue. But there does not seem much force in this explanation. The *door,* or *well,* or any other of the five things in the regular sacrifices, might take the place of the *furnace.* The old explanation which makes no reference to sacrifice is simpler. *Âo* might be the more retired and honourable place, but the *tsâo* was the more important for the support and comfort of the household. The prince and his immediate attendants might be more honourable than such a minister as Chiâ, but more benefit might be got from him. 媚, from *woman* and *eyebrows,* = 'to ogle,' 'to flatter.' 2. Confucius's reply was in a high tone. Chû Hsî says, 天即理也, 'Heaven means principle.' But why should Heaven mean principle, if there were not in such a use of the term an instinctive recognition of a supreme government of intelligence and righteousness? We find 天 explained in the 四書拓餘說 by 高高在上者, 'The lofty One who is on high.' A scholar of great ability and research has written to me contending that we ought to find in this chapter a reference to fire-worship as having been by the time of Confucius introduced from Persia into China; but I have not found sufficient reference to such an introduction at so early a period. The ordinary explanation seems to me more satisfactory;—simple and sufficient. Ho Yen quotes the words of K'ung An-kwo of our second century on the passage:—'Chiâ held in his hands the government of the State. Wishing to make Confucius pay court to him, he stirred him up in a gentle way by quoting to him a saying common among the people.'

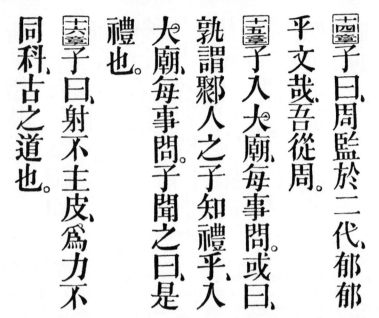

CHAP. XIV. The Master said, 'Châu had the advantage of viewing the two past dynasties. How complete and elegant are its regulations! I follow Châu.'

CHAP. XV. The Master, when he entered the grand temple, asked about everything. Some one said, 'Who will say that the son of the man of Tsâu knows the rules of propriety! He has entered the grand temple and asks about everything.' The Master heard the remark, and said, 'This is a rule of propriety.'

CHAP. XVI. The Master said, 'In archery it is not *going through* the leather which is the principal thing;—because people's strength is not equal. This was the old way.'

14. THE COMPLETENESS AND ELEGANCE OF THE INSTITUTIONS OF THE CHÂU DYNASTY. By the 周 we are specially to understand the founders of the power and polity of the dynasty—the kings Wǎn and Wû, and the duke of Châu. The two past dynasties are the Hsiâ and the Shang or Yin. 文 = 'elegant regulations.'

15. CONFUCIUS IN THE GRAND TEMPLE. 大 (=太) 廟 was the temple dedicated to the duke of Châu (周公), and where he was sacrificed to with royal rites. The thing is supposed to have taken place at the beginning of Confucius's official service in Lû, when he went into the temple with other officers to assist at the sacrifice. He had studied all about ceremonies, but he thought it a mark of sincerity and earnestness to make minute inquiries about them on the occasion spoken of. 鄹 was the name of the town of which Confucius's father had been governor, who was known therefore as 'the man of Tsâu.' Confucius would be styled as in the text, only in his early life, or by very ordinary people.—See on page 59.

16. How THE ANCIENTS MADE ARCHERY A DISCIPLINE OF VIRTUE. We are not to understand 射不主皮 of all archery among the ancients. The characters are found in the 儀禮, 鄉射, par. 315 of the Chû Sû edition. In the edition of the present dynasty, V. iii, par. 81. There were trials of archery where the strength was tested. Probably Confucius was speaking of some archery of his times, when the strength which could go through the 皮, 'skin,' or leather, in the middle of the target, was esteemed more than the skill which could hit it.

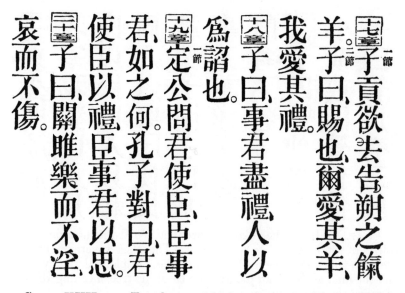

CHAP. XVII. 1. Tsze-kung wished to do away with the offering of a sheep connected with the inauguration of the first day of each month.

2. The Master said, 'Ts'ze, you love the sheep; I love the ceremony.'

CHAP. XVIII. The Master said, 'The full observance of the rules of propriety in serving one's prince is accounted by people to be flattery.'

CHAP. XIX. The duke Ting asked how a prince should employ his ministers, and how ministers should serve their prince. Confucius replied, 'A prince should employ his ministers according to the rules of propriety; ministers should serve their prince with faithfulness.'

CHAP. XX. The Master said, 'The Kwan Tsü is expressive of enjoyment without being licentious, and of grief without being hurtfully excessive.'

17. How CONFUCIUS CLEAVED TO ANCIENT RITES. 1. The king in the last month of the year gave out to the princes a calendar for the first days of the months of the year ensuing. This was kept in their ancestral temples, and on the 1st of every month they offered a sheep and announced the day, requesting sanction for the duties of the month. This idea of requesting sanction is indicated by 告, read *kŭh*. The dukes of Lû now neglected their part of this ceremony, but the sheep was still offered:—a meaningless formality, it seemed to Tsze-kung. Confucius, however, thought that while any part of the ceremony was retained, there was a better chance of restoring the whole. 去, in the 3rd tone, an active verb, 'to put away.' It is disputed whether 餼, in the text, mean a *living* sheep, or a sheep killed but not roasted. 2. 愛, in the sense of 愛惜, 'to grudge,' it is said. But this is hardly necessary.

18. How PRINCES SHOULD BE SERVED :— AGAINST THE SPIRIT OF THE TIMES.

19. THE GUIDING PRINCIPLES IN THE RELATION OF PRINCE AND MINISTER. 定, 'Greatly anxious, tranquillizer of the people,' was the posthumous epithet of 宋, prince of Lû, B.C. 509–495. 如之何, 'As it what?' 之 referring to the two points inquired about.

20. THE PRAISE OF THE FIRST OF THE ODES. 關雎 is the name of the first ode in the Shih-ching, and may be translated—'The murmuring of the ts'ü.' See Shih-ching, I. i. 1.

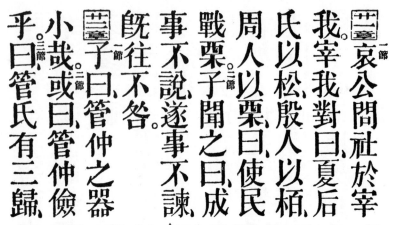

CHAP. XXI. 1. The duke Âi asked Tsâi Wo about the altars of the spirits of the land. Tsâi Wo replied, 'The Hsiâ sovereign planted the pine tree about them; the men of the Yin planted the cypress; and the men of the Châu planted the chestnut tree, meaning thereby to cause the people to be in awe.'

2. When the Master heard it, he said, 'Things that are done, it is needless to speak about; things that have had their course, it is needless to remonstrate about; things that are past, it is needless to blame.'

CHAP. XXII. 1. The Master said, 'Small indeed was the capacity of Kwan Chung!'

2. Some one said, 'Was Kwan Chung parsimonious?' 'Kwan,' was the reply, 'had the *San Kwei*, and his officers performed no double duties; how can he be considered parsimonious?'

3. 'Then, did Kwan Chung know the rules of propriety?' The

---

21. A RASH REPLY OF TSÂI WO ABOUT THE ALTARS TO THE SPIRITS OF THE LAND, AND LAMENT OF CONFUCIUS THEREON. 1. 哀公, see II. xix. Tsâi Wo, by name 子, and styled 子我, was an eloquent disciple of the sage, a native of Lû. His place is the second west among 'the wise ones.' 社, from 示 (*Ch'î*), 'spirit or spirits of the earth,' and 土, 'the soil,' means 土地神主, 'the resting-place or altars of the spirits of the land or ground Wo simply tells the duke that the founders of the several dynasties planted such and such trees about those altars. The reason was that the soil suited such trees; but as 栗, 'the chestnut tree,' the tree of the existing dynasty, is used in the sense of 慄, 'to be afraid,' he suggested a reason for its planting which might lead the duke to severe measures against his people to be carried into effect at the altars. Comp. the Shû-ching, IV. ii. 5, 'I will put you

to death before the 社.' 夏后氏 is the Great Yu, called 后, to distinguish him from his predecessors, the 帝, and 夏氏, to distinguish him from 舜, who was 虞氏, while they were descended from the same ancestor. See chap. i, on 氏. 殷人 and 周人, in parallelism with 夏后氏, must mean the founders of these dynasties; why they are simply styled 人, 'man,' or 'men,' I have not found clearly explained, though commentators feel it necessary to say something on the point. 2. This is all directed against Wo's reply. He had spoken, and his words could not be recalled.

22. CONFUCIUS'S OPINION OF KWAN CHUNG:— AGAINST HIM. 1. Kwan Chung, by name 夷吾, is one of the most famous names in Chinese history. He was chief minister to the duke 桓 of 齊 (B.C. 683–642), the first and greatest

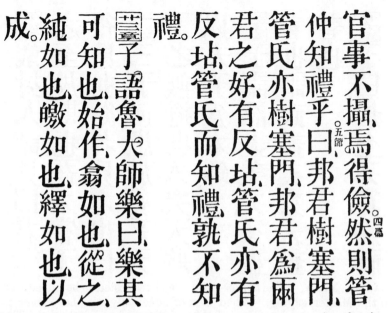

Master said, 'The princes of States have a screen intercepting the view at their gates. Kwan had likewise a screen at his gate. The princes of States on any friendly meeting between two of them, had a stand on which to place their inverted cups. Kwan had also such a stand. If Kwan knew the rules of propriety, who does not know them?'

CHAP. XXIII. The Master instructing the Grand music-master of Lü said, 'How to play music may be known. At the commencement of the piece, all the parts should sound together. As it proceeds, they should be in harmony, *while* severally distinct and flowing without break, and thus on to the conclusion.'

of the five *pá* (伯 or 霸), leaders of the princes of the nation under the Châu dynasty. In the times of Confucius and Mencius, people thought more of Kwan than those sages, no hero-worshippers, would allow. 器, see II. xii, but its significance here is different, and = our *measure* or *capacity*. 2. 三歸, in the dictionary, and the commentary of Chû Hsî, was the name of an extravagant tower built by Kwan. There are other views of the phrase, the oldest and the best supported apparently being that it means 'three wives.' (A woman's marriage is called 歸.) The *San Kwei* and having no pluralists among his officers proved that he could not be parsimonious. 焉, the 1st tone, 'how.' 3. 樹, 'a tree,' here in the sense of 屏, 'a screen,' the screen of a prince, usurped by Kwan, who was only entitled to the 簾 of a great officer. 好, the

4th tone, = 'a friendly meeting.' The 坫, from 土 and 占, was a stand, made originally of earth and turf. Kwan usurped the use of it, as he did of the screen; being as regardless of prescribed forms, as in par. 2 of expense, and he came far short therefore of the Confucian idea of the *Chün-tsze*.

23. ON THE PLAYING OF MUSIC. 語, the 4th tone, = 告, 'to tell,' 'to instruct.' 大 (= 太) 師 樂 was the title of the Grand music-master. 樂 其 可 知 也, 'music, it may be known,' but the subject is not of the principles, but the performance of music. Observe the 如. Prémare says, '*adjectivis addita sensum auget et exprimit modum.*' It is our *ly* or *like*,— 翕 如, 'blended like.' 從, the 4th tone, the same as 縱 = 放, 'let go,' i.e. proceeding, swelling on.

儀封人請見曰君子
之至於斯也吾未嘗不
得見也從者見之出曰
二三子何患於喪乎天
下之無道也久矣天將
以夫子為木鐸。
子謂韶盡美矣又盡
善也謂武盡美矣未盡
善也。
子曰居上不寬為禮

CHAP. XXIV. The border-warden at Î requested to be introduced to the Master, saying, 'When men of superior virtue have come to this, I have never been denied the privilege of seeing them.' The followers *of the sage* introduced him, and when he came out from the interview, he said, 'My friends, why are you distressed by your master's loss of office? The kingdom has long been without the principles *of truth and right;* Heaven is going to use your master as a bell with its wooden tongue.'

CHAP. XXV. The Master said of the Shâo that it was perfectly beautiful and also perfectly good. He said of the Wû that it was perfectly beautiful but not perfectly good.

CHAP. XXVI. The Master said, 'High station filled without indulgent generosity; ceremonies performed without reverence; mourning conducted without sorrow;—wherewith should I contemplate such ways?'

24. A STRANGER'S VIEW OF THE VOCATION OF CONFUCIUS. Î was a small town on the borders of Wei, referred to a place in the present department of K'âi-fǎng, Ho-nan province. Confucius at the beginning of his wanderings after leaving Lû was retiring from Wei, the prince of which could not employ him. This was the 喪°=失位. The 1st and 3rd 見 are read *hsien*, 4th tone, = 通使 得見, 'to introduce,' or 'to be introduced.' 之 in 君子之至於斯也 has its proper possessive power,—'In the case of a Chün-tsze's coming to this.' *Tsung*, the 4th tone, 'to attend upon.' 二三子, 'Two or three sons,' or 'gentlemen,' = 'my friends.' The

same idiom occurs elsewhere. The 木鐸 was a metal bell with a wooden tongue, shaken in making announcements, or to call people together. Heaven would employ Confucius to proclaim the truth and right.

25. THE COMPARATIVE MERITS OF THE MUSIC OF SHUN AND WÛ. 韶 was the name of the music made by Shun, perfect in melody and sentiment. 武 was the music of king Wû, also perfect in melody, but breathing the martial air, indicative of its author.

26. THE DISREGARD OF WHAT IS ESSENTIAL VITIATES ALL SERVICES. The meaning of the chapter turns upon 何以 = 何有, or 以何 者, 'wherewith.' 寬 is essential to rulers, 敬 to ceremonies, and 哀 to mourning.

BOOK IV.　LE JIN.

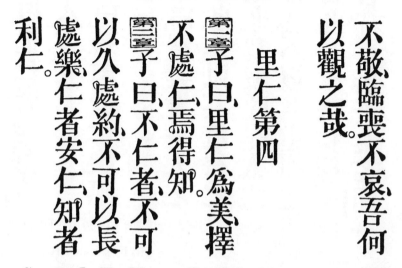

CHAPTER I. The Master said, 'It is virtuous manners which constitute the excellence of a neighbourhood. If a man in selecting a residence, do not fix on one where such prevail, how can he be wise?'

CHAP. II. The Master said, 'Those who are without virtue cannot abide long either in a condition of poverty and hardship, or in a condition of enjoyment. The virtuous rest in virtue; the wise desire virtue.'

HEADING OF THIS BOOK.—里仁第四, 'Virtue in a neighbourhood, No. 4.'—Such is the title of this fourth Book, which is mostly occupied with the subject of 仁. To render that term invariably by *benevolence*, would by no means suit many of the chapters. See II. i. 2. *Virtue*, as a general term, would answer better. The embodiment of virtue demands an acquaintance with ceremonies and music, treated of in the last Book; and this, it is said, is the reason why the one subject immediately follows the other.

1. RULE FOR THE SELECTION OF A RESIDENCE. According to the 周禮, five families made a 鄰, and five 鄰 a 里, which we might style, therefore, *a hamlet* or *village*. There are other estimates of the number of its component households. 處, 3rd tone, a verb, 'to dwell in.' 知, 4th tone, is the same as 智, 'wise,' 'wisdom.' So, not unfrequently, below. Friend-ship, we have seen, is for the aid of virtue (I. viii. 3), and the same should be the object desired in selecting a residence.

2. ONLY TRUE VIRTUE ADAPTS A MAN FOR THE VARIED CONDITIONS OF LIFE. 約, 'to bind,' is used for what binds, as an oath, a covenant; and here, the metaphor being otherwise directed, it denotes a condition of poverty and distress. 利, 'gain,' 'profit,' used as a verb, = 貪, 'to desire,' 'to covet.' 安仁, 'to rest in virtue,' being virtuous without effort. 利仁, 'to desire virtue,' being virtuous because it is the best policy. Observe how 者 following 仁 and 知 makes those terms adjectives or participles. 不可, 'may not,' = 不能, 'cannot.' The inability is moral. See 可 in the Index VII.

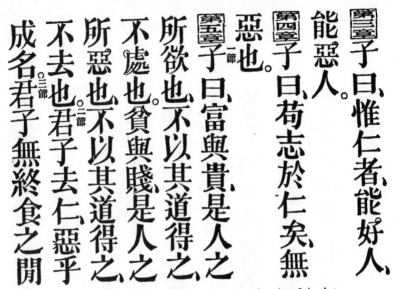

CHAP. III. The Master said, 'It is only the (*truly*) virtuous man, who can love, or who can hate, others.'

CHAP. IV. The Master said, 'If the will be set on virtue, there will be no practice of wickedness.'

CHAP. V. 1. The Master said, 'Riches and honours are what men desire. If it cannot be obtained in the proper way, they should not be held. Poverty and meanness are what men dislike. If it cannot be obtained in the proper way, they should not be avoided.

2. 'If a superior man abandon virtue, how can he fulfil the requirements of that name?

3. 'The superior man does not, even for the space of a single meal, act contrary to virtue. In moments of haste, he cleaves to it. In seasons of danger, he cleaves to it.'

3. ONLY IN THE GOOD MAN ARE EMOTIONS OF LOVE AND HATRED RIGHT, AND TO BE DEPENDED ON. This chapter is incorporated with the 大學 傳, X. xv. 好 and 惡 (read *wû*) are both verbs in the 4th tone.

4. THE VIRTUOUS WILL PRESERVES FROM ALL WICKEDNESS. 苟 = 誠, not merely—'if,' but 'if really.' Comp. the statement, 1 John iii. 9, 'Whosoever is born of God doth not commit sin.'

5. THE DEVOTION OF THE CHÜN-TSZE TO VIRTUE. 1. For the antecedent to 之 in the recurring 得之, we are to look to the following verbs, 處 and 去. We might translate the first 不以道得之, 'if they cannot be obtained, &c.,' but this would not suit the second case. 其道, '*the* way,' i.e. the proper way. If we supply a nom. to 處 and 去, it must be 君子;—he will not 'abide in,' nor 'go away from,' riches and honours. 2. 惡, read *wû*, the 1st tone, 'how.' 名, 'name,' not reputation, but the name of a *chün-tsze*, which he bears. 3. 終食之間, 'The space in which a meal can be *finished*;' meaning a short time. 造次 (interchangeable with 草次) and 顚沛 are well-known expressions, the former for haste and confusion, the latter for change and danger; but it is not easy to trace the attaching of those meanings to the characters. 顚, 'to fall down,' and 沛, the same, but the former with the face up, the other with the face down. 必 於是;—comp. Horace's '*Omnis in hoc sum.*'

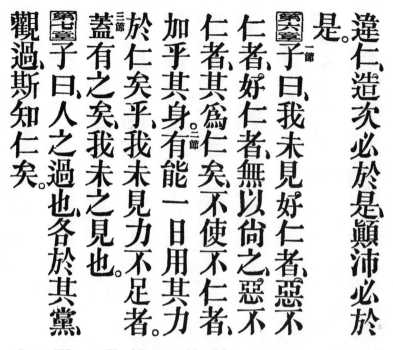

CHAP. VI.　1. The Master said, 'I have not seen a person who loved virtue, or one who hated what was not virtuous.　He who loved virtue, would esteem nothing above it.　He who hated what is not virtuous, would practise virtue in such a way that he would not allow anything that is not virtuous to approach his person.

2. 'Is any one able for one day to apply his strength to virtue? I have not seen the case in which his strength would be insufficient.

3. 'Should there possibly be any such case, I have not seen it.'

CHAP. VII.　The Master said, 'The faults of men are characteristic of the class to which they belong.　By observing a man's faults, it may be known that he is virtuous.'

6. A LAMENT BECAUSE OF THE RARITY OF THE LOVE OF VIRTUE; AND ENCOURAGEMENT TO PRACTISE VIRTUE.　1. The first four 者 belong to the verbs 好 and 惡, and give them the force of participles.　In 使不仁者, 者 belongs to 不仁, and 不仁者＝不仁之事. Commonly, 者 = 'he or those who,' but sometimes also = 'that or those things which.' 尚 ＝加, 'to add to.' Morrison, character 尚 translates the sentence wrongly—'He who loves virtue and benevolence can have nothing more said in his praise.'　3. 蓋 here is 疑辭,

'a particle of doubt;' as often.　未之有, a transposition, as in I. ii. 1.

7. A MAN IS NOT TO BE UTTERLY CONDEMNED BECAUSE HE HAS FAULTS.　Such is the sentiment found in this chapter, in which we may say, however, that Confucius is liable to the charge brought against Tsze-hsiâ, I. vii.　人之過 也 stands absolutely,—'As to the faults of men.'　各＝各人, and 於＝從,—'Each man follows his class.'　Observe the force of 過, 'what goes beyond.'　The faults are the excesses of the general tendencies.　Compare Goldsmith's line, 'And even his failings leant to virtue's side.'

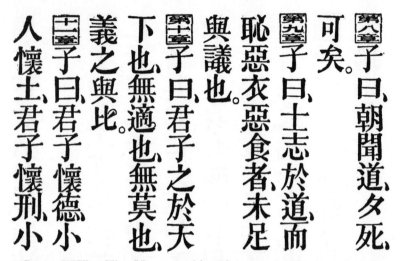

CHAP. VIII. The Master said, 'If a man in the morning hear the right way, he may die in the evening without regret.'

CHAP. IX. The Master said, 'A scholar, whose mind is set on truth, and who is ashamed of bad clothes and bad food, is not fit to be discoursed with.'

CHAP. X. The Master said, 'The superior man, in the world, does not set his mind either for anything, or against anything; what is right he will follow.'

CHAP. XI. The Master said, 'The superior man thinks of virtue; the small man thinks of comfort. The superior man thinks of the sanctions of law; the small man thinks of favours *which he may receive.*'

8. THE IMPORTANCE OF KNOWING THE RIGHT WAY. One is perplexed to translate 道 here. Chû defines it—事物當然之理, 'the principles of what is right in events and things.' Better is the explanation in 四書翼註, 一道卽率性之道, '道 is the path'—i.e. *of action*—'which is in accordance with our nature.' Man is formed for this, and if he die without coming to the knowledge of it, his death is no better than that of a beast. One would fain recognise in such sentences a vague apprehension of some higher truth than Chinese sages have been able to propound.—Ho Yen takes a different view, and makes the whole chapter a lament of Confucius that he was likely to die without hearing of right principles prevailing in the world.—'Could I once hear of the prevalence of right principles, I could die the same evening!' Other views of the meaning have been proposed.

9. THE PURSUIT OF TRUTH SHOULD RAISE A MAN ABOVE BEING ASHAMED OF POVERTY. 與議,—to be discoursed with, i.e. about 道, or 'truth,' which perhaps is the best translation of the term in places like this.

10. RIGHTEOUSNESS IS THE RULE OF THE CHÜN-TSZE'S PRACTICE. 君子之云云, 'The relation of the *Chün-tsze* to the world,' i.e. to all things presenting themselves to him. 適, read *ti*, is explained by 專主, 'to set the mind exclusively on.' We may take the last clause thus :—'his is the according with, and keeping near to (比, the 4th tone, = 從 or 親) righteousness.' This gives each character its signification, the 與 blending its meaning with 比.

11. THE DIFFERENT MINDINGS OF THE SUPERIOR AND THE SMALL MAN. *Hwâi* is here emphatic, = '*cherishes* and plans about.' 土, 'earth,' 'the ground,' is here defined—所處之安, 'the rest or comforts one dwells amidst.' May it not be used somewhat in our sense of earthly? —'thinks of what is earthly.'

人懷惠。

子曰、放於利而行多怨。

子曰、能以禮讓爲國乎、

何有不能以禮讓爲國、如禮何。

子曰、不患無位、患所以立不患莫己知求爲可知也。

子曰、參乎、吾道一以貫之。曾子曰、唯。子出、門人問

CHAP. XII. The Master said, 'He who acts with a constant view to his own advantage will be much murmured against.'

CHAP. XIII. The Master said, 'Is *a prince* able to govern his kingdom with the complaisance proper to the rules of propriety, what difficulty will he have? If he cannot govern it with that complaisance, what has he to do with the rules of propriety?'

CHAP. XIV. The Master said, '*A man should say*, I am not concerned that I have no place, I am concerned how I may fit myself for one. I am not concerned that I am not known, I seek to be worthy to be known.'

CHAP. XV. 1. The Master said, 'Shăn, my doctrine is that of an all-pervading unity.' The disciple Tsăng replied, 'Yes.'

2. The Master went out, and the *other* disciples asked, saying,

12. THE CONSEQUENCE OF SELFISH CONDUCT. 放, the 3rd tone, = 依, 'to accord with,' 'to keep along.'—'He who acts along the line of gain.'

13. THE INFLUENCE IN GOVERNMENT OF CEREMONIES OBSERVED IN THEIR PROPER SPIRIT. 禮讓字是二是一, i.e. they are a hendiadys. 讓 = 禮之實, 'the sincerity and substance of ceremony,' the *spirit* of it. Comp. 和 in I. xii. 爲 = 治, 'to govern.' This meaning is found in the dictionary.

14. ADVISING TO SELF-CULTIVATION. Comp. I. xvi. Here, as there, 不 not being imperative, we must supply a nominative. 位, 'a place,' i.e. an official situation. 所以立 is to be completed 所以立乎其位.

15. CONFUCIUS'S DOCTRINE THAT OF A PERVADING UNITY. This chapter is said to be the most profound in the *Lun Yü*. 1. 吾道一以貫之;—to myself it occurs to translate, 'my doctrines have one thing which goes through them,' but such an exposition has not been approved by any Chinese writer. 一以貫之 are made to contain the copula and predicate of 吾道; and 之, it is said, 'refers to all affairs and all things.' The one thing or unity intended by Confucius was the heart, man's nature, of which all the relations and duties of life are only the development and outgoings.

諫見志不從又敬 子曰事父母幾 省也。 焉見不賢而內自 子曰見賢思齊 義小人喻於利。 子曰君子喻於 已矣。 夫子之道忠恕而 曰何謂也曾子曰

'What do his words mean?' Tsăng said, 'The doctrine of our master is to be true to the principles of our nature and the benevolent exercise of them to others,—this and nothing more.'

CHAP. XVI. The Master said, 'The mind of the superior man is conversant with righteousness; the mind of the mean man is conversant with gain.'

CHAP. XVII. The Master said, 'When we see men of worth, we should think of equalling them; when we see men of a contrary character, we should turn inwards and examine ourselves.'

CHAP. XVIII. The Master said, 'In serving his parents, *a son* may remonstrate with them, but gently; when he sees that they do not incline to follow *his advice*, he shows an increased degree of reverence, but does not abandon *his purpose;* and should they punish him, he does not allow himself to murmur.'

2. 忠 and 恕, which seem to be two things, are both formed from 心, 'the heart,' 忠 being compounded of 中, 'middle,' 'centre,' and 心, and 恕 of 如 'as,' and 心. The 'centre heart' = I, the *ego;* and the 'as heart' = the I in sympathy with others. 忠 is duty-doing, on a consideration, or from the impulse, of one's own self; 恕 is duty-doing, on the principle of reciprocity. The chapter shows that Confucius only claimed to enforce duties indicated by man's mental constitution. He was simply a moral philosopher. Observe 唯 is 3rd tone, = 'yes.' Some say that 門人 must mean Tsăng's own disciples, and that, had they been those of Confucius, we should have read 弟子. The criticism cannot be depended on. 而已矣 is a very emphatic 'and nothing more.'

16. HOW RIGHTEOUSNESS AND SELFISHNESS DISTINGUISH THE SUPERIOR MAN AND THE SMALL MAN.

喻 = 曉, 'to understand.' 於 is here to be dwelt on, and may be compared with the Hebrew *eth.*

17. THE LESSONS TO BE LEARNED FROM OBSERVING MEN OF DIFFERENT CHARACTERS. Of the final particles 焉 and 也, it is said, 二字頗 有抑揚警醒意, 'the two characters have something of a repressive, expansive, warning force.' Ho Yen's text has a 者 after the second 賢 which is not necessary.

18. HOW A SON MAY REMONSTRATE WITH HIS PARENTS ON THEIR FAULTS. See the 禮記, XI. i. 15. 幾, the 1st tone, 'mildly,' = the 下氣, 怡色, 柔聲 of the 內則. 志 is the will of the parents. 又敬 = 更 加孝敬, 'again increasing his filial reverence,' the 起敬起孝 of the 內則. 不違 is not abandoning his purpose of re-

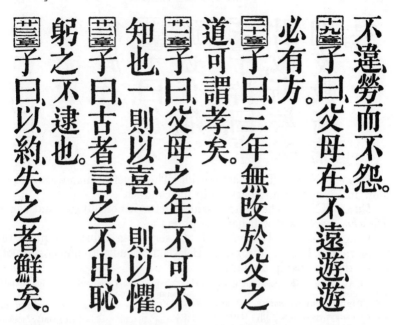

CHAP. XIX. The Master said, 'While his parents are alive, *the son* may not go abroad to a distance. If he does go abroad, he must have a fixed place to which he goes.'

CHAP. XX. The Master said, 'If the son for three years does not alter from the way of his father, he may be called filial.'

CHAP. XXI. The Master said, 'The years of parents may by no means not be kept in the memory, as an occasion at once for joy and for fear.'

CHAP. XXII. The Master said, 'The reason why the ancients did not readily give utterance to their words, was that they feared lest their actions should not come up to them.'

CHAP. XXIII. The Master said, 'The cautious seldom err.'

monstrance, and not as 包咸 says in the comment given by Ho Yen, 不敢違父母意, 'not daring to go against the mind of his parents.' 勞 = 'toiled and pained,' what the 內則 says, 撻之流血, 'should they beat him till the blood flows.'

19. A SON OUGHT NOT TO GO TO A DISTANCE WHERE HE WILL NOT BE ABLE TO PAY THE DUE SERVICES TO HIS PARENTS. 方 = 一定向, 'a fixed direction or quarter,' whence he may be recalled, if necessary.

20. A REPETITION OF PART OF I. xi.

21. WHAT EFFECT THE AGE OF PARENTS SHOULD HAVE ON THEIR CHILDREN. 知, it is said, conveys here 念念不忘意, 'the meaning of unforgetting thoughtfulness.'

22. THE VIRTUE OF THE ANCIENTS SEEN IN THEIR SLOWNESS TO SPEAK. Observe the force of the two 之.—'The not coming forth of the words of the ancients was shame about the not coming up to them of their actions.'

23. ADVANTAGE OF CAUTION. Collie's version, which I have adopted, is here happy. 約, see chap. ii. The 'binding' here is of one's self, self-restraint, = 'caution.' 失之, 'loses it,' 之 referring to whatever business the cautious may be engaged in. 之, after an active verb, often makes it neuter; at least, a neuter verb renders the expression best in English.

CHAP. XXIV. The Master said, 'The superior man wishes to be slow in his speech and earnest in his conduct.'

CHAP. XXV. The Master said, 'Virtue is not left to stand alone. *He who practises it* will have neighbours.'

CHAP. XXVI. Tsze-yû said, 'In serving a prince, frequent remonstrances lead to disgrace. Between friends, frequent reproofs make the friendship distant.'

24. RULE OF THE CHÜN-TSZE ABOUT HIS WORDS AND ACTIONS.

25. THE VIRTUOUS ARE NOT LEFT ALONE :—AN ENCOURAGEMENT TO VIRTUE. 孤, 'fatherless;' here = solitary, friendless. 德不孤 = 德無孤立之理, 'it is not the nature of virtue to be left to stand alone.' 鄰,

see chap. i; here, generally used for friends, associates of like mind.

26. A LESSON TO COUNSELLORS AND FRIENDS. 數, the 4th tone, read *sho*, 'frequently,' understood here in reference to remonstrating or reproving. 斯 = 'this,' 'this leads to,' or 'thereon is.'

BOOK V. KUNG-YÊ CH'ANG.

CHAPTER I. 1. The Master said of Kung-yê Ch'ang that he might be wived; although he was put in bonds, he had not been guilty of any crime. *Accordingly*, he gave him his own daughter to wife.

2. Of Nan Yung he said that if the country were well-governed,

HEADING OF THIS BOOK.—公冶長第 五. Kung-yê Ch'ang, the surname and name of the first individual spoken of in it, heads this Book, which is chiefly occupied with the judgment of the sage on the character of several of his disciples and others. As the decision

frequently turns on their being possessed of that zän, or perfect virtue, which is so conspicuous in the last Book, this is the reason, it is said, why the one immediately follows the other. As Tsze-kung appears in the Book several times, some have fancied that it was compiled by his disciples.

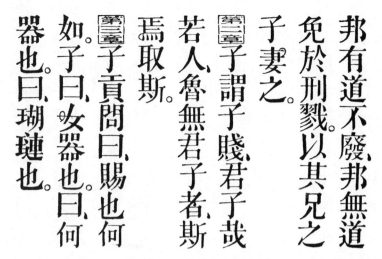

he would not be out of office, and if it were ill-governed, he would escape punishment and disgrace. He gave him the daughter of his own elder brother to wife.

CHAP. II. The Master said of Tsze-chien, 'Of superior virtue indeed is such a man! If there were not virtuous men in Lû, how could this man have acquired this character?'

CHAP. III. Tsze-kung asked, 'What do you say of me, Ts'ze? The Master said, 'You are a utensil.' 'What utensil?' 'A gemmed sacrificial utensil.'

1. CONFUCIUS IN MARRIAGE-MAKING WAS GUIDED BY CHARACTER AND NOT BY FORTUNE. 1. Of Kung-yê Ch'ang, though the son-in-law of Confucius, nothing certain is known, and his tablet is only 3rd on the west, among the οἱ πολλοί. Silly legends are told of his being put in prison from his bringing suspicion on himself by his knowledge of the language of birds. Chŭ Hsî approves the interpretation of 縲 as meaning 'a black rope,' with which criminals were anciently bound (縲) in prison. 妻, and in par. 2, the 3rd tone, 'to wive,' 'to give a wife to one.' 子, in both paragraphs, = 'a daughter.' Confucius's brother would be the cripple Măng-p'î ;—see p. 58.   2. Nan Yung, another of the disciples, is now 4th, east, in the outer hall. The discussions about who he was, and whether he is to be identified with 南宮适 and several other aliases, are very perplexing. 廢, 'to lay, or be laid aside,' from office. 戮, 'to put to death,' has also the lighter meaning of 'disgrace.' We cannot tell whether Confucius is giving his impression of Yung's character, or referring to events that had taken place.

2. THE CHÜN-TSZE FORMED BY INTERCOURSE WITH OTHER CHÜN-TSZE. Tsze-chien, by sur-name 宓 (= 虙, and said to be i.q. 伏), and named 不齊, appears to have been of some note among the disciples of Confucius as an administrator, though his tablet is now only 2nd, west, in the outer hall. See the Narratives of the School, chap. xxxviii. What chiefly distinguished him, as appears here, was his cultivation of the friendship of men of ability and virtue. 若人=若此人, 'a man such as this.' See the 註疏 in loc. The first 斯 is 'this man;' the second, 'this virtue.' The paraphrasts complete the last clause thus:—斯將何所取以成斯德乎, 'what friends must this man have chosen to complete this virtue!'

3. WHERETO TSZE-KUNG HAD ATTAINED. See I. x; II. xiii. The 瑚璉 were vessels richly adorned, used to contain grain-offerings in the royal ancestral temples. Under the Hsiâ dynasty they were called 璉, and 瑚 under the Yin. See the Lî Chî, XII. ii. While the sage did not grant to Ts'ze that he was a Chün-tsze (II. xii), he made him 'a vessel of honour,' valuable and fit for use on high occasions.

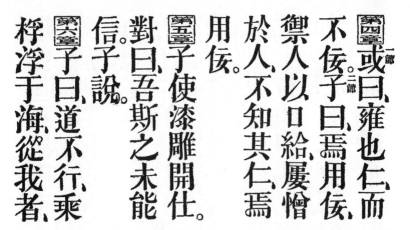

CHAP. IV. 1. Some one said, 'Yung is truly virtuous, but he is not ready with his tongue.'

2. The Master said, 'What is the good of being ready with the tongue? They who encounter men with smartnesses of speech for the most part procure themselves hatred. I know not whether he be truly virtuous, but why should he show readiness of the tongue?'

CHAP. V. The Master was wishing Ch'î-tiâo K'âi to enter on official employment. He replied, 'I am not yet able to rest in the assurance of THIS.' The Master was pleased.

CHAP. VI. The Master said, 'My doctrines make no way. I will get upon a raft, and float about on the sea. He that will accompany me will be Yû, I dare to say.' Tsze-lû hearing this was glad,

4. OF ZAN YUNG :—READINESS WITH THE TONGUE NO PART OF VIRTUE. 1. 冉雍, styled 仲弓, has his tablet the 2nd, on the east, among 'the wise ones.' His father was a worthless character (see VI. iv), but he himself was the opposite. 佞 means 'ability,' generally ; then, 'ability of speech,' often, though not here, with the bad sense of artfulness and flattery. 2. Confucius would not grant that Yung was 仁, but his not being 佞 was in his favour rather than otherwise. 口給 (read chieh : see dict.), 'smartnesses of speech.' 焉 is here 'why,' rather than 'how.' The first 焉用仁 is a general statement, not having special reference to Zan Yung. In the 註疏, 不知其仁焉用佞 is read as one sentence :—'I do not know how the virtuous should also use readiness of speech.'

5. CH'Î-TIÂO K'ÂI'S OPINION OF THE QUALIFICATIONS NECESSARY TO TAKING OFFICE. Ch'î-tiâo, now 6th, on the east, in the outer hall, was styled 子若. His name originally was 啟,

changed into 開 on the accession of the emperor 孝景, B.C. 156, whose name was also 啟. The difficulty is with 斯—what does it refer to? and with 信—what is its force? In the chapter about the disciples in the 家語, it is said that K'âi was reading in the Shû-ching, when Confucius spoke to him about taking office, and he pointed to the book, or some particular passage in it, saying, 'I am not yet able to rest in the assurance of (信＝眞知確見) this.' It may have been so. Obs. the force of the 之.

6. CONFUCIUS PROPOSING TO WITHDRAW FROM THE WORLD :—A LESSON TO TSZE-LÛ. Tsze-lû supposed his master really meant to leave the world, and the idea of floating along the coasts pleased his ardent temper. But Confucius only expressed in this way his regret at the backwardness of men to receive his doctrines. 無所取材 is difficult of interpretation. Chû Hsî takes 材 as being for 裁, 'to cut out clothes,' 'to estimate, dis-

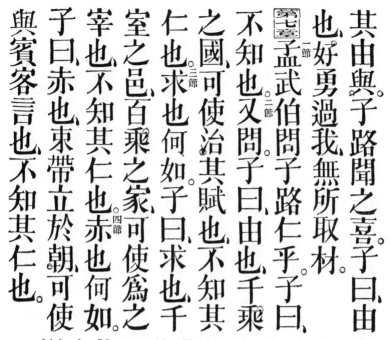

其由與子路聞之喜子曰由
也好勇過我無所取材。

第七章　一節　孟武伯問子路仁乎子曰由也千乘
不知也又問子路曰由也千乘　二節
之國可使治其賦也不知其
仁也求也何如子曰求也　三節
室之邑百乘之家可使爲之
宰也不知其仁也赤也何如　四節
子曰赤也束帶立於朝可使
與賓客言也不知其仁也。

upon which the Master said, 'Yû is fonder of daring than I am. He does not exercise his judgment upon matters.'

CHAP. VII. 1. Măng Wŭ asked about Tsze-lû, whether he was perfectly virtuous. The Master said, 'I do not know.'

2. He asked again, when the Master replied, 'In a kingdom of a thousand chariots, Yû might be employed to manage the military levies, but I do not know whether he be perfectly virtuous.'

3. 'And what do you say of Ch'iû?' The Master replied, 'In a city of a thousand families, or a clan of a hundred chariots, Ch'iû might be employed as governor, but I do not know whether he is perfectly virtuous.'

4. 'What do you say of Ch'ih?' The Master replied, 'With his sash girt and standing in a court, Ch'ih might be employed to converse with the visitors and guests, but I do not know whether he is perfectly virtuous.'

criminate,' and hence the meaning in the translation. 鄭玄, keeping the meaning of 材, explains—無所取於桴材, = 'my meaning is not to be found in the *raft*.' Another old writer makes 材 = 哉, and putting a stop at 勇 explains—'Yû is fond of daring; he cannot go beyond himself to find my meaning.'

7. OF TSZE-LÛ, TSZE-YÛ, AND TSZE-HWÂ. 1.

孟武伯, see II. vi. 2. 千乘之國, see I. v. 賦, properly 'revenues,' 'taxes,' but the quota of soldiers contributed being regulated by the amount of the revenue, the term is used here for the forces, or *military levies*. 3. 求, see III. vi. 百乘之家, in opposition to 千乘之國, was the secondary fief, the territory appropriated to the highest nobles or officers in a 國 or state, supposed also to comprehend 1000 families

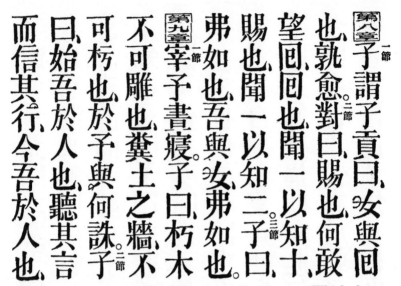

CHAP. VIII. 1. The Master said to Tsze-kung, 'Which do you consider superior, yourself or Hûi?'

2. Tsze-kung replied, 'How dare I compare myself with Hûi? Hûi hears one point and knows all about a subject; I hear one point and know a second.'

3. The Master said, 'You are not equal to him. I grant you, you are not equal to him.'

CHAP. IX. 1. Tsâi Yü being asleep during the day time, the Master said, 'Rotten wood cannot be carved; a wall of dirty earth will not receive the trowel. This Yü!—what is the use of my reproving him?'

2. The Master said, 'At first, my way with men was to hear their words, and give them credit for their conduct. Now my way is to hear their words, and look at their conduct. It is from Yü that I have learned to make this change.'

爲之宰, 'to be its governor.' This is a peculiar idiom, something like the double object in Latin. 4. Ch'ih, surnamed 公西, and styled 子華, having now the 14th place, west, in the outer hall, was famous among the disciples for his knowledge of rules of ceremony, and those especially relating to dress and intercourse. 朝, in 2nd tone. 賓 and 客 may be distinguished, the former indicating neighbouring princes visiting the court; the latter, ministers and officers of the State present as guests.

8. SUPERIORITY OF YEN HÛI TO TSZE-KUNG. 2. 望, 'to look to,' 'to look up to,' here = 比, 'to compare with.' 'One' is the beginning of numbers, and 'ten' the completion; hence the meaning of 聞一以知十, as in the translation. 3. 與 = 許, 'to allow,' 'to grant to.' Ho Yen gives here the comm. of 包咸 (about A.D. 50), who interprets strangely,—'I and you are both not equal to him,' saying that Confucius thus comforted Tsze-kung.

9. THE IDLENESS OF TSÂI YÜ AND ITS REPROOF. 1. 於予與, 'In the case of Yü!' 與 has here the force of an exclamation; so below. 誅, a strong term, to mark the severity of the reproof. 2. 子曰 is superfluous. The characters were probably added by a transcriber. If not, they should head another chapter. Tsâi Yü,—the same as Tsâi Wo in III. xxi.

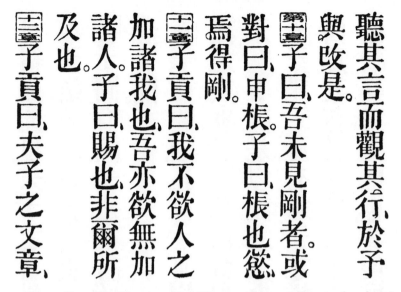

CHAP. X. The Master said, 'I have not seen a firm and unbending man.' Some one replied, 'There is Shăn Ch'ang.' 'Ch'ang,' said the Master, 'is under the influence of his passions; how can he be pronounced firm and unbending?'

CHAP. XI. Tsze-kung said, 'What I do not wish men to do to me, I also wish not to do to men.' The Master said, 'Ts'ze, you have not attained to that.'

CHAP. XII. Tsze-kung said, 'The Master's *personal* displays *of his principles* and *ordinary* descriptions of them may be heard. His discourses about *man's* nature, and the way of Heaven, cannot be heard.'

10. UNBENDING VIRTUE CANNOT CO-EXIST WITH INDULGENCE OF THE PASSIONS. Shăn Ch'ang (there are several *aliases*, but they are disputed) was one of the minor disciples, of whom little or nothing is known. He was styled 子周, and his place is 31st, east, in the outer ranges. 剛 is to be understood with reference to virtue. 慾 is 情所好, 'what the passions love,' 'lusts.' 焉得 are said to = 不是, and not 不能. I have translated accordingly.

11. THE DIFFICULTY OF ATTAINING TO THE NOT WISHING TO DO TO OTHERS AS WE WISH THEM NOT TO DO TO US. It is said—此章見無我之不易及, 'this chapter shows that the *no I* (freedom from selfishness) is not easily reached.' In the 中庸, XIII. iii, it is said—施諸己而不願亦勿施諸人, 'what you do not like when done to yourself, do not do to others.' The difference between it and the sentence here is said to be that of 恕, 'reciprocity;' and 仁, 'benevolence,' or the highest virtue, apparent in the adverbs 勿 and 無, the one prohibitive, and the other a simple, unconstrained negation. The golden rule of the Gospel is higher than both,—'Do ye unto others as ye would that others should do unto you.' 諸 = 於; 加諸, or 加於, 'to add upon,' 'to do to.'

12. THE GRADUAL WAY IN WHICH CONFUCIUS COMMUNICATED HIS DOCTRINES. So the lesson of this chapter is summed up, but there is hardly another more perplexing to a translator. 文章 is the common name for essays, elegant literary compositions. Of course that meaning is out of the question. Whatever is *figured* and *brilliant* is 文; whatever is *orderly* and *defined* is 章. The comm., accordingly, make 文 to be the deportment and manners of the sage, and 章 his ordinary discourses, but 聞 is an in-

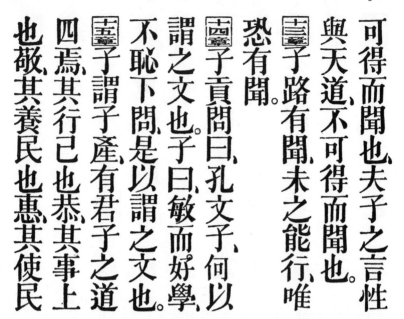

CHAP. XIII. When Tsze-lû heard anything, if he had not yet succeeded in carrying it into practice, he was only afraid lest he should hear *something else.*

CHAP. XIV. Tsze-kung asked, saying, 'On what ground did Kung-wăn get that title of WĂN?' The Master said, 'He was of an active nature and yet fond of learning, and he was not ashamed to ask *and learn of* his inferiors!—On these grounds he has been styled WĂN.'

CHAP. XV. The Master said of Tsze-ch'an that he had four of the characteristics of a superior man:—in his conduct of himself, he was humble; in serving his superiors, he was respectful; in nourishing the people, he was kind; in ordering the people, he was just.'

appropriate term with reference to the former. These things, however, were level to the capacities of the disciples generally, and they had the benefit of them. As to his views about man's nature, as the gift of Heaven, and the way of Heaven generally; these he only communicated to those who were prepared to receive them, and Tsze-kung is supposed to have expressed himself thus, after being on some occasion so privileged.

13. THE ARDOUR OF TSZE-LÛ IN PRACTISING THE MASTER'S INSTRUCTIONS. The concluding 唯 恐有聞 is to be completed 唯恐復 有所聞, as in the translation.

14. AN EXAMPLE OF THE PRINCIPLE ON WHICH HONORARY POSTHUMOUS TITLES WERE CONFERRED. 文, corresponding nearly to our 'accomplished,' was the posthumous title given to

子圉, an officer of the same surname of the State of Wei, and a contemporary of Confucius. Many of his actions had been of a doubtful character, which made Tsze-kung stumble at the application to him of so honourable an epithet. But Confucius shows that, whatever he might otherwise have been, he *had* those qualities which justified his being so denominated. The rule for posthumous titles in China has been, and is, very much—' *De mortuis nil nisi bonum.*'

15. THE EXCELLENT QUALITIES OF TSZE-CH'AN. Tsze-ch'an, named 公孫僑, was the chief minister of the State of Chăng (鄭), the ablest, perhaps, and most upright of all the statesmen among Confucius's contemporaries. The sage wept when he heard of his death. The old interpreters take 使 in the sense of 'employing,' but it seems to express more, and = 'ordering,' 'regulating.'

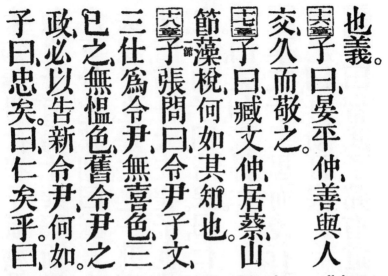

CHAP. XVI. The Master said, 'Yen P'ing knew well how to maintain friendly intercourse. The acquaintance might be long, but he showed the *same* respect *as at first*.'

CHAP. XVII. The Master said, 'Tsang Wăn kept a large tortoise in a house, on the capitals of the pillars of which he had hills made, with representations of duckweed on the small pillars *above the beams supporting the rafters.*—Of what sort was his wisdom?'

CHAP. XVIII. 1. Tsze-chang asked, saying, 'The minister Tsze-wăn thrice took office, and manifested no joy in his countenance. Thrice he retired from office, and manifested no displeasure. He made it a point to inform the new minister of the way in which he had conducted the government;—what do you say of him?' 'The Master replied, 'He was loyal.' 'Was he perfectly virtuous?' 'I do not know. How can he be pronounced perfectly virtuous?'

16. HOW TO MAINTAIN FRIENDSHIP. 'Familiarity breeds contempt,' and with contempt friendship ends. It was not so with Yen P'ing, another of the worthies of Confucius's time. He was a principal minister of Ch'î (齊), by name 嬰. P'ing (= 'Ruling and averting calamity') was his posthumous title. If we were to render 仲, the name would be 'Yen P'ing, *secundus.*' The antecedent to 之 is 人.

17. THE SUPERSTITION OF TSANG WĂN. Tsang Wăn (Wăn is the honorary epithet, and 仲, see last chapter) had been a great officer in Lû, and left a reputation for wisdom, which Confucius did not think was deserved. His full name was 臧孫辰. He was descended from the duke 孝 (B.C. 794-767), whose son was styled 子臧. This Tsang

was taken by his descendants as their surname. Such was one of the ways in which surnames were formed among the Chinese. 蔡, 'a large tortoise,' so called, because the State of Ts'âi was famous for its tortoises. 居 is used as an active verb, = 臧. The 節 = 柱頭斗栱, 'the capitals of the pillars.' The 梲 may be seen in any Chinese house where the whole structure of the roof is displayed, and these small pillars are very conspicuous. The old critics make the keeping such a tortoise an act of usurpation on the part of Tsang Wăn. Chû Hsî finds the point of Confucius's words in the keeping it in such a style.

18. THE PRAISE OF PERFECT VIRTUE IS NOT TO BE LIGHTLY ACCORDED. 1. Ling-yin, lit. 'good corrector,' was the name given to the chief minister of Ch'û (楚). 尹 is still applied

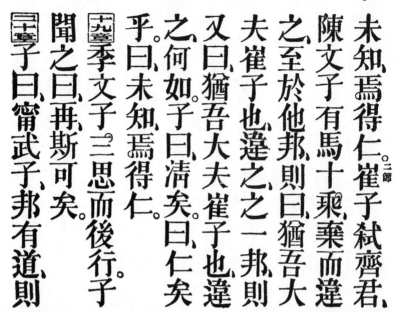

2. *Tsze-chang* proceeded, 'When the officer Ch'ûi killed the
prince of Ch'î, Ch'ǎn Wǎn, though he was the owner of forty horses,
abandoned them and left the country. Coming to another State, he
said, "They are here like our great officer, Ch'ûi," and left it. He
came to a second State, and with the same observation left it also;
—what do you say of him?' The Master replied, 'He was pure.'
'Was he perfectly virtuous?' 'I do not know. How can he be
pronounced perfectly virtuous?'

CHAP. XIX. Chî Wǎn thought thrice, and then acted. When
the Master was informed of it, he said, 'Twice may do.'

CHAP. XX. The Master said, 'When good order prevailed in his
country, Ning Wû acted the part of a wise man. When his country
was in disorder, he acted the part of a stupid man. Others may
equal his wisdom, but they cannot equal his stupidity.'

to officers; e.g. the prefect of a department
is called 府尹. Tsze-wǎn, surnamed 鬬,
and named 穀於菟 ('suckled by a tiger'),
had been noted for the things mentioned by
Tsze-chang, but the sage would not concede
that he was therefore 仁. 2. 崔 was a great
officer of Ch'î. Yen P'ing (chap. xvi) distinguished himself on the occasion of the murder
(B.C. 547) here referred to. Ch'ǎn Wǎn was likewise an officer of Ch'î. 之一邦, 之 is a
verb, = 往. 乘, 4th tone, as in I. vi, but with
a different meaning, = 'a team of four horses.'

19. PROMPT DECISION GOOD. Wǎn was the
posthumous title of 季行父, a faithful

and disinterested officer of Lû. 三, 4th tone,
'three times,' but some say it = 二三, 'again
and again.' Comp. Robert Hall's remark—'In
matters of conscience first thoughts are best.'

20. THE UNCOMMON BUT ADMIRABLE STUPIDITY
OF NING WÛ. Ning Wû (武, honorary epithet; see II. vi) was an officer of Wei in the
time of Wǎn (B.C. 660–635). In the first part
of his official life the State was quiet and prosperous, and he 'wisely' acquitted himself of
his duties. Afterwards came confusion. The
prince was driven from the throne, and Ning
Yü (俞 was his name) might, like other wise
men, have retired from the danger. But he
'foolishly,' as it seemed, chose to follow the

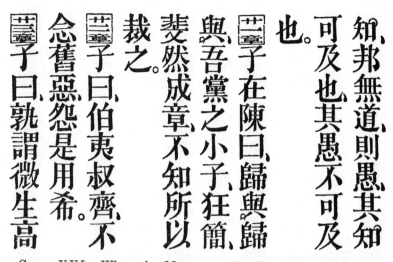

CHAP. XXI. When the Master was in Ch'ăn, he said, 'Let me return! Let me return! The little children of my school are ambitious and too hasty. They are accomplished and complete so far, but they do not know how to restrict and shape themselves.'

CHAP. XXII. The Master said, 'Po-î and Shû-ch'î did not keep the former wickednesses of men in mind, and hence the resentments directed towards them were few.'

CHAP. XXIII. The Master said, 'Who says of Wei-shang Kâo

fortunes of his prince, and yet adroitly brought it about in the end, that the prince was reinstated and order restored.

21. THE ANXIETY OF CONFUCIUS ABOUT THE TRAINING OF HIS DISCIPLES. Confucius was thrice in Ch'ăn. It must have been the third time, when he thus expressed himself. He was then over 60 years, and being convinced that he was not to see for himself the triumph of his principles, he became the more anxious about their transmission, and the training of the disciples in order to that. Such is the common view of the chapter. Some say, however, that it is not to be understood of all the disciples. Compare Mencius, VII. ii. ch. 37. 吾黨之小子, an affectionate way of speaking of the disciples. 狂, 'mad,' also 'extravagant,' 'high-minded.' The 狂 are naturally 簡, hasty and careless of minutiæ. 斐然, 'accomplished-like.' 章, see chap. xii. 成章, 'something complete.' 裁, see chap. vi, but its application here is somewhat different. The antecedent to 之 is all the preceding description.

22. THE GENEROSITY OF Po-î AND SHÛ-CH'Î, AND ITS EFFECTS. These were ancient worthies of the closing period of the Shang dynasty.

Compare Mencius, II. i. ch. 2, et al. They were brothers, sons of the king of Kû-chû (孤竹), named respectively 允 and 致. î and Ch'î are·their honorary epithets, and 伯 and 叔 only indicate their relation to each other as elder and younger. Po-î and Shû-ch'î, however, are in effect their names in the mouths and writings of the Chinese. Kû-chû was a small State, included in the present department of 永平, in Pei-chih-lî. Their father left his kingdom to Shû-ch'î, who refused to take the place of his elder brother. Po-î in turn declined the throne; so they both abandoned it, and retired into obscurity. When king Wû was taking his measures against the tyrant Châu, they made their appearance, and remonstrated against his course. Finally, they died of hunger, rather than live under the new dynasty. They were celebrated for their purity, and aversion to men whom they considered bad, but Confucius here brings out their generosity. 怨是用希 = 怨是以希, 'Resentments thereby were few.'

23. SMALL MEANNESSES INCONSISTENT WITH UPRIGHTNESS. It is implied that Kâo gave the vinegar as from himself. He was a native of Lû, with a reputation better than he deserved to have.

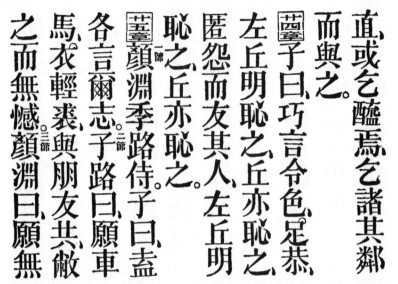

that he is upright? One begged some vinegar of him, and he begged
it of a neighbour and gave it to the man.'

CHAP. XXIV. The Master said, 'Fine words, an insinuating
appearance, and excessive respect;—Tso Ch'iû-ming was ashamed of
them. I also am ashamed of them. To conceal resentment against
a person, and appear friendly with him;—Tso Ch'iû-ming was
ashamed of such conduct. I also am ashamed of it.'

CHAP. XXV. 1. Yen Yüan and Chî Lû being by his side, the
Master said to them, 'Come, let each of you tell his wishes.'

2. Tsze-lû said, 'I should like, having chariots and horses, and
light fur dresses, to share them with my friends, and though they
should spoil them, I would not be displeased.'

3. Yen Yüan said, 'I should like not to boast of my excellence,
nor to make a display of my meritorious deeds.'

24. PRAISE OF SINCERITY, AND OF Tso Ch'iû-
MING. 巧言令色, see I. iii. 足恭, 'ex-
cessive respect,' 足 being in 4th tone read *tsŭ*.
Some of the old commentators, keeping the
usual tone and meaning of 足, interpret the
phrase of movements of the 'feet' to indicate
respect. The discussions about Tso Ch'iû-ming
are endless. See 拓餘說, I. xxx. It is
sufficient for us to rest in the judgment of the
commentator 程, that 'he was an ancient of
reputation.' It is not to be received that he
was a disciple of Confucius, the same whose
supplement to the Ch'un Ch'iû chronicles the
death of the sage, and carries on the history
for many subsequent years. 丘 was the name

of Confucius. The Chinese decline pronouncing
it, always substituting *Mâu* (某), 'such an
one,' for it.

25. THE DIFFERENT WISHES OF YEN YÜAN, TSZE-
LÛ, AND CONFUCIUS. 1. 盍各言爾志,
'why not each tell your will?' 2. A student is
apt to translate—'I should like to have chariots
and horses, &c.,' but 共 is the important word
in the paragraph, and under the regimen of
願. 衣, the 4th tone, 'to wear.' Several
writers carry the regimen of 願 on to 之, and
removing the comma at 共, read 共敝 together, but this construction is not so good. 3.
In Ho Yen's compilation 施勞 is interpreted,
'not to impose troublesome affairs on others.'

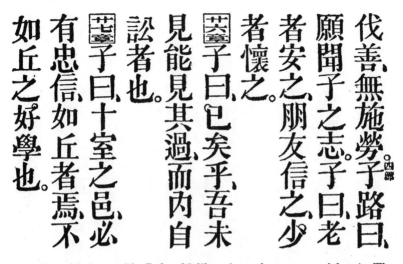

4. Tsze-lû then said, 'I should like, sir, to hear your wishes.' The Master said, '*They are*, in regard to the aged, to give them rest; in regard to friends, to show them sincerity; in regard to the young, to treat them tenderly.'

CHAP. XXVI. The Master said, 'It is all over! I have not yet seen one who could perceive his faults, and inwardly accuse himself.'

CHAP. XXVII. The Master said, 'In a hamlet of ten families, there may be found one honourable and sincere as I am, but not so fond of learning.'

Chû Hsî's view is better. 4. 信之 = 與之 以信, 'To be with them with sincerity.'— The Master and the disciples, it is said, agreed in being devoid of selfishness. Hûi's, however, was seen in a higher style of mind and object than Yû's. In the sage there was an unconsciousness of self, and without any effort he proposed acting in regard to his classification of men just as they ought severally to be acted to.

26. A LAMENT OVER MEN'S PERSISTENCE IN ERROR. The 乎 has an exclamatory force. 訟, 'to litigate.' 內自訟者, 'one who brings himself before the bar of his conscience.' The remark affirms a fact, inexplicable on Confucius's view of the nature of man. But perhaps such an exclamation should not be pressed too closely.

27. THE HUMBLE CLAIM OF CONFUCIUS FOR HIMSELF. 邑 (人聚會之稱也) is 'the designation of the place where men are collected together,' and may be applied from a hamlet upwards to a city. 忠 = 忠厚, 'honourable,' 'substantial.' Confucius thus did not claim higher natural and moral qualities than others, but sought to perfect himself by learning.

BOOK VI. YUNG YÊY.

CHAPTER I. 1. The Master said, 'There is Yung!—He might occupy the place of a prince.'

2. Chung-kung asked about Tsze-sang Po-tsze. The Master said, 'He may pass. He does not mind small matters.'

3. Chung-kung said, 'If a man cherish in himself a reverential feeling *of the necessity of attention to business*, though he may be easy in small matters in his government of the people, that may be allowed. But if he cherish in himself that easy feeling, and also carry it out in his practice, is not such an easy mode of procedure excessive?'

4. The Master said, 'Yung's words are right.'

HEADING OF THIS BOOK.—雍也第六. 'There is Yung!' commences the first chapter, and stands as the title of the Book. Its subjects are much akin to those of the preceding Book, and therefore, it is said, they are in juxtaposition.

1. THE CHARACTERS OF ZAN YUNG AND TSZE-SANG PO-TSZE, AS REGARDS THEIR APTITUDE FOR GOVERNMENT. 1. Yung, V. iv, 可使南面, 'might be employed with his face to the south.' In China the sovereign sits facing the south. So did the princes of the States in their several courts in Confucius's time. An explanation of the practice is attempted in the Yî-ching, 說卦, chap. ix, 離也者明也, 萬物皆相見, 南方之卦也, 聖人南面而聽天下, 向明而治蓋取此也, 'The diagram Lî conveys the idea of brightness, when all things are exhibited to one another. It is the diagram of the south. The custom of the sages (i.e. monarchs) to sit with their faces to the south, *and listen to the representations* of all in the kingdom, governing towards the bright region, was taken from this.' 2. Chung-kung was the designation of Zan Yung, see V. iv. 簡 has here substantially the same meaning as in V. xxi, = 不煩, 'not troubling,' i.e. one's self about small matters. With reference to that place, however, the dict., after the old comm., explains it by 大, 'great.' Of Tsze-sang Po-tsze we know nothing certain but what is here stated. Chû Hsî seems to be wrong in approving the identification of him with the Tsze-sang Hû of Chwang-tsze, VI. par. 11. 3. 居敬, 'to dwell in respect,' to have the mind imbued with it. 敬 = 敬事 as in I. v.

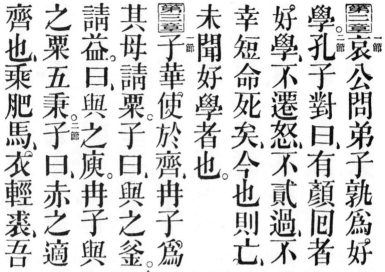

CHAP. II. The duke Âi asked which of the disciples loved to learn. Confucius replied to him, 'There was Yen Hûi; HE loved to learn. He did not transfer his anger; he did not repeat a fault. Unfortunately, his appointed time was short and he died; and now there is not *such another*. I have not yet heard of any one who loves to learn *as he did*.'

CHAP. III. 1. Tsze-hwâ being employed on a mission to Ch'î, the disciple Zan requested grain for his mother. The Master said, 'Give her a *fû*.' *Yen* requested more. 'Give her an *yü*,' said the Master. Yen gave her five *ping*.

2. The Master said, 'When Ch'ih was proceeding to Ch'î, he had fat horses to his carriage, and wore light furs. I have heard that

2. THE RARITY OF A TRUE LOVE TO LEARN. HÛI'S SUPERIORITY TO THE OTHER DISCIPLES. In 有顏回者, 者 = 'that.'—'There was that Yen Hûi.' 'He did not transfer his anger,' i.e. his anger was no tumultuary passion in the mind, but was excited by some specific cause, to which alone it was directed. 短命死矣 = 'he died an early death,' but 命 conveys also the idea in the translation. The two last clauses are completed thus: 一今也，則亡 (read as, and = 無) 是人，未聞如是之好學者也.

3. DISCRIMINATION OF CONFUCIUS IN REWARDING OR SALARYING OFFICERS. Kung-hsî Ch'ih, styled Tsze-hwâ;—see V. vii. 3. 1. 使, in 4th tone, 'to commission,' or 'to be commissioned.' Chû Hsî says the commission was a private one from Confucius, but this is not likely. The old interpretation makes it a public one from the court of Lû; see 四書改錯,

III. ix. 冉子, 'the disciple Zan;' see III. vi. Zan is here styled 子, like 有子, in I. ii, but only in narrative, not as introducing any wise utterance. A *fû* contained 6 *tâu* (斗) and 4 *shăng* (升), or 64 *shăng*. The *yü* contained 160 *shăng*, and the *ping* 16 *hŏ* (斛), or 1600 *shăng*. A *shăng* of the present day is about one-fourth less than an English pint. 2. The 之 in 吾聞之 refers to what follows. 3. In Ho Yen's edition, another chapter commences here. Yüan Sze, named 憲, is now the 3rd, east, in the outer hall of the temples. He was noted for his pursuit of truth, and carelessness of worldly advantages. After the death of Confucius, he withdrew into retirement in Wei. It is related by Chwang-tsze that Tsze-kung, high in official station, came one day in great style to visit him. Sze received him in a tattered coat, and Tsze-kung asking him if he were ill, he replied, 'I have heard

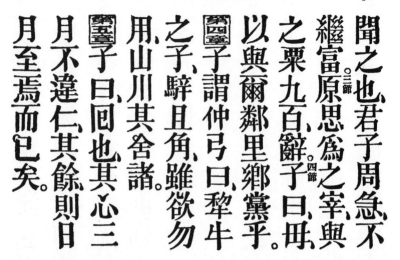

聞之也君子周急不
繼富原思爲之宰與
之粟九百辭子曰毋
以與爾鄰里鄉黨乎。
子謂仲弓曰犂牛
之子騂且角雖欲勿
用山川其舍諸。
子曰回也其心三
月不違仁其餘則日
月至焉而已矣。

a superior man helps the distressed, but does not add to the wealth of the rich.'

3. Yüan Sze being made governor *of his town by the Master*, he gave him nine hundred measures of grain, but Sze declined them.

4. The Master said, 'Do not decline them. May you not give them away in the neighbourhoods, hamlets, towns, and villages?'

CHAP. IV. The Master, speaking of Chung-kung, said, 'If the calf of a brindled cow be red and horned, although men may not wish to use it, would *the spirits of* the mountains and rivers put it aside?'

CHAP. V. The Master said, 'Such was Hûi that for three months there would be nothing in his mind contrary to perfect virtue. The others may attain to this on some days or in some months, but nothing more.'

that to have no money is to be poor, and that to study truth and not be able to find it is to be ill.' This answer sent Tsze-kung away in confusion. The 900 measures (whatever they were) was the proper allowance for an officer in Sze's station. 爲之宰, see V. vii, though it is not easy to give the 之 the same reference here as in that passage. 4. According to ancient statutes, a *lin*, a *li*, a *hsiang*, and a *tang*, had each their specific number of component families, but the meaning is no more than— 'the poor about you.' 乎 makes the remark = 'may you not, &c.'

4. THE VICES OF A FATHER SHOULD NOT DISCREDIT A VIRTUOUS SON. The father of Chung-kung (see V. ii) was a man of bad character, and some would have visited this upon his son, which drew forth Confucius's remark. The rules of the Châu dynasty required that sacrificial victims should be red, and have

good horns. An animal with those qualities, though it might spring from one not possessing them, would certainly not be unacceptable on that account to the spirits sacrificed to. I translate 子 by 'calf,' but it is not implied that the victim was young. 舍, the 3rd tone, = 捨, 'to lay aside,' 'to put away.' 其 舍諸 = 其舍之乎.

5. THE SUPERIORITY OF HÛI TO THE OTHER DISCIPLES. It is impossible to say whether we should translate here about Hûi in the past or present tense. 違 is not 違背, 'to oppose,' but 違去, 'to depart from.' 日月至, 'come to it,' i.e. the line of perfect virtue, 'in the course of a day, or a month.' 日月 may also be, 'for a day or a month.' So in the 註疏.

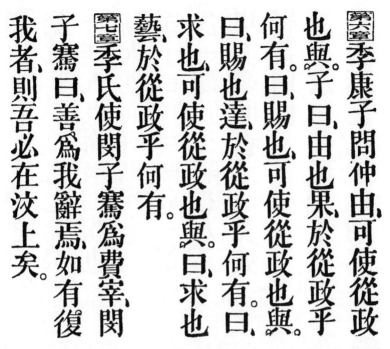

CHAP. VI. Chî K'ang asked about Chung-yû, whether he was fit to be employed as an officer of government. The Master said, 'Yû is a man of decision; what difficulty would he find in being an officer of government?' K'ang asked, 'Is Ts'ze fit to be employed as an officer of government?' and was answered, 'Ts'ze is a man of intelligence; what difficulty would he find in being an officer of government?' And to the same question about Ch'iû the Master gave the same reply, saying, 'Ch'iû is a man of various ability.'

CHAP. VII. The chief of the Chî family sent to ask Min Tsze-ch'ien to be governor of Pî. Min Tsze-ch'ien said, 'Decline the offer for me politely. If any one come again to me with a second invitation, I shall be *obliged to go and live* on the banks of the Wăn.'

6. THE QUALITIES OF TSZE-LÛ, TSZE-KUNG, AND TSZE-YÛ, AND THEIR COMPETENCY TO ASSIST IN GOVERNMENT. The prince is called 爲政者, 'the *doer* of government:' his ministers and officers are styled 從政者, 'the *followers* of government.' 也與 and 何有 are set, the one expression against the other, the former indicating a doubt of the competency of the disciples, the latter affirming their more than competency.

7. MIN TSZE-CH'IEN REFUSES TO SERVE THE CHÎ FAMILY. The tablet of Tsze-ch'ien (his name was 損) is now the first on the east among 'the wise ones' of the temple. He was among the foremost of the disciples. Confucius praises

his filial piety, and we see here, how he could stand firm in his virtue, and refuse the proffers of the powerful but unprincipled families of his time. 使＝使人來召, in the translation, and in 復 (*fâu*, 4th tone) 我者, we must similarly understand 復來召我者. 費, read Pî, was a place belonging to the Chî family. Its name is still preserved in 費縣 in the department of 沂州, in Shantung. The Wăn stream divided Ch'î and Lû. Tsze-ch'ien threatens, if he should be troubled again, to retreat to Ch'î, where the Chî family could not reach him.

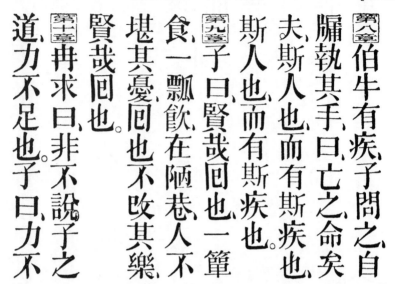

CHAP. VIII. Po-niû being ill, the Master went to ask for him. He took hold of his hand through the window, and said, 'It is killing him. It is the appointment *of Heaven*, alas! That such a man should have such a sickness! That such a man should have such a sickness!'

CHAP. IX. The Master said, 'Admirable indeed was the virtue of Hûi! With a single bamboo dish of rice, a single gourd dish of drink, and living in his mean narrow lane, while others could not have endured the distress, he did not allow his joy to be affected by it. Admirable indeed was the virtue of Hûi!'

CHAP. X. Yen Ch'iû said, 'It is not that I do not delight in your doctrines, but my strength is insufficient.' The Master said, 'Those whose strength is insufficient give over in the middle of the way, but now you limit yourself.'

8. LAMENT OF CONFUCIUS OVER THE MORTAL SICKNESS OF PO-NIÛ. Po-niû, 'elder or uncle Niû,' was the denomination of 冉耕, one of the disciples of the sage. In the old interpretation, his sickness is said to have been 惡疾, 'an evil disease,' by which name leprosy, called 癩, is intended, though that character is now employed for 'itch.' Suffering from such a disease, Po-niû would not see people, and Confucius took his hand through the window. A different explanation is given by Chû Hsî. He says that sick persons were usually placed on the north side of the apartment; but when the prince visited them, in order that he might appear to them with his face to the south (see chap. i), they were moved to the south. On this occasion, Po-niû's friends wanted to receive Confucius after this royal fashion, which he avoided by not entering the house. 亡之 = 'It is killing him.' 夫, the 2nd tone, generally an initial particle = 'now.' It is here final, and = 'alas!'

9. THE HAPPINESS OF HÛI INDEPENDENT OF HIS POVERTY. The 簞 was simply a piece of the stem of a bamboo, and the 瓢 half of a gourd cut into two. 食, see II. viii. The eulogy turns much on 其 in 其樂, as opposed to 其憂, 'his joy,' the delight which he had in the doctrines of his master, contrasted with the grief others would have felt under such poverty.

10. A HIGH AIM AND PERSEVERANCE PROPER TO A STUDENT. Confucius would not admit Ch'iû's apology for not attempting more than he did. 'Give over in the middle of the way,' i. e. they go as long and as far as they can, and are pursuing when they stop.

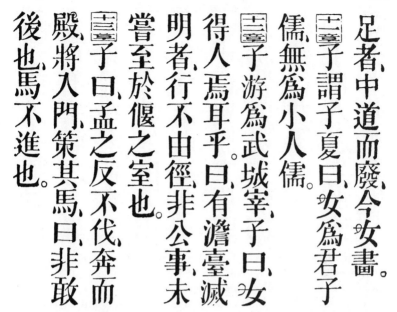

CHAP. XI. The Master said to Tsze-hsiâ, 'Do you be a scholar after the style of the superior man, and not after that of the mean man.'

CHAP. XII. Tsze-yû being governor of Wû-ch'ăng, the Master said to him, 'Have you got *good* men *there?*' He answered, 'There is Tan-t'âi Mieh-ming, who never in walking takes a short cut, and never comes to my office, excepting on public business.'

CHAP. XIII. The Master said, 'Măng Chih-fan does not boast of his merit. Being in the rear on an occasion of flight, when they were about to enter the gate, he whipped up his horse, saying, "It is not that I dare to be last. My horse would not advance."'

11. How LEARNING SHOULD BE PURSUED. 君子 and 小人 here = adjectives, qualifying 儒. The 君子, it is said, learns 爲己 for his own real improvement and from duty; the 小人, 爲人, 'for men,' with a view to their opinion, and for his own material benefit. We should hardly have judged such a counsel necessary for Tsze-hsiâ.

12. THE CHARACTER OF TAN-T'ÂI MIEH-MING. The chapter shows, according to Chinese commentators, the advantage to people in authority of their having good men about them. In this way after their usual fashion, they seek for a profound meaning in the remark of Confucius. Tan-t'âi Mieh-ming, who was styled 子羽, has his tablet the 2nd, east, outside the hall. The accounts of him are conflicting. According to one, he was very good-looking, while another says he was so bad-looking that Confucius at first formed an unfavourable opinion of him, an error which he afterwards confessed on

Mieh-ming's becoming eminent. He travelled southwards with not a few followers, and places near Sû-châu and elsewhere retain names indicative of his presence. 焉爾乎, three particles coming together, are said to indicate the slow and deliberate manner in which the sage spoke. 滅明者, compare 顏回者 in chap. ii. 室 is said to = 公堂.

13. THE VIRTUE OF MĂNG CHIH-FAN IN CONCEALING HIS MERIT. But where was his virtue in deviating from the truth? And how could Confucius commend him for doing so? These questions have never troubled the commentators, nor is it wise to bring a railing accusation against the sage for his words here. Măng Chih-fan, named 側, was an officer of Lû. The defeat referred to was in the eleventh year of duke Âi. To lead the van of an army is called 啓, to bring up the rear is 殿. In retreat, the rear is of course the place of honour.

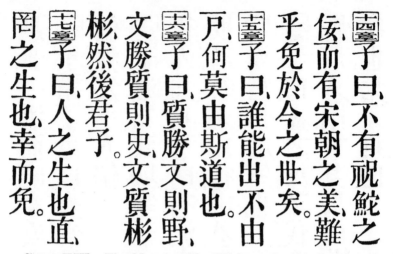

CHAP. XIV. The Master said, 'Without the specious speech of the litanist T'o, and the beauty of *the prince* Châo of Sung, it is difficult to escape in the present age.'

CHAP. XV. The Master said, 'Who can go out but by the door? How is it that men will not walk according to these ways?'

CHAP. XVI. The Master said, 'Where the solid qualities are in excess of accomplishments, we have rusticity; where the accomplishments are in excess of the solid qualities, we have the manners of a clerk. When the accomplishments and solid qualities are equally blended, we then have the man of virtue.'

CHAP. XVII. The Master said, 'Man is born for uprightness. If a man lose his uprightness, and yet live, his escape *from death* is the effect of mere good fortune.'

14. THE DEGENERACY OF THE AGE ESTEEMING GLIBNESS OF TONGUE AND BEAUTY OF PERSON. 祝, 'to pray,' 'prayers;' here, in the concrete, the officer charged with the prayers in the ancestral temple. I have coined the word *litanist* to come as near to the meaning as possible. This T'o was an officer of the State of Wei, styled 子魚. Prince Châo had been guilty of incest with his half-sister Nan-tsze (see chap. xxvi), and afterwards, when she was married to the duke Ling of Wei, he served as an officer there, carrying on his wickedness. He was celebrated for his beauty of person. 而 is a simple connective, = 與, and the 不 is made to belong to both clauses. The old commentators construe differently:—'If a man have not the speech of T'o, though he may have the beauty of Châo, &c.,' making the degeneracy of the age all turn on its fondness for specious talk. This cannot be right.

15. A LAMENT OVER THE WAYWARDNESS OF MEN'S CONDUCT. 斯道, 'these ways,' in a moral sense;—not deep doctrines, but rules of life.

16. THE EQUAL BLENDING OF SOLID EXCELLENCE AND ORNAMENTAL ACCOMPLISHMENTS IN A COMPLETE CHARACTER. 史, 'an historian,' an officer of importance in China. The term, however, is to be understood here of 'a clerk,' one that is of a class sharp and well informed, but insincere.

17. LIFE WITHOUT UPRIGHTNESS IS NOT TRUE LIFE, AND CANNOT BE CALCULATED ON. 'No more serious warning than this,' says one commentator, 'was ever addressed to men by Confucius.' A distinction is made by Chû Hsî and others between the two 生;—the 1st is 始生, 'birth,' or 'the beginning of life,' and the 2nd is 生存, 'preservation in life.' 人之生 也直, 'The being born of man is upright,' which may mean either that man at his birth is upright, or that he is born for uprightness. I prefer the latter view. 罔之生也, 'The living without it,' if we take 罔=無, or 'to

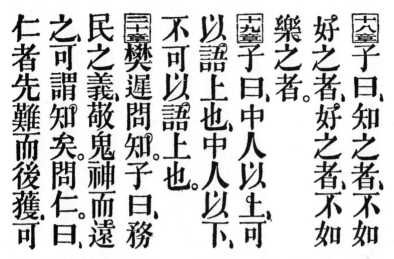

CHAP. XVIII. The Master said, 'They who know *the truth* are not equal to those who love it, and they who love it are not equal to those who delight in it.'

CHAP. XIX. The Master said, 'To those whose talents are above mediocrity, the highest subjects may be announced. To those who are below mediocrity, the highest subjects may not be announced.

CHAP. XX. Fan Ch'ih asked what constituted wisdom. The Master said, 'To give one's self earnestly to the duties due to men, and, while respecting spiritual beings, to keep aloof from them, may be called wisdom.' He asked about perfect virtue. The Master said, 'The man of virtue makes the difficulty *to be overcome* his first business, and success only a subsequent consideration;—this may be called perfect virtue.'

defame it,' if 罔=誣. We long here as else-where for more perspicuity and fuller develop-ment of view. Without uprightness the end of man's existence is not fulfilled, but his pre-servation in such case is not merely a fortunate accident.

18. DIFFERENT STAGES OF ATTAINMENT. The four 之 have all one reference, which must be 道 or 理, the subject spoken of.

19. TEACHERS MUST BE GUIDED IN COMMUNI-CATING KNOWLEDGE BY THE SUSCEPTIVITY OF THE LEARNERS. In 以上, 上 is read 2nd tone, a verbal word, and not the prep. 'upon,' so the 下 in 以下 is also verbal as in III. vii. The 中人, 'or mediocre people,' may have all classes of subjects announced to them, I suppose. 語 is in the 4th tone, 'to tell to.'

20. CHIEF ELEMENTS IN WISDOM AND VIRTUE. Fan Ch'ih, II. v. The modern comm. take

民 here as = 人, and 民之義 as = 人 道之宜, 'what is right according to the principles of humanity.' With some hesita-tion I have assented to this view, though 民 properly means 'the multitude,' 'the people,' and the old interpreters explain—'Strive to perfect the righteousness of the people.' We may suppose from the second clause that Fan Ch'ih was striving after what was uncommon and superhuman. For a full exhibition of the phrase 鬼神, see 中庸, XVI. Here it = 'spiritual beings,' *manes* and others. 遠, the 4th tone; 遠之, 'keep at a distance from them,' not 'keep them at a distance.' The sage's advice therefore is—'attend to what are plainly human duties, and do not be super-stitious.' 先 and 後 are, as frequently, verbs, 'put first,' 'put last.' The old inter-preters take them differently, but not so well.

之曰井有仁焉其從之　宰我問曰仁者雖告　哉。　魯子曰觚不觚觚哉觚　子一變至於道。　子曰齊一變至於魯、　者樂仁者壽。　樂山知者動仁者靜知　子曰知者樂水仁者　謂仁矣。

CHAP. XXI. The Master said, 'The wise find pleasure in water; the virtuous find pleasure in hills. The wise are active; the virtuous are tranquil. The wise are joyful; the virtuous are long-lived.'

CHAP. XXII. The Master said, 'Ch'î, by one change, would come to the State of Lû. Lû, by one change, would come to a State where true principles predominated.'

CHAP. XXIII. The Master said, 'A cornered vessel without corners.—A strange cornered vessel! A strange cornered vessel!'

CHAP. XXIV. Tsâi Wo asked, saying, 'A benevolent man, though it be told him,—"There is a man in the well," will go in after him, I suppose.' Confucius said, 'Why should he do so?' A superior

21. CONTRASTS OF THE WISE AND THE VIRTUOUS. The two first 樂 are read *áo*, 4th tone, = 喜好, 'to find pleasure in.' The wise or knowing are active and restless, like the waters of a stream, ceaselessly flowing and advancing. The virtuous are tranquil and firm, like the stable mountains. The pursuit of knowledge brings joy. The life of the virtuous may be expected to glide calmly on and long. After all, the saying is not very comprehensible.

22. THE CONDITION OF THE STATES CH'Î AND LÛ. Ch'î and Lû were both within the present Shan-tung. Ch'î lay along the coast on the north, embracing the present department of 青州 and other territory. Lû was on the south, the larger portion of it being formed by the present department of 兗州. At the rise of the Châu dynasty, king Wû invested Lü-shang, a counsellor of king Wû and the commander of his army, with the principality of Ch'î. King Wû at his first interview with Lü-shang addressed him as Thâi-kung Wang, 'grandfather Hope,' the man long looked for

in his family. This successor, king Ch'äng, constituted the son of his uncle, the famous duke of Châu, prince of Lû. In Confucius's time, Ch'î had degenerated more than Lû. 道 is 先王盡善盡美之道, 'the entirely good and admirable ways of the former kings.'

23. THE NAME WITHOUT THE REALITY IS FOLLY. This was spoken (see the 註疏) with reference to the governments of the time, retaining ancient names without ancient principles. The 觚 was a drinking-vessel; others say a wooden tablet. The latter was a later use of the term. It was made with corners as appears from the composition of the character, which is formed from 角, 'a horn,' 'a sharp corner.' In Confucius's time the form was changed, while the name was kept.—See the translation in Williams's Syllabic Dictionary, under syllable *kû*.

24. THE BENEVOLENT EXERCISE THEIR BENEVOLENCE WITH PRUDENCE. Tsâi Wo could see no limitation to acting on the impulses of bene-

至矣乎、民鮮久矣。 子曰、中庸之爲德也、其 之、天厭之。 子矢之曰、予所否者、天厭 子見南子、子路不說、夫 之以禮、亦可以弗畔矣夫。 子曰、君子博學於文、約 不可罔也。 可逝也、不可陷也、可欺也、 也。子曰、何爲其然也。君子

man may be made to go *to the well*, but he cannot be made to go down into it. He may be imposed upon, but he cannot be befooled.'

CHAP. XXV. The Master said, 'The superior man, extensively studying all learning, and keeping himself under the restraint of the rules of propriety, may thus likewise not overstep what is right.'

CHAP. XXVI. The Master having visited Nan-tsze, Tsze-lû was displeased, on which the Master swore, saying, 'Wherein I have done improperly, may Heaven reject me! may Heaven reject me!'

CHAP. XXVII. The Master said, 'Perfect is the virtue which is

volence. We are not to suppose with modern scholars that he wished to show that benevolence was impracticable. 雖 belongs to the whole following clause, especially to the mention of a well. The 仁 of 仁焉 should be 人. This happy correction of the text is due to a contemporary and teacher of Chû Hsî whom he calls Liû P'ing-chün. 其...也 indicate some doubt in Wo's mind. Observe the *hophal* force of 逝 and 陷.

25. THE HAPPY EFFECT OF LEARNING AND PROPRIETY COMBINED. 君子 has here its lighter meaning, = 'the student of what is right and true.' The 之 in 約之 we naturally refer to 文, but comparing IX. x. 2—約我以禮—we may assent to the observation that 我指己身, '*me* refers to the learner's own person.' See note on IV. xxiii. 畔, 'the boundary of a field;' also, 'to overstep a

boundary.' 矣夫, as in V. xxvi, but the force here is more 'ah!' than 'alas!'

26. CONFUCIUS VINDICATES HIMSELF FOR VISITING THE UNWORTHY NAN-TSZE. Nan-tsze was the wife of the duke of Wei, and half-sister of prince Châo, mentioned in chap. xiv. Her lewd character was well known, and hence Tsze-lû was displeased, thinking an interview with her was disgraceful to the Master. Great pains are taken to explain the incident. 'Nan-tsze,' says one, 'sought the interview from the stirrings of her natural conscience.' 'It was a rule,' says another, 'that stranger officers in a State should visit the prince's wife.' 'Nan-tsze,' argues a third, 'had all influence with her husband, and Confucius wished to get currency by her means for his doctrine.' Whether 矢 is to be understood in the sense of 'to swear,' = 誓, or 'to make a declaration,' = 陳, is much debated. Evidently the thing is an oath, or solemn protestation against the suspicions of Tsze-lû. 說, as in I. i. 1.

27. THE DEFECTIVE PRACTICE OF THE PEOPLE IN CONFUCIUS'S TIME. See the *Chung Yung*.

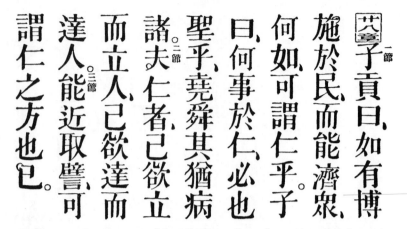

according to the Constant Mean! Rare for a long time has been its practice among the people.'

CHAP. XXVIII. 1. Tsze-kung said, 'Suppose the case of a man extensively conferring benefits on the people, and able to assist all, what would you say of him? Might he be called perfectly virtuous?' The Master said, 'Why speak only of virtue in connexion with him? Must he not have the qualities of a sage? Even Yâo and Shun were still solicitous about this.

2. 'Now the man of perfect virtue, wishing to be established himself, seeks also to establish others; wishing to be enlarged himself, he seeks also to enlarge others.

3. 'To be able to judge *of others* by what is nigh *in ourselves;*— this may be called the art of virtue.'

28. THE TRUE NATURE AND ART OF VIRTUE. There are no higher sayings in the Analects than we have here. 1. 施, the 4th tone, 'to confer benefits.' 聖乎,—乎 is said to be 'a particle of doubt and uncertainty,' but it is rather the interrogative affirmation of opinion. Tsze-kung appears to have thought that great doings were necessary to virtue, and propounds a case which would transcend the achievements of the ancient model sovereigns Yâo and Shun. From such extravagant views the Master recalls him. 2. This is the description of 仁者之心體, 'the mind of the perfectly virtuous man,' as void of all selfishness. 3. It is to be wished that the idea intended by 能近取譬 had been more clearly expressed. Still we seem to have here a near approach to a positive enunciation of 'the golden rule.'

BOOK VII. SHÛ *R*.

逑而第七

第一章 子曰逑而不作、信而好古竊比於我老彭。

第二章 子曰默而識之、學而不厭誨人不倦何有於我哉。

第三章 子曰德之不脩、學之不講聞義不能徙不善不能改、

CHAPTER I. The Master said, 'A transmitter and not a maker, believing in and loving the ancients, I venture to compare myself with our old P'ăng.'

CHAP. II. The Master said, 'The silent treasuring up of knowledge; learning without satiety; and instructing others without being wearied:—which one of these things belongs to me?'

CHAP. III. The Master said, 'The leaving virtue without proper cultivation; the not thoroughly discussing what is learned; not being able to move towards righteousness of which a knowledge is gained; and not being able to change what is not good:—these are the things which occasion me solicitude.'

HEADING OF THIS BOOK.—逑而第七, 'A transmitter, and —— Book VII.' We have in this Book much information of a personal character about Confucius, both from his own lips, and from the descriptions of his disciples. The two preceding Books treat of the disciples and other worthies, and here, in contrast with them, we have the sage himself exhibited.

1. CONFUCIUS DISCLAIMS BEING AN ORIGINATOR OR MAKER. 逑＝傳舊而已, 'simply to hand down the old.' Commentators say the Master's language here is from his extreme humility. But we must hold that it expresses his true sense of his position and work. Who the individual called endearingly 'our old P'ăng' was, can hardly be ascertained. Some make 老彭 to be Lâo-tsze, the founder of the Tâo sect, and others again make two individuals, one Lâo-tsze, and the other that 彭祖, of whom we read much in Chwang-tsze. A P'ăng Hsien appears in the Lî Sâo, st. 21, where Chû Hsî describes him as a worthy of the Yin (or Shang) dynasty, and he supposes him to be the Lâo P'ăng here.

2. CONFUCIUS'S HUMBLE ESTIMATE OF HIMSELF. 識, here by most scholars read *chih*, 4th tone, 'to remember.' 之 refers, it is said, to 理, 'principles,' the subjects of the silent observation and reflection. 何有於我哉, cannot be,—'what difficulty do these occasion me?' but ＝ 何者能有於我, as in the translation. 'The language,' says Chû Hsî, 'is that of humility upon humility.' Some insert, in their explanation, 此外 before 何—'Besides these, what is there in me?' But this is quite arbitrary. The profession may be inconsistent with what we find in other passages, but the inconsistency must stand rather than violence be done to the language. Ho Yen gives the singular exposition of 鄭康成 (about A.D. 150–200)—'Other men have not these things, I only have them.'

3. CONFUCIUS'S ANXIETY ABOUT HIS SELF-CULTIVATION:—ANOTHER HUMBLE ESTIMATE OF HIMSELF. Here again commentators find only the

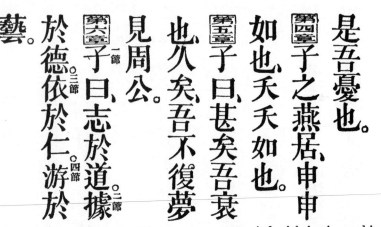

藝。　於德依於仁游於　第六章 子曰志於道據　見周公。　也久矣吾不復夢　第五章 子曰甚矣吾衰　如也夭夭如也。　第四章 子之燕居申申　是吾憂也。

一節　二節　三節　四節

CHAP. IV. When the Master was unoccupied with business, his manner was easy, and he looked pleased.

CHAP. V. The Master said, 'Extreme is my decay. For a long time, I have not dreamed, as I was wont to do, that I saw the duke of Châu.'

CHAP. VI. 1. The Master said, 'Let the will be set on the path of duty.

2. 'Let every attainment in what is good be firmly grasped.

3. 'Let perfect virtue be accorded with.

4. 'Let relaxation and enjoyment be found in the polite arts.'

expressions of humility, but there can be no reason why we should not admit that Confucius was anxious lest these things, which are only put forth as possibilities, should become in his case actual facts. 講 is in the sense explained in the dictionary by the terms 習 and 究, 'practising,' 'examining.'

4. THE MANNER OF CONFUCIUS WHEN UNOCCUPIED. The first clause, which is the subject of the other two, is literally—'The Master's dwelling at ease.' Observe 燕, in the 4th tone; 夭, in the 1st; 如, as in III. xxiii.

5. HOW THE DISAPPOINTMENT OF CONFUCIUS'S HOPES AFFECTED EVEN HIS DREAMS. 周公 is now to all intents a proper name, but the characters mean 'the duke of Châu.' Châu was the name of the seat of the family from which the dynasty so called sprang, and, on the enlargement of this territory, king Wăn divided the original seat between his son 旦 (Tan) and the minister 奭 (Shih). Tan was Châu-kung, in wisdom and politics, what his elder brother, the first sovereign, Wû, was in arms. Confucius had longed to bring the principles and institutions of Châu-kung into practice, and in his earlier years, while hope animated him, had often dreamt of the former sage. The original territory of Châu was what is now the district of Ch'i-shan (岐 山), department of Fung-hsiang in Shen-hsî.

6. RULES FOR THE FULL MATURING OF CHARACTER. 2. 德 might be translated virtue, but 仁 = 'perfect virtue' following, we require another term. 4. 游, 'to ramble for amusement,' here = 'to seek recreation.' 藝, see note on 文, in I. vi. A full enumeration makes 'six arts,' viz. ceremonies, music, archery, charioteering, the study of characters or language, and figures or arithmetic. The ceremonies were ranged in five classes: lucky or sacrifices; unlucky or those of mourning; military; those of host and guest; and festive. Music required the study of the music of Hwang-tî, of Yâo, of Shun, of Yü, of T'ang, and of Wû. Archery had a fivefold classification. Charioteering had the same. The study of the characters required the examination of them to determine whether there predominated in their formation resemblance to the object, combination of ideas, indication of properties, a phonetic principle, a principle of contrariety, or metaphorical accommodation. Figures were managed according to nine rules, as the object was the measurement of land, capacity, &c. These six subjects were the business of the highest and most liberal education, but we need not suppose that Confucius had them all in view here.

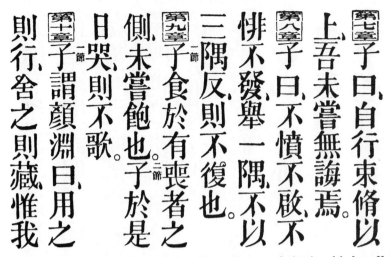

CHAP. VII. The Master said, 'From the man bringing his bundle of dried flesh *for my teaching* upwards, I have never refused instruction to any one.'

CHAP. VIII. The Master said, 'I do not open up the truth to one who is not eager *to get knowledge*, nor help out any one who is not anxious to explain himself. When I have presented one corner of a subject to any one, and he cannot from it learn the other three, I do not repeat my lesson.'

CHAP. IX. 1. When the Master was eating by the side of a mourner, he never ate to the full.

2. He did not sing on the same day in which he had been weeping.

CHAP. X. 1. The Master said to Yen Yüan, 'When called to office, to undertake its duties; when not so called, to lie retired;—it is only I and you who have attained to this.'

7. THE READINESS OF CONFUCIUS TO IMPART INSTRUCTION. It was the rule anciently that when one party waited on another, he should carry some present or offering with him. Pupils did so when they first waited on their teacher. Of such offerings, one of the lowest was a bundle of strips of 脩, 'dried flesh.' The wages of a teacher are now called 脩金, 'the money of the dried flesh.' However small the offering brought to the sage, let him only see the indication of a wish to learn, and he imparted his instructions. 以上 may be translated 'upwards,' i.e. 'to such a man and others with larger gifts,' 上 being in the 3rd tone; or the character may be understood in the sense of 'coming to my instructions.' I prefer the former interpretation.

8. CONFUCIUS REQUIRED A REAL DESIRE AND ABILITY IN HIS DISCIPLES. The last chapter tells of the sage's readiness to teach; this shows that he did not teach where his teaching was likely

to prove of no avail. 悱, in the comm. and dict., is explained 口欲言而未能之貌, 'the appearance of one with mouth wishing to speak and yet not able to do so.' This being the meaning, we might have expected the character to be 啡. 反, 'to turn,' is explained 還以相證之義, 'going round for mutual testimony.' 不復＝不復有所告, 'I tell him nothing more.'

9. CONFUCIUS'S SYMPATHY WITH MOURNERS. The weeping is understood to be on occasion of offering his condolences to a mourner, which was 'a rule of propriety.'

10. THE ATTAINMENTS OF HÛI LIKE THOSE OF CONFUCIUS. THE EXCESSIVE BOLDNESS OF TSZE-LÛ. 1. In 用之, 舍之, 之 is explained by 我, but we have seen that 之 following active verbs imparts to them a sort of neuter

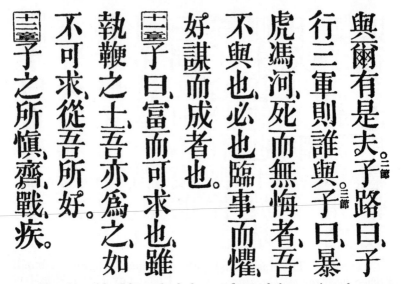

2. Tsze-lû said, 'If you had the conduct of the armies of a great State, whom would you have to act with you?'

3. The Master said, 'I would not have him to act with me, who will unarmed attack a tiger, or cross a river without a boat, dying without any regret. My associate must be the man who proceeds to action full of solicitude, who is fond of adjusting his plans, and then carries them into execution.'

CHAP. XI. The Master said, 'If the search for riches is sure to be successful, though I should become a groom with whip in hand to get them, I will do so. As the search may not be successful, I will follow after that which I love.'

CHAP. XII. The things in reference to which the Master exercised the greatest caution were—fasting, war, and sickness.

signification. 用之 = 'used.' 舍之 = 'neglected.' 2. A *Chün*, according to the 周禮, consisted of 12,500 men. The royal forces consisted of six such bodies, and those of a great State of three. 3. 暴虎馮河, see Shih-ching, II. v. 1, st. 6. 懼 does not indicate *timidity*, but *solicitude*.—Tsze-lû, it would appear, was jealous of the praise conferred on Hûi, and, pluming himself on his bravery, put in for a share of the Master's approbation. But he only brought on himself this rebuke.

11. THE UNCERTAINTY AND FOLLY OF THE PURSUIT OF RICHES. It occurs to a student to understand the first clause—'If it be *proper* to search for riches,' and the third—'I will do it.' But the translation is according to the modern commentaries, and the conclusion agrees better with it. In explaining 執鞭之士, some refer us to the attendants who cleared the street with

their whips when the prince went abroad, but we need not seek any particular allusion of the kind. Observe 而 = 若, 'if,' and then 如 = 'since.' Still we may bring out the meaning from 而 taken in its usual significance of '*and*.' In this construction the previous 富 = 'given riches,' and 而可求 = 'and such as can surely be found.'—An objection to the pursuit of wealth may be made on the ground of righteousness, or on that of its uncertainty. It is the latter on which Confucius here rests.

12. WHAT THINGS CONFUCIUS WAS PARTICULARLY CAREFUL ABOUT. 齊, read *châi*, and = 齋, 'to fast,' or, rather, denoting the whole religious adjustment, enjoined before the offering of sacrifice, and extending over the ten days previous to the great sacrificial seasons. 齊 means 'to equalize' (see II. iii), and the effect of those pre-

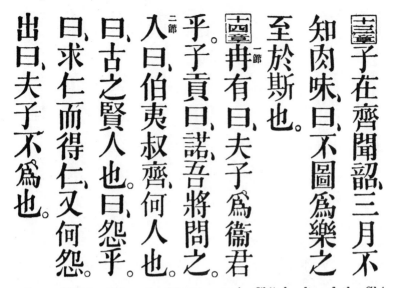

CHAP. XIII. When the Master was in Ch'î, he heard the Shâo, and for three months did not know the taste of flesh. 'I did not think,' he said, 'that music could have been made so excellent as this.'

CHAP. XIV. 1. Yen Yû said, 'Is our Master for the ruler of Wei?' Tsze-kung said, 'Oh! I will ask him.'

2. He went in *accordingly*, and said, 'What sort of men were Po-î and Shû-ch'î?' 'They were ancient worthies,' said the Master. 'Did they have any repinings *because of their course?*' The Master again replied, 'They sought to act virtuously, and they did so; what was there for them to repine about?' On this, *Tsze-kung* went out and said, 'Our Master is not for him.'

vious exercises was 齊不齊以致齊, 'to adjust what was not adjusted, so as to produce a perfect adjustment.' Sacrifices presented in such a state of mind were sure to be acceptable. Other people, it is said, might be heedless in reference to sacrifices, to war, and to sickness, but not so the sage.

13. THE EFFECT OF MUSIC ON CONFUCIUS. The *shâo*, see III. xxv. This incident must have happened in the thirty-sixth year of Confucius, when he followed the duke Châo in his flight from Lû to Ch'î. As related in the 史記, 'Historical Records,' before the characters 三月, we have 學之, 'he learned it three months,' which may relieve us from the necessity of extending the three months over all the time in which he did not know the taste of his food. In Ho Yen's compilation, the 不知 is explained by 忽忘, 'he was careless about and forgot.' The last clause is also explained there—'I did not think that this music had reached this country of Ch'î.'

14. CONFUCIUS DID NOT APPROVE OF A SON OPPOSING HIS FATHER. 1. The eldest son of duke Ling of Wei had planned to kill his mother (? stepmother), the notorious Nan-tsze (VI. xxvi). For this he had to flee the country, and his son, on the death of Ling, became duke (出公), and subsequently opposed his father's attempts to wrest the State from him. This was the matter argued among the disciples,—Was Confucius for (為, 4th tone) the son, the ruling duke? 2. In Wei it would not have been according to *propriety* to speak by name of its ruler, and therefore Tsze-kung put the case of Po-î and Shû-ch'î, see V. xxii. They having given up a throne, and finally their lives, rather than do what they thought wrong, and Confucius fully approving of their conduct, it was plain he could not approve of a son's holding by force what was the rightful inheritance of the father. 求仁而得仁, 'They sought for virtue, and they got virtue;' i.e. such was the character of their conduct.

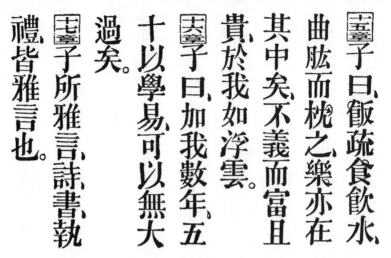

CHAP. XV. The Master said, 'With coarse rice to eat, with water to drink, and my bended arm for a pillow;—I have still joy in the midst of these things. Riches and honours acquired by unrighteousness are to me as a floating cloud.'

CHAP. XVI. The Master said, 'If some years were added to my life, I would give fifty to the study of the Yî, and then I might come to be without great faults.'

CHAP. XVII. The Master's frequent themes of discourse were— the Odes, the History, and the maintenance of the Rules of Propriety. On all these he frequently discoursed.

15. THE JOY OF CONFUCIUS INDEPENDENT OF OUTWARD CIRCUMSTANCES. 飯, in 3rd tone, 'a meal;' also, as here, a verb, 'to eat.' 枕, 4th tone, 'to pillow,' 'to use as a pillow.' Critics call attention to 亦, making the sentiment = 'My joy is everywhere. It is amid other circumstances. It is *also* here.' 不義云云, = 'By unrighteousness I might get riches and honours, but such riches and honours are to me as a floating cloud. It is vain to grasp at them, so uncertain and unsubstantial,'

16. THE VALUE WHICH CONFUCIUS SET UPON THE STUDY OF THE Yî. Chû Hsî supposes that this was spoken when Confucius was about seventy, as he was in his sixty-eighth year when he ceased his wanderings, and settled in Lû to the adjustment and compilation of the Yî and other *Ching*. If the remark be referred to that time, an error may well be found in 五十, for he would hardly be speaking at seventy of having fifty years added to his life. Chû also mentions the report of Liû P'ing-chün, referred to by him under V. xxiv, that he had been told of a copy of the Lun Yü, which read 假 for 加, and 卒 for 五.

Amended thus, the meaning would be—'If I had some *more* years to finish the study of the Yî, &c.' Ho Yen interprets the chapter quite differently. Referring to the saying, II. iv. 4, 'At fifty, I knew the decrees of Heaven,' he supposes this to have been spoken when Confucius was forty-seven, and explains—'In a few years more I will be fifty, and have finished the Yî, when I may be without great faults.'—One thing remains upon both views :—Confucius never claimed, what his followers do for him, to be a perfect man.

17. CONFUCIUS'S MOST COMMON TOPICS. 書, 'The History,' i.e. the historical documents which were compiled into the Shû-ching that has come down to us in a mutilated condition. 詩 also, and much more 禮, must not be understood of the now existing Shih-ching and Lî Chî. Chû Hsî explains 雅 (3rd tone) by 常, 'constantly.' The old interpreter Chǎng explains it by 正, 'correctly,'—'Confucius would speak of the Odes, &c., with attention to the correct enunciation of the characters.' This does not seem so good.

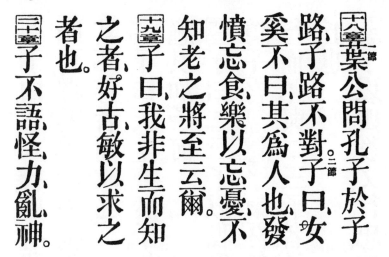

CHAP. XVIII. 1. The duke of Sheh asked Tsze-lû about Confucius, and Tsze-lû did not answer him.

2. The Master said, 'Why did you not say to him,—He is simply a man, who in his eager pursuit (of knowledge) forgets his food, who in the joy *of its attainment* forgets his sorrows, and who does not perceive that old age is coming on?'

CHAP. XIX. The Master said, 'I am not one who was born in the possession of knowledge; I am one who is fond of antiquity, and earnest in seeking it *there.*'

CHAP. XX. The subjects on which the Master did not talk, were—extraordinary things, feats of strength, disorder, and spiritual beings.

18. CONFUCIUS'S DESCRIPTION OF HIS OWN CHARACTER, AS BEING SIMPLY A CHEERFUL, EARNEST LEARNER. 1. 葉 (read *sheh*) was a district of Ch'û (楚), the governor or prefect of which was styled *kung*, after the usurping fashion of Ch'û. Its name is still preserved in a district of the department of 南陽, in the south of Ho-nan. 2. 云 sometimes finishes a sentence (Prémare, '*claudit orationem*'), as here. The 爾 after it = 耳, imparting to all the preceding description a meaning indicated by our *simply* or *only*. Wang Yin-chih, in his treatise on the particles, gives instances of 云 used as a particle, now initial, now medial, and again final.

19. CONFUCIUS'S KNOWLEDGE NOT CONNATE, BUT THE RESULT OF HIS STUDY OF ANTIQUITY. Here again, according to the commentators, is a wonderful instance of the sage's humility disclaiming what he really had. The comment of a Mr. Yin, subjoined to Chû Hsî's own, is to the effect that the knowledge born with a man is only 義 and 理, while ceremonies, music, names of things, history, &c., must be learned. This would make what we may call connate or innate knowledge the moral sense, and those intuitive principles of reason, on and by which all knowledge is built up. But Confucius could not mean to deny his being possessed of these. 'I love antiquity;' i.e. the ancients and all their works.

20. SUBJECTS AVOIDED BY CONFUCIUS IN HIS CONVERSATION. 亂, 'confusion,' meaning rebellious disorder, parricide, regicide, and such crimes. Chû Hsî makes 神 here = 鬼神造化之迹, 'the mysterious, or spiritual operations apparent in the course of nature.' 王肅 (died A.D. 266), as given by Ho Yen, simply says—鬼神之事, 'the affairs of spiritual beings.' For an instance of Confucius avoiding such a subject, see XI. xi.

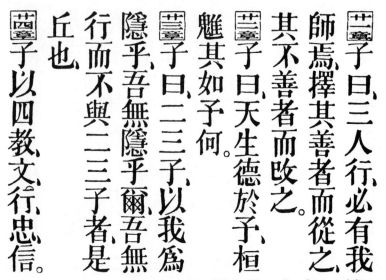

CHAP. XXI. The Master said, 'When I walk along with two others, they may serve me as my teachers. I will select their good qualities and follow them, their bad qualities and avoid them.'

CHAP. XXII. The Master said, 'Heaven produced the virtue that is in me. Hwan T'ûi—what can he do to me?'

CHAP. XXIII. The Master said, 'Do you think, my disciples, that I have any concealments? I conceal nothing from you. There is nothing which I do that is not shown to you, my disciples;—that is my way.'

CHAP. XXIV. There were four things which the Master taught,— letters, ethics, devotion of soul, and truthfulness.

21. How a man may find instructors for himself. 三人行, 'three men walking;' but it is implied that the speaker is himself one of them. The commentators all take 擇 in the sense of 'to distinguish,' 'to determine.' —'I will determine the one who is good, and follow him, &c.' I prefer to understand as in the translation. 改之, 'change them,' i.e. correct them in myself, avoid them.

22. Confucius calm in danger, through the assurance of having a divine mission. According to the historical accounts, Confucius was passing through Sung in his way from Wei to Ch'ǎn, and was practising ceremonies with his disciples under a large tree, when they were set upon by emissaries of Hwan (or Hsiang) T'ûi, a high officer of Sung. These pulled down the tree, and wanted to kill the sage. His disciples urged him to make haste and escape, when he calmed their fears by these words. At the same time, he disguised himself till he had got past Sung. This story may be apocryphal, but the saying remains,— a remarkable one.

23. Confucius practised no concealment with his disciples. 二三子, see III. xxiv. 與 is explained by Chû Hsî by 示, 'to show,' as if the meaning were, 'There is not one of my doings in which I am not showing my doctrines to you.' But the common signification of 與 may be retained, as in Ho Yen,— 'which is not given to, shared with, you.' To what the concealment has reference we cannot tell. Observe the force of 者 followed by 也 at the end;—'To have none of my actions not shared with you,—that is I, Ch'iû.'

24. The subjects of Confucius's teaching. 以四教, 'took four things and taught.' There were four things which—not four ways in which—Confucius taught. 文 here = our use of letters. 行 = 人倫日用, 'what is daily used in the relations of life.' 忠 = 無一念之不盡, 'not a single thought not

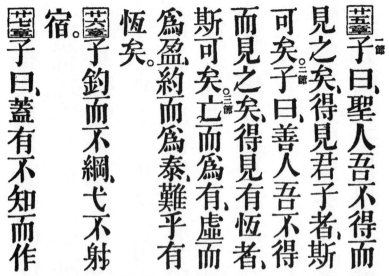

CHAP. XXV. 1. The Master said, 'A sage it is not mine to see; could I see a man of real talent and virtue, that would satisfy me.'

2. The Master said, ' A good man it is not mine to see ; could I see a man possessed of constancy, that would satisfy me.

3. 'Having not and yet affecting to have, empty and yet affecting to be full, straitened and yet affecting to be at ease :—it is difficult with such characteristics to have constancy.'

CHAP. XXVI. The Master angled,—but did not use a net. He shot,—but not at birds perching.

CHAP. XXVII. The Master said, 'There may be those who act without knowing why. I do not do so. Hearing much and selecting what is good and following it; seeing much and keeping it in memory:—this is the second style of knowledge.'

exhausted.' 信＝無一事之不實, 'not a single thing without its reality.' These are the explanations in the 四書備旨. I confess to apprehend but vaguely the two latter subjects as distinguished from the second.

25. THE PAUCITY OF TRUE MEN IN, AND THE PRETENTIOUSNESS OF, CONFUCIUS'S TIME. 子曰, par. 2, is supposed by some to be an addition to the text. That being so, we have in the chapter a climax of character :—the man of constancy, or the single-hearted, stedfast man ; the good man, who on his single-heartedness has built up his virtue ; the *Chün-tsze*, the man of virtue in large proportions, and intellectually able besides ; and the sage, or highest style of man. 聖, from 耳, 口, and 壬, 'ear, mouth, and good,'＝intuitively apprehensive of truth, and correct in utterance and action. Comp. Mencius, VII. Pt. ii. ch. xxv.

26. THE HUMANITY OF CONFUCIUS. 綱 is properly the large rope attached to a net, by means of which it may be drawn so as to sweep a stream. 弋, 'to shoot with a string tied to the arrow, by which it may be drawn back again.' 射, applied to such shooting, in the 4th tone, is read *shih*. Confucius would only destroy what life was necessary for his use, and in taking that he would not take advantage of the inferior creatures. This chapter is said to be descriptive of him in his early life.

27. AGAINST ACTING HEEDLESSLY. Pâo Hsien, in Ho Yen, says that this was spoken with reference to heedless compilers of records. Chû Hsî makes 作之 simply＝作事, 'to do things,' 'to act.' The paraphrasts make the latter part descriptive of Confucius—'I hear much, &c.' This is not necessary, and the translation had better be as indefinite as the original.

曰知禮孔子退揖巫馬期而進

陳司敗問昭公知禮乎孔子

至矣

子曰仁遠乎哉我欲仁斯仁

保其往也

何甚人潔已以進與其潔也不

子曰與其進也不與其退也唯

互鄉難與言童子見門人惑

而從之多見而識之知之次也

之者我無是也多聞擇其善者

CHAP. XXVIII. 1. It was difficult to talk (profitably and reputably) with the people of Hû-hsiang, and a lad of that place having had an interview with the Master, the disciples doubted.

2. The Master said, 'I admit people's approach to me without committing myself *as to what they may do* when they have retired. Why must one be so severe? If a man purify himself to wait upon me, I receive him so purified, without guaranteeing his past conduct.'

CHAP. XXIX. The Master said, 'Is virtue a thing remote? I wish to be virtuous, and lo! virtue is at hand.'

CHAP. XXX. 1. The minister of crime of Ch'ăn asked whether the duke Châo knew propriety, and Confucius said, 'He knew propriety.'

2. Confucius having retired, the minister bowed to Wû-mâ Ch'î

28. THE READINESS OF CONFUCIUS TO MEET APPROACHES TO HIM THOUGH MADE BY THE UNLIKELY. 1. In 互鄉, the 鄉 appears to be like our local termination *ham*.—'The people of Hû-ham.' Its site is now sought in three different places. 2. Chû Hsî would here transpose the order of the text, and read 人潔 已云云 immediately after 子曰. He also supposes some characters lost in the sentence 唯何甚. This is hardly necessary.

與, as in V. vii. 3, = 許, 'to allow,' 'to concede to.'

29. VIRTUE IS NOT FAR TO SEEK. 哉, after 乎, implies the negative answer to be given.

30. HOW CONFUCIUS ACKNOWLEDGED HIS ERROR. 1. Ch'ăn, one of the States of China in Confucius's time, is to be referred probably to the present department of Ch'ăn-châu in Ho-nan province. 司敗 was the name given in Ch'ăn and Ch'û to the minister elsewhere called 司寇, which terms Morrison and Medhurst

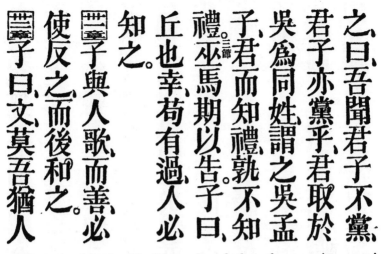

to come forward, and said, 'I have heard that the superior man is not a partizan. May the superior man be a partizan also? The prince married a daughter of *the house of* Wû, of the same surname with himself, and called her,—"The elder *Tsze* of Wû." If the prince knew propriety, who does not know it?'

3. Wû-mâ Ch'î reported these remarks, and the Master said, 'I am fortunate! If I have any errors, people are sure to know them.'

CHAP. XXXI. When the Master was in company with a person who was singing, if he sang well, he would make him repeat the song, while he accompanied it with his own voice.

CHAP. XXXII. The Master said, 'In letters I am perhaps equal to other men, but *the character of* the superior man, carrying out in his conduct what he professes, is what I have not yet attained to.'

translate—'criminal judge.' But *judge* does not come up to his functions, which were legislative as well as executive. He was the adviser of his sovereign on all matters relating to crime. See the 周禮, 秋官司寇 Châo was the honorary epithet of Châu (稠), duke of Lû, B.C. 541-509. He had a reputation for the knowledge and observance of ceremonies, and Confucius answered the minister's question accordingly, the more readily that he was speaking to the officer of another State, and was bound, therefore, to hide any failings that his own sovereign might have had. 2. With all his knowledge of proprieties, the duke Châo had violated an important rule,—that which forbids the intermarriage of parties of the same surname. The ruling houses of Lû and Wû were branches of the imperial house of Châu, and consequently had the same surname—Chî (姬). To conceal his violation of the rule, Châo called his wife by the surname *Tsze* (子), as if she had belonged to the ducal house of Sung.

取, the 4th tone = 娶. 3. Confucius takes the criticism of his questioner very lightly.

31. THE GOOD FELLOWSHIP OF CONFUCIUS. On this chapter, see the 四書合講, which states very distinctly the interpretation which I have followed, making only two singings and not three. 和, 4th tone, here = 'to sing in unison with.'

32. ACKNOWLEDGMENT OF CONFUCIUS IN ESTIMATING HIMSELF. 莫 here occasions some difficulty. Ho Yen takes it, as it often is, = 無, and explains, 'I am not better than others in letters.' In the dictionary, with reference to this passage, it is explained by 强, so that the meaning would be—'By effort, I can equal other men in letters.' Chû Hsî makes it 疑辭, a 'particle of doubt,' = 'perhaps.' But this is formed for the occasion. 躬行君子, 'an in-person-acting *chün-tsze*.'

之禱久矣。
禱爾于上下神祇。子曰丘
有諸子路對曰、有之誄曰、
子疾病子路請禱子曰、
曰正唯弟子不能學也。
則可謂云爾已矣。公西華
敢抑爲之不厭、誨人不倦、
子曰若聖與仁、則吾豈
得。
也躬行君子、則吾未之有

CHAP. XXXIII. The Master said, 'The sage and the man of perfect virtue ;—how dare I *rank myself with them?* It may simply be said of me, that I strive to become such without satiety, and teach others without weariness.' Kung-hsî Hwâ said, 'This is just what we, the disciples, cannot imitate you in.'

CHAP. XXXIV. The Master being very sick, Tsze-lû asked leave to pray for him. He said, 'May such a thing be done?' Tsze-lû replied, 'It may. In the Eulogies it is said, "Prayer has been made for thee to the spirits of the upper and lower worlds."' The Master said, 'My praying has been for a long time.'

33. WHAT CONFUCIUS DECLINED TO BE CONSIDERED, AND WHAT HE CLAIMED. 若 and 抑 are said to be correlatives, in which case they = our 'although' and 'yet.' More naturally, we may join 若 directly with 聖與仁, and take 抑 as = our 'but.' 云爾, see chap. xviii.

2. 已矣, added to 云爾, increases its emphasis, = 'just this and nothing more.' Kung-hsî Hwâ, see V. vii. 4.

34. CONFUCIUS DECLINES TO BE PRAYED FOR. 疾病 together mean 'very sick.' 有諸;—諸 is interrogative, as we find it frequently in Mencius. 誄, 'to write a eulogy, and confer the posthumous honorary title ;' also, 'to eulogise in prayer,' i. e. to recite one's excellences as the ground of supplication. Lêi is a special form of composition corresponding to the French *éloge*, specimens of which are to be found in the Wăn Hsüan (文選), of prince Hsiâo

T'ung. Wylie, 'Notes on Chinese Literature,' p. 192, calls them ' obituaries.' Tsze-lû must have been referring to some well-known collection of such compositions. In 禱爾, 爾 may be taken as the pronoun. 上下 = heaven and earth, 神 being the appropriate designation of the spirits of the former, and 祇 of the latter.

—Chû Hsî says, 'Prayer is the expression of repentance and promise of amendment, to supplicate the help of the spirits. If there be not those things, then there is no need for praying. In the case of the sage, he had committed no errors, and admitted of no amendment. In all his conduct he had been in harmony with the spiritual intelligences, and therefore he said,—*my praying has been for a long time.*' We must demur to some of these expressions ; but the declining to be prayed for, and the concluding remark, seem to indicate the satisfaction of Confucius with himself. We wish that our information about him were not so stinted and fragmentary.

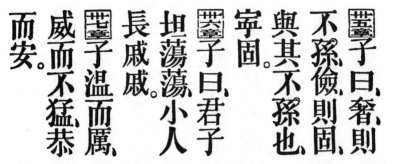

子曰、奢則
不孫儉則
固。

與其不孫
寗固。

子曰、君子
坦蕩蕩、小人
長戚戚。

子溫而厲、
威而不猛、恭
而安。

CHAP. XXXV. The Master said, 'Extravagance leads to insubordination, and parsimony to meanness. It is better to be mean than to be insubordinate.'

CHAP. XXXVI. The Master said, 'The superior man is satisfied and composed; the mean man is always full of distress.'

CHAP. XXXVII. The Master was mild, and yet dignified; majestic, and yet not fierce; respectful, and yet easy.

35. MEANNESS NOT SO BAD AS INSUBORDINATION. 孫, read *sun*, like 遜, and with the same meaning.

36. CONTRAST IN THEIR FEELINGS BETWEEN THE CHÜN-TSZE AND THE MEAN MAN. 坦, 'a level plain,' used adverbially with 然, = 'lightsomely.' This is its force here. 長=常時, 'constantly.'

37. How VARIOUS ELEMENTS MODIFIED ONE ANOTHER IN THE CHARACTER OF CONFUCIUS.

BOOK VIII. TʻÂI-PO.

而稱
焉。

民無
得、

天下
讓、

矣三
以、

德也
已。

可謂
其至

泰伯
其

子曰、

第八

泰伯

CHAPTER I. The Master said, 'Tʻâi-po may be said to have reached the highest point of virtuous action. Thrice he declined the kingdom, and the people *in ignorance of his motives* could not express their approbation of his conduct.'

THE HEADING OF THIS BOOK.—泰伯第八, 'Tʻâi-po, Book VIII.' As in other cases, the first words of the Book give the name to it. The subjects of the chapter are miscellaneous, but it begins with the chapter and ends with the character and deeds of ancient sages and worthies, and on this account it follows the seventh chapter, where we have Confucius himself described.

1. THE EXCEEDING VIRTUE OF TʻÂI-PO. Tʻâi-po was the eldest son of king Tʻâi (大°), the grandfather of Wăn, the founder of the Châu dynasty. Tʻâi had formed the intention of upsetting the Yin dynasty, of which Tʻâi-po disapproved. Tʻâi moreover, because of the sage virtues of his grandson Chʻang (昌), who afterwards became king Wăn, wished to hand down his principality to his third son, Chʻang's father. Tʻâi-po observing this, and to escape opposing

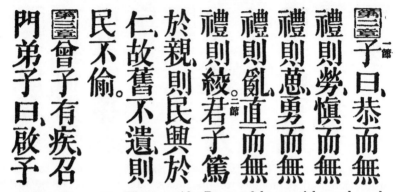

CHAP. II. 1. The Master said, 'Respectfulness, without the rules of propriety, becomes laborious bustle; carefulness, without the rules of propriety, becomes timidity; boldness, without the rules of propriety, becomes insubordination; straightforwardness, without the rules of propriety, becomes rudeness.

2. 'When those who are in high stations perform well all their duties to their relations, the people are aroused to virtue. When old friends are not neglected by them, the people are preserved from meanness.'

CHAP. III. The philosopher Tsăng being ill, he called to him the disciples of his school, and said, 'Uncover my feet, uncover my hands. It is said in the Book of Poetry, "We should be apprehensive and cautious, as if on the brink of a deep gulf, as if treading on thin ice," *and so have I been.* Now and hereafter, I know my escape *from all injury to my person,* O ye, my little children.'

his father's purpose, retired with his second brother among the barbarous tribes of the south, and left their youngest brother in possession of the State. The motives of his conduct T'âi-po kept to himself, so that the people 不得而稱之, 'could not find how to praise him.' There is a difficulty in making out the refusal of the empire *three* times, there being different accounts of the times and ways in which he did so. Chû Hsî cuts the knot, by making 'thrice' = 'firmly,' in which solution we may acquiesce. There is as great difficulty to find out a declining of the kingdom in T'âi-po's withdrawing from the petty State of Châu. It may be added that king Wû, the first sovereign of the Châu dynasty, subsequently conferred on T'âi-po the posthumous title of Chief of Wû (吳), the country to which he had withdrawn, and whose rude inhabitants gathered round him. His second brother succeeded him in the government of them, and hence the ruling house of Wû had the same surname as the royal house of Châu, that namely of Chî (姬);—see VII. xxx. 也已矣 give emphasis to the preceding declaration;—compare I. xiv.

2. THE VALUE OF THE RULES OF PROPRIETY ;

AND OF EXAMPLE IN THOSE IN HIGH STATIONS. 1. We must bear in mind that the ceremonies, or rules of propriety, spoken of in these Books, are not mere conventionalities, but the ordinations of man's moral and intelligent nature in the line of what is *proper.* 絞, 'to strangle,' is here explained by Chû Hsî by 急切. Ho Yen, after Mâ Yung (early part of 2nd century), makes it = 絞刺, 'sarcasm.' 2. There does not seem any connexion between the former paragraph and this, and hence this is by many considered to be a new chapter, and assigned to the philosopher Tsăng. 君子 differs here from its previous usage, having reference more to the 位 or station of the individuals indicated, than to their 德 or virtue. 故舊=舊臣舊交, 'old ministers and old intimacies.' 偷, often a verb, 'to steal;' here an adjective, 'mean.'

3. THE PHILOSOPHER TSĂNG'S FILIAL PIETY SEEN IN HIS CARE OF HIS PERSON. We get our bodies perfect from our parents, and should so preserve them to the last. This is a great branch of filial piety with the Chinese, and this chapter is said

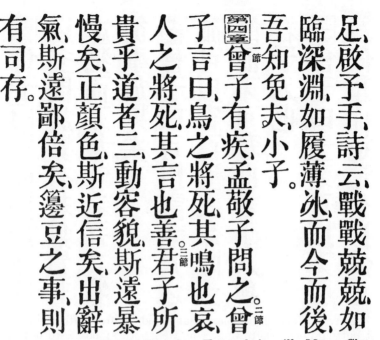

CHAP. IV. 1. The philosopher Tsăng being ill, Măng Chăng went to ask how he was.

2. Tsăng said to him, 'When a bird is about to die, its notes are mournful; when a man is about to die, his words are good.

3. 'There are three principles of conduct which the man of high rank should consider specially important :—that in his deportment and manner he keep from violence and heedlessness; that in regulating his countenance he keep near to sincerity; and that in his words and tones he keep far from lowness and impropriety. As to such matters as attending to the sacrificial vessels, there are the proper officers for them.'

to illustrate how Tsăng-tsze (I. iv) had made this his life-long study. He made the disciples uncover his hands and feet to show them in what preservation those members were. 詩云，— see the Shih-ching, II. v. I. st. 6. In 而今, we must take 而＝自. Wang Yin-chih, however, takes the first 而 as＝乃, and adduces other instances of 乃＝而. Still the usage is remarkable.

4. THE PHILOSOPHER TSĂNG'S DYING COUNSELS TO A MAN OF HIGH RANK. 1. 敬 was the honorary epithet of 仲孫捷, a great officer of Lû, and son of Măng-wû, II. vi. From the conclusion of this chapter, we may suppose that he descended to small matters below his rank.

之 refers to 疾. 2. 言, in 曾子言曰, intimates that Tsăng commenced the conversation. 3. 動, 正, and 出 are all = verbs governing the nouns following. 倍 is read like 背, and with the same meaning, 'to rebel against,' 'to be contrary to,' that here opposed being 道, 'the truth and right.' 籩 was a bamboo dish with a stand, made to hold fruits and seeds at sacrifice ; 豆 was like it, and of the same size, only made of wood, and used to contain pickled vegetables and sauces. 君子 is used as in chap. ii.—In Ho Yen's compilation, the three clauses, beginning 斯遠, are taken not so well, and = 'thus he will not suffer from men's being violent and insulting, &c. &c.'

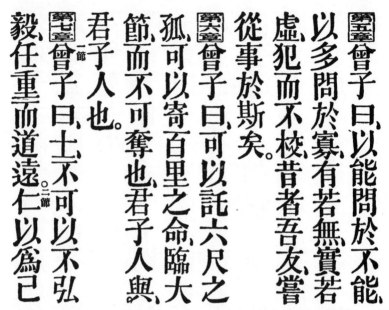

CHAP. V. The philosopher Tsăng said, 'Gifted with ability, and yet putting questions to those who were not so; possessed of much, and yet putting questions to those possessed of little; having, as though he had not; full, and yet counting himself as empty; offended against, and yet entering into no altercation: formerly I had a friend who pursued this style of conduct.'

CHAP. VI. The philosopher Tsăng said, 'Suppose that there is an individual who can be entrusted with the charge of a young orphan *prince*, and can be commissioned with authority over *a State of* a hundred *li*, and whom no emergency however great can drive from his principles:—is such a man a superior man? He is a superior man indeed.'

CHAP. VII. 1. The philosopher Tsăng said, 'The officer may not be without breadth of mind and vigorous endurance. His burden is heavy and his course is long.

5. THE ADMIRABLE SIMPLICITY AND FREEDOM FROM EGOTISM OF A FRIEND OF THE PHILOSOPHER TSĂNG. This friend is supposed to have been Yen Yüan. 校, 'imprisonment by means of wood,' 'stocks.' The dictionary, after the old writers, explains it with reference to this passage, by 角也, 報也, 'altercation,' 're-torting.' 從事於斯, literally, 'followed things in this *way*.'

6. A COMBINATION OF TALENTS AND VIRTUE CONSTITUTING A CHÜN-TSZE. 六尺之孤, 'an orphan of six cubits.' By a comparison of a passage in the Châu Lî and other references, it is established that 'of six cubits' is equiva-

lent to 'of fifteen years or less,' and that for every cubit more or less we should add or deduct five years. See the 經註集證, where it is also said that the ancient cubit was shorter than the modern, and only = 7·4 in., so that six cubits = 4·44 cubits of the present day. But this estimate of the ancient cubit is probably still too high. King Wăn, it is said, was ten cubits high! 百里之命, see Mencius, V. Pt. ii. ch. ii. 6. 與 amounts nearly to a question, and is answered by 也, —'Yes, indeed.'

7. THE NECESSITY TO THE OFFICER OF COMPASS AND VIGOUR OF MIND. 1. 士, a learned man, 'a

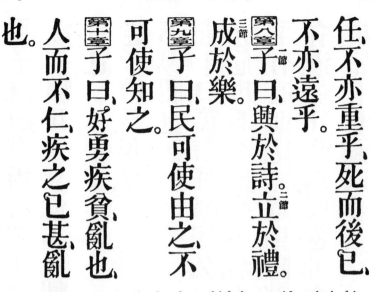

2. 'Perfect virtue is the burden which he considers it is his to sustain;—is it not heavy? Only with death does his course stop;—is it not long?'

CHAP. VIII. 1. The Master said, 'It is by the Odes that the mind is aroused.

2. 'It is by the Rules of Propriety that the character is established.

3. 'It is from Music that the finish is received.'

CHAP. IX. The Master said, 'The people may be made to follow a path of action, but they may not be made to understand it.'

CHAP. X. The Master said, 'The man who is fond of daring and is dissatisfied with poverty, will proceed to insubordination. So will the man who is not virtuous, when you carry your dislike of him to an extreme.'

scholar;' but in all ages learning has been the qualification for, and passport to, official employment in China, hence it is also a general designation for 'an officer.' 任, 4th tone, a noun, = 'an office,' 'a burden borne;' with the 2nd tone, it is the verb 'to bear.'

8. THE EFFECTS OF POETRY, PROPRIETIES, AND MUSIC. These three short sentences are in form like the four, 志於道, &c., in VII. vi, but must be interpreted differently. There the first term in each sentence is a verb in the imperative mood; here it is rather in the indicative. There the 於 is to be joined closely to the 1st character and here to the 3rd. There it=our preposition *to*; here it = *by*. The terms 詩, 禮, 樂 have all specific reference to the Books so called.

9. WHAT MAY, AND WHAT MAY NOT BE ATTAINED TO WITH THE PEOPLE. According to Chû Hsî, the first 之 is 理之所當然, —*duty*, what principles require, and the second is 理之所以然, 'the *principle* of duty.' He also takes 可 and 不可 as = 能 and 不能. If the meaning were so, then the sentiment would be much too broadly expressed. See 四書改錯, XVI. xv. As often in other places, the 冀註 gives the meaning here happily; viz. that a knowledge of the reasons and principles of what they are called to do need not be required from the people,— 不可責之民.

10. DIFFERENT CAUSES OF INSUBORDINATION;— A LESSON TO RULERS.

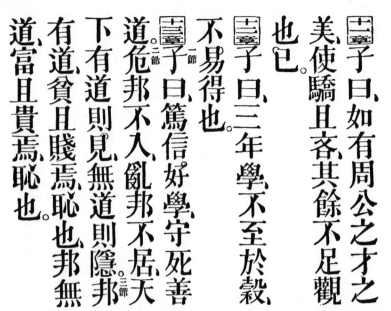

CHAP. XI. The Master said, 'Though a man have abilities as admirable as those of the duke of Châu, yet if he be proud and niggardly, those other things are really not worth being looked at.'

CHAP. XII. The Master said, 'It is not easy to find a man who has learned for three years without coming to be good.'

CHAP. XIII. 1. The Master said, 'With sincere faith he unites the love of learning; holding firm to death, he is perfecting the excellence of his course.

2. '*Such an one* will not enter a tottering State, nor dwell in a disorganized one. When right principles of government prevail in the kingdom, he will show himself; when they are prostrated, he will keep concealed.

3. 'When a country is well-governed, poverty and a mean condition are things to be ashamed of. When a country is ill-governed, riches and honour are things to be ashamed of.'

11. THE WORTHLESSNESS OF TALENT WITHOUT VIRTUE. 'The duke of Châu;'—see VII. v. 其餘, 'the overplus,' 'the superfluity,' referring to the 'talents,' and indicating that ability is not the 本, or root of character, not what is essential. 也已, as in chap. i.

12. HOW QUICKLY LEARNING MAKES MEN GOOD. This is the interpretation of K'ung Ân-kwo, who takes 穀 in the sense of 善. Chû Hsî takes the term in the sense of 祿, 'emolument,' and would change 至 into 志, making the whole a lamentation over the rarity of the disinterested pursuit of learning. But we are not at liberty to admit alterations of the text, unless, as received, it is absolutely unintelligible.

13. THE QUALIFICATIONS OF AN OFFICER, WHO WILL ALWAYS ACT RIGHT IN ACCEPTING AND DECLINING OFFICE. 1. This paragraph is taken as descriptive of character, the effects of whose presence we have in the next, and of its absence in the last. 2. 見 in opposition to 隱, read *hsien*, in 4th tone. The whole chapter seems to want the warmth of generous principle and feeling. In fact, I doubt whether its parts bear the relation and connexion which they are supposed to have.

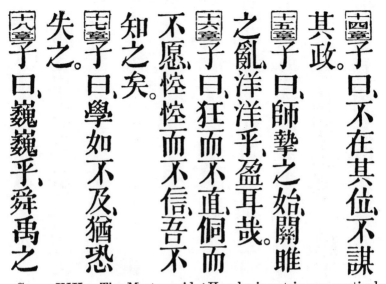

CHAP. XIV. The Master said, 'He who is not in any particular office, has nothing to do with plans for the administration of its duties.'

CHAP. XV. The Master said, 'When the music-master Chih first entered on his office, the finish of the Kwan Tsü was magnificent;—how it filled the ears!'

CHAP. XVI. The Master said, 'Ardent and yet not upright; stupid and yet not attentive; simple and yet not sincere:—such persons I do not understand.'

CHAP. XVII. The Master said, 'Learn as if you could not reach your object, and were *always* fearing also lest you should lose it.'

CHAP. XVIII. The Master said, 'How majestic was the manner in which Shun and Yü held possession of the empire, as if it were nothing to them!'

14. EVERY MAN SHOULD MIND HIS OWN BUSINESS. So the sentiment of this chapter is generalized by the paraphrasts, and perhaps correctly. Its letter, however, has doubtless operated to prevent the spread of right notions about political liberty in China.

15. THE PRAISE OF THE MUSIC-MASTER CHIH. Neither Morrison nor Medhurst gives what appears to be the meaning of 亂 in this chapter. The K'ang-hsî dictionary has it—樂 之 卒 章 曰 亂, 'The last part in the musical services is called *lwan*.' The programme on those occasions consisted of four parts, in the last of which a number of pieces from the *Fäng* or songs of the States was sung, commencing with the *Kwan Tsü*. The name *lwan* was also given to a sort of refrain, at the end of each song.—The old interpreters explain differently, —'when the music-master Chih first corrected the confusion of the Kwan Tsü,' &c.

16. A LAMENTATION OVER MORAL ERROR ADDED TO NATURAL DEFECT. 吾 不 知 之, 'I do not know them;' that is, say commentators, natural defects of endowment are generally associated with certain redeeming qualities, as hastiness with straightforwardness, &c., but in the parties Confucius had in view, those redeeming qualities were absent. He did not understand them, and could do nothing for them.

17. WITH WHAT EARNESTNESS AND CONTINUOUSNESS LEARNING SHOULD BE PURSUED.

18. THE LOFTY CHARACTER OF SHUN AND YÜ. Shun received the empire from Yâo, B.C. 2255, and Yü received it from Shun, B.C. 2205. The throne came to them not by inheritance. They were called to it through their talents and virtue. And yet the possession of it did not affect them at all. 不 與,—'it did not concern them,' was as if nothing to them. Ho Yen takes 與 = 求,—'they had the empire without seeking for it.' This is not according to usage.

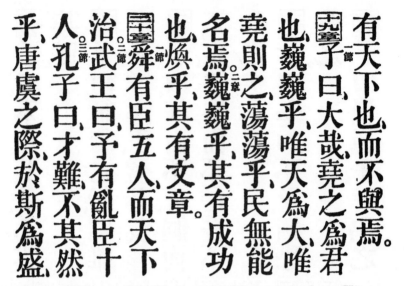

CHAP. XIX. 1. The Master said, 'Great indeed was Yâo as a sovereign! How majestic was he! It is only Heaven that is grand, and only Yâo corresponded to it. How vast *was his virtue!* The people could find no name for it.

2. 'How majestic was he in the works which he accomplished! How glorious in the elegant regulations which he instituted!'

CHAP. XX. 1. Shun had five ministers, and the empire was well-governed.

2. King Wû said, 'I have ten able ministers.'

3. Confucius said, 'Is not *the saying* that talents are difficult to find, true? *Only* when the dynasties of T'ang and Yü met, were they more abundant than in this *of Châu, yet* there was a woman among them. *The able ministers* were no more than nine men.

19. THE PRAISE OF YÂO. 1. No doubt, Yâo, as he appears in Chinese annals, is a fit object of admiration, but if Confucius had had a right knowledge of, and reverence for, Heaven, he could not have spoken as he does here. Grant that it is only the visible heaven overspreading all, to which he compares Yâo, even that is sufficiently absurd. 則之, not simply = 法之, 'imitated it,' but 能與之準, 'could equalize with it.' 2. 其有成功 = 其所有之成功, the great achievements of his government. 文章 (see V. xii) = the music, ceremonies, &c., of which he was the author.

20. THE SCARCITY OF MEN OF TALENT, AND PRAISE OF THE HOUSE OF CHÂU. 1. Shun's five ministers were 禹, Superintendent of Works; 稷, Superintendent of Agriculture; 契 (hsieh), Minister of Instruction; 皐陶, Minister of Justice; and 伯益, Warden of Woods and Marshes. Those five, as being eminent above all their compeers, are mentioned. 2. See the Shû-ching, V. i. sect. ii. 6. 亂臣, 'governing, i. e. able ministers.' In the dictionary, the first meaning given of 亂 is 'to regulate,' and the second is just the opposite,—'to confound,' 'confusion.' Of the ten ministers, the most distinguished of course was the duke of Châu. One of them, it is said next paragraph, was a woman, but whether she was the mother of king Wăn, or his wife, is much disputed. The ten men were:—the duke of Châu, the duke of Shâo, Grandfather Hope, the duke of Pî, the duke of Yung, T'âi-tien, Hung-yâo, San-î Shăng, Nan-kung Kwo, and the wife or mother of king Wăn. 3. Instead of the usual 'The Master said,' we have here 孔子曰, 'The philosopher K'ung said.'

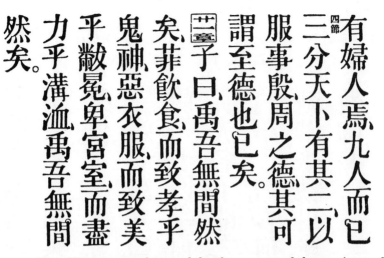

4. '*King Wăn* possessed two of the three parts of the empire, and with those he served the dynasty of Yin. The virtue of the house of Châu may be said to have reached the highest point indeed.'

CHAP. XXI. The Master said, 'I can find no flaw in the character of Yü. He used himself coarse food and drink, but displayed the utmost filial piety towards the spirits. His ordinary garments were poor, but he displayed the utmost elegance in his sacrificial cap and apron. He lived in a low mean house, but expended all his strength on the ditches and water-channels. I can find nothing like a flaw in Yü.'

This is accounted for on the ground that the words of *king* Wû having been quoted immediately before, it would not have been right to crown the sage with his usual title of 'the *Master*.' The style of the whole chapter, however, is different from that of any previous one, and we may suspect that it is corrupt. 才難 is a sort of proverb, or common saying, which Confucius quotes and illustrates. 唐虞之際 (Yâo is called T'ang, having ascended the throne from the marquisate of that name, and Yü became a sort of accepted surname or style of Shun) 於斯爲盛 is understood by Chû Hsî as in the translation, while the old writers take exactly the opposite view. The whole is obscure. 4. This paragraph must be spoken of king Wăn.

21. THE PRAISE OF YÜ. 間, read *chien*, 4th tone, 'a crevice,' 'a crack.' The form 間 in the text is not so correct. 禹吾無間然

矣, '*In* Yü, *I find* no crevice so,' i.e. I find nothing in him to which I can point as a flaw. 鬼神 is interpreted of the spirits of heaven and earth, as well as those sacrificed to in the ancestral temple, but the saying that the rich offerings were filial (孝) would seem to restrict the phrase to the latter. The 黻 was an apron made of leather, and coming down over the knees, and the 冕 was a sort of cap or crown, flat on the top, and projecting before and behind, with a long fringe on which gems and pearls were strung, exactly like the Christ-Church cap of Oxford. They were both used in sacrificing. 溝洫, generally the water-channels by which the boundaries of the fields were determined, and provision made for their irrigation, and to carry off the water of floods. The 溝 were four cubits wide and deep, and arranged so as to flow into the 洫, which were double the size.

BOOK IX. TSZE HAN.

子罕第九

第一章 子罕言利與命、與仁。

第二章 一節 達巷黨人曰、大哉孔子、博學而無所成名。二節 子聞之、謂門弟子曰、吾何執、執御乎、執射乎、吾執御矣。

CHAPTER I. The subjects of which the Master seldom spoke were—profitableness, and also the appointments *of Heaven*, and perfect virtue.

CHAP. II. 1. A man of the village of Tâ-hsiang said, 'Great indeed is the philosopher K'ung! His learning is extensive, and yet he does not render his name famous by any *particular* thing.'

2. The Master heard the observation, and said to his disciples, 'What shall I practise? Shall I practise charioteering, or shall I practise archery? I will practise charioteering.'

HEADING OF THIS BOOK.—子罕第九, 'The Master seldom, No. 9.' The thirty chapters of this Book are much akin to those of the seventh. They are mostly occupied with the doctrine, character, and ways of Confucius himself.

1. SUBJECTS SELDOM SPOKEN OF BY CONFUCIUS. 利 is mostly taken here in a good sense, not as selfish gain, but as it is defined under the first of the diagrams in the Yî-ching,—義之和, 'the harmoniousness of all that is righteous;' that is, how what is right is really what is truly profitable. Compare Mencius, I. i. 1. Yet even in this sense Confucius seldom spoke of it, as he would not have the consideration of the profitable introduced into conduct at all. With his not speaking of 仁 there is a difficulty which I know not how to solve. The fourth Book is nearly all occupied with it, and no doubt it was a prominent topic in Confucius's teachings. 命 is not = our *fate*, unless in the primary meaning of that term,—'*Fatum est quod dii fantur.*' Nor is it *decree*, or antecedent purpose and determination, but the decree embodied and realised in its object.

2. AMUSEMENT OF CONFUCIUS AT THE REMARK OF AN IGNORANT MAN ABOUT HIM. Commentators, old and new, say that the chapter shows the exceeding humility of the sage, educed by his being praised, but his observation on the man's remark was evidently ironical. 1. For want of another word, I render 黨 by 'village.' According to the statutes of Châu, 'five families made a 比, four *pi* a 閭, and five *lü* or 500 families a *tang*.' Who the villager was is not recorded, though some would have him to be the same with 項橐, the boy of whom it is said in the 三字經, 昔仲尼師項橐, 'of old Confucius was a scholar of Hsiang T'o.' The man was able to see that Confucius was very extensively learned, but his idea of fame, common to the age, was that it must be acquired by excellence in some one particular art. In his lips, 孔子 was not more than our 'Mr. K'ung.'

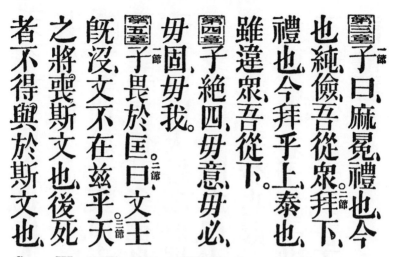

CHAP. III. 1. The Master said, 'The linen cap is that prescribed by the rules of ceremony, but now a silk one is worn. It is economical, and I follow the common practice.

2. 'The rules of ceremony prescribe the bowing below *the hall*, but now the practice is to bow *only* after ascending it. That is arrogant. I *continue to* bow below the hall, though I oppose the common practice.'

CHAP. IV. There were four things from which the Master was entirely free. He had no foregone conclusions, no arbitrary pre-determinations, no obstinacy, and no egoism.

CHAP. V. 1. The Master was put in fear in K'wang.

2. He said, 'After the death of king Wăn, was not the cause of truth lodged here *in me?*

3. SOME COMMON PRACTICES INDIFFERENT AND OTHERS NOT. 1. The cap here spoken of was that prescribed to be worn in the ancestral temple, and made of very fine linen dyed of a deep dark colour. It had fallen into disuse, and was superseded by a simpler one of silk. Rather than be singular, Confucius gave in to a practice, which involved no principle of right, and was economical. 2. Chû Hsî explains the 拜下, 拜乎上, thus: 'In the ceremonial intercourse between ministers and their prince, it was proper for them to bow below the raised hall. This the prince declined, on which they ascended and completed the homage.' See this illustrated in the 經註集證, *in loc.* The prevailing disregard of the first part of the ceremony Confucius considered inconsistent with the proper distance to be observed between prince and minister, and therefore he would be singular in adhering to the rule.

4. FRAILTIES FROM WHICH CONFUCIUS WAS FREE. 毋, it is said, is not prohibitive here, but simply negative;—to make it appear that it was not by any effort, as 絶 and 毋 more naturally suggest, that Confucius attained to these things.

5. CONFUCIUS ASSURED IN A TIME OF DANGER BY HIS CONVICTION OF A DIVINE MISSION. Compare VII. xxii, but the adventure to which this chapter refers is placed in the sage's history before the other, not long after he had resigned office, and left Lû. 1. There are different opinions as to what State K'wang belonged to. The most likely is that it was a border town of Chăng, and its site is now to be found in the department of K'âi-fäng in Ho-nan. It is said that K'wang had suffered from 陽虎, an officer of Lû, to whom Confucius bore a resemblance. As he passed by the place, moreover, a disciple, 顔刻, who had been associated with Yang Hû in his measures against K'wang, was driving him. These circumstances made the people think that Confucius was their old enemy, so they attacked him, and kept him prisoner for five days. The accounts of his escape vary, some of them

天之未喪斯文也匡人
其如予何。

第六章
大宰問於子貢曰、夫
子聖者與、何其多能也。
子貢曰、固天縱之將聖、
又多能也。子聞之曰、大
宰知我乎、吾少也賤、故
多能鄙事、君子多乎哉、
不多也。牢曰、子云、吾不
試故藝。

3. 'If Heaven had wished to let this cause of truth perish, then I, a future mortal, should not have got such a relation to that cause. While Heaven does not let the cause of truth perish, what can the people of K'wang do to me?'

CHAP. VI. 1. A high officer asked Tsze-kung, saying, 'May we not say that your Master is a sage? How various is his ability!'

2. Tsze-kung said, 'Certainly Heaven has endowed him unlimitedly. He is about a sage. And, moreover, his ability is various.'

3. The Master heard of the conversation and said, 'Does the high officer know me? When I was young, my condition was low, and therefore I acquired my ability in many things, but they were mean matters. Must the superior man have such variety of ability? He does not need variety of ability.'

4. Lâo said, 'The Master said, "Having no official employment, I acquired many arts."'

being evidently fabulous. The disciples were in fear. 畏 would indicate that Confucius himself was so, but this is denied. 2. The *wăn* I render by 'the cause of truth.' More exactly, it is the truth embodied in literature, ceremonies, &c., and its use instead of *tâo*, 'truth in its principles,' is attributed to Confucius's modesty. 在兹, 'in this,' referring to himself. 3. There may be modesty in his use of *wăn*, but he here identifies himself with the line of the great sages, to whom Heaven has intrusted the instruction of men. In all the six centuries between himself and king Wăn, he does not admit of another. 後死者, 'he who dies afterwards,' = a future mortal.

6. ON THE VARIOUS ABILITY OF CONFUCIUS :— HIS SAGEHOOD NOT THEREIN. 1. According to

the 周禮, the 大宰 was the chief of the six great officers of State, but the use of the designation in Confucius's time was confined to the States of Wû and Sung, and hence the officer in the text must have belonged to one of them. See the 註疏, *in loc.* The force of 與 is as appears in the translation. 2. 與 is responded to by Tsze-kung with 固, 'certainly,' while yet by the use of 將 he gives his answer an air of hesitancy. 縱之, 'lets him go,' i.e. does not restrict him at all. The officer had found the sagehood of Confucius in his various ability;—by the *yŭ*, 'moreover,' Tsze-kung makes that ability only an additional circumstance. 3. Confucius ex-

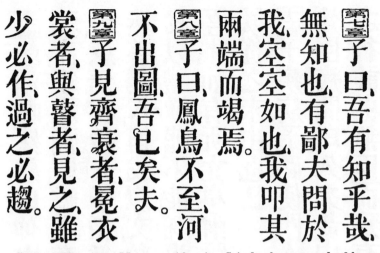

CHAP. VII. The Master said, 'Am I indeed possessed of knowledge? I am not knowing. But if a mean person, who appears quite empty-like, ask anything of me, I set it forth from one end to the other, and exhaust it.'

CHAP. VIII. The Master said, 'The FĂNG bird does not come; the river sends forth no map:—it is all over with me!'

CHAP. IX. When the Master saw a person in a mourning dress, or any one with the cap and upper and lower garments of full dress, or a blind person, on observing them *approaching*, though they were younger than himself, he would rise up, and if he had to pass by them, he would do so hastily.

plains his possession of various ability, and repudiates its being essential to the sage, or even to the *chŭn-tsze*. 4. Lâo was a disciple, by surname Ch'in (琴), and styled Tsze-k'âi (子開), or Tsze-chang (子張). It is supposed that when these conversations were being digested into their present form, some one remembered that Lâo had been in the habit of mentioning the remark given, and accordingly it was appended to the chapter. 子云 indicates that it was a frequent saying of Confucius.

7. CONFUCIUS DISCLAIMS THE KNOWLEDGE ATTRIBUTED TO HIM, AND DECLARES HIS EARNESTNESS IN TEACHING. The first sentence here was probably an exclamation with reference to some remark upon himself as having extraordinary knowledge. 叩其兩端, 'exhibit (叩 = 發動, 'to agitate') its two ends,' i.e. discuss it from beginning to end.

·8. FOR WANT OF AUSPICIOUS OMENS, CONFUCIUS GIVES UP THE HOPE OF THE TRIUMPH OF HIS DOCTRINES. The *fäng* is the male of a fabulous bird, which has been called the Chinese phœnix, said to appear when a sage ascends the throne

or when right principles are going to triumph in the world. The female is called 凰. In the days of Shun, they gambolled in his hall, and were heard singing on mount Ch'î in the time of king Wän. The river and the map carry us farther back still,—to the time of Fû-hsî, to whom a monster with the head of a dragon, and the body of a horse, rose from the water, being marked on the back so as to give that first of the sages the idea of his diagrams. Confucius indorses these fables. 吾已矣夫, —see V. xxvi, and observe how 乎 and 夫 are interchanged.

9. CONFUCIUS'S SYMPATHY WITH SORROW, RESPECT FOR RANK, AND PITY FOR MISFORTUNE. 齊, read *tsze*, is 'the lower edge of a garment,' and joined with 衰, read *ts'âi*, 'mourning garments,' the two characters indicate the mourning of the second degree of intensity, where the edge is unhemmed, but cut *even*, instead of being ragged, the terms for which are 斬衰. The phrase, however, seems to be for 'in mourning' generally. 少, in 4th tone, 'young.'

CHAP. X. 1. Yen Yüan, *in admiration of the Master's doctrines*, sighed and said, 'I looked up to them, and they *seemed to become* more high; I tried to penetrate them, and they *seemed to become* more firm; I looked at them before me, and suddenly they *seemed to be* behind.

2. 'The Master, by orderly method, skilfully leads men on. He enlarged my mind with learning, and taught me the restraints of propriety.

3. 'When I wish to give over *the study of his doctrines*, I cannot do so, and having exerted all my ability, there seems something to stand right up before me; but though I wish to follow *and lay hold of it*, I really find no way to do so.'

CHAP. XI. 1. The Master being very ill, Tsze-lû wished the disciples to act as ministers to him.

2. During a remission of his illness, he said, 'Long has the conduct of Yû been deceitful! By pretending to have ministers when I have them not, whom should I impose upon? Should I impose upon Heaven?

10. YEN YÜAN'S ADMIRATION OF HIS MASTER'S DOCTRINES; AND HIS OWN PROGRESS IN THEM. 1. 喟然歎, 'sighingly sighed.' 仰 and the other verbs here are to be translated in the past tense, as the chapter seems to give an account of the progress of Hûi's mind. 忽焉=忽然, 'suddenly.' 2. 誘=引進, 'to lead forward.' 博我 云云,—comp. VI. xxv. 3. 卓爾=卓然, an adverb, 'uprightly,' 'loftily.' 末, in the sense of 無.

末由=無所由以用其力, 'I find myself unable to use my strength.' 也已, 'yea, indeed.'—It was this which made him sigh.

11. CONFUCIUS'S DISLIKE OF PRETENSION, AND CONTENTMENT WITH HIS CONDITION. 1. 使, 'was causing,' or wanted to cause. Confucius had been a great officer, and enjoyed the services of ministers, as in a petty court. Tsze-lû would have surrounded him in his great sickness with the illusions of his former state, and brought on himself this rebuke. 3. 縱

臣吾誰欺欺天乎且予與其

死於臣之手也無寧死於二

三子之手乎且予縱不得大

葬予死於道路乎。

子貢曰有美玉於斯韞匱

而藏諸求善賈而沽諸子曰、

沽之哉沽之哉我待賈者也。

子欲居九夷或曰陋如之

何子曰君子居之何陋之有。

子曰吾自衞反魯然後樂

3. 'Moreover, than that I should die in the hands of ministers, is
it not better that I should die in the hands of you, my disciples?
And though I may not get a great burial, shall I die upon the road?'

CHAP. XII. Tsze-kung said, 'There is a beautiful gem here.
Should I lay it up in a case and keep it? or should I seek for a
good price and sell it?' The Master said, 'Sell it! Sell it! But
I would wait for one to offer the price.'

CHAP. XIII. 1. The Master was wishing to go and live among
the nine wild tribes of the east.

2. Some one said, 'They are rude. How can you do such a thing?'
The Master said, 'If a superior man dwelt among them, what rudeness would there be?'

CHAP. XIV. The Master said, 'I returned from Wei to Lû, and
then the music was reformed, and the pieces in the Royal songs and
Praise songs all found their proper places.'

= 縱然, as a conjunction, 'letting it be
that,' = although.

12. HOW THE DESIRE FOR OFFICE SHOULD BE
QUALIFIED BY SELF-RESPECT. 諸 is interrogative here, as in VII. xxxiv. There being no
nominative to 韞, like the 'I' in the translation, we might render, 'should it be put,' &c.
賈, read *chiǎ*, 4th tone = 價, 'price,' 'value.'
The disciple wanted to elicit from Confucius
why he declined office so much, and insinuated
his question in this way. It seems better to

translate *yü* here by 'a gem,' or a 'precious
stone,' than by 'a piece of jade.'

13. HOW BARBARIANS CAN BE CIVILIZED. This
chapter is to be understood, it is said, like
V. vi, not as if Confucius really wished to go
among the Î, but that he thus expressed his
regret that his doctrine did not find acceptance
in China. 1. The Î,—see III. v. There were
nine tribes or varieties (種) of them, the
yellow, white, red, &c. 2. 如之何,—the
之 refers to his purpose to go among the Î.

14. CONFUCIUS'S SERVICES IN CORRECTING THE

正雅頌各得其所。

子曰、出則事公卿、入則
事父兄、喪事不敢不勉、不
爲酒困、何有於我哉。

子在川上曰、逝者如斯
夫、不舍晝夜。

子曰、吾未見好德如好
色者也。

子曰、譬如爲山、未成一
簣、止吾止也、譬如平地、雖

CHAP. XV. The Master said, 'Abroad, to serve the high ministers and nobles; at home, to serve one's father and elder brothers; in all duties to the dead, not to dare not to exert one's self; and not to be overcome of wine:—which one of these things do I attain to?'

CHAP. XVI. The Master standing by a stream, said, 'It passes on just like this, not ceasing day or night!'

CHAP. XVII. The Master said, 'I have not seen one who loves virtue as he loves beauty.'

CHAP. XVIII. The Master said, '*The prosecution of learning* may be compared to what may happen in raising a mound. If there want but one basket *of earth* to complete the work, and I stop, the

MUSIC OF HIS NATIVE STATE AND ADJUSTING THE BOOK OF POETRY. Confucius returned from Wei to Lû in his 69th year, and died five years after. The 雅 (read *yâ*, 3rd tone) and the 頌 are the names of two, or rather three, of the divisions of the Shih-ching, the former being the 'elegant' or 'correct' odes, to be used with music at royal festivals, and the latter the praise songs, celebrating principally the virtues of the founders of different dynasties, to be used in the services of the ancestral temple.

15. CONFUCIUS'S VERY HUMBLE ESTIMATE OF HIMSELF. Comp. VII. ii, but the things which Confucius here disclaims are of a still lower character than those there mentioned. Very remarkable is the last, as from the sage. The old interpreters treat 何有於我哉, as they do in VII. ii;—compare VII. xxv, xxvii, xxxiii, et al. 公卿 stand together, indicating men of superior rank. If we distinguish be-tween them, the 公 may express the princes, high officers in the royal court, and the 卿, the high officers in the princes' courts.

16. HOW CONFUCIUS WAS AFFECTED BY A RUN-NING STREAM. What does the *it* in the translation refer to? 者 and 如 indicate something in the sage's mind, suggested by the ceaseless movement of the water. Chû Hsî makes it 天地之化, = our 'course of nature.' In the 註疏 we find for it 時事, 'events,' 'the things of time.' Probably Chû Hsî is correct. Comp. Mencius, IV. Pt. ii. ch. xviii.

17. THE RARITY OF A SINCERE LOVE OF VIRTUE. 色, as in I. vii.

18. THAT LEARNERS SHOULD NOT CEASE NOR INTERMIT THEIR LABOURS. This is a fragment, like many other chapters, of some conversation, and the subject thus illustrated must be supplied, after the modern commentator, as in the translation, or, after the old, by 'the

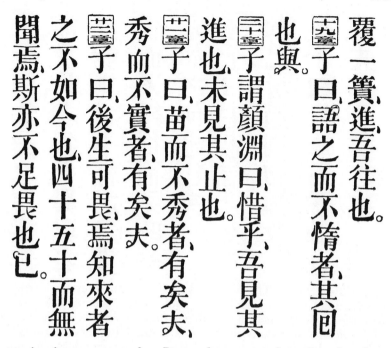

覆一簣進吾往也。

也與。

子曰語之而不惰者其回

子謂顏淵曰惜乎吾見其

進也未見其止也。

子曰苗而不秀者有矣夫

秀而不實者有矣夫。

子曰後生可畏焉知來者

之不如今也四十五十而無

聞焉斯亦不足畏也已。

stopping is my own work. It may be compared to *throwing down the earth* on the level ground. Though *but* one basketful is thrown *at a time*, the advancing with it is my own going forward.'

CHAP. XIX. The Master said, 'Never flagging when I set forth anything to him;—ah! that is Hûi.'

CHAP. XX. The Master said of Yen Yüan, 'Alas! I saw his constant advance. I never saw him stop in his progress.'

CHAP. XXI. The Master said, 'There are cases in which the blade springs, but the plant does not go on to flower! There are cases where it flowers, but no fruit is subsequently produced!'

CHAP. XXII. The Master said, 'A youth is to be regarded with respect. How do we know that his future will not be equal to our present? If he reach the age of forty or fifty, and has not made himself heard of, then indeed he will not be worth being regarded with respect.'

following of virtue.' See the Shû-ching, V. v. 9, where the subject is virtuous consistency. We might expect 平 in 平地 to be a verb, like 爲 in 爲山, but a good sense cannot be made out by taking it so. 雖, = 'though only,' as many take it in VI. xxiv. The lesson of the chapter is—that repeated acquisitions individually small will ultimately amount to much, and that the learner is never to give over.

19. HÛI THE EARNEST STUDENT.

20. CONFUCIUS'S FOND RECOLLECTION OF HÛI

AS A MODEL STUDENT. This is said to have been spoken after Hûi's death. 惜乎 looks as if it were so. The 未, 'not yet,' would rather make us think differently.

21. IT IS THE END WHICH CROWNS THE WORK.

22. HOW AND WHY A YOUTH SHOULD BE REGARDED WITH RESPECT. The same person is spoken of throughout the chapter, as is shown by the 亦 in the last sentence. This is not very conclusive, but it brings out a good enough meaning. With Confucius's remark compare that of John Trebonius, Luther's schoolmaster

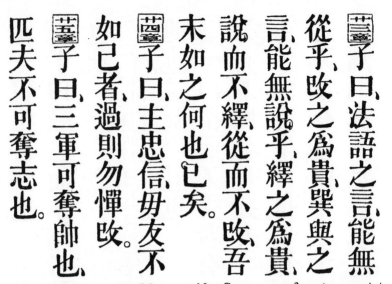

CHAP. XXIII. The Master said, 'Can men refuse to assent to the words of strict admonition? But it is reforming the conduct because of them which is valuable. Can men refuse to be pleased with words of gentle advice? But it is unfolding their aim which is valuable. If a man be pleased with these words, but does not unfold their aim, and assents to those, but does not reform his conduct, I can really do nothing with him.'

CHAP. XXIV. The Master said, 'Hold faithfulness and sincerity as first principles. Have no friends not equal to yourself. When you have faults, do not fear to abandon them.'

CHAP. XXV. The Master said, 'The commander of the forces of a large State may be carried off, but the will of even a common man cannot be taken from him.'

at Eisenach, who used to raise his cap to his pupils on entering the schoolroom, and gave as the reason—'There are among these boys men of whom God will one day make burgomasters, chancellors, doctors, and magistrates. Although you do not yet see them with the badges of their dignity, it is right that you should treat them with respect.' 後生, 'after born,' a youth. See 先生, II. viii.

23. THE HOPELESSNESS OF THE CASE OF THOSE WHO ASSENT AND APPROVE WITHOUT REFORMATION OR SERIOUS THOUGHT. 法語之言, 'words of law-like admonition.' 巽 is the name of the 5th trigram, to which the element of 'wind' is attached. Wind enters everywhere, hence the character is interpreted by 'entering,' and also by 'mildness,' 'yielding.' 巽 與之言, 'words of gentle insinuation.'

In 繹之為貴, an antecedent to 之 is readily found in the preceding 言, but in 改 之為貴, such an antecedent can only be found in a roundabout way. This is one of the cases which shows the inapplicability to Chinese composition of our strict syntactical apparatus. 末 as in chap. x.

24. This is a repetition of part of I. viii.

25. THE WILL UNSUBDUABLE. 三軍, see VII. x. 帥, read shwâi, 4th tone, = 將帥 'a general.' 匹, 'mate.' We find in the dictionary—'Husband and wife of the common people are a pair (相匹),' and the application of the term being thus fixed, an individual man is called 匹夫, an individual woman 匹婦.

子曰、可與共學、未可與

憂、勇者不懼。

子曰、知者不惑、仁者不

之後彫也。

子曰、歲寒然後知松栢

何足以臧。

路終身誦之、子曰、是道也、三節

與不忮不求、何用不臧、子

貉者立而不恥者其由也 二節

子曰、衣敝緼袍與衣狐 一節

CHAP. XXVI.　1. The Master said, 'Dressed himself in a tattered robe quilted with hemp, yet standing by the side of men dressed in furs, and not ashamed;—ah! it is Yû who is equal to this!

2. ' " He dislikes none, he covets nothing;—what can he do but what is good?"'

3. Tsze-lû kept continually repeating these *words of the ode*, when the Master said, 'Those things are by no means sufficient to constitute (*perfect*) excellence.'

CHAP. XXVII.　The Master said, 'When the year becomes cold, then we know how the pine and the cypress are the last to lose their leaves.'

CHAP. XXVIII.　The Master said, 'The wise are free from perplexities; the virtuous from anxiety; and the bold from fear.'

CHAP. XXIX.　The Master said, 'There are some with whom we may study in common, but we shall find them unable to go along

26. Tsze-lû's brave contentment in poverty, but failure to seek the highest aims.　1. On the construction of this paragraph, compare chap. xviii. The 狐 is the fox. The 貉, read *heh*, is probably the badger. It is described as nocturnal in its habits, having a soft, warm fur. It sleeps much, and is carnivorous. This last characteristic is not altogether inapplicable to the badger. See the 本草獸部. 2. See the Shih-ching, I. iii. Ode VIII. 4. 3. 終身, not 'all his life,' as frequently, but 'continually.' Tsze-lû was a man of impulse, with many fine points, but not sufficiently reflective.

27. Men are known in times of adversity. 後彫, 'the after-withering,' a meiosis for their being evergreens.

28. The sequences of wisdom, virtue, and bravery. 仁者不憂,—this is one of the sayings about virtue, which is only true when it is combined with trust in God.

29. How different individuals stop at different stages of progress. More literally rendered, this chapter would be—'It may be possible with *some parties* together to study, *but* it may not yet be possible with them to go on to principles, &c.' 權, the weight of a steel-yard, then 'to weigh.' It is used here with

遠之有。
之思也夫何
遠而子曰未
不爾思室是
偏其反而豈
三十章 唐棣之華、
與權。
可與立未可
道未可與立
適道可與適

with us to principles. *Perhaps* we may go on with them to principles, but we shall find them unable to get established in those along with us. Or if we may get so established along with them, we shall find them unable to weigh *occurring events* along with us.'

CHAP. XXX. 1. How the flowers of the aspen-plum flutter and turn! Do I not think of you? But your house is distant.

2. The Master said, 'It is the want of thought about it. How is it distant?'

reference to occurring events,—to weigh them and determine the application of principles to them. In the old commentaries, 權 is used here in opposition to 經, the latter being that which is always, and everywhere right, the former a deviation from that in particular circumstances, to bring things right. This meaning of the term here is denied. The ancients adopted it probably from their interpretation of the second clause in the next chapter, which they made one with this.

30. THE NECESSITY OF REFLECTION. 1. This is understood to be from one of the pieces of poetry, which were not admitted into the collection of the Shih, and no more of it being preserved than what we have here, it is not altogether intelligible. There are long disputes about the 唐棣. Chû Hsî makes it a kind of small plum or cherry tree, whose leaves are constantly quivering, even when there is no wind; and adopting a reading, in a book of the Tsin (晉) dynasty, of 翩 for 偏, and changing 翻 into 反, he makes out the meaning in the translation. The old commentators keep the text, and interpret,—'How perversely contrary are the flowers of the T'angtâi!' saying that those flowers are first open and then shut. This view made them take 權 in the last chapter, as we have noticed. Who or what is meant by 爾 in 爾思, we cannot tell. The two 而 are mere expletives, completing the rhythm. 2. With this paragraph Chû Hsî compares VII. xxix.—The whole piece is like the 20th of the last Book, and suggests the thought of its being an addition by another hand to the original compilation.

BOOK X. HEANG TANG.

CHAPTER I. 1. Confucius, in his village, looked simple and sincere, and as if he were not able to speak.

2. When he was in the *prince's* ancestorial temple, or in the court, he spoke minutely on every point, but cautiously.

CHAP. II. 1. When he was waiting at court, in speaking with the great officers of the lower grade, he spake freely, but in a straightforward manner; in speaking with those of the higher grade, he did so blandly, but precisely.

2. When the ruler was present, his manner displayed respectful uneasiness; it was grave, but self-possessed.

HEADING OF THIS BOOK.—鄉黨第十, 'The village, No. 10.' This Book is different in its character from all the others in the work. It contains hardly any sayings of Confucius, but is descriptive of his ways and demeanour in a variety of places and circumstances. It is not uninteresting, but, as a whole, it hardly heightens our veneration for the sage. We seem to know him better from it, and perhaps to Western minds, after being viewed in his bedchamber, his undress, and at his meals, he becomes divested of a good deal of his dignity and reputation. There is something remarkable about the style. Only in one passage is its subject styled 子, '*The Master*.' He appears either as 孔子, 'The philosopher K'ung,' or as 君子, 'The superior man.' A suspicion is thus raised that the chronicler had not the same relation to him as the compilers of the other Books. Anciently, the Book formed only one chapter, but it is now arranged under seventeen divisions. Those divisions, for convenience in the translation, I continue to denominate chapters, which is done also in some native editions.

1. DEMEANOUR OF CONFUCIUS IN HIS VILLAGE, IN THE ANCESTRAL TEMPLE, AND IN THE COURT. 1.

According to the dictionary, quoting from a record of 'the former Han dynasty, the 鄉 contained 2,500 families, and the 黨 only 500;' but the two terms are to be taken here together, indicating the residence of the sage's relatives. His native place in Lû is doubtless intended, rather than the original seat of his family in Sung. 恂恂如 is explained by Wang Sû 'mild-like,' and by Chû Hsî, as in the translation, thinking probably that, with that meaning, it suited the next clause better. 2. 便, read *p'ien*, the 2nd tone = 辯, 'to debate,' 'to discriminate accurately.' 爾=耳. In those two places of high ceremony and of government, it became the sage, it is said, to be precise and particular. Compare III. xv.

2. DEMEANOUR OF CONFUCIUS AT COURT WITH OTHER GREAT OFFICERS, AND BEFORE THE PRINCE. 1. 朝 may be taken here as a verb, literally = 'courting.' It was the custom for all the officers to repair at daybreak to the court, and wait for the ruler to give them audience. 大夫, 'Great officer,' was a general name, applicable to all the higher officers in a

第三章
一節　君召使擯、色勃如也、足躩如也。
二節　揖所與立、左右手、衣前後襜如也。
三節　趨進翼如也。
四節　賓退必復命曰、賓不顧矣。

第四章
一節　入公門、鞠

CHAP. III. 1. When the prince called him to employ him in the reception of a visitor, his countenance appeared to change, and his legs to move forward with difficulty.

2. He inclined himself to the *other officers* among whom he stood, moving his left or right arm, *as their position required*, but keeping the skirts of his robe before and behind evenly adjusted.

3. He hastened forward, *with his arms* like the wings of a bird.

4. When the guest had retired, he would report to the prince, 'The visitor is not turning round any more.'

CHAP. IV. 1. When he entered the palace gate, he seemed to bend his body, as if it were not sufficient to admit him.

court. At the royal court they were divided into three classes,—'highest,' 'middle,' and 'lowest,' 上, 中, 下, but the various princes had only the first and third. Of the first order there were properly three, 卿, or nobles of the State, who were in Lû the chiefs of the 'three families.' Confucius belonged himself to the lower grade. 2. 踧踖 = 'the feet moving uneasily,' indicating the respectful anxiety of the mind. 與, 2nd tone, here appears in the phrase 與與如也, in a new sense.

3. DEMEANOUR OF CONFUCIUS AT THE OFFICIAL RECEPTION OF A VISITOR. 1. The visitor is supposed to be the ruler of another State. On the occasion of two princes meeting there was much ceremony. The visitor having arrived, he remained outside the front gate, and the host inside his reception room, which was in the ancestral temple. Messages passed between them by means of a number of officers called 介, on the side of the visitor, and 擯, on the side of the host, who formed a zigzag line of communication from the one to the other, and passed their questions and answers along, till an understanding about the visit was thus officially effected. 足躩如 probably has the meaning which I have given in the translation. 2. This shows Confucius's manner when engaged in the transmission of the messages between the prince and his visitor. The prince's nuncio, in immediate communication with himself, was the 上擯, the next was the

承擯, and below were one or more 紹擯. Confucius must have been the *ch'äng pin*, bowing to the right as he transmitted a message to the *shang pin*, who was an officer of the higher grade, and to the left as he communicated one from him to the *shâo pin*. 3. The host having come out to receive his visitor, proceeded in with him, it is said, followed by all their internuncios in a line, and to his manner in this movement this paragraph is generally referred. But the duty of seeing the guest off, the subject of next paragraph, belonged to the *shang pin*, and could not be performed by Confucius as merely a *ch'äng pin*. Hence arises a difficulty. Either it is true that Confucius was at one time raised to the rank of the highest dignitaries of the State, or he was temporarily employed, from his knowledge of ceremonies, after the first act in the reception of visitors, to discharge the duties of one. Assuming this, the 趨進 is to be explained of some of his movements in the reception room. How could he hurry forward when walking in file with the other internuncios? See the 拓餘說, II. xxiii. 4. 必復命, 'would return the commission,' i. e. he had seen the guest off, according to his duty, and reported it. The ways of China, it appears, were much the same anciently as now. A guest turns round and bows repeatedly in leaving, and the host cannot return to his place, till these salutations are ended.

4. DEMEANOUR OF CONFUCIUS IN THE COURT AT AN AUDIENCE. 1. The royal court consisted of five divisions, each having its peculiar gate. That of a prince of a State consisted only of

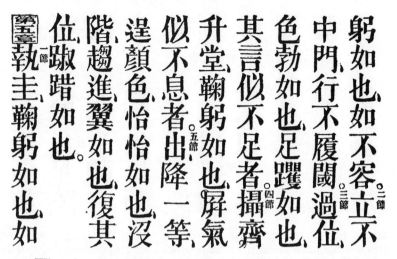

2. When he was standing, he did not occupy the middle of the gate-way; when he passed in or out, he did not tread upon the threshold.

3. When he was passing the *vacant* place *of the prince*, his countenance appeared to change, and his legs to bend under him, and his words came as if he hardly had breath to utter them.

4. He ascended the reception hall, holding up his robe with both his hands, and his body bent; holding in his breath also, as if he dared not breathe.

5. When he came out *from the audience*, as soon as he had descended one step, he began to relax his countenance, and had a satisfied look.   When he had got to the bottom of the steps, he advanced rapidly to his place, *with his arms* like wings, and on occupying it, his manner *still* showed respectful uneasiness.

CHAP. V.   1. When he was carrying the sceptre *of his ruler*, he seemed to bend his body, as if he were not able to bear its weight. He did not hold it higher than the position of the hands in making

three, whose gates were named 庫, 雉, and 路. The 公門 is the k'ú, or first of these. The bending his body when passing through, high as the gate was, is supposed to indicate the great reverence which Confucius felt.   2. 不中門＝不中於門, 'He did not stand opposite the middle of the gate-way.' Each gate had a post in the centre, called 闑, by which it was divided into two halves, appropriated to ingress and egress.   The prince only could stand in the centre of either of them, and *he* only could tread on the threshold or sill.   3. At the early formal audience at day-break, when the prince came out of the inner apartment, and received the homage of the officers, he occupied a particular spot called 宁.

This is the 位, now empty, which Confucius passes in his way to the audience in the inner apartment.   4. 齊, see IX. ix. He is now ascending the steps to the 堂, 'the dais,' or raised platform in the inner apartment, where the prince held his council, or gave entertainments, and from which the family rooms of the palace branched off.   5. The audience is now over, and Confucius is returning to his usual place at the formal audience.   K'ung Ân-kwo makes the 位 to be the 宁 in par. 3, but improperly. 進 after 趨 is an addition that has somehow crept into the ordinary text.

5. DEMEANOUR OF CONFUCIUS WHEN EMPLOYED ON A FRIENDLY EMBASSY.   1. 圭 may be trans-

裘素衣麑裘黃衣　服當暑袗絺綌　飾紅紫不以為褻　第六章 君子不以紺緅　也。　容色私覿愉愉如　蹜如有循享禮有　授勃如戰色足躇　不勝上如揖下如

表而出之。緇衣羔

a bow, nor lower than their position in giving anything to another. His countenance seemed to change, and look apprehensive, and he dragged his feet along as if they were held by something to the ground.

2. In presenting the presents *with which he was charged*, he wore a placid appearance.

3. At his private audience, he looked highly pleased.

CHAP. VI. 1. The superior man did not use a deep purple, or a puce colour, in the ornaments of his dress.

2. Even in his undress, he did not wear anything of a red or reddish colour.

3. In warm weather, he had a single garment either of coarse or fine texture, but he wore it displayed over an inner garment.

4. Over lamb's fur he wore a garment of black; over fawn's fur one of white; and over fox's fur one of yellow.

lated 'sceptre,' in the sense simply of 'a badge of authority.' It was a piece of jade, conferred by the sovereign on the princes, and differed in size and shape, according to their rank. They took it with them when they attended the king's court, and, according to Chû Hsî and the old interpreters, it was carried also by their representatives, as their voucher, on occasions of embassies among themselves. In the 拓餘說, II. xxxiii, however, it is contended, apparently on sufficient grounds, that the sceptre then employed was different from the other. 勝, 1st tone, 'to be equal to,' 'able for.' 2. The preceding paragraph describes Confucius's manner in the friendly court, at his first interview, showing his credentials and delivering his message. That done, he had to deliver the various presents with which he was charged. This was called 享,＝獻. 3. After all the public presents were delivered, the ambassador had others of his own to give, and his interview for that purpose was called 私覿.

—Chû Hsî remarks that there is no record of Confucius ever having been employed on such a mission, and supposes that this chapter and the preceding are simply summaries of the manner in which he used to say duties referred to in them ought to be discharged.

6. RULES OF CONFUCIUS IN REGARD TO HIS DRESS.—The discussions about the colours here mentioned are lengthy and tedious. I am not confident that I have given them all correctly in the translation. 1. 君子, used here to denote Confucius, can hardly have come from the hand of a disciple. 紺＝深青揚赤色, 'a deep azure flushed with carnation.' 緅＝絳色, 'a deep red;' it was dipped thrice in a red dye, and then twice in a black. 飾, 'for ornament,' i.e. for the edgings of the collar and sleeves. The *kan*, it is said, if the *kan*, it is said, after K'ung Ân-kwo, was worn in fasting, and the *tsâu* in mourning, on which account Confucius would not use them. See

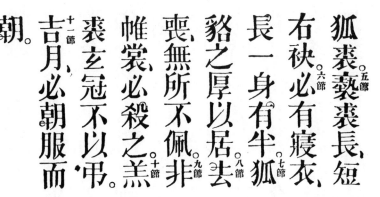

狐裘。〔五節〕褻裘長，短右袂。〔六節〕必有寢衣，長一身有半。狐〔七節〕貉之厚以居。去〔八節〕喪無所不佩。非〔九節〕帷裳必殺之。〔十節〕羔裘玄冠不以弔。〔十一節〕吉月，必朝服而朝。

5. The fur robe of his undress was long, with the right sleeve short.

6. He required his sleeping dress to be half as long again as his body.

7. When staying at home, he used thick furs of the fox or the badger.

8. When he put off mourning, he wore all the appendages of the girdle.

9. His under-garment, except when it was required to be of the curtain shape, was made of silk cut narrow above and wide below.

10. He did not wear lamb's fur or a black cap, on a visit of condolence.

11. On the first day of the month he put on his court robes, and presented himself at court.

this and the account of the colours denied in the 拓餘說, *in loc.* 2. There are five colours which go by the name of 正, 'correct,' viz. 青, 黃, 赤, 白, 黑, 'azure, yellow, carnation, white, and black;' others, among which are 紅 and 紫, go by the name of 間, or 'intermediate.' See the 集證, *in loc.* Confucius would use only the correct colours, and moreover, Chû Hsî adds, red and reddish-blue are liked by women and girls. 褻服, his dress, when in private. 3. 絺 and 綌 were made from the fibres of a creeping plant, the 葛. See the Shih-ching, I. i. Ode II. 必表而出之, 'he must display and have it outwards.' The interpretation of this, as in the translation, after Chû Hsî, though differing from the old commentators, seems to be correct. 4. The lamb's fur belonged to the court dress, the fawn's was worn on embassies, the fox's on occasions of sacrifice, &c. 5. Confucius knew how to blend comfort and convenience. 6. This paragraph, it is supposed, belongs to the next chapter, in which case it is not the usual sleeping garment of Confucius that is spoken of, but the one he used in fasting. 長, 2nd tone, 'over,' 'overplus.' 7. These are the 褻裘 of paragraph 5. 8. The appendages of the girdle were, the handkerchief, a small knife, a spike for opening knots, &c. 去, 3rd tone, 'to put away.' 9. The 裳 was the lower garment, reaching below the knees like a kilt or petticoat. For court and sacrificial dress, it was made curtain-like, as wide at top as at bottom. In that worn on other occasions, Confucius saved the cloth in the way described. So, at least, says K'ung Ân-kwo. 殺, read *shâi*, 4th tone. 10. Lamb's fur was worn with black (par. 4), but white is the colour of mourning in China, and Confucius would not visit mourners, but in a sympathising colour. 11. 吉月, 'the fortunate day of the moon,' i. e. the first of the month. This was Confucius's practice, after he had ceased to be in office.

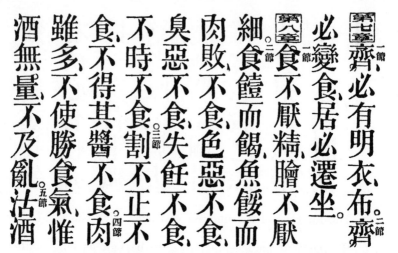

酒無量不及亂沽酒。五節
雖多不使勝食氣惟
食不得其醬不食肉。四節
不時不食割不正不
臭惡不食失飪不食
肉敗不食色惡不食
細食饐而餲魚餒而
第八章 食不厭精膾不厭 一節
必變食居必遷坐。
第七章 齊必有明衣布。齊 二節

CHAP. VII. 1. When fasting, he thought it necessary to have his clothes brightly clean and made of linen cloth.

2. When fasting, he thought it necessary to change his food, and also to change the place where he commonly sat in the apartment.

CHAP. VIII. 1. He did not dislike to have his rice finely cleaned, nor to have his minced meat cut quite small.

2. He did not eat rice which had been injured by heat or damp and turned sour, nor fish or flesh which was gone. He did not eat what was discoloured, or what was of a bad flavour, nor anything which was ill-cooked, or was not in season.

3. He did not eat meat which was not cut properly, nor what was served without its proper sauce.

4. Though there might be a large quantity of meat, he would not allow what he took to exceed the due proportion for the rice. It was only in wine that he laid down no limit for himself, but he did not allow himself to be confused by it.

5. He did not partake of wine and dried meat bought in the market.

7. RULES OBSERVED BY CONFUCIUS WHEN FASTING. 1. 齊, read *châi*, 1st tone; see VII. xii. The 6th paragraph of the last chapter should come in as the 2nd here. 2. The fasting was not from all food, but only from wine or spirits, and from pot herbs. Observe the difference between 變 and 遷, the former 'to change,' the latter 'to change from,' 'to remove.'—The whole chapter may be compared with Matt. vi. 16-18.

8. RULES OF CONFUCIUS ABOUT HIS FOOD. 1. 膾, 'minced meat,' the commentators say, was made of beef, mutton, or fish, *uncooked*. 100 *shing* of paddy were reduced to 30, to bring it to the state of 精 rice. 2. 飪 in the dictionary is 'overdone,' hence 失飪 = 'wrong in being overdone.' Some, however, make the phrase to mean 'badly cooked,' either underdone or overdone. 4. 食 *(tsze)* 氣, 'the breath of the rice,' or perhaps, 'the life-sustaining power of it,' but 氣 can hardly be translated here. 唯 = 惟, 'only,' showing, it is said, that in other things he had a limit, but the use of wine being to make glad, he could not beforehand set a limit to the quantity of it. See, however, the singular note in IX. xv. 6. Literally, 'He did not take away ginger in eating.' 8. The prince, anciently (and it is still a custom), distributed among the assisting ministers the flesh of his sacrifice. Each would only get a little, and so it could be

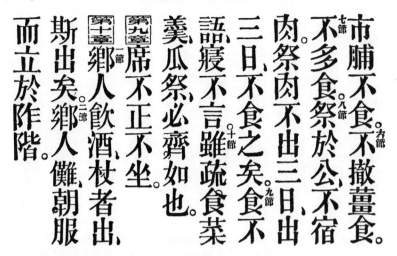

6. He was never without ginger when he ate.

7. He did not eat much.

8. When he had been *assisting* at the prince's sacrifice, he did not keep the flesh *which he received* over night. The flesh of his *family* sacrifice he did not keep over three days. If kept over three days, people could not eat it.

9. When eating, he did not converse. When in bed, he did not speak.

10. Although his food might be coarse rice and vegetable soup, he would offer *a little of it* in sacrifice with a grave respectful air.

CHAP. IX. If his mat was not straight, he did not sit on it.

CHAP. X. 1. When the villagers were drinking together, on those who carried staffs going out, he went out immediately after.

2. When the villagers were going through their ceremonies to drive away pestilential influences, he put on his court robes and stood on the eastern steps.

used at once. 10. 瓜 should be changed into 必, according to Chû Hsî. Ho Yen, however, retains it, and putting a comma after it, joins it with the two preceding specimens of spare diet. The 'sacrificing' refers to a custom something like our saying grace. The master took a few grains of rice, or part of the other provisions, and placed them on the ground, among the sacrificial vessels, a tribute to the worthy or worthies who first taught the art of cooking. The Buddhist priests in their monasteries have a custom of this kind, and on public occasions, as when Ch'î-ying gave an entertainment in Hongkong in 1845, something like it is sometimes observed, but any such ceremony is unknown among the common habits of the people. However poor might be his fare, Confucius always observed it. 齊 (*châi*) = 齋, the grave demeanour appropriate to fasting.

9. RULE OF CONFUCIUS ABOUT HIS MAT.

10. OTHER WAYS OF CONFUCIUS IN HIS VILLAGE. 1. At sixty, people carried a staff. Confucius here showed his respect for age. 斯 has here an adverbial force, = 即. 2. There were three 儺 ceremonies every year, but that in the text was called 'the great *no*,' being observed in the winter season, when the officers led all the people of a village about, searching every house to expel demons, and drive away pestilence. It was conducted with great uproar, and little better than a play, but Confucius saw a good old idea in it, and when the mob was in his house, he stood on the eastern steps (the place of a host receiving guests) in full dress. Some make the steps those of his ancestral temple, and his standing there to be to assure the spirits of his shrine.

CHAP. XI. 1. When he was sending complimentary inquiries to any one in another State, he bowed twice as he escorted the messenger away.

2. Chî K'ang having sent him a present of physic, he bowed and received it, saying, 'I do not know it. I dare not taste it.'

CHAP. XII. The stable being burned down, when he was at court, on his return he said, 'Has any man been hurt?' He did not ask about the horses.

CHAP. XIII. 1. When the prince sent him a gift of *cooked* meat, he would adjust his mat, *first* taste it, *and then give it away to others.* When the prince sent him a gift of undressed meat, he would have it cooked, and offer it *to the spirits of his ancestors.* When the prince sent him a gift of a living animal, he would keep it alive.

2. When he was in attendance on the prince and joining in the entertainment, the prince only sacrificed. He first tasted everything.

11. TRAITS OF CONFUCIUS'S INTERCOURSE WITH OTHERS. 1. The two bows were not to the messenger, but intended for the distant friend to whom he was being sent. 2. 康 was the 季 康子 of II. xx *et al.* Confucius accepted the gift, but thought it necessary to let the donor know he could not, for the present at least, avail himself of it.

12. HOW CONFUCIUS VALUED HUMAN LIFE. A ruler's 廐 was fitted to accommodate 216 horses. See the 集證, *in loc.* It may be used indeed for a private stable, but it is more natural to take it here for the 國 or State *chiû.* This is the view in the 家語.

13. DEMEANOUR OF CONFUCIUS IN RELATION TO HIS PRINCE. 1. He would not offer the cooked meat to the spirits of his ancestors, not knowing but it might previously have been offered by the prince to the spirits of his. But he reverently tasted it, as if he had been in the prince's presence. He 'honoured' the gift of cooked food, 'glorified' the undressed, and 'was kind' to the living animal. 2. The 祭 here is that in chapter viii. 10. Among parties of equal rank, all performed the ceremony, but Confucius, with his prince, held that the prince sacrificed for all. He tasted everything, as if he had been a *cook,* it being the cook's duty to taste every dish, before the prince partook of it. 3. 首, in the 4th tone, 頭向, 'the direction of the head.' The head to the east was the proper position for a person in bed; a sick man might for comfort be lying differently, but Confucius would not see the prince but in the correct position, and also in the court dress, so far as he could accomplish it. 4. He would not wait a moment, but let his carriage follow him.

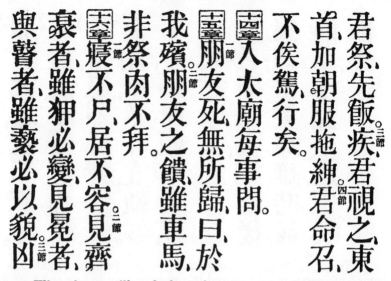

3. When he was ill and the prince came to visit him, he had his head to the east, made his court robes be spread over him, and drew his girdle across them.

4. When the prince's order called him, without waiting for his carriage to be yoked, he went at once.

CHAP. XIV. When he entered the ancestral temple of the State, he asked about everything.

CHAP. XV. 1. When any of his friends died, if he had no relations who could be depended on for the necessary offices, he would say, 'I will bury him.'

2. When a friend sent him a present, though it might be a carriage and horses, he did not bow.

3. The only present for which he bowed was that of the flesh of sacrifice.

CHAP. XVI. 1. In bed, he did not lie like a corpse. At home, he did not put on any formal deportment.

2. When he saw any one in a mourning dress, though it might be an acquaintance, he would change countenance; when he saw any one wearing the cap of full dress, or a blind person, though he might be in his undress, he would salute them in a ceremonious manner.

14. A repetition of III. xv. Compare also chap. ii. These two passages make the explanation, given at III. xv, of the questioning being on his first entrance on office very doubtful.

15. TRAITS OF CONFUCIUS IN THE RELATION OF A FRIEND. 1. 殯, properly, 'the closing up of the coffin,' is here used for all the expenses and services necessary to interment. 2, 3. Between friends there should be a community of goods. 'The flesh of sacrifice,' however, was that which had been offered by his friend to the spirits of his parents or ancestors. That demanded acknowledgment.

16. CONFUCIUS IN BED, AT HOME, HEARING THUNDER, &c. 2. Compare IX. ix, which is here repeated, with heightening circumstances. 3. 式 is the front bar of a cart or carriage. In fact, the carriage of Confucius's time was only

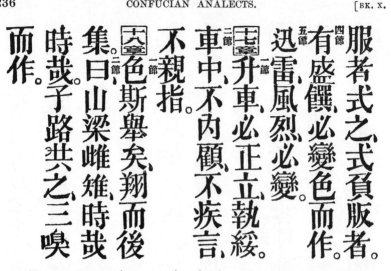

3. To any person in mourning he bowed forward to the cross-bar of his carriage; he bowed in the same way to any one bearing the tables of population.

4. When he was at an entertainment where there was an abundance of provisions set before him, he would change countenance and rise up.

5. On a sudden clap of thunder, or a violent wind, he would change countenance.

CHAP. XVII. 1. When he was about to mount his carriage, he would stand straight, holding the cord.

2. When he was in the carriage, he did not turn his head quite round, he did not talk hastily, he did not point with his hands.

CHAP. XVIII. 1. *Seeing* the countenance, it instantly rises. It flies round, and by and by settles.

2. *The Master* said, 'There is the hen-pheasant on the hill bridge. At its season! At its season!' Tsze-lû made a motion to it. Thrice it smelt him and then rose.

what we call a cart. In saluting, when riding, parties bowed forward to this bar. 4. He showed these signs, with reference to the generosity of the provider.

17. CONFUCIUS AT AND IN HIS CARRIAGE. 1. The 綏 was a strap or cord, attached to the carriage to assist in mounting it. 2. 不內顧, 'He did not look round within,' i. e. turn his head quite round. See the Lî Chî, I. i. Pt. v. 43.

18. A fragment, which seemingly has no connexion with the rest of the Book. Various alterations of characters are proposed, and various views of the meaning given. Ho Yen's view of the conclusion is this:—'Tsze-lû took it and served it up. The Master thrice smelt it and rose.' 共, in 3rd tone, = 向.

BOOK XI. HSIEN TSIN.

宰　冉　德二　蔡　第　之　禮　樂　第　先
我　伯　行節　者　三　則　樂　野　二　進
子　牛　顏　皆　章　吾　君　人　章　第
貢　仲　淵　不　子　從　子　也　子　十
政　弓　閔　及　曰　我　也　後二　曰　一
事　言　子　門　從　於　如節　進　先
冉　語　騫　也　我　陳　用　於　進
　　　　　　　　於　　　　　　　於
　　　　　　　　　　　　　　　禮

CHAPTER I. 1. The Master said, 'The men of former times, in the matters of ceremonies and music, were rustics, *it is said*, while the men of *these* latter times, in ceremonies and music, are accomplished gentlemen.

2. 'If I have occasion to use those things, I follow the men of former times.'

CHAP. II. 1. The Master said, 'Of those who were with me in Ch'ăn and Ts'âi, there are none to be found to enter my door.'

2. Distinguished for their virtuous principles and practice, there were Yen Yûan, Min Tsze-ch'ien, Zan Po-niû, and Chung-kung; for their ability in speech, Tsâi Wo and Tsze-kung; for their adminis-

HEADING OF THIS BOOK.—先進第 十一, 'The former men, No. 11.' With this Book there commences the second part of the Analects, commonly called the *Hsiâ Lun* (下論). There is, however, no important authority for this division. It contains 25 chapters, treating mostly of various disciples of the Master, and deciding the point of their worthiness. Min Tsze-ch'ien appears in it four times, and on this account some attribute the compilation of it to his disciples. There are indications in the style of a peculiar hand.

1. CONFUCIUS'S PREFERENCE OF THE SIMPLER WAYS OF FORMER TIMES. 1. 先進, 後進 are said by Chû Hsî to=先輩, 後輩. Literally, the expressions are,—'those who first advanced,' 'those who afterwards advanced,' i. e. on the stage of the world. In Ho Yen, the chapter is said to speak of the disciples who had first advanced to office, and those who had advanced subsequently,—評

其弟子之中仕進先後之輩. But the 2nd paragraph is decidedly against this interpretation. 進 is not to be joined to the succeeding 於禮樂, but 於 = *quoad*. It is supposed that the characterising the 先進 as rustics, and their successors as *chün-tsze*, was a style of his times, which Confucius quotes ironically. We have in it a new instance of the various application of the name *chün-tsze*. In the 備旨, it is said, 'Of the words and actions of men in their mutual intercourse and in the business of government, whatever indicates *respect* is here included in *ceremonies*, and whatever is expressive of *harmony* is here included in *music*.'

2. CONFUCIUS'S REGRETFUL MEMORY OF HIS DISCIPLES' FIDELITY:—CHARACTERISTICS OF TEN OF THE DISCIPLES. 1. This utterance must have been made towards the close of Confucius's life, when many of his disciples had been removed by death, or separated from him by other causes.

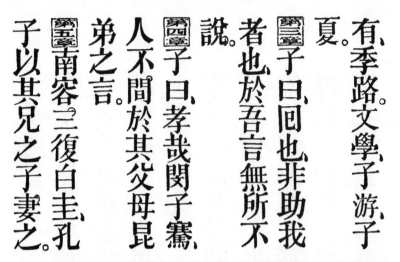

trative talents, Zan Yû and Chî Lû; for their literary acquirements, Tsze-yû and Tsze-hsiâ.

CHAP. III. The Master said, 'Hûi gives me no assistance. There is nothing that I say in which he does not delight.'

CHAP. IV. The Master said, 'Filial indeed is Min Tsze-ch'ien! Other people say nothing of him different from the report of his parents and brothers.'

CHAP. V. Nan Yung was frequently repeating the *lines about a* white sceptre-stone. Confucius gave him the daughter of his elder brother to wife.

In his 62nd year or thereabouts, as the accounts go, he was passing, in his wanderings from Ch'än to Ts'âi, when the officers of Ch'än, afraid that he would go on into Ch'û, endeavoured to stop his course, and for several days he and the disciples with him were cut off from food. Both Ch'än and Ts'âi were in the present province of Ho-nan, and are referred to the departments of 陳州 and 汝寧. 2. This paragraph is to be taken as a note by the compilers of the Book, enumerating the principal followers of Confucius on the occasion referred to, with their distinguishing qualities. They are arranged in four classes (四科), and, amounting to ten, are known as the 十哲. The 'four classes' and 'ten wise ones' are often mentioned in connexion with the sage's school. The ten disciples have all appeared in the previous Books.

3. HÛI'S SILENT RECEPTION OF THE MASTER'S TEACHINGS. A teacher is sometimes *helped* by the doubts and questions of learners, which lead him to explain himself more fully. Compare III. viii. 3. 說 for 悅 as in I. i. 1, but K'ung Ân-kwo takes it in its usual pronunciation=解, 'to explain.'

4. THE FILIAL PIETY OF MIN TSZE-CH'IEN. 閒, as in VIII. xxi, 'could pick out no crevice or flaw in the words, &c.' 陳羣 (about A. D. 200–250), as given in Ho Yen, explains—'Men had no words of disparagement for his conduct in reference to his parents and brothers.' This is the only instance where Confucius calls a disciple by his designation. The use of 子騫 is supposed, in the 合講, to be a mistake of the compilers. 'Brothers' includes cousins, indeed=kindred.

5. CONFUCIUS'S APPROBATION OF NAN YUNG. Nan Yung, see V. i. 三, as in V. xix. I have translated it by 'frequently;' but, in the 'Family Sayings,' it is related that Yung repeated the lines thrice in one day. 白圭, see the Shih-ching, III. iii. Ode II. 5. The lines there are—'A flaw in a white sceptre-stone may be ground away; but for a flaw in speech, nothing can be done.' In his repeating of these lines, we have, perhaps, the ground-virtue of the character for which Yung is commended in V. i. Observe 孔子, where we might expect 子.

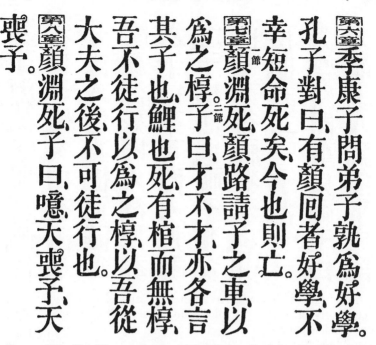

CHAP. VI. Chî K'ang asked which of the disciples loved to learn. Confucius replied to him, 'There was Yen Hûi; he loved to learn. Unfortunately his appointed time was short, and he died. Now there is no one *who loves to learn, as he did.*'

CHAP. VII. 1. When Yen Yüan died, Yen Lû begged the carriage of the Master to *sell* and get an outer shell for his *son's* coffin.

2. The Master said, 'Every one calls his son his son, whether he has talents or has not talents. There was Lî; when he died, he had a coffin but no outer shell. I would not walk on foot to get a shell for him, because, having followed in the rear of the great officers, it was not proper that I should walk on foot.'

CHAP. VIII. When Yen Yüan died, the Master said, 'Alas! Heaven is destroying me! Heaven is destroying me!'

6. How Hûi LOVED TO LEARN. See VI. ii, where the same question is put by the duke Âi, and the same answer is returned, only in a more extended form.

7. How CONFUCIUS WOULD NOT SELL HIS CARRIAGE TO BUY A SHELL FOR YEN YÜAN. 1. There is a chronological difficulty here. Hûi, according to the 'Family Sayings,' and the 'Historical Records,' must have died several years before Confucius's son, Lî. Either the dates in them are incorrect, or this chapter is spurious.—Yen Lû, the father of Hûi, had himself been a disciple of the sage in former years. 爲之槨 (i. q. char. in text),—this is the idiom noticed in V. vii. 3. 爲 would almost seem to be an active verb followed by a double objective. In burying, they used a coffin, called 棺, and an outer shell without a bottom, which was called 槨. 2. 吾從大夫之後, literally, 'I follow in rear of the great officers.' This is said to be an expression of humility. Confucius, retired from office, might still present himself at court, in the robes of his former dignity, and would still be consulted on emergencies. He would no doubt have a foremost place on such occasions.

8. CONFUCIUS FELT HÛI'S DEATH AS IF IT HAD BEEN HIS OWN. The old interpreters make this simply the exclamation of bitter sorrow. The modern, perhaps correctly, make the chief in-

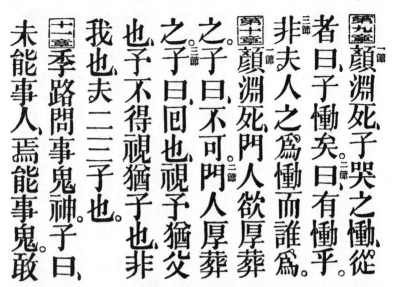

未能事人焉能事鬼敢
季路問事鬼神子曰
我也夫二三子也
之子曰回也視予猶父
也予不得視猶子也非
之子曰不可門人厚葬
顏淵死門人欲厚葬
非夫人之為慟而誰為
者曰子慟矣曰有慟乎
顏淵死子哭之慟從

CHAP. IX. 1. When Yen Yüan died, the Master bewailed him exceedingly, and the disciples who were with him said, 'Master, your grief is excessive?'

2. 'Is it excessive?' said he.

3. 'If I am not to mourn bitterly for this man, for whom should I mourn?'

CHAP. X. 1. When Yen Yüan died, the disciples wished to give him a great funeral, and the Master said, 'You may not do so.'

2. The disciples did bury him in great style.

3. The Master said, 'Hûi behaved towards me as his father. I have not been able to treat him as my son. The fault is not mine; it belongs to you, O disciples.'

CHAP. XI. Chî Lû asked about serving the spirits *of the dead.* The Master said, 'While you are not able to serve men, how can you serve *their spirits?*' *Chî Lû added,* 'I venture to ask about

gredient to be grief that the man was gone to whom he looked most for the transmission of his doctrines.

9. CONFUCIUS VINDICATES HIS GREAT GRIEF FOR THE DEATH OF HÛI. 1. 哭 is the loud wail of grief. Moaning with tears is called 泣.

3. 夫人 = 斯人, 'this man.' The third definition of 夫 in the dictionary is 有所指之辭, 'a term of definite indication.'

10. CONFUCIUS'S DISSATISFACTION WITH THE GRAND WAY IN WHICH HÛI WAS BURIED. 1. The old interpreters take 門人 as being the disciples of Yen Yüan. This is not natural, and yet we can hardly understand how the disciples of Confucius would act so directly contrary to his express wishes. Confucius objected to a grand funeral as inconsistent with the poverty of the family (see chap. vii). 3. 視, literally, '*regarded* me,' but that term would hardly suit the next clause. 夫, as in the last chapter. This passage, indeed, is cited in the dictionary, in illustration of that use of the term. 二三子, see III. xxiv.

11. CONFUCIUS AVOIDS ANSWERING QUESTIONS ABOUT SERVING SPIRITS, AND ABOUT DEATH. 鬼神 are here to be taken together, and understood of the spirits of the dead. This appears from Confucius using only 鬼 in his reply, and from the opposition between 人 and 鬼.

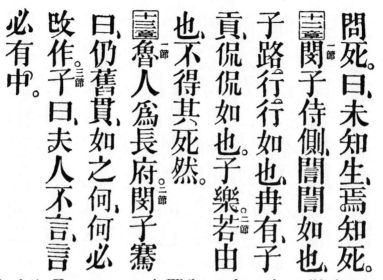

問死。曰、未知生、焉知死。

閔子侍側、誾誾如也、子路行行如也、冉有、子貢侃侃如也。子樂若由也、不得其死然。

魯人爲長府、閔子騫曰、仍舊貫、如之何、何必改作、子曰、夫人不言、言必有中。

death?'　He was answered, 'While you do not know life, how can you know about death?'

Chap. XII.　1. The disciple Min was standing by his side, looking bland and precise; Tsze-lû, looking bold and soldierly; Zan Yû and Tsze-kung, with a free and straightforward manner.　The Master was pleased.

2. (He said), 'Yû there!—he will not die a natural death.'

Chap. XIII.　1. Some parties in Lû were going to take down and rebuild the Long treasury.

2. Min Tsze-chi'en said, 'Suppose it were to be repaired after its old style;—why must it be altered and made anew?'

3. The Master said, 'This man seldom speaks; when he does, he is sure to hit the point.'

人 is man alive, while 鬼 is man dead—a ghost, a spirit.　Two views of the replies are found in commentators.　The older ones say —'Confucius put off Chî Lû, and gave him no answer, because spirits and death are obscure and unprofitable subjects to talk about.'　With this some modern writers agree, as the author of the 翼註; but others, and the majority, say—'Confucius answered the disciple profoundly, and showed him how he should prosecute his inquiries in the proper order.　The service of the dead must be in the same spirit as the service of the living.　Obedience and sacrifice are equally the expression of the filial heart.　Death is only the natural termination of life.　We are born with certain gifts and principles, which carry us on to the end of our course.'　This is ingenious refining, but, after all, Confucius avoids answering the important questions proposed to him.

12. Confucius happy with his disciples about him.　He warns Tsze-lû.　1. 閔子, like 冉子, VI. iii. 1.　行, read hang, 4th tone.

2. There being wanting here 子曰 at the commencement, some, unwisely, would change the 樂 at the end of the first paragraph into 曰, to supply the blank.　若由也,—若 is used with reference to the appearance and manner of Tsze-lû.　然, in the 註疏, is taken as = the final 焉.　Some say that it indicates some uncertainty as to the prediction.　But it was verified;—see on II. xvii.

13. Wise advice of Min Sun against useless expenditure.　1. 魯人, not 'the people of Lû,' but as in the translation—certain officers, disapprobation of whom is indicated by simply calling them 人.　The full meaning of 爲 is collected from the rest of the chapter.

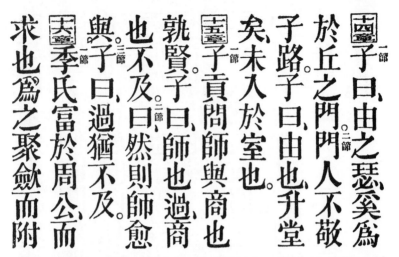

CHAP. XIV. 1. The Master said, 'What has the lute of Yû to do in my door?'

2. The other disciples *began* not to respect Tsze-lû. The Master said, 'Yû has ascended to the hall, though he has not yet passed into the inner apartments.'

CHAP. XV. 1. Tsze-kung asked which of the two, Shih or Shang, was the superior. The Master said, 'Shih goes beyond *the due mean*, and Shang does not come up to it.'

2. 'Then,' said Tsze-kung, 'the superiority is with Shih, I suppose.'

3. The Master said, 'To go beyond is as wrong as to fall short.'

CHAP. XVI. 1. The head of the Chî family was richer than the duke of Châu had been, and yet Ch'iû collected his imposts for him, and increased his wealth.

府 is 'a treasury,' as distinguished from 倉, 'a granary,' and from 庫, 'an arsenal.' 'The Long Treasury' was the name of the one in question. We read of it in the Tso Chwan under the 25th year of duke Châo (par. 5), as being then the duke's residence. 2. The use of 貫 is perplexing. Chû Hsî adopts the explanation of it by the old commentators as = 事, 'affair,' but with what propriety I do not see. The character means 'a string of cowries, or cash,' then 'to thread together,' 'to connect.' May not its force be here,—'suppose it were to be carried on—continued—as before?' 3. 夫 as in chapter ix. 中, 4th tone, a verb, 'to hit the mark,' as in shooting.

14. CONFUCIUS'S ADMONITION AND DEFENCE OF TSZE-LÛ. 1. The form of the harpsichord or lute seems to come nearer to that of the *shih* than any other of our instruments. The 瑟 is a kindred instrument with the 琴, commonly called 'the scholar's lute.' See the Chinese Repository, vol. viii. p. 38. The music made by Yû was more martial in its air than befitted the peace-inculcating school of the sage. 2. This contains a defence of Yû, and an illustration of his real attainments.

15. COMPARISON OF SHIH AND SHANG. EXCESS AND DEFECT EQUALLY WRONG. Shang was the name of Tsze-hsiâ, I. vii, and Shih, that of Twansun, styled Tsze-chang. 1. 賢, here = 勝, 'to overcome,' 'be superior to,' being interchanged with 愈 in par. 2. We find this meaning of the term also in the dictionary.

16. CONFUCIUS'S INDIGNATION AT THE SUPPORT OF USURPATION AND EXTORTION BY ONE OF HIS DISCIPLES. 1. 季氏, see III. 1. Many illustrations might be collected of the encroachments of the Chî family and its great wealth. 爲之 聚歛 'for him collected and ingathered,' i. e. all his imposts. This clause and the next imply that Ch'iû was aiding in the matter of laying imposts on the people. 2. 'Beat the

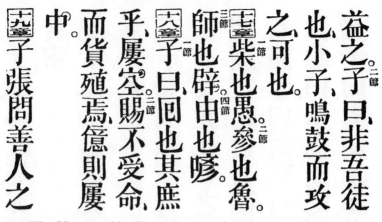

2. The Master said, 'He is no disciple of mine. My little children, beat the drum and assail him.'

CHAP. XVII. 1. Ch'âi is simple.

2. Shăn is dull.

3. Shih is specious.

4. Yû is coarse.

CHAP. XVIII. 1. The Master said, 'There is Hûi! He has nearly attained *to perfect virtue.* He is often in want.'

2. 'Ts'ze does not acquiesce in the appointments *of Heaven,* and his goods are increased by him. Yet his judgments are often correct.'

CHAP. XIX. Tsze-chang asked what were the characteristics of

drum and assail him,'—this refers to the practice of executing criminals in the market-place, and by beat of drum collecting the people to hear their crimes. We must, however, say that the Master only required the disciples here to tell Ch'iû of his faults and recover him.

17. CHARACTERS OF THE FOUR DISCIPLES— CH'ÂI, SHĂN, SHIH, AND YÛ. It is supposed that 子曰 is missing from the beginning of this chapter. Admitting this, the sentences are to be translated in the present tense, and not in the past, which would be required if the chapter were simply the record of the compilers. 1. Ch'âi, by surname 高, and styled 子羔 (of 羔 there are several *aliases*), has his tablet now the 5th west, in the outer court of the temples. He was small and ugly, but distinguished for his sincerity, filial piety, and justice. Such was the conviction of his impartial justice, that in a time of peril he was saved by a man, whom he had formerly punished with cutting off his feet. All the other names have already occurred and been explained. 3. 辟, read *p'i,* is defined in the dictionary,—'practising airs with little sincerity.'—Confucius certainly does not here flatter his followers.

18. HÛI AND TS'ZE CONTRASTED. In Ho Yen's compilation, this chapter is joined with the

preceding as one. 1. 庶, here = 近, 'nearly,' 'near to.' It is often found with 乎 following, both terms together being = our 'nearly.' To make out a meaning, the old commentators supply 聖道, 'the way or doctrines of the sages,' and the modern supply 道, 'the truth and right.' 空, 4th tone, 'emptied,' i. e. brought to extremity, poor, distressed. Hûi's being brought often to this state is mentioned merely as an additional circumstance about him, intended to show that he was happy in his deep poverty. Ho Yen preserves the comment of some one, which is worth giving here, and according to which, 空 = 虚中, 'empty-hearted,' free from all vanities and ambitions. Then 屢 = 每, 'always.' In this sense 屢空 was the formative element of Hûi's character. 2. 受, 'to receive,' here = 'to acquiesce in.' 億 = 度, 'to form a judgment.' Ts'ze, of course, is Tsze-kung.

19. THE GOOD MAN. Compare VII. xxv. By 善人 Chû Hsî understands—質美而 未學者, 'one of fine natural capacity, but

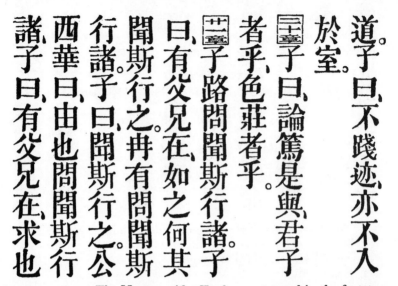

諸子曰、有父兄在、求也

西華曰、由也問聞斯行

行諸子曰聞斯行之公

聞斯行之冉有問聞斯

曰、有父兄在、如之何其

〇二十一章子路問聞斯行諸子

者乎色莊者乎。

〇二十章子曰、論篤是與君子

於室。

道子曰不踐迹亦不入

the GOOD man. The Master said, 'He does not tread in the footsteps of others, but, moreover, he does not enter the chamber *of the sage.*'

CHAP. XX. The Master said, 'If, because a man's discourse appears solid and sincere, we allow him *to be a good man,* is he *really* a superior man? or is his gravity only in appearance?'

CHAP. XXI. Tsze-lû asked whether he should immediately carry into practice what he heard. The Master said, 'There are your father and elder brothers *to be consulted;*—why should you act on that principle of immediately carrying into practice what you hear?' Zan Yû asked the same, whether he should immediately carry into practice what he heard, and the Master answered, 'Immediately carry into practice what you hear.' Kung-hsî Hwâ said, 'Yû asked whether he should carry immediately into practice what he heard, and you said, "There are your father and elder brothers *to be consulted.*" Ch'iû asked whether he should immediately carry into practice what he heard, and you said, "Carry it immediately into practice." I, Ch'ih, am perplexed, and venture to ask you for an explanation.' The Master said, 'Ch'iû is retiring and slow; therefore,

who has not learned.' Such a man will in many things be a law to himself, and needs not to follow in the wake of others, but after all his progress will be limited. The text is rather enigmatical. 入室, compare chap. xiv. 2. Tsze-chang was the Shih of chap. xv.

20. WE MAY NOT HASTILY JUDGE A MAN TO BE GOOD FROM HIS DISCOURSE. 論 is here 'speech,' 'conversation.' In Ho Yen this chapter is joined to the preceding one, and is said to give additional characteristics of 'the good man,' mentioned on a different occasion.—The construction, however, on that view is all but inextricable.

21. AN INSTANCE IN TSZE-LÛ AND ZAN YÛ OF HOW CONFUCIUS DEALT WITH HIS DISCIPLES ACCORDING TO THEIR CHARACTERS. On Tsze-lû's question, compare V. 13. 聞斯行諸, 'Hearing *this* (=anything), should I do it *at once* or not?' 行諸=行之乎, like 舍諸, in VI. iv. 兼人,—兼 is explained by Chû Hsî with 勝, 'to overcome,' 'to be superior to.' But we can well take it in its radical signification of 'to unite,' as a hand grasps two sheaves of corn. The phrase is equivalent to our English one in the transla-

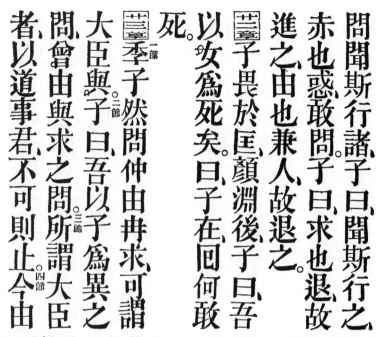

I urged him forward. Yû has more than his own share of energy; therefore, I kept him back.'

CHAP. XXII. The Master was put in fear in K'wang and Yen Yüan fell behind. The Master, *on his rejoining him,* said, 'I thought you had died.' *Hûi* replied, 'While you were alive, how should I presume to die?'

CHAP. XXIII. 1. Chî Tsze-zan asked whether Chung Yû and Zan Ch'iû could be called great ministers.

2. The Master said, 'I thought you would ask about some extraordinary individuals, and you only ask about Yû and Ch'iû!

3. 'What is called a great minister, is one who serves his prince according to what is right, and when he finds he cannot do so, retires.

tion. Similarly, the best pure gold is called 兼金.

22. YEN YÜAN'S ATTACHMENT TO CONFUCIUS, AND CONFIDENCE IN HIS MISSION. See IX. v. If Hûi's answer was anything more than pleasantry, we must pronounce it foolish. The commentators, however, expand it thus:—'I knew that you would not perish in this danger, and therefore I would not rashly expose my own life, but preserved it rather, that I might continue to enjoy the benefit of your instructions.' If we inquire how Hûi knew that Confucius would not perish, we are informed that he shared his master's assurance that he had a divine mission.—See VII. xxii, IX. v.

23. A GREAT MINISTER. CHUNG-YÛ AND ZAN CH'IÛ ONLY ORDINARY MINISTERS. The paraphrasts sum up the contents thus:—'Confucius represses the boasting of Chî Tsze-zan, and indicates an acquaintance with his traitorous purposes.' 1. Chî Tsze-zan was a younger brother of Chî Hwan, who was the 季氏 of III. i. Having an ambitious purpose on the rulership of Lû, he was increasing his officers, and having got the two disciples to enter his service, he boastingly speaks to Confucius about them. 2. 吾以云云, literally, 'I supposed you were making a question of (=about) extraordinary *men*, and lo! it is a question about Yû and Ch'iû.' 曾=乃; its force is rather different from what it has in II. viii, but is much akin to that in III. vi. 4. 具臣 is explained 備臣數而已, 'simply

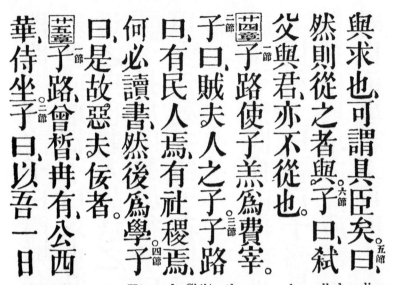

4. 'Now, as to Yû and Ch'iû, they may be called ordinary ministers.'

5. Tsze-zan said, 'Then they will always follow their chief;— will they?'

6. The Master said, 'In an act of parricide or regicide, they would not follow him.'

CHAP. XXIV. 1. Tsze-lû got Tsze-kâo appointed governor of Pî.

2. The Master said, 'You are injuring a man's son.'

3. Tsze-lû said, 'There are (there) common people and officers; there are the altars of the spirits of the land and grain. Why must one read books before he can be considered to have learned?'

4. The Master said, 'It is on this account that I hate your glib-tongued people.'

CHAP. XXV. 1. Tsze-lû, Tsǎng Hsî, Zan Yû, and Kung-hsî Hwâ were sitting by *the Master*.

2. He said to them, 'Though I am a day or so older than you, do not think of that.

fitted to rank among the number of officers.' 具 often means what is merely 'official.' 具文, 'an official paper.' 具臣, 'mere officials.' 5. 之 supposes an antecedent, such as 主, 'their master.'

24. HOW PRELIMINARY STUDY IS NECESSARY TO THE EXERCISE OF GOVERNMENT:—A REPROOF OF TSZE-LÛ. 1. 費,—see VI. vii. Tsze-lû had entered into the service of the Chî family (see last chapter), and recommended (使) Tsze-kâo (see chap. xvii) as likely to keep the turbulent Pî in order, thereby withdrawing him from his studies. 2. 賊, in the sense of 害, 'to injure.' 夫 as in chap. ix. 3. It qualifies the whole phrase 人之子, and not only the Zǎn. By denominating Tsze-kâo—'a man's son,' Confucius intimates, I suppose, that the father was injured as well. His son ought not to be so dealt with. 3. The absurd defence of Tsze-lû. It is to this effect:—'The whole duty of man is in treating other men right, and rendering what is due to spiritual beings, and it may be learned practically without the study you require.' 4. 是故, 'on this account,' with reference to Tsze-lû's reply.

25. THE AIMS OF TSZE-LÛ, TSǍNG HSÎ, ZAN YÛ,

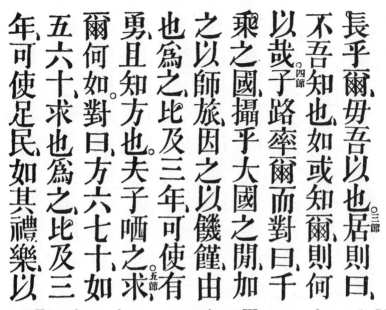

長乎爾毋吾以也居則曰、○三節
不吾知也如或知爾則何
以哉○四節子路率爾而對曰千
乘之國攝乎大國之閒加
之以師旅因之以饑饉由
也爲之比及三年可使有
勇且知方也。夫子哂之。○五節
爾何如。對曰方六七十、如
五六十求也爲之比及三
年可使足民如其禮樂以

3. 'From day to day you are saying, "We are not known." If some *ruler* were to know you, what would you like to do?'

4. Tsze-lû hastily and lightly replied, 'Suppose the case of a State of ten thousand chariots; let it be straitened between *other* large States; let it be suffering from invading armies; and to this let there be added a famine in corn and in all vegetables:—if I were intrusted with the government of it, in three years' time I could make the people to be bold, and to recognise the rules of righteous conduct.' The Master smiled at him.

5. *Turning to Yen Yû, he said*, 'Ch'iû, what are your wishes?' Ch'iû replied, 'Suppose a State of sixty or seventy *li* square, or one of fifty or sixty, and let me have the government of it;—in three years' time, I could make plenty to abound among the people. As to *teaching them* the principles of propriety, and music, I must wait for the rise of a superior man *to do that*.'

AND KUNG-HSÎ HWÂ, AND CONFUCIUS'S REMARKS ABOUT THEM. Compare V. vii and xxv. 1. The disciples mentioned here are all familiar to us excepting Tsäng Hsî. He was the father of Tsäng Shän, and himself by name Tien (點). The four are mentioned in the order of their age, and Tien would have answered immediately after Tsze-lû, but that Confucius passed him by, as he was occupied with his harpsichord. 2. 長, 3rd tone, 'senior.' Many understand 爾 輩, 'ye,' as nominative to the first 以, but it is better to take 以 = 雖, 'although.' 一日, 'one day,' would seem to indicate the importance which the disciples attached to the seniority of their Master, and his wish that they should attach no importance to it. In 勿吾以也 we have a not uncommon inversion;—'do not consider me to be your senior.' 3. 居 = 平居之時, 'the level, ordinary course of your lives.' 何以哉 = 何以爲用哉, 'what would you consider to be your use?' i. e. what course of action would you pursue? 4. 率爾, an adverb, = 'hastily.' 攝, according to Chû Hsî, = 管束; according to Pâo Hsien, = 迫, 'straitened,' 'urged.' In the

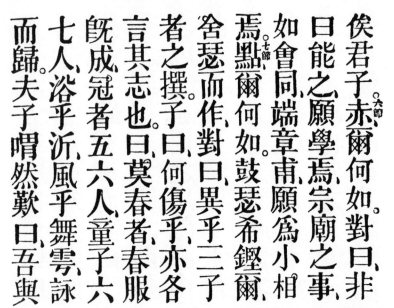

6. 'What are your wishes, Ch'ih,' *said the Master next to Kung-hsî Hwâ.* Ch'ih replied, 'I do not say that my ability extends to these things, but I should wish to learn them. At the services of the ancestral temple, and at the audiences of the princes with the sovereign, I should like, dressed in the dark square-made robe and the black linen cap, to act as a small assistant.'

7. *Last of all, the Master asked Tsǎng Hsî,* 'Tien, what are your wishes?' *Tien,* pausing as he was playing on his lute, while it was yet twanging, laid the instrument aside, and rose. 'My wishes,' he said, 'are different from the cherished purposes of these three gentlemen.' 'What harm is there in that?' said the Master; 'do you also, as well as they, speak out your wishes.' *Tien* then said, 'In *this,* the last month of spring, with the dress of the season all complete, along with five or six young men who have assumed the cap, and six or seven boys, I would wash in the Î, enjoy the breeze among the rain altars, and return home singing.' The Master heaved a sigh and said, 'I give my approval to Tien.'

Châu Lî, 500 men make a 旅, and 5 旅, or 2,500 men, make a 師. The two terms together have here the meaning given in the translation. 為之, 'managed it.' 比, 3rd tone, blends its force with the following 及. 方＝向, 'towards.' 知方, 'know the quarter to which to turn, the way in which to go.' 5. At the beginning of this paragraph and the two following, we must supply 子曰. 如＝或, 'or.' 6. 能之,—之 refers to the 禮樂,

in par. 5. 會 is the name for occasional or incidental interviews of the princes with the sovereign, what are called 時見. 同 belongs to occasions when they all presented themselves together at court. The 端 (and from its colour called 玄端) was a robe of ceremony, so called from its *straight* make, its component parts having no gathers nor slanting cuttings. 章甫 was the name of a cap of ceremony. It had different names under different dynasties. 甫 means a MAN. The cap

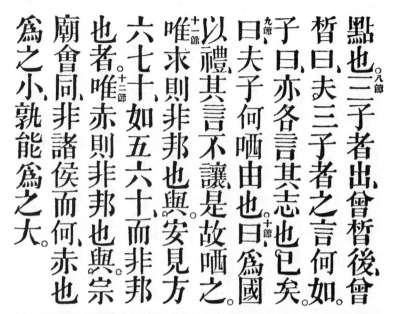

8. The three others having gone out, Tsăng Hsî remained behind, and said, 'What do you think of the words of these three friends?' The Master replied, 'They simply told each one his wishes.'

9. *Hsî* pursued, 'Master, why did you smile at Yû?'

10. He was answered, 'The management of a State demands the rules of propriety. His words were not humble; therefore I smiled at him.'

11. *Hsî again said,* 'But was it not a State which Ch'iû proposed for himself?' *The reply was,* '*Yes;* did you ever see a territory of sixty or seventy *lî*, or one of fifty or sixty, which was not a State?'

12. *Once more, Hsî inquired,* 'And was it not a State which Ch'ih proposed for himself?' *The Master again replied,* '*Yes;* who but princes have to do with ancestral temples, and with audiences but the sovereign? If Ch'ih were to be a small *assistant* in these *services,* who could be a great one?'

---

was so named, as 'displaying the MAN.' 7. 希 = 止, 'pausing,' 'stopping.' 鏗, an adverb, expressing the twanging sound of the instrument. 莫, read *mû*, 4th tone, the same as 暮, 'sunset,' 'the close of a period of time.' 冠 (4th tone) 者, 'capped men.' Capping was in China a custom similar to the assuming the *toga virilis* among the Romans. It took place at 20. 浴 is not 'to bathe,' but is used with reference to a custom of washing the hands and clothes at some stream in the 3rd month, to put away evil influences. 雩 was the name of the

summer sacrifice for rain (Lî Chî, IV. ii. Pt. ii. 8). Dancing movements were employed at it, hence the name—舞雩. 11. 曾皙曰 is to be supplied before 唯, and 子曰 before 安. Similar supplements must be made in the next paragraph.—It does not appear whether Hsî, even at the last, understood why Confucius had laughed at Tsze-lû, and not at the others. 'It was not,' say the commentators, 'because Tsze-lû was extravagant in his aims. They were all thinking of great things, yet not greater than they were able for. Tsze-lû's fault was his levity. That was his offence against *propriety.*'

BOOK XII.　YEN YÜAN.

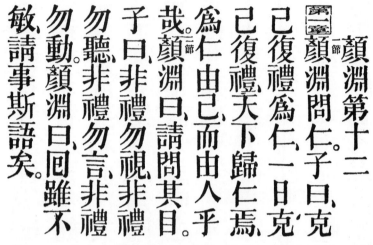

CHAPTER I. 1. Yen Yüan asked about perfect virtue. The Master said, 'To subdue one's self and return to propriety, is perfect virtue. If a man can for one day subdue himself and return to propriety, all under heaven will ascribe perfect virtue to him. Is the practice of perfect virtue from a man himself, or is it from others?'

2. Yen Yüan said, 'I beg to ask the steps of that process.' The Master replied, 'Look not at what is contrary to propriety; listen not to what is contrary to propriety; speak not what is contrary to propriety; make no movement which is contrary to propriety.' Yen Yüan *then* said, 'Though I am deficient in intelligence and vigour, I will make it my business to practise this lesson.'

HEADING OF THIS BOOK.—顏淵第十二, 'The twelfth Book, beginning with "Yen Yüan."' It contains 24 chapters, conveying lessons on perfect virtue, government, and other questions of morality and policy, addressed in conversation by Confucius chiefly to his disciples. The different answers, given about the same subject to different questioners, show well how the sage suited his instructions to the characters and capacities of the parties with whom he had to do.

1. HOW TO ATTAIN TO PERFECT VIRTUE:—A CONVERSATION WITH YEN YÜAN. 1. In Ho Yen, 克己 is explained by 約身, 'to restrain the body.' Chû Hsî defines 克 by 勝, 'to overcome,' and 己 by 身之私欲, 'the selfish desires of the body.' In the 合講, it is said—己非即是私, 但私即附 身而存, 故謂私爲己, '己 here is not exactly selfishness, but selfishness is what abides by being attached to the body, and hence it is said that selfishness is 己.' And again, 克己非克去其己, 乃克 去己中之私欲也, '克己 is not subduing and putting away the *self*, but subduing and putting away the selfish desires *in the self*.' This 'selfishness in the self' is of a threefold character:—first, 氣稟, said by Morrison to be 'a person's natural constitution and disposition of mind:' it is, I think, very much the ψυχικὸς ἄνθρωπος or 'animal man;' second, 耳, 目, 口, 鼻之欲, 'the desires of the ears, the eyes, the mouth, the nose;' i. e. the dominating influences of the senses; and third, 爾我, 'Thou and I,' i. e. the lust of superiority. More concisely, the 己 is said, in the

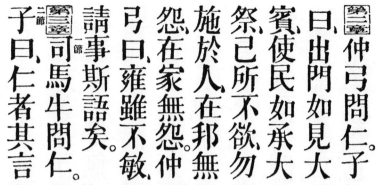

CHAP. II. Chung-kung asked about perfect virtue. The Master said, 'It is, when you go abroad, to behave to every one as if you were receiving a great guest; to employ the people as if you were assisting at a great sacrifice; not to do to others as you would not wish done to yourself; to have no murmuring against you in the country, and none in the family.' Chung-kung said, 'Though I am deficient in intelligence and vigour, I will make it my business to practise this lesson.'

CHAP. III. 1. Sze-mâ Niû asked about perfect virtue.

2. The Master said, 'The man of perfect virtue is cautious and slow in his speech.'

翼註, to be the 人心 as opposed to the 道心, 'the mind of man' in opposition to 'the mind of reason;'—see the Shû-ching, II. ii. 15. This refractory 'mind of man,' it is said, 與生俱生, 'is innate,' or, perhaps, 'connate.' In all these statements there is an acknowledgment of the fact—the morally abnormal condition of human nature—which underlies the Christian doctrine of original sin. With reference to the above threefold classification of selfish desires, the second paragraph shows that it was the second order of them—the influence of the senses—which Confucius specially intended. 復禮,—see note on 禮 VIII. ii. It is not here ceremonies. Chû Hsî defines it—天理之節文, 'the specific divisions and graces of heavenly principle or reason.' This is continually being departed from, on the impulse of selfishness, but there is an ideal of it as proper to man, which is to be sought—'returned to'—by overcoming that. 歸 is explained by Chû Hsî by 與, 'to allow.' The gloss of the 備旨 is—稱其仁, 'will praise his perfect virtue.' Perhaps 天下 is only = our 'everybody,' or 'anybody.' Some editors take kwei in the sense of 'to return,'—'the empire will return to perfect virtue;'—supposing the exemplifier to be a prince.' In the next sentence, which is designed to teach

that every man may attain to this virtue for himself, 而 is equivalent to our 'or,' and implies a strong denial of what is asked. 2. 其 refers to 克己復禮. 目 = 條件, 'a list of particulars.' 事 is used as an active verb;—'I beg to make my business these words.'

2. WHEREIN PERFECT VIRTUE IS REALIZED :—A CONVERSATION WITH CHUNG-KUNG. Chung-kung, see VI. i. From this chapter it appears that reverence (敬) and reciprocity (恕), on the largest scale, constitute perfect virtue. 使民,—'ordering the people,' is apt to be done with haughtiness. This part of the answer may be compared with the apostle's precept—'Honour all men,' only the 'all men' is much more comprehensive there. 己所云云, —compare V. xi. 在邦, 在家, = 'abroad,' 'at home.' Pâo Hsien, in Ho Yen, however, takes the former as denoting 'the prince of a State,' and the latter, 'the chief of a great officer's establishment.' This is like the interpretation of 歸 in last chapter.—The answer, the same as that of Hûi in last chapter, seems to betray the hand of the compiler.

3. CAUTION IN SPEAKING A CHARACTERISTIC OF PERFECT VIRTUE :—A CONVERSATION WITH TSZE-NIÛ. 1. Tsze-niû was the designation of Sze-mâ Käng, alias Lî Käng (犂耕), whose

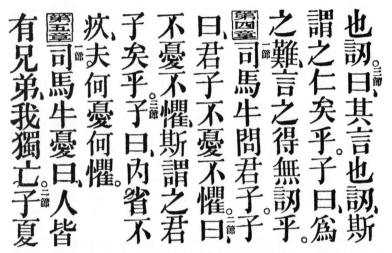

3. 'Cautious and slow in his speech!' said Niû;—'is this what is meant by perfect virtue?' The Master said, 'When a man feels the difficulty of doing, can he be other than cautious and slow in speaking?'

CHAP. IV. 1. Sze-mâ Niû asked about the superior man. The Master said, 'The superior man has neither anxiety nor fear.'

2. 'Being without anxiety or fear!' said Niû;—'does this constitute what we call the superior man?'

3. The Master said, 'When internal examination discovers nothing wrong, what is there to be anxious about, what is there to fear?'

CHAP. V. 1. Sze-mâ Niû, full of anxiety, said, '*Other* men all have their brothers, I only have not.'

2. Tsze-hsiâ said to him, 'There is the following saying which I have heard:—

tablet is now the 7th east in the outer ranges of the disciples. He belonged to Sung, and was a brother of Hwan T'ûi, VII. xxii. Their ordinary surname was Hsiang (向), but that of Hwan could also be used by them, as they were descended from the duke so called. The office of 'Master of the horse' (司馬) had long been in the family, and that title appears here as if it were Niû's surname. 2. 訒 = 言難出, 'the words coming forth with difficulty.' 3. 爲之, 言之,—comp. on 之 in the note on VII. x, *et al.*—'Doing being difficult, can speaking be without difficulty of utterance.'

4. HOW THE CHÜN-TSZE HAS NEITHER ANXIETY NOR FEAR, AND CONSCIOUS RECTITUDE FREES FROM THESE. 1. 憂 is our 'anxiety,' trouble about coming troubles; 懼 is 'fear,' when the troubles have arrived. 2. 疚 is 'a chronic

illness;' here it is understood with reference to the mind, *that* displaying no symptom of disease.

5. CONSOLATION OFFERED BY TSZE-HSIÂ TO TSZE-NIÛ, ANXIOUS ABOUT THE WAYS OF HIS BROTHER. 1. Tsze-niû's anxiety was occasioned by the conduct of his eldest brother Hwan T'ûi, who, he knew, was contemplating rebellion, which would probably lead to his death. 兄弟 'elder brothers' and 'younger brothers,' but Tsze-niû was himself the youngest of his family. The phrase simply = 'brothers.' 'All have their brothers,'—i.e. all can rest quietly without anxiety in their relation. 2. It is naturally supposed that the author of the observation was Confucius. Tsze-hsiâ, see I. vii. 4. The 翼 註 says that the expression, 'all within the four seas are brothers,' 不是通天譜 'does not mean that all under heaven have the same genealogical register.' Chû Hsî's interpretation is that, when a man so acts, other

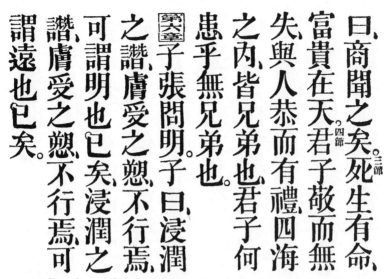

曰、商聞之矣。死生有命、

富貴在天。君子敬而無

失與人恭而有禮四海

之內、皆兄弟也君子何

患乎無兄弟也。

子張問明子曰、浸潤

之譖、膚受之愬不行焉、

可謂明也已矣浸潤之

譖、膚受之愬不行焉可

謂遠也已矣。

3. '"Death and life have their determined appointment; riches
and honours depend upon Heaven."

4. 'Let the superior man never fail reverentially to order his
own conduct, and let him be respectful to others and observant of
propriety:—then all within the four seas will be his brothers. What
has the superior man to do with being distressed because he has no
brothers?'

CHAP. VI. Tsze-chang asked what constituted intelligence. The
Master said, 'He with whom neither slander that gradually soaks
into the mind, nor statements that startle like a wound in the flesh,
are successful, may be called intelligent indeed. Yea, he with whom
neither soaking slander, nor startling statements, are successful, may
be called far-seeing.'

men will love and respect him as a brother.
This, no doubt, is the extent of the saying. I
have found no satisfactory gloss on the phrase
—'the four seas.' It is found in the Shû-ching,
the Shih-ching, and the Lî Chî. In the 爾雅
a sort of Lexicon, very ancient, which was once
reckoned among the *Ching*, it is explained as a
territorial designation, the name of the dwelling-place of all the barbarous tribes. But the
great Yü is represented as having made the
four seas as four ditches, to which he drained
the waters inundating 'the Middle Kingdom.'
Plainly, the ancient conception was of their
own country as the great habitable tract, north,
south, east, and west of which were four seas
or oceans, between whose shores and their own
borders the intervening space was not very
great, and occupied by wild hordes of inferior
races. See the 四書釋地續, II. xxiv.
—Commentators consider Tsze-hsiâ's attempt
at consolation altogether wide of the mark.

6. WHAT CONSTITUTES INTELLIGENCE:—AD-

DRESSED TO TSZE-CHANG. Tsze-chang (II. xvii),
it is said, was always seeking to be wise about
things lofty and distant, and therefore Confucius brings him back to things near at hand,
which it was more necessary for him to attend
to. 浸潤之譖, 'soaking, moistening,
slander,' which unperceived sinks into the
mind. 膚受之愬 (= and interchanged
with 訴), 'statements of wrongs which startle
like a wound in the flesh,' to which in the surprise credence is given. He with whom these
things 不行,—are 'no go,' is intelligent,—
yea, far-seeing. 遠=明之至. So Chû
Hsî. The old interpreters differ in their view
of 膚受之愬. The 註疏 says—'The
skin receives dust which gradually accumulates.' This makes the phrase synonymous
with the former.

而己矣何以文爲子

棘子成曰君子質

民無信不立。

曰去食自古皆有死、

而去於斯二者何先。

兵子貢曰必不得己

於斯三者何先。

貢曰必不得己而去

食足兵民信之矣子

子貢問政子曰足

CHAP. VII. 1. Tsze-kung asked about government. The Master said, '*The requisites of government are* that there be sufficiency of food, sufficiency of military equipment, and the confidence of the people in their ruler.'

2. Tsze-kung said, 'If it cannot be helped, and one of these must be dispensed with, which of the three should be foregone first?' 'The military equipment,' said the Master.

3. Tsze-kung *again* asked, 'If it cannot be helped, and one of the remaining two must be dispensed with, which of them should be foregone?' The Master answered, 'Part with the food. From of old, death has been the lot of all men; but if the people have no faith *in their rulers*, there is no standing *for the State*.'

CHAP. VIII. 1. Chî Tsze-ch'ǎng said, 'In a superior man it is only the substantial qualities which are wanted;—why should we seek for ornamental accomplishments?'

7. REQUISITES IN GOVERNMENT:—A CONVERSATION WITH TSZE-KUNG. 1. 兵 primarily means 'weapons.' 'A soldier,' the bearer of such weapons, is a secondary meaning. There were no standing armies in Confucius's time. The term is to be taken here, as ='military equipment,' 'preparation for war.' 信之,-之 refers to 其上, 'their ruler.' 3. The difficulty here is with the concluding clause—無 信不立. Transferring the meaning of 信 from paragraph 1, we naturally render as in the translation, and 不立=國不立, 'the State will not stand.' This is the view, moreover, of the old interpreters. Chû Hsî and his followers, however, seek to make much more of 信. On the 1st paragraph he comments, —'The granaries being full, and the military preparation complete, then let the influence of instruction proceed. So shall the people have faith in their ruler, and will not leave him or rebel.' On the 3rd paragraph he says,—'If the people be without food, they must die, but death is the inevitable lot of men. If they are without 信, though they live, they have not wherewith to establish themselves. It is better for them in such case to die. Therefore it is better for the ruler to die, not losing faith to his people, so that the people will prefer death rather than lose faith to him.'

8. SUBSTANTIAL QUALITIES AND ACCOMPLISHMENTS IN THE CHÜN-TSZE. 1. Tsze-ch'ǎng was an officer of the State of Wei, and, distressed by the pursuit in the times of what was merely external, made this not sufficiently well-considered remark, to which Tsze-kung replied, in, according to Chû Hsî, an equally one-sided manner. 1. 何以文爲 is thus expanded in the 註疏—何用文章乃爲君 子, 'why use accomplishments in order to make a *Chün-tsze?*' 2. We may interpret this

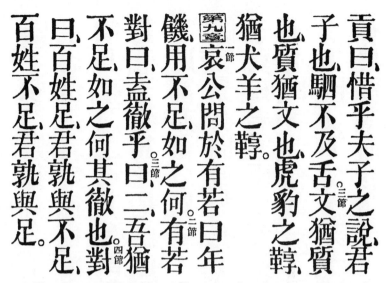

2. Tsze-kung said, 'Alas! Your words, sir, show you to be a superior man, but four horses cannot overtake the tongue.

3. 'Ornament is as substance; substance is as ornament. The hide of a tiger or leopard stripped of its hair, is like the hide of a dog or goat stripped of its hair.'

CHAP. IX. 1. The duke Âi inquired of Yû Zo, saying, 'The year is one of scarcity, and *the returns for* expenditure are not sufficient;—what is to be done?'

2. Yû Zo replied to him, 'Why not *simply* tithe the people?'

3. 'With two-tenths,' said the duke, 'I find them not enough;—how could I do with that system of one-tenth?'

4. Yû Zo answered, 'If the people have plenty, their prince will not be left to want alone. If the people are in want, their prince cannot enjoy plenty alone.'

paragraph, as in the translation, putting a comma after 說. So, Chû Hsî. But the old interpreters seem to have read right on, without any comma, to 也, in which case the paragraph would be—'Alas! sir, for the way in which you speak of the superior man!' And this is the most natural construction. 3. The modern commentators seem hypercritical in condemning Tsze-kung's language here. He shows the desirableness of the ornamental accomplishments, but does not necessarily put them on the same level with the substantial qualities.

9. LIGHT TAXATION THE BEST WAY TO SECURE THE GOVERNMENT FROM EMBARRASSMENT FOR WANT OF FUNDS. 1. Duke Âi, II. xx. Yû Zo, I. ii. 2. By the statutes of the Châu dynasty, the ground was divided into allotments cultivated in common by the families located upon them, and the produce was divided equally, nine-tenths being given to the farmers, and one-tenth being reserved as a contribution to the State. This was called the law of 徹, which term = 通, 'pervading,' 'general,' with reference, apparently, to the system of *common* labour. 3. A former duke of Lû, Hsüan (B.C. 609–591), had imposed an additional tax of another tenth from each family's portion. 4. The meaning of this paragraph is given in the translation. Literally rendered, it is,—'The people having plenty, the prince—with whom not plenty? The people not having plenty, with whom can the prince have plenty?' Yû Zo wished to impress on the duke that a sympathy and common condition should unite him and his people. If he lightened his taxation to the regular tithe, then they would cultivate their allotments with so much vigour, that his receipts would be abundant. They would be able, moreover, to help their kind ruler in any emergency.

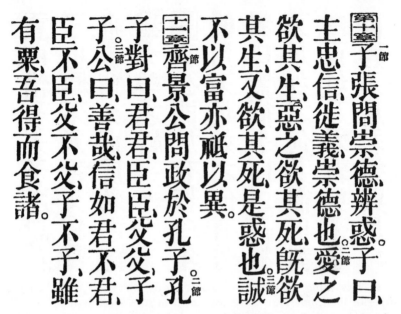

CHAP. X. 1. Tsze-chang having asked how virtue was to be exalted, and delusions to be discovered, the Master said, 'Hold faithfulness and sincerity as first principles, and be moving continually to what is right;—this is the way to exalt one's virtue.

2. 'You love a man and wish him to live; you hate him and wish him to die. Having wished him to live, you also wish him to die. This is a case of delusion.

3. '"It may not be on account of her being rich, yet you come to make a difference."'

CHAP. XI. 1. The duke Ching, of Ch'î, asked Confucius about government.

2. Confucius replied, '*There is government*, when the prince is prince, and the minister is minister; when the father is father, and the son is son.'

3. 'Good!' said the duke; 'if, indeed; the prince be not prince, the minister not minister, the father not father, and the son not son, although I have my revenue, can I enjoy it?'

10. HOW TO EXALT VIRTUE AND DISCOVER DELUSIONS. 1. Tsze-chang, see chap. vi. The Master says nothing about the 辨, 'discriminating,' or 'discovering,' of delusions, but gives an instance of a twofold delusion. Life and death, it is said, are independent of our wishes. To desire for a man either the one or the other, therefore, is one delusion. And on the change of our feelings to change our wishes in reference to the same person, is another. 之＝此人.—But in this Confucius hardly appears to be the sage. 3. See the Shih-ching, II. iv. Ode IV. 3. I have

translated according to the meaning in the Shih-ching. The quotation may be twisted into some sort of accordance with the preceding paragraph, as a case of delusion, but the commentator Ch'ǎng (程) is probably correct in supposing that it should be transferred to XVI. xii. Then 祇 should be in the text, not 祗.

11. GOOD GOVERNMENT OBTAINS ONLY WHEN ALL THE RELATIVE DUTIES ARE MAINTAINED. 1. Confucius went to Ch'î in his 36th year, B. C. 517, and finding the reigning duke—styled *ching* after his death—overshadowed by his ministers, and thinking of setting aside his eldest son from the

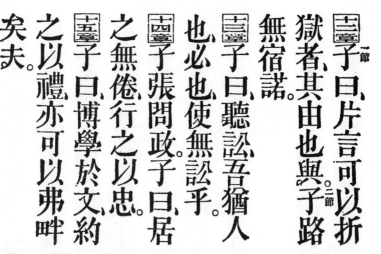

CHAP. XII. 1. The Master said, 'Ah! it is Yû, who could with half a word settle litigations!'

2. Tsze-lû never slept over a promise.

CHAP. XIII. The Master said, 'In hearing litigations, I am like any other body. What is necessary, *however*, is to cause *the people* to have no litigations.'

CHAP. XIV. Tsze-chang asked about government. The Master said, '*The art of governing* is to keep *its affairs* before the mind without weariness, and to practise them with undeviating consistency.'

CHAP. XV. The Master said, 'By extensively studying all learning, and keeping himself under the restraint of the rules of propriety, *one* may thus likewise not err from what is right.'

succession, he shaped his answer to the question about government accordingly. 3. 'Although I have the grain,' i.e. my revenue, the tithe of the produce of the country. 吾得而食諸 (食諸, compare 行諸, XI. xxi), 'shall I be able to eat it?'—intimating the danger the State was exposed to from insubordinate officers.

12. WITH WHAT EASE TSZE-LÛ COULD SETTLE LITIGATIONS. 1. We translate here—'could,' and not—'can,' because Confucius is simply praising the disciple's character. Tsze-lû, see II. xvii. 片言 = 半言, 'half a word.'

2. This paragraph is from the compilers, stating a fact about Tsze-lû, to illustrate what the Master said of him. 宿 is explained by Chû Hsî by 留, 'to leave,' 'to let remain.' Its primary meaning is—'to pass a night.' We have in English, as given in the translation, a corresponding idiom.—In Ho Yen, 片言 is taken as = 偏言, 'one-sided words,' meaning that Tsze-lû could judge rightly on hearing half

a case. 宿 again is explained by 豫, 'beforehand.'—'Tsze-lû made no promises beforehand.'

13. TO PREVENT BETTER THAN TO DETERMINE LITIGATIONS. See the 大學傳, IV. 訟, as opposed to 獄 (preceding chapter), is used of civil causes (爭財曰訟), and the other of criminal (爭罪曰獄). Little stress is to be laid on the 'I;' much on 使, as = 'to influence to.'

14. THE ART OF GOVERNING. 居, as opposed to 行, must be used as an active verb, and is explained by Chû Hsî as in the translation. 之 refers to that aspect of government about which Tsze-chang was inquiring. 無倦 = 始終如一, 'first and last the same;' 以忠 = 表裏如一, 'externally and internally the same.'

15. HARDLY DIFFERENT FROM VI. xxv.

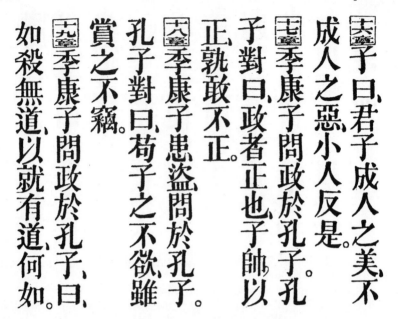

CHAP. XVI. The Master said, 'The superior man *seeks to* perfect the admirable qualities of men, and does not *seek to* perfect their bad qualities. The mean man does the opposite of this.'

CHAP. XVII. Chî K'ang asked Confucius about government. Confucius replied, 'To govern means to rectify. If you lead on *the people* with correctness, who will dare not to be correct?'

CHAP. XVIII. Chî K'ang, distressed about the number of thieves *in the State*, inquired of Confucius *how to do away with them.* Confucius said, 'If you, sir, were not covetous, although you should reward them to do it, they would not steal.'

CHAP. XIX. Chî K'ang asked Confucius about government, saying, 'What do you say to killing the unprincipled for the good of the principled?' Confucius replied, 'Sir, in carrying on your government, why should you use killing at all? Let your *evinced* desires be for what is good, and the people will be good. The relation

16. OPPOSITE INFLUENCE UPON OTHERS OF THE SUPERIOR MAN AND THE MEAN MAN.

17. GOVERNMENT MORAL IN ITS END, AND EFFICIENT BY EXAMPLE.

18. THE PEOPLE ARE MADE THIEVES BY THE EXAMPLE OF THEIR RULERS. This is a good instance of Confucius's boldness in reproving men in power. Chî K'ang (II. xx) had made himself head of the Chî family, and entered into all its usurpations, by taking off the infant nephew, who should have been its rightful chief. 不欲＝不貪, 'did not covet,' i.e. a position and influence to which you have no right. 苟子之不欲＝'given the fact

of your not being ambitious.' 賞之＝賞 民.

19. KILLING NOT TO BE TALKED OF BY RULERS; THE EFFECT OF THEIR EXAMPLE. In 就 有道, 就 is an active verb, ＝成, or 成 就, 'to complete,' 'to perfect.' 德 is used in a vague sense, not positive virtue, but ＝'nature,' 'character.' Some for 上 would read 尚＝加, 'to add upon,' but 上 itself must here have substantially that meaning. 草上之風

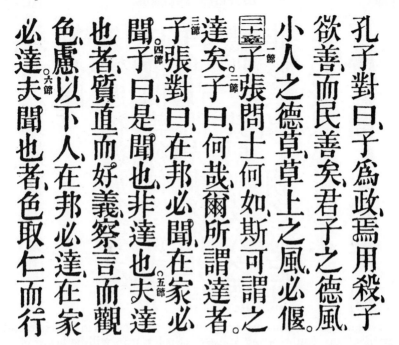

between superiors and inferiors, is like that between the wind and the grass. The grass must bend, when the wind blows across it.'

CHAP. XX. 1. Tsze-chang asked, 'What must the officer be, who may be said to be distinguished?'

2. The Master said, 'What is it you call being distinguished?'

3. Tsze-chang replied, 'It is to be heard of through the State, to be heard of throughout his clan.'

4. The Master said, 'That is notoriety, not distinction.

5. 'Now the man of distinction is solid and straightforward, and loves righteousness. He examines people's words, and looks at their countenances. He is anxious to humble himself to others. Such a man will be distinguished in the country; he will be distinguished in his clan.

6. 'As to the man of notoriety, he assumes the appearance of

=草，加之以風, 'the grass, having the wind upon it.'

20. THE MAN OF TRUE DISTINCTION, AND THE MAN OF NOTORIETY. 1. The ideas of 'a scholar' and an 'officer' blend together in China. 達=通達, 'to reach all round;'—being influential, and that influence being acknowledged. 3. If 士 be 'an officer,' then 在邦 assumes him to be the minister of a prince of a State, and 在家, that he is only the minister of a great officer, who is the head of a clan.

If, however, 士 be understood of 'a scholar,' 邦 will = 州里, 'the country,' 'people generally,' and 家 will = 族黨, 'the circle of relatives and neighbours.' 5. 下人，— 下 is the verb. The dictionary explains it by 'to descend. From being on high to become low.' But it is here rather more still, = 'to come down below other men.' 6. The condemnation here might be more fully and clearly expressed.

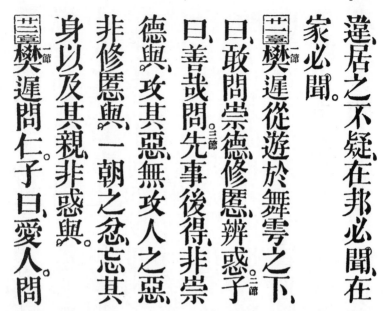

virtue, but his actions are opposed to it, and he rests in this character without any doubts *about himself.* Such a man will be heard of in the country; he will be heard of in the clan.'

CHAP. XXI. 1. Fan Ch'ih rambling with the Master under *the trees* about the rain altars, said, 'I venture to ask how to exalt virtue, to correct cherished evil, and to discover delusions.'

2. The Master said, 'Truly a good question!

3. 'If doing what is to be done be made the first business, and success a secondary consideration;—is not this the way to exalt virtue? To assail one's own wickedness and not assail that of others; —is not this the way to correct cherished evil? For a morning's anger to disregard one's own life, and involve that of his parents;— is not this a case of delusion?'

CHAP. XXII. 1. Fan Ch'ih asked about benevolence. The Master said, 'It is to love *all* men.' He asked about knowledge. The Master said, 'It is to know *all* men.'

21. HOW TO EXALT VIRTUE, CORRECT VICE, AND DISCOVER DELUSIONS. Compare chap. x. Here, as there, under the last point of the inquiry, Confucius simply indicates a case of delusion, and perhaps that is the best way to teach how to discover delusions generally. 1. Fan Ch'ih, see II. v. 舞雩, see XI. xxv. 7; followed here by 之下, there must be reference to the trees growing about the altars. 慝 formed from 'heart' and 'to conceal,' = secret vice.

3. 先事後得,—compare with 先難 後獲, in VI. xx, which also is the report of a conversation with Fan Ch'ih. 其惡,— 其 = 己, 'himself,' 'his own.' 'A morning's anger' must be a small thing, but the consequences of giving way to it are very terrible. The case is one of great delusion.

22. ABOUT BENEVOLENCE AND WISDOM;—HOW KNOWLEDGE SUBSERVES BENEVOLENCE. Fan Ch'ih might well deem the Master's replies enigmatical, and, with the help of Tsze-hsiá's explanations, the student still finds it difficult to understand the chapter. 1. 仁 here, being opposed to, or distinct from, 知, is to be taken as meaning 'benevolence,' and not as 'perfect

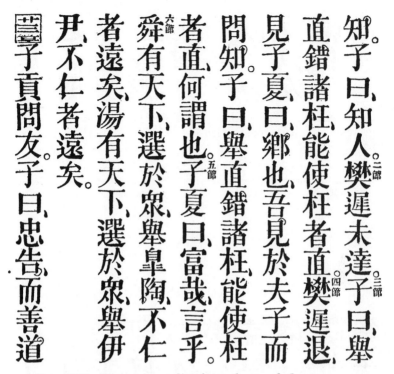

2. Fan Ch'ih did not immediately understand *these answers*.

3. The Master said, 'Employ the upright and put aside all the crooked;—in this way the crooked can be made to be upright.'

4. Fan Ch'ih retired, and, seeing Tsze-hsiâ, he said to him, 'A little while ago, I had an interview with our Master, and asked him about knowledge.   He said, "Employ the upright, and put aside all the crooked;—in this way, the crooked will be made to be upright." What did he mean?'

5. Tsze-hsiâ said, 'Truly rich is his saying!

6. 'Shun, being in possession of the kingdom, selected from among all the people, and employed Kâo-yâo, on which all who were devoid of virtue disappeared.   T'ang, being in possession of the kingdom, selected from among all the people, and employed Î Yin, and all who were devoid of virtue disappeared.'

CHAP. XXIII.   Tsze-kung asked about friendship.   The Master said, 'Faithfully admonish *your friend*, and skilfully lead him on. If you find him impracticable, stop.   Do not disgrace yourself.'

---

virtue.' 2. 未, 'not yet,' i.e. not immediately.

3. Compare II. xix.   4. 鄉, 4th tone, in the dictionary defined by 昔, 'formerly.' 6. See the names here in the Shû-ching, Parts II, III, and IV.   Shun and T'ang showed their wisdom

—their knowledge of men—in the selection of the ministers who were named.   That was their employment of the upright, and therefore all devoid of virtue disappeared.   That was their making the crooked upright;—and so their love reached to all.

CHAP. XXIV. The philosopher Tsăng said, 'The superior man on grounds of culture meets with his friends, and by their friendship helps his virtue.'

23. PRUDENCE IN FRIENDSHIP. 告, read *kŭ*, as in III. xvii, implying some degree of deference. 道＝導, as in II. iii. 1.

24. THE FRIENDSHIP OF THE CHÜN-TSZE. 以文, 'by means of letters,' i. e. common literary studies and pursuits.

BOOK XIII. TSZE-LÛ.

CHAPTER I. 1. Tsze-lû asked about government. The Master said, 'Go before the people *with your example,* and be laborious in their affairs.'

2. He requested further instruction, and was answered, 'Be not weary (in these things).'

CHAP. II. 1. Chung-kung, being chief minister to the Head of the Chî family, asked about government. The Master said, 'Employ

HEADING OF THIS BOOK.—子路第十三, 'Tsze-lû, No. 13.' Here, as in the last Book, we have a number of subjects touched upon, all bearing more or less directly on the government of the State, and the cultivation of the person. The Book extends to thirty chapters.

1. THE SECRET OF SUCCESS IN GOVERNING IS THE UNWEARIED EXAMPLE OF THE RULERS :—A LESSON TO TSZE-LÛ. 1. To what understood antecedents do the 之 refer? For the first, we may suppose 民;—先之＝率民, or 道民, 'precede the people,' 'lead the people,' that is, do so by the example of your personal conduct. But we cannot in the second clause bring

之(＝民) in the same way under the regimen of 勞. 勞之＝爲他勤勞, 'to be laborious for them;' that is, to set them the example of diligence in agriculture, &c. It is better, however, according to the idiom I have several times pointed out, to take 之 as giving a sort of neuter and general force to the preceding words, so that the expressions are＝ 'example and laboriousness.'—K'ung Ân-kwo understands the meaning differently :—'set the people an example, and then you may make them labour.' But this is not so good.

2. 無 in the old copies is 毋. The meaning comes to be the same.

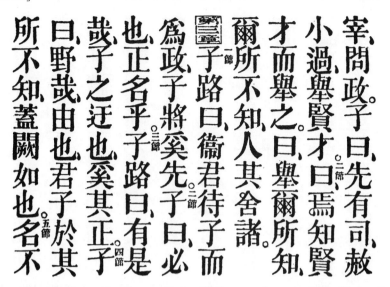

宰、問政。子曰、先有司、赦
小過、舉賢才。曰、焉知賢
才而舉之。曰、舉爾所知
爾所不知、人其舍諸。
子路曰、衞君待子而
為政、子將奚先。子曰、必
也正名乎。子路曰、有是
哉、子之迂也、奚其正。
曰、野哉由也、君子於其
所不知、蓋闕如也。名不

first the services of your various officers, pardon small faults, and raise to office men of virtue and talents.'

2. *Chung-kung* said, 'How shall I know the men of virtue and talent, so that I may raise them to office?' He was answered, 'Raise to office those whom you know. As to those whom you do not know, will others neglect them?'

CHAP. III. 1. Tsze-lû said, 'The ruler of Wei has been waiting for you, in order with you to administer the government. What will you consider the first thing to be done?'

2. The Master replied, 'What is necessary is to rectify names.'

3. 'So, indeed!' said Tsze-lû. 'You are wide of the mark! Why must there be such rectification?'

4. The Master said, 'How uncultivated you are, Yû! A superior man, in regard to what he does not know, shows a cautious reserve.

5. 'If names be not correct, language is not in accordance with

2. THE DUTIES CHIEFLY TO BE ATTENDED TO BY A HEAD MINISTER :—A LESSON TO ZAN YUNG. 1. 先有司,—compare VIII. iv. 3. The 有司 are the various smaller officers. A head minister should assign them their duties, and not be interfering in them himself. His business is to examine into the manner in which they discharge them. And in doing so, he should overlook small faults. 2. 其 舍諸,—compare 山川其舍諸, in VI. iv, though the force of 舍 here is not so great as in that chapter. Confucius's meaning is, that Chung-kung need not trouble himself about *all* men of worth. Let him advance those he knew. There was no fear that the others would be neglected. Compare what is said on 'knowing men,' in XII. xxii.

3. THE SUPREME IMPORTANCE OF NAMES BEING CORRECT. 1. This conversation is assigned by Chû Hsî to the 11th year of the duke Âi of Lû, when Confucius was 69, and he returned from his wanderings to his native State. Tsze-lû had then been some time in the service of the duke Ch'û of Wei, who, it would appear, had been wishing to get the services of the sage himself, and the disciple did not think that his Master would refuse to accept office, as he had not objected to *his* doing so. 2. 名 must have here a special reference, which Tsze-lû did not apprehend. Nor did the old interpreters, for Mâ Yung explains the 正名 by 正百事 之名, 'to rectify the names of all things.'

不如老農請學爲圃曰

第四章
一節
樊遲請學稼子曰吾

而已矣。

也君子於其言無所苟

必可言也言之必可行

所措手足故君子名之
〇七節

不中刑罰不中則民無

不興禮樂不興則刑罰

事不成事不成則禮樂
〇六節

正則言不順言不順則

the truth of things. If language be not in accordance with the truth of things, affairs cannot be carried on to success.

6. 'When affairs cannot be carried on to success, proprieties and music will not flourish. When proprieties and music do not flourish, punishments will not be properly awarded. When punishments are not properly awarded, the people do not know how to move hand or foot.

7. 'Therefore a superior man considers it necessary that the names he uses may be spoken *appropriately*, and also that what he speaks may be carried out *appropriately*. What the superior man requires, is just that in his words there may be nothing incorrect.'

CHAP. IV. 1. Fan Ch'ih requested to be taught husbandry. The Master said, 'I am not so good for that as an old husbandman.' He

On this view, the reply would indeed be 'wide of the mark.' The answer is substantially the same as the reply to duke Ching of Ch'î about government in XII. xi, that it obtains when the prince is prince, the father father, &c.; that is, when each man in his relations is what the *name* of his relation would require. Now, the duke Ch'û held the rule of Wei against his father; see VII. xiv. Confucius, from the necessity of the case and peculiarity of the circumstances, allowed his disciples, notwithstanding that, to take office in Wei; but at the time of this conversation, Ch'û had been duke for nine years, and ought to have been so established that he could have taken the course of a filial son without subjecting the State to any risks. On this account, Confucius said he would begin with rectifying the name of the duke, that is, with requiring him to resign the dukedom to his father, and be what his name of *son* required him to be. See the 翼註, *in loc.* This view enables us to understand

better the climax that follows, though its successive steps are still not without difficulty. 正名乎,—乎 may be taken as an exclamation, or as='is it not?' 4. 闕如,—闕 is used in the same sense as in II. xviii. The *kâi* is the introductory hypothetical particle. The phrase='is putting-aside-like,' i. e. the superior man reserves and revolves what he is in doubt about, and does not rashly speak. 6. 'Proprieties' here are not ceremonial rules, but='*order*,' what such rules are designed to display and secure. So, 'music' is equivalent to 'harmony.' 中, 4th tone, is the verb.

4. A RULER HAS NOT TO OCCUPY HIMSELF WITH WHAT IS PROPERLY THE BUSINESS OF THE PEOPLE. It is to be supposed that Fan Ch'ih was at this time in office somewhere, and thinking of the Master, as the villager and high officer did, IX. ii and vi, that his knowledge embraced almost every subject, he imagined that he might get

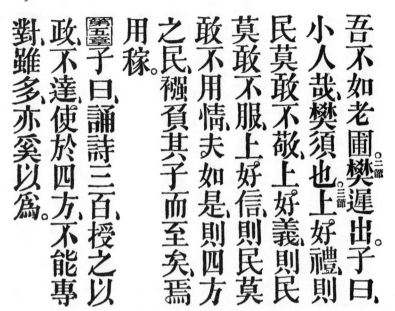

requested *also* to be taught gardening, and was answered, 'I am not so good for that as an old gardener.'

2. Fan Ch'ih having gone out, the Master said, 'A small man, indeed, is Fan Hsü!

3. 'If a superior love propriety, the people will not dare not to be reverent. If he love righteousness, the people will not dare not to submit *to his example*. If he love good faith, the people will not dare not to be sincere. Now, when these things obtain, the people from all quarters will come to him, bearing their children on their backs;—what need has he of a knowledge of husbandry?'

CHAP. V. The Master said, 'Though a man may be able to recite the three hundred odes, yet if, when intrusted with a governmental charge, he knows not how to act, or if, when sent to any quarter on a mission, he cannot give his replies unassisted, notwithstanding the extent *of his learning*, of what practical use is it?'

lessons from him on the two subjects he specifies, which he might use for the benefit of the people. 1. 稼 is properly the 'seed-sowing,' and 圃, 'a kitchen-garden,' but they are used generally, as in the translation. 3. 情, 'the feelings,' 'desires,' but sometimes, as here, in the sense of 'sincerity.' 褓, often joined with *pâo* (made of the classifier 衣 and 保), is a cloth with strings by which a child is strapped upon the back of its mother or nurse.—This paragraph shows what people in office should learn. Confucius intended that it should be repeated to Fan Ch'ih.

5. LITERARY ACQUIREMENTS USELESS WITHOUT PRACTICAL ABILITY. 詩三百,—see II. ii. 誦, 'to croon over,' as Chinese students do; here, = 'to have learned.' 專=獨, 'alone,' i.e. unassisted by the individuals of his suite. 多, 'many,' refers to the 300 odes. 亦, 'also,' here and in other places, = our 'yet,' 'after all.' 奚以為,—以, it is said, = 用, 'use,' and 為 is a mere expletive,—是語助詞. See in Wang Yǎn-chih's Treatise on the Particles under the heading 為語助也; chap. ii.

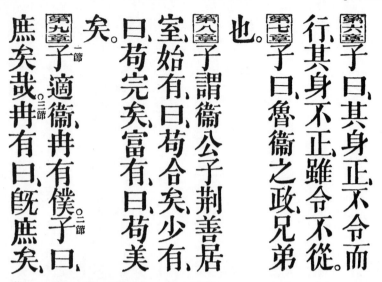

CHAP. VI. The Master said, 'When a prince's personal conduct is correct, his government is effective without the issuing of orders. If his personal conduct is not correct, he may issue orders, but they will not be followed.'

CHAP. VII. The Master said, 'The governments of Lû and Wei are brothers.'

CHAP. VIII. The Master said of Ching, a scion of the ducal family of Wei, that he knew the economy of a family well. When he began to have means, he said, 'Ha! here is a collection!' When they were a little increased, he said, 'Ha! this is complete!' When he had become rich, he said, 'Ha! this is admirable!'

CHAP. IX. 1. When the Master went to Wei, Zan Yû acted as driver of his carriage.

2. The Master observed, 'How numerous are the people!'

3. Yû said, 'Since they are thus numerous, what more shall be done for them?' 'Enrich them,' was the reply.

6. HIS PERSONAL CONDUCT ALL IN ALL TO A RULER. A translator finds it impossible here to attain to the terse conciseness of his original.

7. THE SIMILAR CONDITION OF THE STATES OF LÛ AND WEI. Compare VI. xxii. Lû's State had been directed by the influence of Châu-kung, and Wei was the fief of his brother Fung (封), commonly known as K'ang-shû (康叔). They had, similarly, maintained an equal and brotherly course in their progress, or, as it was in Confucius's time, in their degeneracy. That portion of the present Ho-nan, which runs up and lies between Shan-hsî and Pei-chih-lî, was the bulk of Wei.

8. THE CONTENTMENT OF THE OFFICER CHING, AND HIS INDIFFERENCE ON GETTING RICH. Ching was a great officer of Wei, a scion of its ducal house. 善居室 is a difficult expression. Literally it is—'dwelt well in his house.' 室 implies that he was a married man, the head of a family. The 合講 says the phrase is equivalent to 處家, 'managed his family.' Chû Hsî explains 苟 by 聊且粗畧之意,—'it is significant of indifference and carelessness.' Our word 'ha!' expressing surprise and satisfaction corresponds to it pretty nearly. We are not to understand that Ching really made these utterances, but Confucius thus vividly represents how he felt. Compare Burns's line, 'Contented wi' little, and cantie wi' mair.'

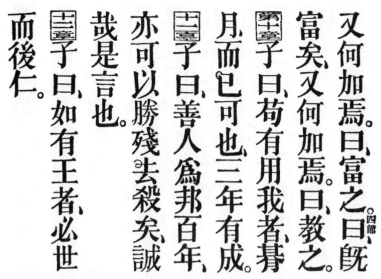

4. 'And when they have been enriched, what more shall be done ?' The Master said, 'Teach them.'

CHAP. X. The Master said, 'If there were (any of the princes) who would employ me, in the course of twelve months, I should have done something considerable. In three years, *the government* would be perfected.'

CHAP. XI. The Master said, '"If good men were to govern a country *in succession* for a hundred years, they would be able to transform the violently bad, and dispense with capital punishments." True indeed is this saying!'

CHAP. XII. The Master said, 'If a truly royal ruler were to arise, it would *still* require a generation, and then virtue would prevail.'

9. A PEOPLE NUMEROUS, WELL-OFF, AND EDU-CATED, IS THE GREAT ACHIEVEMENT OF GOVERN-MENT. I. 僕, 'a servant,' but here with the meaning in the translation. That, indeed, is the second meaning of the character given in the dictionary.

10. CONFUCIUS'S ESTIMATE OF WHAT HE COULD DO, IF EMPLOYED TO ADMINISTER THE GOVERNMENT OF A STATE. 朞 is to be distinguished from 期, and = 'a revolution of the year.' There is a comma at 月, and 而已可 are read together. 而已 does not signify, as it often does, 'and nothing more,' but = 'and have,' 已 being 已經, a sign of the perfect tense. —'Given twelve months, and there would be a passable result. In three years there would be a completion.'

11. WHAT A HUNDRED YEARS OF GOOD GOVERN-

MENT COULD EFFECT. Confucius quotes here a saying of his time, and approves of it. 勝, 1st tone, 'to be equal to.' 勝殘, 'would be equal to the violent,' that is, to transform them. 去殺, 'to do away with killing,' that is, with capital punishments, unneces-sary with a transformed people.

12. IN WHAT TIME A ROYAL RULER COULD TRANS-FORM THE KINGDOM. 王者, 'one who was a king.' The character 王 is formed by three straight lines representing the three powers of Heaven, Earth, and Man, and a perpendicular line, going through and uniting them, and thus conveys the highest idea of power and influence. See the dictionary, *sub voc.*, character 玉. Here it means the highest wisdom and virtue in the highest place. 世, 'a genera-tion,' or thirty years. See note on II. xxiii. I.

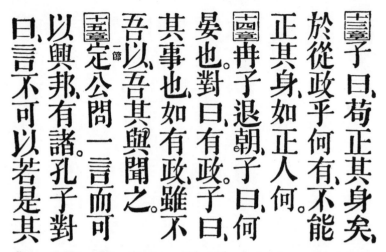

CHAP. XIII.　The Master said, 'If a minister make his own conduct correct, what difficulty will he have in assisting in government? If he cannot rectify himself, what has he to do with rectifying others?'

CHAP. XIV.　The disciple Zan returning from the court, the Master said to him, 'How are you so late?' He replied, 'We had government business.' The Master said, 'It must have been *family* affairs. If there had been government business, though I am not *now* in office, I should have been consulted about it.'

CHAP. XV.　1. The duke Ting asked whether there was a single sentence which could make a country prosperous. Confucius replied, 'Such an effect cannot be expected from one sentence.

The old interpreters take 仁 as = 仁政, 'virtuous government.'—To save Confucius from the charge of vanity in what he says, in chap. x, that he could accomplish in three years, it is said, that the perfection which he predicates there would only be the foundation for the virtue here realised.

13. THAT HE BE PERSONALLY CORRECT ESSENTIAL TO AN OFFICER OF GOVERNMENT. Compare chap. vi. That the subject is here an officer of government, and not the ruler, appears from the phrase 從政; see note on VI. vi. With reference to the other phraseology of the chapter, the 備旨 says that 從政 embraces 正君, 'the rectification of the prince,' and 正民, 'the rectification of the people.'

14. AN IRONICAL ADMONITION TO ZAN YÛ ON THE USURPING TENDENCIES OF THE CHÎ FAMILY. The point of the chapter turns on the opposition of the phrases 有政 and 其事也;—at the court of the Chî family, that is, they had really been discussing matters of government, affecting the State, and proper only for the prince's court. Confucius affects not to believe it, and says that at the chief's court they could only have been discussing the affairs of his house. 不吾以,—an inversion, and 以 = 用, 'although I am *now* not employed.' 與, in 4th tone.—'I should have been present and heard it.' Superannuated officers might go to court on occasions of emergency, and might also be consulted on such, though the general rule was to allow them to retire at 70. See the Lî Chî, I. i. Pt. i. 28. The 其 after 吾 makes a double subject, and = an emphatic I; a style more common in the Shû than in these Analects.

15. HOW THE PROSPERITY AND RUIN OF A COUNTRY MAY DEPEND ON THE RULER'S VIEW OF HIS POSITION, HIS FEELING ITS DIFFICULTY, OR ONLY CHERISHING A HEADSTRONG WILL. 1. I should suppose that 一言可以興邦 and the corresponding sentence below were common sayings, about which the duke asks, in a way to intimate his disbelief of them,—有諸. 幾 is

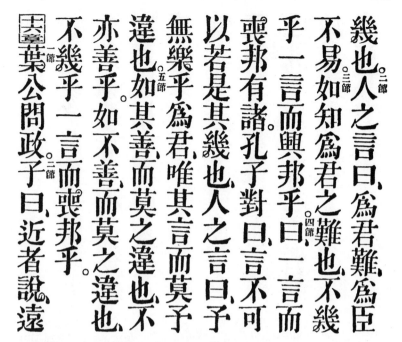

幾也人之言曰、爲君難、爲臣

不易如知爲君之難也、不幾

乎一言而興邦乎。曰、一言而

喪邦有諸孔子對曰、言不可

以若是其幾也、人之言曰子

無樂乎爲君唯其言而莫予

違也。如其善而莫之違也、不

亦善乎如不善而莫之違也、

不幾乎一言而喪邦乎。

葉公問政子曰、近者說、遠

2. 'There is a saying, however, which people have—"To be a prince is difficult; to be a minister is not easy."'

3. 'If a *ruler* knows this,—the difficulty of being a prince,—may there not be expected from this one sentence the prosperity of his country?'

4. *The duke then* said, 'Is there a single sentence which can ruin a country?' Confucius replied, 'Such an effect as that cannot be expected from one sentence. There is, *however*, the saying which people have—"I have no pleasure in being a prince, but only in that no one can offer any opposition to what I say!"'

5. 'If a *ruler's* words be good, is it not also good that no one oppose them? But if they are not good, and no one opposes them, may there not be expected from this one sentence the ruin of his country?'

CHAP. XVI. 1. The duke of Sheh asked about government.

2. The Master said, '*Good government obtains, when* those who are near are made happy, and those who are far off are attracted.'

not here in the sense of 'a spring,' or '*primum mobile*,' but = 期, in the sense of 'to expect,' 'to be expected from.' 一言 = 一句, as in II. ii. 2. It is only the first part of the saying on which Confucius dwells. That is called 主, the principal sentence; the other is only 帶說, 'an accessory.' 3. Some put a comma

at the first 乎, but it is better to take that 乎 as a preposition;—'May it not be expected that *from* this one word, &c.?' Similarly, par. 4, 乎 is a preposition = our *in*. 其言、一言 is here used specially of the orders, rules, &c., which a ruler may issue.

16. GOOD GOVERNMENT SEEN FROM ITS EFFECTS.

1. 葉, read *shêh*; see VII. xviii. 2. Confucius

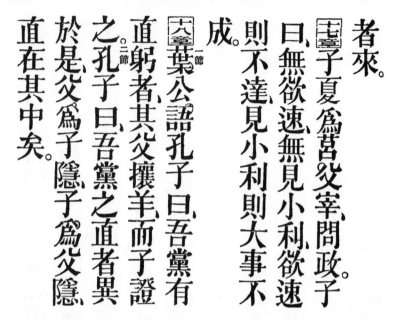

CHAP. XVII. Tsze-hsiâ, being governor of Chü-fû, asked about government. The Master said, 'Do not be desirous to have things done quickly; do not look at small advantages. Desire to have things done quickly prevents their being done thoroughly. Looking at small advantages prevents great affairs from being accomplished.'

CHAP. XVIII. 1. The duke of Sheh informed Confucius, saying, 'Among us here there are those who may be styled upright in their conduct. If their father have stolen a sheep, they will bear witness to the fact.'

2. Confucius said, 'Among us, in our part of the country, those who are upright are different from this. The father conceals the misconduct of the son, and the son conceals the misconduct of the father. Uprightness is to be found in this.'

is supposed to have in view the oppressive and aggressive government of Ch'û, to which Shih belonged.

17. HASTE AND SMALL ADVANTAGES NOT TO BE DESIRED IN GOVERNING. Chü-fû (fû 3rd tone) was a small city in the western border of Lû. 無=毋, the prohibitive particle.

18. NATURAL DUTY AND UPRIGHTNESS IN COLLISION. 1. 吾黨, 'our village,' 'our neighbourhood,' but 黨 must be taken vaguely, as in the translation; compare V. xxi. We cannot say whether the duke is referring to one or more actual cases, or giving his opinion of what his people would do. Confucius's reply would

incline us to the latter view. In the 集證, accounts are quoted of such cases, but they are probably founded on this chapter. 攘 is 'to steal on occasion,' i. e. on some temptation, as when another person's animal comes into my grounds, and I appropriate it. 證 seems to convey here the idea of accusation, as well as of witnessing. 2. 直在其中,—compare II. xviii. 2. The expression does not absolutely affirm that this is upright, but that in this there is a better principle than in the other conduct.—Anybody but a Chinese will say that both the duke's view of the subject and the sage's were incomplete.

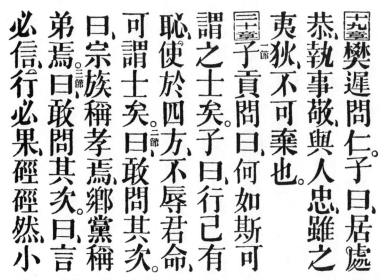

CHAP. XIX. Fan Ch'ih asked about perfect virtue. The Master said, 'It is, in retirement, to be sedately grave; in the management of business, to be reverently attentive; in intercourse with others, to be strictly sincere. Though a man go among rude, uncultivated tribes, these *qualities* may not be neglected.'

CHAP. XX. 1. Tsze-kung asked, saying, 'What qualities must a man possess to entitle him to be called an officer?' The Master said, 'He who in his conduct of himself maintains a sense of shame, and when sent to any quarter will not disgrace his prince's commission, deserves to be called an officer.'

2. *Tsze-kung* pursued, 'I venture to ask who may be placed in the next lower rank?' and he was told, 'He whom the circle of his relatives pronounce to be filial, whom his fellow-villagers and neighbours pronounce to be fraternal.'

3. *Again the disciple* asked, 'I venture to ask about the class still next in order.' *The Master* said, 'They are determined to be sincere in what they say, and to carry out what they do. They are obstinate little men. Yet perhaps they may make the next class.'

19. CHARACTERISTICS OF PERFECT VIRTUE. This is the third time that Fan Ch'ih is represented as questioning the Master about 仁, and it is supposed by some to have been the first in order. 居處 (in 3rd tone), in opposition to 執事 = 'dwelling alone,' 'in retirement.' The rude tribes here are the Î and the Tî. The Î we met with in IX. xiii. Here it is associated with Tî, the name of tribes on the north.

20. DIFFERENT CLASSES OF MEN WHO IN THEIR SEVERAL DEGREES MAY BE STYLED OFFICERS, AND THE INFERIORITY OF THE MASS OF THE OFFICERS OF CONFUCIUS'S TIME. 1. 士,—compare on XII.

xx. Here it denotes—not the scholar, but the officer. 有恥, 'has shame,' i. e. will avoid all bad conduct which would subject him to reproach. 2. 宗族 is 'a designation for all who form one body having the same ancestor.' They are also called 九族, 'nine branches of kindred,' being all of the same surname from the great-great-grandfather to the great-great-grandson. 弟 = 悌, meaning 'submissive,' giving due honour to all older than himself. 3. 硜, 'the sound of stones.' 硜然, 'stone-like.' The dictionary, with

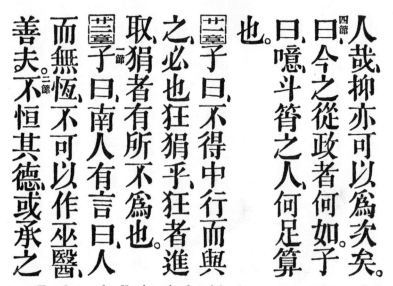

4. *Tsze-kung finally* inquired, 'Of what sort are those of the present day, who engage in government?' The Master said, 'Pooh! they are so many pecks and hampers, not worth being taken into account.'

CHAP. XXI. The Master said, 'Since I cannot get men pursuing the due medium, to whom I might communicate *my instructions*, I must find the ardent and the cautiously-decided. The ardent will advance and lay hold *of truth*; the cautiously-decided will keep themselves from what is wrong.'

CHAP. XXII. 1. The Master said, 'The people of the south have a saying—"A man without constancy cannot be either a wizard or a doctor." Good!

2. 'Inconstant in his virtue, he will be visited with disgrace.'

reference to this passage, explains it—小人貌, 'the appearance of a small man.' 4. 斗筲之人, i.e. mere utensils. Compare on II. xii. Dr. Williams translates the expression fairly well by 'peck-measure men.'

21. CONFUCIUS OBLIGED TO CONTENT HIMSELF WITH THE ARDENT AND CAUTIOUS AS DISCIPLES. Compare V. xxi, and Mencius VII. ii. 37. 與之 is explained as in the translation—以道傳之. The 註疏, however, gives simply—與之同處, 'dwell together with them.' 必也, 狂狷乎,—comp. VIII. xvi. 2. 狷 is explained in the dictionary by 褊急, 'contracted and urgent.' Opposed to 狂, it would seem to denote caution, but

yet not a caution which may not be combined with decision. 有所不爲, 'have what they will not do.'

22. THE IMPORTANCE OF FIXITY AND CONSTANCY OF MIND. 1. I translate 巫 by 'wizard,' for want of a better term. In the Châu Lî, Bk. XXVI, the *wû* appear sustaining a sort of official status, regularly called in to bring down spiritual beings, obtain showers, &c. They are distinguished as men and women, though 巫 is often feminine, 'a witch,' as opposed to 覡, 'a wizard.' Confucius's use of the saying, according to Chû Hsî, is this :—'Since such small people must have constancy, how much more ought others to have it !' The ranking of the doctors and wizards together sufficiently shows what was the position of the healing art in those days.—Chang K'ang-ch'ăng interprets this paragraph quite inadmissibly :—'Wizards and doctors cannot manage people who have

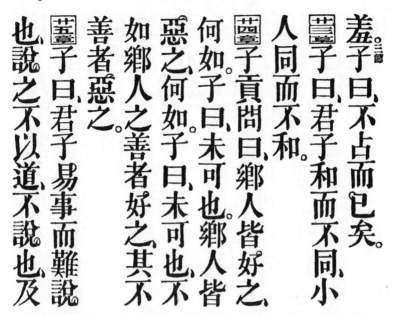

3. The Master said, 'This arises simply from not attending to the prognostication.'

CHAP. XXIII. The Master said, 'The superior man is affable, but not adulatory; the mean man is adulatory, but not affable.'

CHAP. XXIV. Tsze-kung asked, saying, 'What do you say of a man who is loved by all the people of his neighbourhood?' The Master replied, 'We may not for that accord our approval of him.' 'And what do you say of him who is hated by all the people of his neighbourhood?' The Master said, 'We may not for that conclude that he is bad. It is better than either of these cases that the good in the neighbourhood love him, and the bad hate him.'

CHAP. XXV. The Master said, 'The superior man is easy to serve and difficult to please. If you try to please him in any way which is not accordant with right, he will not be pleased. But in his

no constancy.' 2. This is a quotation from the Yî-ching, diagram 極; hexagram XXXII, line 3. 3. This is inexplicable to Chû Hsî. Some bring out from it the meaning in the translation.—Chăng K'ang-ch'ăng says:—'By the Yî we prognosticate good and evil, but in it there is no prognostication of people without constancy.'

23. THE DIFFERENT MANNERS OF THE SUPERIOR AND THE MEAN MAN. Compare II. xiv, but here the parties are contrasted in their more private intercourse with others. 同, 'agreeing with,' = flattering.

24. How, TO JUDGE OF A MAN FROM THE LIKINGS AND DISLIKINGS OF OTHERS, WE MUST KNOW THE CHARACTERS OF THOSE OTHERS. 未可,—liter-

ally, 'not yet may.' The general meaning of a Chinese sentence is often plain, and yet we are puzzled to supply exactly the subjects, auxiliaries, &c., which other languages require. In rendering the phrase, I have followed many of the paraphrasts, who complete it thus :— 未可信其爲賢也 and 未可信其爲惡也. In the 註疏, however, the second occurrence of it is expanded in the same way as the first. Compare Luke's Gospel, vi. 21, 26.

25. DIFFERENCE BETWEEN THE SUPERIOR AND THE MEAN MAN IN THEIR RELATION TO THOSE EMPLOYED BY THEM. 易事而難說 (= 悅),—as in the translation, or we may render,

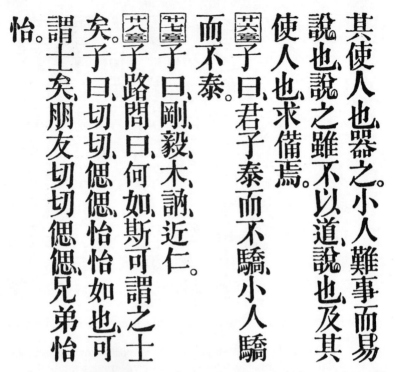

employment of men, he uses them according to their capacity. The mean man is difficult to serve, and easy to please. If you try to please him, though it be in a way which is not accordant with right, he may be pleased. But in his employment of men, he wishes them to be equal to everything.'

CHAP. XXVI. The Master said, 'The superior man has a dignified ease without pride. The mean man has pride without a dignified ease.'

CHAP. XXVII. The Master said, 'The firm, the enduring, the simple, and the modest are near to virtue.'

CHAP. XXVIII. Tsze-lù asked, saying, 'What qualities must a man possess to entitle him to be called a scholar?' The Master said, 'He must be thus,—earnest, urgent, and bland:—among his friends, earnest and urgent; among his brethren, bland.'

'is easily served, but is pleased with difficulty.' 器之,—see II. xii, 器 being here a verb. 求備 is the opposite of 器之, and = 以全材責備一人身上, 'he requires all capabilities from a single man.'

26. THE DIFFERENT AIR AND BEARING OF THE SUPERIOR AND THE MEAN MAN.

27. NATURAL QUALITIES WHICH ARE FAVOURABLE TO VIRTUE. 木, 'wood,' here an adjec-

tive, but not our 'wooden.' It = 質樸, 'simple,' 'plain.' 訥, see IV. xxiv. The gloss on it here is—遲鈍, 'slow and blunt.' 'Modest' seems to be the idea.

28. QUALITIES THAT MARK THE SCHOLAR IN SOCIAL INTERCOURSE. This is the same question as in chap. xx. 1, but 士 is here 'the scholar,' the gentleman of education, without reference to his being in office or not.

CHAP. XXIX. The Master said, 'Let a good man teach the people seven years, and they may then likewise be employed in war.'

CHAP. XXX. The Master said, 'To lead an uninstructed people to war, is to throw them away.'

29. How THE GOVERNMENT OF A GOOD RULER WILL PREPARE THE PEOPLE FOR WAR. 善人, 'a good man,'—spoken with reference to him as a ruler. The teaching is not to be understood of military training, but of the duties of life and citizenship ; a people so taught are morally fitted to fight for their government. What military training may be included in the teaching, would merely be the hunting and drilling in the people's repose from the toils of agriculture. 戎, 'weapons of war.' 可以 即戎,—'they may go to their weapons.'

30. THAT PEOPLE MUST BE TAUGHT, TO PREPARE THEM FOR WAR. Compare the last chapter. The language is very strong, and 敎 being understood as in the last chapter, shows how Confucius valued education for all classes.

BOOK XIV. HSIEN WĂN.

CHAPTER I. Hsien asked what was shameful. The Master said, 'When good government prevails in a State, *to be thinking only of salary* ; and, when bad government prevails, *to be thinking, in the same way, only of salary* ;—this is shameful.'

HEADING OF THIS BOOK.—憲問第十四, 'Hsien asked, No. 14.' The glossarist Hsing Ping (邢昺) says, 'In this Book we have the characters of the *Three Kings*, and *Two Chiefs*, the courses proper for princes and great officers, the practice of virtue, the knowledge of what is shameful, personal cultivation, and the tranquillizing of the people ;—all subjects of great importance in government. They are therefore collected together, and arranged after the last Book which commences with an inquiry about government.' Some writers are of opinion that the whole Book with its 47 chapters was compiled by Hsien or Yüan Sze, who appears in the first chapter. That only the name of the inquirer is given, and not his surname, is said to be our proof of this.

1. IT IS SHAMEFUL IN AN OFFICER TO BE CARING ONLY ABOUT HIS EMOLUMENT. Hsien is the Yüan Sze of VI. iii, and if we suppose Confucius's answer designed to have a practical application to himself, it is not easily reconcileable with what appears of his character in that other place. 穀 here = 祿, 'emolument,' but its meaning must be pregnant and intensive, as in the translation. If we do not take it so, the sentiment is contradictory to VIII. xiii. 3. K'ung Ân-kwo, however, takes the following view of the reply :—'When a country is well-governed, emolument is right ; when a country is ill-governed, to take office and emolument is shameful.' I prefer the construction of Chû Hsî, which appears in the translation.

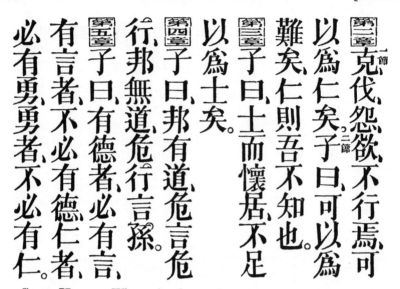

CHAP. II. 1. 'When the love of superiority, boasting, resentments, and covetousness are repressed, this may be deemed perfect virtue.'

2. The Master said, 'This may be regarded as the achievement of what is difficult. But I do not know that it is to be deemed perfect virtue.'

CHAP. III. The Master said, 'The scholar who cherishes the love of comfort is not fit to be deemed a scholar.'

CHAP. IV. The Master said, 'When good government prevails in a State, language may be lofty and bold, and actions the same. When bad government prevails, the actions may be lofty and bold, but the language may be with some reserve.'

CHAP. V. The Master said, 'The virtuous will be sure to speak *correctly*, but those whose speech is good may not always be virtuous. Men of principle are sure to be bold, but those who are bold may not always be men of principle.'

2. THE PRAISE OF PERFECT VIRTUE IS NOT TO BE ALLOWED FOR THE REPRESSION OF BAD FEELINGS. In Ho Yen, this chapter is joined to the preceding, and Chû Hsî also takes the first paragraph to be a question of Yuǎn Hsien. 1. 克, 'overcoming,' i. e. here = 'the love of superiority.' 伐, as in V. xxv. 3. 不行, 'do not go,' i. e. are not allowed to have their way, = are repressed. 2. 難, 'difficult,'—the doing what is difficult. 仁 is *quoad* 仁;—'as to its being perfect virtue, that I do not know.'

3. A SCHOLAR MUST BE AIMING AT WHAT IS HIGHER THAN COMFORT OR PLEASURE. Compare

IV. xi. The 懷居 here is akin to the 懷土 there. Compare also IV. ix.

4. WHAT ONE DOES MUST ALWAYS BE RIGHT; WHAT ONE FEELS NEED NOT ALWAYS BE SPOKEN :— A LESSON OF PRUDENCE. 孫, for 遜, as in VII. xxxv. 危, 'terror from being in a high position;' then 'danger,' 'dangerous.' It is used here in a good sense, meaning 'lofty, and what may seem to be, or really be, dangerous,' under a bad government, where good principles do not prevail.

5. WE MAY PREDICATE THE EXTERNAL FROM THE INTERNAL, BUT NOT VICE VERSÂ. The 有言 must be understood of virtuous speaking and

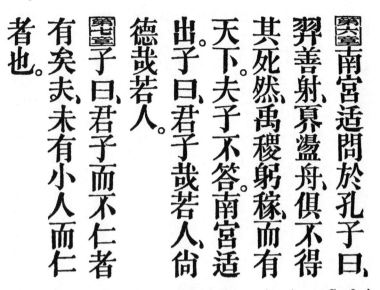

CHAP. VI. Nan-kung Kwo, submitting an inquiry to Confucius, said, 'Î was skilful at archery, and Âo could move a boat along upon the land, but neither of them died a natural death. Yü and Chî personally wrought at the toils of husbandry, and they became possessors of the kingdom.' The Master made no reply; but when Nan-kung Kwo went out, he said, 'A superior man indeed is this! An esteemer of virtue indeed is this!'

CHAP. VII. The Master said, 'Superior men, and yet not *always* virtuous, there have been, alas! But there never has been a mean man, and, *at the same time*, virtuous.'

'virtuously,' or 'correctly,' be supplied to bring out the sense. A translator is puzzled to render 仁者 differently from 有德者. I have said 'men of principle,' the opposition being between moral and animal courage; yet the men of principle may not be without the other, in order to their doing justice to themselves.

6. EMINENT PROWESS CONDUCTING TO RUIN; EMINENT VIRTUE LEADING TO DIGNITY. THE MODESTY OF CONFUCIUS. Nan-kung Kwo is said by Chû Hsî to have been the same as Nan Yung in V. i. But this is doubtful. See on Nan Yung there. Kwo, it is said, insinuated in his remark an inquiry whether Confucius was not like Yü or Chî, and the great men of the time so many Î and Âo; and the sage was modestly silent upon the subject. Î and Âo carry us back to the 22nd century before Christ. The first belonged to a family of princelets, famous, from the time of the emperor 嚳 (B.C. 2432), for their archery, and dethroned the emperor Hâu-hsiang (后相), B.C. 2145. Î was afterwards slain by his minister, Han

Cho (寒浞), who then married his wife, and one of their sons (澆, *Chiâo*) was the individual here named Âo, who was subsequently destroyed by the emperor Shâo-k'ang, the posthumous son of Hâu-hsiang. Chî was the son of the emperor 嚳, of whose birth many prodigies are narrated, and appears in the Shû-ching as Hâu-chî, the minister of agriculture to Yâo and Shun, by name 棄. The Châu family traced their descent lineally from him, so that though the throne only came to his descendants more than a thousand years after his time, Nan-kung Kwo speaks as if he had got it himself, as Yü did. 君子哉若人,— compare V. ii. The name Âo in the text should be 臭.

7. THE HIGHEST VIRTUE NOT EASILY ATTAINED TO, AND INCOMPATIBLE WITH MEANNESS. Compare IV. iv. We must supply the 'always,' to bring out the meaning.

駢邑三百、飯疏食沒齒、

三節 問管仲。曰、人也奪伯氏

二節 也、問子西。曰、彼哉彼哉。

一節 或問子產。子曰、惠人

第十章 色之。

羽修飾之、東里子產潤

之、世叔討論之、行人子

第九章 子曰、爲命裨諶草創

忠焉、能勿誨乎。

第八章 子曰、愛之、能勿勞乎、

CHAP. VIII. The Master said, 'Can there be love which does not lead to strictness with its object? Can there be loyalty which does not lead to the instruction of its object?'

CHAP. IX. The Master said, 'In preparing the governmental notifications, P'î Shăn first made the rough draught; Shî-shŭ examined and discussed its contents; Tsze-yü, the manager of Foreign intercourse, then polished the style; and, finally, Tsze-ch'ân of Tung-lî gave it the proper elegance and finish.'

CHAP. X. 1. Some one asked about Tsze-ch'ân. The Master said, 'He was a kind man.'

2. He asked about Tsze-hsî. The Master said, 'That man! That man!'

3. He asked about Kwan Chung. 'For him,' said the Master, 'the city of Pien, with three hundred families, was taken from the chief of the Po family, who did not utter a murmuring word, though, to the end of his life, he had only coarse rice to eat.'

8. A LESSON FOR PARENTS AND MINISTERS, THAT THEY MUST BE STRICT AND DECIDED. *Lǎo*, being parallel with *hǎi*, is to be construed as a verb, and conveys the meaning in the translation different from the meaning of the term in XIII. i. K'ung Ân-kwo takes it in the sense of 'to soothe,' 'comfort,' in the 3rd tone, but that does not suit the parallelism.

9. THE EXCELLENCE OF THE OFFICIAL NOTIFICATIONS OF CHĂNG, OWING TO THE ABILITY OF FOUR OF ITS OFFICERS. The State of Chăng, small and surrounded by powerful neighbours, was yet fortunate in having able ministers, through whose mode of conducting its government it enjoyed considerable prosperity. 命, with reference to this passage, is explained in the dictionary by 政令盟會之辭, 'the language of government orders, covenants, and conferences;' see the Châu Lî, XXV. par. 11. Tsze-ch'ân (see V. xv) was the chief minister of the State, and in preparing such documents first used the services of P'î Shăn, who was noted for his wise planning of matters. Shî-shŭ shows the relation of the officer indicated to the ruling family. His name was Yû-chî (游吉). The province of the 行人 was 'to superintend the ceremonies of communication with other States;' see the Châu Lî, Bk. XXXVIII.

10. THE JUDGMENT OF CONFUCIUS CONCERNING TSZE-CH'ÂN, TSZE-HSÎ, AND KWAN CHUNG. 1. See V. xv. 2. Tsze-hsî was the chief minister of Ch'û. He had refused to accept the nomination to the sovereignty of the State in preference to the rightful heir, but did not oppose the usurp-

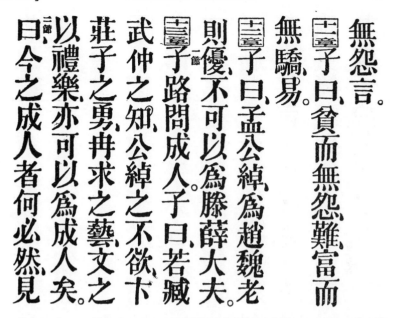

CHAP. XI. The Master said, ' To be poor without murmuring is difficult. To be rich without being proud is easy.'

CHAP. XII. The Master said, ' Măng Kung-ch'o is more than fit to be chief officer in the families of Châo and Wei, but he is not fit to be great officer to either of *the States* T'ăng or Hsieh.'

CHAP. XIII. 1. Tsze-lû asked what constituted a COMPLETE man. The Master said, ' Suppose a man with the knowledge of Tsang Wû-chung, the freedom from covetousness of Kung-ch'o, the bravery of Chwang of Pien, and the varied talents of Zăn Ch'iû; add to these the accomplishments of the rules of propriety and music :—such an one might be reckoned a COMPLETE man.'

2. *He then* added, ' But what is the necessity for a complete man of the present day to have all these things ? The man, who in the

ing tendencies of the rulers of Ch'û. He had moreover opposed the wish of king Châo (of Ch'û) to employ the sage. 3. Kwan Chung,— see III. xxii. To reward his merits, the duke Hwan conferred on him the domain of the officer mentioned in the text, who had been guilty of some offence. His submitting as he did to his changed fortunes was the best tribute to Kwan's excellence.

11. IT IS HARDER TO BEAR POVERTY ARIGHT THAN TO CARRY RICHES. This sentiment may be controverted. Compare I. xv.

12. THE CAPACITY OF MĂNG KUNG-CH'O. Kungch'o was the head of the Măng, or Chung-sun family, and, according to the 'Historical Records,' was regarded by Confucius more than any other great man of the times in Lû. His estimate of him, however, as appears here, was

not very high. In the sage's time, the government of the State of Tsin (晉) was in the hands of the three families, Châo, Wei, and Han (韓), which afterwards divided the whole State among themselves ; but meanwhile they were not States, and Kung-ch'o, as their *lâo*, or chief officer, could have managed their affairs. T'ăng and Hsieh were small States, whose great officers would have to look after their relations with greater States, to which function Kung-ch'o's abilities were not equal.

13. OF THE COMPLETE MAN :—A CONVERSATION WITH TSZE-LÛ. 1. Tsang Wû-chung had been an officer of Lû in the reign anterior to that in which Confucius was born. So great was his reputation for wisdom that the people gave him the title of a 聖人, or 'sage.' Wû was his

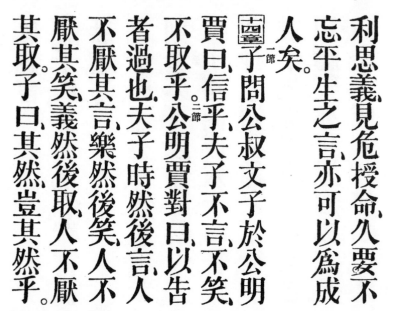

view of gain thinks of righteousness; who in the view of danger is prepared to give up his life; and who does not forget an old agreement however far back it extends:—such a man may be reckoned a COMPLETE man.'

CHAP. XIV. 1. The Master asked Kung-ming Chiâ about Kung-shû Wǎn, saying, 'Is it true that your master speaks not, laughs not, and takes not?'

2. Kung-ming Chiâ replied, 'This has arisen from the reporters going beyond *the truth.*—My master speaks when it is the time to speak, and so men do not get tired of his speaking. He laughs when there is occasion to be joyful, and so men do not get tired of his laughing. He takes when it is consistent with righteousness to do so, and so men do not get tired of his taking.' The Master said, 'So! But is it so with him?'

honorary epithet, and 仲 denotes his family place, among his brothers. Chwang, it is said by Chû Hsî, after Châu (周), one of the oldest commentators, whose surname only has come down to us, was 卞邑大夫, 'great officer of the city of Pien.' According to the 'Great Collection of Surnames,' a secondary branch of a family of the State of Ts'âo (曹) having settled in Lû, and being gifted with Pien, its members took their surname thence. For the history of Chwang and of Wû-chung, see the 集證, *in loc.* 亦可云云,—亦 implies that there was a higher style of man still, to whom the epithet *complete* would be more fully applic-

able. 2. The 曰 is to be understood of Confucius, though some suppose that Tsze-lû is the speaker. 要, 1st tone, = 約, 'an agreement,' 'a covenant;'—'a long agreement, he does not forget the words of his whole life.' The meaning is what appears in the translation.

14. THE CHARACTER OF KUNG-SHÛ WǍN, WHO WAS SAID NEITHER TO SPEAK, NOR LAUGH, NOR TAKE. 1. Wǎn was the honorary epithet of the individual in question, by name Chih (枝), or, as some say, Fa (發), an officer of the State of Wei. He was descended from the duke 獻, and was himself the founder of the Kung-shû family, being so designated, I suppose, because of his relation to the reigning duke. Of Kung-

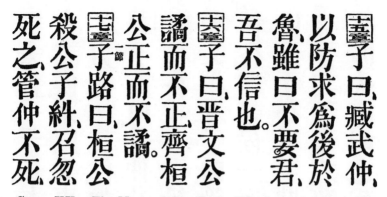

CHAP. XV. The Master said, 'Tsang Wû-chung, keeping possession of Fang, asked of *the duke of* Lû to appoint a successor to him *in his family.* Although it may be said that he was not using force with his sovereign, I believe he was.'

CHAP. XVI. The Master said, 'The duke Wăn of Tsin was crafty and not upright. The duke Hwan of Ch'î was upright and not crafty.'

CHAP. XVII. 1. Tsze-lû said, 'The duke Hwan caused his brother Chiû to be killed, when Shâo Hû died *with his master,* but Kwan Chung did not die. May not I say that he was wanting in virtue?'

ming Chiâ nothing seems to be known; he would seem from this chapter to have been a disciple of Kung-shû Wăn. 2. 其然,—with reference to Chiâ's account of Kung-shû Wăn. 豈其然乎 intimates Confucius's opinion that Chiâ was himself going beyond the truth.

15. CONDEMNATION OF TSANG WÛ-CHUNG FOR FORCING A FAVOUR FROM HIS PRINCE. Wû-chung (see chap. xiii) was obliged to fly from Lû, by the animosity of the Măng family, and took refuge in Chû (邾). As the head of the Tsang family, it devolved on him to offer the sacrifices in the ancestral temple, and he wished one of his half-brothers to be made the Head of the family, in his room, that those might not be neglected. To strengthen the application for this, which he contrived to get made, he returned himself to the city of Fang, which belonged to his family, and thence sent a message to the court, which was tantamount to a threat, that if the application were not granted, he would hold possession of the place. This was what Confucius condemned,—the 以防 in a matter which should have been left to the duke's grace. See all the circumstances in the 左傳, 襄公二十三年. 要, in 1st tone, as in chap. xiii, but with a different meaning, = 勒, 'to force to do.'

16. THE DIFFERENT CHARACTERS OF THE DUKES WĂN OF TSIN AND HWAN OF CH'Î. Hwan and Wăn were the two first of the five leaders of the princes of the empire, who play an important part in Chinese history, during the period of the Châu dynasty known as the Ch'un Ch'iû (春秋). Hwan ruled in Ch'î, B.C. 681–643, and Wăn in Tsin, B.C. 636–628. Of duke Hwan, see the next chapter. The attributes mentioned by Confucius are not to be taken absolutely, but as respectively predominating in the two chiefs.

17. THE MERIT OF KWAN CHUNG:—A CONVERSATION WITH TSZE-LÛ. 1. 公子糾, 'the duke's son Ch'iû,' but, to avoid the awkwardness of that rendering, I say—'his brother.' Hwan (the honorary epithet; his name was 小白) and Ch'iû had both been refugees in different States, the latter having been carried into Lû, away from the troubles and dangers of Ch'î, by the ministers, Kwan Chung and Shâo Hû. On the death of the prince of Ch'î, Hwan anticipated Ch'iû, got to Ch'î, and took possession of the State. Soon after, he required the duke of Lû to put his brother to death, and to deliver up the two ministers, when Shâo (召 here = 邵) Hû chose to dash his brains out, and die with his master, while Kwan Chung returned gladly to Ch'î, took service with Hwan, became his prime minister, and made him supreme arbiter among the various chiefs of the empire. Such conduct was condemned by Tsze-lû. 死之 is a peculiar ex-

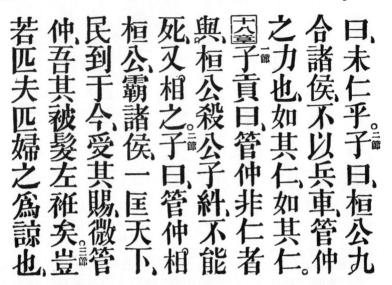

曰、未仁乎。子曰、桓公九
合諸侯不以兵車管仲
之力也。如其仁如其仁。
子貢曰、管仲非仁者、
與桓公殺公子糾不能
死又相之子曰、管仲相
桓公霸諸侯一匡天下、
民到于今受其賜微管
仲吾其被髮左衽矣。豈
若匹夫匹婦之爲諒也、

2. The Master said, 'The duke Hwan assembled all the princes together, and that not with weapons of war and chariots :—it was all through the influence of Kwan Chung. Whose beneficence was like his? Whose beneficence was like his?'

CHAP. XVIII. 1. Tsze-kung said, 'Kwan Chung, I apprehend, was wanting in virtue. When the duke Hwan caused his brother Chiû to be killed, Kwan Chung was not able to die with him. Moreover, he became prime minister to Hwan.'

2. The Master said, 'Kwan Chung acted as prime minister to the duke Hwan, made him leader of all the princes, and united and rectified the whole kingdom. Down to the present day, the people enjoy the gifts which he conferred. But for Kwan Chung, we should now be wearing our hair unbound, and the lappets of our coats buttoning on the left side.

3. 'Will you require from him the small fidelity of common

pression＝爲子糾而死. 2. Confucius defends Kwan Chung, on the ground of the services which he rendered, using 仁 in a different acceptation from that intended by the disciple. 九, 1st tone, explained in the dictionary by 聚, synonymous with 合, though the 註疏 makes out more than nine assemblages of princes under the presidency of duke Hwan. 如其仁＝誰如其仁者, as in the translation.

18. THE MERIT OF KWAN CHUNG :—A CONVERSATION WITH TSZE-KUNG. 1. Tsze-lû's doubts about Kwan Chung arose from his not dying with the prince Chiû; Tsze-kung's turned principally on his subsequently becoming pre-

mier to Hwan. 2. 匡＝正, 'to rectify,' 're-duce to order.' —— blends with 匡 its own verbal force, = 'to unite.' 微＝無, 'not,' 'if not.' 被 (the 4th tone) 髮,—see the Lî Chî, III. iii. 14, where this is mentioned as a characteristic of the eastern barbarians. 左衽,—see the Shû-ching, V. xxiv. 13. A note in the 集證 says, that anciently the right was the position of honour, and the right hand, moreover, is the more convenient for use, but the practice of the barbarians was contrary to that of China in both points. The sentiment of Confucius is, that but for Kwan Chung, his countrymen would have sunk to the state of the rude tribes about them. 3. 匹夫,匹

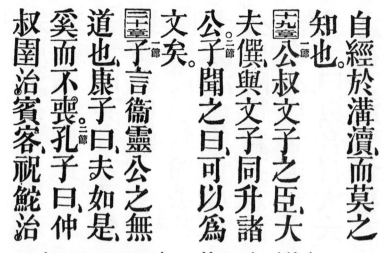

men and common women, who would commit suicide in a stream or ditch, no one knowing anything about them?'

CHAP. XIX. 1. The great officer, Hsien, who had been *family*-minister to Kung-shû Wăn, ascended to the prince's *court* in company with Wăn.

2. The Master, having heard of it, said, 'He deserved to be considered WĂN (the accomplished).'

CHAP. XX. 1. The Master was speaking about the unprincipled course of the duke Ling of Wei, when Ch'î K'ang said, 'Since he is of such a character, how is it he does not lose his State?'

2. Confucius said, 'The Chung-shû Yü has the superintendence of his guests and of strangers; the litanist, T'o, has the management

婦,—see IX. xxv. 諒=小信, 'small fidelity,' by which is intended the faithfulness of a married couple of the common people, where the husband takes no concubine in addition to his wife. The argument is this:—'Do you think Kwan Chung should have considered himself bound to Chiû, as a common man considers himself bound to his wife? And would you have had him commit suicide, as common people will do on any slight occasion?' Commentators say that there is underlying the vindication this fact:—that Kwan Chung and Shâo Hû's adherence to Chiû was wrong in the first place, Chiû being the younger brother. Chung's conduct, therefore, was not to be judged as if Chiû had been the senior. There is nothing of this, however, in Confucius's words. He vindicates Chung simply on the ground of his subsequent services, and his reference to 'the small fidelity' of husband and wife among the common people is very unhappy. 自經 (3rd tone), 'to strangle one's self,' but in connexion with 溝瀆, the phrase must be understood generally = 'to commit suicide.'

19. THE MERIT OF KUNG-SHÛ WĂN IN RECOMMENDING TO HIGH OFFICE, WHILE IN AN INFERIOR POSITION, A MAN OF WORTH. 1. Kung-shû Wăn, —see chap. xiv. This paragraph is to be understood as intimating that Kung-shû, seeing the worth and capacity of his minister, had recommended him to his sovereign, and afterwards was not ashamed to appear in the same rank with him at court. 公, = our 'duke's,' i. e. the duke's court. 2. The meaning of the chapter turns on the signification of the title Wăn. For the conferring of this on Kung-shû, see the Lî Chî, II. Sect. ii. Pt. ii. 13. The name Hsien generally appears in the form 僎.

20. THE IMPORTANCE OF GOOD AND ABLE MINISTERS :—SEEN IN THE STATE OF WEI. 1. *Ling* was the honorary epithet of Yüan (元), duke of Wei, B.C. 533-492. He was the husband of Nan-tsze, VI. xxvi. See 莊子, Bk. XXV. 9. 2. The Chung-shû Yü is the K'ung Wăn of V. xiv. 仲叔 express his family position, according to the degrees of kindred. 'The litanist, T'o,'—see VI. xiv. Wang-sun Chiâ,—see III. xiii.

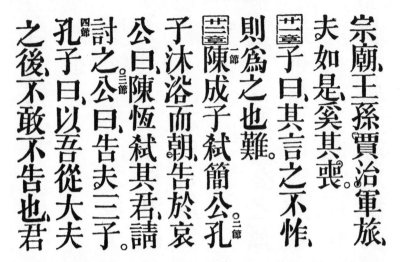

of his ancestral temple; and Wang-sun Chiâ has the direction of the army and forces:—with such officers as these, how should he lose his State?'

CHAP. XXI. The Master said, 'He who speaks without modesty will find it difficult to make his words good.'

CHAP. XXII. 1. Chăn Ch'ăng murdered the duke Chien *of* Ch'î.

2. Confucius bathed, went to court, and informed the duke Âi, saying, 'Chăn Hăng has slain his sovereign. I beg that you will undertake to punish him.'

3. The duke said, 'Inform the chiefs of the three families of it.'

4. Confucius *retired, and* said, 'Following in the rear of the great officers, I did not dare not to represent such a matter, and my prince says, "Inform the chiefs of the three families of it."'

21. EXTRAVAGANT SPEECH HARD TO BE MADE GOOD. Compare IV. xxii.

22. HOW CONFUCIUS WISHED TO AVENGE THE MURDER OF THE DUKE OF CH'Î:—HIS RIGHTEOUS AND PUBLIC SPIRIT. 1. *Chien*,—'not indolent in a single virtue,' and 'tranquil, not speaking unadvisedly,' are the meanings attached to 簡, as an honorary epithet, while 成 (the honorary epithet of Chăn Hăng) indicates, 'tranquillizer of the people, and establisher of government.' The murder of the duke Chien by his minister, Chăn Hăng (恆), took place B.C. 481, barely two years before Confucius's death. 2. 沐浴 implies all the fasting and all the solemn preparation, as for a sacrifice or other great occasion. Properly, 沐 is to wash the hair with the water in which rice has been washed, and 浴 is to wash the body with hot water. 請討之,—according to the account of this matter in the 左傳, Confucius meant that the duke Âi should himself, with the forces of Lû, undertake the punishment of the criminal. Some modern commentators cry out against this. The sage's advice, they say, would have been that the duke should report the thing to the king, and with his authority associate other princes with himself to do justice on the offender. 3. 告夫三子,—this is the use of 夫 in XI. xxiv, *et al.* 4. This is taken as the remark of Confucius, or his colloquy with himself, when he had gone out from the duke. 以吾從大夫之後, —see XI. vii. The 者 leaves the sentence incomplete;—'my prince says, "Inform the three chiefs of it;"'—this circumstance. The paraphrasts complete the sentence by —'How is it that the prince, &c.?' 5. 之三子,—之 is the verb—'to go to.'

曰、告夫三子者之三子告不

可、孔子曰、以吾從大夫之後

不敢不告也。

子路問事君子、曰、勿欺也、

而犯之。

子曰、君子上達小人下達。

子曰、古之學者爲己今之

學者爲人。

蘧伯玉使人於孔子孔子

與之坐而問焉曰、夫子何爲。

5. He went to the chiefs, and informed them, but they would not act. Confucius *then* said, 'Following in the rear of the great officers, I did not dare not to represent such a matter.'

CHAP. XXIII. Tsze-lû asked how a ruler should be served. The Master said, 'Do not impose on him, and, moreover, withstand him to his face.'

CHAP. XXIV. The Master said, 'The progress of the superior man is upwards; the progress of the mean man is downwards.'

CHAP. XXV. The Master said, 'In ancient times, men learned with a view to their own improvement. Now-a-days, men learn with a view to the approbation of others.'

CHAP. XXVI. 1. Chü Po-yü sent a messenger *with friendly inquiries* to Confucius.

2. Confucius sat with him, and questioned him. 'What,' said he, 'is your master engaged in?' The messenger replied, 'My master is

曰、云云,—this was spoken to the chiefs to reprove them for their disregard of a crime, which concerned every public man, or perhaps it is merely the reflection of the sage's own mind.

23. HOW THE MINISTER OF A PRINCE MUST BE SINCERE AND BOLDLY UPRIGHT. 犯之 is well expressed by the phrase in the translation. Many passages in the Lî Chî show that to 犯 was required by the duty of a minister, but not allowed to a son with his father.

24. THE DIFFERENT PROGRESSIVE TENDENCIES OF THE SUPERIOR MAN AND THE MEAN MAN. Ho Yen takes 達 in the sense of 曉, 'to understand.' The modern view seems better.

25. THE DIFFERENT MOTIVES OF LEARNERS IN OLD TIMES, AND IN THE TIMES OF CONFUCIUS. 爲己, 爲人, 'for themselves, for *other* men.' The meaning is as in the translation.

26. AN ADMIRABLE MESSENGER. 1. Po-yü was the designation of Chü Yüan (瑗), an officer of the State of Wei, and a disciple of the sage.

不懼。子貢曰、夫子自道也。　焉、仁者不憂、知者不惑、勇者　子曰、君子道者三、我無能　行。　子曰、君子恥其言而過其　曾子曰、君子思不出其位。　子曰、不在其位不謀其政。　也、使者出、子曰、使乎、使乎。　對曰、夫子欲寡其過、而未能

anxious to make his faults few, but he has not yet succeeded.' He then went out, and the Master said, 'A messenger indeed! A messenger indeed!'

CHAP. XXVII. The Master said, 'He who is not in any particular office, has nothing to do with plans for the administration of its duties.'

CHAP. XXVIII. The philosopher Tsăng said, 'The superior man, in his thoughts, does not go out of his place.'

CHAP. XXIX. The Master said, 'The superior man is modest in his speech, but exceeds in his actions.'

CHAP. XXX. 1. The Master said, 'The way of the superior man is threefold, but I am not equal to it. Virtuous, he is free from anxieties; wise, he is free from perplexities; bold, he is free from fear.

2. Tsze-kung said, 'Master, that is what you yourself say.'

His place is now 1st east in the outer court of the temples. Confucius had lodged with him when in Wei, and it was after his return to Lû that Po-yü sent to inquire for him.

27. A repetition of VIII. xiv.

28. THE THOUGHTS OF A SUPERIOR MAN IN HARMONY WITH HIS POSITION. Tsäng here quotes from the 象, or Illustrations, of the 52nd diagram of the Yî-ching, but he leaves out one character,—以 before 思, and thereby alters the meaning somewhat. What is said in the Yî, is—'The superior man is thoughtful, and so does not go out of his place.'—The chapter, it is said, is inserted here, from its analogy with the preceding.

29. THE SUPERIOR MAN MORE IN DEEDS THAN IN WORDS. 恥其言,—literally, 'is ashamed of his words.' Compare chaps. xxi and IV. xxii.

30. CONFUCIUS'S HUMBLE ESTIMATE OF HIMSELF, WHICH TSZE-KUNG DENIES. 1. We have the greatest part of this paragraph in IX. xxviii, but the translation must be somewhat different, as 仁者, 知者, 勇者 are here in apposition with 君子. 君子道者＝君子所以爲道者, 'what the superior man takes to be his path.' 2. 道＝言, 'to say.'

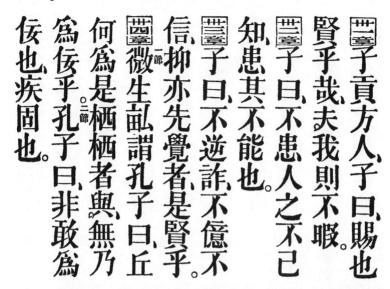

CHAP. XXXI. Tsze-kung was *in the habit of* comparing men together. The Master said, 'Tsze must have reached a high pitch of excellence! Now, I have not leisure *for this.*'

CHAP. XXXII. The Master said, 'I will not be concerned at men's not knowing me; I will be concerned at my own want of ability.'

CHAP. XXXIII. The Master said, 'He who does not anticipate attempts to deceive him, nor think beforehand of his not being believed, and yet apprehends these things readily (*when they occur*); —is he not a man of superior worth?'

CHAP. XXXIV. 1. Wei-shǎng Mâu said to Confucius, 'Ch'iû, how is it that you keep roosting about? Is it not that you are an insinuating talker?'

2. Confucius said, 'I do not dare to play the part of such a talker, but I hate obstinacy.'

31. ONE'S WORK IS WITH ONE'S SELF :—AGAINST MAKING COMPARISONS. 賢乎哉 = 'Ha! is he not superior?' The remark is ironical.

32. CONCERN SHOULD BE ABOUT OUR PERSONAL ATTAINMENT, AND NOT ABOUT THE ESTIMATION OF OTHERS. See I. xvi, *et al.* A critical canon is laid down here by Chû Hsî :—'All passages, the same in meaning and in words, are to be understood as having been spoken only once, and their recurrence is the work of the compilers. Where the meaning is the same and the language a little different, they are to be taken as having been repeated by Confucius himself with the variations.' According to this rule, the sentiment in this chapter was repeated by the Master in four different utterances.

33. QUICK DISCRIMINATION WITHOUT SUSPICIOUS-NESS IS HIGHLY MERITORIOUS. 逆, 'to be disobedient,' 'to rebel;' also, 'to meet,' and here

'to anticipate,' i.e. in judgment. 抑亦, see XIII. xix, but the meaning is there 'perhaps,' while here the 抑 is adversative, and = 'but.' 先覺者 is used in opposition to 後覺者, and = 'a quick apprehender, one who understands things before others.' So, Chû Hsî. K'ung Ân-kwo, however, takes 抑 as conjunctive, and 先覺 in apposition with the two preceding characteristics, and interprets the conclusion—'Is such a man of superior worth?' On Chû Hsî's view, the 乎 is exclamatory.

34. CONFUCIUS NOT SELF-WILLED, AND YET NO GLIB-TONGUED TALKER :—DEFENCE OF HIMSELF FROM THE CHARGE OF AN AGED REPROVER. 1. From Wei-shang's addressing Confucius by his

子曰、驥、不稱其
力、稱其德也。
或曰、以德報怨
何如。子曰、何以報
德、以直報怨、以
報德。
子曰、莫我知也
夫。子貢曰、何爲其
莫知子也。子曰、不
怨天、不尤人、下學

CHAP. XXXV. The Master said, 'A horse is called a ch'î, not because of its strength, but because of its *other* good qualities.'

CHAP. XXXVI. 1. Some one said, 'What do you say concerning the principle that injury should be recompensed with kindness?'

2. The Master said, 'With what then will you recompense kindness?

3. 'Recompense injury with justice, and recompense kindness with kindness.'

CHAP. XXXVII. 1. The Master said, 'Alas! there is no one that knows me.'

2. Tsze-kung said, 'What do you mean by thus saying—that no one knows you?' The Master replied, 'I do not murmur against

---

name, it is presumed that he was an old man. Such a liberty in a young man would have been impudence. It is presumed also, that he was one of those men who kept themselves retired from the world in disgust. 栖, 'to perch or roost,' as a bird, used contemptuously with reference to Confucius going about among the princes and wishing to be called to office. 2. 固＝執一不通, 'holding one idea without intelligence.'

35. VIRTUE, AND NOT STRENGTH, THE FIT SUBJECT OF PRAISE. 驥 was the name of a famous horse of antiquity who could run 1000 *lî* in one day. See the dictionary *in voc.* It is here used generally for 'a good horse.'

36. GOOD IS NOT TO BE RETURNED FOR EVIL; EVIL TO BE MET SIMPLY WITH JUSTICE. 1. 德＝恩惠, 'kindness.' 怨, 'resentment,' 'hatred,' here put for what awakens resentment, 'wrong,' 'injury.' The phrase 以德報怨 is found in the 道德經 of Lâo-tsze, II. chap. lxiii, but it is possible that Confucius's questioner simply consulted him about it as a saying which he had himself heard and was inclined to approve. 2. 以直, 'with straightness,' i.e.

with justice.—How far the ethics of Confucius fall below our Christian standard is evident from this chapter, and even below Lâo-tsze. The same expressions are attributed to Confucius in the Lî Chî, XXIX. xii, and it is there added 子曰、以德報怨、則寬身之仁(＝人), which is explained,—'He who returns good for evil is a man who is careful of his person,' i.e. will try to avert danger from himself by such a course. The author of the 翼註 says, that the injuries intended by the questioner were only trivial matters, which perhaps might be dealt with in the way he mentioned, but great offences, as those against a sovereign or a father, may not be dealt with by such an inversion of the principles of justice. The Master himself, however, does not fence his deliverance in any way.

37. CONFUCIUS, LAMENTING THAT MEN DID NOT KNOW HIM, RESTS IN THE THOUGHT THAT HEAVEN KNEW HIM. 1. 莫我知,—the inversion for 莫知我, 'does not know me.' He referred, commentators say, to the way in which he pursued his course, simply 爲已, out of his own conviction of duty, and for his own improvement, without regard to success, or the opinions

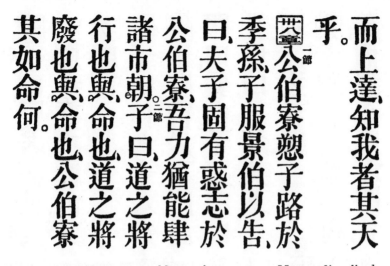

Heaven. I do not grumble against men. My studies lie low, and my penetration rises high. But there is Heaven;—that knows me!'

CHAP. XXXVIII. 1. The Kung-po Liâo, having slandered Tsze-lû to Chî-sun, Tsze-fû Ching-po informed Confucius of it, saying, 'Our master is certainly being led astray by the Kung-po Liâo, but I have still power enough left to cut *Liâo* off, and expose his corpse in the market and in the court.'

2. The Master said, 'If *my* principles are to advance, it is so ordered. If they are to fall to the ground, it is so ordered. What can the Kung-po Liâo do where such ordering is concerned?'

of others. 2. 何爲其莫知子也, 'what is that which you say—no man knows you?' 下學, 上達,—'beneath I learn, above I penetrate;'—the meaning appears to be that he contented himself with the study of men and things, common matters as more ambitious spirits would deem them, but from those he rose to understand the high principles involved in them,—'the appointments of Heaven (天命);'—according to one commentator. 知我者, 其天乎,—'He who knows me, is not that Heaven?' The 日講 paraphrases this, as if it were a soliloquy,—上天, 於冥冥之中, 能知我耳.

38. HOW CONFUCIUS RESTED, AS TO THE PROGRESS OF HIS DOCTRINES, ON THE ORDERING OF HEAVEN:—ON OCCASION OF TSZE-LÛ'S BEING SLANDERED. I. Liâo, called Kung-po (literally,

duke's uncle), probably from an affinity with the ducal House, is said by some to have been a disciple of the sage, but that is not likely, as we find him here slandering Tsze-lû, that he might not be able, in his official connexion with the Chî family, to carry the Master's lessons into practice. 景 was the hon. epithet of Tsze-fû Ching, a great officer of Lû. 夫子 refers to Chî-sun. 有惑志,—'is having his will deceived.' Exposing the bodies (陳尸) of criminals, after their execution, was called 肆. The bodies of 'great officers' were so exposed in the court, and those of meaner criminals in the market-place. 市朝 came to be employed together, though the exposure could take place only in one place, just as we have seen 兄弟 used generally for 'brother.'

2. 與 makes the preceding clause conditional, ='if.' 命=天命, 'Heaven's ordering.'

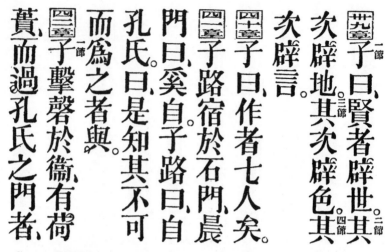

CHAP. XXXIX. 1. The Master said, '*Some* men of worth retire from the world.

2. 'Some retire from *particular* States.

3. 'Some retire because of *disrespectful* looks.

4. 'Some retire because of *contradictory* language.'

CHAP. XL. The Master said, 'Those who have done this are seven men.'

CHAP. XLI. Tsze-lû happening to pass the night in Shih-măn, the gate-keeper said to him, 'Whom do you come from?' Tsze-lû said, 'From Mr. K'ung.' 'It is he,—is it not?'—said the other, 'who knows the impracticable nature of the times, and yet will be doing in them.'

CHAP. XLII. 1. The Master was playing, *one day*, on a musical stone in Wei, when a man, carrying a straw basket, passed the door

39. DIFFERENT CAUSES WHY MEN OF WORTH WITHDRAW FROM PUBLIC LIFE, AND DIFFERENT EXTENTS TO WHICH THEY SO WITHDRAW THEMSELVES. 1. 辟 *pi*, 4th tone, = 避. 2. 其次,—'the next class,' but commentators say that the meaning is no more than 'some,' and that the terms do not indicate any comparison of the parties on the ground of their worthiness. 地, 'the earth,' here = territories or States. 3. The 'looks,' and 'language' in par. 4, are to be understood of the princes whom the worthies wished to serve.—Confucius himself could never bear to withdraw from the world.

40. THE NUMBER OF MEN OF WORTH WHO HAD WITHDRAWN FROM PUBLIC LIFE IN CONFUCIUS'S TIME. This chapter is understood in connexion with the preceding;—as appears in the translation. Chû, however, explains 作 by 起, 'have arisen.' Others explain it by 爲, 'have done this.' They also give the names of the

seven men, which Chû calls 鑿, 'chiselling.'

41. CONDEMNATION OF CONFUCIUS'S COURSE IN SEEKING TO BE EMPLOYED, BY ONE WHO HAD WITHDRAWN FROM PUBLIC LIFE. The site of Shih-măn is referred to the district of Ch'ang-ch'ing, department of Chî-nan, in Shan-tung. 晨門, 'morning gate,'—a designation of the keeper, as having to open the gate in the morning,—perhaps one of the seven worthies of the preceding chapter. We might translate 石門 by 'Stony-gate.' It seems to have been one of the passes between Ch'î and Lû. 孔氏, 'the K'ung,' or Mr. K'ung. Observe the force of the final 與.

42. THE JUDGMENT OF A RETIRED WORTHY ON CONFUCIUS'S COURSE, AND REMARK OF CONFUCIUS THEREON. 1. The *ch'ing* was one of the eight musical instruments of the Chinese; see Medhurst's dictionary, *in voc.* 過, 1st tone, 'to go

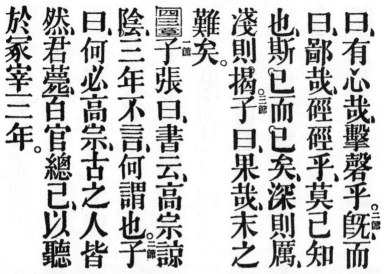

of the house where Confucius was, and said, 'His heart is full who *so* beats the musical stone.'

2. A little while after, he added, 'How contemptible is the one-ideaed obstinacy *those sounds display!* When one is taken no notice of, he has simply at once to give over *his wish for public employment.* "Deep water must be crossed with the clothes on; shallow water may be crossed with the clothes held up."'

3. The Master said, 'How determined is he in his purpose! *But* this is not difficult!'

CHAP. XLIII. 1. Tsze-chang said, 'What is meant when the Shû says that Kâo-tsung, while observing the usual imperial mourning, was for three years without speaking?'

2. The Master said, 'Why must Kâo-tsung *be referred to as an example of this?* The ancients all did so. When the sovereign died, the officers all attended to their several duties, taking instructions from the prime minister for three years.'

by.' Meaning 'to go beyond,' 'to exceed,' it is in the 4th tone. 有心哉擊磬乎 is to be read as one sentence, and understood as if there were a 之 after the 哉. 2. 硜硜乎,—see XIII. xx. 3. The 備旨 interprets this clause also, as if a 之 were after the 哉, and 硜硜 had reference to the sounds of the *ch'ing*. 深則云云,—see the Shih, I. iii. 9, stanza 1. The quotation was intended to illustrate that we must act according to circumstances. 3. 末＝無. 之 seems to be a mere expletive. The case is one where the meaning is plain while the characters can hardly be construed satisfactorily. I have not found this example of 之 in Wang Yin-chih.

43. HOW GOVERNMENT WAS CARRIED ON DURING THE THREE YEARS OF SILENT MOURNING BY THE SOVEREIGN. 1. 書云,—see the Shû, IV. viii. Sect. I. 1, but the passage there is not exactly as in the text. It is there said that Kâo-tsung, after the three years' mourning, still did not speak. 高宗 was the honorary title of the king Wû-ting (武丁, B.C. 1324–1264). 諒 (*Shû*, 亮) 陰 (read *an*), according to the dictionary, means 'the shed where the mourner lived the three years.' Chû Hsî does not know the meaning of the terms.—

四六章　原壤夷俟子曰幼

諸。

己以安百姓堯舜其猶病

己以安百姓脩己以

曰如斯而已乎。曰脩

已乎。曰脩己以安人、

脩己以敬。曰如斯而

四五章　子路問君子子曰、

易使也。

四四章　子曰上好禮則民

CHAP. XLIV. The Master said, 'When rulers love *to observe*
the rules of propriety, the people respond readily to the calls on
them for service.'

CHAP. XLV. Tsze-lû asked what constituted the superior man.
The Master said, 'The cultivation of himself in reverential carefulness.' 'And is this all?' said *Tsze-lû*. 'He cultivates himself so as
to give rest to others,' was the reply. 'And is this all?' *again*
asked *Tsze-lû*. *The Master* said, 'He cultivates himself so as to give
rest to all the people. He cultivates himself so as to give rest to all
the people:—even Yâo and Shun were still solicitous about this.'

CHAP. XLVI. Yüan *Z*ang was squatting on his heels, and

Tsze-chang was perplexed to know how government could be carried on during so long
a period of silence. 2. 古之人,—the
人 embraces the sovereigns, and subordinate
princes who had their own petty courts. 總
已,—in the 備旨 it is said, 一總,攝也,
不敢放縱意也, '總 is to manage.
The meaning is, that they did not dare to allow
themselves any license.' The expression is not
an easy one. I have followed the paraphrasts.

44. How a love of the rules of propriety
in rulers facilitates government.

45. Reverent self-cultivation the distinguishing characteristic of the Chün-tsze.
以 敬, it is said, are not to be taken as the
wherewith of the *Chün-tsze* in cultivating himself, but as the chief thing which he keeps
before him in the process. I translate 以,
therefore, by *in*, but in the other sentences, it
indicates the realizations, or consequences, of
the 修 已. 百 姓,—'the hundred sur-
names,' as a designation for the mass of the
people, occurs as early as in the *Yâo-tien* (堯

典). It is = 百家姓, 'the surnames of
the hundred families,' into which number the
families of the people were perhaps divided at
a very early time. The surnames of the Chinese
now amount to several hundreds. The small
work 百家姓帖, made in the Sung
dynasty, contains nearly 450. The number
of them given in an appendix to Williams's
Syllabic Dictionary, as compiled by the Rev.
Dr. Blodget, is 1863. In the 集證, *in loc.*,
we find a ridiculous reason given for the surnames being a hundred, to the effect that
the ancient sages gave a surname for each of
the five notes of the scale in music, and of the
five great relations of life and of the four seas;
consequently 5 × 5 × 4 = 100. It is to be
observed, that in the Shû we find 'a hundred surnames,' interchanged with 萬 姓,
'ten thousand surnames,' and it would seem
needless, therefore, to seek to attach a definite
explanation to the number. 堯舜其猶
病諸,—see VI. xxviii.

46. Confucius's conduct to an unmannerly
old man of his acquaintance. Yüan *Z*ang was an
old acquaintance of Confucius, but had adopted

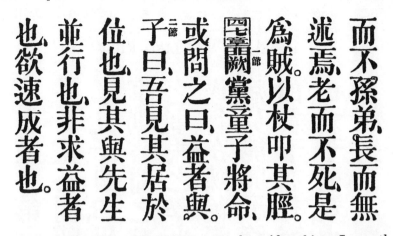

so waited *the approach of* the Master, who said to him, 'In youth, not humble as befits a junior; in manhood, doing nothing worthy of being handed down; and living on to old age:—this is to be a pest.' With this he hit him on the shank with his staff.

CHAP. XLVII. 1. A youth of the village of Ch'üeh was employed *by Confucius* to carry the messages between him and his visitors. Some one asked about him, saying, 'I suppose he has made great progress.'

2. The Master said, 'I observe that he is fond of occupying the seat *of a full-grown man;* I observe that he walks shoulder to shoulder with his elders. He is not one who is seeking to make progress *in learning.* He wishes quickly to become a man.'

the principles of Lâo-tsze, and gave himself extraordinary license in his behaviour.—See an instance in the Lî Chî, II. Sect. II. iii. 24, and the note there. 夷俟,—the dictionary explains the two words together by 展足箕坐, but that is the meaning of 夷 alone, and 俟＝待, 'to wait for.' So, the commentators, old and new. The use of 夷 in this sense is thus explained:— 'The 鴄鳥 is fond of squatting, and is therefore called the squatting *ch'ih* (蹲鴄), but it is called by some the *ch'ih î* (鴄夷), and hence 夷 is used for 蹲, *to squat!*' See the 集證, *in loc.* 孫 for 遜, and 弟 for 悌. 賊,—in the sense of 賊害,＝our 'pest,' rather than 'thief.' The address of Confucius might be translated in the 2nd person, but it is perhaps better to keep to the 3rd, leaving the application to be understood. From several references to Yüan Zang in the Lî Chî, it appears

he was a very old acquaintance of Confucius, and mentally somewhat weak. Confucius felt kindly to him, but was sometimes provoked by him to very candid expressions of his judgment about him,—as here.

47. CONFUCIUS'S EMPLOYMENT OF A FORWARD YOUTH. 1. 闕黨,—there is a tradition that Confucius lived and taught in 闕里, but it is much disputed. 將命謂傳賓主之言, '將命 means to convey the messages between visitors and the host.' 益者與,— the inquirer supposed that Confucius's employment of the lad was to distinguish him for the progress which he had made. 2. According to the rules of ceremony, a youth must sit in the corner, the body of the room being reserved for full-grown men;—see the Lî Chî, II. Sect. I. i. 18. In walking with an elder, a youth was required to keep a little behind him;—see the Lî Chî, I. Sect. I. ii. chap. 4. 7. Confucius's employment of the lad, therefore, was to teach him the courtesies required by his years.

BOOK XV. WEI LING KUNG.

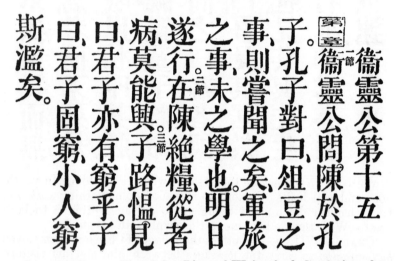

CHAPTER I. 1. The duke Ling of Wei asked Confucius about tactics. Confucius replied, 'I have heard all about sacrificial vessels, but I have not learned military matters.' On this, he took his departure the next day.

2. When he was in Chǎn, their provisions were exhausted, and his followers became so ill that they were unable to rise.

3. Tsze-lû, with evident dissatisfaction, said, 'Has the superior man likewise to endure *in this way?*' The Master said, 'The superior man may indeed have to endure want, but the mean man, when he is in want, gives way to unbridled license.'

HEADING OF THIS BOOK.—衞靈公第 十五, 'The duke Ling of Wei, No. 15.' The contents of the Book, contained in forty chapters, are as miscellaneous as those of the former. Rather they are more so, some chapters bearing on the public administration of government, several being occupied with the superior man, and others containing lessons of practical wisdom. 'All the subjects,' says Hsing Ping, 'illustrate the feeling of the sense of shame and consequent pursuit of the correct course, and therefore the Book immediately follows the preceding one.'

1. CONFUCIUS REFUSES TO TALK ON MILITARY AFFAIRS. IN THE MIDST OF DISTRESS, HE SHOWS THE DISCIPLES HOW THE SUPERIOR MAN IS ABOVE DISTRESS. 1. 陳, read *chǎn*, in 4th tone, 'the arrangement of the ranks of an army,' here = *tactics* generally. 俎豆之事,—comp.

俎豆之事, VIII. iv. 3. The 俎 was a dish, 18 inches long and 8 inches broad, on a stand 8½ inches high, upon which the flesh of victims was laid, but the meaning is sacrificial vessels generally, = the business of ceremonies. It is said of Confucius, in the 'Historical Records,' that when a boy, he was fond of playing at 俎 and 豆. He wished by his reply and departure, to teach the duke that the rules of propriety, and not war, were essential to the government of a State. 2. From Wei, Confucius proceeded to Chǎn, and there met with the distress here mentioned. It is probably the same which is referred to in XI. ii. 1, though there is some chronological difficulty about the subject. (See the note by Chû Hsî in his preface to the Analects.) 3. 固 = 'yes, indeed,' with reference to Tsze-lû's question. Some take it in its sense of 'firm.'—The superior man firmly endures want.'—Duke Ling,— see XIV. xx, also in Chwang-tsze, xxv. 9, *et al.*

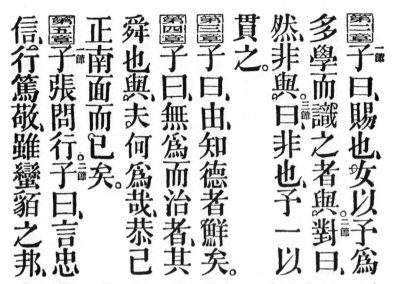

CHAP. II. 1. The Master said, 'Ts'ze, you think, I suppose, that I am one who learns many things and keeps them in memory?'

2. Tsze-kung replied, 'Yes,—but perhaps it is not so?'

3. 'No,' was the answer; 'I seek a unity all-pervading.'

CHAP. III. The Master said, 'Yû, those who know virtue are few.'

CHAP. IV. The Master said, 'May not Shun be instanced as having governed efficiently without exertion? What did he do? He did nothing but gravely and reverently occupy his royal seat.'

CHAP. V. 1. Tsze-chang asked how a man should conduct himself, *so as to be everywhere appreciated.*

2. The Master said, 'Let his words be sincere and truthful, and his actions honourable and careful;—such conduct may be practised among the rude tribes of the South or the North. If his words be

2. HOW CONFUCIUS AIMED AT THE KNOWLEDGE OF AN ALL-PERVADING UNITY. This chapter is to be compared with IV. xv; only, says Chû Hsî, 'that is spoken with reference to practice, and this with reference to knowledge.' But the design of Confucius was probably the same in them both; and I understand the first paragraph here as meaning—'Ts'ze, do you think that I am aiming, by the exercise of memory, to acquire a varied and extensive knowledge?' Then the 3rd paragraph is equivalent to:—'I am not doing this. My aim is to know myself,—the mind which embraces all knowledge, and regulates all practice.' This is the view of the chapter given in the 日講:— 此一章書言學貴乎知要, 'This chapter teaches that what is valuable in learning is the knowledge of that which is important.'

3. FEW REALLY KNOW VIRTUE. This is under-

stood as spoken with reference to the dissatisfaction manifested by Tsze-lû in chapter i. If he had possessed a right knowledge of virtue, he would not have been so affected by distress.

4. HOW SHUN WAS ABLE TO GOVERN WITHOUT PERSONAL EFFORT. 恭已, 'made himself reverent.' 正南面, 'correctly adjusted his southwards face;' see VI. i. Shun succeeding Yâo, there were many ministers of great virtue and ability to occupy all the offices of the government. All that Shun did was by his grave and sage example. This is the lesson, —the influence of a ruler's personal character.

5. CONDUCT THAT WILL BE APPRECIATED IN ALL PARTS OF THE WORLD. 1. We must supply a good deal to bring out the meaning here. Chû Hsî compares the question with that other of Tsze-chang about the scholar who may be called 達; see XII. xx. 2. 貊 may be regarded as

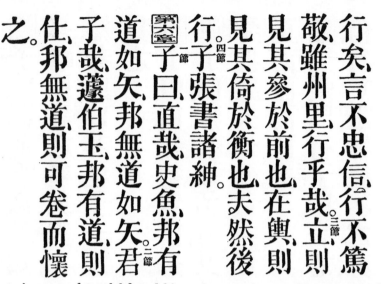

not sincere and truthful, and his actions not honourable and careful, will he, with such conduct, be appreciated, even in his neighbourhood?

3. 'When he is standing, let him see those two things, as it were, fronting him. When he is in a carriage, let him see them attached to the yoke. Then may he subsequently carry them into practice.'

4. Tsze-chang wrote these counsels on the end of his sash.

CHAP. VI. 1. The Master said, 'Truly straightforward was the historiographer Yü. When good government prevailed in his State, he was like an arrow. When bad government prevailed, he was like an arrow.

2. 'A superior man indeed is Chü Po-yü! When good government prevails in his State, he is to be found in office. When bad government prevails, he can roll his principles up, and keep them in his breast.'

another name for the 北狄, the rude tribes on the North (III. v). 2500 families made up a 州, and 25 made up a 里, but the meaning of the phrase is that given in the translation. 3. 其, 'them,' i. e. such words and actions.— Let him see them 參於前, 'before him, with himself making a trio.' 輿 is properly 'the bottom of a carriage,' planks laid over wheels, a simple 'hackery,' but here it = 'a carriage.' 4. 紳 denotes the ends of the sash that hang down.

6. THE ADMIRABLE CHARACTERS OF TSZE-YÜ AND CHÜ PO-YÜ. 1. 子魚 was the designation of 魚子, the historiographer of Wei,

generally styled Shih Ch'iû. On his deathbed, he left a message for his prince, and gave orders that his body should be laid out in a place and manner likely to attract his attention when he paid the visit of condolence. It was so, and the message then delivered had the desired effect. Perhaps it was on hearing this that Confucius made this remark. 如矢, 'as an arrow,' i. e. straight and decided. 2. Chü Po-yü,—see XIV. xxvi. 可 = 能. 卷而懷之,—之 is to be understood as referring to 'his principles,' or perhaps the clause = 'he could roll himself up and keep himself to himself,' i. e. he kept aloof from office.—Commentators say that Tsze-yû's uniform straightforwardness was not equal to Po-yü's rightly adapting himself to circumstances.—Chwang-tsze continually mentions Tsäng Shän and Shih Yü together.

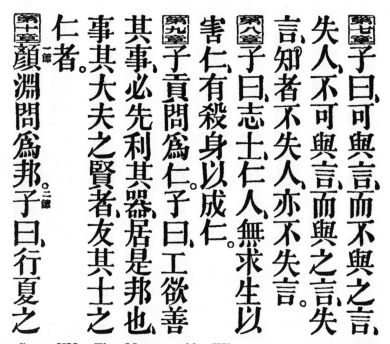

CHAP. VII. The Master said, 'When a man may be spoken with, not to speak to him is to err in reference to the man. When a man may not be spoken with, to speak to him is to err in reference to our words. The wise err neither in regard to their man nor to their words.'

CHAP. VIII. The Master said, 'The determined scholar and the man of virtue will not seek to live at the expense of injuring their virtue. They will even sacrifice their lives to preserve their virtue complete.'

CHAP. IX. Tsze-kung asked about the practice of virtue. The Master said, 'The mechanic, who wishes to do his work well, must first sharpen his tools. When you are living in any State, take service with the most worthy among its great officers, and make friends of the most virtuous among its scholars.'

CHAP. X. 1. Yen Yüan asked how the government of a country should be administered.

2. The Master said, 'Follow the seasons of Hsiâ.

7. THERE ARE MEN WITH WHOM TO SPEAK, AND MEN WITH WHOM TO KEEP SILENCE. THE WISE KNOW THEM. 失言 may be translated, literally and properly,—'to lose our words,' but in English we do not speak of 'losing men.'

8. HIGH NATURES VALUE VIRTUE MORE THAN LIFE. The two different classes here are much the same as in IV. ii. The first word of the second sentence may be naturally translated—

'They will kill themselves.' No doubt suicide is included in the expression (see K'ung Ân-kwo's explanation, given by Ho Yen), and Confucius here justifies that act, as in certain cases expressive of high virtue.

9. HOW INTERCOURSE WITH THE GOOD AIDS THE PRACTICE OF VIRTUE. Compare 'Iron sharpeneth iron; so a man sharpeneth the countenance of his friend.'

10. CERTAIN RULES, EXEMPLIFIED IN THE ANCIENT

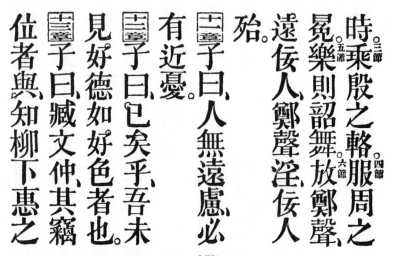

3. 'Ride in the state carriage of Yin.

4. 'Wear the ceremonial cap of Châu.

5. 'Let the music be the Shâo with its pantomimes.

6. 'Banish the songs of Chăng, and keep far from specious talkers. The songs of Chăng are licentious; specious talkers are dangerous.'

CHAP. XI. The Master said, 'If a man take no thought about what is distant, he will find sorrow near at hand.'

CHAP. XII. The Master said, 'It is all over! I have not seen one who loves virtue as he loves beauty.'

CHAP. XIII. The Master said, 'Was not Tsang Wăn like one who had stolen his situation? He knew the virtue and the talents

DYNASTIES, TO BE FOLLOWED IN GOVERNING :—A REPLY TO YEN YÜAN. 1. The disciple modestly put his question with reference to the government of a State (邦), but the Master answers it according to the disciple's ability, as if it had been about the ruling of the kingdom (治天下). 2. The three great ancient dynasties began the year at different times. According to an ancient tradition, 'Heaven was opened at the time 子; Earth appeared at the time 丑; and Man was born at the time 寅.' 子 commences in our December, at the winter solstice; 丑 a month later; and 寅 a month after 丑. The Châu dynasty began its year with 子; the Shang with 丑; and the Hsiâ with 寅. As human life thus began, so the year, in reference to human labours, naturally proceeds from the spring, and Confucius approved the rule of the Hsiâ dynasty. His decision has been the law of all dynasties since the Ch'in. See the 'Discours Preliminaire, Chap. I,' in Gaubil's Shû-ching. 3. The state carriage of the Yin

dynasty was plain and substantial, which Confucius preferred to the more ornamented one of Châu. 4. Yet he does not object to the more elegant cap of that dynasty, 'the cap,' says Chû Hsî, 'being a small thing, and placed over all the body.' 5. The *shâo* was the music of *Shun*; see III. xxv. 舞,—the 'dancers,' or 'pantomimes,' who kept time to the music. See the Shû-ching, II. ii. 21. 6. 鄭聲, 'the sounds of Chăng,' meaning both the songs of Chăng, and the music to which they were sung. Those songs form the 7th book of the 1st division of the Shih-ching, and are here characterized justly.

11. THE NECESSITY OF FORETHOUGHT AND PRECAUTION.

12. THE RARITY OF A TRUE LOVE OF VIRTUE. 已矣乎,—see V. xxvi; the rest is a repetition of IX. xvii, said to have been spoken by Confucius when he was in Wei and saw the duke riding out openly in the same carriage with Nan-tsze.

13. AGAINST JEALOUSY OF OTHERS' TALENTS :—THE CASE OF TSANG WĂN, AND HÛI OF LIÛ-HSIÂ. Tsang Wăn-chung,—see V. xvii. 竊位 is explained—'as if he had got it by theft, and

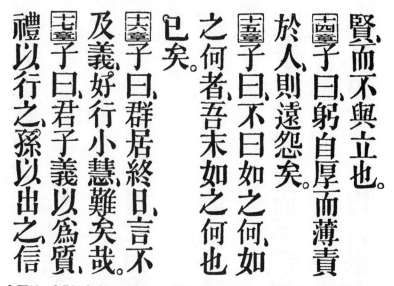

of Hûi of Liû-hsiâ, and yet did not *procure that he should* stand with him *in court*.'

CHAP. XIV. The Master said, 'He who requires much from himself and little from others, will keep himself from *being the object of* resentment.'

CHAP. XV. The Master said, 'When a man is not *in the habit of* saying—"What shall I think of this? What shall I think of this?" I can indeed do nothing with him!'

CHAP. XVI. The Master said, 'When a number of people are together, for a whole day, without their conversation turning on righteousness, and when they are fond of carrying out *the suggestions of* a small shrewdness;—theirs is indeed a hard case.'

CHAP. XVII. The Master said, 'The superior man *in everything* considers righteousness to be essential. He performs it according to the rules of propriety. He brings it forth in humility. He completes it with sincerity. This is indeed a superior man.'

secretly held possession of it.' Tsang Wǎn would not recommend Hûi because he was an abler and better man than himself. Hûi is a famous name in China. He was an officer of Lû, so styled after death, whose name was 展獲, and designation 禽. He derived his revenue from a town called Liû-hsiâ, or from a *liû* or willow-tree, overhanging his house, which made him be called Liû-hsiâ Hûi—'Hûi that lived under the willow-tree.' See Mencius, II. Pt. i. chap. 9.

14. THE WAY TO WARD OFF RESENTMENTS. 責 it is said, is here 'to require from,' and not 'to reprove.'

15. NOTHING CAN BE MADE OF PEOPLE WHO TAKE THINGS EASILY, NOT GIVING THEMSELVES THE TROUBLE TO THINK. Compare VII. viii.

16. AGAINST FRIVOLOUS TALKERS AND SUPERFICIAL SPECULATORS. Chû explains 難矣哉 by 'they have no ground from which to become virtuous, and they will meet with calamity.' Ho Yen gives Chǎng's explanation, 'they will never complete anything.' Our nearly literal translation appears to convey the meaning. 'A hard case,' i. e. they will make nothing out, and nothing can be made of them.

17. THE CONDUCT OF THE SUPERIOR MAN IS RIGHTEOUS, COURTEOUS, HUMBLE, AND SINCERE. 質 is explained by Chû Hsî by 'the substance and stem;' and in the 'Complete Digest' by

以成之君子哉。

之不已知也。

六章 子曰君子病無能焉不病人

焉。

五章 子曰君子疾沒世而名不稱

人。

子曰君子求諸己小人求諸

黨。

子曰君子矜而不爭群而不

子曰君子不以言舉人不以

CHAP. XVIII. The Master said, 'The superior man is distressed by his want of ability. He is not distressed by men's not knowing him.'

CHAP. XIX. The Master said, 'The superior man dislikes the thought of his name not being mentioned after his death.'

CHAP. XX. The Master said, 'What the superior man seeks, is in himself. What the mean man seeks, is in others.

CHAP. XXI. The Master said, 'The superior man is dignified, but does not wrangle. He is sociable, but not a partizan.'

CHAP. XXII. The Master said, 'The superior man does not promote a man *simply* on account of his words, nor does he put aside *good* words because of the man.'

'foundation.' The antecedent to all the 之 is 義, or rather the thing, whatever it be, done righteously.

18. OUR OWN INCOMPETENCY, AND NOT OUR REPUTATION, THE PROPER BUSINESS OF CONCERN TO US. See XIV. xxxii, *et al.*

19. THE SUPERIOR MAN WISHES TO BE HAD IN REMEMBRANCE. Not, say the commentators, that the superior man cares about fame, but fame is the invariable concomitant of merit. He cannot have been the superior man, if he be not remembered. 沒世,—see 大學傳

II. In the 備旨, 日講, and many other paraphrases, 沒世 is taken as = 終身; 'all his life.' Still, I let the translation suggested by the use of the phrase in the 'Great Learning' keep its place.

20. HIS OWN APPROBATION IS THE SUPERIOR MAN'S RULE. THE APPROBATION OF OTHERS IS THE MEAN MAN'S. Compare XIV. xxv.

21. THE SUPERIOR MAN IS DIGNIFIED AND AFFABLE, WITHOUT THE FAULTS TO WHICH THOSE QUALITIES OFTEN LEAD. Compare II. xiv and VII. xxx. 2. 矜 is here = 莊以持己, 'grave in self-maintenance.'

22. THE SUPERIOR MAN IS DISCRIMINATING IN HIS EMPLOYMENT OF MEN AND JUDGING OF STATFMENTS.

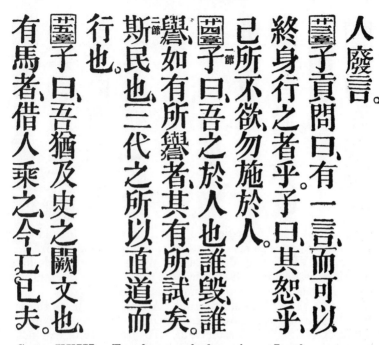

CHAP. XXIII. Tsze-kung asked, saying, 'Is there one word which may serve as a rule of practice for all one's life?' The Master said, 'Is not RECIPROCITY such a word? What you do not want done to yourself, do not do to others.'

CHAP. XXIV. 1. The Master said, 'In my dealings with men, whose evil do I blame, whose goodness do I praise, beyond what is proper? If I do sometimes exceed in praise, there must be ground for it in my examination *of the individual.*

2. 'This people supplied the ground why the three dynasties pursued the path of straightforwardness.'

CHAP. XXV. The Master said, 'Even in my *early* days, a historiographer would leave a blank in his text, and he who had a horse would lend him to another to ride. Now, alas! there are no such things.'

23. THE GREAT PRINCIPLE OF RECIPROCITY IS THE RULE OF LIFE. Compare V. xi. It is singular that Tsze-kung professes there to act on the principle here recommended to him. *Altruism* may be substituted for *reciprocity.*

24. CONFUCIUS SHOWED HIS RESPECT FOR MEN BY STRICT TRUTHFULNESS IN AWARDING PRAISE OR CENSURE. 1. I have not marked 'beyond what is proper' with italics, because there is really that force in the verbs—毀 and 譽. 'Ground for it in my examination of the individual;'— i. e. from my examination of him I believe he will yet verify my words. 2. 斯民也, re-

sumes the 人 of the 1st paragraph, which the 也 indicates. 所以 is to be taken as = 'the reason why,' and 行 as a neuter verb of general application. 三代, 'the three dynasties,' with special reference to their great founders, and the principles which they inaugurated.— The truth-approving nature of the people was a rule even to those sages. It was the same to Confucius.

25. INSTANCES OF THE DEGENERACY OF CONFUCIUS'S TIMES. Most paraphrasts supply a 見 after 及;—'even in my time I have seen.'

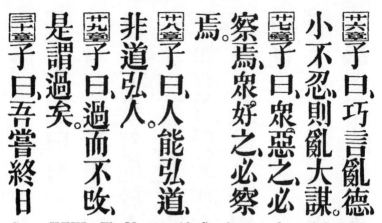

子曰、巧言亂德
小不忍則亂大謀。

子曰、衆惡之必
察焉、衆好之必察
焉。

子曰、人能弘道
非道弘人。

子曰、過而不改、
是謂過矣。

子曰、吾嘗終日

CHAP. XXVI. The Master said, 'Specious words confound virtue. Want of forbearance in small matters confounds great plans.'

CHAP. XXVII. The Master said, 'When the multitude hate a man, it is necessary to examine into the case. When the multitude like a man, it is necessary to examine into the case.'

CHAP. XXVIII. The Master said, 'A man can enlarge the principles *which he follows;* those principles do not enlarge the man.'

CHAP. XXIX. The Master said, 'To have faults and not to reform them,—this, indeed, should be pronounced having faults.'

CHAP. XXX. The Master said, ' I have been the whole day

The appointment of the historiographer is referred to Hwang-tî, or 'The Yellow sovereign,' the inventor of the cycle. The statutes of Châu mention no fewer than five classes of such officers. They were attached also to the feudal courts, and what Confucius says, is that, in his early days, a historiographer, on any point about which he was not sure, would leave a blank; so careful were they to record only truth.

吾猶及 extends on to 有馬云云. This second sentence is explained in Ho Yen:—'If any one had a horse which he could not tame, he would lend it to another to ride and exercise it!'—The commentator Hû (胡氏) says well, that the meaning of the chapter must be left in uncertainty (the second part of it especially).

26. THE DANGER OF SPECIOUS WORDS, AND OF IMPATIENCE. 小不忍 is not 'a little impatience,' but impatience in little things; 'the hastiness,' it is said, 'of women and small people.'

27. IN JUDGING OF A MAN, WE MUST NOT BE GUIDED BY HIS BEING GENERALLY LIKED OR DISLIKED. Compare XIII. xxiv.

28. PRINCIPLES OF DUTY AN INSTRUMENT IN THE HAND OF MAN. This sentence is quite mystical in its sententiousness. The 翼註 says:—'道 here is the path of duty, which all men, in their various relations, have to pursue, and man

has the three virtues of knowledge, benevolence, and fortitude, wherewith to pursue that path, and so he enlarges it. That virtue remote, occupying an empty place, cannot enlarge man, needs not to be said.' That writer's account of 道 here is probably correct, and 'duty unapprehended,' 'in an empty place,' can have no effect on any man; but this is a mere truism. Duty apprehended is constantly enlarging, elevating, and energizing multitudes, who had previously been uncognizant of it. The first clause of the chapter may be granted, but the second is not in accordance with truth. Generally, however, man may be considered as the measure of the truth in morals and metaphysics which he holds; but after all, systems of men are for the most part beneath the highest capacities of the model men, the *Chün-tsze.*

29. THE CULPABILITY OF NOT REFORMING KNOWN FAULTS. Compare I. viii. Chû Hsi's commentary appears to make the meaning somewhat different. He says:—'If one having faults can change them, he comes back to the condition of having no faults. But if he do not change them, then they go on to their completion, and will never come to be changed.'

30. THE FRUITLESSNESS OF THINKING, WITHOUT READING. Compare II. xv, where the dependence of acquisition and reflection on each other is set forth.—Many commentators say that Confucius merely transfers the things which he here mentions to himself for the sake of others, not that it ever was really thus with himself.

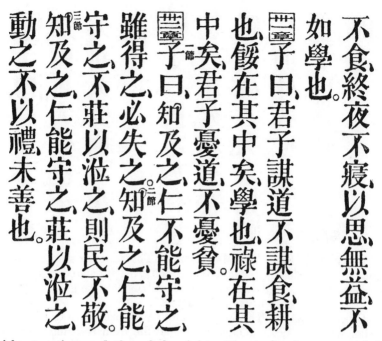

without eating, and the whole night without sleeping:—occupied with thinking. It was of no use. The better plan is to learn.'

CHAP. XXXI. The Master said, 'The object of the superior man is truth. Food is not his object. There is ploughing;—even in that there is *sometimes* want. So with learning;—emolument may be found in it. The superior man is anxious lest he should not get truth; he is not anxious lest poverty should come upon him.'

CHAP. XXXII. 1. The Master said, 'When a man's knowledge is sufficient to attain, and his virtue is not sufficient to enable him to hold, whatever he may have gained, he will lose again.

2. 'When his knowledge is sufficient to attain, and he has virtue enough to hold fast, if he cannot govern with dignity, the people will not respect him.

3. 'When his knowledge is sufficient to attain, and he has virtue enough to hold fast; when he governs also with dignity, yet if he try to move the people contrary to the rules of propriety:—full excellence is not reached.'

31. THE SUPERIOR MAN SHOULD NOT BE MERCENARY, BUT HAVE TRUTH FOR HIS OBJECT. Here again we translate 道 by 'truth,' as the best term that offers. 餒, 'hunger,'=want. 'Want may be in the midst of ploughing,'—i.e. husbandry is the way to plenty, and yet a famine or scarcity sometimes occurs. The application of this to the case of learning, however, is not apt. Is the emolument that sometimes comes with learning a calamity like famine? The contrast of the two cases is not well maintained.

32. HOW KNOWLEDGE WITHOUT VIRTUE IS NOT LASTING, AND TO KNOWLEDGE AND VIRTUE A RULER SHOULD ADD DIGNITY AND THE RULES OF PROPRIETY. 1. Here the various *chih* and the two first in the other paragraphs have *le*, or principle, for their reference. In Ho Yen,

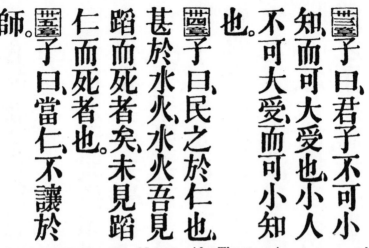

CHAP. XXXIII. The Master said, 'The superior man cannot be known in little matters; but he may be intrusted with great concerns. The small men may not be intrusted with great concerns, but he may be known in little matters.'

CHAP. XXXIV. The Master said, 'Virtue is more to man than either water or fire. I have seen men die from treading on water and fire, but I have never seen a man die from treading the course of virtue.'

CHAP. XXXV. The Master said, 'Let every man consider virtue as what devolves on himself. He may not yield the performance of it *even* to his teacher.'

however, Pâo Hsien says:—'A man may have knowledge equal to the management of his office (治其官), but if he have not virtue which can hold it fast, thòugh he get it, he will lose it.' 2. In 泣之, and 動之 below, 之指民言, 'the 之 have 民, or people, for their reference.' 3. The phrase—'to move the people' is analogous to several others, such as 鼓之, 舞之, 與之, 'to drum the people,' 'to dance them,' 'to rouse them.'

33. How to know the superior man and the mean man; and their capacities. Chû Hsî says—知, 我知之, 'the knowing here is our knowing the individuals.' The 'little matters' are ingenious but trifling arts and accomplishments, in which a really great man may sometimes be deficient, while a small man will be familiar with them. The 'knowing' is not that the parties are *chŭn-tsze* and *hsiâo-zăn*, but what attainments they have, and for what they are fit. The difficulty, on this view, is with the conclusion—而可小知.—Ho Yen says:—'The way of the *chŭn-tsze* is profound and far-reaching. He will not let his

knowledge be small, and he may be trusted with what is great. The way of the *hsiâo-zăn* is shallow and near. He will let his knowledge be small, and he may not be trusted with what is great.'

34. Virtue more to man than water or fire, and never hurtful to him. 民 is here = 人, 'man,' as in VI. xx. 民之於仁也—'the people's relation to, or dependence on, virtue.' The case is easily conceivable of men's suffering death on account of their virtue. There have been martyrs for their loyalty and other virtues, as well as for their religious faith. Chû Hsî provides for this difference in his remarks:—'The want of fire and water is hurtful only to man's body, but to be without virtue is to lose one's mind (the higher nature), and so it is more to him than water or fire.' See on IV. viii.

35. Virtue personal and obligatory on every man. The old interpreters take 當 in the sense of 'ought.' Chû Hsî certainly improves on them by taking it in the sense of 擔當, as in the translation. A student at first takes 當 to be in the 2nd person, but the 不 following recalls him to the 3rd.

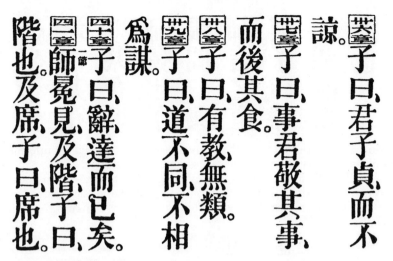

CHAP. XXXVI. The Master said, 'The superior man is correctly firm, and not firm merely.'

CHAP. XXXVII. The Master said, 'A minister, in serving his prince, reverently discharges his duties, and makes his emolument a secondary consideration.'

CHAP. XXXVIII. The Master said, 'In teaching there should be no distinction of classes.'

CHAP. XXXIX. The Master said, 'Those whose courses are different cannot lay plans for one another.'

CHAP. XL. The Master said, 'In language it is simply required that it convey the meaning.'

CHAP. XLI. 1. The Music-master, Mien, having called upon him, when they came to the steps, the Master said, 'Here are the steps.' When they came to the mat *for the guest* to sit upon, he

36. THE SUPERIOR MAN'S FIRMNESS IS BASED ON RIGHT. 貞 is used here in the sense which it has throughout the Yî-ching. Both it and 諒 imply firmness, but 貞 supposes a moral and intelligent basis which may be absent from 諒; see XIV. xviii. 3.

37. THE FAITHFUL MINISTER. The 其 refers not to 君, but to the individual who 事君. We have to supply the subject—'a minister.' 後, as in VI. xx.

38. THE COMPREHENSIVENESS OF TEACHING. Chû Hsî says on this :—'The nature of all men is good, but we find among them the different classes of good and bad. This is the effect of physical constitution and of practice. The superior man, in consequence, employs his teaching, and all may be brought back to the state of good, and there is no necessity (the language is 不當復論其類之惡) of speaking any more of the badness of some.' This is extravagant. Teaching is not so omnipotent.—The old interpretation is simply that in teaching there should be no distinction of classes.

39. AGREEMENT IN PRINCIPLE NECESSARY TO CONCORD IN PLANS. 為 is the 4th tone, but I do not see that there would be any great difference in the meaning, if it were read in its usual 2nd tone.

40. PERSPICUITY THE CHIEF VIRTUE OF LANGUAGE. 辭 may be used both of speech and of style.

41. CONSIDERATION OF CONFUCIUS FOR THE BLIND. 1. 師,—i. q. 太師, III. xxiii. Anciently, the blind were employed in the offices of music, partly because their sense of hearing was more than ordinarily acute, and partly that they might be made of some use in

said, 'Here is the mat.' When all were seated, the Master informed him, saying, 'So and so is here; so and so is here.'

2. The Music-master, Mien, having gone out, Tsze-chang asked, saying, 'Is it the rule to tell those things to the Music-master?'

3. The Master said, 'Yes. This is certainly the rule for those who lead the blind.'

the world; see the 集證, *in loc.* 見,—4th tone. Mien had come to Confucius's house, under the care of a guide, but the sage met him, and undertook the care of him himself. 2. 之 is governed by 言, and refers to the words of Confucius to Mien in the preceding paragraph.

BOOK XVI.　KE SHE.

CHAPTER I. 1. The head of the Chî family was going to attack Chwan-yü.

2. Zăn Yû and Chî-lû had an interview with Confucius, and said, '*Our chief*, Chî, is going to commence operations against Chwan-yü.'

HEADING OF THIS BOOK.—季 氏 第 十 六, 'The chief of the Chî, No. 16.' Throughout this Book, Confucius is spoken of as 孔子, 'The philosopher K'ung,' and never by the designation 子, or 'The Master.' Then, the style of several of the chapters (iv–xi) is not like the utterances of Confucius to which we have been accustomed. From these circumstances, one commentator, Hung Kwo (洪 适), supposed that it belonged to the Ch'î (齊) *recensus* of these Analects; the other Books belonging to the Lû (魯) *recensus*. This supposition, however, is not otherwise supported.

1. CONFUCIUS EXPOSES THE PRESUMPTUOUS AND IMPOLITIC CONDUCT OF THE CHIEF OF THE CHÎ FAMILY IN PROPOSING TO ATTACK A MINOR STATE, AND REBUKES ZĂN YÛ AND TSZE-LÛ FOR ABETTING THE DESIGN. 1. 季 氏 and 季 孫 below,—see III. i. Chwan-yü was a small territory in Lû, whose ruler was of the 子, or 4th order of nobility. It was one of the States called 附 庸, or 'attached,' whose chiefs could not appear in

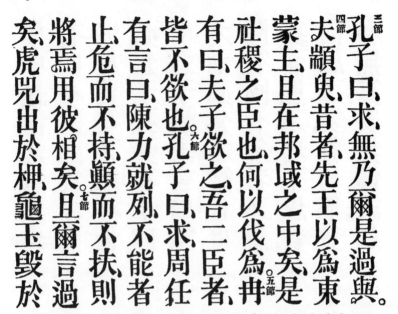

3. Confucius said, 'Ch'iû, is it not you who are in fault here?

4. 'Now, in regard to Chwan-yü, long ago, a former king appointed its ruler to preside over *the sacrifices to* the eastern Măng; moreover, it is in the midst of the territory of our State; and its ruler is a minister in direct connexion with the sovereign:—What has *your chief* to do with attacking it?'

5. Zan Yû said, 'Our master wishes the thing; neither of us two ministers wishes it.'

6. Confucius said, 'Ch'iû, there are the words of Châu Zăn,— "When he can put forth his ability, he takes his place in the ranks *of office;* when he finds himself unable to do so, he retires from it. How can he be used as a guide to a blind man, who does not support him when tottering, nor raise him up when fallen?"

7. 'And further, you speak wrongly. When a tiger or rhinoceros escapes from his cage; when a tortoise or piece of jade is injured in its repository:—whose is the fault?'

the presence of the sovereign, excepting in the train of the prince within whose jurisdiction they were embraced. Their existence was not from a practice like the sub-infeudation, which belonged to the feudal system of Europe. They held of the lord paramount or king, but with the restriction which has been mentioned, and with a certain subservience also to their immediate superior. Its particular position is fixed by its proximity to Pî, and to the Măng hill. 伐 is not merely 'to attack,' but 'to attack and punish,' an exercise of judicial authority, which could emanate only from the sovereign. The term is used here, to show the

nefarious and presumptuous character of the contemplated operations. 2. There is some difficulty here, as, according to the 'Historical Records,' the two disciples were not in the service of the Chî family at the same time. We may suppose, however, that Tsze-lû, returning with the sage from Wei on the invitation of duke Âi, took service a second time, and for a short period, with the Chî family, of which the chief was then Chî K'ang. This brings the time of the transaction to B. c. 483, or 482. 將有事,—literally, 'is going to have an affair.' 3. Confucius addresses himself only to Ch'iû, as he had been a considerable time, and

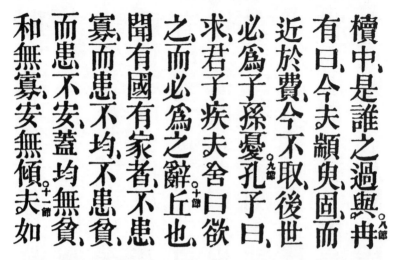

8. Zăn Yû said, 'But at present, Chwan-yü is strong and near to Pî; if *our chief* do not now take it, it will hereafter be a sorrow to his descendants.'

9. Confucius said, 'Ch'iû, the superior man hates that declining to say—"I want such and such a thing," and framing explanations *for the conduct.*

10. 'I have heard that rulers of States and chiefs of families are not troubled lest their people should be few, but are troubled lest they should not keep their several places; that they are not troubled with fears of poverty, but are troubled with fears of a want of contented repose *among the people in their several places.* For when the people keep their several places, there will be no poverty; when harmony prevails, there will be no scarcity of people; and when there is such a *contented* repose, there will be no rebellious upsettings.

11. 'So it is.—Therefore, if remoter people are not submissive, all

very active, in the Chî service. 4. It was the prerogative of the princes to sacrifice to the hills and rivers within their jurisdictions;—here was the chief of Chwan-yŭ, royally appointed (the 'former king' is probably 成, the second sovereign of the Châu dynasty) to be the lord of the Măng mountain, that is, to preside over the sacrifices offered to it. This raised him high above any mere ministers or officers of Lû. The mountain Măng is in the present district of Pî, in the department of Î-châu. It was called eastern, to distinguish it from another of the same name in Shen-hsî, which was the western Măng. 且在邦域之中,—this is mentioned, to show that Chwan-yü was so situated as to give Lû no occasion for apprehension. 社稷之臣, 'a minister of the altars to the spirits of the land and grain.' To those spirits only, the prince had the preroga-

tive of sacrificing. The chief of Chwan-yü having this, how dared an officer of Lû to think of attacking him? The 臣 is used of his relation to the king. Chû Hsî makes the phrase =公家之臣, 'a minister of the ducal house,' saying that the three families had usurped all the dominions proper of Lû, leaving only the chiefs of the attached States to appear in the ducal court. I prefer the former interpretation. 何以伐爲 must be understood with reference to the Chî. See Wang Yin Chih on Wei as a 語助, where he quotes this text (2nd chapter of his treatise on the Particles). 5. 夫子, our 'master,' i.e. the chief of the Chî family. 6. Châu Zăn is by Chû Hsî simply called—'a good historiographer of ancient times.' Some trace him

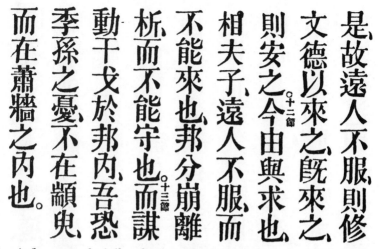

the influences of civil culture and virtue are to be cultivated to attract them to be so; and when they have been so attracted, they must be made contented and tranquil.

12. 'Now, here are you, Yû and Ch'iû, assisting your chief. Remoter people are not submissive, and, *with your help*, he cannot attract them to him. In his own territory there are divisions and downfalls, leavings and separations, and, *with your help*, he cannot preserve it.

13. 'And yet he is planning these hostile movements within the State.—I am afraid that the sorrow of the Chî-sun *family* will not be on account of Chwan-yü, but will be found within the screen of their own court.'

back to the Shang dynasty, and others only to the early times of the Châu. There are other weighty utterances of his in vogue, besides that in the text. 7. Chû Hsî explains 兕 by 野牛, 'a wild bull.' The dictionary says it is like an ox, and goes on to describe it as 'one-horned.' The 本草, 獸 部, says that 兕 and 犀 are different terms for the same animal, i. e. the rhinoceros. I cannot think that 龜 here is the living tortoise. That would not be kept in a 櫝, or 'coffer,' like a gem. Perhaps the character is, by mistake, for 圭. 9. The regimen of 疾 extends down to the end of the paragraph. 夫,—as in XI. xxiv. 爲之辭 is the same idiom as 爲 之宰, V. vii. 10. Confucius uses the term 患 here with reference to the 憂 in par. 8. 均, 'equality.' 謂各得其分 means —'every one getting his own proper name and

place.' From this point, Confucius speaks of the general disorganization of Lû under the management of the three families, and especially of the Chî. By 遠人 we can hardly understand the people of Chwan-yü. 11. 來 is to be understood with a hiphil force, 'to make to come,' 'to attract.' 12. 不能來, 不能 守 are to be understood of the Head of the Chî family, as controlling the government of Lû, and *as being assisted by the two disciples*, so that the reproof falls heavily on them. 13. 在蕭牆 之內,—Chû Hsî simply says 蕭牆, 屏 也, 'hsiâo-ch'iang means a screen.' In the dictionary, after Ho Yen, hsiâo in this passage = 肅, 'reverent,' and 牆 alone means 'screen,' and the phrase is thus explained:— 'Officers, on reaching the screen, which they had only to pass to find themselves in the presence of their ruler, were supposed to become more reverential;' and hence, the expression in the text = 'among his own immediate officers.'

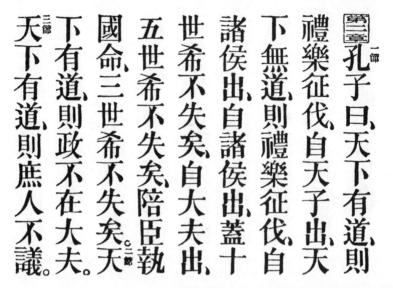

CHAP. II. 1. Confucius said, 'When good government prevails in the empire, ceremonies, music, and punitive military expeditions proceed from the son of Heaven. When bad government prevails in the empire, ceremonies, music, and punitive military expeditions proceed from the princes. When these things proceed from the princes, as a rule, the cases will be few in which they do not lose their power in ten generations. When they proceed from the Great officers *of the princes, as a rule,* the cases will be few in which they do not lose their power in five generations. When the subsidiary ministers *of the Great officers* hold in their grasp the orders of the State, *as a rule,* the cases will be few in which they do not lose their power in three generations.

2. 'When right principles prevail in the kingdom, government will not be in the hands of the Great officers.

3. 'When right principles prevail in the kingdom, there will be no discussions among the common people.'

2. THE SUPREME AUTHORITY OUGHT EVER TO MAINTAIN ITS POWER. THE VIOLATION OF THIS RULE ALWAYS LEADS TO RUIN, WHICH IS SPEEDIER AS THE RANK OF THE VIOLATOR IS LOWER.—In these utterances, Confucius had reference to the disorganized state of the kingdom, when 'the son of Heaven' was fast becoming an empty name, the princes of States were in bondage to their Great officers, and those again at the mercy of their family ministers. 1. 有道, 無道, —compare XIV. i. 征伐 are to be taken together, as in the translation. We read of four 征, i. e. expeditions,—east, west, north, and south; and of nine 伐, i. e. nine grounds on which the sovereign might order such expeditions. On the royal prerogatives, see the 中庸, XXVIII. 蓋 is here= 大約, 'generally speaking,' 'as a rule.' 陪臣 = 家臣, 'family ministers.' 國命 are the same as the previous 禮, 樂, 征, 伐, but having been usurped by the princes, and now again snatched from them by their officers, they can no longer be spoken of as royal affairs, but only as 國之事, 'State matters.' 3. 議 = 私議, 'private discussions;' i. e. about the state of public affairs.

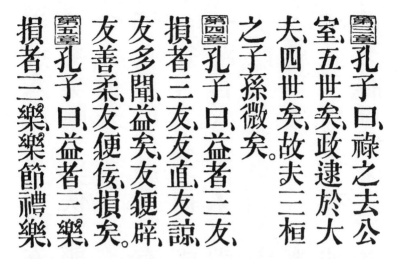

CHAP. III. Confucius said, 'The revenue *of the State* has left the ducal House now for five generations. The government has been in the hands of the Great officers for four generations. On this account, the descendants of the three Hwan are much reduced.'

CHAP. IV. Confucius said, 'There are three friendships which are advantageous, and three which are injurious. Friendship with the upright; friendship with the sincere; and friendship with the man of much observation:—these are advantageous. Friendship with the man of specious airs; friendship with the insinuatingly soft; and friendship with the glib-tongued:—these are injurious.'

CHAP. V. Confucius said, 'There are three things men find enjoyment in which are advantageous, and three things they find enjoyment in which are injurious. To find enjoyment in the discriminating study of ceremonies and music; to find enjoyment in

3. ILLUSTRATION OF THE PRINCIPLES OF THE LAST CHAPTER. In the year B. C. 609, at the death of duke Wän, his rightful heir was killed, and the son of a concubine raised to the ruler's place. He is in the annals as duke Hsüan (宣), and after him came Ch'äng, Hsiang, Ch'âo, and Ting, in whose time this must have been spoken. These dukes were but shadows, pensionaries of their Great officers, so that it might be said the revenue had gone from them. Observe that here and in the preceding chapter 世 is used for 'a reign.' 'The three Hwan' are the three families, as being all descended from duke Hwan; see on II. v.—Chù Hsî appears to have fallen into a mistake in enumerating the four heads of the Chî family who had administered the government of Lû as Wû, Tâo, P'ing, and Hwan, as Tâo (悼) died before his father, and would not be said therefore to have the government in his hands. The right enumeration is

Wän (文), Wû (武), P'ing (平), and Hwan (桓). See the 拓餘說, III. xxvi.

4. THREE FRIENDSHIPS ADVANTAGEOUS, AND THREE INJURIOUS. In the 備旨 it is said— 三友下各友字俱作变字看, 是我去友人, 'after 三友, the character 友 is always verbal and = 变, "*to have intercourse with*."' It is as well to translate the term by 'friendship' throughout. 諒 is 'sincere,' without the subtractions required in XIV. xviii. 3, XV. xxxvi. 便, here = 習熟, 'practised.' 善柔 = 善柔之工, '善 is skilfulness in being bland.'

5. THREE SOURCES OF ENJOYMENT ADVANTAGEOUS, AND THREE INJURIOUS. Here we have 樂 with three pronunciations and in three different

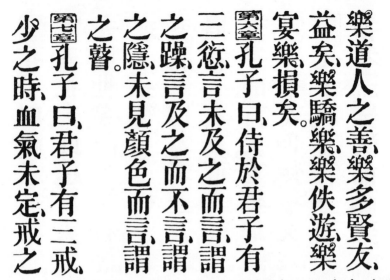

speaking of the goodness of others; to find enjoyment in having
many worthy friends:—these are advantageous. To find enjoyment in extravagant pleasures; to find enjoyment in idleness and
sauntering; to find enjoyment in the pleasures of feasting:—these
are injurious.'

CHAP. VI. Confucius said, 'There are three errors to which
they who stand in the presence of a man of virtue and station are
liable. They may speak when it does not come to them to speak;—
this is called rashness. They may not speak when it comes to them
to speak;—this is called concealment. They may speak without looking at the countenance *of their superior;*—this is called blindness.'

CHAP. VII. Confucius said, 'There are three things which the
superior man guards against. In youth, when the physical powers

meanings. The leading word is read *áo*, 4th
tone, 'to have enjoyment in,' as in VI. xxi.
In 禮樂, it is *yo*, 'music.' The two others
are 樂, *lo* or *lé*, 'joy,' 'to delight in.' 節禮
樂,—節 = 節之, i. e. it is a verb, 'to discriminate;' 'to mark the divisions of.' The idea
is that ceremonies and music containing in them
the principles of propriety and harmony, the
study of them could not but be beneficial to the
student himself, as having to exemplify both of
those things. 驕, primarily, 'a tall horse,'
often used for 'proud;' here = vain and extravagant self-indulgence. 宴, 'feasting,' including, says a gloss, 'eating, drinking, music,
women, &c.'

6. THREE ERRORS IN REGARD TO SPEECH TO BE
AVOIDED IN THE PRESENCE OF THE GREAT. 君子
according to Chû Hsî, denotes here 'a man both

of rank and virtue.' 'Without looking at the
countenance,'—i. e. to see whether he is paying
attention or not.—The general principle is that
there is a time to speak. Let that be observed,
and these three errors will be avoided.

7. THE VICES WHICH YOUTH, MANHOOD, AND AGE
RESPECTIVELY HAVE TO GUARD AGAINST. 血氣,
'blood and breath.' In the 中庸, XXI, 凡
有血氣者 = 'all human beings.' Here
the phrase is equivalent to 'the physical powers.'
On 未定, 'not yet settled,' the gloss in the
備旨 is—方動之時, 'the time when
they are moving most.' As to what causal relation Confucius may have supposed to exist
between the state of the physical powers, and
the several vices indicated, that is not developed. Hsing Ping explains the first caution
thus:—'Youth embraces all the period below
29. Then the physical powers are still weak,

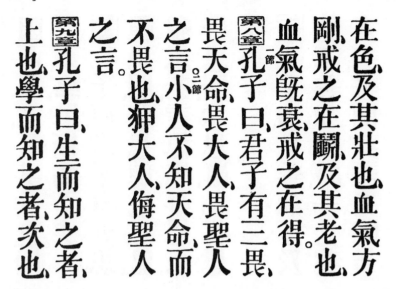

are not yet settled, he guards against lust.　When he is strong, and the physical powers are full of vigour, he guards against quarrelsomeness.　When he is old, and the animal powers are decayed, he guards against covetousness.'

CHAP. VIII.　1. Confucius said, 'There are three things of which the superior man stands in awe.　He stands in awe of the ordinances of Heaven.　He stands in awe of great men.　He stands in awe of the words of sages.

2. 'The mean man does not know the ordinances of Heaven, and *consequently* does not stand in awe of them.　He is disrespectful to great men.　He makes sport of the words of sages.'

CHAP. IX.　Confucius said, 'Those who are born with the possession of knowledge are the highest class of men.　Those who learn, and so, *readily*, get possession of knowledge, are the next.

and the sinews and bones have not reached their vigour, and indulgence in lust will injure the body.'　By the superior man's guarding against these three things, I suppose it is meant that he teaches that they are to be guarded against.

8. CONTRAST OF THE SUPERIOR AND THE MEAN MAN IN REGARD TO THE THREE THINGS OF WHICH THE FORMER STANDS IN AWE. 天命, according to Chû Hsî, means the moral nature of man, conferred by Heaven. High above the nature of other creatures, it lays him under great responsibility to cherish and cultivate himself. The old interpreters take the phrase to indicate Heaven's moral administration by rewards and punishments. The 'great men' are men high in position and great in wisdom and virtue, the royal instructors, who have been raised up by Heaven for the training and ruling of mankind.

So, the commentators; but the 狎 suggests at once a more general and a lower view of the phrase.

9. FOUR CLASSES OF MEN IN RELATION TO KNOWLEDGE. On the 1st clause, see on VII. xix, where Confucius disclaims for himself being ranked in the first of the classes here mentioned. The modern commentators say, that men are differenced here by the difference of their 氣質 or 氣禀, on which see Morrison's Dictionary, part II, vol. i, character 質. 困, in the dictionary, and by commentators, old and new, is explained by 不通, 'not thoroughly understanding.' It is not to be joined with 學, as if the meaning were—'they

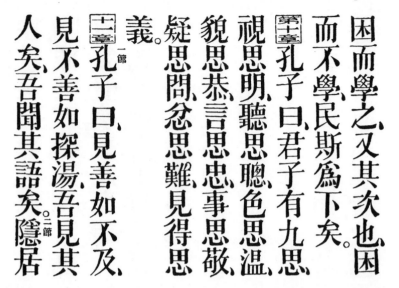

Those who are dull and stupid, and yet compass the learning, are another class next to these. As to those who are dull and stupid and yet do not learn;—they are the lowest of the people.'

CHAP. X. Confucius said, 'The superior man has nine things which are subjects with him of thoughtful consideration. In regard to the use of his eyes, he is anxious to see clearly. In regard to the use of his ears, he is anxious to hear distinctly. In regard to his countenance, he is anxious that it should be benign. In regard to his demeanour, he is anxious that it should be respectful. In regard to his speech, he is anxious that it should be sincere. In regard to his doing of business, he is anxious that it should be reverently careful. In regard to what he doubts about, he is anxious to question others. When he is angry, he thinks of the difficulties (*his anger may involve him in*). When he sees gain to be got, he thinks of righteousness.'

CHAP. XI. 1. Confucius said, 'Contemplating good, *and pursuing it,* as if they could not reach it; contemplating evil, *and shrinking from it,* as they would from thrusting the hand into boiling water:—I have seen such men, as I have heard such words.

2. 'Living in retirement to study their aims, and practising

---

learn with painful effort,' although such effort will be required in the case of the 困.

10. NINE SUBJECTS OF THOUGHT TO THE SUPERIOR MAN :—VARIOUS INSTANCES OF THE WAY IN WHICH HE REGULATES HIMSELF. The conciseness of the text contrasts here with the verbosity of the translation, and yet the many words of the latter seem necessary.

11. THE CONTEMPORARIES OF CONFUCIUS COULD ESCHEW EVIL, AND FOLLOW AFTER GOOD, BUT NO

ONE OF THE HIGHEST CAPACITY HAD APPEARED AMONG THEM. 1. The two first clauses here and in the next paragraph also, are quotations of old sayings, current in Confucius's time. 'Such men' were several of the sage's own disciples.

2. 求其志, 'seeking for their aims;' i. e. meditating on them, studying them, fixing them, to be prepared to carry them out, as in the next clause. Such men among the ancients were the great ministers Î Yin and T'ăi-kung.

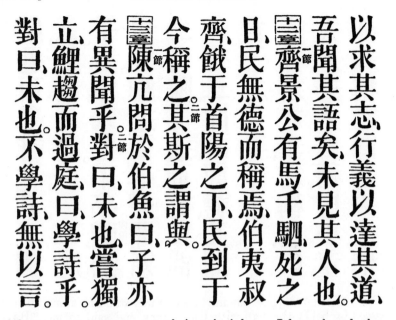

righteousness to carry out their principles :—I have heard these words, but I have not seen such men.'

CHAP. XII. 1. The duke Ching of Ch'î had a thousand teams, each of four horses, but on the day of his death, the people did not praise him for a single virtue. Po-î and Shû-ch'î died of hunger at the foot of the Shâu-yang mountain, and the people, down to the present time, praise them.

2. 'Is not that saying illustrated by this?'

CHAP. XIII. 1. Ch'ăn K'ang asked Po-yü, saying, 'Have you heard any lessons *from your father* different *from what we have all* heard?'

2. Po-yü replied, 'No. He was standing alone once, when I passed below the hall with hasty steps, and said to me, "Have you learned the Odes?" On my replying "Not yet," *he added*, "If you do not learn the Odes, you will not be fit to converse with." I retired and studied the Odes.

Such might the disciple Yen Hûi have been, but an early death snatched him away before he could have an opportunity of showing what was in him.

12. WEALTH WITHOUT VIRTUE AND VIRTUE WITHOUT WEALTH ;—THEIR DIFFERENT APPRECIATIONS. This chapter is plainly a fragment. As it stands, it would appear to come from the compilers and not from Confucius. Then the 2nd paragraph implies a reference to something which has been lost. Under XII. x, I have referred to the proposal to transfer to this place the last paragraph of that chapter which might be explained, so as to harmonize with the sen-

timent of this.—The duke Ching of Ch'î,—see XII. xi. Po-î and Shû-ch'î,—see VI. xxii. The mountain Shâu-yang is to be found probably in the department of 蒲州 in Shan-hsî.

13. CONFUCIUS'S INSTRUCTION OF HIS SON NOT DIFFERENT FROM HIS INSTRUCTION OF THE DISCIPLES GENERALLY. 1. Ch'ăn K'ang is the Tsze-ch'in of I. x. When Confucius's eldest son was born, the duke of Lû sent the philosopher a present of a carp, on which account he named the child 鯉 (the carp), and afterwards gave him the designation of 伯魚. 子亦有

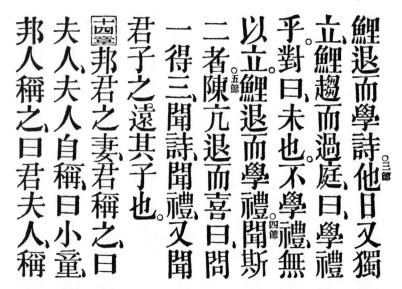

鯉退而學詩他日又獨
○三節

立鯉趨而過庭曰、學禮

乎對曰、未也、不學禮無
○四節

以立鯉退而學禮聞斯

二者陳亢退而喜曰、問
○五節

一得三聞詩聞禮又聞

君子之遠其子也。

邦君之妻君稱之曰

夫人夫人自稱曰小童、

邦人稱之曰君夫人、稱

3. 'Another day, he was in the same way standing alone, when I passed by below the hall with hasty steps, and said to me, "Have you learned the rules of Propriety?" On my replying "Not yet," *he added*, "If you do not learn the rules of Propriety, your character cannot be established." I then retired, and learned the rules of Propriety.

4. 'I have heard only these two things from him.'

5. Ch'ăn K'ang retired, and, quite delighted, said, 'I asked one thing, and I have got three things. I have heard about the Odes. I have heard about the rules of Propriety. I have also heard that the superior man maintains a distant reserve towards his son.'

CHAP. XIV. The wife of the prince of a State is called by him FÛ-ZĂN. She calls herself HSIÂO T'UNG. The people of the State call

異 聞 乎, 'Have you *also* (i.e. as being his son) heard different instructions?' 2. On 詩 here, and 禮 next paragraph, see on VII. xvii. Before 不學, here and below, we must supply a 曰. 3. 立,—see VIII. viii. 4. The force of the 者 is to make the whole = 'what I have heard from him are only these two remarks.' 5. Confucius is, no doubt, intended by 君子, but it is best to translate it generally.

14. APPELLATIONS FOR THE WIFE OF A RULER. This chapter may have been spoken by Confucius to rectify some disorder of the times, but there is no intimation to that effect. The different appellations may be thus explained:—妻 is 與己齊者, 'she who is her husband's equal.' The 夫 in 夫人 is taken as =扶, 'to support,' 'to help,' so that that designation is equivalent to 'help-meet.' 童 means either 'a youth,' or 'a girl.' The wife modestly calls herself 小童, 'the little girl.' The old interpreters take—most naturally—君夫人 as =君之夫人, 'our prince's help-meet,' but the modern commentators take 君 adjectively, as =主, with reference to the office of the wife to 'preside over the internal economy of the palace.' On this view 君夫人 is 'the domestic help-meet.' The ambassador of a prince spoke of him by the style of 寡君, 'our prince of small virtue.' After

人。君 亦 稱 邦 君、寡 邦、諸
夫 曰 之、人 異 小 曰 異

her CHÜN FÛ-ZĂN, and, to the people of other States, they call her
K'WA HSIÂO CHÜN. The people of other States also call her CHÜN
FÛ-ZĂN.

that example of modesty, his wife was styled to the people of other States, 'our small prince of small virtue.' The people of other States	had no reason to imitate her subjects in that, and so they styled her—'your prince's help-meet,' or 'the domestic help-meet.'

BOOK XVII. YANG HO.

乎。迷 言、子 之。其 孔 子
曰 其 曰、曰、遇 亡 子 孔
不 邦 懷 來 諸 也、豚 子
可。可 其 予 塗 而 孔 不
好 謂 寶、與 謂 往 子 見、
從 仁 而 爾 孔 拜 時 歸

陽 貨 第 十 七
陽 貨 欲 見 孔
子 孔 子 不 見、歸 孔

CHAPTER I.   1. Yang Ho wished to see Confucius, but Confucius
would not go to see him. *On this*, he sent a present of a pig to
Confucius, who, having chosen a time when Ho was not at home,
went to pay his respects *for the gift*. He met him, *however*, on the
way.

2. *Ho* said to Confucius, 'Come, let me speak with you.' He then
asked, ' Can he be called benevolent who keeps his jewel in his

HEADING OF THIS BOOK.—陽貨第十七,
'Yang Ho, No. 17.'—As the last Book commenced with the presumption of the Head of
the Chî family, who kept his prince in subjection, this begins with an account of an officer,
who did for the Head of the Chî what he did
for the duke of Lû. For this reason—some
similarity in the subject-matter of the first
chapters—this Book, it is said, is placed after
the former. It contains 26 chapters.

1. CONFUCIUS'S POLITE BUT DIGNIFIED TREAT-
MENT OF A POWERFUL, BUT USURPING AND UN-
WORTHY, OFFICER. 1. Yang Ho, known also as
Yang Hû (虎), was nominally the principal
minister of the Chî family, but its chief was
entirely in his hands, and he was scheming to
arrogate the whole authority of the State of Lû
to himself. He first appears in the Chronicles
of Lû, acting against the exiled duke Châo; in
B. C. 505, we find him keeping his own chief,

與下愚不移。

也習相遠也。

第三章 子曰性相近

第二章 子曰唯上知

吾將仕矣。

我與。日月逝矣歲不

謂知乎曰不可。

事而亟失時。可

bosom, and leaves his country to confusion?' *Confucius* replied, 'No.' 'Can he be called wise, who is anxious to be engaged in public employment, and yet is constantly losing the opportunity of being so?' *Confucius again* said, 'No.' 'The days and months are passing away; the years do not wait for us.' Confucius said, 'Right; I will go into office.'

CHAP. II. The Master said, 'By nature, men are nearly alike; by practice, they get to be wide apart.'

CHAP. III. The Master said, 'There are only the wise of the highest class, and the stupid of the lowest class, who cannot be changed.'

Chì Hwan, a prisoner, and, in 501, he is driven out, on the failure of his projects, a fugitive into Ch'i. At the time when the incidents in this chapter occurred, Yang Ho was anxious to get, or appear to get, the support of a man of Confucius's reputation, and finding that the sage would not call on him, he adopted the expedient of sending him a pig, at a time when Confucius was not at home, the rules of ceremony requiring that when a great officer sent a present to a scholar, and the latter was not in his house on its arrival, he had to go to the officer's house to acknowledge it. See the Lî Chî, XI. Sect. iii. 20. 歸 is in the sense of 饋, 'to present food,' properly 'before a superior.' Confucius, however, was not to be entrapped. He also *timed* (時, as a verb) Hû's being away from home (亡), and went to call on him. 2. 迷其邦, 'deludes, confuses, his country,' but the meaning is only negative, = 'leaves his country to confusion.' 亟, read *k'i*, in 4th tone, 'frequently.' 日月—我與—all this is to be taken as the remark of Yang Ho, and a 曰 supplied before 日. 我與; 與, in the dictionary, and by the old interpreters, is here explained, as in the translation, by 待, 'to wait for.'

2. THE DIFFERENCES IN THE CHARACTERS OF MEN ARE CHIEFLY OWING TO HABIT. 性, it is contended, is here not the moral constitution of man, absolutely considered, but his complex, actual nature, with its elements of the material, the animal, and the intellectual, by association with which, the perfectly good moral nature is continually being led astray. The moral nature is the same in all, and though the material organism and disposition do differ in different individuals, they are, at first, more nearly alike than they subsequently become. In the 註疏 we read:—'The nature is the constitution received by man at birth, and is *then* still. While it has not been acted on by external things, men are all like one another; they are 近. After it has been acted on by external things, then practice forms, as it were, a second nature. He who practises what is good, becomes the superior man ; and he who practises what is not good, becomes the mean man :—men become 相遠.' —No doubt, it is true that many—perhaps most—of the differences among men are owing to habit. This chapter is incorporated with the San Tsze Ching at its commencement.

3. ONLY TWO CLASSES WHOM PRACTICE CANNOT CHANGE. This is a sequel to the last chapter with which it is incorporated in Ho Yen's edition. The case of the 下愚 would seem to be inconsistent with the doctrine of the perfect goodness of the moral nature of all men. Modern

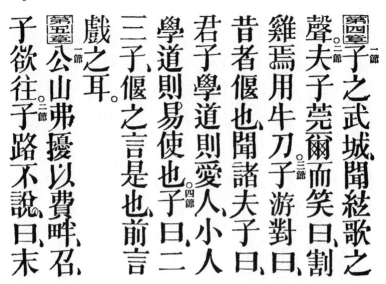

子欲往。子路不說曰、末　公山弗擾以費畔、召。　戲之耳。　三子、偃之言是也。前言　學道則易使也。子曰、二　君子學道則愛人、小人　昔者偃也聞諸夫子曰、　雞焉用牛刀。子游對曰、　聲。夫子莞爾而笑曰、割　子之武城、聞絃歌之

CHAP. IV. 1. The Master having come to Wû-ch'ǎng, heard *there* the sound of stringed instruments and singing.

2. Well pleased and smiling, he said, 'Why use an ox-knife to kill a fowl?'

3. Tsze-yû replied, 'Formerly, Master, I heard you say,—" When the man of high station is well instructed, he loves men; when the man of low station is well instructed, he is easily ruled."

4. The Master said, 'My disciples, Yen's words are right. What I said was only in sport.'

CHAP. V. 1. Kung-shan Fû-zǎo, when he was holding Pî, and in an attitude of rebellion, invited the Master to visit him, who was rather inclined to go.

2. Tsze-lû was displeased, and said, 'Indeed you cannot go! Why must you think of going to see Kung-shan?'

commentators, to get over the difficulty, say that they are the 自暴者 and 自棄者 of Mencius, IV. Pt. I. x.

4. HOWEVER SMALL THE SPHERE OF GOVERNMENT, THE HIGHEST INFLUENCES OF PROPRIETIES AND MUSIC SHOULD BE EMPLOYED. 1. Wû-ch'ang was in the district of Pî. Tsze-yû appears as the commandant of it, in VI. xii. 弦, 'the silken string of a musical instrument,' used here for stringed instruments generally. In the 備 旨 we read, 'The town was named *Wû* (武), from its position, precipitous and favourable to military operations, but Tsze-yû had been able, by his course, to transform the people, and make them change their mail and helmets for stringed instruments and singing. This was what made the Master glad.' 2. 莞 (read *hwan*,

3rd tone) 爾, 'smilingly.' 'An ox-knife,' a large instrument, and not necessary for the death of a fowl. Confucius intends by it the high principles of government employed by Tsze-yû. 3. 君子 and 小人 are here indicative of rank, and not of character. 易使, 'are easily employed,' i. e. 安分從上, 'they rest in their lot, and obey their superiors.' 4. 二三子, as in VII. xxiii, *et al.* Observe the force of the final 耳, = 'only.'

5. THE LENGTHS TO WHICH CONFUCIUS WAS INCLINED TO GO, TO GET HIS PRINCIPLES CARRIED INTO PRACTICE. Kung-shan Fû-zǎo, called also Kung-shan Fû-niù (狃), by designation 子洩, was a confederate of Yang Ho (ch. i), and according

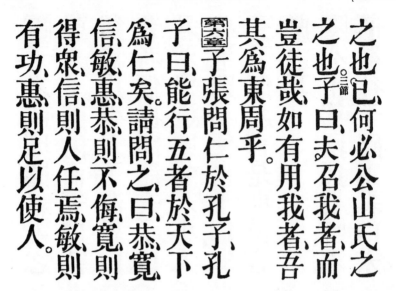

3. The Master said, 'Can it be without some reason that he has invited ME? If any one employ me, may I not make an eastern Châu?'

CHAP. VI. Tsze-chang asked Confucius about perfect virtue. Confucius said, 'To be able to practise five things everywhere under heaven constitutes perfect virtue.' He begged to ask what they were, and was told, 'Gravity, generosity *of soul*, sincerity, earnestness, and kindness. If you are grave, you will not be treated with disrespect. If you are generous, you will win all. If you are sincere, people will repose trust in you. If you are earnest, you will accomplish much. If you are kind, this will enable you to employ the services of others.'

to K'ung Ân-kwo, and the 日講, it was after the imprisonment by them, in common, of Chî Hwan, that Fû-zâo sent this invitation to Confucius. Others make the invitation subsequent to Ho's discomfiture and flight to Ch'î. See the 歷代統紀表, B. C. 501. We must conclude, with Tsze-lû, that Confucius ought not to have thought of accepting the invitation of such a man. 2. The first and last 之 are the verb. 末=無. 末之也已 = 'There is no going there. Indeed there is not.' 何必公山氏之之也, 'why must there be going to (之 here = to) that (such is the force of 氏) Kung-shan?' 3. 夫召我者—者 is to be taken here as referring expressly

to Fû-zâo, while its reference below is more general. The 我 in 用我, and 吾, are emphatic. The original seat of the Châu dynasty lay west from Lû, and the revival of the principles and government of Wăn and Wû in Lû, or even in Pî, which was but a part of it, might make an eastern Châu, so that Confucius would perform the part of king Wăn.—After all, the sage did not go to Pî.

6. FIVE THINGS THE PRACTICE OF WHICH CONSTITUTES PERFECT VIRTUE. 於天下, 'in under heaven' is simply = 'anywhere.' 信則人任,—任, in 4th tone, is explained by Chû Hsî by 倚仗, 'to rely upon,' a meaning of the term not found in the dictionary. See XX. i. 9.

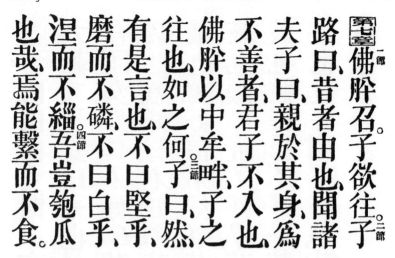

第七章

佛肸召子欲往子

路曰昔者由也聞諸

夫子曰親於其身爲

不善者君子不入也

佛肸以中牟畔子之

往也如之何子曰然

有是言也不曰堅乎

磨而不磷不曰白乎

涅而不緇吾豈匏瓜

也哉焉能繫而不食

CHAP. VII.　1. Pî Hsî inviting him to visit him, the Master was inclined to go.

2. Tsze-lû said, 'Master, formerly I have heard you say, "When a man in his own person is guilty of doing evil, a superior man will not associate with him." Pî Hsî is in rebellion, holding possession of Chung-mâu; if you go to him, what shall be said?'

3. The Master said, 'Yes, I did use these words. But is it not said, that, if a thing be really hard, it may be ground without being made thin? Is it not said, that, if a thing be really white, it may be steeped in a dark fluid without being made black?

4. 'Am I a bitter gourd! How can I be hung up out of the way of being eaten?'

7. CONFUCIUS, INCLINED TO RESPOND TO THE ADVANCES OF AN UNWORTHY MAN, PROTESTS AGAINST HIS CONDUCT BEING JUDGED BY ORDINARY RULES. Compare chap. v; but the invitation of Pî Hsî was subsequent to that of Kung-shan Fû-zâo, and after Confucius had given up office in Lû. 1. 佛 (read Pî) Hsî was commandant of Chung-mâu, for the chief of the Châo family, in the State of Tsin. 2. 親於其身爲不善者, —'he who himself, in his own person, does what is not good.' 不入, —according to K'ung Ân-kwo, = 不入其國, 'does not enter his State;' according to Chû Hsî, it = 不入其黨, 'does not enter his party.' There were two places of the name of Chung-mâu, one belonging to the State of Chäng, and the other to the State of Tsin (晉), which is that intended here, and is referred to the present district of 湯陰, department of 彰德, in Ho-nan province. 3. 不曰 is to be taken interrogatively, as in the translation. Ping's paraphrase is—人豈不曰, 'do not men say?' 堅乎云云,—'Is a thing hard, then,' &c. Nieh is explained—'black earth in water, which may be used to dye a black colour.' The application of these strange proverbial sayings is to Confucius himself, as, from his superiority, incapable of being affected by evil communications. 4. This paragraph is variously explained. By some, 匏瓜 is taken as the name of a star; so that the meaning is —'Am I, like such and such a star, to be hung up, &c.?' But we need not depart from the proper meaning of the characters. Chû Hsî, with Ho Yen, takes 不食 actively:—'A gourd can be hung up, because it does not need to eat. But I must go about, north, south, east, and west, to get food.' This seems to me very unnatural. The expression is taken passively, as in the translation, in the 日講, and other Works.

CHAP. VIII. 1. The Master said, 'Yû, have you heard the six words to which are attached six becloudings?' Yû replied, 'I have not.'

2. 'Sit down, and I will tell them to you.

3. 'There is the love of being benevolent without the love of learning;—the beclouding here leads to a foolish simplicity. There is the love of knowing without the love of learning;—the beclouding here leads to dissipation of mind. There is the love of being sincere without the love of learning;—the beclouding here leads to an injurious disregard of consequences. There is the love of straight-forwardness without the love of learning;—the beclouding here leads to rudeness. There is the love of boldness without the love of learning;—the beclouding here leads to insubordination. There is the love of firmness without the love of learning;—the beclouding here leads to extravagant conduct.'

8. KNOWLEDGE, ACQUIRED BY LEARNING, IS NECESSARY TO THE COMPLETION OF VIRTUE, BY PRESERVING THE MIND FROM BEING BECLOUDED.

1. 六言是六字, 'The six 言 are six characters;' see the 備旨. They are, there-fore, the benevolence, knowledge, sincerity, straightforwardness, boldness, and firmness, mentioned below, all virtues, but yet each, when pursued without discrimination, tending to be-cloud the mind. 蔽=遮掩, 'to cover and screen;' the primary meaning of it is said to be 小草, 'small plants.' 2. 居 = 'sit down.' Tsze-lû had risen, according to the rules of pro-priety, to give his answer; see the Lî Chî, I. Sect. I. iii. 4. 21; and Confucius tells him to re-sume his seat. 3. I give here the paraphrase of the 日講 on the first virtue and its be-clouding, which may illustrate the manner in which the whole paragraph is developed:—'In all matters, there is a perfectly right and un-changeable principle, which men ought care-fully to study, till they have thoroughly ex-amined and apprehended it. Then their actions will be without error, and their virtue may be perfected. For instance, loving is what rules in benevolence. It is certainly a beautiful vir-tue, but if you only set yourself to love men, and do not care to study to understand the principle of benevolence, then your mind will be beclouded by that loving, and you will be following a man into a well to save him, so that both he and you will perish. Will not this be foolish simplicity?'

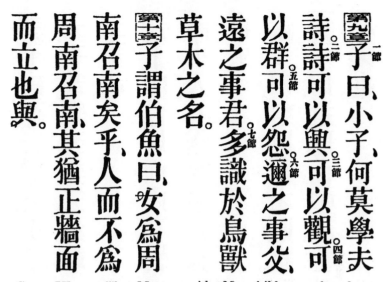

CHAP. IX. 1. The Master said, 'My children, why do you not study the Book of Poetry?

2. '*The Odes* serve to stimulate the mind.

3. 'They may be used for purposes of self-contemplation.

4. 'They teach the art of sociability.

5. 'They show how to regulate feelings of resentment.

6. 'From them you learn the more immediate duty of serving one's father, and the remoter one of serving one's prince.

7. 'From them we become largely acquainted with the names of birds, beasts, and plants.'

CHAP. X. The Master said to Po-yü, 'Do you give yourself to the Châu-nan and the Shâo-nan. The man who has not studied the Châu-nan and the Shâo-nan, is like one who stands with his face right against a wall. Is he not so?'

9. BENEFITS DERIVED FROM STUDYING THE BOOK OF POETRY. 1. 小子;—see V. xxi, VIII. iii. I translate 詩 here by 'the Book of Poetry,' because the lesson is supposed to have been given with reference to the compilation of the Odes. The 夫 is *that*, as in XI. ix. 1, *et al.* 2. The descriptions in them of good and evil may have this effect. 3. Their awarding of praise and blame may show a man his own character. 4. Their exhibitions of gravity in the midst of pleasure may have this effect. 羣, as in XV. xxi. 5. Their blending of pity and earnest desire with reproofs may teach how to regulate our resentments. 7. 草木, 'grasses and trees,' = plants generally.

10. THE IMPORTANCE OF STUDYING THE CHÂU-NAN AND SHÂO-NAN. Châu-nan and Shâo-nan are the titles of the first two Books in the Songs of the States, or first part of the Shih-ching. For the meaning of the titles, see the Shih-ching, I. i. and I. ii. They are supposed to inculcate important lessons about personal virtue and family government. Chû Hsî explains 爲 by 學, 'to learn,' 'to study.' It denotes the entire mastery of the studies. 女 (for 汝) 爲云云 is imperative, the 乎 at the end not being interrogative. 正面牆而立 is for 正面對牆而立. In such a situation, one cannot advance a step, nor see anything. I have added—'Is he not so?' to bring out the force of the 與.—This chapter in the old editions is incorporated with the preceding one.

子曰、禮云禮云、玉帛
云乎哉樂云樂云、鐘鼓
云乎哉。

子曰、色厲而內荏、譬
諸小人、其猶穿窬之盜
也與。

子曰、鄉原、德之賊也。

子曰、道聽而塗說德
之棄也。

CHAP. XI. The Master said, '"It is according to the rules of propriety," they say.—"It is according to the rules of propriety," they say. Are gems and silk all that is meant by propriety? "It is music," they say.—"It is music," they say. Are bells and drums all that is meant by music?'

CHAP. XII. The Master said, 'He who puts on an appearance of stern firmness, while inwardly he is weak, is like one of the small, mean people;—yea, is he not like the thief who breaks through, or climbs over, a wall?'

CHAP. XIII. The Master said, 'Your good, careful people of the villages are the thieves of virtue.'

CHAP. XIV. The Master said, 'To tell, as we go along, what we have heard on the way, is to cast away our virtue.'

11. IT IS NOT THE EXTERNAL APPURTENANCES WHICH CONSTITUTE PROPRIETY, NOR THE SOUND OF INSTRUMENTS WHICH CONSTITUTES MUSIC. 禮 云＝所稱爲禮者, 'as to what they say is propriety.' The words approach the quotation of a common saying. So 樂云 Having thus given the common views of propriety and music, he refutes them in the questions that follow, 樂 and 禮 being present to the mind as the expressions of respect and harmony.

12. THE MEANNESS OF PRESUMPTION AND PUSILLANIMITY CONJOINED. 色 is here not the countenance merely, but the whole outward appearance. 小人 is explained by 細民, and the latter clause shows emphatically to whom, among the low, mean people, the individual spoken of is like—a thief, namely, who is in constant fear of being detected.

13. CONTENTMENT WITH VULGAR WAYS AND VIEWS INJURIOUS TO VIRTUE. See the sentiment of this chapter explained and expanded by Mencius, VII. Pt. II. xxxvii. 7, 8. 原, 4th tone, the same as 愿. See the dictionary, character 愿. 賊, as in XIV. xlvi, though it may be translated here, as generally, by the term 'thief.'

14. SWIFTNESS TO SPEAK INCOMPATIBLE WITH THE CULTIVATION OF VIRTUE. It is to be understood that what has been heard contains some good lesson. At once to be talking of it without revolving it, and striving to practise it, shows an indifference to our own improvement. 道 is 'the way' or 'road.' 塗 is the same 'way,' a little farther on.—The glossarist on Ho Yen's work explains 德之棄 as meaning— 'is what the virtuous do not do.' But this is evidently incorrect.

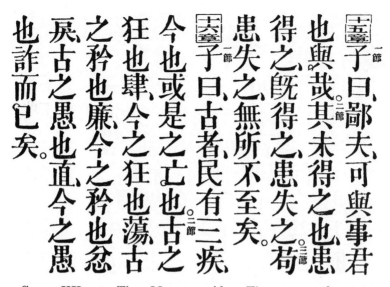

CHAP. XV. 1. The Master said, 'There are those mean creatures! How impossible it is along with them to serve one's prince!

2. 'While they have not got their aims, their anxiety is how to get them. When they have got them, their anxiety is lest they should lose them.

3. 'When they are anxious lest such things should be lost, there is nothing to which they will not proceed.'

CHAP. XVI. 1. The Master said, 'Anciently, men had three failings, which now perhaps are not to be found.

2. 'The high-mindedness of antiquity showed itself in a disregard of small things; the high-mindedness of the present day shows itself in wild license. The stern dignity of antiquity showed itself in grave reserve; the stern dignity of the present day shows itself in quarrelsome perverseness. The stupidity of antiquity showed itself in straightforwardness; the stupidity of the present day shows itself in sheer deceit.'

15. THE CASE OF MERCENARY OFFICERS, AND HOW IT IS IMPOSSIBLE TO SERVE ONE'S PRINCE ALONG WITH THEM. 1. 與字作共字看, '與 = 共,' i. e. 'together with.' 與哉是深慨其不可與意, '與哉 = a deep-felt lamentation on the unfitness of such persons to be associated with.' So, the 備旨. But as the remaining paragraphs are all occupied with describing the mercenaries, we must understand Confucius's object as being to condemn the employment of such creatures, rather than to set forth the impossibility of serving with them. 2. The 之 here, and in par. 3, are all to be understood of place and emolument.

16. THE DEFECTS OF FORMER TIMES BECOME VICES IN THE TIME OF CONFUCIUS. 1. 疾, 'bodily sickness,' here used metaphorically for 'errors,' 'vices.' 或是之亡 (wû),—'perhaps there is the absence of them.' The next paragraph shows that worse things had taken their place. 2. That 肆 is only 'a disregard of smaller matters,' or conventionalisms, appears from its opposition to 蕩, which has a more intense signification than in chap. viii. 矜,

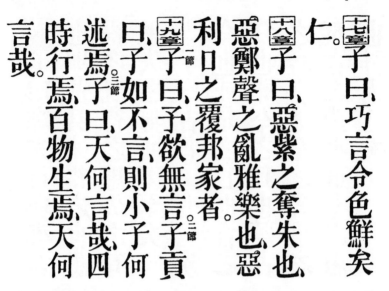

CHAP. XVII. The Master said, 'Fine words and an insinuating appearance are seldom associated with virtue.'

CHAP. XVIII. The Master said, 'I hate the manner in which purple takes away *the lustre of* vermilion. I hate the way in which the songs of Chăng confound the music of the Yâ. I hate those who with their sharp mouths overthrow kingdoms and families.'

CHAP. XIX. 1. The Master said, 'I would prefer not speaking.'

2. Tsze-kung said, 'If you, Master, do not speak, what shall we, your disciples, have to record?'

3. The Master said, 'Does Heaven speak? The four seasons pursue their courses, and all things are *continually* being produced, *but* does Heaven say anything?'

as in XV. xxi, also with an intenser meaning. 廉, 'an angular corner,' which cannot be impinged against without causing pain. It is used for 'purity,' 'modesty,' but the meaning here appears to be that given in the translation.

17. A repetition of I. iii.

18. CONFUCIUS'S INDIGNATION AT THE WAY IN WHICH THE WRONG OVERCAME THE RIGHT. 紫 之奪朱,—see X. vi. 2. 朱 is here as 'a correct' colour, though it is not among the five such colours mentioned in the note there. 紫 I have here translated—'purple.' 'Black and carnation mixed,' it is said, 'give 紫.' 'The songs or sounds of Chăng,'—see XV. x. 'The yâ,'—see on IX. xiv. 國家 is a common

designation for 'a State,' the 國, or kingdom of the prince, embracing the 家, 'families or clans,' of his great officers. For 國 we here have 邦.

19. THE ACTIONS OF CONFUCIUS WERE LESSONS AND LAWS, AND NOT HIS WORDS MERELY. Such is the scope of this chapter, according to Chû Hsî and his School. The older commentators say that it is a caution to men to pay attention to their conduct rather than to their words. This interpretation is far-fetched, but, on the other hand, it is not easy to defend Confucius from the charge of presumption in comparing himself to Heaven. 3. 天何言哉, 'Does Heaven speak,'—better than 'what does Heaven say?'

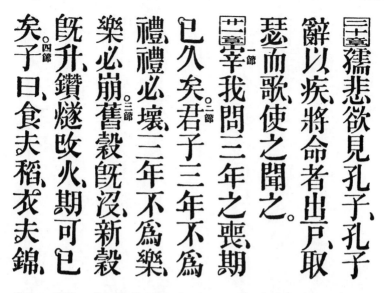

CHAP. XX. *Zû* Pei wished to see Confucius, but Confucius declined, on the ground of being sick, to see him. When the bearer of this message went out at the door, (the master) took his lute and sang to it, in order that Pei might hear him.

CHAP. XXI. 1. Tsâi Wo asked about the three years' mourning *for parents, saying* that one year was long enough.

2. 'If the superior man,' said he, 'abstains for three years from the observances of propriety, those observances will be quite lost. If for three years he abstains from music, music will be ruined.

3. '*Within a year* the old grain is exhausted, and the new grain has sprung up, and, in procuring fire by friction, we go through all the changes of wood for that purpose. After a complete year, the mourning may stop.'

4. The Master said, 'If you were, *after a year*, to eat good rice, and wear embroidered clothes, would you feel at ease?' 'I should,' replied Wo.

20. How CONFUCIUS COULD BE 'NOT AT HOME,' AND YET GIVE INTIMATION TO THE VISITOR OF HIS PRESENCE. Of *Zû* Pei little is known. He was a small officer of Lû, and had at one time been in attendance on Confucius to receive his instructions. There must have been some reason—some fault in him—why Confucius would not see him on the occasion in the text; and that he might understand that it was on that account, and not because he was really sick, that he declined his visit, the sage acted as we are told;—see the Lî Chî, XVIII. Sect. II. i. 22. It is said that his fault was in trying to see the Master without using the services of an internuncius (將命者);—see XIV. xlvii.

I translate the last 之 by *him*, but it refers generally to the preceding sentence, and might be left untranslated.

21. THE PERIOD OF THREE YEARS' MOURNING FOR PARENTS ; IT MAY NOT ON ANY ACCOUNT BE SHORTENED ; THE REASON OF IT. 1. We must understand a 日, either before 三, or, as I prefer, before 期, which is read *chî*, in 1st tone, the same as 朞, XIII. x. On the three years' mourning, see the 35th Book of the Lî Chî. Nominally extending to three years, that period compre-

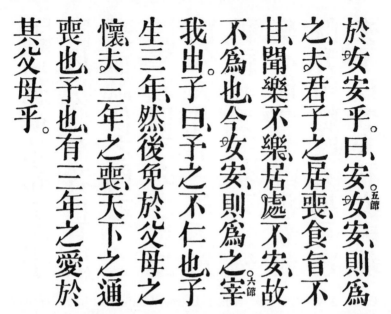

5. The Master said, 'If you can feel at ease, do it. But a superior man, during the whole period of mourning, does not enjoy pleasant food which he may eat, nor derive pleasure from music which he may hear. He also does not feel at ease, if he is comfortably lodged. Therefore he does not do *what you propose*. But now you feel at ease and may do it.'

6. Tsâi Wo then went out, and the Master said, 'This shows Yü's want of virtue. It is not till a child is three years old that it is allowed to leave the arms of its parents. And the three years' mourning is universally observed throughout the empire. Did Yü enjoy the three years' love of his parents?'

hended properly but 25 months, and at most 27 months. 2. 此以人事言之,—Tsze-wo finds here a reason for his view in the necessity of 'human affairs.' 3. 此以天時言之,—he finds here a reason for his view in 'the seasons of heaven.' 燧 means either 'a piece of metal,'—a speculum, with which to take fire from the sun, or 'a piece of wood,' with which to get fire by friction or 'boring' (鑽). It has here the latter meaning. Certain woods were assigned to the several seasons, to be employed for this purpose, the elm and willow, for instance, to spring, the date and almond trees to summer, &c. 鑽燧改火＝鑽燧以取火, 又改乎四

時之木, 'In boring with the 燧 to get fire, we have changed from wood to wood through the trees appropriate to the four seasons.' 4. Coarse food and coarse clothing were appropriate, though in varying degree, to all the period of mourning. Tsze-wo is strangely insensible to the home-put argument of the Master. 稻 is to be understood here as 穀之美者, 'the most excellent grain.' The 夫 are demonstrative. 6. 予之不仁也 responds to all that has gone before, and forms a sort of *apodosis*. Confucius added, it is said, the remarks in this paragraph that they might be reported to Tsâi Wo (called also Tsze-wo), lest he should 'feel at ease' to go and do as he said he could. Still the reason which the Master finds for the statute-period of mourning for parents must be pronounced puerile.

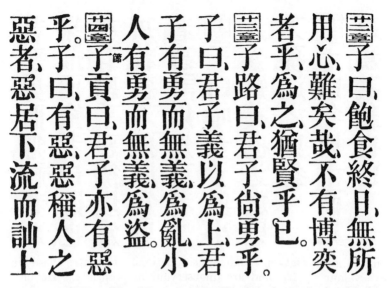

惡者、惡居下流而訕上

平。子曰、有惡惡稱人之

子貢曰、君子亦有惡

人有勇而無義爲盜。

子有勇而無義爲亂小

子曰、君子義以爲上君

子路曰、君子尚勇乎。

者乎、爲之猶賢乎已。

用心難矣哉不有博奕

子曰、飽食終日、無所

CHAP. XXII. The Master said, 'Hard is it to deal with him, who will stuff himself with food the whole day, without applying his mind to anything *good!* Are there not gamesters and chessplayers? To be one of these would still be better than doing nothing at all.'

CHAP. XXIII. Tsze-lû said, 'Does the superior man esteem valour?' The Master said, 'The superior man holds righteousness to be of highest importance. A man in a superior situation, having valour without righteousness, will be guilty of insubordination; one of the lower people, having valour without righteousness, will commit robbery.'

CHAP. XXIV. 1. Tsze-kung said, 'Has the superior man his hatreds also?' The Master said, 'He has his hatreds. He hates those who proclaim the evil of others. He hates the man who,

22. THE HOPELESS CASE OF GLUTTONY AND IDLENESS. 難矣哉.—XV. xvi. 博 and 弈 are two things. To the former I am unable to give a name; but see some account of it quoted in the 集證, *in loc.* 弈 is 'to play at chess,' of which there are two kinds,—the 圍棋, played with 361 pieces, and referred to the ancient Yâo as its inventor, and the 象棋, or ivory chess, played with 32 pieces, and having a great analogy to our European game. Its invention is attributed to the emperor Wû, of the later Châu dynasty, in our 6th century. It was probably borrowed from India. 爲之. —之 refers to 博弈. 賢 for 勝, as in XI. xv. 1.

23. VALOUR TO BE VALUED ONLY IN SUBORDINATION TO RIGHTEOUSNESS; ITS CONSEQUENCES APART FROM THAT. The first two 君子 are to be understood of the man superior in virtue. The third brings in the idea of rank, with 小人 as its correlate.

24. CHARACTERS DISLIKED BY CONFUCIUS AND TSZE-KUNG. 1. Tsze-kung is understood to have intended Confucius himself by 'the superior man.' 流 is here in the sense of 'class.' 下流=下位之人, 'men of low station.' In 君子亦有惡乎 the force of 亦 is to oppose 惡 to 愛, 'hatreds,' to 'loves.' 2. Hsing Ping takes 子貢 as the nominative to 曰,—'he went on to say, I, Ts'ze, *also,*' &c.

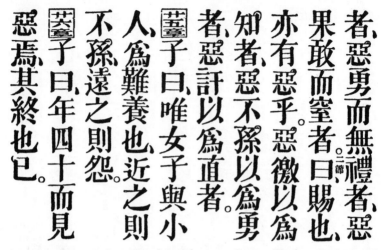

being in a low station, slanders his superiors. He hates those who have valour *merely*, and are unobservant of propriety. He hates those who are forward and determined, and, *at the same time*, of contracted understanding.'

2. *The Master then* inquired, 'Ts'ze, have you also your hatreds?' *Tsze-kung replied*, 'I hate those who pry out matters, and ascribe the knowledge to their wisdom. I hate those who are *only* not modest, and think that they are valorous. I hate those who make known secrets, and think that they are straightforward.'

CHAP. XXV. The Master said, 'Of all people, girls and servants are the most difficult to behave to. If you are familiar with them, they lose their humility. If you maintain a reserve towards them, they are discontented.'

CHAP. XXVI. The Master said, 'When a man at forty is the object of dislike, he will always continue what he is.'

The modern commentators, however, more correctly, understand 子, 'the Master,' as nominative to 曰, and supply another 曰 before 惡徼.

25. THE DIFFICULTY HOW TO TREAT CONCUBINES AND SERVANTS. 女子 does not mean *women* generally, but girls, i. e. concubines. 小人, in the same way, is here boys, i. e. servants. 養, 'to nourish,' 'to keep,'=to behave to. The force of 唯, 'only,' is as indicated in

the translation.—We hardly expect such an utterance, though correct in itself, from Confucius.

26. THE DIFFICULTY OF IMPROVEMENT IN ADVANCED YEARS. According to Chinese views, at forty a man is at his best in every way. After 惡 we must understand 于君子,—'the object of dislike to the superior man.' 其終=其終于此, 'he will end in this.' —Youth is doubtless the season for improvement, but the sentiment of the chapter is too broadly stated.

BOOK XVIII.　WEI TSZE.

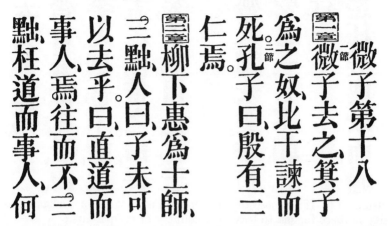

CHAPTER I.　1. The viscount of Wei withdrew *from the court.* The viscount of Chî became a slave *to Châu.* Pî-kan remonstrated with him and died.

2. Confucius said, 'The Yin dynasty possessed *these* three men of virtue.'

CHAP. II.　Hûi of Liû-hsiâ being chief criminal judge, was thrice dismissed from his office. Some one said to him, 'Is it not yet time for you, Sir, to leave this?' He replied, 'Serving men in an upright way, where shall I go to, and not experience such a thrice-repeated

HEADING OF THIS BOOK.—微子第十八, 'The viscount of Wei, No. 18.' This Book, consisting of only eleven chapters, treats of various individuals famous in Chinese history, as eminent for the way in which they discharged their duties to their sovereign, or for their retirement from public service. It commemorates also some of the worthies of Confucius's days, who lived in retirement rather than be in office in so degenerate times. The object of the whole is to illustrate and vindicate the course of Confucius himself.

1. THE VISCOUNTS OF WEI AND CHÎ, AND PÎ-KAN:—THREE WORTHIES OF THE YIN DYNASTY. 1. Wei-tsze and Chî-tsze are continually repeated by Chinese, as if they were proper names. But Wei and Chî were the names of two small States, presided over by chiefs of the Tsze, or fourth, degree of nobility, called *viscounts,* for want of a more exact term. They both appear to have been within the limits of the present Shan-hsî, Wei being referred to the district of 潞城, department 潞安, and Chî to 榆社, department 遼州. The chief of Wei was an elder brother (by a concubine) of the tyrant Châu,

the last sovereign of the Yin dynasty, B. C. 1154–1122. The chief of Chî, and Pî-kan, were both uncles of the tyrant. The first, seeing that remonstrances availed nothing, withdrew from court, wishing to preserve the sacrifices of their family amid the ruin which he saw was impending. The second was thrown into prison, and, to escape death, feigned madness. He was used by Châu as a buffoon. Pî-kan, persisting in his remonstrances, was put barbarously to death, the tyrant having his heart torn out, that he might see, he said, a sage's heart. The 之 in 去之 is explained by 其位, 'his place.' Its reference may also be to 紂, the tyrant himself. On 爲之奴, compare 爲之宰, V. vii. 3, *et al.*

2. HOW HÛI OF LIÛ-HSIÂ, THOUGH OFTEN DISMISSED FROM OFFICE, STILL CLAVE TO HIS COUNTRY. Liû-hsiâ Hûi,—see XV. xiii. The office of the 士師 is described in the Châu-lî, XXXIV. iii. He was under the 司寇, or minister of Crime, but with many subordinate magistrates under him. 三, 4th tone, as in V. xix, XI. v.

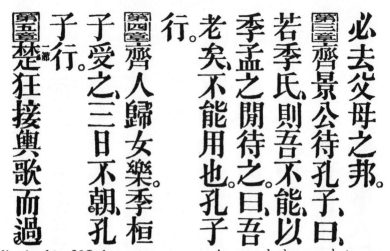

必去父母之邦。

第三章齊景公待孔子曰、若季氏則吾不能以季孟之閒待之曰吾老矣不能用也。孔子行。

第四章齊人歸女樂季桓子受之三日不朝孔子行。

第五章楚狂接輿歌而過

dismissal? If I choose to serve men in a crooked way, what necessity is there for me to leave the country of my parents?'

CHAP. III. The duke Ching of Ch'î, *with reference to the manner in which* he should treat Confucius, said, 'I cannot treat him as I would the chief of the Chî family. I will treat him in a manner between that accorded to the chief of the Chî, and that given to the chief of the Măng family.' He *also* said, 'I am old; I cannot use *his doctrines.*' Confucius took his departure.

CHAP. IV. The people of Ch'î sent *to Lû* a present of female musicians, which Chî Hwan received, and for three days no court was held. Confucius took his departure.

CHAP. V. 1. The madman of Ch'û, Chieh-yü, passed by Confucius, singing and saying, 'O FĂNG! O FĂNG! How is your

We may translate 黜, 'was dismissed from office,' or 'retired from office.' 人 = 或人. —Some remarks akin to that in the text are ascribed to Hûi's wife. It is observed by the commentator Hû (胡), that there ought to be another paragraph, giving Confucius's judgment upon Hûi's conduct, but it has been lost.

3. HOW CONFUCIUS LEFT CH'Î, WHEN THE DUKE COULD NOT APPRECIATE AND EMPLOY HIM. It was in the year B. C. 517 that Confucius went to Ch'î. The remarks about how he should be treated, &c., are to be understood as having taken place in consultation between the duke and his ministers, and being afterwards reported to the sage. The Măng family (see II. v) was in the time of Confucius much weaker than the Chî. The chief of it was only the 下卿, lowest noble of Lû, while the Chî was the highest. Yet for the duke of Ch'î to treat Confucius better than the duke of Lû treated the chief of the Măng family, was not dishonouring the sage. We must suppose that Confucius left Ch'î because of the duke's concluding remarks.

4. HOW CONFUCIUS GAVE UP OFFICIAL SERVICE IN LÛ. In the ninth year of the duke Ting, Confucius reached the highest point of his official service. He was minister of Crime, and also, according to the general opinion, acting premier. He effected in a few months a wonderful renovation of the State, and the neighbouring countries began to fear that under his administration, Lû would overtop and subdue them all. To prevent this, the duke of Ch'î sent a present to Lû of fine horses and of 80 highly accomplished beauties. The duke of Lû was induced to receive these by the advice of the Head of the Chî family, Chî Sze (斯), or Chî Hwan. The sage was forgotten; government was neglected. Confucius, indignant and sorrowful, withdrew from office, and for a time, from the country too. 歸 as in XVII. i. 1. 齊人, 'the people of Ch'î,' is to be understood of the duke and his ministers.

5. CONFUCIUS AND THE MADMAN OF CH'Û, WHO BLAMES HIS NOT RETIRING FROM THE WORLD. 1. Chieh-yü was the designation of one Lû T'ung (陸通), a native of Ch'û, who feigned him-

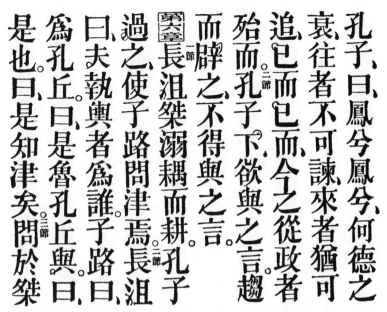

是也。曰、是知津矣。問於桀   為孔丘。曰、是魯孔丘與。曰、   曰、夫執輿者為誰。子路   過之、使子路問津焉。長沮   長沮桀溺耦而耕。孔子   而辟之、不得與之言。   殆而。孔子下、欲與之言、趨   追、已而、已而、今之從政者   衰、往者不可諫、來者猶可   孔子曰、鳳兮鳳兮、何德之

virtue degenerated! As to the past, reproof is useless; but the future may still be provided against. Give up *your vain pursuit*. Give up *your vain pursuit*. Peril awaits those who now engage in affairs of government.'

2. Confucius alighted and wished to converse with him, but Chieh-yü hastened away, so that he could not talk with him.

CHAP. VI. 1. Ch'ang-tsü and Chieh-nî were at work in the field together, when Confucius passed by them, and sent Tsze-lû to inquire for the ford.

2. Ch'ang-tsü said, 'Who is he that holds the reins in the carriage there?' Tsze-lû told him, 'It is K'ung Ch'iû.' 'Is it not K'ung Ch'iû of Lû?' asked he. 'Yes,' was the reply, to which the other rejoined, 'He knows the ford.'

3. *Tsze-lû then* inquired of Chieh-nî, who said to him, 'Who

self mad, to escape being importuned to engage in public service. There are several notices of him in the 集證, *in loc.* It must have been about the year B.C. 489 that the incident in the text occurred. By the *fäng*, which we commonly translate by *phœnix*, his satirizer or adviser intended Confucius; see IX. viii. The three 而 in the song are simply expletives, pauses for the voice to help out the rhythm. 道, 'to overtake,' generally with reference to the past, but here it has reference to the future. In the dictionary, with reference to this passage, it is explained by 及, 'to come up to,' and 救, 'to save,' = to provide against.

6. CONFUCIUS AND THE TWO RECLUSES, CH'ANG-TSÜ AND CHIEH-NÎ; WHY HE WOULD NOT WITHDRAW FROM THE WORLD. 1. The surnames and names of these worthies are not known. It is supposed that they belonged to Ch'û, like the hero of the last chapter, and that the interview with them occurred about the same time. The designations in the text are descriptive of their character, and = 'the long Rester (沮者止 而不出)' and 'the firm Recluse (溺者 沉而不返).' What kind of field labour is here denoted by 耕 cannot be determined.

2. 執輿者, 'he who holds the carriage,' =

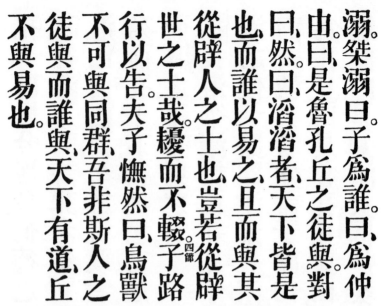

are you, Sir?' He answered, 'I am Chung Yû.' 'Are you not the disciple of K'ung Ch'iû of Lû?' asked the other. 'I am,' replied he, and then Chieh-nî said to him, 'Disorder, like a swelling flood, spreads over the whole empire, and who is he that will change its state *for you*? Than follow one who merely withdraws from this one and that one, had you not better follow those who have withdrawn from the world altogether?' *With this* he fell to covering up the seed, *and proceeded with his work*, without stopping.

4. Tsze-lû went and reported their remarks, when the Master observed with a sigh, 'It is impossible to associate with birds and beasts, as if they were the same with us. If I associate not with these people,—with mankind,—with whom shall I associate? If right principles prevailed through the empire, there would be no use for me to change its state.'

執轡在車者, as in the translation. It is supposed that it was the remarkable appearance of Confucius which elicited the inquiry. In 是知津, 是 = '*he*;' i. e. he, going about everywhere, and seeking to be employed, ought to know the ford. 3. 滔滔者天下,—the speaker here probably pointed to the surging waters before them, for the ford to cross which the travellers were asking. Translating literally, we should say—'swelling and surging, such is all the empire.' 且而,—而 = 汝, 'you.' 辟人, 辟世,—comp. XIV. xxxix. 耰, 'an implement for drawing

the soil over the seed.' It may have been a hoe, or a rake. 4. 徒 is here = 類, 'class.' 吾非斯人之徒與而誰與, = 'If I am not to associate with the class of these men, i. e. with mankind, with whom am I to associate? I cannot associate with birds and beasts.' 丘不與易,—不與, it is said, 作無用,—'there would be no use.' Literally, 'I should not have for whom to change *the state of the empire*.'—The use of 夫子 in this paragraph is remarkable. It must mean 'his Master' and not 'the Master.' The compiler of this chapter can hardly have been a disciple of the sage.

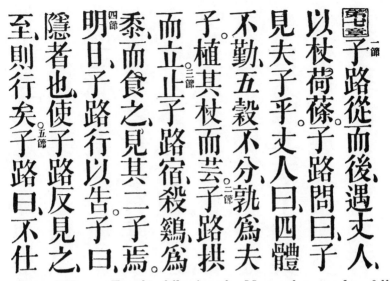

CHAP. VII. 1. Tsze-lû, following the Master, happened to fall behind, when he met an old man, carrying across his shoulder on a staff a basket for weeds. Tsze-lû said to him, 'Have you seen my master, Sir!' The old man replied, 'Your four limbs are unaccustomed to toil; you cannot distinguish the five kinds of grain:—who is your master?' With this, he planted his staff in the ground, and proceeded to weed.

2. Tsze-lû joined his hands across his breast, and stood *before him*.

3. The old man kept Tsze-lû to pass the night in his house, killed a fowl, prepared millet, and feasted him. He also introduced to him his two sons.

4. Next day, Tsze-lû went on his way, and reported *his adventure*. The Master said, 'He is a recluse,' and sent Tsze-lû back to see him again, but when he got to the place, the old man was gone.

5. Tsze-lû then said *to the family*, 'Not to take office is not

7. TSZE-LÛ'S RENCONTRE WITH AN OLD MAN, A RECLUSE: HIS VINDICATION OF HIS MASTER'S COURSE. This incident in this chapter was probably nearly contemporaneous with those which occupy the two previous ones. Some say that the old man belonged to Sheh, which was a part of Ch'û. 1. 後, as in XI. xxii,—顏淵後. 丈人 is used for 'an old man' as early as in the Yî-ching, hexagram 師; perhaps by taking 丈 as = 杖, 'a staff,' the phrase comes to have that signification. 蓧 is simply called by Chû Hsî—竹器, 'a bamboo basket.' The 說文 defines it as in the translation,—芸田器. 四體, 'the four bodies,' i.e. the arms and legs, the four limbs of the body. 'The five grains' are 稻, 黍, 稷, 麥, and 菽, 'rice, millet, pannicled millet, wheat, and pulse.' But they are sometimes otherwise enumerated. We have also 'the six kinds,' 'the eight kinds,' 'the nine kinds,' and perhaps other classifications. 2. Tsze-lû, standing with his arms across his breast, indicated his respect, and won upon the old man. 3. 食 (*tsze*), the 4th tone, 'entertained,' 'feasted.' The dictionary defines it with this meaning, 以食與人, 'to give food to people.' 5. Tsze-lû is to be understood as here speaking the sentiments of the Master, and vindicating his course. 長幼之節 refers to the manner in which the old man had introduced his sons to him the evening before, and

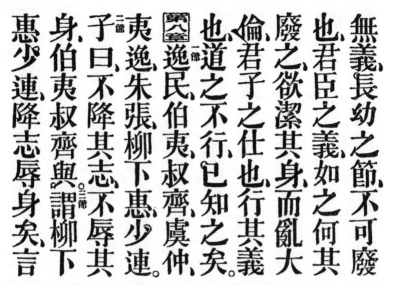

righteous. If the relations between old and young may not be neglected, how is it that he sets aside the duties that should be observed between sovereign and minister? Wishing to maintain his personal purity, he allows that great relation to come to confusion. A superior man takes office, and performs the righteous duties belonging to it. As to the failure of right principles to make progress, he is aware of that.'

CHAP. VIII. 1. The men who have retired to privacy from the world have been Po-î, Shû-ch'î, Yü-chung, Î-yî, Chû-chang, Hûi of Liû-hsiâ, and Shâo-lien.

2. The Master said, 'Refusing to surrender their wills, or to submit to any taint in their persons;—such, I think, were Po-î and Shû-ch'î.

3. 'It may be said of Hûi of Liû-hsiâ, and of Shâo-lien, that they surrendered their wills, and submitted to taint in their persons,

to all the orderly intercourse between old and young, which he had probably seen in the family. 何其廢之,—其 refers to the old man, but there is an indefiniteness about the Chinese construction, which does not make it so personal as our 'he.' So Confucius is intended by 君子, though that phrase may be taken in its general acceptation. ' He is aware of that;'—but will not therefore shrink from his righteous service.

8. CONFUCIUS'S JUDGMENT OF FORMER WORTHIES WHO HAD KEPT FROM THE WORLD. HIS OWN GUIDING PRINCIPLE. 1. 逸民,—'retired people.'

民 is used here just as we sometimes use *people*, without reference to the rank of the in-

dividuals spoken of. The 備旨 quotes, upon the phrase, from the 說統 to the following effect :—'逸 here is not the 逸 of seclusion, but is characteristic of men of large souls, who cannot be measured by ordinary rules. They may display their character by retiring from the world. They may display it also in the manner of their discharge of office.' The phrase is guarded in this way, I suppose, because of its application to Hûi of Liû-hsiâ, who did not obstinately withdraw from the world. Po-î and Shû-ch'î,—see V. xxii. Yü-chung should probably be Wû (吳)-chung. He was the brother of T'âi-po, called Chung-yung (仲雍), and is mentioned in the note on VIII. i.

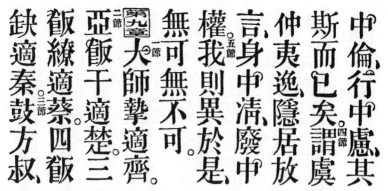

but their words corresponded with reason, and their actions were such as men are anxious to see. This is all that is to be remarked in them.

4. 'It may be said of Yü-chung and Î-yî, that, while they hid themselves in their seclusion, they gave a license to their words; but, in their persons, they succeeded in preserving their purity, and, in their retirement, they acted according to the exigency of the times.

5. 'I am different from all these. I have no course for which I am predetermined, and no course against which I am predetermined.'

CHAP. IX. 1. The grand music-master, Chih, went to Ch'î.

2. Kan, *the master of the band at* the second meal, went to Ch'û. Liâo, *the band-master at* the third meal, went to Ts'âi. Chüĕh, *the band-master* at the fourth meal, went to Ch'in.

3. Fang-shû, the drum-master, withdrew to *the north of* the river.

He retired with T'âi-po among the barbarous tribes, then occupying the country of Wû, and succeeded to the chieftaincy of them on his brother's death. 'Î-yî and Chû-chang,' says Chû Hsî, 'are not found in the *ching* and *chwan* (經傳).' See, however, the 集證, *in loc.* From a passage in the Lî Chî, XVIII. ii. 14, it appears that Shâo-lien belonged to one of the barbarous tribes on the east, but was well acquainted with, and observant of, the rules of Propriety, particularly those relating to mourning. 3. The 謂 at the beginning of this paragraph and the next are very perplexing. As there is neither 謂 nor 曰 at the beginning of par. 5, the 子曰 of par. 2 must evidently be carried on to the end of the chapter. Commentators do not seem to have felt the difficulty, and understand 謂 in the 3rd person.— 'He, i. e. the Master, said,' &c. I have made the best of it I could. 倫=義理之次第, 'the order and series of righteousness and principles.' 慮=人心之思慮, 'the thoughts and solicitudes of men's hearts.' 4. 'Living in retirement, they gave a license to

their words,'—this is intended to show that in this respect they were inferior to Hûi and Shâo-lien, who 言中倫. 權,—see note on IX. xxix. 5. Confucius's openness to act according to circumstances is to be understood as being always in subordination to right and propriety.

9. THE DISPERSION OF THE MUSICIANS OF LÛ. The dispersion here narrated is supposed to have taken place in the time of duke Âi. When once Confucius had rectified the music of Lû (IX. xiv), the musicians would no longer be assisting in the prostitution of their art; and so, as the disorganization and decay proceeded, the chief among them withdrew to other States, or from society altogether. 1. 大=太, as opposed to 少, par. 5, 'grand,' and 'assistant.' 'The music-master, Chih,'—see VIII. xv. 2. The princes of China, it would appear, had music at their meals, and a separate band performed at each meal, or, possibly, the band might be the same, but under the superintendence of a separate officer at each meal. The king had four meals a day, and the princes of States only three, but it was the prerogative of the duke of Lû to use the ceremonies of the royal court. Nothing is said here of the bandmaster at the first meal, perhaps because he

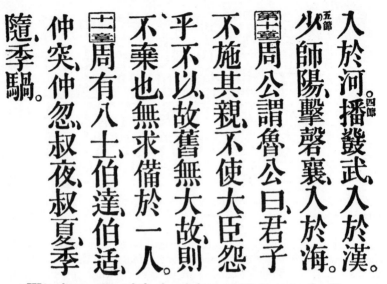

4. Wû, the master of the hand-drum, withdrew to the Han.

5. Yang, the assistant music-master, and Hsiang, master of the musical stone, withdrew to *an island in* the sea.

CHAP. X. The duke of Châu addressed *his son*, the duke of Lû, saying, 'The virtuous prince does not neglect his relations. He does not cause the great ministers to repine at his not employing them. Without some great cause, he does not dismiss from their offices the members of old families. He does not seek in one man talents for every employment.'

CHAP. XI. To Châu belonged the eight officers, Po-tâ, Po-

did not leave Lû, or nothing may have been known of him. 3. 'The river' is, of course, 'the Yellow river.' According to the 四書 釋地, article LVII, the expressions 入於 河, 入於漢 are to be taken as meaning simply,—'lived on the banks of the Ho, the Han.' The interpretation in the translation is after Chû Hsî, who follows the glossarist Hsing Ping. The ancient sovereigns had their capitals mostly north and east of 'the river,' hence, the country north of it was called 河內, and to the south of it was called 河外. I do not see, however, the applicability of this to the Han, which is a tributary of the Yang-tsze, flowing through Hû-pei. 5. It was from Hsiang that Confucius learned to play on the 琴.

10. INSTRUCTIONS OF CHÂU-KUNG TO HIS SON ABOUT GOVERNMENT; A GENEROUS CONSIDERATION OF OTHERS TO BE CHERISHED. 周公,—see VII. v. The facts of the case seem to be that the duke of Châu was himself appointed to the principality of Lû, but being detained at court

by his duties to the young king 成, he sent his son 伯禽, here called 'the duke of Lû,' to that State as his representative. 君子 contains here the ideas both of rank and virtue. 施 is read in the 3rd tone, with the same meaning as 弛. Chû Hsî, indeed, seems to think that 弛 should be in the text, but we have 施 in Ho Yen, who gives K'ung Ân-kwo's interpretation:—施易也,不以他人 之親易己之親, '施 is to change. He does not substitute the relatives of other men in the room of his own relatives.' 以,—here = 用, 'to use,' 'to employ.' 求備,—see XIII. xxv.

11. THE FRUITFULNESS OF THE EARLY TIME OF THE CHÂU DYNASTY IN ABLE OFFICERS. The eight individuals mentioned here are said to have been brothers, four pairs of twins by the same mother. This is intimated in their names, the

kwô, Chung-tû, Chung-hwû, Shû-yâ, Shû-hsiâ, Chî-sui, and Chî-kwa.

two first being 伯, or *primi*, the next pair 仲, or *secundi*, the third 叔, or *tertii*, and the last two 季. One mother, bearing twins four times in succession, and all proving distinguished

men, showed the vigour of the early days of the dynasty in all that was good.—It is disputed to what reign these brothers belonged, nor is their surname ascertained. 達, 适, 突, 云云 seem to be honorary designations.

BOOK XIX. TSZE-CHANG.

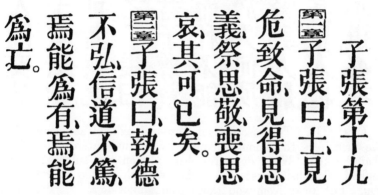

CHAPTER I. Tsze-chang said, 'The scholar, *trained for public duty*, seeing threatening danger, is prepared to sacrifice his life. When the opportunity of gain is presented to him, he thinks of righteousness. In sacrificing, his thoughts are reverential. In mourning, his thoughts are about the grief *which he should feel*. Such a man commands our approbation indeed.'

CHAP. II. Tsze-chang said, 'When a man holds fast virtue, but without seeking to enlarge it, and believes right principles, but without firm sincerity, what account can be made of his existence or non-existence?'

HEADING OF THIS BOOK.— 子張第十九, 'Tsze-chang, No. 19.' Confucius does not appear personally in this Book at all. Chû Hsî says :—'This Book records the words of the disciples, Tsze-hsiâ being the most frequent speaker, and Tsze-kung next to him. For in the Confucian school, after Yen Yüan there was no one of such discriminating understanding as Tsze-kung, and after Tsǎng Shăn no one of such firm sincerity as Tsze-hsiâ.' The disciples deliver their sentiments very much after the manner of their master, and yet we can discern a falling off from him.

1. TSZE-CHANG'S OPINION OF THE CHIEF ATTRIBUTES OF THE TRUE SCHOLAR. 士,—see note on XII. xx. 1. Tsze-chang there asks Confucius

about the scholar-officer. 見危,—the danger is to be understood as threatening his country. Hsing Ping, indeed, confines the danger to the person of the sovereign, for whom the officer will gladly sacrifice his life. 致命 is the same as 致其身 in I. vii. 已 is not to be explained by 止, as in 而已. The combination 已矣 has occurred before, and = 也已 in I. xiv. It greatly intensifies the preceding 可.

2. TSZE-CHANG ON NARROW-MINDEDNESS AND A HESITATING FAITH. Hsing Ping interprets this chapter in the following way :—'If a man grasp hold of his virtue, and is not widened and

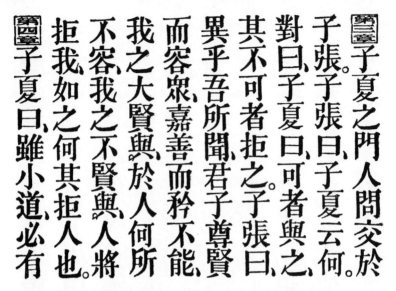

子夏之門人問交於
子張。子張曰子夏云何。
對曰子夏曰可者與之。
其不可者拒之。子張曰、
異乎吾所聞君子尊賢
而容眾、嘉善而矜不能、
我之大賢與、於人何所
不容我之不賢與、人將
拒我如之何其拒人也。
⬚四⬚子夏曰、雖小道必有

CHAP. III. The disciples of Tsze-hsiâ asked Tsze-chang about the principles that should characterize mutual intercourse. Tsze-chang asked, 'What does Tsze-hsiâ say on the subject?' They replied, 'Tsze-hsiâ says:—"Associate with those who can *advantage you*. Put away from you those who cannot *do so*."' Tsze-chang observed, 'This is different from what I have learned. The superior man honours the talented and virtuous, and bears with all. He praises the good, and pities the incompetent. Am I possessed of great talents and virtue?—who is there among men whom I will not bear with? Am I devoid of talents and virtue?—men will put me away from them. What have we to do with the putting away of others?'

CHAP. IV. Tsze-hsiâ said, 'Even in inferior studies and employments there is something worth being looked at; but if it be

enlarged by it, although he may believe good principles, he cannot be sincere and generous.' But it is better to take the clauses as co-ordinate, and not dependent on each other. With 執德不弘 we may compare XV. xxviii, which suggests the taking 弘 actively. The two last clauses are perplexing. Chû Hsî, after Ân-kwo apparently, makes them equivalent to—'is of no consideration in the world' (猶言不足輕重).

3. THE DIFFERENT OPINIONS OF TSZE-HSIÂ AND TSZE-CHANG ON THE PRINCIPLES WHICH SHOULD REGULATE OUR INTERCOURSE WITH OTHERS. On the disciples of Tsze-hsiâ, see the 集證, *in loc.* It is strange to me that they should begin their answer to Tsze-chang with the designation 子夏, instead of saying 夫子, 'our

Master.' 変,—see V. xvi. In 可者不 可者, the 可 is taken differently by the old interpreters and the new. Hsing Ping expounds:—'If the man be worthy, fit for you to have intercourse with, then have it; but if he be not worthy,' &c. On the other hand, we find:—'If the man will advantage you, he is a fit person (是可者); then maintain intercourse with him,' &c. This seems to be merely carrying out Confucius's rule, I. viii. 3. Chû Hsî, however, approves of Tsze-chang's censure of it, while he thinks also that Tsze-chang's own view is defective.—Pâo Hsien says,—'Our intercourse with friends should be according to Tsze-hsiâ's rule; general intercourse according to Tsze-chang's.'

4. TSZE-HSIÂ'S OPINION OF THE INAPPLICABILITY OF SMALL PURSUITS TO GREAT OBJECTS. Gardening, husbandry, divining, and the healing art, are

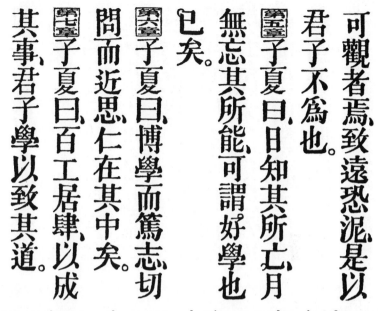

可觀者焉致遠恐泥是以
君子不爲也。

第五章 子夏曰日知其所亡月
無忘其所能可謂好學也
已矣。

第六章 子夏曰博學而篤志切
問而近思仁在其中矣。

第七章 子夏曰百工居肆以成
其事君子學以致其道。

attempted to carry them out to what is remote, there is a danger of
their proving inapplicable. Therefore, the superior man does not
practise them.'

CHAP. V. Tsze-hsiâ said, 'He, who from day to day recognises
what he has not yet, and from month to month does not forget what
he has attained to, may be said indeed to love to learn.'

CHAP. VI. Tsze-hsiâ said, 'There are learning extensively, and
having a firm and sincere aim; inquiring with earnestness, and
reflecting with self-application:—virtue is in such a course.'

CHAP. VII. Tsze-hsiâ said, 'Mechanics have their shops to dwell
in, in order to accomplish their works. The superior man learns, in
order to reach to the utmost of his principles.'

all mentioned by Chû Hsî as instances of the
小道, 'small ways,' here intended, having
their own truth in them, but not available for
higher purposes, or what is beyond themselves.
致 is imperative and emphatic, = 推極,
'push them to an extreme.' What is intended
by 遠 is the far-reaching object of the *Chün-
tsze*, 'to cultivate himself and regulate others.'
泥, in the 4th tone, explained in the dictionary by 滯, 'water impeded.'—Ho Yen makes
the 小道 to be 異端, 'strange principles.'

5. THE INDICATIONS OF A REAL LOVE OF LEARN-
ING :—BY TSZE-HSIÂ.

6. HOW LEARNING SHOULD BE PURSUED TO LEAD
TO VIRTUE :—BY TSZE-HSIÂ. K'ung Ân-kwo ex-

plains 志 as if it were 識, 'to remember.'
On 切問而近思, the 備旨 says—
所問, 皆切己之事, 所思, 皆
身心之要, 'what are inquired about are
things essential to one's self; what are thought
about are the important personal duties.' Probably it is so, but all this cannot be put in a
translation. On 近思, compare VI. xxviii.

3. 仁在其中,—compare VII. xv ; XIII.
xviii.

7. LEARNING IS THE STUDENT'S WORKSHOP :—BY
TSZE-HSIÂ. 肆 is here 'a place for the display
and sale of goods.' A certain quarter was
assigned anciently in Chinese towns and cities
for mechanics, and all of one art were required

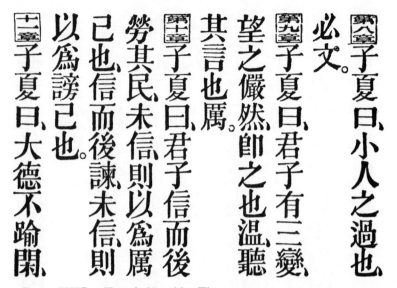

CHAP. VIII. Tsze-hsiâ said, 'The mean man is sure to gloss his faults.'

CHAP. IX. Tsze-hsiâ said, 'The superior man undergoes three changes. Looked at from a distance, he appears stern; when approached, he is mild; when he is heard to speak, his language is firm and decided.'

CHAP. X. Tsze-hsiâ said, 'The superior man, having obtained their confidence, may then impose labours on his people. If he have not gained their confidence, they will think that he is oppressing them. Having obtained the confidence *of his prince*, one may then remonstrate with him. If he have not gained his confidence, *the prince* will think that he is vilifying him.'

CHAP. XI. Tsze-hsiâ said, 'When a person does not transgress the boundary-line in the great virtues, he may pass and repass it in the small virtues.'

to have their shops together. This is still very much the case. A son must follow his father's profession, and, seeing nothing but the exercise of that around him, it was supposed that he would not be led to think of anything else, and become very proficient in it.

8. GLOSSING HIS FAULTS THE PROOF OF THE MEAN MAN :—BY TSZE-HSIÂ. Literally, 'The faults of the mean man, must gloss,' i. e. *he* is sure to gloss. *Wăn*, in this sense, a verb, in the 4th tone.

9. CHANGING APPEARANCES OF THE SUPERIOR MAN TO OTHERS :—BY TSZE-HSIÂ. Tsze-hsiâ probably intended Confucius by the *Chŭn-tsze*, but there is a general applicability in his language and sentiments. 望之,即之,—literally, 'look towards him,' 'approach him.'—The description is about equivalent to our '*fortiter in re, suaviter in modo*.'

10. THE IMPORTANCE OF ENJOYING CONFIDENCE TO THE RIGHT SERVING OF SUPERIORS AND ORDERING OF INFERIORS :—BY TSZE-HSIÂ. Chû Hsî gives to 信 here the double meaning of 'being sincere,' and 'being believed in.' The last is the proper force of the term, but it requires the possession of the former quality.

11. THE GREAT VIRTUES DEMAND THE CHIEF ATTENTION, AND THE SMALL ONES MAY BE SOMEWHAT VIOLATED :—BY TSZE-HSIÂ. The sentiment here is very questionable. A different turn, however, is given to the chapter in the older interpreters. Hsing Ping, expanding K'ung Ân-kwo, says :—'Men of great virtue never go beyond the boundary-line; it is enough for those who are virtuous in a less degree to keep near to it, going beyond and coming back.' We adopt the more natural interpretation of Chû

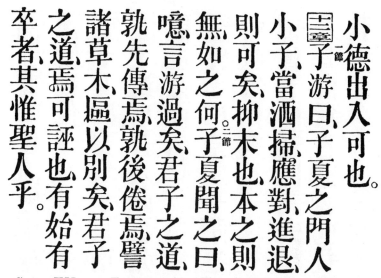

小德出入可也。

二章

子游曰子夏之門人

二節

小子當洒掃應對進退

則可矣抑末也本之則

無如之何子夏聞之曰

噫言游過矣君子之道

孰先傳焉孰後倦焉譬

諸草木區以別矣君子

之道焉可誣也有始有

卒者其惟聖人乎。

CHAP. XII. 1. Tsze-yû said, 'The disciples and followers of Tsze-hsiâ, in sprinkling and sweeping the ground, in answering and replying, in advancing and receding, are sufficiently accomplished. But these are only the branches *of learning*, and they are left ignorant of what is essential.—How can they be acknowledged as sufficiently taught?'

2. Tsze-hsiâ heard of the remark and said, 'Alas! Yen Yû is wrong. According to the way of the superior man *in teaching*, what departments are there which he considers of prime importance, and delivers? what are there which he considers of secondary importance, and allows himself to be idle about? *But* as in the case of plants, which are assorted according to their classes, *so he deals with his disciples*. How can the way of a superior man be such as to make fools of *any of* them? Is it not the sage alone, who can unite in one the beginning and the consummation *of learning?*'

Hsî. 閑, 'a piece of wood, in a doorway, obstructing ingress and egress;' then, 'an inclosure' generally, 'a railing,' whatever limits and confines.

12. Tsze-hsiâ's defence of his own graduated method of teaching:—against Tsze-yû. 1. 小子 is to be taken in apposition with 門人, being merely, as we have found it previously, an affectionate method of speaking of the disciples. The sprinkling, &c., are the things which boys were supposed anciently to be taught, the rudiments of learning, from which they advanced to all that is inculcated in the 大學. But as Tsze-hsiâ's pupils were not boys, but men, we should understand, I suppose, these specifications as but a contemptuous reference to his instructions, as embracing merely what was external. 洒, read *shâi* and *shâ*, 1st tone, 'to sprinkle the ground before sweeping.' 應, in the 4th tone, 'to answer a call.' 對, 'to answer a question.' 抑 = 'but,' as in VII. xxxiii. 本之 is expanded by the paraphrasts—若本之所在, 'as to that in which the root (or, what is essential) is.' This is, no doubt, the meaning, but the phrase itself is abrupt and enigmatical. 如之何 = 如之何其可哉, in opposition to the 則可矣. 2. The general scope of Tsze-hsiâ's reply is sufficiently plain, but the old interpreters and new differ in explaining the several sentences. After dwelling

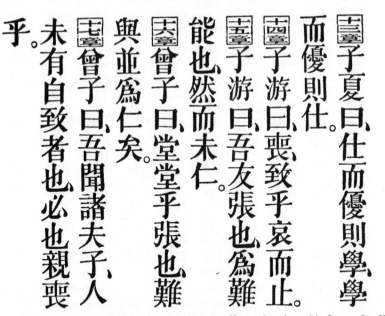

CHAP. XIII. Tsze-hsiâ said, 'The officer, *having discharged all his duties*, should devote his leisure to learning. The student, having completed his learning, should apply himself to be an officer.'

CHAP. XIV. Tsze-hsiâ said, 'Mourning, having been carried to the utmost degree of grief, should stop with that.'

CHAP. XV. Tsze-hsiâ said, 'My friend Chang can do things which are hard to be done, but yet he is not perfectly virtuous.'

CHAP. XVI. The philosopher Tsăng said, 'How imposing is the manner of Chang! It is difficult along with him to practise virtue.'

CHAP. XVII. The philosopher Tsăng said, 'I heard this from our Master:—"Men may not have shown what is in them to the full extent, and yet they will be found to do so, on occasion of mourning for their parents."'

long on it, I have agreed generally with the new school, and followed Chû Hsî in the translation. 區 is explained in the dictionary by 類, 'classes.'

13. THE OFFICER AND THE STUDENT SHOULD ATTEND EACH TO HIS PROPER WORK IN THE FIRST INSTANCE :—BY TSZE-HSIÂ. 優＝有餘力, in I. vi.—The saying needs to be much supplemented in translating, in order to bring out its meaning.

14. THE TRAPPINGS OF MOURNING MAY BE DISPENSED WITH :—BY TSZE-YÛ. The sentiment here is perhaps the same as that of Confucius in III. iv, but the sage guards and explains his utterance.—K'ung Ân-kwo, following an expression in the 孝經, makes the meaning

to be that the mourner may not endanger his health or life by excessive grief and abstinence.

15. TSZE-YÛ'S OPINION OF TSZE-CHANG, AS MINDING HIGH THINGS TOO MUCH.

16. THE PHILOSOPHER TSĂNG'S OPINION OF TSZE-CHANG, AS TOO HIGH-PITCHED FOR FRIENDSHIP. 堂堂 is explained in the dictionary by 盛也, 正也, 'exuberant,' 'correct.' It is to be understood of Chang's manner and appearance, keeping himself aloof from other men in his high-pitched course.

17. HOW GRIEF FOR THE LOSS OF PARENTS BRINGS OUT THE REAL NATURE OF MAN :—BY TSĂNG SHĂN. 自 is said to indicate the ideas both of 自已, 'one's self,' and 自然, 'naturally.' 自致, 'to put forth one's self to the utmost,' as we

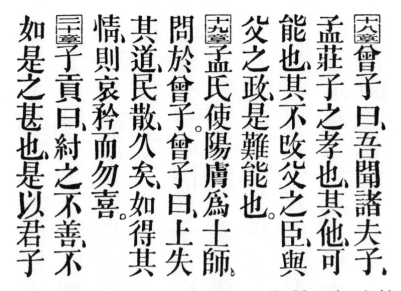

曾子曰、吾聞諸夫子、
孟莊子之孝也、其他可
能也、其不改父之政、是難能也。
孟氏使陽膚為士師。問於曾子。曾子曰、上失
其道、民散久矣、如得其
情、則哀矜而勿喜。
子貢曰、紂之不善、不
如是之甚也、是以君子

CHAP. XVIII. The philosopher Tsăng said, 'I have heard this from our Master:—"The filial piety of Măng Chwang, in other matters, was what other men are competent to, but, as seen in his not changing the ministers of his father, nor his father's mode of government, it is difficult to be attained to."'

CHAP. XIX. The chief of the Măng family having appointed Yang Fû to be chief criminal judge, the latter consulted the philosopher Tsăng. Tsăng said, 'The rulers have failed in their duties, and the people consequently have been disorganised, for a long time. When you have found out the truth *of any accusation*, be grieved for and pity them, and do not feel joy *at your own ability.*'

CHAP. XX. Tsze-kung said, 'Chău's wickedness was not so great *as that name implies.* Therefore, the superior man hates to dwell

should say—'to come out fully,' i. e. in one's proper nature and character. On the construction of 必也, 親喪乎, compare XII. xiii. 吾聞諸夫子—諸 seems to= 之, *it*, so that 諸 and 夫子 are like two objectives, both governed by 聞.

18. THE FILIAL PIETY OF MĂNG CHWANG:—BY TSĂNG SHĂN. Chwang was the honorary epithet of Sŭ (速), the head of the Măng family, not long anterior to Confucius. His father, according to Chû Hsî, had been a man of great merit, nor was he inferior to him, but his virtue especially appeared in what the text mentions.—Ho Yen gives the comment of Mâ Yung, that though there were bad men among his father's ministers, and defects in his government, yet Chwang made no change in the one or the other,

during the three years of mourning, and that it was this which constituted his excellence.

19. HOW A CRIMINAL JUDGE SHOULD CHERISH COMPASSION IN HIS ADMINISTRATION OF JUSTICE:—BY TSĂNG SHĂN. Seven disciples of Tsăng Shăn are more particularly mentioned, one of them being this Yang Fû. 散 is to be understood of the moral state of the people, and not, physically, of their being scattered from their dwellings. 情 has occurred before in the sense of—'the truth,' which it has here.

20. THE DANGER OF A BAD NAME:—BY TSZE-KUNG. 如是之甚, 'so very bad as this;'—the *this* (是) is understood by Hsing Ping as referring to the epithet—紂, which cannot be called honorary in this instance. According to the rules for such terms, it means—殘忍損

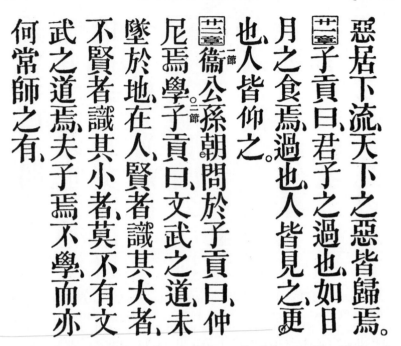

in a low-lying situation, where all the evil of the world will flow in upon him.'

CHAP. XXI. Tsze-kung said, 'The faults of the superior man are like the eclipses of the sun and moon. He has his faults, and all men see them; he changes again, and all men look up to him.'

CHAP. XXII. 1. Kung-sun Ch'âo of Wei asked Tsze-kung, saying, 'From whom did Chung-nî get his learning?'

2. Tsze-kung replied, 'The doctrines of Wăn and Wû have not yet fallen to the ground. They are to be found among men. Men of talents and virtue remember the greater principles of them, and others, not possessing such talents and virtue, remember the smaller. *Thus*, all possess the doctrines of Wăn and Wû. Where could our Master go that he should not have an opportunity of learning them? And yet what necessity was there for his having a regular master?'

義, 'cruel and unmerciful, injurious to right-eousness.' If the 是 does not in this way refer to the name, the remark would seem to have occurred in a conversation about the wickedness of Châu. 下流 is a low-lying situation, to which the streams flow and waters drain, representing here a bad reputation, which gets the credit of every vice.

21. THE SUPERIOR MAN DOES NOT CONCEAL HIS ERRORS, NOR PERSIST IN THEM:—BY TSZE-KUNG. Such is the lesson of this chapter, as expanded in the 日講. The sun and the moon being here spoken of together, the 食 must be confined to 'eclipses,' but the term is also applied to the ordinary waning of the moon.

22. CONFUCIUS'S SOURCES OF KNOWLEDGE WERE THE RECOLLECTIONS AND TRADITIONS OF THE PRINCIPLES OF WĂN AND WÛ:—BY TSZE-KUNG. 1. Of the questioner here we have no other memorial. His surname indicates that he was a descendant of some of the dukes of Wei. Observe how he calls Confucius by his designation of 仲尼 or 'Nî *secundus*.' (There was an elder brother, a concubine's son, who was called 伯

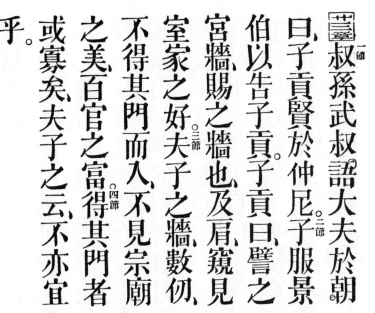

CHAP. XXIII.   1. Shû-sun Wû-shû observed to the great officers in the court, saying, 'Tsze-kung is superior to Chung-nî.'

2. Tsze-fû Ching-po reported the observation to Tsze-kung, who said, 'Let me use the comparison of a house and its *encompassing* wall. My wall *only* reaches to the shoulders. One may peep over it, and see whatever is valuable in the apartments.

3. 'The wall of my master is several fathoms high. If one do not find the door and enter by it, he cannot see the ancestral temple with its beauties, nor all the officers in their rich array.

4. 'But I may assume that they are few who find the door. Was not the observation of the chief only what might have been expected?'

仲尼 焉 學, 'How did Chung-nî learn?' but the 'how' = 'from whom?' The expression, however, in par. 2, —夫子 焉 不 學, expounded as in the translation, might suggest, from 'what quarter?' rather than 'from what person?' as the proper rendering. The last clause is taken by modern commentators, as asserting Confucius's connate knowledge, but Ân-kwo finds in it only a repetition of the statement that the sage found teachers everywhere.

23. TSZE-KUNG REPUDIATES BEING THOUGHT SUPERIOR TO CONFUCIUS, AND, BY THE COMPARISON OF A HOUSE AND WALL, SHOWS HOW ORDINARY PEOPLE COULD NOT UNDERSTAND THE MASTER.

1. 武 was the honorary epithet of Châu Ch'âu (州仇), one of the chiefs of the Shû-sun family. From a mention of him in the 家語,

顏回篇, we may conclude that he was given to envy and detraction. 賢,—used here as in XI. xv. 1. 2. Tsze-fû Ching-po,—see XIV. xxxviii. 譬之宮牆,—宮 is to be taken generally for a house or building, and not in its now common acceptation of 'a palace.' It is a poor house, as representing the disciple, and a ducal mansion as representing his master. Many commentators make the wall to be the sole object in the comparison, and 宮牆 = 宮之牆. It is better, with the 合講, to take both the house and the wall as members of the comparison, and 宮牆 = 宮與牆. The wall is not a part of the house, but one enclosing it. 3. 仞 means 7 cubits. I have translated it—'fathoms.' 4. The 夫子 here refers to Wû-shû.

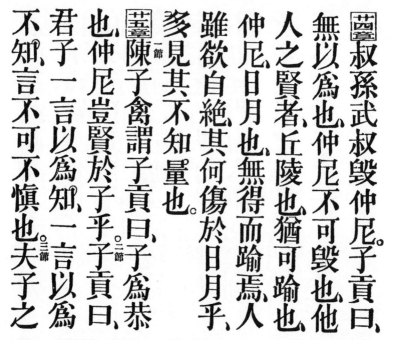

不知言不可不愼也夫子之

君子一言以爲知一言以爲

也仲尼豈賢於子乎子貢曰

陳子禽謂子貢曰子爲恭

多見其不知量也。

雖欲自絶其何傷於日月乎

仲尼日月也無得而踰焉人

人之賢者丘陵也猶可踰也

無以爲也仲尼不可毀也他

叔孫武叔毀仲尼子貢曰

CHAP. XXIV. Shû-sun Wû-shû having spoken revilingly of Chung-nî, Tsze-kung said, 'It is of no use doing so. Chung-nî cannot be reviled. The talents and virtue of other men are hillocks and mounds, which may be stepped over. Chung-nî is the sun or moon, which it is not possible to step over. Although a man may wish to cut himself off *from the sage*, what harm can he do to the sun or moon? He only shows that he does not know his own capacity.'

CHAP. XXV. 1. Ch'ăn Tsze-ch'in, addressing Tsze-kung, said, 'You are too modest. How can Chung-nî be said to be superior to you?'

2. Tsze-kung said to him, 'For one word a man is *often* deemed to be wise, and for one word he is *often* deemed to be foolish. We ought to be careful indeed in what we say.

3. 'Our Master cannot be attained to, just in the same way as the heavens cannot be gone up to by the steps of a stair.

24. CONFUCIUS IS LIKE THE SUN OR MOON, HIGH ABOVE THE REACH OF DEPRECIATION :—BY TSZE-KUNG. 無以爲 is explained by Chû Hsî (and the gloss of Hsing Ping is the same) as= 無用爲此, 'it is of no use to do this.' 他人之賢者,—他人 is to be understood, according to the 備旨, as embracing all other sages. 自絶,—I have supplied 'from the sage,' after most modern paraphrasts.

Hsing Ping, however, supplies '*from the sun and moon*.' The meaning comes to the same. Chû Hsî says that 多 here is the same with 祇, 'only;' and Hsing Ping takes it as= 適, 'just.' This meaning of the character is not given in the dictionary, but it is necessary here; —see supplement to Hsing Ping's 疏, *in loc.*

25. CONFUCIUS CAN NO MORE BE EQUALLED THAN THE HEAVENS CAN BE CLIMBED :—BY TSZE-KUNG. We find it difficult to conceive of the sage's disciples speaking to one another, as Tsze-ch'in does

何其可及也。 其死也哀如之 斯和其生也榮 綏之斯來動之 斯立道之斯行 家者所謂立之 也夫子之得邦 之不可階而升 不可及也猶天

四節

4. 'Were our Master in the position of the ruler of a State or the chief of a Family, we should find verified the description *which has been given of a sage's rule*:—he would plant the people, and forthwith they would be established; he would lead them on, and forthwith they would follow him; he would make them happy, and forthwith *multitudes* would resort to *his dominions*; he would stimulate them, and forthwith they would be harmonious. While he lived, he would be glorious. When he died, he would be bitterly lamented. How is it possible for him to be attained to?'

here to Tsze-kung, and Hsing Ping says that this was not the disciple Tsze-ch'in, but another man of the same surname and designation. But this is inadmissible, especially as we find the same parties, in I. x, talking about the character of their Master. 1. 子爲恭, 'you are doing the modest.' 2. 君子 has here its lightest meaning. The 備旨 makes it = 學者, 'a student,' but 'a man,' as in

the translation, is quite as much as it denotes. Compare its use in I. viii, *et al.* 4. 夫子之 得邦家者 must be understood hypothetically, because he never was in the position here assigned to him. 斯,—as in X. x. 1. 道 is for 導, as in I. v. 來,—as in XVI. i. 11. 動之,—as in XV. xxxii. 3. 之, *them*, 'the people' being always understood.

BOOK XX. YÂO YÜEH.

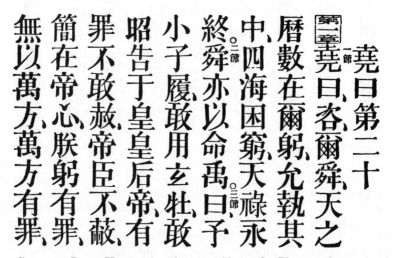

CHAPTER I. 1. Yâo said, 'Oh! you, Shun, the Heaven-determined order of succession now rests in your person. Sincerely hold fast the due Mean. If there shall be distress and want within the four seas, the Heavenly revenue will come to a perpetual end.'

2. Shun also used the same language in giving charge to Yü.

3. *T'ang* said, 'I, the child Lî, presume to use a dark-coloured victim, and presume to announce to Thee, O most great and sovereign God, that the sinner I dare not pardon, and thy ministers, O God, I do not keep in obscurity. The examination of them is by thy mind, O God. If, in my person, I commit offences, they are not to be attributed to you, *the people of* the myriad regions. If you in the myriad regions commit offences, these offences must rest on my person.'

HEADING OF THIS BOOK.—堯曰第二十, 'Yâo said, No. 20.' Hsing Ping says: —'This Book records the words of the two sovereigns, the three kings, and of Confucius, throwing light on the excellence of the ordinances of Heaven, and the transforming power of government. Its doctrines are all those of sages, worthy of being transmitted to posterity. On this account, it brings up the rear of all the other Books, without any particular relation to the one immediately preceding.'

1. PRINCIPLES AND WAYS OF Yâo, SHUN, Yü, T'ANG, AND Wû. The first five paragraphs here are mostly compiled from different parts of the Shû-ching. But there are many variations of language. The compiler may have thought it sufficient, if he gave the substance of the original in his quotations, without seeking to observe a verbal accuracy, or, possibly, the Shû-ching, as it was in his days, may have contained the passages as he gives them, and the variations be owing to the burning of most of the classical books by the founder of the Ch'in dynasty, and their recovery and restoration in a mutilated state. 1. We do not find this address of Yâo to Shun in the Shû-ching, Pt. I, but the different sentences may be gathered from Pt. II. ii. 14, 15, where we have the charge of Shun to Yü. Yâo's reign commenced B.C. 2357, and after reigning 73 years, he resigned the administration to Shun. He died B.C. 2257, and, two years after, Shun occupied the throne, in obedience to the will of the people. 天之曆數, literally, 'the represented and calculated numbers of heaven,' i. e. the divisions of the

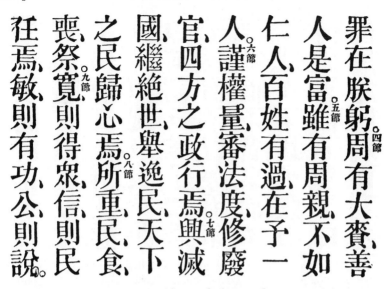

4. Châu conferred great gifts, and the good were enriched.

5. 'Although he has his near relatives, they are not equal to *my* virtuous men. The people are throwing blame upon me, the One man.'

6. He carefully attended to the weights and measures, examined the body of the laws, restored the discarded officers, and the good government of the kingdom took its course.

7. He revived States that had been extinguished, restored families whose line of succession had been broken, and called to office those who had retired into obscurity, so that throughout the kingdom the hearts of the people turned towards him.

8. What he attached chief importance to, were the food of the people, the duties of mourning, and sacrifices.

9. By his generosity, he won all. By his sincerity, he made the people repose trust in him. By his earnest activity, his achievements were great. By his justice, all were delighted.

year, its terms, months, and days, all described in a calendar, as they succeed one another with determined regularity. Here, ancient and modern interpreters agree in giving to the expression the meaning which appears in the translation. I may observe here, that Chû Hsî differs often from the old interpreters in explaining these passages of the Shû-ching, but I have followed him, leaving the correctness or incorrectness of his views to be considered in the annotations on the Shû-ching. 3. Before 曰 here we must understand 湯, the designation of the founder of the Shang dynasty. The sentences here may in substance be collected from the Shû-ching, Pt. IV. iii. 4, 8. Down to 簡在帝心 is a prayer addressed to God by T'ang, on his undertaking the overthrow of the Hsiâ dynasty, which he rehearses to his nobles and people, after the completion of his work. T'ang's name was 履. We do not find in the Shû-ching the remarkable designation of God—皇皇后帝. For the grounds on which I translate 帝 by *God*, see my work on 'The Notions of the Chinese concerning God and Spirits.' 后, now generally used for 'empress,' was anciently used for 'sovereign,' and applied to the kings. Here it is an adjective, or in apposition with 帝. The sinner is Chieh (桀), the tyrant, and last

子張問於孔子、曰、

何如、斯可以從政矣。子

曰、尊五美、屏四惡、

斯可以從政矣。子張曰、

曰、何謂五美。子

子惠而不費、勞而不

怨、欲而不貪、泰而不

驕、威而不猛。子張

何謂惠而不費。子曰、

因民之所利而利之、

第二章
一節

二節

CHAP. II. 1. Tsze-chang asked Confucius, saying, 'In what way should *a person in authority* act in order that he may conduct government properly?' The Master replied, 'Let him honour the five excellent, and banish away the four bad, things;—then may he conduct government properly.' Tsze-chang said, 'What are meant by the five excellent things?' The Master said, 'When the person in authority is beneficent without great expenditure; when he lays tasks *on the people* without their repining; when he *pursues what he* desires without being covetous; when he maintains a dignified ease without being proud; when he is majestic without being fierce.'

2. Tsze-chang said, 'What is meant by being beneficent without great expenditure?' The Master replied, 'When *the person in authority* makes more beneficial to the people the things from which

sovereign of the Hsiâ dynasty. 'The ministers of God' are the able and virtuous men, whom T'ang had called, or would call, to office. By 簡在帝心, T'ang indicates that, in his punishing or rewarding, he only wanted to act in harmony with the mind of God. 無以萬方＝萬方小民何預焉, as in the translation. In the dictionary, it is said that 以 and 與 are interchanged. This is a case in point. 4. In the Shû-ching, Pt. V. iii. 9, we find king Wû saying 大賚於四海而萬姓悅服, 'I distributed great rewards through the kingdom, and all the people were pleased and submitted.' 5. See the Shû-ching, Pt. V. i. sect. II. 6, 7. The subject in 雖有周親 is 受 or 紂, tyrant of the Yin dynasty. 周,—in the sense of 至. 過 is used in the sense of 咎, 'to blame.'—The people found fault with him, because he did

not come to save them from their sufferings by destroying their oppressor. The remaining paragraphs are descriptive of the policy of king Wû, but cannot, excepting the 8th one, be traced in the present Shû-ching. 任, paragraph 9, is in the 4th tone. See XVII. vi, which chapter, generally, resembles this paragraph.

2. HOW GOVERNMENT MAY BE CONDUCTED WITH EFFICIENCY, BY HONOURING FIVE EXCELLENT THINGS, AND PUTTING AWAY FOUR BAD THINGS:— A CONVERSATION WITH TSZE-CHANG. It is understood that this chapter, and the next, give the ideas of Confucius on government, as a sequel to those of the ancient sages and emperors, whose principles are set forth in the preceding chapter, to show how Confucius was their proper successor. 1. On 從政, see VI. vi, but the gloss of the 備旨 says—從政只泛說行政, 不作爲大夫, '從政 here denotes generally the practice of government. It is not to be taken as indicating a minister.' We may, however, retain the proper

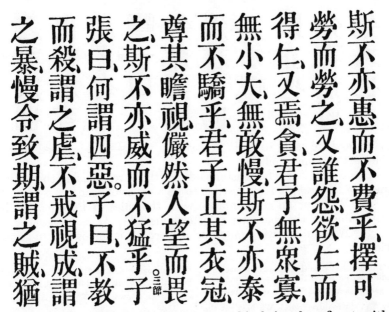

斯不亦惠而不費乎擇可
勞而勞之又誰怨欲仁而
得仁又焉貪君子無眾寡
無小大無敢慢斯不亦泰
而不驕乎君子正其衣冠
尊其瞻視儼然人望而畏
之斯不亦威而不猛乎子　○三節
張曰何謂四惡。子曰不教
而殺謂之虐不戒視成謂
之暴慢令致期謂之賊猶

they naturally derive benefit;—is not this being beneficent without *great* expenditure? When he chooses the labours which are proper, and makes them labour on them, who will repine? When his desires are set on benevolent *government*, and he secures it, who will accuse him of covetousness? Whether he has to do with many people or few, or with things great or small, he does not dare to indicate any disrespect;—is not this to maintain a dignified ease without any pride? He adjusts his clothes and cap, and throws a dignity into his looks, so that, thus dignified, he is looked at with awe;—is not this to be majestic without being fierce?'

3. Tsze-chang then asked, 'What are meant by the four bad things?' The Master said, 'To put the people to death without having instructed them;—this is called cruelty. To require from them, *suddenly*, the full tale of work, without having given them warning;—this is called oppression. To issue orders as if without urgency, *at first*, and, when the time comes, *to insist on them with severity;*—this is called injury. And, generally, in the giving *pay*

meaning of the phrase, Confucius describing principles to be observed by all in authority, and which will find in the highest their noblest embodiment. The 日講 favours this view. See its paraphrase *in loc.* I have therefore translated 君子 by—'a person in authority.' 勞而不怨,—see IV. xviii, though the application of the terms there is different. 泰而不驕,—see XIII. xxvi. 威而不猛,—see VII. xxxvii.

2. 因民云云 is instanced by the promotion of agriculture. 擇可勞云云 is instanced by the employment of the people in advantageous public works. 欲仁云云 is explained:—'Desire for what is not proper is covetousness, but if, while the wish to have the kingdom overshadowed by his benevolence has not reached to universal advantaging, his desire does not cease, then, with a heart impatient of people's evils, he administers a government impatient

or rewards to men, to do it in a stingy way;—this is called acting the part of a mere official.'

CHAP. III. 1. The Master said, 'Without recognising the ordinances *of Heaven*, it is impossible to be a superior man.

2. 'Without an acquaintance with the rules of Propriety, it is impossible for the character to be established.

3. 'Without knowing *the force of* words, it is impossible to know men.'

of those evils. What he desires is benevolence; and what he gets is the same;—how can he be regarded as covetous?' 3. 視 is explained here by 責, 'to require from.' We may get that meaning out of the character, which = 'to examine,' 'to look for.' A good deal has to be supplied, here and in the sentences below, to bring out the meaning as in the translation. 猶之 is explained by 均之, and seems to me to be nearly = our 'on the whole.' 出納, —'giving out,' i.e. *from this*, and 'presenting,' i.e. *to that*. The whole is understood to refer to rewarding men for their services, and doing it in an unwilling and stingy manner.

3. THE ORDINANCES OF HEAVEN, THE RULES OF PROPRIETY, AND THE FORCE OF WORDS, ALL NECESSARY TO BE KNOWN. 1. 知 here is not only 'knowing,' but 'believing and resting in.' 命 is the will of Heaven regarding right and wrong, of which man has the standard in his own moral nature. If this be not recognised, a man is the slave of passion, or the sport of feeling. 2. Compare VIII. viii. 2. 3. 知 here supposes much thought and examination of principles. Words are the voice of the heart. To know a man, we must attend well to what and how he thinks.

THE GREAT LEARNING.

——

大學
子程子曰大學
孔氏之遺書而
初學入德之門
也於今可見古
人爲學次第者
獨賴此篇之存
而論孟次之學
者必由是而學
焉則庶乎其不

My master, the philosopher Ch'ăng, says:—'The Great Learning is a Book transmitted by the Confucian School, and forms the gate by which first learners enter into virtue. That we can now perceive the order in which the ancients pursued their learning is solely owing to the preservation of this work, the Analects and Mencius coming after it. Learners must commence their course with this, and then it may be hoped they will be kept from error.'

TITLE OF THE WORK.—大學, 'The Great Learning.' I have pointed out, in the prolegomena, the great differences which are found among Chinese commentators on this Work, on almost every point connected with the criticism and interpretation of it. We encounter them here on the very threshold. The name itself is simply the adoption of the two commencing characters of the treatise, according to the custom noticed at the beginning of the Analects ; but in explaining those two characters, the old and new schools differ widely. Anciently, 大 was read as 太, and the oldest commentator whose notes on the work are preserved, Chăng K'ang-ch'ăng, in the last half of the 2nd century, said that the Book was called 大學, 以其記博學, 可以爲政, 'because it recorded that extensive learning, which was available for the administration of government.' This view is approved by K'ung Ying-tă (孔穎達), whose expansion of K'ang-ch'ăng's notes, written in the first half of the 7th century, still remains. He says—大學, 至道矣, '大 學 means the highest principles.' Chû Hsî's definition, on the contrary, is—大學者大人之學也, '大學 means the Learning of Adults.' One of the

paraphrasts who follow him says—大是 大人, 與小子對, '大 means adults, in opposition to children.' The grounds of Chû Hsî's interpretation are to be found in his very elegant preface to the Book, where he tries to make it out, that we have here the subjects taught in the advanced schools of antiquity. I have contented myself with the title—'The Great Learning,' which is a literal translation of the characters, whether read as 太學 or 大學.

THE INTRODUCTORY NOTE.—I have thought it well to translate this, and all the other notes and supplements appended by Chû Hsî to the original text, because they appear in nearly all the editions of the work, which fall into the hands of students, and his view of the classics is what must be regarded as the orthodox one. The translation, which is here given, is also, for the most part, according to his views, though my own differing opinion will be found freely expressed in the notes. Another version, following the order of the text, before it was transposed by him and his masters, the Ch'ăng, and without reference to his interpretations, will be found in the translation of the Lî Chî.—子程子,—see note to the Analects, I. i. 1. The Ch'ăng here is the second of the two brothers, to whom reference is made in the prolegomena. 孔氏, 'Confucius,' = the K'ung,

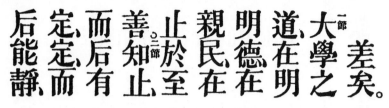

THE TEXT OF CONFUCIUS.

1. What the Great Learning teaches, is—to illustrate illustrious virtue; to renovate the people; and to rest in the highest excellence.

2. The point where to rest being known, the object of pursuit is then determined; and, that being determined, a calm unperturbedness may be attained to. To that calmness there will succeed a tranquil repose. In that repose there may be careful deliberation,

as 季氏 is found continually in the Analects for *the* Chî, i. e. the chief of the Chî family. For how can we say that 'The Great Learning' is a work left by Confucius? Even Chû Hsî ascribes only a small portion of it to the Master, and makes the rest to be the production of the disciple Tsäng, and before his time, the whole work was attributed generally to the sage's grandson. I must take 孔氏 as = 孔門, the Confucian school.

THE TEXT OF CONFUCIUS. Such Chû Hsî, as will be seen from his concluding note, determines this chapter to be, and it has been divided into two sections (段), the first containing three paragraphs, occupied with the *heads* (綱領) of the Great Learning, and the second containing four paragraphs, occupied with the *particulars* (條目) of those.

Par. 1. *The heads of the Great Learning.* 大學之道,—'the way of the Great Learning,' 道 being = 修爲之方法, 'the methods of cultivating and practising it,'—the Great Learning, that is. 在, 'is in.' The first 明 is used as a verb; the second as an adjective, qualifying 德. The illustrious virtue is the virtuous nature which man derives from Heaven. This is perverted as man grows up, through defects of the physical constitution, through inward lusts, and through outward seductions; and the great business of life should be, to bring the nature back to its original purity.—'To renovate the people,'—this object of the Great Learning is made out, by changing the character 親 of the old text into 新. The Ch'äng first proposed the alteration, and Chû Hsî approved of it. When a man has entirely illustrated his own illustrious nature, he has to proceed to bring about the same result in every other man, till 'under heaven' there be not an individual, who is

not in the same condition as himself.—'The highest excellence' is understood of the two previous matters. It is not a third and different object of pursuit, but indicates a perseverance in the two others, till they are perfectly accomplished.—According to these explanations, the objects contemplated in the Great Learning are not three, but two. Suppose them realised, and we should have the whole world of mankind perfectly good, every individual what he ought to be!

Against the above interpretation, we have to consider the older and simpler. 德 is there not the *nature*, but simply virtue, or virtuous conduct, and the first object in the Great Learning is the making of one's self more and more illustrious in virtue, or the practice of benevolence, reverence, filial piety, kindness, and sincerity. See the 故本大學註辨, *in loc.*—There is nothing, of course, of the *renovating of the people*, in this interpretation. The second object of the Great Learning is 親民 = 親愛於民, 'to love the people. —The third object is said by Ying-tâ to be 'in resting in conduct which is perfectly good (在止處於至善之行),' and here also, there would seem to be only two objects, for what essential distinction can we make between the first and third? There will be occasion below to refer to the reasons for changing 親 into 新, and their unsatisfactoriness. 'To love the people' is, doubtless, the second thing taught by the Great Learning.—Having the heads of the Great Learning now before us, according to both interpretations of it, we feel that the student of it should be a sovereign, and not an ordinary man.

Par. 2. *The mental process by which the point of rest may be attained.* I confess that I do not well understand this paragraph, in the relation of its parts in itself, nor in relation to the rest of the chapter. Chû Hsî says :—' 止 is the ground where we ought to rest;'—namely, the highest excellence mentioned above. But if

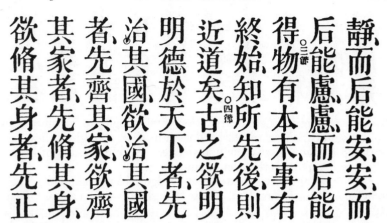

and that deliberation will be followed by the attainment *of the desired end.*

3. Things have their root and their branches. Affairs have their end and their beginning. To know what is first and what is last will lead near to what is taught *in the Great Learning.*

4. The ancients who wished to illustrate illustrious virtue throughout the kingdom, first ordered well their own States. Wishing to order well their States, they first regulated their families. Wishing to regulate their families, they first cultivated their persons. Wishing to cultivate their persons, they first rectified their hearts.

this be known in the outset, where is the necessity for the 慮, or 'careful deliberation,' which issues in its attainment? The paraphrasts make 知止 to embrace even all that is understood by 格物致知 below.— Ying-tă is perhaps rather more intelligible. He says :—'When it is known that the rest is to be in the perfectly good, then the mind has fixedness. So it is free from concupiscence, and can be still, not engaging in disturbing pursuits. That stillness leads to a repose and harmony of the feelings. That state of the feelings fits for careful thought about affairs (能思慮於事), and thence it results that what is right in affairs is attained.' Perhaps, the paragraph just intimates that the objects of the Great Learning being so great, a calm, serious thoughtfulness is required in proceeding to seek their attainment.

Par. 3. The order of things and methods in the two preceding paragraphs. So, according to Chû Hsî, does this paragraph wind up the two preceding. 'The illustration of virtue,' he says, 'is the *root,* and the renovation of the people is the *completion* (literally, *the branches*). Knowing where to rest is the *beginning,* and being able to attain is the end. The root and the beginning are *what is first.* The completion and end are *what is last.*'—The adherents of the old commentators say, on the contrary, that this paragraph is introductory to the succeeding ones. They contend that the illustration of virtue and renovation of the people are *doings* (事), and not *things* (物). According to them, the *things* are the person, heart, thoughts, &c., mentioned below, which are 'the root,' and the family, kingdom, and empire, which are 'the branches.' The *affairs* or *doings* are the various processes put forth on those things.'—This, it seems to me, is the correct interpretation.

Par. 4. The different steps by which the illustration of illustrious virtue throughout the kingdom may be brought about. 明明德於天下 is understood by the school of Chû Hsî as embracing the two first objects of the Great Learning, the illustration, namely, of virtue, and the renovation of the people. We are not aided in determining the meaning by the synthetic arrangement of the different steps in the next paragraph, for the result arrived at there is simply—天下平, 'the whole kingdom was made tranquil.'—Ying-tă's comment is— 章明已之明德使徧於天下, 'to display illustriously their own illustrious virtue (or virtues), making them reach through the whole kingdom.' But the influence must be very much transformative. Of the several steps described, the central one is 修身, 'the cultivation of the person,' which, indeed, is called 本, 'the root,' in par. 6. This re-

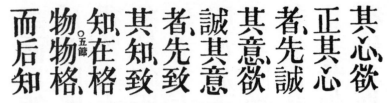

Wishing to rectify their hearts, they first sought to be sincere in their thoughts. Wishing to be sincere in their thoughts, they first extended to the utmost their knowledge. Such extension of knowledge lay in the investigation of things.

5. Things being investigated, knowledge became complete. Their knowledge being complete, their thoughts were sincere. Their

quires 'the heart to be correct,' and that again 'that the thoughts be sincere.' Chû Hsî defines 心 as 身之所主, 'what the body has for its lord,' and 意 as 心之所發, 'what the 心 sends forth.' Ying-tâ says :—總包 萬慮謂之心, 'that which comprehends and embraces all considerings is called the 心;' 爲情所意念謂之意, 'the thoughts under emotion are what is called 意.' 心 is then the metaphysical part of our nature, all that we comprehend under the terms of mind or soul, heart, and spirit. This is conceived of as quiescent, and when its activity is aroused, then we have thoughts and purposes relative to what affects it. The 'being sincere' is explained by 實, 'real.' The sincerity of the thoughts is to be obtained by 致知, which means, according to Chû Hsî, carrying our knowledge to its utmost extent, with the desire that there may be nothing which it shall not embrace.' This knowledge, finally, is realised 在格物. The same authority takes 物, 'things,' as embracing, 事, 'affairs,' as well. 格 sometimes =至, 'to come or extend to,' and assuming that the 'coming to' here is by study, he makes it= 窮究 'to examine exhaustively,' so that '格物 means exhausting by examination the principles of things and affairs, with the desire that their uttermost point may be reached.'—We feel that this explanation cannot be correct, or that, if it be correct, the teaching of the Chinese sage is far beyond and above the condition and capacity of men. How can we suppose that, in order to secure sincerity of thought and our self-cultivation, there is necessarily the study of all the phenomena of physics and metaphysics, and of the events of history ? Moreover, Chû Hsî's view of the two last clauses is a consequence of the alterations which he adopts in the order of the text.

As that exists in the Lî Chî, the 7th paragraph of this chapter is followed by 此爲知本, 此爲知之至也, which he has transferred and made the 5th chapter of annotations. Ying-tâ's comment on it is :—' The root means the person. The person (i. e. personal character) being regarded as the root, if one can know his own person, this is the knowledge of the root ; yea, this is the very extremity of knowledge.' If we apply this conclusion to the clauses under notice, it is said that wishing to make our thoughts sincere we must first carry to the utmost our self-knowledge, and this extension of self-knowledge 在格物. Now, the change of the style indicates that the relation of 致知 and 格物 is different from that of the parts in the other clauses. It is not said that to get the one thing we must first do the other. Rather it seems to me that the 格物 is a consequence of 致知, that in it is seen the other. Now, 式, 'a rule or pattern,' and 正, 'to correct,' are accepted meanings of 格, and 物 being taken generally and loosely as = things, 在格物 will tell us that, when his self-knowledge is complete, a man is a law to himself, measuring, and measuring correctly, all things with which he has to do, not led astray or beclouded by them. This is the interpretation strongly insisted on by 羅仲藩, the author of the 古本大學註莽. It is the only view into any sympathy with which I can bring my mind. In harmony with it, I would print 致知在格物 as a paragraph by itself, between the analytic and synthetic processes described in paragraphs 4, 5. Still there are difficulties connected with it, and I leave the vexed questions, regretting my own inability to clear them up.

Par. 5. The synthesis of the preceding processes.
Observe the 致 of the preceding paragraph is

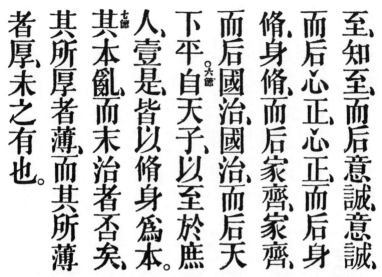

至知至而后意誠意誠
而后心正心正而后身
脩身脩而后家齊家齊
而后國治國治而后天
下平自天子以至於庶
人壹是皆以脩身為本。
其本亂而未治者否矣、
其所厚者薄、而其所薄
者厚、未之有也。

thoughts being sincere, their hearts were then rectified. Their hearts being rectified, their persons were cultivated. Their persons being cultivated, their families were regulated. Their families being regulated, their States were rightly governed. Their States being rightly governed, the whole kingdom was made tranquil and happy.

6. From the Son of Heaven down to the mass of the people, all must consider the cultivation of the person the root of *everything besides*.

7. It cannot be, when the root is neglected, that what should spring from it will be well ordered. It never has been the case that what was of great importance has been slightly cared for, and, at the same time, that what was of slight importance has been greatly cared for.

changed into 至, and how 治 (the second, or lower first tone) now becomes 治, the 4th tone. 治 is explained by 攻理, 'the work of ruling,' and 治 by 理效, 'the result.' 后 is used for 後, as in par. 2.

Par. 6. *The cultivation of the person is the prime, radical thing required from all.* I have said above that the Great Learning is adapted only to a sovereign, but it is intimated here that *the people* also may take part in it in their degree. 天子, 'Son of Heaven,' a designation of the sovereign, 以其命于天, 'because he is ordained by Heaven.' 壹是 = 一切, 'all.' Chăng K'ang-ch'ăng, however, says:— 壹是, 專行是也, '壹是 means that they uniformly do this.'

Par. 7. *Reiteration of the importance of attending* to the root. Chû Hsî makes the *root* here to be the person, but according to the preceding paragraph, it is 'the cultivation of the person' which is intended. By the 末 or 'branches' is intended the proper ordering of the family, the State, the kingdom. 'The family,' however, must be understood in a wide sense, as meaning not a household, but a *clan*, embracing all of the same surname. 厚薄, 'thick,' and 'thin,'—used here metaphorically. 所厚, according to Chû Hsî, means 'the family,' and 所薄, 'the State and the kingdom,' but that I cannot understand. 所厚 is the same as the *root*. Mencius has a saying which may illustrate the second part of the paragraph.— 於所厚者薄, 無所不薄, 'He, who is careless in what is important, will be careless in everything.'

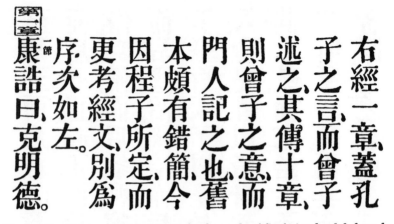

第二章

第一章

一節

康誥曰克明德。

序次如左。

更考經文別為

因程子所定而

本頗有錯簡今

門人記之也舊

則曾子之意而

述之其傳十章

子之言而曾子

右經一章蓋孔

The preceding chapter of classical text is in the words of Confucius, handed down by the philosopher Tsăng. The ten chapters of explanation which follow contain the views of Tsăng, and were recorded by his disciples. In the old copies of the work, there appeared considerable confusion in these, from the disarrangement of the tablets. But now, availing myself of the decisions of the philosopher Ch'ăng, and having examined anew the classical text, I have arranged it in order, as follows:—

COMMENTARY OF THE PHILOSOPHER TSĂNG.

CHAPTER I.   1. In the Announcement to K'ang, it is said, 'He was able to make his virtue illustrious.'

CONCLUDING NOTE. It has been shown in the prolegomena that there is no ground for the distinction made here between so much *ching* attributed to Confucius, and so much 傳, or commentary, ascribed to his disciple Tsăng. The invention of paper is ascribed to Ts'ai Lun (蔡倫), an officer of the Han dynasty, in the time of the emperor Hwo (和), A. D. 89–105. Before that time, and long after also, slips of wood and of bamboo (簡) were used to write and engrave upon. We can easily conceive how a collection of them might get disarranged, but whether those containing the Great Learning did so is a question vehemently disputed. 右經一章, 'the chapter of classic on the right;' 如左, 'on the left;'—these are expressions = our 'preceding,' and 'as follows,' indicating the Chinese method of writing and printing from the right side of a manuscript or book on to the left.

COMMENTARY OF THE PHILOSOPHER TSĂNG.

1. THE ILLUSTRATION OF ILLUSTRIOUS VIRTUE. The student will do well to refer here to the text of 'The Great Learning,' as it appears in the Lî Chî. He will then see how a considerable portion of it has been broken up, and transposed to form this and the five succeeding chapters. It was, no doubt, the occurrence of 明, in the four paragraphs here, and of the phrase 明德, which determined Chû Hsî to form them into one chapter, and refer them to the first head in the classical text. The old commentators connect them with the great business of making the thoughts sincere. 1. See the Shû-ching, V. ix. 3. The words are part of the address of king Wû to his brother Făng (封), called also K'ang-shû (康叔; 康, the honorary epithet) on appointing him to the marquisate of 衞. The subject of 克 is king Wăn, to whose example K'ang-shû is referred.—We cannot determine, from this paragraph, between the old interpretation of 德, as = 'virtues,' and the new which understands by it,—'the heart or nature, all-virtuous.' 2. See the Shû-ching, IV. v. Sect. I. 2. Chû Hsî takes 諟 as = 此, 'this,' or 審, 'to judge,' 'to examine.' The old interpreters explain it by 正, 'to correct.' The sentence is part of the address of the premier, Î Yin, to T'ai-chiǎ, the second emperor of the Shang dynasty, B. C. 1753–1719. The subject of 顧 is T'ai-chiǎ's father, the great T'ang. Chû Hsî

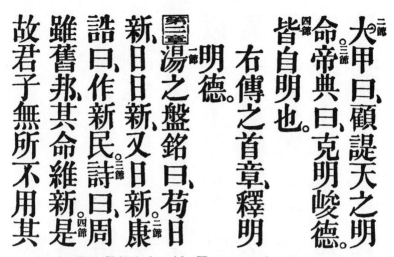

2. In the Tʻâi Chiâ, it is said, 'He contemplated and studied the illustrious decrees of Heaven.'

3. In the Canon of the emperor (Yâo), it is said, 'He was able to make illustrious his lofty virtue.'

4. These *passages* all *show how those sovereigns* made themselves illustrious.

The above first chapter of commentary explains the illustration of illustrious virtue.

CHAP. II. 1. On the bathing-tub of Tʻang, the following words were engraved :—'If you can one day renovate yourself, do so from day to day. Yea, let there be daily renovation.'

2. In the Announcement to Kʻang, it is said, 'To stir up the new people.'

3. In the Book of Poetry, it is said, 'Although Châu was an ancient State, the ordinance which lighted on it was new.'

4. Therefore, the superior man in everything uses his utmost endeavours.

understands by 明命, the Heaven-given, illustrious nature of man. The other school take the phrase more generally, = the 顯道, 'displayed ways' of Heaven. 3. See the Shû-ching, I. i. 2. It is of the emperor Yâo that this is said. 4. The 皆 must be referred to the three quotations.

2. THE RENOVATION OF THE PEOPLE. Here the character 新, 'new,' 'to renovate,' occurs five times, and it was to find something corresponding to it at the commencement of the work, which made the Chʻäng change the 親 of 親民 into 新. But the 新 here have nothing to do with the renovation of the people. This is self-evident in the 1st and 3rd paragraphs. The description of the chapter, as above, is a misnomer. 1. This fact about Tʻang's bathing-tub had come down by tradition. At least, we do not now find the mention of it anywhere but here. It was customary among the ancients, as it is in China at the present day, to engrave, all about them, on the articles of their furniture, such moral aphorisms and lessons. 2. See the *Kʻang Kâo*, par. 7, where Kʻang-shû is exhorted to assist the king 'to settle the decree of Heaven, and 作新民,' which may mean to make the bad people of Yin into good people, or to stir up the new people, i. e. *new*, as recently subjected to Châu. 3. See the Shih-ching, III. i. Ode I. st. 1. The subject of the ode is the praise of king Wän, whose virtue led to the possession of the kingdom by his

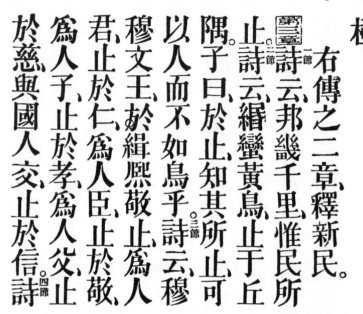

極。

右傳之二章、釋新民。

詩云、邦畿千里、惟民所[一節]

止。詩云、緡蠻黃鳥、止于丘[二節]

隅。子曰、於止、知其所止、可

以人而不如鳥乎。詩云、穆[三節]

穆文王、於緝熙敬止、爲人

君、止於仁、爲人臣、止於敬、

爲人子、止於孝、爲人父、止

於慈、與國人交、止於信。詩[四節]

The above second chapter of commentary explains the renovating of the people.

CHAP. III. 1. In the Book of Poetry, it is said, 'The royal domain of a thousand lî is where the people rest.'

2. In the Book of Poetry, it is said, 'The twittering yellow bird rests on a corner of the mound.' The Master said, 'When it rests, it knows where to rest. Is it possible that a man should not be equal to this bird?'

3. In the Book of Poetry, it is said, 'Profound was king Wăn. With how bright and unceasing a feeling of reverence did he regard his resting-places!' As a sovereign, he rested in benevolence. As a minister, he rested in reverence. As a son, he rested in filial piety. As a father, he rested in kindness. In communication with his subjects, he rested in good faith.

4. In the Book of Poetry, it is said, 'Look at that winding-course

House, more than a thousand years after its first rise. 4. 君子 is here the man of rank and office probably, as well as the man of virtue; but I do not, for my own part, see the particular relation of this to the preceding paragraphs, nor the work which it does in relation to the whole chapter.

3. ON RESTING IN THE HIGHEST EXCELLENCE. The frequent occurrence of 止 in these paragraphs, and of 至善, in par. 4, led Chû Hsî to combine them in one chapter, and connect them with the last clause in the opening paragraph of the work. 1. See the Shih-ching, IV. iii. Ode III. st. 4. The ode celebrates the

rise and establishment of the Shang or Yin dynasty. 畿 is the 1000 lî around the capital, and constituting the royal demesne. The quotation shows, according to Chû Hsî, that 物各有所當止之處, 'everything has the place where it ought to rest.' But that surely is a very sweeping conclusion from the words. 2. See the Shih-ching, II. viii. Ode VI. st. 2, where we have the complaint of a down-trodden man, contrasting his position with that of a bird. For 緡 here, we have 綿 in the Shih-ching. 緡蠻 are intended to express the

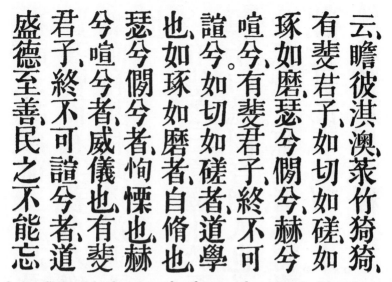

云、瞻彼淇澳、菉竹猗猗、有斐君子、如切如磋、如琢如磨瑟兮僴兮、赫兮喧兮。有斐君子、終不可諠兮。如切如磋者、道學也。如琢如磨者、自脩也瑟兮僴兮者、恂慄也赫兮喧兮者、威儀也有斐君子、終不可諠兮者道盛德至善民之不能忘

of the Ch'î, with the green bamboos so luxuriant! Here is our elegant and accomplished prince! As we cut and then file; as we chisel and then grind: *so has he cultivated himself*. How grave is he and dignified! How majestic and distinguished! Our elegant and accomplished prince never can be forgotten.' *That expression*— 'As we cut and then file,' indicates the work of learning. 'As we chisel and then grind,' indicates that of self-culture. 'How grave is he and dignified!' indicates the feeling of cautious reverence. 'How commanding and distinguished!' indicates an awe-inspiring deportment. 'Our elegant and accomplished prince never can be forgotten,' indicates how, when virtue is complete and excellence extreme, the people cannot forget them.

sound of the bird's singing or chattering. 'The yellow bird' is known by a variety of names. A common one is 倉庚, or, properly, 鶬鶊 (*ts'ang kăng*). It is a species of oriole. The 子曰 are worthy of observation. If the first chapter of the classical text, as Chû Hsî calls it, really contains the words of Confucius, we might have expected it to be headed by these characters. 於止, literally, 'in resting.' 3. See the Shih-ching, III. i. Ode I. st. 4. All the stress is here laid upon the final 止, which does not appear to have any force at all in the original, Chû Hsî himself saying there that it is 語詞, 'a mere supplemental particle.' In 於緝, 於 is read *wû*, and is an interjection. 4. See the Shih-ching, I. v. Ode I. st. 1. The ode celebrates the virtue of the

duke *Wû* (武) of Wei (衞), in his laborious endeavours to cultivate his person. There are some verbal differences between the ode in the Shih-ching, and as here quoted; namely, 奧 for 澳; 綠 for 菉; 匪 for 斐. 猗, here, *poetice*, read O. 道 is used as = 言, 'says,' or 'means.' It is to be understood before 自脩, 恂慄, and 威儀.—The transposition of this paragraph by Chû Hsî to this place does seem unhappy. It ought evidently to come in connexion with the work of 脩身. 5. See the Shih-ching, IV. i. Sect. I. Ode IV. st. 3. The former kings are Wăn and Wû, the founders of the Châu dynasty. 於戲 are an interjection, read *wû hû*. In the Shih-ching we have 於乎. 烏呼 are found with the same meaning. I translate 其賢, 其親 by

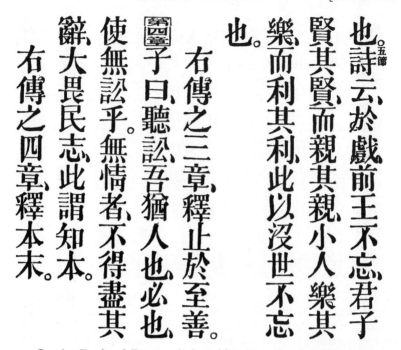

5. In the Book of Poetry, it is said, 'Ah! the former kings are not forgotten.' *Future* princes deem worthy what they deemed worthy, and love what they loved. The common people delight in what delighted them, and are benefited by their beneficial arrangements. It is on this account that the former kings, after they have quitted the world, are not forgotten.

The above third chapter of commentary explains resting in the highest excellence.

CHAP. IV. The Master said, 'In hearing litigations, I am like any other body. What is necessary is to cause the people to have no litigations?' *So*, those who are devoid of principle find it impossible to carry out their speeches, and a great awe would be struck into men's minds;—this is called knowing the root.

The above fourth chapter of commentary explains the root and the issue.

'what they deemed worthy,' 'what they loved.' When we try to determine *what* that what was, we are perplexed by the varying views of the old and new schools. 沒世,—see Analects, XV. xix.—According to Ying-tâ, 'this paragraph illustrates the business of having the thoughts sincere.' According to Chû Hsî, it tells that how the former kings renovated the people was by their resting in perfect excellence, so as to be able, throughout the kingdom and to future ages, to effect that there should not be a single thing but got its proper place.

4. EXPLANATION OF THE ROOT AND THE BRANCHES.

See the Analects, XII. xiii, from which we understand that the words of Confucius terminate at 訟乎, and that what follows is from the compiler. According to the old commentators, this is the conclusion of the chapter on having the thoughts made sincere, and that 誠其意 is the *root*. But according to Chû, it is the illustration of illustrious virtue which is the *root*, while the renovation of the people is the *result* therefrom. Looking at the words of Confucius, we must conclude that *sincerity* was the subject in his mind.

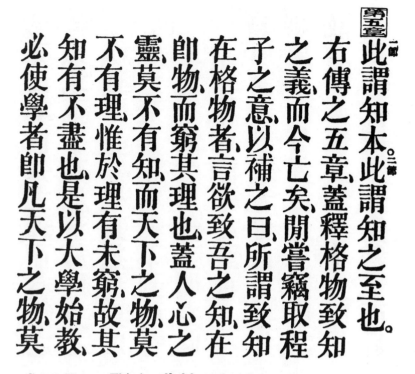

CHAP. V.   1. This is called knowing the root.

2. This is called the perfecting of knowledge.

The above fifth chapter of the commentary explained the meaning of 'investigating things and carrying knowledge to the utmost extent,' but it is now lost. I have ventured to take the views of the scholar Ch'ăng to supply it, as follows:—The meaning of the expression, 'The perfecting of knowledge depends on the investigation of things,' is this:—If we wish to carry our knowledge to the utmost, we must investigate the principles of all things we come into contact with, for the intelligent mind of man is certainly formed to know, and there is not a single thing in which its principles do not inhere. But so long as all principles are not investigated, man's knowledge is incomplete. On this account, the Learning for Adults, at the outset of its lessons, instructs the learner, in regard to all things in the world, to proceed from what knowledge he has of their principles, and pursue his investigation of them, till he reaches the extreme point. After exerting himself in this

5. ON THE INVESTIGATION OF THINGS, AND CARRYING KNOWLEDGE TO THE UTMOST EXTENT. 1. This is said by one of the Ch'ăng to be 衍文, 'superfluous text.' 2. Chû Hsî considers this to be the conclusion of a chapter which is now lost. But we have seen that the two sentences come in, as the work stands in the Lî Chî, at the conclusion of what is deemed the classical text. It is not necessary to add anything here to what has been said there, and in the prolegomena, on the new dispositions of the work from the time of the Sung scholars, and the manner in which Chû Hsî has supplied this supposed missing chapter.

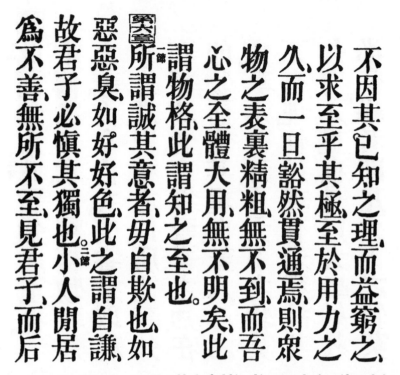

way for a long time, he will suddenly find himself possessed of a wide and far-reaching penetration. Then, the qualities of all things, whether external or internal, the subtle or the coarse, will all be apprehended, and the mind, in its entire substance and its relations to things, will be perfectly intelligent. This is called the investigation of things. This is called the perfection of knowledge.

CHAP. VI. 1. What is meant by 'making the thoughts sincere,' is the allowing no self-deception, as *when* we hate a bad smell, and as *when* we love what is beautiful. This is called self-enjoyment. Therefore, the superior man must be watchful over himself when he is alone.

2. There is no evil to which the mean man, dwelling retired, will not proceed, but when he sees a superior man, he instantly tries to

6. ON HAVING THE THOUGHTS SINCERE. 1. *The sincerity of the thoughts obtains, when they move without effort to what is right and wrong, and, in order to this, a man must be specially on his guard in his solitary moments.* 自謙 is taken as if it were 自慊, = repose or enjoyment in one's self. 慊, according to Chû Hsî, is in the entering tone, but the dictionary makes it in the 2nd.

2. *An enforcement of the concluding clause in the last paragraph.* 厭, 3rd tone, the same as 掩, meaning 閉藏貌, 'the appearance of concealing.' 人之視 已,─一人 refers to the superior man mentioned above, = 'the other.' 已 = 他, 'him,' and not = *himself*, which is its common signification. 肺肝,─literally,

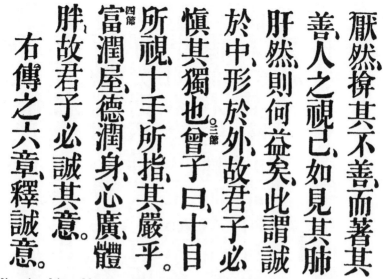

厭然揜其不善、而著其
善、人之視己、如見其肺
肝然、則何益矣、此謂誠
於中、形於外、故君子必
慎其獨也。曾子曰、十目
所視、十手所指、其嚴乎。
富潤屋、德潤身、心廣體
胖、故君子必誠其意。
右傳之六章釋誠意。

disguise himself, concealing his evil, and displaying what is good. The other beholds him, as if he saw his heart and reins;—of what use *is his disguise?* This is an instance of the saying—'What truly is within will be manifested without.' Therefore, the superior man must be watchful over himself when he is alone.

3. The disciple Tsăng said, 'What ten eyes behold, what ten hands point to, is to be regarded with reverence!'

4. Riches adorn a house, and virtue adorns the person. The mind is expanded, and the body is at ease. Therefore, the superior man must make his thoughts sincere.

The above sixth chapter of commentary explains making the thoughts sincere.

'the lungs and liver,' but with the meaning which we attach to the expression substituted for it in the translation. The Chinese make the lungs the seat of righteousness, and the liver the seat of benevolence. Compare 今子其敷心腹腎腸 in the Shû-ching, IV. vii. Sect. III. 3. 3. The use of 曾子 at the beginning of this paragraph (and extending, perhaps, over to the next) should suffice to show, that the whole work is not his, as assumed by Chû Hsî. 'Ten' is a round number, put for *many*. The recent commentator, Lo Chung-fan, refers Tsăng's expressions to the multitude of spiritual beings, servants of Heaven or God, who dwell in the regions of the air, and are continually beholding men's conduct. But they are probably only an emphatic way of exhibiting what is said in the preceding paragraph. 4. This paragraph is commonly ascribed to Tsăng Shăn, but whether correctly so or not cannot be positively affirmed. It is of the same purport as the two preceding,

showing that hypocrisy is of no use. Compare Mencius, VII. Pt. I. xxi. 4. Chăng K'ang-ch'ăng explains 胖 (read *p'ang*) by 大, 'large,' and Chû Hsî by 安舒, as in the translation. The meaning is probably the same.—It is only the first of these paragraphs from which we can in any way ascertain the views of the writer on making the thoughts sincere. The other paragraphs contain only illustration or enforcement. Now the gist of the first paragraph seems to be in 毋自欺, 'allowing no self-deception.' After knowledge has been carried to the utmost, this remains to be done, and it is not true that, when knowledge has been completed, the thoughts become sincere. This fact overthrows Chû Hsî's interpretation of the vexed passages in what he calls the text of Confucius. Let the student examine his note appended to this chapter, and he will see that Chû was not unconscious of this pinch of the difficulty.

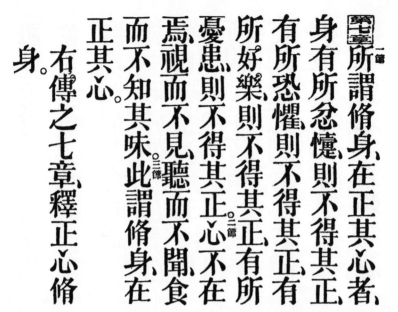

正其心。右傳之七章、釋正心脩
身。

CHAP. VII.　1. What is meant by, 'The cultivation of the person depends on rectifying the mind,' *may be thus illustrated :*—If a man be under the influence of passion, he will be incorrect in his conduct. He will be the same, if he is under the influence of terror, or under the influence of fond regard, or under that of sorrow and distress.

2. When the mind is not present, we look and do not see; we hear and do not understand; we eat and do not know the taste of what we eat.

3. This is what is meant by saying that the cultivation of the person depends on the rectifying of the mind.

The above seventh chapter of commentary explains rectifying the mind and cultivating the person.

7. ON PERSONAL CULTIVATION AS DEPENDENT ON THE RECTIFICATION OF THE MIND. 1. Here Chû Hsî, following his master Ch'äng, would again alter the text, and change the second 身 into 心. But this is unnecessary. The 身 in 脩身 is not the mere material body, but the person, the individual man, in contact with things, and intercourse with society, and the 2nd paragraph shows that the evil conduct in the first is a consequence of the mind not being under control. In 忿懥, 恐懼, 好樂 (*ào*), 憂患, the 2nd term rises on the signification of the first, and intensifies it.

Thus, 忿 is called 'a burst of anger,' and 懥, 'persistence in anger,' &c. &c.—I have said above that 身 here is not the material body. Lo Chung-fan, however, says that it is :—身謂肉身, '身 is the body of flesh.' See his reasonings, *in loc.*, but they do not work conviction in the reader. 2. 心不在焉, —this seems to be a case in point, to prove that we cannot tie 心 in this Work to any very definite application. Lo Chung-fan insists that it is 'the God-given *moral* nature,' but 心不在焉 is evidently = 'when the thoughts are otherwise engaged.'

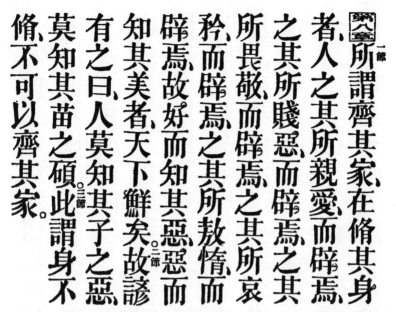

CHAP. VIII. 1. What is meant by 'The regulation of one's family depends on the cultivation of his person,' is this:—Men are partial where they feel affection and love; partial where they despise and dislike; partial where they stand in awe and reverence; partial where they feel sorrow and compassion; partial where they are arrogant and rude. Thus it is that there are few men in the world, who love and at the same time know the bad qualities of *the object of their love*, or who hate and yet know the excellences of *the object of their hatred*.

2. Hence it is said, in the common adage, 'A man does not know the wickedness of his son; he does not know the richness of his growing corn.'

3. This is what is meant by saying that if the person be not cultivated, a man cannot regulate his family.

8. THE NECESSITY OF CULTIVATING THE PERSON, IN ORDER TO THE REGULATION OF THE FAMILY. The lesson here is evidently, that men are continually falling into error, in consequence of the partiality of their feelings and affections. How this error affects their personal cultivation, and interferes with the regulating of their families, is not specially indicated. 1. The old interpreters seem to go far astray in their interpretation. They take 之 in 之其所親愛, and the other clauses, as = 適, 'to go to,' and 辟 as synonymous with 譬, 'to compare.' Ying-tâ thus expands K'ang-ch'äng on 人之其所親愛而辟焉:—

'Suppose I go to that man. When I see that he is virtuous, I feel affection for, and love him. I ought then to turn round and compare him with myself. Since he is virtuous and I love him, then, if I cultivate myself and be virtuous, I shall so be able in like manner to make all men feel affection for and love me.' In a similar way the other clauses are dealt with. Chû Hsî takes 之 as = 於, 'in regard to,' and 辟 (read *p'i*) as = 偏, 'partial,' 'one-sided.' Even his opponent, Lo Chung-fan, interprets here in the same way. But 之 is evidently the common sign of possession, the clause that follows it being construed as the regent after 人之. 敖 = 傲, 'proud,'

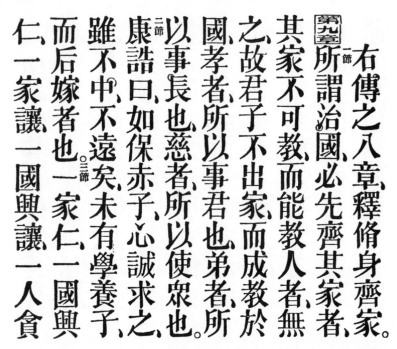

The above eighth chapter of commentary explains cultivating the person and regulating the family.

CHAP. IX. 1. What is meant by 'In order rightly to govern the State, it is necessary first to regulate the family,' is this :—It is not possible for one to teach others, while he cannot teach his own family. Therefore, the ruler, without going beyond his family, completes the lessons for the State. There is filial piety :—therewith the sovereign should be served. There is fraternal submission : —therewith elders and superiors should be served. There is kindness :—therewith the multitude should be treated.

2. In the Announcement to K'ang, it is said, '_Act_ as if you were watching over an infant.' If (_a mother_) is really anxious about it, though she may not hit _exactly the wants of her infant_, she will not be far from doing so. There never has been _a girl_ who learned to bring up a child, that she might afterwards marry.

3. From the loving _example_ of one family a whole State becomes loving, and from its courtesies the whole State becomes courteous,

'uncivil.' 2. 碩,—'great,' 'tall;' 苗之 碩,—'the tallness (richness, abundance) of his growing crop.' Farmers were noted, it would appear, in China, so long ago, for grumbling about their crops.

9. ON REGULATING THE FAMILY AS THE MEANS TO THE WELL-ORDERING OF THE STATE. 1. _There is here implied the necessity of self-cultivation to the_ rule both of the family and of the State, and that being supposed to exist,—which is the force of the 故,—it is shown how the virtues that secure the regulation of the family have their corresponding virtues in the wider sphere of the State. 君子 has here both the moral and the political meaning ; it is 治國之君子, 'the superior man

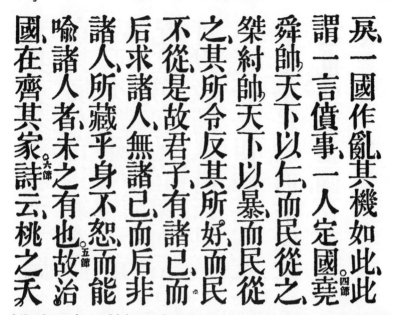

戾一國作亂其機如此此
謂一言僨事一人定國。四節
舜帥天下以仁而民從之
桀紂帥天下以暴而民從
之其所令反其所好而民
不從是故君子有諸己而
后求諸人無諸己而后非
諸人所藏乎身不恕而能
喻諸人者未之有也。五節故治
國在齊其家詩云桃之夭

while, from the ambition and perverseness of the One man, the whole State may be led to rebellious disorder;—such is the nature of the influence. This verifies the saying, 'Affairs may be ruined by a single sentence; a kingdom may be settled by its One man.'

4. Yâo and Shun led on the kingdom with benevolence, and the people followed them. Chieh and Châu led on the kingdom with violence, and the people followed them. The orders which these issued were contrary to the practices which they loved, and so the people did not follow them. On this account, the ruler must himself be possessed of the *good* qualities, and then he may require them in the people. He must not have *the bad qualities* in himself, and then he may require that they shall not be in the people. Never has there been a man, who, not having reference to his own character and wishes in dealing with others, was able effectually to instruct them.

5. Thus we see how the government of the State depends on the regulation of the family.

with whom is the government of the State.' It being once suggested to Chû Hsî that 不可教 should be 不能教, he replied— 彼之不可教, 即我之不能教, 'The *impossibility* of another's being taught is just my *inability* to teach.' 2. See the Shû-ching, V. x. 7. Both in the Shû and here, some verb, like *act*, must be supplied. This paragraph seems designed to show that *the ruler must be carried on to his object by an inward, unconstrained feeling, like that of the mother for her infant.* Lo Chung-fan insists on this as harmonizing with

親民, 'to love the people,' as the second object proposed in the Great Learning. 3. *How certainly and rapidly the influence of the family extends to the State.* 一家 is the one family of the ruler, and 一人 is the ruler. 一人, = 'I, the One man,' is a way in which the sovereign speaks of himself; see Analects, XX. i. 5. 一言＝一句, as in Analects, II. ii. 一言僨事, 一人定國,—compare Analects, XIII. xv. 仁 and 讓 have reference to the

6. In the Book of Poetry, it is said, 'That peach tree, so delicate and elegant! How luxuriant is its foliage! This girl is going to her husband's house. She will rightly order her household.' Let the household be rightly ordered, and then the people of the State may be taught.

7. In the Book of Poetry, it is said, 'They can discharge their duties to their elder brothers. They can discharge their duties to their younger brothers.' Let the ruler discharge his duties to his elder and younger brothers, and then he may teach the people of the State.

8. In the Book of Poetry, it is said, 'In his deportment there is nothing wrong; he rectifies all the people of the State.' *Yes;* when the ruler, as a father, a son, and a brother, is a model, then the people imitate him.

9. This is what is meant by saying, 'The government of his kingdom depends on his regulation of the family.'

孝, 弟 (＝悌), 慈, in par. 1. 4. *An illustration of the last part of the last paragraph.* But from the examples cited, the sphere of influence is extended from the State to the kingdom, and the family, moreover, does not intervene between the kingdom and the ruler. In 其 所令, 其 must be understood as referring to the tyrants Chieh and Châu. Their orders were good, but unavailing, in consequence of their own contrary example. 諸＝於 所 藏乎身, 'what is kept in one's own person,' i. e. his character and mind. 恕—see Analects, V. xi; XV. xxiii. Ying-tâ seems to take 不恕 as simply ＝ 'good.' 6. See the Shih-ching, I. i. Ode VI. st. 3. The ode celebrates the wife of king Wăn, and the happy influence of their family government. 之子 ＝是子. Observe 子 is feminine, as in Analects, V. i. 歸, 'going home,' a term for marriage, used by women. 7. See the Shih, II. ii. Ode VI. st. 3. The ode was sung at entertainments, when the king feasted the princes. It celebrates their virtues. 8. See the Shih, I. xiv. Ode III. st. 3. It celebrates, according to Chû Hsî, the praises of some *chün-tsze,* or ruler. 四國,—not 'four States,' but the four quarters of the State, the whole of it.

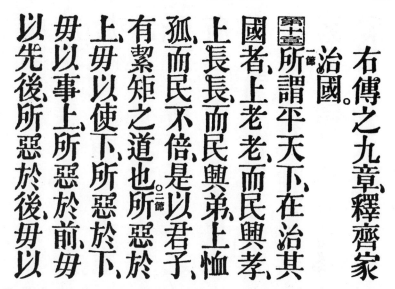

以先後所惡於後毋以
毋以事上所惡於前毋
上毋以使下所惡於下
有絜矩之道也所惡於
孤而民不倍是以君子
上長長而民興弟上恤
國者上老老而民興孝
所謂平天下在治其
治國。
右傳之九章釋齊家

The above ninth chapter of commentary explains regulating the family and governing the kingdom.

CHAP. X. 1. What is meant by 'The making the whole kingdom peaceful and happy depends on the government of his State,' is this:—When the sovereign behaves to his aged, as the aged should be behaved to, the people become filial; when the sovereign behaves to his elders, as the elders should be behaved to, the people learn brotherly submission; when the sovereign treats compassionately the young and helpless, the people do the same. Thus the ruler has a principle with which, as with a measuring-square, he may regulate his conduct.

2. What a man dislikes in his superiors, let him not display in the treatment of his inferiors; what he dislikes in inferiors, let him not display in the service of his superiors; what he hates in those who are before him, let him not therewith precede those who are behind him; what he hates in those who are behind him, let him

10. ON THE WELL-ORDERING OF THE STATE, AND MAKING THE WHOLE KINGDOM PEACEFUL AND HAPPY. The key to this chapter is in the phrase 絜矩之道, the principle of reciprocity, the doing to others as we would that they should do to us, though here, as elsewhere, it is put forth negatively. It is implied in the expression of the last chapter,—所藏乎身不恕, but it is here discussed at length, and shown in its highest application. The following analysis of the chapter is translated freely from the 四書輯要:—'This chapter explains the well-ordering of the State, and the tranquillization of the kingdom. The greatest stress is to be laid on the phrase—*the measuring-square.* That, and the expression in the general commentary—*loving and hating what the people love and hate, and not thinking only of the profit,* exhaust the teaching of the chapter. It is divided into five parts. The *first,* embracing the first two paragraphs, teaches, that the way to make the kingdom tranquil and happy is in the principle of the measuring-square. The *second* part embraces three paragraphs, and teaches that the application of the measuring-square is seen in loving and hating, in common with the people. The consequences of *losing* and *gaining* are mentioned for the first time in the 5th paragraph, to wind up the chapter so far, showing that the decree of Heaven goes or remains, according as the people's hearts are

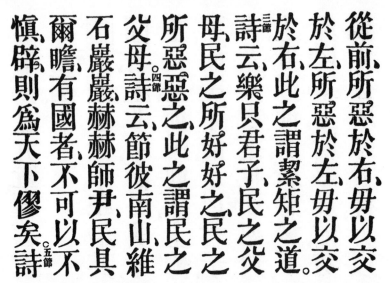

從前所惡於右、毋以交
於左、所惡於左、毋以交
於右、此之謂絜矩之道。
詩云、樂只君子民之父
母、民之所好好之民之
所惡惡之、此之謂民之
父母。詩云節彼南山維
石巖巖赫赫師尹、民具
爾瞻有國者不可以不
慎辟則為天下僇矣。詩

not therewith follow those who are before him; what he hates to receive on the right, let him not bestow on the left; what he hates to receive on the left, let him not bestow on the right:—this is what is called 'The principle with which, as with a measuring-square, to regulate one's conduct.'

3. In the Book of Poetry, it is said, 'How much to be rejoiced in are these princes, the parents of the people!' When *a prince* loves what the people love, and hates what the people hate, then is he what is called the parent of the people.

4. In the Book of Poetry, it is said, 'Lofty is that southern hill, with its rugged masses of rocks! Greatly distinguished are you, O *grand*-teacher Yin, the people all look up to you.' Rulers of States may not neglect to be careful. If they deviate *to a mean selfishness*, they will be a disgrace in the kingdom.

lost or gained. The *third* part embraces eight paragraphs, and teaches that the most important result of loving and hating in common with the people is seen in making the *root* the primary subject, and the *branch* only secondary. Here, in par. 11, mention is again made of *gaining* and *losing*, illustrating the meaning of the quotation in it, and showing that to the collection or dissipation of the people the decree of Heaven is attached. The *fourth* part consists of five paragraphs, and exhibits the extreme results of loving and hating, as shared with the people, or on one's own private feeling, and it has special reference to the sovereign's employment of ministers, because there is nothing in the principle more important than that. The 19th paragraph speaks of *gaining* and *losing*, for the third time, showing that from the 4th paragraph downwards, in reference both to the hearts of the people and the decree of Heaven, the application or non-application of the principle of the *measuring-square* depends on the mind of the sovereign. The *fifth* part embraces the other paragraphs. Because the root of the evil of a sovereign's not applying that principle lies in his not knowing how wealth is produced, and employing mean men for that object, the distinction between righteousness and profit is here much insisted on, the former bringing with it all advantages, and the latter leading to all evil consequences. Thus the sovereign is admonished, and it is seen how to be careful of his virtue is the root of the principle of the *measuring-square*; and his loving and hating, in common sympathy with the people, is its reality.'

1. There is here no progress of thought, but a repetition of what has been insisted on in the two last chapters. In 老老，長長, the first characters are verbs, with the meaning which it requires so many words to bring out

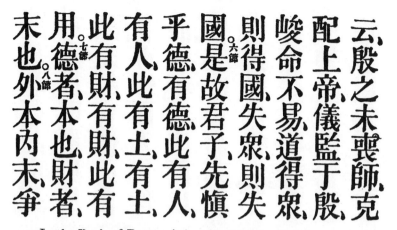

5. In the Book of Poetry, it is said, 'Before the sovereigns of the Yin *dynasty* had lost the *hearts of the* people, they could appear before God. Take warning from *the house of* Yin. The great decree is not easily *preserved*.' This shows that, by gaining the people, the kingdom is gained, and, by losing the people, the kingdom is lost.

6. On this account, the ruler will first take pains about *his own* virtue. Possessing virtue will give him the people. Possessing the people will give him the territory. Possessing the territory will give him its wealth. Possessing the wealth, he will have resources for expenditure.

7. Virtue is the root; wealth is the result.

8. If he make the root his secondary object, and the result his primary, he will *only* wrangle with his people, and teach them rapine.

in the translation. 弟=悌. 孤,—properly, 'fatherless;' here = 'the young and helpless.' 倍, read as, and = 背, 'to rebel,' 'to act contrary to.' 君子, here and throughout the chapter, has reference to office, and specially to the royal or highest. 絜矩之道,—絜 is a verb, read *hsieh*, according to Chû Hsî, = 度, 'to measure;' 矩,—the mechanical instrument, 'the carpenter's square.' It having been seen that the ruler's example is so influential, it follows that the minds of all men are the same in sympathy and tendency. He has then only to take his own mind, and measure therewith the minds of others. If he act accordingly, the grand result—the kingdom tranquil and happy—will ensue. 2. *A lengthened description of the principle of reciprocity.* 先,—4th tone, 'to precede.' 3. See the Shih-ching, II. ii. Ode V. st. 3. The ode is one that was sung at festivals, and celebrates the virtues of the princes present. Chû Hsî makes 只 (read *chih*, 3rd tone) an exple-

tive. Chǎng's gloss, in 毛詩註疏, takes it as = 是, and the whole is—'I gladden these princes, the parents of the people.' 4. See the Shih-ching, II. iv. Ode VII. st. 1. The ode complains of the king Yû (幽), for his employing unworthy ministers. 節, read *ts'ieh*, meaning 'rugged and lofty-looking.' 具 = 俱, 'all.' 辟, read *p'i*, as in chap. viii. is explained in the dictionary by 辱, 'disgrace.' Chû Hsî seems to take it as = 戮, 'to kill,' as did the old commentators. They say:—'He will be put to death by the people, as were the tyrants Chieh and Châu.' 5. See the Shih, III. i. st. 6, where we have 宜 for 儀, and 駿 for 峻. The ode is supposed to be addressed to king Ch'ǎng (成), to stimulate him to imitate the virtues of his grandfather Wăn. 殷, = 'the sovereigns of the Yin dynasty.' The capital of the Shang dynasty was changed

9. Hence, the accumulation of wealth is the way to scatter the people; and the letting it be scattered among them is the way to collect the people.

10. And hence, the ruler's words going forth contrary to right, will come back to him in the same way, and wealth, gotten by improper ways, will take its departure by the same.

11. In the Announcement to K'ang, it is said, 'The decree indeed may not always rest on *us;*' that is, goodness obtains the decree, and the want of goodness loses it.

12. In the Book of Ch'û, it is said, 'The kingdom of Ch'û does not consider that to be valuable. It values, *instead*, its good men.'

to Yin by P'an-kǎng, about B.C. 1400, after which the dynasty was so denominated. 配 上帝, according to Chû Hsî, means 'they were the sovereigns of the realm, and corresponded to (fronted) God.' K'ang-ch'ăng says:—'Before they lost their people, from their virtue, they were also able to appear before Heaven; that is, Heaven accepted their sacrifices.' Lo Chung-fan makes it:—'They harmonized with God; that is, in loving the people.' K'ang-ch'ăng's interpretation is, I apprehend, the correct one. 6. 愼乎德—德 here, according to Chû Hsî, is the 'illustrious virtue' at the beginning of the book. His opponents say that it is the exhibition of virtue; that is, of filial piety, brotherly submission, &c. This is more in harmony with the first paragraph of the chapter. 8. 外 and 內 are used as verbs, = 輕重, 'to consider slight,' 'to consider important.' 爭民,—'will wrangle the (i. e. with the) people.' The ruler will be trying to take, and the people will be trying to hold. 施奪,—'he will give'—(i. e. lead the people to, = teach them)—'rapine.' The two phrases = he will be against the people, and will set them against himself, and against

one another. Ying-tâ explains them—'people wrangling for gain will give reins to their rapacious disposition.' 9. 財散 'wealth being scattered,'—that is, diffused, and allowed to be so by the ruler, among the people. The collecting and scattering of the people are to be understood with reference to their feelings towards their ruler. 10. The 'words' are to be understood of governmental orders and enactments. 悖, read *pei*, = 逆, 'to act contrary to,' 'to rebel,' that which is outraged being 理, 'what is right,' or, in the first place, 民心, 'the people's hearts,' and, in the second place, 君心, 'the ruler's heart.' Our proverb—'goods ill-gotten go ill-spent'— might be translated by 貨悖而入者, 亦悖而出, but those words have a different meaning in the text. 11. See the *K'ang Kâo*, par. 23. The only difficulty is with 于. K'ang-ch'ăng and Ying-tâ do not take it as an expletive, but say it = 於, 'in,' or 'on;'—'The appointment of Heaven may not constantly rest on one family.' Treating 于 in this way, the supplement in the Shû should be 'us.' 12. The

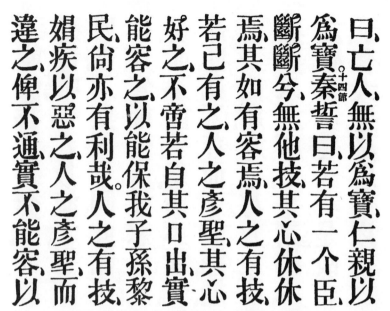

違之俾不通實不能容以
娟疾以惡之人之彥聖而
民尙亦有利哉。
能容之以能保我子孫黎
好之不啻若自其口出實
若己有之人之彥聖其心
焉其如有容焉人之有技
斷斷兮無他技其心休休
爲寶。秦誓曰若有一个臣
曰、亡人、無以爲寶、仁親以

○十四節

13. *Duke Wăn's* uncle, Fan, said, 'Our fugitive does not account that to be precious. What he considers precious, is the affection due to his parent.'

14. In the Declaration *of the duke of* Ch'in, it is said, 'Let me have but one minister, plain and sincere, not *pretending to* other abilities, but with a simple, upright, mind; and possessed of generosity, *regarding* the talents of others as though he himself possessed them, and, where he finds accomplished and perspicacious men, loving them in his heart more than his mouth expresses, and really showing himself able to bear them *and employ them:*—such a minister will be able to preserve my sons and grandsons and black-haired people, and benefits likewise to the kingdom may well be looked for from him. But if *it be his character,* when he finds men of ability, to be jealous and hate them; and, when he finds accomplished and perspicacious men, to oppose them and not allow their advancement, showing himself really not able to bear them:—such a minister will not be able to protect my sons and grandsons

Book of Ch'û is found in the 國語, 'Narratives of the States,' a collection purporting to be of the Châu dynasty, and, in relation to the other States, what Confucius's 'Spring and Autumn' is to Lû. The exact words of the text do not occur, but they could easily be constructed from the narrative. An officer of Ch'û being sent on an embassy to Tsin, the minister who received him asked about a famous girdle of Ch'û, called 白珩, how much it was worth. The officer replied that his country did not look on such things as its treasures, but on its able and virtuous ministers. 13. 舅犯, 'uncle Fan;' that is, uncle to Wăn, subsequently marquis, commonly described as duke, of Tsin. Wăn is the 亡人, or, 'fugitive.' In the early part of his life, he was a fugitive, and suffered many vicissitudes of fortune. Once, the duke of Ch'in (秦) having offered to help him, when he was in mourning for his father who had expelled him, to recover Tsin, his uncle Fan gave the reply in the text. The *that* in the translation refers to 得國, 'getting the kingdom.' 14.

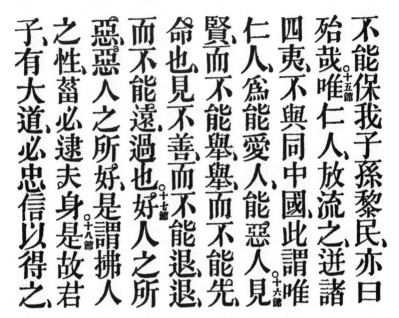

and black-haired people; and may he not also be pronounced dangerous *to the State*?'

15. It is only the truly virtuous man who can send away such a man and banish him, driving him out among the barbarous tribes around, determined not to dwell along with him in the Middle Kingdom. This is in accordance with the saying, 'It is only the truly virtuous man who can love or who can hate others.'

16. To see men of worth and not be able to raise them to office; to raise them to office, but not to do so quickly:—this is disrespectful. To see bad men and not be able to remove them; to remove them, but not to do so to a distance:—this is weakness.

17. To love those whom men hate, and to hate those whom men love:—this is to outrage the natural feeling of men. Calamities cannot fail to come down on him who does so.

18. Thus *we see that* the sovereign has a great course *to pursue*. He must show entire self-devotion and sincerity to attain it, and by pride and extravagance he will fail of it.

'The declaration *of the duke of* Ch'in' is the last book in the Shû-ching. It was made by one of the dukes of Ch'in to his officers, after he had sustained a great disaster, in consequence of neglecting the advice of his most faithful minister. Between the text here, and that which we find in the Shû, there are some differences, but they are unimportant. 15. 仁

人 is here, according to Chû Hsî and his followers, the prince who applies the principle of reciprocity, expounded in the second paragraph. Lo Chung-fan contends that it is 親民者, 'the lover of the people.' The paragraph is closely connected with the preceding. In 放流之, 之 refers to the bad minister, there described. The 四夷, 'four î;' see the Lî Chî, III. iii. 14. 不與同中國 =不與之同處中國, 'will not dwell

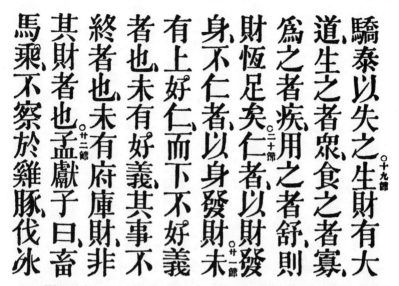

馬乘不察於雞豚伐冰

其財者也孟獻子曰畜

終者也未有府庫財非

者也未有好義其事不

有上好仁而下不好義

身不仁者以身發財。廿一節

財恆足矣仁者以財發

爲之者疾用之者舒則

道生之者衆食之者寡

驕泰以失之生財有大 十九節

19. There is a great course *also* for the production of wealth. Let the producers be many and the consumers few. Let there be activity in the production, and economy in the expenditure. Then the wealth will always be sufficient.

20. The virtuous *ruler*, by means of his wealth, makes himself more distinguished. The vicious ruler accumulates wealth, at the expense of his life.

21. Never has there been a case of the sovereign loving benevolence, and the people not loving righteousness. Never has there been a case where the people have loved righteousness, and the affairs of the sovereign have not been carried to completion. And never has there been a case where the wealth in such a State, collected in the treasuries and arsenals, did not continue in the sovereign's possession.

22. The officer Măng Hsien said, 'He who keeps horses and a carriage does not look after fowls and pigs. The family which

together with him in the Middle Kingdom.' China is evidently so denominated, from its being thought to be surrounded by barbarous tribes. 惟仁人能云云,—see Analects, IV. iii. 16. I have translated 命 as if it were 慢, which K'ang-ch'äng thinks should be in the text. Ch'äng Î (頤) would substitute 怠, 'idle,' instead of 慢, and Chû Hsî does not know which suggestion to prefer. Lo Chung-fan stoutly contends for retaining 命, and interprets it as = 'fate,' but he is obliged to supply a good deal himself, to make any sense of the passage. See his argument, *in loc.*

The paraphrasts all explain 先 by 早, 'early.' 遠, 3rd tone, but with a hiphil force. 退 is referred to 放流 in last paragraph, and 遠 to 不與同中國. 17. This is spoken of the ruler not having respect to the common feelings of the people in his employment of ministers, and the consequences thereof to himself. 夫, 1st tone, is used as in Analects, XI. ix. 4, or = the preposition 乎. *This paragraph speaks generally of the primal cause of gaining and losing, and shows how the principle of the measuring-square must have its root in the ruler's mind.* So, in the 日講. The great course is explained

亦　蓄　之　必　長　利　有　與　之　之
無　害　小　自　國　爲　盜　其　家　家
如　並　人　小　家　利　臣　有　不　不
之　至　之　人　而　以　此　聚　畜　畜
何　雖　使　矣　務　義　謂　斂　聚　牛
矣　有　爲　彼　財　爲　國　之　斂　羊
此　善　國　爲　用　利　不　臣　之　百
謂　者　家　善　者　也。　以　寧　臣、　乘

keeps its stores of ice does not rear cattle or sheep. *So*, the house which possesses a hundred chariots should not keep a minister to look out for imposts that he may lay them on the people. Than to have such a minister, it were better for that house to have one who should rob it *of its revenues.*' This is in accordance with the saying:—' In a State, *pecuniary* gain is not to be considered to be prosperity, but its prosperity *will* be found in righteousness.'

23. When he who presides over a State or a family makes his revenues his chief business, he must be under the influence of some small, mean man. He may consider this man to be good; but when such a person is employed in the administration of a State or family, calamities *from Heaven*, and injuries *from men*, will befal it together, and, though a good man may take his place, he will not be able to

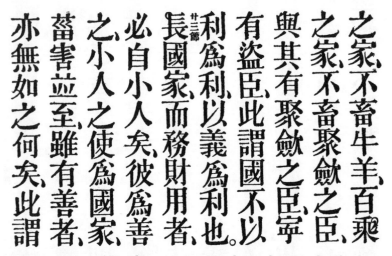

by Chû as—'the art of occupying the throne, and therein cultivating himself and governing others.' Ying-tâ says it is—'the course by which he practises filial piety, fraternal duty, benevolence, and righteousness.' 驕 and 泰 are here qualities of the same nature. They are not contrasted as in Analects, XIII. xxvi. 19. This is understood by K'ang-ch'äng as requiring the promotion of agriculture, and that is included, but does not exhaust the meaning. The consumers are the salaried officers of the government. The sentiment of the whole is good;—where there is cheerful industry in the people, and an economical administration of the government, the finances will be flourishing. 20. The sentiment here is substantially the same as in paragraphs 7, 8. The old interpretation is different:—'The virtuous man uses his wealth so as to make his person distinguished. He who is not virtuous, toils with his body to increase his wealth.' 21. This shows how the people respond to the influence of the ruler, and that benevolence, even to the scattering of his wealth on the part of the latter, is the way to permanent prosperity and wealth. 22. Hsien was the honorary epithet of Chung-sun Mieh (獻), a worthy minister of Lû under the two dukes, who ruled before the birth of Confucius. His sayings, quoted here, were preserved by tradition, or recorded in some Work which is now lost. 畜 (read *ch'ú*) 乘馬, —on a scholar's being first called to office, he was gifted by his prince with a carriage and four horses. He was then supposed to withdraw from petty ways of getting wealth. The 卿, or high officers of a State, kept ice for use in their funeral rites and sacrifices. 伐冰, —with reference to the *cutting* the ice to store it; see the Shih, I. xv. Ode I. 8. 聚斂之臣,—see Analects, XI. xvi. 23. 彼爲善之,—善 is used as a verb, = 以爲善, 'considers to be good.' 不以利爲利, 以義爲利,—see Mencius, I. Pt. I. i, *et passim.*

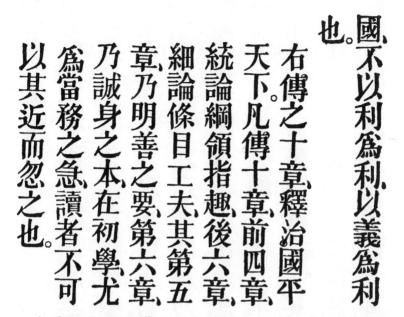

也。國不以利爲利以義爲利

右傳之十章釋治國平
天下。凡傳十章前四章
統論綱領指趣後六章
細論條目工夫其第五
章乃明善之要第六章
乃誠身之本在初學尤
爲當務之急讀者不可
以其近而忽之也。

remedy the evil. This illustrates *again* the saying, 'In a State, gain is not to be considered prosperity, but its prosperity will be found in righteousness.'

The above tenth chapter of commentary explains the government of the State, and the making the kingdom peaceful and happy.

There are thus, in all, ten chapters of commentary, the first four of which discuss, in a general manner, the scope of the principal topic of the Work ; while the other six go particularly into an exhibition of the work required in its subordinate branches. The fifth chapter contains the important subject of comprehending true excellence, and the sixth, what is the foundation of the attainment of true sincerity. Those two chapters demand the especial attention of the learner. Let not the reader despise them because of their simplicity.

THE DOCTRINE OF THE MEAN.

—•—

中庸

子程子曰、不偏之謂
中、不易之謂庸、中者、天
下之正道、庸者、天
下之定理、此篇乃孔
門傳授心法、子思恐
其久而差也、故筆之
於書、以授孟子、其書
始言一理、中散爲萬
事、末復合爲一理、放

My master, the philosopher Ch'ang, says:—'Being without inclination to either side is called CHUNG; *admitting of no change is called* YUNG. *By* CHUNG *is denoted the correct course to be pursued by all under heaven; by* YUNG *is denoted the fixed principle regulating all under heaven. This work contains the law of the mind, which was handed down from one to another, in the Confucian school, till Tsze-sze, fearing lest in the course of time errors should arise about it, committed it to writing, and delivered it to Mencius. The Book first speaks of one principle; it next spreads this out, and embraces all things; finally, it returns and gathers them all up under the one principle. Unroll it, and it fills*

THE TITLE OF THE WORK.—中庸, 'The Doctrine of the Mean.' I have not attempted to translate the Chinese character 庸, as to the exact force of which there is considerable difference of opinion, both among native commentators, and among previous translators. Chǎng K'ang-ch'ǎng said—名曰中庸者、以其記中和之爲用也, 'The Work is named 中庸, because it records the practice of the non-deviating mind and of harmony.' He takes 庸 in the sense of 用, 'to use,' 'to employ,' which is the first given to it in the dictionary, and is found in the Shû-ching, I. i. par. 9. As to the meaning of 中 and 和, see chap. i. par. 4. This appears to have been the accepted meaning of 庸 in this

combination, till Ch'ang Î introduced that of 不易, 'unchanging,' as in the introductory note, which, however, the dictionary does not acknowledge. Chû Hsî himself says—中者 不偏不倚、無過不及之名、庸、平常也, '*Chung* is the name for what is without inclination or deflection, which neither exceeds nor comes short. *Yung* means ordinary, constant.' The dictionary gives another meaning of *Yung*, with special reference to the point before us. It is said—又和也, 'It also means harmony;' and then reference is made to K'ang-ch'ǎng's words given above, the compilers not having observed that he immediately subjoins—庸、用也, showing that he takes *Yung* in the sense of 'to employ,' and not of 'harmony.' Many, however, adopt this mean-

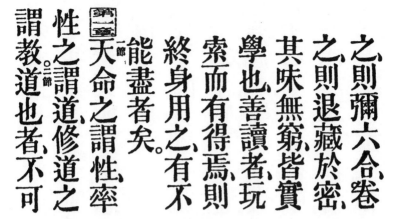

謂教道也者、不可
性之謂道、修道之
第一章
天命之謂性率
能盡者矣。
終身用之有不
索而有得焉則
學也善讀者玩
其味無窮皆實
之則退藏於密
之則彌六合卷

二節

一節

the universe; roll it up, and it retires and lies hid in mysteriousness. The relish of it is inexhaustible. The whole of it is solid learning. When the skilful reader has explored it with delight till he has apprehended it, he may carry it into practice all his life, and will find that it cannot be exhausted.'

CHAPTER I. 1. What Heaven has conferred is called THE NATURE; an accordance with this nature is called THE PATH *of duty;* the regulation of this path is called INSTRUCTION.

ing of the term in chap. ii, and my own opinion is decidedly in favour of it, here in the title. The work then treats of the human mind:—in its state of *chung*, absolutely correct, as it is in itself; and in its state of *hwo*, or harmony, acting *ad extra*, according to its correct nature. —In the version of the work, given in the collection of '*Mémoires concernant l'histoire, les sciences, &c., des Chinois*,' vol. i, it is styled—'*Juste Milieu.*' Rémusat calls it '*L'invariable Milieu*,' after Ch'äng Î. Intorcetta and his coadjutors call it—'*Medium constans vel sempiternum.*' The Book treats, they say, '*De MEDIO SEMPITERNO, sive de aurea mediocritate illa, quæ est, ut ait Cicero, inter nimium et parum, constanter et omnibus in rebus tenenda.*' Morrison, character 庸, says, '*Chung Yung*, the constant (golden) Medium.' Collie calls it— 'The golden Medium.' The objection which I have to all these names is, that from them it would appear as if 中 were a noun, and 庸 a qualifying adjective, whereas they are co-ordinate terms. My own version of the title in the translation published in the Sacred Books of the East is, '*The State of Equilibrium and Harmony.*'

INTRODUCTORY NOTE. 子程子,—see on introductory note to the 大學. On Tsze-sze, and his authorship of this work, see the prolegomena. 六合 is a phrase denoting —'the zenith and nadir, and the four cardinal points,' = the universe. 善讀者,—not our ' good reader,' but as in the translation.—I will

not here anticipate the judgment of the reader on the eulogy of the enthusiastic Ch'äng.

1. It has been stated, in the prolegomena, that the current division of the Chung Yung into chapters was made by Chû Hsî, as well as their subdivision into paragraphs. The thirty-three chapters which embrace the work, are again arranged by him in five divisions, as will be seen from his supplementary notes. The first and last chapters are complete in themselves, as in the introduction and conclusion of the treatise. The second part contains ten chapters ; the third, nine ; and the fourth, twelve.

Par. 1. The principles of duty have their root in the evidenced will of Heaven, and their full exhibition in the teaching of sages. By 性, or ' nature,' is to be understood the nature of man, though Chû Hsî generalizes it so as to embrace that of brutes also; but only *man* can be cognizant of the *táo* and *chiáo*. 命 he defines by 令, 'to command,' ' to order.' But we must take it as in a gloss on a passage from the Yi-ching, quoted in the dictionary.—命 者 人 所 禀 受, '*Ming* is what men are endowed with.' Chû also says that 性 is just 理, the ' principle,' characteristic of any particular nature. But this only involves the subject in mystery. His explanation of 道 by 路, 'a path,' seems to be correct, though some modern writers object to it.—What is taught seems to be this :— To man belongs a moral nature, conferred on him by Heaven or God, by which he is consti-

天　節　謂　喜　故　見　懼　愼　道　須
下　謂　之　怒　君　乎　乎　乎　也　臾
之　之　中　哀　子　隱　其　其　是　離
大　和　發　樂　愼　莫　所　所　故　也
本　中　而　之　其　顯　不　不　君　可
也　也　皆　未　獨　乎　聞　睹　子　離
和　者　中　發　也。　微　莫　恐　戒　非

（四節）　（三節）

2. The path may not be left for an instant. If it could be left, it would not be the path. On this account, the superior man does not wait till he sees things, to be cautious, nor till he hears things, to be apprehensive.

3. There is nothing more visible than what is secret, and nothing more manifest than what is minute. Therefore the superior man is watchful over himself, when he is alone.

4. While there are no stirrings of pleasure, anger, sorrow, or joy, the mind may be said to be in the state of EQUILIBRIUM. When those feelings have been stirred, and they act in their due degree, there ensues what may be called the state of HARMONY. This EQUILIBRIUM is the great root *from which grow all the human actings* in the world, and this HARMONY is the universal path *which they all should pursue.*

tuted a law to himself. But as he is prone to deviate from the path in which, according to his nature, he should go, wise and good men—sages—have appeared, to explain and regulate this, helping all by their instructions to walk in it.

Par. 2. *The path indicated by the nature may never be left, and the superior man*—體道之人 *he who would embody all principles of right and duty—exercises a most sedulous care that he may attain thereto.* 須臾 is a name for a short period of time, of which there are thirty in the twenty-four hours; but the phrase is commonly used for 'a moment,' 'an instant.' K'ung Ying-tâ explains 可離非道，—'what may be left is a wrong way,' which is not admissible. 離, 4th tone, = 去, 'to be, or go, away from.' If we translate the two last clauses literally,— 'is cautious and careful in regard to what he does not see ; is fearful and apprehensive in regard to what he does not hear,'—they will not be intelligible to an English reader. A question arises, moreover, whether 其所不睹

其所不聞, ought not to be understood passively, = 'where he is not seen,' 'where he is not heard.' They are so understood by Ying-tâ, and the 大學傳, chap. vi, is much in favour, by its analogy, of such an interpretation.

Par. 3. Chû Hsî says that 隱 is 'a dark place ;' that 細 means 'small matters ;' and that 獨 is 'the place which other men do not know, and is known only to one's self.' There would thus hardly be any advance from the last paragraph. It seems to me that the secrecy must be in the recesses of one's own heart, and the minute things, the springs of thought and stirrings of purpose there. The full development of what is intended here is probably to be found in all the subsequent passages about 誠, or 'sincerity.' See 西河 合集, 中庸說, *in loc.*

Par. 4. 'This,' says Chû Hsî, 'speaks of the virtue of the nature and passions, to illustrate the meaning of the statement that the path may not be left.' It is difficult to translate the para-

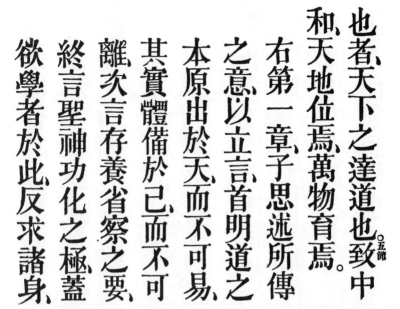

也者天下之達道也。致中
和天地位焉萬物育焉。
右第一章子思述所傳
之意以立言首明道之
本原出於天而不可易、
其實體備於己而不可
離次言存養省察之要、
終言聖神功化之極蓋
欲學者於此反求諸身、

5. Let the states of equilibrium and harmony exist in perfection, and a happy order will prevail throughout heaven and earth, and all things will be nourished and flourish.

In the first chapter which is given above, Tsze-sze states the views which had been handed down to him, as the basis of his discourse. First, it shows clearly how the path of duty is to be traced to its origin in Heaven, and is unchangeable, while the substance of it is provided in ourselves, and may not be departed from. Next, it speaks of the importance of preserving and nourishing this, and of exercising a watchful self-scrutiny with reference to it. Finally, it speaks of the meritorious achievements and transforming influence of sage and spiritual men in their highest extent. The wish of Tsze-sze was that hereby the learner should direct his thoughts inwards, and by searching in himself, there find these

graph because it is difficult to understand it. 謂 之 is different from 之 謂 in par. 1. That *defines;* this *describes.* What is described in the first clause, seems to be 性, 'the nature,' capable of all feelings, but unacted on, and in equilibrium.

Par. 5. On this Intorcetta and his colleagues observe:—'*Quis non videt eo dumtaxat collimasse philosophum, ut hominis naturam, quam ab origine sua rectam, sed deinde lapsam et depravatam passim Sinenses docent, ad primævum innocentiæ statum reduceret? Atque ita reliquas res creatas, homini jam rebelles, et in ejusdem ruinam armatas, ad pristinum obsequium veluti revocaret. Hoc caput primum libri Ta Heŏ, hoc item hic et alibi non semel indicat. Etsi autem nesciret philosophus nos a prima felicitate propter peccatum primi parentis excidisse, tamen et tot rerum quæ adversantur et infestæ sunt homini, et ipsius naturæ humanæ ad deteriora tam pronæ, longo usu et contemplatione didicisse videtur, non posse hoc*

universum, quod homo vitiatus quodam modo vitiarat, connaturali suæ integritati et ordini restitui, nisi prius ipse homo per victoriam sui ipsius, eam, quam amiserat, integritatem et ordinem recuperaret.' I fancied something of the same kind, before reading their note. According to Chû Hsî, the paragraph describes the work and influence of sage and spiritual men in their highest issues. The subject is developed in the 4th part of the work, in very extravagant and mystical language. The study of it will modify very much our assent to the views in the above passage. There is in this whole chapter a mixture of sense and mysticism,—of what may be grasped, and what tantalizes and eludes the mind. 位, according to Chû Hsî, = 安其位, 'will rest in their positions.' K'ang-ch'ǎng explained it by 正, —'will be rectified.' 'Heaven and earth' are here the parent powers of the universe. Thus

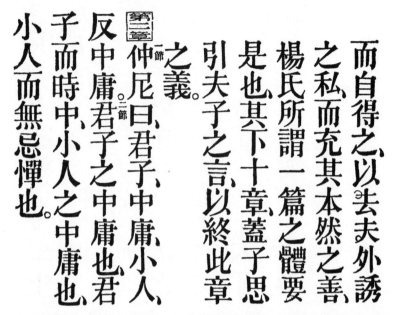

小人而無忌憚也。

子而時中小人之中庸也、

反中庸君子之中庸也君

二節

仲尼曰君子中庸小人、

一節

第二章

之義。

引夫子之言以終此章

是也其下十章蓋子思

楊氏所謂一篇之體要

之私而充其本然之善、

而自得之以去夫外誘

truths, so that he might put aside all outward temptations appealing to his selfishness, and fill up the measure of the goodness which is natural to him. This chapter is what the writer Yang called it,—'The sum of the whole work.' In the ten chapters which follow, Tsze-sze quotes the words of the Master to complete the meaning of this.

CHAP. II.　1. Chung-nî said, 'The superior man *embodies* the course of the Mean; the mean man acts contrary to the course of the Mean.

2. 'The superior man's embodying the course of the Mean is because he is a superior man, and so always maintains the Mean. The mean man's acting contrary to the course of the Mean is because he is a mean man, and has no caution.'

Ying-tâ expounds :—'Heaven and earth will get their correct place, and the processes of production and completion will go on according to their principles, so that all things will be nourished and fostered.'

CONCLUDING NOTE. The writer Yang, A.D. 1053-1135, quoted here, was a distinguished scholar and author in the Sung dynasty. He was a disciple of Ch'ǎng Hâo, and a friend both of him and his brother î. 體要, 'the substance and the abstract,' = the sum.

2. ONLY THE SUPERIOR MAN CAN FOLLOW THE MEAN ; THE MEAN MAN IS ALWAYS VIOLATING IT. 1. Why Confucius should here be quoted by his designation, or marriage name, is a moot-point. It is said by some that disciples might in this way refer to their teacher, and a grandson to his grandfather, but such a rule is constituted

probable on the strength of this instance, and that in chap. xxx. Others say that it is the honorary designation of the sage, and = the 尼父, which duke Âi used in reference to Confucius, in eulogizing him after his death. See the Lî Chî, II. Sect. I. iii. 44. Some verb must be understood between 君子 and 中庸, and I have supposed it to be 體, with most of the paraphrasts. Nearly all seem to be agreed that 中庸 here is the same as 中和 in the last chapter. On the change of terms, Chû Hsî quotes from the scholar Yû (遊), to the effect that 中和 is said with the nature and feelings in view, and 中庸, with reference to

CHAP. III. The Master said, 'Perfect is the virtue which is according to the Mean! Rare have they long been among the people, who could practise it!'

CHAP. IV. 1. The Master said, 'I know how it is that the path *of the Mean* is not walked in :—The knowing go beyond it, and the stupid do not come up to it. I know how it is that the path of the Mean is not understood :—The men of talents and virtue go beyond it, and the worthless do not come up to it.

2. 'There is no body but eats and drinks. But they are few who can distinguish flavours.'

virtue and conduct. 2. 君子而時中 is explained by Chû :—'Because he has the virtue of a superior man, and moreover is able always to manage the *chung*.' But I rather think that the *chün-tsze* here is specially to be referred to the same as described in I. ii, and 中＝正中. Wang Sû, the famous scholar of the Wei (魏) dynasty, in the first part of the third century, quotes 小人之中庸, with 反 before 中, of which Chû Hsî approves. If 反 be not introduced into the text, it must certainly be understood. 忌憚 is the opposite of 戒愼, 恐懼, in I. ii.— This, and the ten chapters which follow, all quote the words of Confucius with reference to the 中庸, to explain the meaning of the first chapter; and 'though there is no connexion of composition between them,' says Chû Hsî, 'they are all related by their meaning.'

3. THE RARITY, LONG EXISTING IN CONFUCIUS'S TIME, OF THE PRACTICE OF THE MEAN. See the Analects, VI. xxvii. K'ang-ch'ǎng and Ying-tâ take the last clause as = 'few can practise it long.' But the view in the translation is better.

The change from 仲尼曰 to 子曰 is observable.

4. HOW IT WAS THAT FEW WERE ABLE TO PRACTISE THE MEAN. 1. 道 may be referred to the 道 in the first chapter; immediately following 中庸 in the last, I translate it here—'the path of the Mean.' 知者 and 賢者 are not to be understood as meaning the truly wise and the truly worthy, but only those who in the degenerate times of Confucius deemed themselves to be such. The former thought the course of the Mean not worth their study, and the latter thought it not sufficiently exalted for their practice. 肖,—'as,' 'like.' 不肖 following 賢, indicates individuals of a different character, not equal to them. 2. We have here not a comparison, but an illustration, which may help to an understanding of the former paragraph, though it does not seem very apt. People do not know the true flavour of what they eat and drink, but they need not go beyond that to learn it. So the Mean belongs to all the actions of ordinary life, and might be discerned and practised in them, without looking for it in extraordinary things.

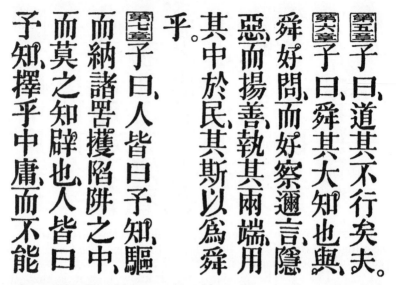

第五章 子曰、道其不行矣夫。

第六章 子曰、舜其大知也與、舜好問而好察邇言、隱惡而揚善、執其兩端、用其中於民、其斯以爲舜乎。

第七章 子曰、人皆曰予知、驅而納諸罟擭陷阱之中、而莫之知辟也、人皆曰予知、擇乎中庸而不能

CHAP. V. The Master said, 'Alas! How is the path of the Mean untrodden!'

CHAP. VI. The Master said, 'There was Shun:—He indeed was greatly wise! Shun loved to question *others*, and to study their words, though they might be shallow. He concealed what was bad *in them,* and displayed what was good. He took hold of their two extremes, *determined* the Mean, and employed it in *his government of* the people. It was by this that he was Shun!'

CHAP. VII. The Master said, 'Men all say, "We are wise;" but being driven forward and taken in a net, a trap, or a pitfall, they know not how to escape. Men all say, "We are wise;" but happening to choose the course of the Mean, they are not able to keep it for a round month.'

5. Chû Hsî says:—'From not being understood, therefore it is not practised.' According to K'ang-ch'äng, the remark is a lament that there was no intelligent sovereign to teach the path. But the two views are reconcileable.

6. How SHUN PURSUED THE COURSE OF THE MEAN. This example of Shun, it seems to me, is adduced in opposition to the knowing of chap. iv. Shun, though a sage, invited the opinions of all men, and found truth of the highest value in their simplest sayings, and was able to determine from them the course of the Mean. 執其兩端—'the two extremes,' are understood by K'ang-ch'äng of the two errors of exceeding and coming short of the Mean. Chû Hsî makes them—'the widest differences in the opinions which he received.' I conceive the meaning to be that he examined the answers which he got, in their entirety, from beginning to end. Compare 扣其兩

端, Analects, IX. vii. His concealing what was bad, and displaying what was good, was alike to encourage people to speak freely to him. K'ang-ch'äng makes the last sentence to turn on the meaning of 舜, when applied as an honorary epithet of the dead, = 'Full, all-accomplished;' but Shun was so named when he was alive.

7. THEIR CONTRARY CONDUCT SHOWS MEN'S IGNORANCE OF THE COURSE AND NATURE OF THE MEAN. The first 予知 is to be understood with a general reference,—'We are wise,' i. e. we can very well take care of ourselves. Yet the presumption of such a profession is seen in men's not being able to take care of themselves. The application of this illustration is then made to the subject in hand, the second 予知 requiring to be specially understood with reference to the subject of the Mean. The conclusion in

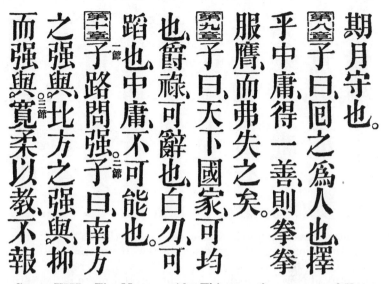

而強與　○三節　之強與　○二節　子路問強子曰南方　蹈也中庸不可能也。　也爵祿可辭也白刃可　第九章 子曰天下國家可均　服膺而弗失之矣。　乎中庸得一善則拳拳　第八章 子曰囘之爲人也擇　期月守也。　寬柔以教不報　北方之強與抑　一節

CHAP. VIII. The Master said, 'This was the manner of Hûi:—he made choice of the Mean, and whenever he got hold of what was good, he clasped it firmly, as if wearing it on his breast, and did not lose it.'

CHAP. IX. The Master said, 'The kingdom, its States, and its families, may be perfectly ruled; dignities and emoluments may be declined; naked weapons may be trampled under the feet;—but the course of the Mean cannot be attained to.'

CHAP. X. 1. Tsze-lû asked about energy.

2. The Master said, 'Do you mean the energy of the South, the energy of the North, or the energy which you should cultivate yourself?

3. 'To show forbearance and gentleness in teaching others;

both parts is left to be drawn by the reader for himself. 攫, read *hwâ*, 4th tone, 'a trap for catching animals.' 期, read *ch'î*, like 朞, in Analects, XIII. x, though it is here applied to a month, and not, as there, to a year.

8. How Hûi HELD FAST THE COURSE OF THE MEAN. Here the example of Hûi is likewise adduced, in opposition to those mentioned in chap. iv. All the rest is exegetical of the first clause—囘之爲人也, 'Hûi's playing the man.' 一善 is not 'one good point,' so much as any one. 拳 is 'the closed fist;' 拳拳,—'the appearance of holding firm.'

9. THE DIFFICULTY OF ATTAINING TO THE COURSE OF THE MEAN. 天下,—'the kingdom;' we should say—'kingdoms,' but the Chinese know only of *one* kingdom, and hence this name for

it—'all under the sky,' embracing by right, if not in fact, all kingdoms. The kingdom was made up of States, and each State of Families. See the Analects, V. vii; XII. xx. 均, 'level;' here a verb = 平治, 'to bring to perfect order.' 刃,—'a sharp, strong weapon,' used of swords, spears, javelins, &c. 不可能,—literally, 'cannot be *canned*.'

10. ON ENERGY IN ITS RELATION TO THE MEAN. In the Analects we find Tsze-lû, on various occasions, putting forward the subject of his valour (勇), and claiming, on the ground of it, such praise as the Master awarded to Hûi. We may suppose, with the old interpreters, that hearing Hûi commended, as in chap. viii, he wanted to know whether Confucius would not allow that he also could, with his forceful character, seize and hold fast the Mean. 1. For

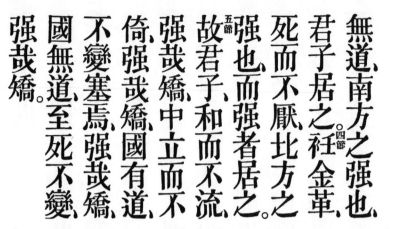

強哉矯。國無道至死不變、不變塞焉強哉矯、倚強哉矯國有道、強哉矯中立而不故君子、和而不流。^{五節}死而不厭比方之強也、而強者居之。君子居之。^{四節}無道南方之強也、

and not to revenge unreasonable conduct:—this is the energy of Southern regions, and the good man makes it his study.

4. 'To lie under arms; and meet death without regret:—this is the energy of Northern regions, and the forceful make it their study.

5. 'Therefore, the superior man cultivates *a friendly* harmony, without being weak.—How firm is he in his energy! He stands erect in the middle, without inclining to either side.—How firm is he in his energy! When good principles prevail in the government of his country, he does not change from what he was in retirement. —How firm is he in his energy! When bad principles prevail in the country, he maintains his course to death without changing.— How firm is he in his energy!'

強 I have been disposed to coin the term 'forcefulness.' Chû defines it correctly—力 足以勝人之名, 'the name of strength sufficient to overcome others.' 2. 而(=汝) 強 must be—'the energy which you should cultivate,' not 'which you have.' If the latter be the meaning, no farther notice of it is taken in Confucius's reply, while he would seem, in the three following paragraphs, to describe the three kinds of energy which he specifies. K'ang-ch'äng and Ying-tä say that 而強 means the energy of the Middle Kingdom, the North being 'the sandy desert,' and the South, 'the country south of the Yang-tsze.' But this is not allowable. 3. That climate and situation have an influence on character is not to be denied, and the Chinese notions on the subject may be seen in the amplification of the 9th of the K'ang-hsî celebrated Precepts (聖諭廣訓). But to speak of their effects as Confucius here does is extravagant. The barbarism of the South, according to the interpretation mentioned above, could not have been described by him in these terms. The energy of mildness and forbearance, thus described, is held to come short of the Mean; and therefore 君子 is taken with a low and light meaning, far short of what it has in par. 5. This practice of determining the force of phrases from the context makes the reading of the Chinese classics perplexing to a student. 居之,—see the Analects, XII. xiv. 4. 衽, 'the lappel in front of a coat;' also 'a mat.' 衽金革, 'to make a mat of the leather dress (革) and weapons (金).' This energy of the North, it is said, is in excess of the Mean, and the 故, at the beginning of par. 5, 'therefore,'='those two kinds of energy being thus respectively in defect and excess.' 矯 is 強貌, 'the appearance of being energetic.' This illustrates the energy which is in exact accord with the Mean, in the individual's treatment of others, in his regulation of himself, and in relation to public affairs. 有道, 無道;—often in the Analects. I have followed Chû Hsî in translating 塞. Ying-tä paraphrases:—守直不變, 德 行充實, 'He holds to what is upright, and

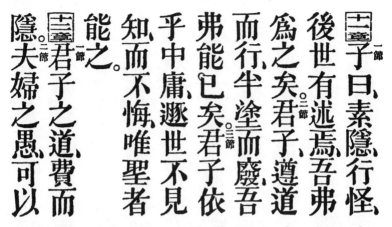

子曰、素隱行怪、後世有述焉、吾弗爲之矣。君子遵道而行、半塗而廢、吾弗能已矣。君子依乎中庸、遯世不見知而不悔、唯聖者能之。

君子之道費而隱。夫婦之愚、可以

CHAP. XI. 1. The Master said, 'To live in obscurity, and yet practise wonders, in order to be mentioned with honour in future ages:—this is what I do not do.

2. 'The good man tries to proceed according to the right path, but when he has gone halfway, he abandons it :—I am not able *so* to stop.

3. 'The superior man accords with the course of the Mean. Though he may be all unknown, unregarded by the world, he feels no regret.—It is only the sage who is able for this.'

CHAP. XII. 1. The way which the superior man pursues, reaches wide and far, and yet is secret.

2. Common men and women, however ignorant, may intermeddle

does not change, his virtuous conduct being all-complete.' A modern writer makes the meaning :—'He does not change through being puffed up by the fulness of office.' Both of these views go on the interpretation of 塞 as = 實.

11. ONLY THE SAGE CAN COME UP TO THE REQUIREMENTS OF THE MEAN. 1. 素 is found written 索, 'to examine,' 'to study,' in a work of the Han dynasty, and Chû adopts that character as the true reading, and explains accordingly :—'To study what is obscure and wrong (隱僻).' K'ang-ch'äng took it as = 傃, 'towards,' or, 'being inclined to,' and both he and Ying-tâ explain as in the translation. It is an objection to Chû's view, that, in the next chapter, 隱 is given as one of the characteristics of the Mean. The 遯世云云, in par. 3, moreover, agree well with the older view. 2. 君子 is here the same as in the last chapter, par. 3. A distinction is made between 遵道 here and 依道 below.

The former, it is said, implies endeavour, while the latter is natural and unconstrained accordance. 3. 君子 here has its very highest signification, and = 聖者 in the last clause.

避世 is said to be different from 遯世, the latter being applicable to the recluse who withdraws from the world, while the former may describe one who is in the world, but does not act with a reference to its opinion of him. It will be observed how Confucius declines saying that he had himself attained to this highest style.—'With this chapter,' says Chû Hsî, 'the quotations by Tsze-sze of the Master's words, to explain the meaning of the first chapter, stop. The great object of the work is to set forth wisdom, benevolent virtue, and valour, as the three grand virtues whereby entrance is effected into the path of the Mean, and therefore, at its commencement, they are illustrated by reference to Shun, Yen Yüan, and Tsze-lû ; Shun possessing the wisdom, Yen Yüan the benevolence, and Tsze-lû the valour. If one of these virtues be absent, there is no way of advancing to the path, and perfecting the virtue. This will be found fully treated of in the 20th chapter.' So, Chû Hsî. The student forming a judgment for himself, however, will not see

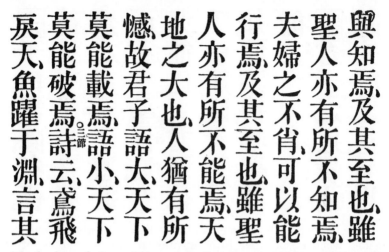

with the knowledge of it; yet in its utmost reaches, there is that which even the sage does not know. Common men and women, however much below the ordinary standard of character, can carry it into practice; yet in its utmost reaches, there is that which even the sage is not able to carry into practice. Great as heaven and earth are, men still find some things in them with which to be dissatisfied. Thus it is that, were the superior man to speak of his way in all its greatness, nothing in the world would be found able to embrace it, and were he to speak of it in its minuteness, nothing in the world would be found able to split it.

3. It is said in the Book of Poetry, 'The hawk flies up to heaven; the fishes leap in the deep.' This expresses how this *way* is seen above and below.

very distinctly any reference to these cardinal virtues. The utterances of the sage illustrate the phrase 中庸, showing that the course of the Mean had fallen out of observance, some overshooting it, and others coming short of it. When we want some precise directions how to attain to it, we come finally to the conclusion that only the sage is capable of doing so. We greatly want teaching, more practical and precise.

12. THE COURSE OF THE MEAN REACHES FAR AND WIDE, BUT YET IS SECRET. With this chapter, the third part of the work commences, and the first sentence,—君子之道, 費而隱, may be regarded as its text. If we could determine satisfactorily the signification of those two terms, we should have a good clue to the meaning of the whole, but it is not easy to do so. The old view is inadmissible. K'ang-ch'äng takes 費 as = 佹, 'doubly involved,' 'perverted,' and both he and Ying-tâ explain :—'When right principles are opposed and disallowed, the superior man retires into obscurity, and does not hold office.' On this view of it,

the sentence has nothing to do with the succeeding chapters. The two meanings of 費 in the dictionary are—'the free expenditure of money,' and 'dissipation,' or 'waste.' According to Chû, in this passage, 費即用之廣也, '費 indicates the wide range of the *tâo* in practice.' Something like this must be its meaning :—the course of the Mean, requiring everywhere to be exhibited. Chû then defines 隱 as 體之微, 'the minuteness of the *tâo* in its nature or essence.' The former answers to the *what* of the *tâo*, and the latter to the *why*. But it rather seems to me, that the 隱 here is the same with the 隱 and 微, i. 4, and that the author simply intended to say that the way of the superior man reaching everywhere, —embracing all duties,—yet had its secret spring and seat in the Heaven-gifted nature, the individual consciousness of duty in every man. 2. 夫婦 = 匹夫, 匹婦, Ana-

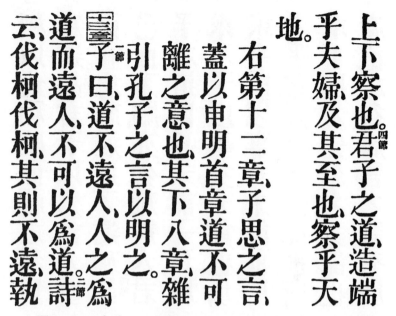

云伐柯伐柯其則不遠執　道而遠人、不可以為道。詩　子曰道不遠人人之為　引孔子之言以明之。　離之意也其下八章雜　蓋以申明首章道不可　右第十二章子思之言、　地。乎夫婦及其至也察乎天　上下察也君子之道造端

4. The way of the superior man may be found, in its simple elements, in the intercourse of common men and women; but in its utmost reaches, it shines brightly through heaven and earth.

The twelfth chapter above contains the words of Tsze-sze, and is designed to illustrate what is said in the first chapter, that 'The path may not be left.' In the eight chapters which follow, he quotes, in a miscellaneous way, the words of Confucius to illustrate it.

CHAP. XIII. 1. The Master said, 'The path is not far from man. When men try to pursue a course, which is far from the common indications of consciousness, this course cannot be considered THE PATH.

2. 'In the Book of Poetry, it is said, "In hewing an axe-handle, in hewing an axe-handle, the pattern is not far off." We grasp one

lects, XIV. xviii. 3. But I confess to be all at sea in the study of this paragraph. Chû quotes from the scholar Hâu (侯氏), that what the superior man fails to know was exemplified in Confucius's having to ask about ceremonies and offices, and what he fails to practise was exemplified in Confucius not being on 'the throne, and in Yâo and Shun's being dissatisfied that they could not make every individual enjoy the benefits of their rule. He adds his own opinion, that what men complained of in Heaven and Earth, was the partiality of their operations in overshadowing and supporting, producing and completing, the heat of summer, the cold of winter, &c. If such things were intended by the writer, we can only regret the vagueness of his language, and the want of

coherence in his argument. In translating 君子語大云云, I have followed Mâo Hsî-ho. 3. See the Shih, III. i. Ode V. st. 3. The ode is in praise of the virtue of king Wǎn. 察 is in the sense of 昭著, 'brightly displayed.' The application of the words of the ode does appear strange.

13. THE PATH OF THE MEAN IS NOT FAR TO SEEK. EACH MAN HAS THE LAW OF IT IN HIMSELF, AND IT IS TO BE PURSUED WITH EARNEST SINCERITY.

1. 人之為道而遠人, 'When men practise a course, and *wish to be* far from men.' The meaning is as in the translation. 2. See the Shih-ching, I. xv. Ode V. st. 2. The object of the paragraph seems to be to show that the rule for dealing with men, according to the

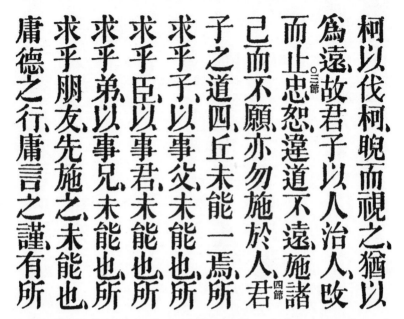

庸德之行、庸言之謹、有所　求乎朋友、先施之、未能也、　求乎弟以事兄、未能也、所　求乎臣以事君、未能也、所　求乎子以事父、未能也、所　子之道四、丘未能一焉、所　己而不願、亦勿施於人、君四節　而止忠恕違道不遠施諸　爲遠、故君子以人治人、改〇三節　柯以伐柯、睨而視之、猶以

axe-handle to hew the other; and yet, if we look askance from the one to the other, we may consider them as apart. Therefore, the superior man governs men, according to their nature, with what is proper to them, and as soon as they change *what is wrong*, he stops.

3. 'When one cultivates to the utmost the principles of his nature, and exercises them on the principle of reciprocity, he is not far from the path. What you do not like when done to yourself, do not do to others.

4. 'In the way of the superior man there are four things, to not one of which have I as yet attained.—To serve my father, as I would require my son to serve me: to this I have not attained; to serve my prince, as I would require my minister to serve me: to this I have not attained; to serve my elder brother, as I would require my younger brother to serve me: to this I have not attained; to set the example in behaving to a friend, as I would require him to behave to me: to this I have not attained. Earnest in practising the ordinary virtues, and careful in speaking about them, if, in his practice, he has anything defective, the superior man

principles of the Mean, is nearer to us than the one axe is to the other. The branch is hewn, and its form altered from its natural one. Not so with man. The change in him only brings him to his proper state. 3. Compare Analects, IV. xv. 違 is here a neuter verb = 'to be distant from.' 4. The admissions made by Confucius here are remarkable, and we do not think the less of him because of them. Those who find it necessary to insist, with the Chinese, on his

having been, like other men, compassed with infirmity, dwell often on them; but it must be allowed that the cases, as put by him, are in a measure hypothetical, his father having died when he was a child. He passes from speaking of himself by his name (丘), to speak of the *chün-tsze*, and the change is most naturally made after the last 能也. 庸德之行、庸言之謹,—'in the practice of ordinary

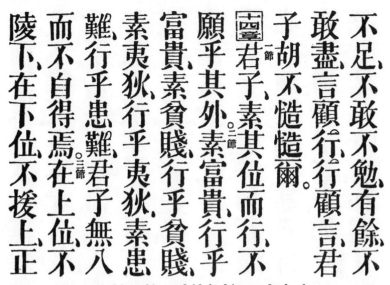

dares not but exert himself; and if, in his words, he has any excess, he dares not allow himself such license. Thus his words have respect to his actions, and his actions have respect to his words; is it not just an entire sincerity which marks the superior man?'

CHAP. XIV. 1. The superior man does what is proper to the station in which he is; he does not desire to go beyond this.

2. In a position of wealth and honour, he does what is proper to a position of wealth and honour. In a poor and low position, he does what is proper to a poor and low position. Situated among barbarous tribes, he does what is proper to a situation among barbarous tribes. In a position of sorrow and difficulty, he does what is proper to a position of sorrow and difficulty. The superior man can find himself in no situation in which he is not himself.

3. In a high situation, he does not treat with contempt his inferiors. In a low situation, he does not court the favour of his

virtues,' i.e. the duties of a son, minister, &c., mentioned above, and 'in the carefulness of ordinary speech,' i.e. speaking about those virtues. To the practice belong the clauses 有所不足, 不敢不勉, and to the speaking, the two next clauses. 爾,—as a final particle, = 耳, 'simply,' 'just.'

14. HOW THE SUPERIOR MAN, IN EVERY VARYING SITUATION, PURSUES THE MEAN, DOING WHAT IS RIGHT, AND FINDING HIS RULE IN HIMSELF. 1. Chû Hsî takes 素 as = 見在, 'at present,' 'now;' but that meaning was made to meet the exigency of the present passage. K'ang-ch'ăng takes it, as in chap. xi, as = 傃, 'being inclined to.' Mâo endeavours to establish this view:—素位者, 即本來故有之位, '素位 is the proper station in which he has been.' The meaning comes to much the same in all these interpretations. 不願乎其外,—compare Analects, XIV. xxviii.

2. 行乎富貴 = 行乎富貴所當行之道, 'He pursues the path, which ought to be pursued amid riches and honours.' So, in the other clauses. 自得,—literally = 'self-possessing.' The paraphrasts make it—'happy in conforming himself to his position.' I consider it equivalent to what is said in chap. ii,—君子之中庸也, 君子而時

瑟琴、兄弟既翕、和樂且

卑。詩曰、妻子好合、如鼓【三節】【二節】

必自邇、辟如登高、必自

【圖書】君子之道、辟如行遠【一節】

求諸其身。

似乎君子、失諸正鵠、反

行險以徼幸子曰、射有【五節】

君子居易以俟命、小人、

上不怨天下不尤人。故【四節】

己而不求於人、則無怨、

superiors. He rectifies himself, and seeks for nothing from others, so that he has no dissatisfactions. He does not murmur against Heaven, nor grumble against men.

4. Thus it is that the superior man is quiet and calm, waiting for the appointments *of Heaven*, while the mean man walks in dangerous paths, looking for lucky occurrences.

5. The Master said, 'In archery we have something like the way of the superior man. When the archer misses the centre of the target, he turns round and seeks for the cause of his failure in himself.'

CHAP. XV. 1. The way of the superior man may be compared to what takes place in travelling, when to go to a distance we must first traverse the space that is near, and in ascending a height, when we must begin from the lower ground.

2. It is said in the Book of Poetry, 'Happy union with wife and children, is like the music of lutes and harps. When there is concord among brethren, the harmony is delightful and enduring. *Thus*

中. 3. 援 is explained in the dictionary, after K'ang-ch'äng, by 牽持, 'to drag and cling to.' The opposition of the two clauses makes the meaning plain. 4. 易, according to K'ang-ch'äng, 猶平安, 'is equivalent to peaceful and tranquil.' Chû Hsî says,—易 平地也, '易 means level ground.' This is most correct, but we cannot so well express it in the translation. 5. 正, the 1st tone, and 鵠 are both names of birds, small and alert, and difficult to be hit. On this account, a picture of the former was painted on the middle of the target, and a figure of the latter was attached to it in leather. It is not meant, however, by this, that they were both used in the same target, at the same time. For another illustration of the way of the superior man from the customs of archery, see Analects, III. vii.

15. IN THE PRACTICE OF THE MEAN THERE IS AN ORDERLY ADVANCE FROM STEP TO STEP. 1. 辟 is read as, and = 譬. 2. See the Shih, II. i. Ode IV. st. 7, 8. The ode celebrates, in a regretful tone, the dependence of brethren on one another, and the beauty of brotherly harmony. Mâo says :—'Although there may be the happy union of wife and children, like the music of lutes and harps, yet there must also be the harmonious concord of brethren, with its exceeding delight, and then may wife and children be regulated and enjoyed. Brothers

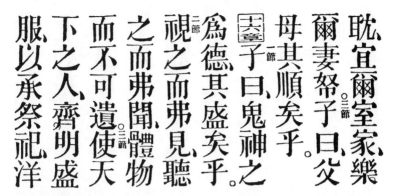

耽。宜爾室家、樂爾妻帑。子曰、父母其順矣乎。○三節

六章 子曰、鬼神之爲德、其盛矣乎。視之而弗見、聽之而弗聞、體物而不可遺、使天下之人、齊明盛服、以承祭祀、洋 二節 ○三節

may you regulate your family, and enjoy the pleasure of your wife and children.'

3. The Master said, 'In such a state of things, parents have entire complacence!'

CHAP. XVI. 1. The Master said, 'How abundantly do spiritual beings display the powers that belong to them!

2. 'We look for them, but do not see them; we listen to, but do not hear them; yet they enter into all things, and there is nothing without them.

3. 'They cause all the people in the kingdom to fast and purify themselves, and array themselves in their richest dresses, in order to

are near to us, while wife and children are more remote. Thus it is, that from what is near we proceed to what is remote.' He adds that anciently the relationship of husband and wife was not among the five relationships of society, because the union of brothers is from Heaven, and that of husband and wife is from man! 3. This is understood to be a remark of Confucius on the ode. From wife, and children, and brothers, parents at last are reached, illustrating how from what is low we ascend to what is high.—But all this is far-fetched and obscure.

16. AN ILLUSTRATION, FROM THE OPERATION AND INFLUENCE OF SPIRITUAL BEINGS, OF THE WAY OF THE MEAN. What is said of the *kwei-shăn* in this chapter is only by way of illustration. There is no design, on the part of the sage, to develop his views on those beings or agencies. The key of it is to be found in the last paragraph, where the 夫微之顯 evidently refers to 莫顯乎微 in chap. i. This paragraph, therefore, should be separated from the others, and not interpreted specially of the *kwei-shăn*. I think that Dr. Medhurst, in rendering it (Theology of the Chinese, p. 22)— 'How great then is the manifestation of *their* abstruseness! Whilst displaying their sincerity, they are not to be concealed,' was wrong, notwithstanding that he may be defended by the example of many Chinese commentators. The second clause of par. 5,—誠之不可

揜如此, appears altogether synonymous with the 誠於中必形於外, in the 大學傳, chap. vi. 2, to which chapter we have seen that the whole of chap. i, pars. 2, 3, has a remarkable similarity. However we may be driven to find a recondite, mystical, meaning for 誠 in the 4th part of this work, there is no necessity to do so here. With regard to what is said of the *kwei-shăn*, it is only the first two paragraphs which occasion difficulty. In the 3rd par., the sage speaks of the spiritual beings that are sacrificed to. 齊,— read *châi*; see Analects, VII. xii. The same is the subject of the 4th par.; or rather, spiritual beings generally, whether sacrificed to or not, invisible themselves and yet able to behold our conduct. See the Shih-ching, III. iii. Ode II. st. 7, which is said to have been composed by one of the dukes of Wei, and was repeated daily in his hearing for his admonition. In the context of the quotation, he is warned to be careful of his conduct, when alone as when in company. For in truth we are never alone. 'Millions of spiritual beings walk the earth,' and can take note of us. The 思 is a final particle here, without meaning. It is often used so in the Shih-ching. 度, read *to*, 4th tone, 'to conjecture,' 'to surmise.' 射, read *yî*, 4th tone, 'to dislike.' What now are the

大　七　此　之　五　思　格　右　上　洋
孝　章　夫。　不　節　矧　思　四　如　乎、
也　子　一　可　夫　可　不　節　在　如
與、　曰、　節　揜、　微　射　可　詩　其　在
德　舜　　　如　之　思。　度　曰、　左　其
　　其　　　　　顯、　　　　　神
　　　　　　　　誠　　　　　之

attend at their sacrifices. Then, like overflowing water, they seem
to be over the heads, and on the right and left *of their worshippers.*

4. 'It is said in the Book of Poetry, "The approaches of the spirits,
you cannot surmise ;—and can you treat them with indifference ?"'

5. 'Such is the manifestness of what is minute! Such is the
impossibility of repressing the outgoings of sincerity!'

CHAP. XVII. 1. The Master said, 'How greatly filial was

kwei-shǎn in the first two paragraphs. Are we
to understand by them something different
from what they are in the third par., to which
they run on from the first as the nominative
or subject of 使 ? I think not. The precise
meaning of what is said of them in 體物
而不可遺 cannot be determined. The
old interpreters say that 體＝生, 'to give
birth to ;' that 可＝所, 'that which ;' that
不可遺＝不有所遺, 'there is no-
thing which they neglect;' and that the meaning of the whole is—'that of all things there
is not a single thing which is not produced by
the breath (or energy ; 氣) of the *kwei-shǎn.*'
This is all that we learn from them. The Sung
school explain the terms with reference to their
physical theory of the universe, derived, as
they think, from the *Yi-ching.* Chû's master,
Ch'ǎng, explains :—'The *kwei-shǎn* are the energetic operations of Heaven and Earth, and the
traces of production and transformation.' The
scholar Chǎng (張氏) says :—'The *kwei-shǎn*
are the easily acting powers of the two breaths
of nature (二氣).' Chû Hsî's own account
is :—'If we speak of two breaths, then by *kwei*
is denoted the efficaciousness of the secondary
or inferior one, and by *shǎn,* that of the superior
one. If we speak of one breath, then by *shǎn*
is denoted its advancing and developing, and
by *kwei,* its returning and reverting. They are
really only one thing.' It is difficult—not to
say impossible—to conceive to one's self exactly what is meant by such descriptions. And
nowhere else in the Four Books is there an
approach to this meaning of the phrase. Mâo
Hsî-ho is more comprehensible; though, after
all, it may be doubted whether what he says

is more than a play upon words. His explanation is :—'But in truth, the *kwei-shǎn* are
道. In the *Yi-ching* the 陰 and 陽 are considered to be the *kwei-shǎn ;* and it is said—"one
陰 and *one* 陽 are called 道." Thus the *kwei-
shǎn* are the 道, embodied in Heaven (體天)
for the nourishment of things. But in the text
we have the term 德 instead of 道, because
the latter is the name of the absolute as embodied in Heaven, and the former denotes the
same not only embodied, but operating to the
nourishing of things, for Heaven considers the
production of things to be 德.' See the 中
庸說, *in loc.*
Rémusat translates the first paragraph :—
'*Que les vertus des esprits sont sublimes !*' His Latin
version is :—'*Spirituum geniorumque est virtus : ea
capax !*' Intorcetta renders :—'*Spiritibus inest
operativa virtus et efficacitas, et hæc o quam præstans
est ! quam multiplex ! quam sublimis !*' In a note,
he and his friends say that the dignitary of the
kingdom who assisted them, rejecting other
interpretations, understood by *kwei-shǎn* here—
'those spirits for the veneration of whom, and
imploring their help, sacrifices were instituted.'
神 signifies 'spirits,' 'a spirit,' 'spirit ;' and
鬼, 'a ghost,' or 'demon.' The former is used
for the *animus,* or intelligent soul separated
from the body, and the latter for the *anima,* or
animal, grosser, soul, so separated. In the
text, however, they blend together, and are not
to be separately translated. They are together
equivalent to 神 in par. 4, 'spirits,' or
'spiritual beings.'

17. THE VIRTUE OF FILIAL PIETY, EXEMPLIFIED
IN SHUN AS CARRIED TO THE HIGHEST POINT, AND
REWARDED BY HEAVEN. 1. One does not readily

嘉樂君子、憲憲令

之傾者覆之。四節之詩曰、

而篤焉、故栽者培

之生物必因其材

名必得其壽故天

必得其祿、必得其

故大德必得其位、

廟饗之、子孫保之。二節

富有四海之內、宗

爲聖人、尊爲天子、

Shun! His virtue was that of a sage; his dignity was the throne; his riches were all within the four seas. He offered his sacrifices in his ancestral temple, and his descendants preserved the sacrifices to himself.

2. 'Therefore having such great virtue, it could not but be that he should obtain the throne, that he should obtain those riches, that he should obtain his fame, that he should attain to his long life.

3. 'Thus it is that Heaven, in the production of things, is sure to be bountiful to them, according to their qualities. Hence the tree that is flourishing, it nourishes, while that which is ready to fall, it overthrows.

4. 'In the Book of Poetry, it is said, "The admirable, amiable prince displayed conspicuously his excelling virtue, adjusting his

see the connexion between Shun's great filial piety, and all the other predicates of him that follow. The paraphrasts, however, try to trace it in this way :—'A son without virtue is insufficient to distinguish his parents. But Shun was born with all knowledge and acted without any effort;—in virtue, a sage. How great was the distinction which he thus conferred on his parents!' And so with regard to the other predicate. See the 日講 四海之內; —on this expression it is said in the encyclopædia called 博物志:—'The four cardinal points of heaven and earth are connected together by the waters of seas, the earth being a small space in the midst of them. Hence, he who rules over the kingdom (天下) is said to govern all within the four seas.' See also note on Analects, XII. v. 4. The characters 宗廟 are thus explained:—'Tsung means honourable. Miâo means figure. The two together mean the place where the figures of one's ancestors are.' Chû Hsî says nothing on 宗廟 饗之, because he had given in to the views of some who thought that Shun sacrificed

merely in the ancestral temple of Yâo. But it is capable of proof that he erected one of his own, and ascended to Hwang-tî, as his great progenitor. See Mâo Hsî-ho's 中庸說, in loc. 饗,—'to entertain a guest ;' and sometimes for 享, 'to enjoy.' So we must take it here,—'enjoyed him ;' that is, his sacrifices. As Shun resigned the throne to Yü, and it did not run in the line of his family, we must take 保之 as in the translation. In the time of the Châu dynasty, there were descendants of Shun, possessed of the State of Ch'ăn (陳), and of course sacrificing to him. 2. The 其 must refer in every case to 大德;—'its place, its emolument,' &c.; that is, what is appropriate to such great virtue. The whole is to be understood with reference to Shun. He died at the age of 100 years. The word 'virtue' takes here the place of 'filial piety,' in the last paragraph, according to Mâo, because that is the root, the first and chief, of all virtues. 3. 材 and 篤 (according to Chû = 厚, 'thick,' 'liberal ') are

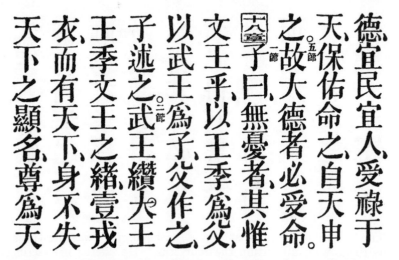

德宜民宜人受祿于
天保佑命之自天申
之故大德者必受命。○五節
【六章】子曰無憂者其惟
文王乎以王季為父
以武王為子父作之
子述之武王纘大王○二節
王季文王之緒壹戎
衣而有天下身不失
天下之顯名尊為天

people, and adjusting his officers. *Therefore*, he received from Heaven the emoluments of dignity. It protected him, assisted him, decreed him the throne; sending from Heaven these favours, *as it were* repeatedly."

5. '*We may say* therefore that he who is greatly virtuous will be sure to receive the appointment of Heaven.'

CHAP. XVIII. 1. The Master said, 'It is only king Wăn of whom it can be said that he had no cause for grief! His father was king Chĭ, and his son was king Wŭ. His father laid the foundations of his dignity, and his son transmitted it.

2. 'King Wŭ continued the enterprise of king T'âi, king Chĭ, and king Wăn. He once buckled on his armour, and got possession of the kingdom. He did not lose the distinguished personal reputation which he had throughout the kingdom. His dignity was the royal throne. His riches were the possession of all within the

explained by most commentators as equally capable of a good and bad application. This may be said of 材, but not of 篤, and the 生 in 天之生物 would seem to determine the meaning of both to be only good. If this be so, then the last clause 傾者覆之 is only an after-thought of the writer, and, indeed, the sentiment of it is out of place in the chapter. 栽 is best taken, with K'ang-ch'äng, as = 殖, and not, with Chû Hsî, as merely = 植. 4. See the Shih-ching, III. ii. Ode V. st. 1, where we have two slight variations of 假 for 嘉 and 顯 for 憲. The prince spoken of is king Wăn, who is thus brought forward to confirm the lesson taken from Shun. That lesson, however, is stated much too broadly in the last paragraph. It is well to say that only virtue is a

solid title to eminence, but to hold forth the certain attainment of wealth and position as an inducement to virtue is not favourable to morality. The case of Confucius himself, who attained neither to power nor to long life, may be adduced as inconsistent with these teachings.

18. ON KING WĂN, KING WŬ, AND THE DUKE OF CHÂU. 1. Shun's father was bad, and the fathers of Yâo and Yü were undistinguished. Yâo and Shun's sons were both bad, and Yü's not remarkable. But to Wăn neither father nor son gave occasion but for satisfaction and happiness. King Chĭ was the duke Chĭ-lĭ (季歷), the most distinguished by his virtues, and prowess, of all the princes of his time. He prepared the way for the elevation of his family. In 父作之, 子述之, the 之 is made to refer to 基業, 'the foundation of the kingdom,' but it may as well be referred to Wăn himself. 2. 大王,—this was the duke

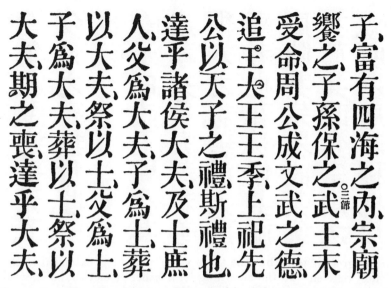

四大夫，期之喪，達乎大夫。

子爲大夫，葬以大夫，祭以士。

以大夫，祭以士。

人父爲大夫，子爲士，葬

達乎諸侯大夫，及士庶

公以天子之禮，斯禮也。

追王大王王季，上祀先

受命，周公成文武之德，

饗之，子孫保之。武王末

子，富有四海之內，宗廟

○三節

four seas. He offered his sacrifices in his ancestral temple, and his descendants maintained the sacrifices to himself.

3. 'It was in his old age that king Wû received the appointment *to the throne*, and the duke of Châu completed the virtuous course of Wăn and Wû. He carried up the title of king to T'âi and Chî, and sacrificed to all the former dukes above them with the royal ceremonies. And this rule he extended to the princes of the kingdom, the great officers, the scholars, and the common people. If the father were a great officer and the son a scholar, then the burial was that due to a great officer, and the sacrifice that due to a scholar. If the father were a scholar and the son a great officer, then the burial was that due to a scholar, and the sacrifice that due to a great officer. The one year's mourning was made to extend *only*

T'an-fû (亶父), the father of Chî-lî, a prince of great eminence, and who, in the decline of the Yin dynasty, drew to his family the thoughts of the people. 緒,—'the end of a cocoon.' It is used here for the beginnings of supreme sway, traceable to the various progenitors of king Wû. 壹戎衣 is interpreted by K'ang-ch'ǎng:—'He destroyed the great Yin;' and recent commentators defend his view. It is not worth while setting forth what may be said for and against it. 'He did not lose his distinguished reputation;' that is, though he proceeded against his rightful sovereign, the people did not change their opinion of his virtue. 3. 末=老, 'when old.' Wû was 87 when he became emperor, and he only reigned 7 years. His brother Tan (旦), the duke of Châu (see Analects, VI. xxii; VII. v) acted as his chief minister. In 追王, 王 is in the 4th tone, in which the character means—'to exercise the sovereign power.' 上祀先公云云, —the house of Châu traced their lineage up to the Tî K'û (帝嚳), B.C. 2432. But in various passages of the Shû, king T'âi and king Chî are spoken of, as if the conference of those titles had been by king Wû. On this there are very long discussions. See the 中庸說, *in loc.* The truth seems to be, that Châu-kung, carrying out his brother's wishes by laws of State, confirmed the titles, and made the general rule about burials and sacrifices which is described. From 斯禮也 to the end, we are at first inclined to translate in the present tense, but the past with a reference to Châu-kung is more correct. The 'year's mourning' is that principally for uncles, and it did not extend beyond

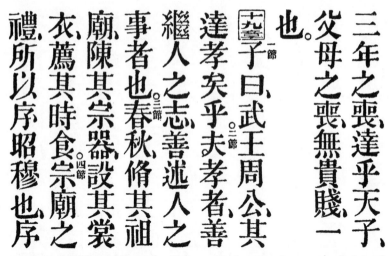

三年之喪達乎天子、父母之喪無貴賤一也。

六章
一節 子曰武王周公其
二節 達孝矣乎夫孝者善
繼人之志善述人之
三節 事者也春秋脩其祖
廟陳其宗器設其裳
四節 衣薦其時食宗廟之
禮所以序昭穆也序

to the great officers, but the three years' mourning extended to the Son of Heaven. In the mourning for a father or mother, he allowed no difference between the noble and the mean.'

CHAP. XIX. 1. The Master said, 'How far-extending was the filial piety of king Wû and the duke of Châu!

2. 'Now filial piety is seen in the skilful carrying out of the wishes of our forefathers, and the skilful carrying forward of their undertakings.

3. 'In spring and autumn, they repaired and beautified the temple-halls of their fathers, set forth their ancestral vessels, displayed their various robes, and presented the offerings of the several seasons.

4. 'By means of the ceremonies of the ancestral temple, they distinguished the royal kindred according to their order of descent. By ordering the parties present according to their rank, they distinguished the more noble and the less. By the arrangement of the

the great officers, because their uncles were the subjects of the princes and the sovereign, and feelings of kindred must not be allowed to come into collision with the relation of governor and governed. On the 'three years' mourning,' see Analects, XVII. xxi.

19. THE FAR-REACHING FILIAL PIETY OF KING Wû, AND OF THE DUKE OF CHÂU. 1. 達 is taken by Chû as meaning—'universally acknowledged;' 'far-extending' is better, and accords with the meaning of the term in other parts of the Work. 2. This definition of 孝, or 'filial piety,' is worthy of notice. Its operation ceases not with the lives of parents and parents' parents. 人=前人, 'antecedent men;' but English idiom seems to require the addition of our. 3. 春秋,—the sovereigns of China sacrificed, as they still do, to their ancestors every season. Reckoning from the

spring, the names of the sacrifices appear to have been—祠, 禴 or 礿, 嘗, and 烝. Others, however, give the names as 礿, 禘, 嘗, 烝, while some affirm that the spring sacrifice was 禘. Though spring and autumn only are mentioned in the text, we are to understand that what is said of the sacrifices in those seasons applies to all the others. 祖廟, —'halls or temples of ancestors,' of which the sovereign had seven (see the next paragraph), all included in the name of 宗廟. 宗器, 'ancestral,' or 'venerable, vessels.' Chû Hsî understands by them relics, something like our regalia. Chäng K'ang-ch'äng makes them, and apparently with more correctness, simply 'the sacrificial vessels.' 裳衣,—'lower and upper garments,' with the latter of which the

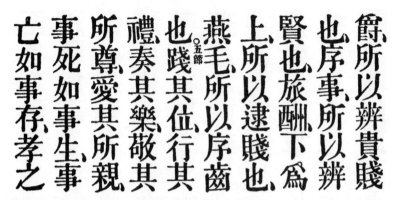

亡如事存孝之
事死如事生事
所尊愛其所親
禮奏其樂敬其
也。踐其位行其
燕毛所以序齒
上所以逮賤也
賢也旅酬下爲
也序事所以辨
爵所以辨貴賤

〔五節〕

services, they made a distinction of talents and worth. In the ceremony of general pledging, the inferiors presented the cup to their superiors, and thus something was given the lowest to do. At the *concluding* feast, places were given according to the hair, and thus was made the distinction of years.

5. 'They occupied the places of their forefathers, practised their ceremonies, and performed their music. They reverenced those whom they honoured, and loved those whom they regarded with affection. Thus they served the dead as they would have served them alive; they served the departed as they would have served them had they been continued among them.

parties personating the deceased were invested.
4. It was an old interpretation that the sacrifices and accompanying services, spoken of here, were not the seasonal services of every year, which are the subject of the preceding paragraph, but the great 禘 and 祫 sacrifices; and to that view I would give in my adhesion. The sovereign, as mentioned above, had seven 廟. One belonged to the remote ancestor to whom the dynasty traced its origin. At the great sacrifices, his spirit-tablet was placed fronting the east, and on each side were ranged, three in a row, the tablets belonging to the six others, those of them which fronted the south being, in the genealogical line, the fathers of those who fronted the north. As fronting the south, the region of *brilliancy*, the former were called 昭; the latter, from the north, the *sombre* region, were called 穆. As the dynasty was prolonged, and successive sovereigns died, the older tablets were removed, and transferred to what was called the 祧廟, yet so that one in the 昭 line displaced the topmost 昭, and so with the 穆. At the sacrifices, the royal kindred arranged themselves as they were descended from a 昭 on the left, and from a 穆 on the right, and thus a genealogical correct-

ness of place was maintained among them. The ceremony of 'general (旅=衆) pledging' occurred towards the end of the sacrifice. Chû Hsî takes 爲 in the 3rd tone, saying that to have anything to do at those services was accounted honourable, and after the sovereign had commenced the ceremony by taking 'a cup of blessing,' all the juniors presented a similar cup to the seniors, and thus were called into employment. Ying-tâ takes 爲 in its ordinary tone, 下爲上, 'the inferiors were the superiors,' i.e. the juniors did present a cup to their elders, but had the honour of drinking first themselves. The 燕 was a concluding feast confined to the royal kindred. 5. 踐其位, according to K'ang-ch'äng, is—'ascended their thrones;' according to Chû, it is 'trod on—i.e. occupied—their places in the ancestral temple.' On either view, the statement must be taken with allowance. The ancestors of king Wû had not been kings, and their places in the temples had only been those of princes. The same may be said of the four particulars which follow. By 'those whom they'—i. e. their progenitors—'honoured' are intended their ancestors, and by 'those whom they loved,' their descendants, and indeed all the people of their government. The two concluding sentences are important, as the Jesuits

三哀公問政。　乎。其如示諸掌　嘗之義治國　郊社之禮禘　其先也明乎　禮所以祀乎　帝也宗廟之　禮所以事上　至也。郊社之

6. 'By the ceremonies of the sacrifices to Heaven and Earth they served God, and by the ceremonies of the ancestral temple they sacrificed to their ancestors. He who understands the ceremonies of the sacrifices to Heaven and Earth, and the meaning of the several sacrifices to ancestors, would find the government of a kingdom as easy as to look into his palm!'

CHAP. XX. 1. The duke Âi asked about government.

mainly based on them the defence of their practice in permitting their converts to continue the sacrifices to their ancestors. We read in 'Confucius Sinarum philosophus,'—the work of Intorcetta and others, to which I have made frequent reference:—'Ex plurimis et clarissimis textibus Sinicis probari potest, legitimum prædicti axiomatis sensum esse, quod eadem intentione et formali motivo Sinenses naturalem pietatem et politicum obsequium erga defunctos exerceant, sicuti erga eosdem adhuc superstites exercebant, ex quibus et ex infra dicendis prudens lector facile deducet, hos ritus circa defunctos fuisse mere civiles, institutos dumtaxat in honorem et obsequium parentum, etiam post mortem non intermittendum; nam si quid illic divinum agnovissent, cur diceret Confucius—Priscos servire solitos defunctis, uti iisdem serviebant viventibus.' This is ingenious reasoning, but does it meet the fact that sacrifice is an entirely new element introduced into the service of the dead? 6. What is said about the sacrifices to God, however, is important, in reference to the views which we should form about the ancient religion of China. K'ang-ch'ǎng took 郊 to be the sacrifice to Heaven, offered, at the winter solstice, in the southern suburb (郊) of the imperial city; and 社 to be that offered to the Earth, at the summer solstice, in the northern. Chû agrees with him. Both of them, however, add that after 上帝 we are to understand 后土, 'Sovereign Earth (不言后土者省文).' This view of 社 here is vehemently controverted by Mâo and many others. But neither the opinion of the two great commentators that 后土 is suppressed for the sake of brevity, nor the opinion of others that by 社 we are to understand the tutelary deities of the soil, affects the judgment of the Sage himself, that the service of one being—even of God —was designed by all those ceremonies. See my 'Notions of the Chinese concerning God and Spirits,' pp. 50-52. The ceremonies of the ancestral temple embrace the great and less frequent services of the 禘 and 祫 (see the Analects, III. x. 11) and the seasonal sacrifices, of which only the autumnal one (嘗) is specified here. The old commentators take 示 as = 寘, with the meaning of 置, 'to place,' and interpret—'the government of the kingdom would be as easy as to place anything in the palm.' This view is defended in the 中庸說. It has the advantage of accounting better for the 諸. We are to understand 'the meaning of the sacrifices to ancestors,' as including all the uses mentioned in par. 4. It is not easy to understand the connexion between the first part of this paragraph and the general object of the chapter. Taking the paragraph by itself, it teaches that a proper knowledge and practice of the duties of religion and filial piety would amply equip a ruler for all the duties of his government.

20. ON GOVERNMENT: SHOWING PRINCIPALLY HOW IT DEPENDS ON THE CHARACTER OF THE OFFICERS ADMINISTERING IT, AND HOW THAT DEPENDS ON THE CHARACTER OF THE SOVEREIGN HIMSELF. We have here one of the fullest expositions of Confucius's views on this subject, though he unfolds them only as a description of the government of the kings Wǎn and Wû. In the chapter there is the remarkable intermingling, which we have seen in 'The Great Learning,' of what is peculiar to a ruler, and what is of universal application. From the concluding paragraphs, the transition is easy to the next and most difficult part of the Work. This chapter is found also in the 家語, but with considerable additions.

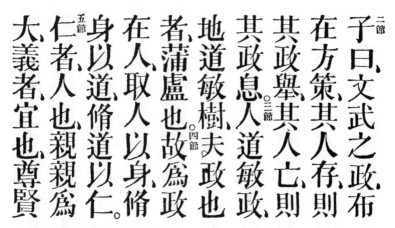

2. The Master said, 'The government of Wăn and Wŭ is displayed in *the records,*—the tablets of wood and bamboo. Let there be the men and the government will flourish; but without the men, their government decays and ceases.

3. 'With the *right* men the growth of government is rapid, just as vegetation is rapid in the earth ; and moreover *their* government *might be called* an easily-growing rush.

4. 'Therefore the administration of government lies in *getting proper* men. Such men are to be got by means of *the ruler's own* character. That character is to be cultivated by his treading in the ways *of duty*. And the treading those ways of duty is to be cultivated by the cherishing of benevolence.

5. 'Benevolence is *the characteristic element of* humanity, and the great exercise of it is in loving relatives. Righteousness is *the accordance of actions with what is* right, and the great exercise of

1. 哀公,—see Analects, II. xix, *et al.* 2. The 方 were tablets of wood, one of which might contain up to 100 characters. The 策 were 簡, or slips of bamboo tied together. In 其人, 其 = *such,* i.e. rulers like Wăn and Wŭ, and ministers such as they had. 3. K'ang-ch'äng and Ying-tâ take 敏 as = 勉, 'to exert one's self,' and interpret:—'A ruler ought to exert himself in the practice of government, as the earth exerts itself to produce and to nurture (樹 = 殖).' Chû Hsî takes 敏 as = 速, 'hasty,' 'to make haste.' 人道敏政,— 'man's way hastens government;' but the 人 must be taken with special reference to the preceding paragraph, as in the translation. The old commentators took 蒲盧 as the name of an insect (so it is defined in the 爾訝), a kind of bee, said to take the young of the mul-

berry caterpillar, and keep them in its hole, where they are transformed into bees. So, they said, does government transform the people. This is in accordance with the paragraph, as we find it in the 家語,—天道敏生, 人道敏政, 地道敏樹, 夫政者猶蒲盧也, 待化以成. This view is maintained also in the 中庸說. But we cannot hesitate in preferring Chû Hsî's, as in the translation. The other is too absurd. He takes 盧, as if it were 盧 = 葦, which, as well as 蒲, is the name of various rushes or sedges. 4. In the 家語, for 在人, we have 在於得人, which is, no doubt, the meaning. By 道 here, says Chû Hsî, are intended 'the duties of universal obligation,' in par. 8, 'which,' adds Mâo, 'are the ways of the Mean, in accordance with the nature.' 5. 仁

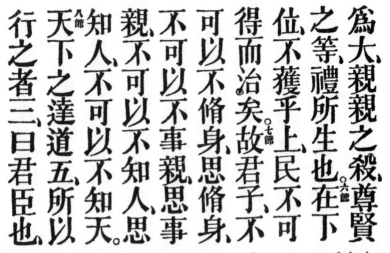

行之者三、曰君臣也、〔八節〕天下之達道五、所以知人不可以不知天。親不可以不知人、思不可以不事親思事可以不脩身、思脩身、得而治矣。〔七節〕故君子、不位不獲乎上民不可之等、禮所生也。〔六節〕在下爲大親親之殺尊賢

it is in honouring the worthy. The decreasing measures of the love due to relatives, and the steps in the honour due to the worthy, are produced by *the principle of* propriety.

6. 'When those in inferior situations do not possess the confidence of their superiors, they cannot retain the government of the people.

7. 'Hence the sovereign may not neglect the cultivation of his own character. Wishing to cultivate his character, he may not neglect to serve his parents. In order to serve his parents, he may not neglect to acquire a knowledge of men. In order to know men, he may not dispense with a knowledge of Heaven.

8. 'The duties of universal obligation are five, and the virtues wherewith they are practised are three. The duties are those between sovereign and minister, between father and son, between

者人也, 'Benevolence is man.' We find the same language in Mencius, VII. Pt. ii. 16. This virtue is called MAN, 'because loving, feeling, and the forbearing nature, belong to man, as he is born. They are that whereby man is man.' See the 中庸說, *in loc.* 殺,—in the 3rd tone, read *shâi*. It is opposed to 隆, and means 'decreasing,' 'growing less.' For 禮所生 we have, in the 家語, 禮所 以生, which would seem to mean—'are that whereby ceremonies are produced.' But there follow the words—禮者政之本也. The 'produced' in the translation can only = 'distinguished.' Ying-tâ explains 生 by 辨 明. 6. This has crept into the text here by mistake. It belongs to par. 17, below. We do not find it here in the 家語. 7. 君子 is

here the *ruler* or *sovereign*. I fail in trying to trace the connexion between the different parts of this paragraph. 'He may not be without knowing men.'—Why? 'Because,' we are told, 'it is by honouring, and being courteous to the worthy, and securing them as friends, that a man perfects his virtue, and is able to serve his relatives.' 'He may not be without knowing Heaven.'—Why? 'Because,' it is said, 'the gradations in the love of relatives and the honouring the worthy, are all heavenly arrangements and a heavenly order,—natural, necessary, principles.' But in this explanation, 知人 has a very different meaning from what it has in the previous clause. 親, too, is here *parents*, its meaning being more restricted than in par. 5. 8. From this down to par. 11, there is brought before us the character of the '*men*,' mentioned in par. 2, on whom depends the flourishing of '*government*,' which government is exhibited in paragraphs 12-15. 天下之達道,—'the paths proper to be

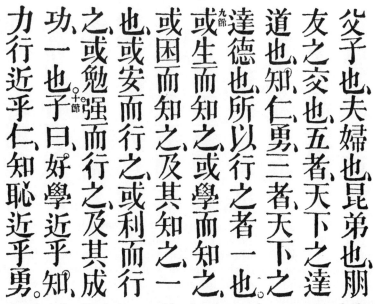

husband and wife, between elder brother and younger, and those belonging to the intercourse of friends. Those five are the duties of universal obligation. Knowledge, magnanimity, and energy, these three, are the virtues universally binding. And the means by which they carry *the duties* into practice is singleness.

9. 'Some are born with the knowledge *of those duties;* some know them by study; and some acquire the knowledge after a painful feeling of their ignorance. But the knowledge being possessed, it comes to the same thing. Some practise them with a natural ease; some from a desire for their advantages; and some by strenuous effort. But the achievement being made, it comes to the same thing.'

10. The Master said, 'To be fond of learning is to be near to knowledge. To practise with vigour is to be near to magnanimity. To possess the feeling of shame is to be near to energy.

trodden by all under heaven,' = the path of the Mean. 知 = 智, is the *knowledge* necessary to choose the detailed course of duty. 仁 (= 心之公, 'the unselfishness of the heart') is the *magnanimity* (so I style it for want of a better term) to pursue it. 勇 is the *valiant energy*, which maintains the permanence of the choice and the practice. 所以行之者 一也,—this, according to Ying-tâ, means— 'From the various kings (百王) downwards, in the practising of these five duties, and three

virtues, there has been but one method. There has been no change in modern times and ancient.' This, however, is not satisfactory. We want a substantive meaning, for 一. This Chû Hsî gives us. He says:— 一則誠而 已, '一 is simply sincerity;' the sincerity, that is, on which the rest of the work dwells with such strange predication. I translate, therefore, 一 here by *singleness*. There seems a reference in the term to 獨, chap. i. p. 3. The singleness is that of the soul in the apprehension and practice of the duties of the Mean, which is attained to by watchfulness over one's

知斯三者、則知所以脩身、知所以脩身、則知所以治人、知所以治人、則知所以治天下國家矣。凡爲天下國家有九經、曰脩身也、尊賢也、親親也、敬大臣也、體群臣也、子庶民也、來百工

11. 'He who knows these three things, knows how to cultivate his own character. Knowing how to cultivate his own character, he knows how to govern other men. Knowing how to govern other men, he knows how to govern the kingdom with all its States and families.

12. 'All who have the government of the kingdom with its States and families have nine standard rules to follow;—viz. the cultivation of their own characters; the honouring of men of virtue and talents; affection towards their relatives; respect towards the great ministers; kind and considerate treatment of the whole body of officers; dealing with the mass of the people as children; encouraging the resort of all classes of artisans; indulgent treat-

self, when *alone*. 行之 I understand as in the second clause of the paragraph. 9. Compare Analects, XVI. ix. 利,—compare Analects, XX. ii. 強, 2nd tone, 'to force,' 'to employ violent efforts.' Chû Hsî says:—'The 之 in 知之, and 行之, refers to the duties of universal obligation.' But is there the three-fold difference in the *knowledge* of those duties? And who are they who can practise them with entire ease? 10. Chû Hsî observes that 子曰 is here superfluous. In the 家語, however, we find the last paragraph followed by—'The duke said, Your words are beautiful and perfect, but I am stupid, and unable to accomplish this.' Then comes this paragraph, 'Confucius said,' &c. The 子曰, therefore, prove that Tsze-sze took this chapter from some existing document, that which we have in the 家語, or some other. Confucius's words were intended to encourage and stimulate the duke, telling him that the three grand virtues might be nearly, if not absolutely, attained to. 知恥,—'knowing to be ashamed,' i. e. being ashamed at being below others, leading to the determination not to be so. 11. 'These three things' are the three things in the last para-

graph, which makes an approximation at least to the three virtues which connect with the discharge of duty attainable by every one. What connects the various steps of the climax is the unlimited confidence in the power of the example of the ruler, which we have had occasion to point out so frequently in 'The Great Learning.' 12. These nine standard rules, it is to be borne in mind, constitute the government of Wǎn and Wǔ, referred to in par. 2. Commentators arrange the 4th and 5th rules under the second; and the 6th, 7th, 8th, and 9th under the third, so that after 'the cultivation of the person,' we have here an expansion of 親親 and 尊賢, in par. 5. 凡爲—爲=治, 'to govern.' The student will do well to understand a 者 after 家. 尊賢—by the 賢 here are understood specially the officers called 師, 傅, and 保, the 三公 and the 三孤, who, as teachers and guardians, were not styled 臣, 'ministers,' or 'servants.' See the Shû-ching, V. xxi. 5, 6. 敬大臣,—by the 大臣 are understood the six 卿,—the minister of Instruction, the minister of Religion, &c. See the Shû, V. xxi.

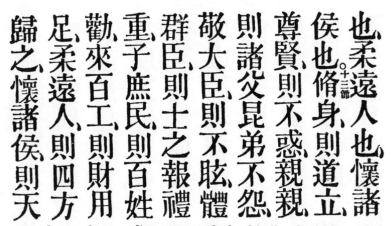

歸之懷諸侯則天　足柔遠人則四方　勸來百工則財用　重子庶民則百姓　群臣則士之報禮　敬大臣則不眩體　則諸父昆弟不怨　尊賢則不惑親親　侯也。脩身則道立　也、柔遠人也、懷諸

ment of men from a distance; and the kindly cherishing of the princes of the States.

13. 'By the ruler's cultivation of his own character, the duties *of universal obligation* are set forth. By honouring men of virtue and talents, he is preserved from errors of judgment. By showing affection to his relatives, there is no grumbling nor resentment among his uncles and brethren. By respecting the great ministers, he is kept from errors in the practice of government. By kind and considerate treatment of the whole body of officers, they are led to make the most grateful return for his courtesies. By dealing with the mass of the people as his children, they are led to exhort one another to what is good. By encouraging the resort of all classes of artisans, his resources for expenditure are rendered ample. By indulgent treatment of men from a distance, they are brought to resort to him from all quarters. And by kindly cherishing the princes of the States, the whole kingdom is brought to revere him.

7-13. 體羣臣,—the 羣臣 are the host of subordinate officers after the two preceding classes. K'ang-ch'äng says,—體猶接納, '體＝to receive,' to which Ying-tâ adds—與之同體, 'being of the same body with them.' Chû Hsî brings out the force of the term in this way:—體謂設以身處其地, 而察其心也, '體 means that he places himself in their place, and so examines their feelings.' 子庶民,—子 is a verb, 'to make children of,' 'to treat kindly as children.' 來百工,—來＝招來, 'to call to come,'＝'to encourage.' The 百工, or 'various artisans,' were, by the statutes of Châu, under the superintendence of a special officer, and it was his business to draw them out and forth from among the people. See the

Châu-lî, XXXIX. 1-5. 柔遠人,—Chû Hsî by 遠人 understands 賓旅, 'guests or envoys, and travellers, or travelling merchants;' K'ang-ch'äng understands by them 蕃國之諸侯, 'the princes of surrounding kingdoms,' i. e. of the tribes that lay beyond the six *fû* (服), or feudal tenures of the Châu rule. But these would hardly be spoken of before the 諸侯. And among *them*, in the 9th rule, would be included the 賓, or guests, the princes themselves at the royal court, or their envoys. I doubt whether any others beside the 旅, or travelling merchants, are intended by the 遠人. If we may adopt, however, K'ang-ch'äng's view, this is the rule for the treatment of foreigners by the government of China. 13. This paragraph describes the happy effects of

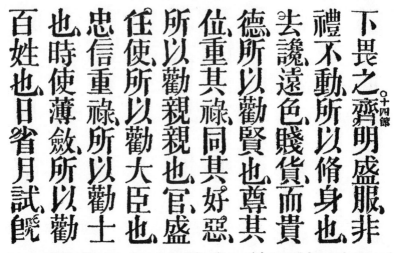

下畏之齊明盛服、非
禮不動所以脩身也、
去讒遠色賤貨而貴
德所以勸賢也、尊其
位重其祿、同其好惡
所以勸親親也、官盛
任使所以勸大臣也、
忠信重祿所以勸士
也、時使薄斂所以勸
百姓也、日省月試餼

14. 'Self-adjustment and purification, with careful regulation of his dress, and the not making a movement contrary to the rules of propriety :—this is the way for a ruler to cultivate his person. Discarding slanderers, and keeping himself from *the seductions of* beauty; making light of riches, and giving honour to virtue :—this is the way for him to encourage men of worth and talents. Giving them places *of honour* and large emolument, and sharing with them in their likes and dislikes :—this is the way for him to encourage his relatives to love him. Giving them numerous officers to discharge their orders and commissions :—this is the way for him to encourage the great ministers. According to them a generous confidence, and making their emoluments large :—this is the way to encourage the body of officers. Employing them only at the proper times, and making the imposts light :—this is the way to encourage the people. By daily examinations and monthly trials, and by making their rations in accordance with their labours :—this is the

observing the above nine rules. 道立,—by 道 are understood the five duties of universal obligation. We read in the 日講 :—'About these nine rules, the only trouble is that sovereigns are not able to practise them strenuously. Let the ruler be really able to cultivate his person, then will the universal duties and universal virtues be all-complete, so that he shall be an example to the whole kingdom, with its States and families. Those duties will be set up (道立), and men will know what to imitate.' 不惑 means, according to Chû Hsî, 不疑於理, 'he will have no doubts as to principle.' K'ang-ch'ang explains it by 謀者良, 'his counsels will be good.' This latter is the meaning, the worthies being those

specified in the note on the preceding paragraph, their sovereign's counsellors and guides. The addition of 諸 determines the 父 to be uncles. See the 爾雅, I. iv. 昆弟 are all the younger branches of the ruler's kindred. 不眩 = 不惑; but the deception and mistake will be in the affairs in charge of those great ministers. 羣臣 and 士 are the same parties. 勸,—as in Analects, II. xx. Ying-tâ explains it here—'They will exhort and stimulate one another to serve their ruler.' On 財用足, Chû Hsî says :—'The resort of all classes of artisans being encouraged, there is an intercommunication of the productions of labour, and an interchange of men's services, and the husbandman and the trafficker' (it is

豫則廢言前定則不　一也凡事豫則立不○十六節　有九經所以行之者　侯也凡爲天下國家○十五節　往而薄來所以懷諸　亂持危朝聘以時厚　也繼絕世舉廢國治　矜不能所以柔遠人　也送往迎來嘉善而　稟稱事所以勸百工

way to encourage the classes of artisans. To escort them on their departure and meet them on their coming; to commend the good among them, and show compassion to the incompetent:—this is the way to treat indulgently men from a distance. To restore families whose line of succession has been broken, and to revive States that have been extinguished; to reduce to order States that are in confusion, and support those which are in peril; to have fixed times for their own reception at court, and the reception of their envoys; to send them away after liberal treatment, and welcome their coming with small contributions:—this is the way to cherish the princes of the States.

15. 'All who have the government of the kingdom with its States and families have the above nine standard rules. And the means by which they are carried into practice is singleness.

16. 'In all things success depends on previous preparation, and without such previous preparation there is sure to be failure. If what is to be spoken be previously determined, there will be no

this class which is designed by 末), 'are aiding to one another. Hence the resources for expenditure are sufficient.' I suppose that Chû felt a want of some mention of agriculture in connexion with these rules, and thought to find a place for it here. Mâo would make 財 = 材, and 用 = 器物. See the 中庸 說, in loc. Compare also 大學傳, x. 19. K'ang-ch'äng understands 四方 as meaning 蕃國, 'frontier kingdoms,' but the usage of the phrase is against such an interpretation. 14. After 天下畏之, we have in the 家語,—公曰,爲之奈何 'The duke said, How are these rules to be practised?' and then

follows this paragraph, preceded by 孔子曰,'Confucius said.' 齊明盛服,—as in chap. xvi. 3. The blending together, as equally important, attention to inward purity and to dress, seems strange enough to a western reader. 勸, throughout, = 'to stimulate in a friendly way.' I have translated 親親 after the 合講, which says 勸親親謂親之親我, the upper 親 being the noun, and the second the verb. The use of 忠 in reference to the prince's treatment of the officers is strange, but the translation gives what appears to be the meaning. K'ang-ch'äng explained:—'Making large the emolument of the loyal and sincere;' but, according to the

不誠不順乎親矣誠
順乎親有道反諸身
平親不信乎朋友矣
信乎朋友有道不順
乎朋友不獲乎上矣
矣獲乎上有道不信
乎上民不可得而治
則不窮在下位不獲
前定則不疚道前定
跲事前定則不困行

○十七節

stumbling. If affairs be previously determined, there will be no difficulty with them. If one's actions have been previously determined, there will be no sorrow in connexion with them. If principles of conduct have been previously determined, the practice of them will be inexhaustible.

17. 'When those in inferior situations do not obtain the confidence of the sovereign, they cannot succeed in governing the people. There is a way to obtain the confidence of the sovereign;—if one is not trusted by his friends, he will not get the confidence of his sovereign. There is a way to being trusted by one's friends; —if one is not obedient to his parents, he will not be true to friends. There is a way to being obedient to one's parents;—if one, on turning his thoughts in upon himself, finds a want of sincerity, he will

analogy of all the other clauses, 患 and 信 must be descriptive of the ruler. 時使,— compare Ana. I. v. For 既稟 we have in the 家語, 餼稟, which K'ang-ch'äng explains by 稍食, 'rations allowed by government;'—see Morrison, character 稍. Chû follows K'ang-ch'äng, but I agree with Mâo, that 餼 and not 餼 is to be substituted here for 既 稱, 4th tone, 'to weigh,' 'to be according to.' The trials and examinations, with these rations, show that the artisans are not to be understood as dispersed among the people. Ambassadors from foreign countries have been received up to the present century, according to the rules here prescribed, and the two last regulations are quite in harmony with the superiority that China claims over the countries which they may represent. But in

the case of travellers, and travelling merchants, passing from one State to another, there were anciently regulations, which may be adduced to illustrate all the expressions here;—see the 中庸說, and the 日講, in loc. 繼絕世, 舉廢國, as in Ana. XX. i. 7. 15. We naturally understand the last clause as meaning—'the means by which they are carried into practice is one and the same.' Then this means will be the 豫, or 'previous preparation' of the next paragraph. This is the interpretation of K'ang-ch'äng and Ying-tâ, who take the two paragraphs together. But according to Chû, 'the one thing' is sincerity, as in par. 8. 16. The 'all things' has reference to the above duties, virtues, and standard rules. 17. The object here seems to be to show that the singleness, or sincerity, lies at the basis of that previous preparation, which is essential to success in any and every thing. The steps of the climax conduct us to it, and this sincerity is again made dependent on the understanding

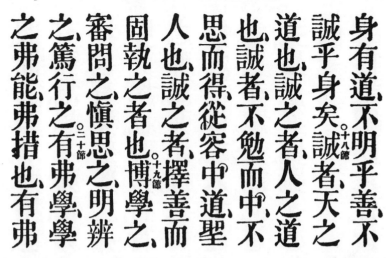

之弗能弗措也有弗
之篤行之有弗學學
審問之慎思之明辨
固執之者也。博學之
人也誠之者擇善而
思而得從容中道聖
也誠者不勉而中不
道也誠之者人之道
誠乎身矣。誠者天之
身有道不明乎善不

not be obedient to his parents. There is a way to the attainment of sincerity in one's self;—if a man do not understand what is good, he will not attain sincerity in himself.

18. 'Sincerity is the way of Heaven. The attainment of sincerity is the way of men. He who possesses sincerity, is he who, without an effort, hits what is right, and apprehends, without the exercise of thought;—he is the sage who naturally and easily embodies the *right* way. He who attains to sincerity, is he who chooses what is good, and firmly holds it fast.

19. 'To this attainment there are requisite the extensive study of what is good, accurate inquiry about it, careful reflection on it, the clear discrimination of it, and the earnest practice of it.

20. 'The superior man, while there is anything he has not studied, or while in what he has studied there is anything he cannot understand, will not intermit his labour. While there is any-

of what is good, upon which point see the next chapter. 不獲乎上, = according to Ying-tâ, 'do not get the mind—pleased feeling—of the sovereign.' We use 'to gain,' and 'to win,' sometimes, in a similar way. 18. Prémare (p. 156) says:—'誠者 *est in abstracto, et* 誠之者 *est in concreto.*' 誠者 is in the concrete, as much as the other, and is said, below, to be characteristic of the sage. 誠者 is the quality possessed absolutely. 誠之者 is the same acquired. 'The way of Heaven,'—this, according to Ying-tâ, = 'the way which Heaven pursues.' Chû Hsî explains it, 'the fundamental, natural course of heavenly principle.' Mâo says:—'this is like the accordance of nature in the Mean, considered to be THE PATH, having its root in Heaven.' We might ac-

quiesce in this, but for the opposition of 人之道, on which Mâo says:—此猶中庸之修道以爲道者也, 成乎人也;—'this is like the cultivation of the path in the Doctrine of the Mean, considered to be THE PATH, having its completion from man.' But this takes the second and third utterances in the Work as independent sentiments, which they are not. I do not see my way to rest in any but the old interpretation, extravagant as it is.—At this point, the chapter in the 家語 ceases to be the same with that before us, and diverges to another subject. 19. The different processes which lead to the attainment of sincerity. The gloss in the 備旨 says that 'the five 之 all refer to the *what is good* in the last chapter, the five universal duties,

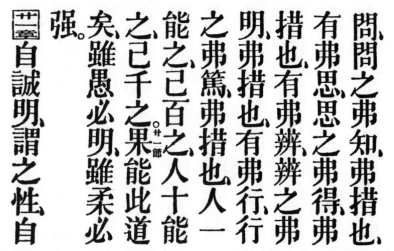

thing he has not inquired about, or anything in what he has inquired about which he does not know, he will not intermit his labour. While there is anything which he has not reflected on, or anything in what he has reflected on which he does not apprehend, he will not intermit his labour. While there is anything which he has not discriminated, or his discrimination is not clear, he will not intermit his labour. If there be anything which he has not practised, or his practice fails in earnestness, he will not intermit his labour. If another man succeed by one effort, he will use a hundred efforts. If another man succeed by ten efforts, he will use a thousand.

21. 'Let a man proceed in this way, and, though dull, he will surely become intelligent; though weak, he will surely become strong.'

CHAP. XXI. When we have intelligence resulting from sincerity, this condition is to be ascribed to nature; when we have sincerity

and the nine standard rules being included therein.' Rather it seems to me, that the 之, according to the idiom pointed out several times in the Analects, simply intensifies the meaning of the different verbs, whose regimen it is. 20. Here we have the determination which is necessary in the prosecution of the above processes, and par. 21 states the result of it. Chû Hsî makes a pause at the end of the first clause in each part of the paragraph, and interprets thus:—' If he do not study, well. But if he do, he will not give over till he understands what he studies,' and so on. But it seems more natural to carry the supposition in 有 over the whole of every part, as in the translation, which moreover substantially agrees with Ying-tâ's interpretation.—Here terminates the third part of the Work. It was to illustrate, as Chû Hsî told us, how 'the path of the Mean cannot be left.' The author seems to have kept this point before him in chapters xiii-xvi, but

the next three are devoted to the one subject of filial piety, and the 20th, to the general subject of government. Some things are said worthy of being remembered, and others which require a careful sifting; but, on the whole, we do not find ourselves advanced in an understanding of the argument of the Work.

21. THE RECIPROCAL CONNEXION OF SINCERITY AND INTELLIGENCE. With this chapter commences the fourth part of the Work, which, as Chû observes in his concluding note, is an expansion of the 18th paragraph of the preceding chapter. It is, in a great measure, a glorification of the sage, finally resting in the person of Confucius; but the high character of the sage, it is maintained, is not unattainable by others. He realizes the ideal of humanity, but by his example and lessons, the same ideal is brought within the reach of many, perhaps of all. The ideal of humanity,—the perfect character belonging to the sage, which ranks him on a level with Heaven;—is indicated by 誠,

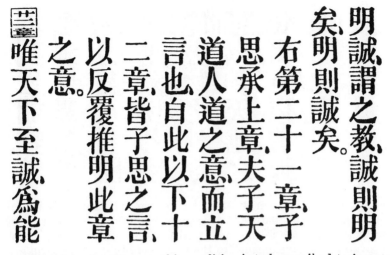

明誠謂之教、誠則明矣、明則誠矣。

右第二十一章、子思承上章夫子天道人道之意而立言也、自此以下十二章、皆子思之言、以反覆推明此章之意。

第二十二章 唯天下至誠爲能

resulting from intelligence, this condition is to be ascribed to instruction. But given the sincerity, and there shall be the intelligence; given the intelligence, and there shall be the sincerity.

The above is the twenty-first chapter. Tsze-sze takes up in it, and discourses from, the subjects of 'the way of Heaven' and 'the way of men,' mentioned in the preceding chapter. The twelve chapters that follow are all from Tsze-sze, repeating and illustrating the meaning of this one.

CHAP. XXII.   It is only he who is possessed of the most com-

and we have no single term in English, which can be considered as the complete equivalent of that character. The Chinese themselves had great difficulty in arriving at that definition of it which is now generally acquiesced in. In the 四書通 (quoted in the 匯參中庸, xvi. 5), we are told that 'the Han scholars were all ignorant of its meaning. Under the Sung dynasty, first came 李邦直, who defined it by 不欺, *freedom from all deception.* After him, 徐仲車 said that it meant 不息, *ceaselessness.* Then, one of the Chăng called it 無妄, *freedom from all moral error;* and finally, Chû Hsî added to this the positive element of 眞實, *truth and reality,* on which the definition of 誠 was complete.' Rémusat calls it—*la perfection,* and *la perfection morale.* Intorcetta and his friends call it—*vera solidaque perfectio.* Simplicity or singleness of soul seems to be what is chiefly intended by the term;—the disposition to, and capacity of, what is good, without any deteriorating element, with no defect of intelligence, or intromission of selfish thoughts. This belongs to Heaven, to Heaven and Earth, and to the Sage. Men, not naturally sages, may, by cultivating the intelligence of what is good, raise themselves to this elevation. 性 and 教 carry us back to the first chapter, but the terms have a different force, and the longer I dwell upon it, the more am I satisfied with Chû Hsî's pronouncement in his 語類, that 性 is here 性之, 'possessing from nature,' and 教＝學之, 'learning it,' and therefore I have translated 謂之 by—'is to be ascribed to.' When, however, he makes a difference in the connexion between the parts of the two clauses—誠則明矣, 明則誠矣, and explains—誠則無不明, 明則可以至誠, 'sincerity is invariably intelligent, and intelligence may arrive at sincerity,' this is not dealing fairly with his text.

Here, at the outset, I may observe that, in this portion of the Work, there are specially the three following dogmas, which are more than questionable:—1st, That there are some men—Sages—naturally in a state of moral perfection; and, That the same moral perfection is attainable by others, in whom its development is impeded by their material organization, and the influence

盡其性能盡其
性則能盡人之
性能盡人之性、
則能盡物之性、
能盡物之性、則
可以贊天地之
化育可以贊天
地之化育則可
以與天地參矣。

plete sincerity that can exist under heaven, who can give its full development to his nature. Able to give its full development to his own nature, he can do the same to the nature of other men. Able to give its full development to the nature of other men, he can give their full development to the natures of animals and things. Able to give their full development to the natures of creatures and things, he can assist the transforming and nourishing powers of Heaven and Earth. Able to assist the transforming and nourishing powers of Heaven and Earth, he may with Heaven and Earth form a ternion.

of external things; and 3rd, That the understanding of what is good will certainly lead to such moral perfection.

22. THE RESULTS OF SINCERITY; AND HOW THE POSSESSOR OF IT FORMS A TERNION WITH HEAVEN AND EARTH. On 天下至誠, Chû Hsî says that it denotes 'the reality of the virtue of the Sage, to which there is nothing in the world that can be added.' This is correct, and if we were to render—'It is only the most sincere man under heaven,' the translation would be wrong. 盡 means simply 'to exhaust,' but, by what processes and in what way, the character tells us nothing about. The 'giving full development to his nature,' however, may be understood, with Mâo, as = 'pursuing THE PATH in accordance with his nature, so that what Heaven has conferred on him is displayed without shortcoming or let.' The 'giving its development to the nature of other men' indicates the Sage's helping them, by his example and lessons, to perfect themselves. 'His exhausting the nature of things,' i.e. of all other beings, animate and inanimate, is, according to Chû, 'knowing them completely, and dealing with them correctly,' 'so,' add the paraphrasts, 'that he secures their prosperous increase and development according to their nature.' Here, however, a Buddhist idea appears in Chû's commentary. He says:— 'The nature of other men and things (=animals) is the same with my nature,' which, it is observed in Mâo's Work, is the same with the Buddhist sentiment, that 'a dog has the nature of Buddha,' and with that of the philosopher Kâo, that 'a dog's nature is the same

as a man's.' Mâo himself illustrates the 'exhausting the nature of things,' by reference to the Shû-ching, IV. iii. 2, where we are told that under the first sovereigns of the Hsiâ dynasty, 'the mountains and rivers all enjoyed tranquillity, and the birds and beasts, the fishes and tortoises, all realized the happiness of their nature.' It is thus that the sage 'assists Heaven and Earth.' K'ang-ch'âng, indeed, explains this by saying:—'The sage, receiving Heaven's appointment to the throne, extends everywhere a happy tranquillity.' Evidently there is a reference in the language to the mystical paragraph in the 1st chapter—致中和, 天地位焉, 萬物育焉. 'Heaven and Earth' take the place here of the single term—'Heaven,' in chap. xx. par. 18. On this Yingtâ observes:—'It is said above, sincerity is the way of Heaven, and here mention is made also of Earth. The reason is, that the reference above, was to the principle of sincerity in its spiritual and mysterious origin, and thence the expression simple,—The way of Heaven; but here we have the transformation and nourishing seen in the production of things, and hence Earth is associated with Heaven.' This is not very intelligible, but it is to bring out the idea of a ternion, that the great, supreme, ruling Power is thus dualized. 參 is 'a file of three,' and I employ 'ternion' to express the idea, just as we use 'quaternion' for a file of four. What is it but extravagance thus to file man with the supreme Power?

其次致曲、曲能有誠、誠則形、形則著、著則明、明則動、動則變、變則化、唯天下至誠為能化。

至誠之道可以前知、國家將興必有禎祥、國家將亡必有妖孽、見乎蓍龜、動乎四體、禍福將至、善必先

CHAP. XXIII. Next to the above is he who cultivates to the utmost the shoots *of goodness* in him. From those he can attain to the possession of sincerity. This sincerity becomes apparent. From being apparent, it becomes manifest. From being manifest, it becomes brilliant. Brilliant, it affects others. Affecting others, they are changed by it. Changed by it, they are transformed. It is only he who is possessed of the most complete sincerity that can exist under heaven, who can transform.

CHAP. XXIV. It is characteristic of the most entire sincerity to be able to foreknow. When a nation or family is about to flourish, there are sure to be happy omens; and when it is about to perish, there are sure to be unlucky omens. *Such events are* seen in the milfoil and tortoise, and affect the movements of the four limbs. When calamity or happiness is about to come, the good

23. THE WAY OF MAN;—THE DEVELOPMENT OF PERFECT SINCERITY IN THOSE NOT NATURALLY POSSESSED OF IT. 其次, 'the next,' or 'his next,' referring to the 自誠明者, of chap. xxi. 曲 is defined by Chû Hsî as 一偏, 'one half,' 'a part.' K'ang-ch'ǎng explains it by 小小之事, 'very small matters.' Mâo defines it by 隅, 'a corner,' and refers to Analects, VII. viii, 舉一隅不以三隅反, as a sentiment analogous to the one in 致曲. There is difficulty about the term. It properly means 'crooked,' and with a bad application, like 偏, often signifies 'deflection from what is straight and right.' Yet it cannot have a bad meaning here, for if it have, the phrase, 致曲, will be, in the connexion, unintelligible. One writer uses this com-

parison:—'Put a stone on a bamboo shoot, or where the shoot would show itself, and it will travel round the stone, and come out *crookedly* at its side.' So it is with the good nature, whose free development is repressed. It shows itself in shoots, but if they be cultivated and improved, a moral condition and influence may be attained, equal to that of the Sage.

24. THAT ENTIRE SINCERITY CAN FOREKNOW. 至誠之道 is the quality in the abstract, while 至誠 at the end, is the entirely sincere individual,—the Sage, by nature, or by attainment. 禎祥, 'lucky omens.' In the dictionary 祥 is used to define 禎. 祥 may be used also of inauspicious omens, but here it cannot embrace such. Distinguishing between the two terms, Ying-tâ says that unusual appearances of things existing in a country are 祥, and appearances of things new are 禎. 妖孽 are 'unlucky omens,' the former being spoken

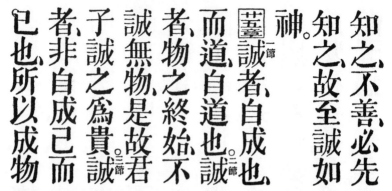

shall certainly be foreknown by him, and the evil also.   Therefore the individual possessed of the most complete sincerity is like a spirit.

CHAP. XXV.   1. Sincerity is that whereby self-completion is effected, and *its* way is that by which man must direct himself.

2. Sincerity is the end and beginning of things; without sincerity there would be nothing.   On this account, the superior man regards the attainment of sincerity as the most excellent thing.

3. The possessor of sincerity does not merely accomplish the self-completion of himself.   With this quality he completes *other men and* things *also*.   The completing himself *shows his* perfect

of 'prodigies of plants, and of strangely dressed boys singing ballads,' and the latter of 'prodigious animals.'   The subject of the verbs 見 and 動 is the events, not the omens.   For the milfoil and tortoise, see the Yî-ching, App. III. ii. 73.   They are there called 神物, 'spiritual things.'   Divination by the milfoil was called 筮; that by the tortoise was called 卜.   They were used from the highest antiquity.   See the Shû-ching, II. ii. 18; V. iv. 20-30.   四體, 'four limbs,' are by K'ang-ch'äng interpreted of the feet of the tortoise, each foot being peculiarly appropriate to divination in a particular season.   Chû Hsî interprets them of the four limbs of the human body.   如神 must be left as indefinite in the translation as it is in the text.—The whole chapter is eminently absurd, and gives a character of ridiculousness to all the magniloquent teaching about 'entire sincerity.'   The foreknowledge attributed to the Sage,—the mate of Heaven,—is only a guessing by means of augury, sorcery, and other follies.

25. HOW FROM SINCERITY COMES SELF-COMPLETION, AND THE COMPLETION OF OTHERS AND OF THINGS.   I have had difficulty in translating this chapter, because it is difficult to understand it.   We wish that we had the writer before us to question him; but if we had, it is not likely that he would be able to afford us much satisfaction.   Persuaded that what he denominates *sincerity* is a figment, we may not wonder at the extravagance of its predicates.   1. All the

commentators of the Sung school say that 誠 is here 天命之性, 'the Heaven-conferred nature,' and that 道 is 率性之道, 'the path which is in accordance with the nature.'   They are probably correct, but the difficulty comes when we go on with this view of 誠 to the next paragraph.   2. I translate the expansion of this in the 日講:—'All that fill up the space between heaven and earth are things (物).   They end and they begin again; they begin and proceed to an end; every change being accomplished by sincerity, and every phenomenon having sincerity unceasingly in it.   So far as the mind of man (人之心) is concerned, if there be not sincerity, then every movement of it is vain and false.   How can an unreal mind accomplish real things?   Although it may do something, that is simply equivalent to nothing.   Therefore the superior man searches out the source of sincerity, and examines the evil of insincerity, chooses what is good, and firmly holds it fast, so seeking to arrive at the place of truth and reality.'   Mâo's explanation is:—'Now, since the reason why the sincerity of spiritual beings is so incapable of being repressed, and why they foreknow, is because they enter into things, and there is nothing without them:—shall there be anything which is without the entirely sincere man, who is as a spirit?'   I have given these specimens of commentary, that the reader may, if he can, by means of them, gather some

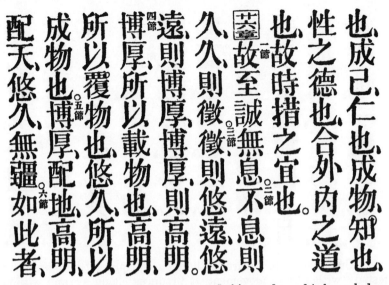

也成己仁也成物知也

性之德也合外內之道

也故時措之宜也

故至誠無息不息則
一節

久久則徵徵則悠遠悠
三節

遠則博厚博厚則高明
四節

博厚所以載物也高明

所以覆物也博厚配
五節

成物也博厚配地高明
六節

配天悠久無疆如此者

virtue. The completing *other men and* things *shows his* knowledge. *Both these are* virtues belonging to the nature, and *this is* the way by which a union is effected of the external and internal. Therefore, whenever he—*the entirely sincere man*—employs them,—*that is, these virtues,*—*their action will be* right.

CHAP. XXVI. 1. Hence to entire sincerity there belongs ceaselessness.

2. Not ceasing, it continues long. Continuing long, it evidences itself.

3. Evidencing itself, it reaches far. Reaching far, it becomes large and substantial. Large and substantial, it becomes high and brilliant.

4. Large and substantial;—this is how it contains *all* things. High and brilliant;—this is how it overspreads *all* things. Reaching far and continuing long;—this is how it perfects *all* things.

5. So large and substantial, *the individual possessing it* is the co-equal of Earth. So high and brilliant, it makes him the co-equal of Heaven. So far-reaching and long-continuing, it makes him infinite.

apprehensible meaning from the text. 3. I have translated 成物 by—'complete *other men and* things *also,*' with a reference to the account of the achievements of sincerity, in chap. xxii. On 性之德也 合外內 之道也, the 日講 paraphrases:—'Now both this perfect virtue and knowledge are virtues certainly and originally belonging to our nature, to be referred for their bestowment to Heaven;—what distinction is there in them of external and internal?'—All this, so far as I can see, is but veiling ignorance by words without knowledge.

26. A PARALLEL BETWEEN THE SAGE POSSESSED OF ENTIRE SINCERITY, AND HEAVEN AND EARTH, SHOWING THAT THE SAME QUALITIES BELONG TO THEM. The first six paragraphs show the way of the Sage; the next three show the way of Heaven and Earth; and the last brings the two ways together, in their essential nature, in a passage from the Shih-ching. The doctrine of the chapter is liable to the criticisms which have been made on the 22nd chapter. And, moreover, there is in it a sad confusion of the visible heavens and earth with the immaterial power and reason which govern them; in a word, with God. 1. Because of the 故, 'hence,' or 'therefore,' Chû Hsî is condemned by recent writers

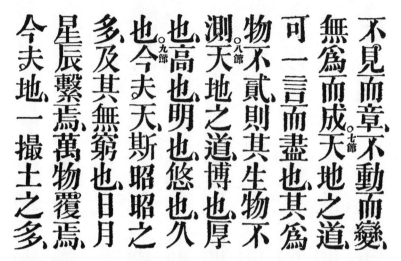

今　星　多　也　也　測　物　可　無　不
夫　辰　及　今　高　天　不　一　爲　見
地　繫　其　夫　也　地　貳　言　而　而
一　焉　無　天　明　之　則　而　成　章
撮　萬　窮　斯　也　道　其　盡　　　不
土　物　也　昭　悠　博　生　也　七節　動
之　覆　日　昭　也　也　物　其　天　而
多　焉　月　之　久　厚　不　爲　地　變
　　　　　　　　　九節　八節　　　　　之

6. Such being its nature, without any display, it becomes manifested; without any movement, it produces changes; and without
any effort, it accomplishes its ends.

7. The way of Heaven and Earth may be completely declared
in one sentence.—They are without any doubleness, and so they
produce things in a manner that is unfathomable.

8. The way of Heaven and Earth is large and substantial, high
and brilliant, far-reaching and long-enduring.

9. The heaven now before us is only this bright shining spot;
but when viewed in its inexhaustible extent, the sun, moon, stars,
and constellations of the zodiac, are suspended in it, and all things
are overspread by it. The earth before us is but a handful of soil;
but when regarded in its breadth and thickness, it sustains

for making a new chapter to commence here.
Yet the matter is sufficiently distinct from that
of the preceding one. Where the 故 takes
hold of the text above, however, it is not easy
to discover. The gloss in the 備旨 says that
it indicates a conclusion from all the preceding
predicates about sincerity. 至誠 is to be
understood, now in the abstract, and now in
the concrete. But the 5th paragraph seems
to be the place to bring out the personal idea,
as I have done. 無疆, 'without bounds,' =
our *infinite*. Surely it is strange to apply
that term in the description of any created
being. 7. What I said was the prime idea in
誠, viz. 'simplicity,' 'singleness of soul,' is
very conspicuous here. 其爲物不貳—
爲 is the substantive verb. It surprises us,
however, to find Heaven and Earth called
'*things*,' at the same time that they are repre-

sented as by their entire sincerity producing
all things. 9. This paragraph is said to illustrate the unfathomableness of Heaven and
Earth in producing things, showing how it
springs from their sincerity, or freedom from
doubleness. I have already observed how it is
only the material heavens and earth which are
presented to us. And not only so;—we have
mountains, seas, and rivers, set forth as acting
with the same unfathomableness as those entire
bodies and powers. The 備旨 says on this:—
'The hills and waters are what Heaven and
Earth produce, and that they should yet be able
themselves to produce *other* things, shows still
more how Heaven and Earth, in the producing
of things, are unfathomable.' The use of 多 in
the several clauses here perplexes the student.
On 斯昭昭之多, Chû Hsî says—此指
其一處而言之, 'This is speaking of
it'—heaven—'as it appears in one point.' In the
中庸說, *in loc.*, there is an attempt to make

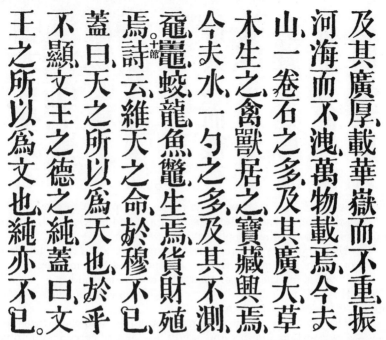

及其廣厚、載華嶽而不重、振
河海而不洩、萬物載焉、今夫
山、一卷石之多、及其廣大、草
木生之禽獸居之寶藏興焉、
今夫水一勺之多、及其不測、
黿鼉蛟龍魚鼈生焉、貨財殖
焉。○十節 詩云維天之命、於穆不已、
蓋曰天之所以為天也、於乎
不顯文王之德之純、蓋曰、文
王之所以為文也、純亦不已。

mountains like the Hwâ and the Yo, without feeling their weight,
and contains the rivers and seas, without their leaking away.   The
mountain now before us appears only a stone; but when contemplated in all the vastness of its size, we see how the grass and trees
are produced on it, and birds and beasts dwell on it, and precious
things which men treasure up are found on it.   The water now
before us appears but a ladleful; yet extending our view to its
unfathomable depths, the largest tortoises, iguanas, iguanodons,
dragons, fishes, and turtles, are produced in them, articles of value
and sources of wealth abound in them.

10. It is said in the Book of Poetry, 'The ordinances of Heaven,
how profound are they and unceasing!'   The meaning is, that it is
thus that Heaven is Heaven.   *And again,* 'How illustrious was it, the
singleness of the virtue of king Wăn!' indicating that it was thus that
king Wăn was what he was.   Singleness likewise is unceasing.

this out by a definition of 多:—多餘也,
言少許耳, '多 is overplus, meaning a
small overplus.'   日月星辰,—compare the
Shû-ching, I. 3.   In that passage, as well as here,
many take 星 as meaning the planets, but we
need not depart from the meaning of 'stars'
generally.   辰 is applied variously, but used
along with the other terms, it denotes the con-
junctions of the sun and moon, which divide
the circumference of the heavens into twelve
parts.   華嶽,—there are five peaks, or 嶽,
celebrated in China, the western one of which
is called 華 (lower 3rd tone).   嶽   Here, however, we are to understand by each term a
particular mountain.   See the 集證 and 中
庸說, *in loc.*   In the 集證, the Yellow
river, and that only, is understood by 河, but
both it and 海 must be taken generally.   卷
read *ch'üan,* the 2nd tone, is in the dictionary,

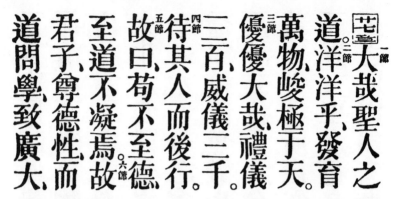

CHAP. XXVII.   1. How great is the path proper to the Sage!

2. Like overflowing water, it sends forth and nourishes all things, and rises up to the height of heaven.

3. All-complete is its greatness! It embraces the three hundred rules of ceremony, and the three thousand rules of demeanour.

4. It waits for the proper man, and then it is trodden.

5. Hence it is said, 'Only by perfect virtue can the perfect path, in all its courses, be made a fact.'

6. Therefore, the superior man honours his virtuous nature, and maintains constant inquiry and study, seeking to carry it out to its breadth and greatness, so as to omit none of the more exquisite and

with reference to this passage, defined by 區, 'a place,' 'a small plot.' In the 中庸說, 黿 is defined as 介蟲之元, 'the first-produced of the chelonia;' 龍 as 麟蟲之長, 'the chief of scaly animals;' 鼉 as being 'a kind of 黿;' 蛟 as being 'a kind of 龍,' while the 鼉 'has scales like a fish, feet like a dragon, and is related to the 黿.' By 貨 are intended pearls and valuable shells; by 財, fish, salt, &c. 10. See the Shih-ching, IV. i. Bk. I. Ode II. st. 1. The attributes of the ordinances of Heaven, and the virtue of king Wăn, are here set forth, as substantially the same. 純 = 'fine and pure,' 'unmixed.' The dictionary gives it the distinct meaning of 'ceaselessness,' quoting the last clause here,—純亦不已, as if it were definition, and not description.

27. THE GLORIOUS PATH OF THE SAGE; AND HOW THE SUPERIOR MAN ENDEAVOURS TO ATTAIN TO IT. The chapter thus divides itself into two parts, one containing five paragraphs, descriptive of the SAGE, and the other two descriptive of the *superior man*, which two appellations are to be here distinguished. 1. 'This paragraph,' says Chû Hsî, 'embraces the two that follow.' They are, indeed, to be taken as exegetical of it. 道, it is said, is here, as

everywhere else in the Work (see the 翼注, *in loc.*), '*the path which is in accordance with the nature.*' The student tries to believe so, and goes on to par. 2, when the predicate about *the nourishing of all things* puzzles and confounds him. 2. 極 is not here the adverb, but = 至, 'reaching to.' 3. By 禮儀 we are to understand the greater and more general principles of propriety, 'such,' says the 備旨, 'as capping, marriage, mourning, and sacrifice;' and by 威儀 are intended all the minuter observances of those. The former are also 經禮, 禮經, and 正經; the latter, 曲禮 and 動禮. See the 集證, *in loc.* 300 and 3000 are round numbers. Reference is made to these rules and their minutiæ, to show how, in every one of them, as proceeding from the Sage, there is a principle, to be referred to the Heaven-given nature. 4. Compare chap. xx. 2. In '*Confucius Sinarum Philosophus*,' it is suggested that there may be here a prophecy of the Saviour, and that the writer may have been 'under the influence of that spirit, by whose moving the Sibyls formerly prophesied of Christ.' There is nothing in the text to justify such a thought. 5. 凝, 'to congeal;' then = 成, 'to complete,' and 定, 'to fix.' The whole paragraph is merely

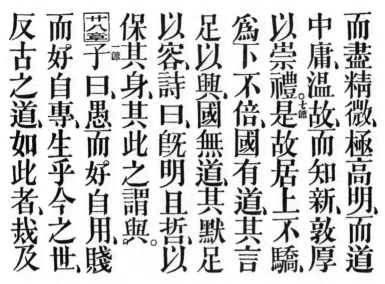

而盡精微、極高明、而道

中庸、溫故、而知新、敦厚

以崇禮。是故居上不驕、　七節

爲下不倍、國有道其言

足以興、國無道其默足

以容、詩曰、既明且哲以

保其身、其此之謂與。

子曰愚而好自用、賤　一節

而好自專、生乎今之世、

反古之道、如此者、栽及

minute points which it embraces, and to raise it to its greatest
height and brilliancy, so as to pursue the course of the Mean. He
cherishes his old knowledge, and is continually acquiring new. He
exerts an honest, generous earnestness, in the esteem and practice
of all propriety.

7. Thus, when occupying a high situation he is not proud, and
in a low situation he is not insubordinate. When the kingdom is
well-governed, he is sure by his words to rise; and when it is ill-
governed, he is sure by his silence to command forbearance to himself. Is not this what we find in the Book of Poetry,—'Intelligent
is he and prudent, and so preserves his person?'

CHAP. XXVIII. 1. The Master said, 'Let a man who is ignorant
be fond of using his own judgment; let a man without rank be fond
of assuming a directing power to himself; let a man who is living
in the present age go back to the ways of antiquity;—on the persons
of all who act thus calamities will be sure to come.'

a repetition of the preceding one, in other
words. 6. 道 in both cases here = 由, 'to
proceed from,' or 'by.' It is said correctly,
that 首句是一節頭腦, 'the first
sentence,—尊德性而道問學, is
the brains of the whole paragraph.' 溫故
而知新,—see Analects, II. xi. 7. This
describes the superior man, largely successful
in pursuing the course indicated in the preceding paragraphs, 倍=背. 詩曰,—see
the Shih, III. iii. Ode VI. st. 4.

28. AN ILLUSTRATION OF THE SENTENCE IN THE
LAST CHAPTER—'IN A LOW SITUATION HE IS NOT

INSUBORDINATE.' There does seem to be a connexion of the kind thus indicated between this
chapter and the last, but the principal object of
what is said here is to prepare the way for the
eulogium of Confucius below,—the eulogium of
him, a Sage without the throne. 1. The different
clauses here may be understood generally, but
they have a special reference to the general
scope of the chapter. Three things are required
to give law to the kingdom: virtue (including
intelligence), rank, and the right time. 愚 is
he who wants the virtue, 賤 is he who wants
the rank, and the last clause describes the
absence of the right time.—In this last clause,
there would seem to be a sentiment, which
should have given course in China to the doc-

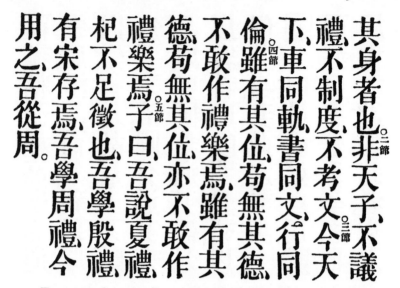

用之吾從周。

有宋存焉吾學周禮今

杞不足徵也吾學殷禮

禮樂焉子曰吾說夏禮　〇五節

德苟無其位亦不敢作

不敢作禮樂焉雖有其

倫雖有其位苟無其德

下車同軌書同文行同　〇四節

禮不制度不考文今天　〇三節

其身者也。非天子不議　〇二節

2. To no one but the Son of Heaven does it belong to order ceremonies, to fix the measures, and to determine the written characters.

3. Now, over the kingdom, carriages have all wheels of the same size; all writing is with the same characters; and for conduct there are the same rules.

4. One may occupy the throne, but if he have not the proper virtue, he may not dare to make ceremonies or music. One may have the virtue, but if he do not occupy the throne, he may not presume to make ceremonies or music.

5. The Master said, 'I may describe the ceremonies of the Hsiâ dynasty, but Chî cannot sufficiently attest my words. I have learned the ceremonies of the Yin dynasty, and in Sung they still continue. I have learned the ceremonies of Châu, which are now used, and I follow Châu.'

trine of Progress. 2. This and the two next paragraphs are understood to be the words of Tsze-sze, illustrating the preceding declarations of Confucius. We have here the royal prerogatives, which might not be usurped. 'Ceremonies' are the rules regulating religion and society; 'the measures' are the prescribed forms and dimensions of buildings, carriages, clothes, &c.; 文 is said by Chû Hsî, after K'ang-ch'ăng, to be 書名, 'the names of the characters.' But 文 is properly the form of the character, representing, in the original characters of the language, the 形, or figure of the object denoted. The character and name together are styled 字; and 書 is the name appropriate to many characters, written or printed. 文, in the text, must denote both the form and sound of the character. 議, 'to discuss,' and 考, 'to examine,' but implying, in each case, the consequent ordering and settling. There is a long and eulogistic note here, in 'Confucius Sinarum Philosophus,' on the admirable uniformity secured by these prerogatives throughout the Chinese empire. It was natural for Roman Catholic writers to regard Chinese uniformity with sympathy. But the value, or, rather, small value, of such a system in its formative influence on the characters and institutions of men may be judged, both in the empire of China, and in the Church of Rome. 3. 今, 'now,' is said with reference to the time of Tsze-sze. The paragraph is intended to account for Confucius's not giving law to the kingdom. It was not the time. 軌, 'the rut of a wheel.' 4. 禮樂;—but

CHAP. XXIX. 1. He who attains to the sovereignty of the kingdom, having *those* three important things, shall be able to effect that there shall be few errors *under his government*.

2. However excellent may have been the regulations of those of former times, they cannot be attested. Not being attested, they cannot command credence, and not being credited, the people would not follow them. However excellent might be the regulations made by one in an inferior situation, he is not in a position to be honoured. Unhonoured, he cannot command credence, and not being credited, the people would not follow his rules.

3. Therefore the institutions of the Ruler are rooted in his own character and conduct, and sufficient attestation of them is given by the masses of the people. He examines them *by comparison* with those of the three kings, and finds them without mistake. He sets

we must understand also 'the measures' and 'characters' in par. 2. This paragraph would seem to reduce most sovereigns to the condition of *rois faineants*. 5. See the Analects, III. ix, xiv, which chapters are quoted here; but in regard to what is said of Sung, with an important variation. The paragraph illustrates how Confucius himself 爲下不倍, 'occupied a low station, without being insubordinate.'

29. AN ILLUSTRATION OF THE SENTENCE IN THE TWENTY-SEVENTH CHAPTER—'WHEN HE OCCUPIES A HIGH SITUATION HE IS NOT PROUD ;' OR RATHER, THE SAGE AND HIS INSTITUTIONS SEEN IN THEIR EFFECT AND ISSUE. 1. Different opinions have obtained as to what is intended by the 三重, 'three important *things*.' K'ang-ch'âng says they are 三王之禮, 'the ceremonies of the three kings,' i. e. the founders of the three dynasties, Hsiâ, Yin, and Châu. This view we may safely reject. Chû Hsî makes them to be the royal prerogatives, mentioned in the last chapter, par. 2. This view may, possibly, be correct. But I incline to the view of the commentator Lû (陸氏), of the T'ang dynasty, that they refer to the virtue, station, and time, which we have seen, in the notes on the last

chapter, to be necessary to one who would give law to the kingdom. Mâo mentions this view, indicating his own approval of it. 寡 is used as a verb, 'to make few.'—'He shall be able to effect that there shall be few errors,' i. e. few errors among his officers and people. 2. By 上焉者 and 下焉者, K'ang-ch'âng understands 'sovereign and minister,' in which, again, I must pronounce him wrong. The translation follows the interpretation of Chû Hsî, it being understood that the subject of the paragraph is the regulations to be followed by the people. 上焉者 having a reference both to *time* and to *rank*, 下焉者 must have the same. Thus there is in it an allusion to Confucius, and the way is still further prepared for his eulogium. 3. By 君子 is intended the 王天下者 in par. 1,—the ruling-sage. By 道 must be intended all his institutions and regulations. 'Attestation of them is given by the masses of the people ;' i. e. the people believe in such a ruler, and follow his regulations, thus attesting their adaptation to the general requirements of humanity. 'The three kings' must be taken

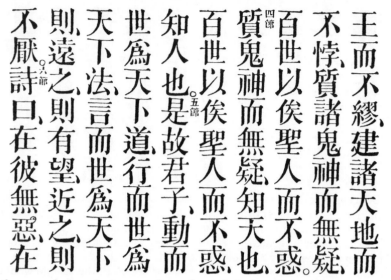

them up before heaven and earth, and finds nothing in them contrary to their mode of operation. He presents himself with them before spiritual beings, and no doubts about them arise. He is prepared to wait for the rise of a sage a hundred ages after, and has no misgivings.

4. His presenting himself *with his institutions* before spiritual beings, without any doubts arising about them, shows that he knows Heaven. His being prepared, without any misgivings, to wait for the rise of a sage a hundred ages after, shows that he knows men.

5. Such being the case, the movements of such a ruler, *illustrating his institutions*, constitute an example to the world for ages. His acts are for ages a law to the kingdom. His words are for ages a lesson to the kingdom. Those who are far from him, look longingly for him; and those who are near him, are never wearied with him.

6. It is said in the Book of Poetry,—'Not disliked there, not

here as the founders of the three dynasties, viz. the great Yü, T'ang, the Completer, and Wän and Wû, who are so often joined together, and spoken of as one. 繆＝謬, and should be read in the 4th tone. I hardly know what to make of 建諸天地. Chû, in his 語類, says:—此天地只是道耳, 謂吾建於此, 而與道不相悖也, 'Heaven and Earth here simply mean right reason. The meaning is—I set up *my institutions* here, and there is nothing in them contradictory to right reason.' This, of course, is explaining the text away. But who can do anything better with it? I interpret 質諸鬼神 (the 諸 is unfortunately left out

in the text) as the general trial of a ruler's institutions by the efficacy of his sacrifices, in being responded to by the various spirits whom he worships. This is the view of a Ho Hî-chan (何屺瞻), and is preferable to any other I have met with. 百世以俟聖人而不惑,—compare Mencius, II. Pt. I. ii. 17.

6. See the Shih-ching, IV. i. Bk. II. Ode III. st. 2. It is a great descent to quote that ode here, however, for it is only praising the feudal princes of Châu. 在彼, 'there,' means their own States; and 在此, 'here,' is the royal court of Châu. For 射, the Shih-ching has 斁.

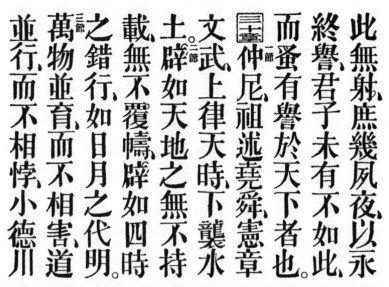

此無射庶幾夙夜以永

終譽君子未有不如此、

而蚤有譽於天下者也。

仲尼祖述堯舜憲章〔一節〕

文武上律天時下襲水

土辟如天地之無不持〔二節〕

載無不覆幬辟如四時

之錯行如日月之代明。〔三節〕

萬物並育而不相害道

並行而不相悖小德川

tired of here, from day to day and night to night, will they perpetuate their praise.' Never has there been a ruler, who did not realise this description, that obtained an early renown throughout the kingdom.

CHAP. XXX. 1. Chung-nî handed down the doctrines of Yâo and Shun, as if they had been his ancestors, and elegantly displayed the regulations of Wăn and Wû, taking them as his model. Above, he harmonized with the times of heaven, and below, he was conformed to the water and land.

2. He may be compared to heaven and earth in their supporting and containing, their overshadowing and curtaining, all things. He may be compared to the four seasons in their alternating progress, and to the sun and moon in their successive shining.

3. All things are nourished together without their injuring one another. The courses *of the seasons, and of the sun and moon,* are pursued without any collision among them. The smaller energies

30. THE EULOGIUM OF CONFUCIUS, AS THE BEAU-IDEAL OF THE PERFECTLY SINCERE MAN, THE SAGE, MAKING A TERNION WITH HEAVEN AND EARTH.

1. 仲尼,—see chap. ii. The various predicates here are explained by K'ang-ch'ăng and Ying-tâ, with reference to the 'Spring and Autumn,' making them descriptive of it, but such a view will not stand examination. In translating the two first clauses, I have followed the editor of the 參匯, who says:—祖述者,以爲祖而纘述之,憲章者,奉爲憲而表章之. In the 紹聞編, it is observed that in what he handed down, Confucius began with Yâo and Shun, because the times of Fû-hsî and Shăn-năng were very remote. Was not the true reason this, that he knew of nothing in China more remote than Yâo and Shun? By 'the times of heaven' are denoted the ceaseless regular movement, which appears to belong to the heavens; and by the 'water and the land,' we are to understand the earth, in contradistinction from heaven, supposed to be fixed and unmoveable. Lü, 'a statute,' 'a law;' here used as a verb, 'to take as a law.' 襲＝因, 'to follow,' 'to accord with.' The scope of the paragraph is, that the qualities of former Sages, of Heaven, and of Earth, were all concentrated in Confucius. 2. 辟 read as, and＝譬. 錯, read ts'oh,＝tieh, 'successively,' 'alternatingly.' 'This describes,' says Chû Hsî, 'the virtue of

以有別也。溥博淵　敬也文理密察足　齊莊中正足以有　剛毅足以有執也　足以有容也發强　有臨也寬裕溫柔　能聰明睿知足以　唯天下至聖足以爲　地之所以爲大也。　流、大德敦化、此天

第三十一章　一節　二節

are like river currents; the greater energies are seen in mighty transformations. It is this which makes heaven and earth so great.

CHAP. XXXI. 1. It is only he, possessed of all sagely qualities that can exist under heaven, who shows himself quick in apprehension, clear in discernment, of far-reaching intelligence, and all-embracing knowledge, fitted to exercise rule; magnanimous, generous, benign, and mild, fitted to exercise forbearance; impulsive, energetic, firm, and enduring, fitted to maintain a firm hold; self-adjusted, grave, never swerving from the Mean, and correct, fitted to command reverence; accomplished, distinctive, concentrative, and searching, fitted to exercise discrimination.

2. All-embracing is he and vast, deep and active as a fountain, sending forth in their due season his virtues.

the Sage.' 3. The wonderful and mysterious course of nature, or—as the Chinese express it —of the operations of Heaven and Earth, are described to illustrate the previous comparison of Confucius.

31. THE EULOGIUM ON CONFUCIUS CONTINUED. Chû Hsî says that this chapter is an expansion of the clause in the last paragraph of the preceding,—'The smaller energies are like river currents.' Even if it be so, it will still have reference to Confucius, the subject of the preceding chapter. K'ang-ch'ǎng's account of the first paragraph is:—言德不如此, 不可以君天下也, 蓋傷孔子有其德而無其命. 'It describes how no one, who has not virtue such as this, can rule the kingdom, being a lamentation over the fact that while Confucius had the virtue, he did not have the appointment;' that is, of Heaven, to occupy the throne. Mâo's account of the whole chapter is:—'Had it been that Chung-nî possessed the throne, then Chung-nî was a perfect Sage. Being a perfect Sage, he would certainly have been able to put forth the greater energies, and the smaller energies, of his virtue, so as to rule the world, and show himself

the co-equal of Heaven and Earth, in the manner here described.' Considering the whole chapter to be thus descriptive of Confucius, I was inclined to translate in the past tense,—'It was only he, who could,' &c. Still the author has expressed himself so indefinitely, that I have preferred translating the whole, that it may read as the description of the ideal man, who found, or might have found, his realisation in Confucius. 1. 唯天下至聖,—see chap. xxi. 聖 here takes the place of 誠. Collie translates:—'It is only the most HOLY man.' Rémusat:—'Il n'y a dans l'univers qu'un SAINT, qui...' So the Jesuits:—'Hic commemorat et commendat summe SANCTI virtutes.' But holiness and sanctity are terms which indicate the humble and pious conformity of human character and life to the mind and will of God. The Chinese idea of the 聖人 is far enough from this. 臨,—以尊適卑曰臨 'the approach of the honourable to the mean is called lin.' It denotes the high drawing near to the low, to influence and rule. 2. 'An abyss, a spring,' equal, according to Chû Hsî, to—靜深而有本, 'still and deep, and having a

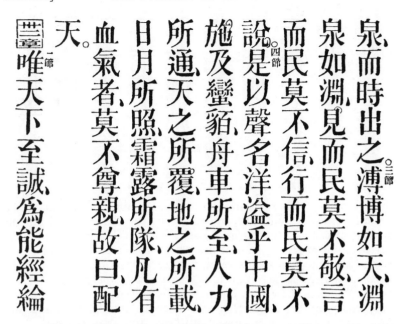

3. All-embracing and vast, he is like heaven. Deep and active as a fountain, he is like the abyss. He is seen, and the people all reverence him; he speaks, and the people all believe him; he acts, and the people all are pleased with him.

4. Therefore his fame overspreads the Middle Kingdom, and extends to all barbarous tribes. Wherever ships and carriages reach; wherever the strength of man penetrates; wherever the heavens overshadow and the earth sustains; wherever the sun and moon shine; wherever frosts and dews fall :—all who have blood and breath unfeignedly honour and love him. Hence it is said,—'He is the equal of Heaven.'

CHAP. XXXII. I. It is only the individual possessed of the most entire sincerity that can exist under heaven, who can adjust

source.' 時出之, 'always,'—or, in season —'puts them forth,' the 之, 'them,' having reference to the qualities described in par. 1. 3. 'He is seen;'—with reference, says the 備旨, to 'the robes and cap,' the visibilities of the ruler. 'He speaks ;'—with reference to his 'instructions, declarations, orders.' 'He acts;'—with reference to his 'ceremonies, music, punishments, and acts of government.' 4. This paragraph is the glowing expression of grand conceptions. 蠻, the general name for the rude tribes south of the Middle Kingdom. 貊 is another name for the 狄, or rude tribes on the north. The two stand here, like 夷狄,

Analects, III. v, and like 四夷, in the *Great Learning*, x. 15, as representatives of all barbarous tribes. 隊, read *chûi*, 4th tone, = 墜, 'to fall.'

32. THE EULOGIUM OF CONFUCIUS CONCLUDED. 'The chapter,' says Chû Hsî, 'expands the clause in the last paragraph of chap. xxix, that the greater energies are seen in mighty transformations.' 1. 經 and 綸 are processes in the manipulation of silk, denoting the first separating of the threads, and the subsequent bringing of them together, according to their kinds. 天下之大經,—'the great invariabilities of the world;' explained of the 達道 and 九經, in chap. xx. 8, 12. 天下

the great invariable relations of mankind, establish the great fundamental virtues of humanity, and know the transforming and nurturing operations of Heaven and Earth;—shall this individual have any being or anything beyond himself on which he depends?

2. Call him man in his ideal, how earnest is he! Call him an abyss, how deep is he! Call him Heaven, how vast is he!

3. Who can know him, but he who is indeed quick in apprehension, clear in discernment, of far-reaching intelligence, and all-embracing knowledge, possessing all heavenly virtue?

CHAP. XXXIII. 1. It is said in the Book of Poetry, 'Over her

之大本,—'the great root of the world;' evidently with reference to the same expression in chap. i. 4. 知 is taken as emphatic;—有 默契焉, 非但聞見之知而已, 'he has an intuitive apprehension of, and agreement with, them. It is not that he knows them merely by hearing and seeing.' 夫焉有所倚. This is joined by K'ang-ch'ang with the next paragraph, and he interprets it of the Master's virtue, universally affecting all men, and not partially deflected, reaching only to those near him or to few. Chû Hsî more correctly, as it seems to me, takes it as = 倚靠, 'to depend on.' I translate the expansion of the clause which is given in 'Confucius Sinarum Philosophus:'—'The perfectly holy man of this kind therefore, since he is such and so great, how can it in any way be, that there is anything in the whole universe, on which he leans, or in which he inheres, or on which he behooves to depend, or to be assisted by it in the first place, that he may afterwards operate?' 2. The three clauses refer severally to the three in the preceding paragraph. 仁 is virtuous humanity in all its dimensions and capacities, existing perfectly in the Sage. Of 淵 I do not know what to say. The old commentators interpret the second and third clauses, as if there were a 如 before 淵 and 天, against which

Chû Hsî reclaims, and justly. In the 紹聞編 we read:—天人本無二, 人只有此形體, 與天便隔, 視聽思慮, 動作, 皆曰由我, 各我其我, 可知其小也, 除却形體, 我便渾是天. 形體如何除得, 只克去有我之私, 便是除也, 天這般廣大, 吾心亦這般廣大, 而造化無間於我, 故曰浩浩其天. 'Heaven and man are not properly two, and man is separate from Heaven only by his having this body. Of their seeing and hearing, their thinking and revolving, their moving and acting, men all say—It is from ME. Every one thus brings out his SELF, and his smallness becomes known. But let the body be taken away, and all would be Heaven. How can the body be taken away? Simply by subduing and removing that self-having of the ego. This is the taking it away. That being done, so wide and great as Heaven is, my mind is also so wide and great, and production and transformation cannot be separated from me. Hence it is said—How vast is his Heaven.' Into such wandering mazes of mysterious speculation are Chinese thinkers conducted by the text:—only to be lost in them. As it is said, in par. 3, that only the sage can know the sage, we may be glad to leave him.

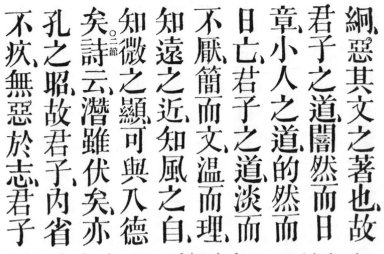

不疚、無惡於志君子
孔之昭故君子內省
矣。詩云潛雖伏矣亦
知微之顯可與入德
知遠之近知風之自、
不厭簡而文温而理、
日亡若子之道淡而
章小人之道的然而
君子之道闇然而日
絅惡其文之著也故

embroidered robe she puts a plain, single garment,' intimating a dislike to the display of the elegance of the former. Just so, it is the way of the superior man to prefer the concealment *of his virtue,* while it daily becomes more illustrious, and it is the way of the mean man to seek notoriety, while he daily goes more and more to ruin. It is characteristic of the superior man, appearing insipid, yet never to produce satiety; while showing a simple negligence, yet to have his accomplishments recognised; while seemingly plain, yet to be discriminating. He knows how what is distant lies in what is near. He knows where the wind proceeds from. He knows how what is minute becomes manifested. Such an one, we may be sure, will enter into virtue.

2. It is said in the Book of Poetry, 'Although *the fish* sink and lie at the bottom, it is still quite clearly seen.' Therefore the superior man examines his heart, that there may be nothing wrong

33. THE COMMENCEMENT AND THE COMPLETION OF A VIRTUOUS COURSE. The chapter is understood to contain a summary of the whole Work, and to have a special relation to the first chapter. There, a commencement is made with Heaven, as the origin of our nature, in which are grounded the laws of virtuous conduct. This ends with Heaven, and exhibits the progress of virtue, advancing step by step in man, till it is equal to that of High Heaven. There are eight citations from the Book of Poetry, but to make the passages suit his purpose, the author allegorises them, or alters their meaning, at his pleasure. Origen took no more license with the Scriptures of the Old and New Testaments than Tsze-sze and even Confucius himself do with the Book of Poetry. 1. *The first requisite in the pursuit of virtue is, that the learner think of his own improvement, and do not act from a regard to others.* 詩曰,—see the Shih-ching, I. v. Ode III. st. 1, where we read, however, 衣錦

褧衣. 褧 and 絅 are synonyms. 惡 (the 4th tone) 其云云 is a gloss by Tsze-sze, giving the spirit of the passage. The ode is understood to express the condolence of the people with the wife of the duke of Wei, worthy of, but denied, the affection of her husband. 君子之道, 小人之道,—道 seems here to correspond exactly to our English *way,* as in the translation. 的然,—the primary meaning of 的 is 明, 'bright,' 'displayed.' 的然, 'displayed-like,' in opposition to 闇然, 'concealed-like.' 知遠之近,—what is *distant,* is the nation to be governed, or the family to be regulated; what is *near,* is the person to be cultivated. 知風

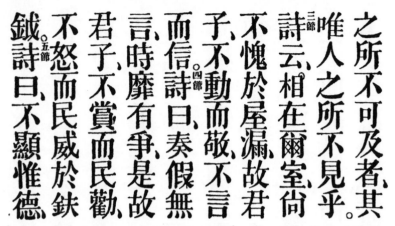

there, and that he may have no cause for dissatisfaction with himself. That wherein the superior man cannot be equalled is simply this,—his *work* which other men cannot see.

3. It is said in the Book of Poetry, 'Looked at in your apartment, be there free from shame as being exposed to the light of heaven.' Therefore, the superior man, even when he is not moving, has *a feeling of* reverence, and while he speaks not, he has *the feeling of* truthfulness.

4. It is said in the Book of Poetry, 'In silence is the offering presented, and *the spirit* approached to; there is not the slightest contention.' Therefore the superior man does not use rewards, and the people are stimulated *to virtue*. He does not show anger, and the people are awed more than by hatchets and battle-axes.

5. It is said in the Book of Poetry, 'What needs no display is

自之,—the *wind* is the influence exerted upon others, the *source* of which is one's own virtue. 顯之徵知,—compare chap. i. 3. 可與 = 'it may be granted to such an one,' 與 being in the sense of 許. 2. *The superior man going on to virtue, is watchful over himself when he is alone.* 云詩,—see the Shih-ching, II. iv. Ode VIII. st. 11. The ode appears to have been written by some officer who was bewailing the disorder and misgovernment of his day. This is one of the comparisons which he uses;—the people are like fish in a shallow pond, unable to save themselves by diving to the bottom. The application of this to the superior man, dealing with himself, in the bottom of his soul, so to speak, and thereby realising what is good and right, is very far-fetched. 志, 'the will,' is here = 心, 'the whole mind,' the self. 3. We have here substantially the same subject as in the last paragraph. The ode is the same which is quoted in chap. xvi. 4, and the citation is from the same stanza of it. 屋漏, according to Chû Hsî, was the north-west corner of ancient apartments, the spot most secret and retired. The single panes, in the roofs of Chinese houses, go now by the name, the light of heaven leaking in (漏) through them. Looking at the whole stanza of the ode, we must conclude that there is reference to the light of heaven, and the inspection of spiritual beings, as specially connected with the spot intended. 4. *The result of the processes described in the two preceding paragraphs.* 詩曰,—see the Shih-ching, IV. iii. Ode II. st. 2, where for 奏 we have 鬷. 假 read as, and = 格. The ode describes the royal worship of T'ang, the founder of the Shang dynasty. The first clause belongs to the sovereign's act and demeanour: the second to the effect of these on his assistants in the service. They were awed to reverence, and had no striving among themselves. The 鈇鉞 were anciently given by the sovereign to a prince, as symbolic of his investiture with a plenipotent authority to

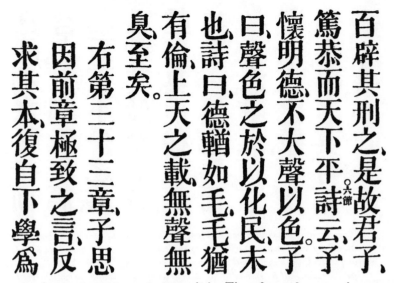

虚。 All the princes imitate it.' Therefore, the superior man being sincere and reverential, the whole world is conducted to a state of happy tranquillity.

6. It is said in the Book of Poetry, 'I regard with pleasure your brilliant virtue, making no great display of itself in sounds and appearances.' The Master said, 'Among the appliances to transform the people, sounds and appearances are but trivial influences. It is said in another ode, "His virtue is light as a hair." Still, a hair will admit of comparison *as to its size.* "The doings of the supreme Heaven have neither sound nor smell."—That is perfect virtue.'

The above is the thirty-third chapter. Tsze-sze having carried his descriptions to the extremest point in the preceding chapters, turns back in this, and examines the source of his subject; and then again from the work of the learner, free from all

punish the rebellious and refractory. The 鉞 is described as a large-handled axe, eight catties in weight. I call it a battle-axe, because it was with one that king Wû despatched the tyrant Châu. 5. *The same subject continued.* 詩曰,—see the Shih-ching, IV. i. Bk. I. Ode IV. st. 3. But in the Shih-ching we must translate,—'There is nothing more illustrious than the virtue *of the sovereign,* all the princes will follow it.' Tsze-sze puts another meaning on the words, and makes them introductory to the next paragraph. 君子 must here be the 王天下者 of chap. xxix. Thus it is that a constant shuffle of terms seems to be going on, and the subject before us is all at once raised to a higher, and inaccessible platform. 6. *Virtue in its highest degree and influence.* 詩云,—see

the Shih-ching, III. i. Ode VII. st. 7. The '*I*' is God, who announces to king Wăn the reasons why he had called him to execute his judgments. Wăn's virtue, not sounded nor emblazoned, might come near to the 不顯 of last paragraph, but Confucius fixes on the 大 to show its shortcoming. It had *some,* though not *large* exhibition. He therefore quotes again from III. iii. Ode VI. st. 6, though away from the original intention of the words. But it does not satisfy him that virtue should be likened even to a *hair.* He therefore finally quotes III. i. Ode I. st. 7, where the imperceptible working of Heaven (載=事), in producing the overthrow of the Yin dynasty, is set forth as without sound or smell. That is his highest conception of the nature and power of virtue.

己謹獨之事推而
言之以馴致乎篤
恭而天下平之盛
又贊其妙至於無
聲無臭而後已焉
蓋舉一篇之要而
約言之其反復丁
寧示人之意至深
切矣學者其可不
盡心乎。

selfishness, and watchful over himself when he is alone, he carries out his description, till by easy steps he brings it to the consummation of the whole kingdom tranquillized by simple and sincere reverentialness.   He farther eulogizes its mysteriousness, till he speaks of it at last as without sound or smell.   He here takes up the sum of his whole Work, and speaks of it in a compendious manner. Most deep and earnest was he in thus going again over his ground, admonishing and instructing men :—shall the learner not do his utmost in the study of the Work ?

INDEXES.

—◆—

INDEX I.

OF SUBJECTS IN THE CONFUCIAN ANALECTS.

Ability, various, of Conf., IX. vi.
Able officers, eight, of Châu, XVIII. xi.
Abroad, when a son may go, IV. xix.
Accomplishments come after duty, I. vi ; blended with solid excellence, VI. xvi.
Achievement of government, the great, XIII. ix.
Acknowledgment of Conf. in estimating himself, VII. xxxii.
Acting heedlessly, against, VII. xxvii.
Actions should always be right, XIV. iv ; of Conf. were lessons and laws, XVII. xix.
Adaptation for government of Zan Yung, &c., VI. i ; of Tsze-lû, &c., VI. vi.
Admiration, Yen Yüan's, of Conf. doctrines, IX. x.
Admonition of Conf. to Tsze-lû, XI. xiv.
Advanced years, improvement difficult in, XVII. xxvi.
Adversity, men are known in times of, IX. xxvii.
Advice against useless expenditure, XI. xiii.
Age, the vice to be guarded against in, XVI. vii.
Aim, the chief, I. xvi.
Aims, of Tsze-lû, Tsäng Hsî, &c., XI. xxv.
An all-pervading unity, the knowledge of, Conf. aim, XV. ii.
Anarchy of Conf. time, III. v.
Ancient rites, how Conf. cleaved to, III. xvii.
Ancients, their slowness to speak, IV. xxii.
Antiquity, Conf. fondness for, VII. xix ; decay of the monuments of, III. ix.
Anxiety of parents, II. vi ; of Conf. about the training of his disciples, V. ii.
Appearances, fair, are suspicious, I. iii ; XVII. xvii.
Appellations for the wife of a prince, XVI. xiv.
Appreciation, what conduct will insure, XV. v.
Approaches of the unlikely, readily met by Conf., VII. xxviii.
Approbation, Conf., of Nan Yung, XI. v.
Aptitude of the *Chün-tsze*, II. xii.
Archery, contention in, III. vii ; a discipline of virtue, III. xvi.
Ardent and cautious disciples, Conf. obliged to be content with, XIII. xxi.
Ardour of Tsze-lû, V. vi.
Art of governing, XII. xiv.
Assent without reformation, a hopeless case, IX. xxiii.
Attachment to Conf. of Yen Yüan, XI. xxiii.
Attainment, different stages of, VI. xviii.
Attainments of Hûi, like those of Conf., VII. x.
Attributes of the true scholar, XIX. i.

Auspicious omens, Conf. gives up hope for want of, IX. viii.
Avenge murder, how Conf. wished to, XIV. xxii.

Bad name, the danger of a, XIX. xx.
Barbarians, how to civilize, IX. xiii.
Becloudings of the mind, XVII. viii.
Bed, manner of Conf. in, X. xvi.
Benefits derived from studying the Odes, XVII. ix.
Benevolence to be exercised with prudence, VI. xxiv ; and wisdom, XII. xxii.
Blind, consideration of Conf. for the, XV. xli.
Boldness, excessive, of Tsze-lû, VII. x.
Burial, Conf. dissatisfaction with Hûi's, XI. x.
Business, every man should mind his own, VIII. xiv ; XIV. xxvii.

Calmness of Conf. in danger, VII. xxii.
Capacities of the superior and inferior man, XV. xxxiii.
Capacity of Mäng Kung-ch'o, XIV. xii.
Careful, about what things Conf. was, VII. xii.
Carriage, Conf. at and in his, X. xvii ; Conf. refuses to sell his, to assist a needless expenditure, XI. vii.
Caution, advantages of, IV. xxiii ; repentance avoided by, I. xiii ; in speaking, XII. iii ; XV. vii.
Ceremonies and music, XI. i ; end of, I. xii ; impropriety in, III. x ; influence of, in government, IV. xiii ; regulated according to their object, III. iv ; secondary and ornamental, III. viii ; vain without virtue, III. iii.
Character(s), admirable, of Tsze-yû, &c., XV. vi ; differences in, owing to habit, XVII. ii ; different, of two dukes, XIV. xvi ; disliked by Conf. and Tsze-kung, XVII. xxiv ; how Conf. dealt with different, XI. xxi ; how to determine, II. x ; lofty, of Shun and Yü, VIII. xviii ; of four disciples, XI. xvii ; of Kung-shû Wän, XIV. xiv ; of Tan-t'âi Mieh-ming, VI. xii ; various elements of, in Conf., VII. xxxvii ; what may be learnt from, IV. xvii.
Characteristics, of perfect virtue, XIII. xix ; of ten disciples, XI. ii.
Claimed, what Conf., VII. xxxiii.
Classes of men, in relation to knowledge, four, XVI. ix ; only two whom practice cannot change, XVII. iii.
Climbing the heavens, equalling Conf. like, XIX. xxv.
Common practices, some indifferent and others not, IX. iii.

INDEX II.

OF PROPER NAMES IN THE CONFUCIAN ANALECTS.

☞ *Names in Italics will be found in their own places in this Index, with additional references.*

Hûi of Liû-hsiâ, posthumous title of Chan Hwo, an officer of Lû, XV. xiii ; XVIII. ii, viii.

Hwan, the three great Houses of Lû, being descended from duke Hwan, are called the descendants of the three Hwan, II. v, note ; XVI. iii.

Hwan, the marquis (or duke) of Ch'î, B. C. 684–643, XIV. xvi, xviii.

Hwan T'ûi, a great officer of Sung, VII. xxii.

Î, a small town or pass on the border of Wei, III. xxiv.

Î, a famous archer in the 22nd century B. C., XIV. vi.

Î-yî, name of a recluse, XVIII. viii.

Î Yin, the minister of T'ang, XII. xxii.

Kan, the master of the band at one of the meals at the court of Lû, XVIII. ix.

Kâo-tsung, honorary epithet of the sovereign Wû-ting, B. C. 1324–1264, XIV. xliii.

Kâo-yâo, Shun's minister of Justice, XII. xxii.

Kung-ch'o, see *Mäng Kung-ch'o*, XIV. xiii.

Kung-hû Hwâ, i. q. *Tsze-hwâ*, a disciple ; see *Ch'ih*, VII. xxxiii ; XI. xxi, xxv.

Kung-ming Chiâ, an officer of Wei, XIV. xiv.

Kung-po Liâo, relative of a marquis of Lû, XIV. xxxviii.

Kung-shan Fû-zâo, a confederate of Yang Ho, XVII. v.

Kung-shû, appellation of a great family in Wei, of which we have Kung-shû Wän (the hon. epithet), XIV. xiv, xix ; and Kung-shû Ch'âo, XIX. xxii.

Kung-wän, honorary posthumous title of Tsze-yü, an officer of Wei, V. xiv.

Kung-yê Ch'ang, the son-in-law of Confucius, V. i.

Kwan-chung, by name Î-wû, chief minister to the marquis (or duke) Hwan of Ch'î, III. xxii ; XIV. x, xvii, xviii.

K'wang, name of a place where Confucius was attacked, IX. v ; XI. xxii.

Lâo, surnamed Ch'in, styled Tsze-k'âi and Tsze-chang, a disciple, IX. vi.

Lî, the name of T'ang, founder of the Shang dynasty, XX. i.

Lî, name of the son of Confucius, XI. vii.

Liâo, one of the bandmasters of Lû, XVIII. ix.

Lin Fang, probably a disciple, a man of Lû, III. iv, vi.

Ling, marquis (or duke) of Wei, XIV. xx ; XV. i.

Lû, the native State of Confucius, II. v, *note ;* III. xxiii ; V. ii ; VI. xxii ; IX. xiv ; XI. xiii ; XIII. vii ; XIV. xv ; XVIII. iv, vi, x.

Mäng, the family, one of the three great families of Lû, XVIII. iii ; XIX. xiv.

Mäng (or Mung), the eastern, name of a mountain, XVI. i.

Mäng Chäng, posthumous title of Mäng-sun (or Chung-sun) Chieh, grandson of Mäng Î, VIII. iv.

Mäng Chih-fan, a brave officer of Lû, VI. xiii.

Mäng Chwang, a head of the Mäng family, before the time of Confucius, XIX. xviii.

Mäng Î, the posthumous name of Ho-chî, head of the Mäng-sun (or Chung-sun) family, a contemporary of Confucius, II. v.

Mäng Kung-ch'o, a head of the Mäng family in the time of Confucius, XIV. xii.

Mäng-sun, named Ho-chî, i. q. Mäng Î, VI. v.

Mäng Wû, the posthumous name of the son of Mäng Î, by name Chih, II. vi ; V. vii.

Mien, a music-master of Lû, XV. xli.

Min, the surname of Min-tsze, XI. xii ; his full name was Min Tsze-ch'ien, VI. vii ; XI. ii, iv, xiii.

Nan-kung Kwo, XVI. vi ; supposed to be the same with Nan Yung.

Nan-tsze, wife of the marquis of Wei, and sister of prince Châo, VI. xxvi.

Nan Yung, a disciple, V. i ; XI. v.

Ning Wû, posthumous title of Ning Yü, an officer of Wei, V. xx.

P'äng, an ancient worthy, VII. i.

Pî, a city of Lû, the stronghold of the Chî family, VI. vii ; XI. xxiv ; XVI. i ; XVII. v.

Pî-kan, an uncle of the tyrant Châu, XVIII. i.

P'î Shän, a minister of the State of Chäng, XIV. ix.

Pien, a city or district of Lû, XIV. x.

Pien, a city in Lû, XIV. xiii.

Po,—the Po family of Ch'î, XIV. x.

Po-î, honorary epithet of a worthy prince of the Shang dynasty, V. xxii ; VII. xiv ; XVI. xii ; XVIII. viii.

Po-kwô and Po-tâ, two eldest sons, probably twins, of the Châu dynasty, XVIII. xi.

Po-niû, the denomination of Tsze-käng, surnamed *Zan*, a disciple, VI. viii ; XI. ii.

Po-yü, the family designation of Confucius's son, XVI. xiii ; XVIII. x.

Shän, name of the disciple *Tsäng-tsze*, IV. xv ; XI. xvii.

Shän Ch'ang, styled Tsze-châu, a disciple, V. x.

Shang, name of the disciple *Tsze-hsiâ*, III. viii ; XI. xv.

Shâo, the music of Shun, III. xxv ; VII. xiii.

Shâo Hû, the minister of duke Hwan of Ch'î's brother, XIV. xvii.

Shâo-lien, a person belonging to a barbarous tribe on the East, who retired from the world, XVIII. viii.

Shâu-yang, a mountain in Shan-hsî, XVI. xii.

Sheh, a district in Ch'û, VII. xviii ; XIII. xxi.

Shih, name of the disciple surnamed Twan-sun, and styled Tsze-chang, XI. xv, xvii.

Shih-män, a frontier pass between Ch'î and Lû, XIV. xli.

Shih-shû, named Yû-chî, an officer of Chäng, XIV. ix.

Shû-ch'î, honorary epithet of a worthy prince of the Shang dynasty, V. xxii ; VII. xiv ; XVI. xii ; XVIII. viii.

Shû-hsiâ and Shû-yê, two brothers, probably twins, of the Châu dynasty, XVIII. xi.

Shun, the ancient sovereign, VI. xxviii ; VIII. xviii, xx ; XII. xxii ; XIV. xlv ; XV. iv ; XX. i.

Shû-sun, gave place to Mäng-sun, as the clan-name of the second of the three great families of Lû, II. v, *note.*

Shû-sun Wu-shû, the honorary epithet of Shû-sun Châu-ch'âu, a chief of the Shû-sun family, XIX. xxiii, xxiv.

Sung, the State, occupied by descendants of the Hsiâ dynasty, III. ix ; VI. xiv.

Sze-mâ Niû, named Käng, a disciple, and brother of Hwan T'ûi, XII. iii, iv, v.

INDEX III.

OF SUBJECTS IN THE GREAT LEARNING.

INDEX IV.

OF PROPER NAMES IN THE GREAT LEARNING.

INDEX V.

OF SUBJECTS IN THE DOCTRINE OF THE MEAN.

Lamentation that the path of the Mean was untrodden, V.

Law to himself, man a, XIII.

Man has the law of the Mean in himself, XIII.

MEAN, only the superior man can follow the, II. 1; the rarity of the practice of the, III; how it was that few were able to practise the, IV; how Shun practised the, VI; men's ignorance of the, shown in their conduct, VII; how Hûi held fast the course of the, VIII; the difficulty of attaining to the, IX; on forcefulness in its relation to the, X; only the sage can come up to the requirements of the, XI. 3; the course of the, reaches far and wide, but yet is secret, XII; common men and women may practise the, XII. 2; orderly advance in the practice of the, XV; Conf. never swerved from the, XXXI. 1.

Middle Kingdom, Conf. fame overspreads the, XXXI. 4.

Nature, definition of, I. 1.

Nine standard rules to be followed in the government of the kingdom, XX. 12, 13, 14, 15.

Odes, quotations from the, XII. 3; XIII. 2; XV. 2; XVI. 4; XVII. 4; XXVI; XXVII. 7; XXIX. 6; XXXIII. 1, 2, 3, 4, 5, 6.

Passions, harmony of the, I. 4.

PATH of duty, definition of, I. 1; may not be left for an instant, I. 2; is not far to seek, XIII.

Praise of Wǎn and Wû, and the duke of Châu, XVIII; XIX.

Preparation necessary to success, XX. 16.

Principles of duty, have their root in the evidenced will of Heaven, I. 1; to be found in the nature of man, XIII.

Progress in the practice of the Mean, XV.

Propriety, the principle of, in relation to the path of duty, XX. 5.

Reciprocity, the law of, XIII. 3, 4.

Righteousness, chiefly exercised in honouring the worthy, XX. 5.

Sacrifices, to spiritual beings, XVI. 3; instituted by Wû and the duke of Châu, XVIII. 2, 3; to Heaven and Earth, XIX. 6; to ancestors, XVIII; XIX.

Sage, a, only can come up to the requirements of the Mean, XI. 3; naturally and easily embodies the right way, XX. 18; the glorious path of, XXVII; Conf. a perfect, XXXI. 1.

Seasons, Confucius compared to the four, XXX. 2, 3.

Secret watchfulness over himself characteristic of the superior man, I. 3.

Self-examination practised by the superior man, XXXIII. 2.

Sincerity, the outgoing of, cannot be repressed, XVI. 5; the way of Heaven, XX. 17, 18; how to be attained, XX. 19; how connected with intelligence, XXI; the most complete, necessary to the full development of the nature, XXII; development of, in those not naturally possessed of it, XXIII; when entire, can foreknow, XXIV; the completion of everything effected by, XXV; the possessor of entire, is the co-equal of Heaven and Earth, and is an infinite and an independent being; a god, XXVI; XXXII. 1.

Singleness necessary to the practice of the relative duties, XX. 8; necessary to the practice of government, XX. 15, 17; of king Wǎn's virtue, XXVI. 10.

Sovereign, a, must not neglect personal and relative duties, XX. 7.

Sovereign-sage, the, described, XXIX.

Spirit, the perfectly sincere man is like a, XXIV.

Spiritual beings, the operation and influence of, XVI; the sovereign-sage presents himself before, without any doubts, XXIX. 3, 4.

Steps in the practice of the Mean, XV.

Superior man is cautious, and watchful over himself, I. 2, 5; only can follow the Mean, II. 2; combines harmony with firmness, X. 5; the way of, is far-reaching and yet secret, XII; distinguished by entire sincerity, XIII. 4; in every variety of situation pursues the Mean, and finds his rule in himself, XIV; pursues his course with determination, XX. 20, 21; endeavours to attain to the glorious path of the sage, XXVII. 6, 7; prefers concealment of his virtue, while the mean man seeks notoriety, XXXIII. 1.

Three hundred rules of ceremony, and three thousand rules of demeanour, XXVII. 3.

Three kings, the founders of the three dynasties, XXIX. 3.

Three things important to a sovereign, XXIX. 1.

Three virtues wherewith the relative duties are practised, XX. 8.

Virtue in its highest degree and influence, XXXIII. 4, 5, 6.

Virtuous course, the commencement and completion of a, XXXIII.

INDEX VI.

OF PROPER NAMES IN THE DOCTRINE OF THE MEAN.

INDEX VII.

OF CHINESE CHARACTERS AND PHRASES;

INTENDED ALSO TO HELP TOWARDS THE FORMATION OF A DICTIONARY AND CONCORDANCE
FOR THE CLASSICS.

A. *stands for Analects*; G.L.T. *for The Great Learning, text*; G.L.C. *for The Great Learning, commentary*; D.M. *for The Doctrine of the Mean. In the references to the Analects, books are separated by a semicolon, and chapters of the same book by a comma.*

THE 1st RADICAL, ——.

一
yi

(1) One, sometimes = a, A., II. ii; IV.vi. 2, xviii. 2; VI. ix, xxii, *et alibi, saepe.* G.L.C., x. 14. D.M., viii, xiii. 4, xxvi. 7, 9. (2) One and the same, D.M., xvii. 3, xx. 9. (3) Singleness = sincerity, D.M., xx. 8, 15. (4) A unity, A., IV. xv. 1; XV. ii. 3. (5) Adverbially = by one effort, D.M., xx. 20. (6) As a verb = to unite in one, A., XIV. xviii. 2. (7) 一人, the One man, a designation of the sovereign, A., XX. i. 5. G.L.C., ix. 3. (8) 一則 … 一則, partly, now… now, A., IV. xxi.

七
ch'i

Seven, A., II. iv. 6; XI. xxv. 5, 7, 10; XIII. xxix; XIV. xl.

三
san

(1) Three, A., I. xi; II. ii, iv. 2; III. ii, *et alibi, saepe.* D.M., xviii. 3, xx. 8, 11, xxvii. 3, xxix. 1. (2) Adverbially = thrice, A., V. xviii. 1; VIII. i; X. xviii. 2. Into three parts, A., VIII. xx. 4. But 三省, A., I. iv, on three points. (3) 三子, ye, disciples, A., III. xxiv; VII. xxiii; IX. xi. 3; XI. x. 3; XVII. iv. 4. (4) 三王, three kings; i. e. the founders of the three great dynasties, D.M., xxix. 3. (5) 三歸, the name of a tower, A., III. xxii. 2. (6) 三飯, A., XVIII. ix. 2 = the band-master at the third meal.

三
san

The 4th tone. Thrice, A., V. xix; XI. v; XVIII. ii.

上
shang

(1) He, she, it, this, that, which is above, with the corresponding plurals, A., I. ii. 1; III. xxvi, *et saepius.* G.L.C., x. 1, 2, 21. D.M., xiv. 3, *et al.* (2) Adverbially = upwards, A., XIV. xxiv, xxxvii. 2 (in these instances some tone it in 2nd tone). D.M., xviii. 3, xxx. 1. (3) 在 … 上, above …, in or on the above of …, A., VI. vii; IX. xvi. D.M., xvi. 3. (4) 上下, above, below, in opposition, applied to heaven and earth, A., VII. xxxiv.

D.M., xii. 3. (5) 草上之風, the grass, when the wind is upon it, A., XII. xix. (6) 上帝, God, the most High God, G.L.C., x. 5. D.M., xix. 6.

上
shang

The 3rd tone. To ascend; proceeding upwards. 以上, A., VI. xix; VII. vii.

下
hsiâ

Anciently, in the 3rd tone. (1) He, she, it, this, that, which is below, with the corresponding plurals; both positive and superlative, A., IX. iii. 2; X. ii. 1; XVI. ix. G.L.C., x. 2, 21. D.M., xiv. 3, xix. 4, xx. 6, 17, xxix. 2. (2) 上下, see on 上. (3) 於 or 于 … 下, under, in or on the beneath of …, A., XII. xxi. 1; XVI. xii. 1. (4) 天下, the world, the kingdom, A., III. xi, xxiv; IV. x, *et al.* G.L.T., 4, 5. G.L.C., viii. 1, ix. 4, x. 1, 4. D.M., i. 4, x. 1, *et al.* (5) Occurs in the proper name 柳下惠, A., XV. xiii; XVIII. ii, viii. 1, 3.

下
hsiâ

A verb, in the 4th tone. (1) To descend, A., III. vii; V. xiv, *et al.* (2) 以下, downwards, A., VI. xix. (3) 下人, to humble one's self to others, A., XII. xx. 5.

丈
chang

丈人, an old man, A., XVIII. vii. 1.

不
pû

Not, *passim.* The simplest negative.

且
ch'ieh

Moreover, and moreover, A., II. iii. 2; VI. iv; VII. xv; VIII. xi, xiii. 3; IX. xi. 3; XI. xxv. 4; XVI. i. 4; XVIII. vi. 3. D.M., xv. 2, xxvii. 7.

世
shih

(1) An age, a generation, A., II. xxiii. 1, 2; VI. xiv; XIII. xii; XVI. i. 8, ii. 1, iii. D.M., xi. 1, xxviii. 1, xxix. 3, 4. (2) To all ages, D.M., xxix. 5. (3) 沒世 = after death, A., XV. xix. G.L.C., iii. 5. This phrase is commonly explained

by 終身—'as long as men live, or to the end of the world.' (4) 絕世, interrupted generations, i.e. families whose line of succession has been broken, A., XX. i. 7. D.M., xx. 14. (5) The world, A., XIV. xxxix. 1; XVIII. vi. 3. G.L.c., xi. 3. (6) 世叔, as a proper name, A., XIV. ix.

丘
ch'iu

(1) A hillock, A., XIX. xxiv. (2) The name of Confucius. Used by himself, A., V. xxvii; VII. xxiii, xxx. 3, xxxiv, *et al.* D.M., xiii. 4. Applied to him contemptuously, A., XIV. xxxiv. 1; XVIII. vi. 2, 3. (3) Part of a double name, A., V. xxiv.

並
ping

Properly written 竝. Together, alongside, A., XIV. xlvii. 2; XIX. xvi. G.L.c., x. 23. D.M., xxx. 3.

THE 2ND RADICAL, 丨.

个
ko

一个人, one man, G.L.c., x. 14.

中
chung

The middle. (1) 中, and 在 or 於… 中, in, in the midst of, A., II. xviii. 2; V. i. 1; VII. xv; X. xvii. 2; XV. xxxi; XVI. i. 4, 7. (2) = the heart, G.L.c., vi. 2. (3) The Mean, A., VI. xxvii; XX. i. 1. D.M., i. 4, 5, ii. 1, 2, *et passim.* (4) 中國, the Middle Kingdom, China, G.L.c., x. 15. D.M., xxxi. 4. (5) 中道, midway, halfway, A., VI. x. (6) 中人, mediocre men, A., VI. xix. (7) 中門, to stand in the middle of the gateway, A., X. iv. 2. (8) 中行, to walk in the Mean, to act entirely right, A., XIII. xxi. Comp. D.M., xxxi. 1. (9) 中牟, the name of a place, A., XVII. vii. 2.

中°
chung

The 4th tone. To hit the mark; hitting the mark; exact, A., XI. xiii. 3; xviii. 2; XIII. iii. 6; XVIII. viii. 3, 4. G.L.c., ix. 2. D.M., i. 4; xx. 18.

THE 3RD RADICAL, 丶.

主
chü

(1) To count as chief or principal, A., I. viii. 2; III. xvi; IX. xxiv; XII. x. (2) A master, president, A., XVI. i. 4.

THE 4TH RADICAL, 丿.

乃
nâi

To be. 無乃…乎 or 與, is it not…? A., VI. i. 3; XIV. xxxiv. 1; XVI. i. 3.

久
chiü

Long, for a long time, A., III. xxiv; IV. ii, *et al.* D.M., iii; xxvi. 2, 4, 5, 8. After a long time, A., V. xvi.

乎
hû

(1) A particle of interrogation. Found alone; preceded by another interrogative particle; preceded by 不亦, A., I. i, iv; II. vii, viii, xvii; VI. xxviii; VII. xiv. 1, 2, *et al., saepe.* G.L.c., iii. 2. (2) A particle

of exclamation, A., VI. vi; VIII. xviii, xix. 1, 2; IX. xx, *et al.* D.M., xvi. 3, xxvii. 2. Followed by 哉, giving emphasis, A., III. xiv; VII. xxix, *et al.* Preceded by 哉, A., XII. xxii. 5; XIV. xlii. 1, 2. (3) Partly interrogatory, partly exclamatory. In this usage it is sometimes preceded by 必也; it is often preceded by 其; and by 矣 immediately before it, A., II. xxi. 2; III. vii, xi; IV. vi. 2; V. xviii. 1, 2, *et al., saepe.* G.L.c., iv. 1, vi. 3. D.M., iii, xvi. 2, xvi. 1, xviii. 1, xix. 1, *et al.* (4) As a preposition, after verbs and adjectives, = *in, to, &c.,* A., I. x. 2; II. xvi; VIII. iv. 3; XVIII. x, *et al., saepe.* G.L.c., ix. 4, x. 6. D.M., i. 2, vii, xiv. 1, 2, 5, *et al., saepe.* (5) Than, in comparison, A., XI. xxv. 2; XVII. xxii. D.M., i. 4, 莫…乎. (6) 惡乎, how, A., IV. v. 2. (7) Observe 焉爾乎, A., VI. xii; and 其庶乎, XI. xviii. 1.

乎
hû
之
chih

The 1st tone. Joined with 於 (*wû*). An exclamation, D.M., xxvi. 10.

(1) Of, A., I. ii. 2, v, xi. 1, *et passim.* G.L.T., 1, 4. G.L.c., iii. 4, *et passim.* D.M., ii. 2, viii, *et passim.* In the construct state, the regent follows the 之, and the regimen precedes. They may be respectively a noun, a phrase, or a larger clause. (2) Him, her, it, them, A., I. vii; XIV. xviii. 1, xx. 2, *et passim.* So in G.L. and D.M. (3) It is often difficult to find the antecedent to 之, and it seems merely to give an active, substantive force to the verb, A., II. xiii; III. xxiii; XV. ii. 3; XVII. ix. 6, *et saepe.* D.M., xx. 18, 19, 20, *et al.* (4) 有之, G.L.c., viii. 2, x. 14, as in (2), but 有之 and 無之 are more like our use of impersonal verbs, G.L.c., ix. 1. A., IV. vi. 3. (5) Where 之 comes in a sentence with 未, it is generally transposed, G.L.T., 7. A., IV. vi. 3, *et al.* So 莫之知避, D.M., vii, *et al.* All negative adverbs seem to exert this attractive force. (6) 之謂, it is called, D.M., i. 1. G.L.c., vi. 1. A., XVI. xii. 2, *et al.* 謂之 is different, and comes under (2). So, 譬之, A., XIX. xxiii. 2. (7) Observe the idiom in A., VI. xii; VII. x. 2; XVIII. i. 1. (Wang Yin-chih explains these cases by taking 之 as = 其.) (8) 如之何, how, A., III. xix; XI. xxi, *et al.* (9) 死之, died with, or for, him, A., XIV. xvii. 1. (10) 末之難, A.,

XIV. xlii. 3. (11) 之＝於, in regard to, G.L.c., viii. 1; but this is doubtful. (12) 之＝是, this, G.L.c., ix. 6. (13) As a verb. To go, or come, to, A., V. xviii. 2; XIII. xix, *et al.* (I do not think that Wang Yin-chih gives this meaning of 之.) (14) Part of a man's name, A., VI. xiii.

乘
shǎng

To mount, to ride; spoken of horses, carriages, boats, A., V. vi; VI. iii. 2; XV. x. 3, xxv.

乘
ch'ǎng

The 3rd tone. (1) A carriage, A., I. v; V. vii. 2, 3, *et al.* G.L.c., x. 22. (2) A team of four horses, A., V. xviii. 2.

THE 5TH RADICAL, 乙.

九
chiǔ

Nine, A., VI. iii. 3; VIII. xx. 3; XVI. x.
九夷, the nine rude tribes on the east, A., IX. xiii. 1. 九經, the nine standard rules of government, D.M., xx. 12, 15.

九
chiǔ

The 1st tone. To collect, A., XIV. xvii. 2.

乞
ch'i

To beg, A., V. xxiii.

也
yě

(1) A particle used at the end of sentences. Sometimes it might be dispensed with, and at others it is felt to be necessary, not only to the euphony and strength of the style, but also to give clearness and definiteness to the meaning, A., I. ii. 1, x. 1; X. i, ii. 1, 2, iii. 1, 2, 3, 4, 5, *et passim.* So also in G.L. and D.M. It closes also the different clauses in a long predicate, where we might use the semicolon in English, D.M., xx. 8, *et al.* (2) It is used after proper names, after some adverbs, and after a clause, in the first member of a sentence, and may be construed as ＝*as to*, the Latin *quoad.* A., I. x. 1, 2, xv. 3; X. 2; XI. xii. 1, xiv. 2, xv, xvi. 1, xvii. 1, 2, 3, 4, *et passim.* So, in G.L. and D.M. In these cases it is followed at the end of the sentence by another particle,—itself, 矣, 焉, 乎.
(3) As correlate of 者, in explanation of terms, G.L.c., iii. 4, vi. 1, x. 7. D.M. xxv. A., III. viii. 3; XII. xvii., *et al., saepe.* (4) At the end of sentences, we find 者也, sometimes preceded by 者, sometimes not. In these cases 者 may often be explained as imparting a participial or adjective power to other characters, but not so always, A., V. xxvi; VI. ii; VII. xix; *et saepe.* So, in G.L. and D.M. (5) 也者 in the first member of a sentence, resuming a previous word, and followed by an explanation or account of it, A., I. ii. 2. D.M., i. 2, 4, *et al., saepe.* (6) 也＝邪, interrogative, A., II. xxiii. 1; V. xvii; VI. xxiv. (7) As a final, it appears often followed by other par-

ticles,—也與; 也已; 也已矣; 也夫; 也哉.

亂
lwan

(1) To confound; unregulated; confusion, insurrection, A., VII. xx; VIII. ii, x, xiii. 2; V. viii. 4; XV. xxvi; XVII. viii. 3, xviii, xxiii; XVIII. vii. 5. 作亂, to raise confusion, or insurrection, A., I. ii. 1. G.L.T., 7. G.L.c., ix. 3. D.M., xx. 14. (2) To put in order; able to govern, A., VIII. xx. 2. (3) The name of a certain part in a musical service, A., VIII. xv.

THE 6TH RADICAL, 亅.

予
yǔ

(1) I, me, my, A., III. viii. 3; VI. xxvi; VII. xxii, *et al.* D.M., vii, xxxiii. 6. (2) Name of a disciple of Confucius, A., V. ix. 1, 2; XVII. xxi. 6.

事
shih

(1) An affair, affairs; business, A., I. v, xiv; III. viii. 2, xv; XV. i. 1, *et al., saepe.* G.L.T., 3. G.L.c., ix. 3, x. 21. D.M., xix. 2; xx. 16. 有事, having troublesome affairs, A., II. viii. Having an affair *with*, A., XVI. i. 2. 從事, to pursue business, A., VIII. v; XVII. i. 2. 執事, to manage business, A., XIII. xix. (2) Labours; the results of labour, A., XII. xxi. 3; XV. ix; XIX. vii. D.M., xx. 14. (3) To serve, A., IX. xv. D.M., xix. 5, *et passim.* (4) 何事於仁 is probably＝何有於仁, what difficulty has he in practising benevolence? so that it may be classed under (1), A., VI. xxviii. 1.

THE 7TH RADICAL, 二.

二
r

(1) Two, A., III. xiv; XII. vii. 3, ix. 3, *et al.* (2) 二三子, see 三 (3).

于
yǔ

In, on, to, from, A., II. iv. 1, xxi. 2; XX. i. 3, *et al.* G.L.c., iii. 2, *et al.* D.M., xvii. 4, *et al.*

云
yǔn

(1) Says, saying, generally in quotations, A., II. xxi. 2; IX. vi. 4; XIV. xliii. 1; XIX. iii; xxiii. 4. 詩云, often in G.L. and D.M. Observe A., XVII. vi. (2) Closing a sentence, and apparently ＝ *so*, A., VII. xviii. 2, xxxiii. It is generally followed by such particles as 爾, 爾已矣.

五
wǔ

Five, D.M., xx. 8. A., II. iv. 1, 4; XX. ii. 1, *et al.*

互
hù

互鄉, the name of a village, A., VII. xxviii.

井
ching

A well, A., VI. xxiv. 1.

亟
chi

The 4th tone. Frequently, A., XVII. i. 2.

亞
yă　亞飯, = the band-master at the second meal, A., XVIII. ix. 2.

THE 8TH RADICAL, 亠.

亡
wang　(1) The dead, D.M., xix. 5, xx. 2. (2) To perish, to go to ruin, D.M., xxiv, xxxiii. 1. (3) To cause to perish, A., VI. viii. (4) Not at home, A., XVII. i. 1. 亡人, a fugitive, G.L.c., x. 13.

亡
wú　Used as 無, not having, being with-●ut, A., III. v; VI. ii; VII. xxv. 3; XI. vi; XII. v. 1; XV. xxv; XVII. xvi. 1; XIX. ii, v.

亢
k'ang　陳亢, a disciple of Confucius, A., XVI. xiii. 1, 5. The same as 子禽.

変
chiáo　(1) Intercourse, to have intercourse with, A., I. iv, vii; V. xvi; XIX. iii. G.L.c., iii. 3. D.M., xx. 8. (2) To give, to bestow, G.L.c., x. 2.

亦
yì　Also; even then, A., I. xii. 2, xiii; III. xxii. 3; V. xi, xxiv, *et saepe*. G.L.c., x. 10, 14, 23. D.M., xii. 2, *et al*. 不亦… 乎, is it not? But the meaning of *also* may often be brought out, A., I. i. 1, 2, 3; XX. ii. 2, *et al*.

享
hsiang　To offer, present, A., X. v. 2.

THE 9TH RADICAL, 人.

人
jên or *zăn*　(1) A man, other men, man, = humanity, A., I. i. 3, iv, v, x. 2, *et passim*. So, in G.L. and D.M. (2) As opposed to 民, meaning officers. D.M., xvii. 4. A., XI. xxiv. 3. (3) 爲人, playing the man, the style of man, A., I. ii; VIII. xix. 1 (爲君). Observe 人君, 人爻, 人子, 人臣, G.L.c., iii. 3. (4) 小人, the mean man, opposed to 君子, *passim.* (5) 聖人, the Sage, A.,VII. xxv; XVI. viii. 1, 2; XIX. xii. 2. D.M., xii. 2, xvii. 1, xx. 18, xxvii. 1, xxix. 3, 4. (6) 門人, disciples, A., IV. xv. 2; VII. xxviii. 1, *et al*. (7) 庶人, all the people, the masses, A., XVI. ii. 3. G.L.T., 6. D.M., xviii. 3. (8) 善人, the good man, A., VII. xxv. 2, *et al*. (9) 成人, the complete man, A., XIV. xiii. (10) 婦人, a woman, A., VIII. xx. 3. (11) 夫人, the designation of the wife of the prince of a State, A., XVI. xiv. (12) Used in designations of officers, like our word man in huntsman. 封人, the border-warden, A., III. xxiv. 行人, the

manager of foreign intercourse, A., XIV. ix.

仁
jên or *zăn*　Is found *passim*. (1) Benevolence. (2) Perfect virtue.

今
chin　(1) Now; the present, modern, time, *saepe*. (2) Used logically, by way of inference, A., XI. xxiii. 4; XVI. i. 8, 12. D.M., xxvi. 9.

仍
jêng or *zăng*　According as, A., XI. xiii. 2.

仕
shih　To take—to be in—office, A.,V. v, xviii; XV. vi. 2; XVII. i. 2; XVIII. vii. 5; XIX. xiii.

他
t'á　Other, another, A., V. xviii. 2; X. xi. 1; XVI. xiii. 3; XIX. xviii, xxiv. G.L.c., x. 14.

仞
jên or *zăn*　A measure of eight cubits, A., XIX. xxiii. 3.

代
tâi　(1) Instead of, alternate, D.M., xxx. 2. (2) A dynasty. 三代, the three dynasties ;—Hsiâ, Shang, and Châu, A., XV. xxiv. 2; III. xiv (二代).

令
ling　(1) To order, A., XIII. vi; XX. ii. 3. G.L.c., ix. 4. (2) Excellent, D.M., xvii. 4. (3) Specious, insinuating, A., I. iii; V. xxiv. (4) 令尹, designation of the chief minister of Ch'û, A., V. xviii. 1.

以
i　(1) To do, A., II. x. 1. Rarely found in this sense. ? A., XI. xxv. 3. (2) By, with, according to, and perhaps other English prepositions, G.L.c., ix. 4. D.M., xviii. 3, xx. 4. A., I. v; II. i, iii. 1, 2, v. 3, *et passim*. To this belong 所以, therefore, that by which; 是以, hence; 何以, whereby ;—which are found *passim*. (3) To take. This use is analogous to the preceding, but the 以 precedes the verb, and is often followed by it without an intervening object, as in 以告, 以與, &c. 以爲, to take to be, to consider, to be considered. Examples occur *passim*. We may refer to it the use of 以 sometimes at the beginning of a sentence, = considering, take it that. (4) To, so as to, G.L.T., 6. G.L.c., x. 18. D.M., x. 3, xxvii. 6, 7; xxix. 3, 4, 6. A., I. v; III. xxiii; VII. 1, 2, *et passim*. Sometimes we might translate in these cases by—*and thereby*. But not so in such cases as 以至, 以上, 以下, &c. (5) It is often found after 可. 可以, may, may be. (6) To use, to be used, A., III. xxi; X. xvi. 2; XIII. xiv; XVIII. x. (7) The following in-

stances are peculiar, G.L.c., iii. 5. D.M., xxxiii. 6. A., XIV. xiv. 2 ; XV. xxx ; XIX. xxv. 2 ; XX. i. 3.

仰 *yang*

To look up to, A., IX. x. 1 ; XIX. xxi.

任 *jên* or *zăn*

The 1st tone. 周任, a man's name, A., XVI. i. 6.

任 *zăn*

(1) An office, a charge, A., VIII. vii. 1, 2. D.M., xx. 14. (2) To repose trust in, A., XVII. vi. 1 ; XX. i. 9.

伐 *fă*

(1) To attack by imperial authority, A., XVI. i. 1, 4, ii. 1. (2) To boast, A., V. xxv. 3 ; VI. xiii ; XIV. ii. 1. (3) To cut down, or out, D.M., xiii. 2. G.L.c., x. 22.

休 *hsiŭ*

休休, simple and upright, G.L.c., x. 14.

伊 *ĭ*

伊伊, the minister of the great T'ang, A., XII. xxii. 6.

伏 *fŭ*

To lie at the bottom, D.M., xxxiii. 2.

仲 *chung*

The second of three ; the second of brothers. Enters very commonly into designations, as in that of Confucius, D.M., ii, xxx. A., XIX. xxii, xxiii, xxiv, xxv. Of others : VI. i. 2, 3, iv ; XI. ii. 2 ; XII. ii ; XIII. ii.—III. xxii. 1, 2, 3 ; XIV. x. 3, xvii. 1, 2, xviii. 1, 2.—V. xvi. —V. xvii ; XV. xiii.—XIV. xiii, xv.— XIV. xx. 2.—XVIII. viii. 1, 4.—XVIII. xi. A surname, A., VI. vi ; XI. xxiii ; XVIII. vi.

伯 *po* or *păi*

The eldest of brothers. Enters into designations, A., XVI. xiii ; XVII. x.— XIV. xxvi ; XV. vi. 2.—II. vi ; V. vii.— V. xxii ; VII. xiv. 2 ; XVI. xii ; XVIII. viii.—VI. i. 2.—XVIII. xi, *bis*.—XIV. xxxviii ; XIX. xxiii. 2.—VIII. i. 1.—VI. viii ; XI. ii. 2. A surname, A., XIV. x. 3. 公伯, see 公.

似 *sze*

Like to, as, A., X. i. 1, iv. 3, 4. D.M., xv. 5.

位 *wei*

Position, status, A., IV. xiv ; X. iv. 3, 5, *et al.* D.M., XIV. 1, 3, *et al.* 天地 位 焉, Heaven and Earth get their places, D.M., i. 5.

佚 *yĭ*

Idleness, A., XVI. v.

佑 *yŭ*

To aid, D.M., xvii. 4.

何 *ho*

(1) What, what kind of, how, A., II. v. 3, vii, xix, xxii. 1 ; XVII. v. 2, ix, xix. 2, 3, *et saepe.* G.L.c., vi. 2. (2) 如何, generally with 之 between. What, im- plying difficulty, indignation, or surprise. Other words are found also between the 如 and 何, and then the phrase = what has . . . to do with . . . ? G.L.c., x. 22.

A., III. xix ; IX. v. 2, xiii. 2, xxiii, *et saepe.* (3) 何 如, what as ? = what do you think of ? how can it be said ? A., I. xv. 1 ; V. iii, xviii. 1, 2, *et saepe.* (4) 何 有, generally, but not always, = will have no difficulty, A., VI. vi ; VII. ii ; XIII. xiii, *et al.* (5) 何 爲, generally = why, A., VI. xxiv ; XIV. xxvi. 2, xxiv, *et al.* 爲 may sometimes be in the 4th tone.

作 *tso*

(1) To make, produce, G.L.c., ix. 3. A., I. ii. 2 ; XI. xiii. 2. To do, A., VII. xxvii. (2) To lay the foundation of, to be a maker or author, A., VII. i. D.M., xviii. 1. (3) To make = to be, A., XIII. xxii. (4) To be begun, A., III. xxiii. (5) To rise, arise, A., IX. ix ; X. xvi. 4, xviii. 2 ; XI. xxv. 7 ; XIV. xl.

佞 *ning*

Glib-tongued, A., V. iv. 1, 2 ; VI. xiv ; XI. xxiv. 4 ; XIV. xxxiv. 1, 2 ; XV. x. 6 ; XVI. iv.

佛 *pĭ*

A surname, A., XVII. vii. 1, 2.

佾 *yĭ*

A row of pantomimes, A., III. i.

使 *shih*

The 4th tone. To send on a mission ; to be commissioned, A., VI. iii. 1 ; XIII. v, xx ; XIV. xxvi. 1, 2.

使 *shih*

The 3rd tone. (1) To cause, G.L.c., iv. D.M., xvi. 3. A., II. xx ; III. xxi ; XVIII. vi. 1, vii. 4, x, *et al.* (2) To employ ; to be employed, G.L.c., x. 23. D.M., xx. 14. A., V. vii. 2, 3, 4 ; VI. vi, vii, *et al.* (3) To treat, behave to, G.L.c., ix. 1, x. 2. A., II. xx ; V. xv. (4) Supposing that, A., VIII. xi.

依 *ĭ*

To accord with, D.M., xi. 3. A., VII. vi. 3.

來 *lăi*

(1) To come, A., I. i. 2, *et al.* (2) To encourage, induce to come, D.M., xx. 12, 13. A., XVI. i. 11, 12 ; XIX. xxv. 4. (3) Coming, future, A., I. xv. 3 ; IX. xxii ; XVIII. v.

侃 *k'an*

Straightforward, bold, 侃侃, A., X. ii. 1 ; XI. xii. 1.

侍 *shih*

To be by, in attendance on, A., V. xxv ; X. xiii. 2 ; XI. xii. 1, xxv. 1 ; XVI. vi.

侗 *t'ung*

Stupid, A., VIII. xvi.

侮 *wŭ*

To contemn ; be contemned, A., XVI. viii. 2 ; XVII. vi.

便 *p'ien*

(1) 便 便, precise, A., X. i. 2. (2) 便辟, with specious airs, A., XVI. iv.

佩 *p'ei*

To wear at the girdle, A., X. vi. 8.

保 *păo*

(1) To watch over, preserve, protect, G.L.c., ix. 2, x. 14. D.M., xvii. 1, 4, xviii. 2, xxvii. 7. (2) To undertake, be security for, A., VII. xxviii. 2.

信
hsin

(1) Sincere, sincerity; to believe, to be believed in, A., I. iv, v, vi, viii. 2, *et saepe.* G.L.c., iii. 3, x. 18.   D.M., xx. 14, 17, xxix. 2, xxxi. 3, xxxiii. 3.   (2) An agreement. A., I. xiii.   (3) Truly, true, A., XII. xi. 3; XIV. xiv. 1.   (4) 信之, to show them sincerity, A., V. xxv. 4.

侯
hâu

諸侯, the princes, a prince, of the kingdom, D.M., xviii. 3, xx. 12, 13, 14. A., XI. xxvii. 12; XIV. xvii. 2, xviii. 2; XVI. ii.

俎
tsû

A vessel used in sacrifice, A., XV. i. 1.

俟
sze

To wait for, D.M., xiv. 4, xxix. 3, 4.   A., X. xiii. 4; XI. xxv. 5.

俱
chü

All of two or more, A., XIV. vi.

俾
pei

To grant, allow, G.L.c., x. 13.

俉
pei

(1) To act contrary to, be insubordinate, G.L.c., x. 1.   D.M., xxvii. 7.   (2) Impropriety, A., VIII. iv. 3.

倚
î

(1) To incline on one side, D.M., x. 5. (2) To depend on, D.M., xxxii. v. 1.   (3) To be close by, attached to, A., XV. v. 3.

倦
chüan

Wearied, A., VII. ii, xxxiii, *et al.*

借
chieh

To lend, A., XV. xxv.

倫
lun

(1) Principles of righteous conduct, D.M., xxviii. 3.   A., XVIII. viii. 3.   (2) Degrees, as of comparison, D.M., xxxiii. 6. (3) The invariable relations of society, A., XVIII. vii. 5.

倩
ch'ien

Charming, A., III. viii. 1.

偃
yen

(1) To bend, or lie down, A., XII. xix. (2) Name of one of Confucius's disciples, A., VI. xii; XVII. iv. 3, 4.

偏
p'ien

Partial, perverse, A., IX. xxx. 1.

假
ko

To approach to, D.M., xxxiii. 4.

偲
sze

偲偲, urgent, A., XIII. xxviii.

偷
t'âu

Mean, A., VIII. ii. 2.

側
châi

By the side, A., VII. ix; XI. xii.

傳
ch'wan

To hand down, as a teacher, A., XIX. xii. 2.   Observe A., I. iv.

傾
ch'ing

Falling, D.M., xvii. 3.

僇
lû

To disgrace, G.L.c., x. 4.

備
pei

All-complete, equal to every service, A., XIII. xxv; XVIII. x.

傷
shang

To hurt, to be hurtfully excessive, A., III. xx; XIX. xxiv. 何傷乎, what harm is there in that? A., XI. xxv. 7.

僕
p'o

To act as driver of a carriage, A., XIII. ix. 1.

僩
ch'ien

Dignified, G.L.c., iii. 4.

僎
hsien

A man's name, A., XIV. xix.

億
yi

To judge, calculate, A., XI. xviii. 2; XIV. xxxiii.

儉
chien

Parsimonious, thrifty, A., III. iv. 3, xxii. 2; VII. xxxv; IX. iii. 1.

僨
fän

To ruin, overturn, G.L.c., ix. 3.

儒
jû or *zû*

A scholar, A., VI. xi.

儀
î

(1) Deportment, G.L.c., ix. 8.   (2) Example, G.L.c., x. 5.   (3) 禮儀, rules of ceremony. 威儀, rules of deportment, D.M., xxvii. 3.   G.L.c., iii. 4.   (4) The name of a place, A., III. xxiv.

優
yû

Abundant, more than adequate, A., XIV. xii; XIX. xiii. 優優, D.M., xxvii. 3.

儺
no

Certain ceremonies to expel evil influences, A., X. x. 2.

儼
yen

儼然, stern, dignified-like, A., XIX. ix; XX. ii. 2.

THE 10TH RADICAL, 儿.

允
yün and *zün*

Sincerely, A., XX. i. 1.

兄
hsiung

An elder brother. 兄弟, elder and younger brothers, often=a brother, A., II. xxi. 2; V. i. 2; XII. v. 1, 4, *et al.* Observe A., XIII. vii. G.L.c., ix. 7, 8. D.M., xiii. 4, xv. 2.

先
hsien

(1) First, former, before, A., II. xiii; X. xiii. 1, *et al.* So in G.L. and D.M. 先王, the ancient kings, A., I. xii. 1, =a former king, A., XVI. i. 4.   (2) Ancestors, D.M., xix. 6.   Compare 先進, A., XI. i.   (3) 先生, elders, II. viii; XIV. xlvii. 2.   (4) To make first or chief, A., VI. xx; XII. xxi. 3; XIII. ii.   (5) 先之, A., XIII. i = to give an example to.

先
hsien

The 4th tone.   To precede.   Quickly, early, G.L.c., x. 2, 15.

克
k'o

(1) To be able, to attain to, G.L.c., i. 1, 3, x. 5.   (2) To subdue, A., XII. i. 1.   (3) The love of superiority, A., XIV. ii.

免 *mien*
(1) To escape, avoid, A., II. iii. 1 ; V. i. 2, *et al.* (2) To dispense with, have done with, A., XVII. xxi. 6.

兕 *hsi*
A rhinoceros, A., XVI. i. 7.

兢 *ching*
兢兢, apprehensive and cautious, A., VIII. iii.

THE 11TH RADICAL, 入.

入 *zŭ*
To enter, G.L.c., x. 10. D.M., xiv. 2. A., III. xv, *et al.* 出, 入, abroad, at home, A., I. vi ; IX. xv. But in A., XIX. xi, 出入 = to pass and repass. 入德, to enter into virtue, become virtuous, D.M., xxxiii. 1.

內 *nêi*
Within, internal, internally, 四海之內, the within of—that which is within—the four seas ; i.e. the kingdom, D.M., xvii. 1, *et al.* Precedes the verb, = internally, A., IV. xvii, *et al.* Observe A., X. xvii. 7. As a verb, G.L.c., x. 7, to make the internal, i. e. of primary importance.

兩 *liang*
The two, D.M., vi. A., III. xxii. 3 ; IX. vii.

THE 12TH RADICAL, 八.

八 *pă*
Eight, A., III. i ; XVIII. xi.

公 *kung*
(1) Public, A., VI. xii. (2) Just, A., XX. i. 9. (3) A duke, dukes, D.M., xviii. 3. A., III. ii, *et al.* It often occurs in connexion with the name and country of the noble spoken of. The title of duke was given to nobles of every order after their death in historical narratives and allusions. *Kung* enters also into double surnames.
公明, A., XIV. xiv. 1, 2 :—公山, XVII. v :—公西, VII. xxxiii ; XI. xxi, xxv :—公冶, A., V. i. 1. Observe 公子, A., XIII. viii.—XIV. xvii, xviii :—公叔, A., XIV. xiv :—公伯, A., XIV. xxxviii ; 公孫, A., XIX. xxii ; 公門, the palace gate, A., X. iv. 1. 於公, in the prince's *temple*, A., X. viii. 8.

六 *liŭ*
Six, A., II. iv. 5, *et al.*

兮 *hsi*
A particle of exclamation. O! how! Much used in poetry, G.L.c., iii. 4. A., III. viii. 1 ; XVIII. v. 1. In G.L.c., x. 13, quoted from the Shû-ching, it appears for 猗.

共 *kung*
Together with, sharing with, A., V. xxv. 2 ; IX. xxix. 1.

共 *kung* c
The 2nd tone. To move towards, A., II. i ; X. xviii. 2.

兵 *ping*
Weapons of war, A., XII. vii. 1, 2 ; XIV. xvii. 2.

其 *ch'i*
The third personal and possessive pronoun, in all genders, numbers, and cases ; the ; that. *Passim.*

具 *chŭ*
(1) 具臣, an ordinary minister, A., XI. xxiii. 4. (2) 具=俱, all, G.L.c., x. 4.

典 *tien*
A classic, a canon. 帝典, G.L.c., i. 3.

兼 *chien*
兼人, A., XI. xxi = to have more than one man's ability.

THE 13TH RADICAL, 冂.

冉 *zan*
A surname. 冉有, A., III. vi ; VII. xiv, *et al.;* the same as 冉求, A., VI. x, *et al.* 冉伯牛, A., XI. ii. 2. Observe 冉子, A., VI. iii ; XIII. xiv.

再 *tsăi*
Repeated, twice, A., V. xix ; X. xi. 1.

冕 *mien*
(1) A cap of full dress or ceremony, A., VIII. xxi ; IX. iii. 1, ix ; X. xvi. 2 ; XV. x. 4. (2) The name of a music-master, A., XV. xli. 1, 2.

THE 14TH RADICAL, 冖.

冠 *kwan*
A cap, A., X. vi. 10 ; XX. ii. 2.

冠 *kwan*
The 4th tone. Capped, i. e. young men about twenty, A., XI. xxv. 7.

冢 *ch'ung*
Great, chief. 冢宰, the prime minister, A., XIV. xliii. 2.

THE 15TH RADICAL, 冫.

冰 *ping*
Ice, G.L.c., x. 22. A., VIII. iii.

冶 *yĕ*
公冶, a double surname, A., V. i.

凝 *ying*
To congeal ; to settle and complete, D.M., xxvii. 5, 道不凝.

THE 16TH RADICAL, 几.

凡 *fan*
All ;—at commencement of clause, D.M., xx. 12, 15, 16, xxxi. 4.

THE 17TH RADICAL, 凵.

凶 *hsiung*
凶服, mourning clothes, A., X. xvi. 3.

出 *ch'u*
(1) To go, or come, forth, A., III. xxiv ; IV. xv, xxii, *et al.* To go beyond. 出家, beyond the family, G.L.c., ix. 1. 出三日, beyond three days, A., X. viii. 8. 出入, see on 入. (2) To put forth, D.M.,

xxxi. 2. A., VIII. iv. 3; IX. viii; XV. xvii. 出納, to give, A., XX. ii. 3. 出之, to put outside, A., X. vi. 3.

THE 18TH RADICAL, 刀.

刀
tâo
A knife, A., XVII. iv. 2.

刃
jên or
zăn
A sharp weapon, D.M., ix.

分
făn
(1) To divide; to be divided, A., VIII. xx. 4; XVI. i. 12. (2) To distinguish, A., XVIII. vii. 1.

切
ch'ieh
(1) To cut, G.L.c., iii. 4. A., I. xv. 2. (2) Earnestly, A., XIX. vi. 切切, earnest, A., XIII. xxviii.

刑
hsing
(1) Punishment, A., II. iii. 1; IV. xi; V. i. 2; XIII. iii. 6. (2) To imitate, D.M., xxxiii. 5.

列
lieh
A rank (as of office), A., XVI. i. 6.

利
li
(1) To sharpen, A., XV. ix. 利口, sharpness of speech, A., XVII. xviii. (2) Gain, profit;—rather in a mean sense, G.L.c., x. 22, 23. A., IV. xii, *et al.* Beneficial arrangements, profitableness, profitable, G.L.c., iii. 5, x. 14, 22, 23. A., IX. i; XX. ii. 2. (3) To get the benefit of, G.L.c., iii. 5. To benefit, A., XX. ii. 2. To desire, A., IV. ii.

別
pieh
The 2nd tone. To discriminate, to differentiate, D.M., xxxi. 1. A., II. vii; XIX. xii. 2.

制
chih
To determine, fix, D.M., xxviii. 2.

到
tâo
Down to, A., XVI. xii.

則
tsê
(1) Then; denoting commonly a logical consequence, and sometimes a sequence of time, *passim.* 然則, so then, well then, A., III. xxii. 3; XI. xv. 3, xxiii. 5. 一則,一則, partly, partly, A., IV. xxi. (2) A rule, a pattern, D.M., xiii. 2. (3) To make a pattern of, to correspond to, A., VIII. xix. 1.

前
ch'ien
(1) Before, the front, G.L.c., x. 2. A., IX. x. 1; X. iii. 2; XV. v. 3. (2) Formerly, A., XVII. iv. 4. (3) Beforehand, D.M., xx. 16, xxiv. (4) Former, G.L.c., iii. 5.

剛
kang
Firm, firmness, D.M., xxxi. 1. A., V. x, *et al.*

割
ko
To cut, A., X. viii. 3; XVII. iv. 2.

創
ch'wang
To make first, A., XIV. ix.

THE 19TH RADICAL, 力.

力
li
Strength, power; opportunity; strongly, strenuously, D.M., xx. 10, xxxi. 4. A., I. vi, vii; VII. 20, *et al.*

功
kung
Achievement, work done, A., VIII. xix. 2; XVII. vi; XX. i. 9. D.M., xx. 9.

加
chiă
To add, A., XIII. ix. 3, 4. To come upon, to affect, IV. vi. To do to, V. xi. To lay upon, X. xiii. 3. To have in addition, XI. xxv. 4.

ᶜ加
chiă
The 3rd tone, supposed to be for 假, if, A., VII. xvi.

助
chû
To help, A., XI. iii.

勃
po
勃如, changing-like, spoken of the countenance, A., X. iii. 1, iv. 3, v. 1.

勇
yung
Valour, physical courage, bold, D.M., xx. 8, 10. A., II. xxiv. 2; XIV. v, xiii, xxx, *et al.*

勉
mien
To exert one's self, use effort, D.M., xiii. 4, xx. 9, 18. A., IX. xv.

動
tung
(1) To move as a neuter verb, D.M., xx. 14, xxix. 5, xxxiii. 3. A., XII. i. 2. 知者動, the wise are active, A., VI. xxi. Observe 動乎四體, D.M., xxiv. (2) To move, excite; as an active verb, D.M., xxiii, xxvi. 6. A., VIII. iv. 3; XV. xxxii. 3. 動干戈, to stir up hostile movements, A., XVI. i. 13.

務
wû
To attend to earnestly, as the chief thing, G.L.c., x. 23. A., I. ii. 2; VI. xx.

勝
shêng
To exceed, surpass, A., VI. xvi; X. viii. 4.

勝
shêng
The 1st tone. To be able for, A., X. v. 1. 勝殘, to transform the violent, A., XIII. xi.

勞
lâo
(1) Toil, toiled, toilsome, A., II. viii; IV. xviii; VIII. ii. 勞之, to toil for the people, A., XIII. i. Compare XIV. viii. (2) Merit, A., V. xxv. 3. (3) To make to labour, A., XIX. x; XX. ii. 1, 2.

勤
ch'in
Laborious, accustomed to toil, A., XVIII. vii. 1.

勸
ch'üan
(1) To encourage, advise, D.M., xx. 14. (2) To rejoice to follow, to exhort one another to good, i. e. to be advised, D.M., xx. 13, xxxiii. 4. A., II. xx.

THE 20TH RADICAL, 勹.

勺
cho
A ladle, a ladleful, D.M., xxvi. 9.

勿
wû
(1) Do not;—prohibitive, D.M., xiii. 3. A., I. viii. 4, *et al.* (2) Not;—negative, or the prohibition indirect, A., VI. iv; XII. ii; XIV. viii.

匏
p'áo

A gourd, A., XVII. vii. 4.

THE 21ST RADICAL, 匕.

化
hwă

To transform; to be transformed. Applied to the operations of Heaven and Earth, and of the sage, D.M., xxii, xxiii, xxx. 3, xxxii. 1, xxxiii. 6.

北
pei

The north, northern, D.M., x. 2, 4. A., II. i.

THE 22ND RADICAL, 匚.

匡
k'wang

(1) To rectify, A., XIV. xviii. 2. (2) The name of a place, A., IX. v. 1; XI. xxii.

匵
tú

A case, a casket, A., IX. xii.

匹
p'i

匹夫, a common man, A., IX. xxv. 匹夫, 匹婦, A., XIV. xviii. 3.

匿
ni

To conceal, A., V. xxiv.

區
ch'ü

Classes, classified, A., XIX. xii. 2.

THE 24TH RADICAL, 十.

十
shih

Ten, G.L.c., vi. 3. A., II. iv. 1, 2, 3, 4, 5, 6, *et al.* Adverbially, at ten times, by ten efforts, D.M., xx. 20.

千
ch'ien

A thousand, G.L.c., iii. 1. D.M., xx. 20. A., I. v, *et al.*

升
shăng

(1) To ascend, go up, A., III. vii, *et al.* (2) To grow up, as grain, A., XVII. xxi. 3.

半
pan

Half, a half, D.M., xi. 2. A., X. vi. 6.

卑
pei

Low, as ground, D.M., xv. 1. 卑宮室, he abased himself to—lived in—a low, mean house, A., VIII. xxi.

卒
tsŭ

The end, completion, A., XIX. xii. 2.

卓
cho

卓爾, uprightly, loftily, A., IX. x. 3.

南
nan

(1) The south, southern, G.L.c., x. 4. D.M., x. 2, 3. A., XIII. xxii. 1. 南面, the face to the south, the position of the sovereign, or of a ruler, A., VI. i. 1; XV. iv. (2) 周南, 召 (read *shâo*) 南, the titles of the two first Books in the Shih-ching, Pt. I, A., XVII. x. (3) A surname, A., V. i. 2; XI. v. 南宮, a double surname, but supposed to be the same man as the preceding, A., XIV. vi. 南子, a duchess of Wei, A., VI. xxvi.

博
po

Extensive, large, extensively, D.M., xxvi. 3, 4, 5, 8, *et al.* A., VI. xxv, *et al.* As a verb, A., IX. ii.

THE 25TH RADICAL, 卜.

卞
pien

The name of a place, A., XIV. xiii. 1.

占
chan

To prognosticate, A., XIII. xxii. 3.

THE 26TH RADICAL, 卩.

危
wei

(1) Lofty, bold, A., XIV. iv. (2) Perilous, tottering, D.M., xx. 14. A., VIII. xiii. 2, *et al.*

卷
chüan

To roll up, A., XV. vi. 2.

卷
ch'üan

The 1st tone. A small plot, D.M., xxvi. 9.

即
chi

To go to, approach, A., XIII. xxix; XIX. ix.

卿
ch'ing

A noble, high officer, A., IX. xv.

THE 27TH RADICAL, 厂.

厚
hău

Thick, A., X. vi. 7. D.M., xxvi. 9. Metaphorically, liberal, generous, in high style, substantial, G.L.T., 7. D.M., xxvi. 3, 4, 5, 8. A., I. ix. 1; XI. x. 1, 2; XV. xiv. 厚往, to depart with liberal presents, D.M., xx. 14. 敦厚, D.M., xxvii. 6.

原
yüan

A surname, A., VI. iii. 3; XIV. xlvi.

原
yüan

The 4th tone. Good, careful people, A., XVII. xiii.

厭
yen

The 4th tone. To dislike, be wearied with, reject, D.M., x. 4, *et al.* A., VI. xxvi; VII. ii, *et al.*

厭
yen

The 3rd tone. 厭然, the appearance of concealing, G.L.c., vi. 2.

厲
li

(1) Dignified, stern, A., VII. xxxvii; XIX. ix, x. (2) To oppress, A., XVII. xii. (3) To keep the clothes on, from above the waist, in crossing a stream, A., XIV. xlii. 2.

THE 28TH RADICAL, 厶.

去
ch'ü

To go away from, leave, A., XVI. iii; XVIII. i, ii.

去
ch'ü

The 3rd tone. To put away, dispense with, D.M., xx. 14. A., III. xvii. 1, *et al.*

參
san

(1) One of three, forming a ternion, D.M., xxii. A., XV. v. 3. (2) Read also *shăn*. The name of one of Confucius's disciples, A., IV. xv; XI. xvii.

THE 29TH RADICAL, 又.

又
yŭ

Moreover, further;—continuing a narrative by the addition of further particulars, G.L.c., II. i. A., III. xxv, *et al.* And so;—a consequence from what precedes, A., IX. vi. 2; XIII. ix. 3; 4.

及
chi

To come to, attain to; coming to, D.M., iv. 1, xxviii. 1, xxxi. 4, xxxiii. 2. A., V. xi, xx, *et al., saepe.* Coming to, = and, but, D.M.,

xii. 2, 4, xviii. 3, xx. 9, xxvi. 2. 比及, by the time it came to, A., XI. xxv. 4, 5.

友
yŭ

(1) A friend, friends, A., I. viii. 3 ; IX. xxiv, *et al.* Combined with 朋, D.M., xiii. 4, xx. 8, 17. A., I. iv, vii, *et al.* Friendship, A., XII. xxiii ; XVI. iv. Friendly with, to make friends of, A., V. xxiv ; XV. ix. (2) Brotherly regard, A., II. xxi. 2.

反
fan

(1) To be, or act, contrary to, G.L.c., ix. 4. D.M., ii. A., XII. xvi. (2) To turn round, on or to, to return, A., IX. xiv ; XVIII. vii. 4. D.M., xiv. 5. 反諸身, to turn round on and examine one's self, D.M., xx. 17. Observe A., VII. viii. 反坫, name of an ancient stand for cups, A., III. xxxii. 3. (3) To repeat, A., VII. xxxi. (4) The 1st tone, for 翻, A., IX. xxx. 1. (5) 之反, a man's name, A., VI. xiii.

取
ch'ŭ

To take, to get, D.M., xx. 4. A., V. ii. Observe V. vi ; VI. xxviii. 3, *et al.* 奚取, what application can it have ? A., III. ii. 色取仁, assuming the appearance of virtue, A., XII. xx. 6.

取
ch'ŭ

The 4th tone. To marry a wife, A., VII. xxx. 3.

叔
shŭ

A father's younger brother. In enumerating brothers, not the oldest nor the youngest. Used in surnames and designations, A., XIV. xx. 2.—XIX. xxiii, xxiv. —XIV. xiv. 1, xix.—V. xxii ; VII. xiv. 2 ; XVI. xii.—XVIII. ix. 2.—XIV. ix ; XVIII. viii. 1, 2.—XVIII. xi, *bis.*

受
shŭu

To receive, D.M., xvii. 4, 5, xviii. 3. A., X. xi. 2, *et al.* To acquiesce in, A., XI. xviii. 2. 受 = to be intrusted with, A., XV. xxxiii.

THE 30TH RADICAL, 口.

口
k'ŏu

The mouth, G.L.c., x. 13. A., XVII. xviii. 口給, smartnesses of speech, A., V. iv. 2.

古
kŭ

Antiquity, G.L.T., 4. D.M., xxviii. 1. A., III. xvi, *et al.* 古者, the ancients; anciently, A., IV. xx ; XVII. xvi. 1.

叩
k'ŏu

(1) To tap, strike, A., XIV. xlvi. (2) To inquire about, A., IX. vii.

召
châo

To call, summon, A., VIII. iii, *et al.* Read *shâo*, in 召南, see 南. 召忽 a name, A., XIV. xvii.

只
chih

These, G.L.c., x. 3.

右
yŭ

The right, on the right hand, G.L.c., x. 2. D.M., xvi. 3. A., X. iii. 2. Observe X. vi. 5.

史
shih

(1) A historiographer, A., XV. xxv. (2) A clerk, a scrivener, A., V. xvi.

司
sze

(1) Always in the phrase 有司, the officers, A., VIII. iv. 3, xx. ii. 3. (2) 司馬, a double surname, A., XII. iii, iv, v. (3) 司敗, the minister of Crime, A., VII. xxx.

可
k'ŏ

May, *passim.* As in English, the *may* may represent possibility, ability, liberty, or moral power, so with the character 可. It is found continually in the combination 可以 = *may* (seldom, if ever, *can*), where we cannot assign much distinctive force to the 以. 可也 is concessive, but does not indicate entire approval, A., I. xv. 1 ; II. xxii ; VI. i. 2, *et al.* 可矣, however, is more concessive, A., V. xix ; VII. xxv. 1, 2, *et al.* Observe A., XIV. xxii. 5 ; XVIII. viii. 5 ; XIX. iii.

各
ko

Each, every one, A., IV. vii ; V. xxv. 1 ; IX. xiv ; XI. vii. 2, xxv. 7, 8.

名
ming

(1) Name, names; to name, A., IV. v. 2 ; VIII. xix ; XIII. iii. 2, 5, 7, *et al.* (2) Fame, reputation, D.M., xvii. 2, xviii. 2, xxxi. 4. 成名, A., IX. ii.

合
ho

To unite, assemble; united; a collection, D.M., xv. 2, xxv. 3. A., XIII. viii ; XIV. xvii. 2.

同
t'ung

(1) The same, D.M., xxviii. 3. A., III. xvi, *et al.* Together with, A., XIV. xix. As a verb, to be together in, to share, G.L.c., x. 15, xx. 14. (2) Applied to a certain imperial audience, A., XI. xxv. 6, 12.

后
hâu

(1) Sovereign, a sovereign, A., III. xxi ; XX. i. 3. (2) Used throughout the G.L. for 後, afterwards.

吉
chî

Fortunate. 吉月, the first day of the month, A., X. vi. 11.

君
chŭn

A ruler, a sovereign, *passim.* 君臣, Ruler and minister, the relation between, *saepe.* 君夫人, 小君, designations of the wife of the prince of a State, A., XVI. xiv. 君子, see on 子. 人君, &c., G.L.c., iii. 3. See 人.

吝
lin

Niggardly, stingy, A., VIII. xi ; XX. ii. 3.

否
fâu

A negation, not, G.L.T., 7. 否 = to do wrong, A., VI. xxvi.

吳
wû

The name of a State, A., VII. xxx. 2.

吾
wû

I, *passim.* In a few cases = *my.* Very rarely plural. Almost always in the nominative.

告
kâo

To tell, report, announce to, A., I. xv. 3 ; II. v. 2 ; XIV. xxii. 2, 3, 4, 5. **告者**, the reporters, A., XIV. xiv. 2.

告
kû

To inform respectfully, A., III. xvii. 1 ; XII. xxiii.

味
wei

Taste, flavours, A., VII. xiii. D.M., iv. 2. G.L.c., vii. 2.

周
châu

(1) Catholic, A., II. xiv. (2) Explained by **至**, A., XX. i. 5. (3) To assist, give charity to, synonymous with **賙**, A., VI. iii. 2. (4) Name of the Châu dynasty or of its original seat, *saepe*. **周公**, the duke of Châu, *saepe*. **周任**, a man's name, A., XVI. i. 6. **周南**, one of the Books of the Shih-ching, XVII. x. 1.

呼
hû

鳴呼, alas! A., III. vi. 1.

命
ming

(1) To order, direct ; what is appointed, spoken of what Heaven appoints,—the throne, our nature, and generally, G.L.c., i. 2, ii. 3, x. 5, 11. D.M., i. 1, xiv. 4, *et al.* A., II. iv. 4 ; VI. ii, viii ; IX. i, *et al.* (2) Spoken of a sovereign's ordering, a commission, A., VIII. vi ; X. iii. 4, xiii. 4 ; XIII. xx. 1 ; XVI. ii. 1 ; XX. i. 2. (3) Life. **致命**, to devote life, A., XIV. xiii. 2 ; XIX. i. (4) Government notifications, A., XIV. ix. (5) Messages between host and guest. **將命**, to convey such messages, A., XIV. xlvii. 1 ; XVII. xx.

命
ming

Used for **慢**, *man*. Disrespectful, G.L.c., x. 16.

和
ho

Harmony, harmonious ; natural ease, affable, D.M., i. 4, 5, x. 5, xv. 2. A., I. xii. 1, 2 ; XIII. xxiii ; XVI. i. 10 ; XIX. xxv. 4.

和
ho

The 4th tone. To accompany in singing, A., VII. xxxi.

咎
chiû

To blame, A., III. xxi. 2.

哂
shăn

To smile at, A., XI. xxv. 4, 8, 9.

咨
tsze

Ho! Oh! A., XX. i. 1.

哀
âi

(1) Sorrow, sorrowful, to feel sorry, G.L.c., viii. 1. D.M., i. 4. A., III. xxvi, *et al.* (2) Honorary epithet of a duke of Lû, D.M., xx. 1. A., II. xix, *et al.*

哉
tsâi

A particle of exclamation, expressing admiration or surprise. (1) It is often at the end of sentences, G.L.c., x. 14. D.M., xxvii. 3. A., III. xxii. 1, *et al.* (2) It is often used at the close of the first clause of a sentence, the subject exclaimed about following, D.M., x. 5, xxvii. 1. A., III. iv. 2 ; V. ii, *et al.* (3) It often closes an interrogative sentence, being preceded by **何, 焉, 乎**, and other interrogative particles, though the **乎** is itself sometimes more exclamatory than interrogative, A., II. x. 4, xxii ; VIII. xv ; IX. vii, *et al.*

哲
chi

Wise, prudent, D.M., xxvii. 7.

唐
t'ang

(1) **唐棣**, a kind of tree, A., IX. xxx. 1. (2) A designation of the emperor Yâo, A., VIII. xx. 2.

哭
k'û

To wail, A., VII. ix. 2 ; XI. ix. 1 (bewail).

唯
wei

Only, *saepe*. It stands at the beginning of the sentence or clause to which it belongs, such instances as A., II. vi ; D.M., xxxiii. 2, being only apparent exceptions. Observe A., VII. xxviii. 2, where Chû thinks that before and after **唯** portions of text must be lost.

唯
wei

The 3rd tone. Yes, A., IV. xv. 1.

問
wăn

(1) To ask, to ask about, to investigate ; a question, *passim.* (2) To inquire for, to visit, A., VI. viii ; VIII. iv. 1. To send a complimentary inquiry, A., X. xi. 1.

啟
ch'i

To open out ; to uncover, A., VII. viii ; VIII. iii.

啻
ch'i

Simply, only, G.L.c., x. 14.

喻
yü

(1) To instruct, G.L.c., ix. 4. (2) To understand, be conversant with, A., IV. xvi.

善
shan

(1) Good, the good :—in both numbers, and all persons, *passim.* (2) Skilful ; ability, D.M., xix. 2. A., V. xvi ; VII. xxxi, *et al.* (3) As a verb, to consider, or make, good, G.L.c., x. 23. A., XV. ix.

嗅
hsiû

To smell, A., X. xviii. 2.

商
shang

Name of Tsze-hsiâ, A., III. viii. 5 ; XI. xv. 1 ; XII. v. 2.

喜
hsi

Joy, joyful, to be joyful, D.M., i. 4. A., IV. xxi ; V. vi, xviii. 1 ; XVI. xiii. 5 ; XIX. xix.

喟
wei

喟然, sighingly, A., IX. x. 1 ; XI. xxv. 7.

喪
sang

To mourn, mourning ; mourning clothes, D.M., xviii. 3. A., III. iv. 3, xxvi ; VII. ix. 1 ; XVII. xxi. 1, 5, 6, *et al.*

喪
sang

The 4th tone. (1) To lose, G.L.c., x. 5. To lose office, a throne, A., III. xxiv ; XIV. xx. 1, 2. (2) To let be lost, to destroy, A., IX. v. 3 ; XI. viii ; XIII. xv. 4, 5.

喧
hsüan

喧兮, how distinguished ! G.L.c., iii. 4.

嘉
chiâ

Admirable, D.M., xvii. 4. To commend, honour, D.M., xx. 14. A., XIX. iii.

嗚
wŭ　嗚呼, alas! A., III. vi.

嗆
ăn　Coarse, rude, A., XI. xvii. 4.

嘗
ch'ang　(1) To taste, A., X. xi. 2, xiii. 1. (2) Name of the autumnal sacrifice, D.M., xix. 6. (3) Indicates the present complete and past tenses, being often joined with 未, A., III. xxiv; VIII. v, *et al.*

器
ch'i　(1) A vessel, a tool, D.M., xix. 3. A., XV. ix. Metaphorically, A., II. xii; V. iii. (2) Capacity, calibre, A., III. xxii. 1. (3) To use according to capacity, A., XIII. xxv.

噫
i　An exclamation of grief, of contempt, A., XI. viii; XIX. xii. 2; XIII. xx. 4.

嚴
yen　Severe, dignified, G.L.c., vi. 3.

THE 31ST RADICAL, 口.

四
sze　Four, *saepe.* Four things which Confucius taught, and four others from which he was free, A., VII. xxiv; IX. iv. 四國, the four parts of the State, G.L.c., ix. 8. 四夷, the barbarians on the four sides of the kingdom, G.L.c., x. 15. 四體, the four limbs, D.M., xxiv. A., XVIII. vii. 四飯, A., XVIII. ix. 2.

因
yin　(1) As a preposition. Because of, taking occasion from, D.M., xvii. 3. A., XX. ii. 2. (2) As a verb. To follow, succeed to, A., II. xxiii. 2 ; XI. xxv. 4. To rely on, A., I. xiii.

回
hŭi　The name of Confucius's favourite disciple, *saepe.* 顏回, A., VI. ii ; XI. vi.

困
k'wăn　(1) Distressed, reduced to straits, D.M., xx. 9. A., XX. i. 1. 酒困, overcome with wine, A., IX. xv. (2) Stupidity and the feeling of it. D.M., xx. 16. A., XVI. ix.

固
kŭ　(1) Firm, strong, A., I. viii ; XVI. i. 8. ? XV. i. 3. (2) Obstinate, obstinacy, A., IX. iv ; XIV. xxxiv. 2. (3) Mean, niggardly, A., VII. xxxv. (4) Firmly, D.M., xx. 18. (5) Certainly, indeed, D.M., xxxii. 3. A., IX. vi. 2 ; XIV. xxxviii. 1; XV. i. 3, xli. 3.

圃
pŭ　A gardener, A., XIII. iv. 1.

圉
yŭ　The name of an officer, A., XIV. xx. 2.

國
kwo　A State, *passim.* 中國, the Middle Kingdom, D.M., xxvii. 4, *et al.* Only in this phrase is the term used for the whole kingdom. 千乘之國, one of the largest States, equipping 1,000 chariots, A., I. v, *et al.* 爲國, to administer a State, A., IV. xiii.

圖
t'ŭ　(1) To think, imagine, A., VII. xiii. (2) A map or scheme, A., IX. viii.

THE 32ND RADICAL, 土.

土
t'ŭ　(1) The ground, ground, earth, D.M., xxvi. 9. A., V. ix. 1. (2) 水土, water and land, D.M., xxx. 1. (3) 土 = comfort, A., IV. xi.

圭
kwei　A precious stone, differently shaped, used as a badge of authority, A., X. v. 1; XI. v. 白圭, see the Shih, III. iii. 2, st. 5.

地
ti　(1) The earth, the ground, D.M., xxx. 3. A., IX. xviii; XIX. xxii. 2. (2) Any particular country, A., XIV. xxxix. 2. (3) Throughout the Doctrine of the Mean, it occurs constantly as the correlative of 天, heaven, the phrase 天地 being now the component parts, and now the great Powers, of the universe.

在
tsâi　(1) To be in, to consist in, depend on, the where and wherein following, *passim.* (2) To be present, G.L.c., vii. 2. A., XI. xxi. (3) To be in life, A., I. xi ; IV. xix. 在 is followed not unfrequently by 上, 中, 内, with words intervening. Observe A., XIX. xxii. 2 ; XX. i. 5.

均
chŭn　Level. An equally adjusted state of society, A., XVI. i. 10. As a verb, to adjust, keep in order, D.M., ix.

坐
tso　To sit, A., X. vii. 2, ix. 1, *et al.*

坦
t'an　Broad and level. Satisfied, A., VII. xxxvi.

坫
tien　An earthen stand for cups. 反坫, A., III. xxii. 3.

城
ch'ăng　In the name of a place. 武城, A., VI. xii ; XVII. iv.

域
yŭ　Boundaries, territory, A., XVI. i. 4.

執
chih　To hold, keep hold of, D.M., vi, xiii. 2, *et al.* A., VI. viii ; VII. xi, *et al.* 執禮, to maintain the rules of propriety, A., VII. xvii. 執御, to practise charioteering, A., IX. ii. 2. 執事, to manage business, A., XIII. xix. 執國命, to grasp the government of a State, A., XVI. ii.

培
pei　To nourish, D.M., xvii. 3.

堂
t'ang　(1) The hall or principal apartment, ascended to by steps, A., III. ii ; X. iv. 4 ; XI. xiv. 2. (2) 堂堂, exuberant; an imposing manner, A., XIX. xvi.

堅
chien　Firm, hard, A., IX. x. 1 ; XVII. vii. 3.

堪
k'an

To be able, to endure, A., VI. ix.

堯
yáo

The name of an ancient sovereign, A., VIII. xix ; XX. i. 1. Coupled with Shun, G.L., ix. 4, *et al.*

報
páo

To revenge, recompense, return, D.M., x. 3, xx. 13. A., XIV. xxxvi. 1, 2, 3.

塗
t'û

A road, the way, D.M., xi. 2. A., XVII. i. 1, xiv.

墜
ch'ui

To fall, be fallen, A., XIX. xxii. 2.

塞
sâi

(1) To shut up, as a screen, A., III. xxii. 3. (2) An unemployed condition, D.M., x. 5.

壞
hwâi

To be ruined, A., XVII. xxi. 2.

壤
zang

A man's name, A., XIV. xlvi.

THE 33RD RADICAL, 士.

士
shih

(1) A scholar, A., IV. ix ; VIII. vii, *et al.* (2) An officer, D.M., xviii. 3, xx. 13, 14. A., XIII. xx. 1, xxviii, *et al.* In many cases these two meanings are united, A., XII. xx ; XV. viii, *et al.* (3) A gillie. 執鞭之士, a groom, A., VII. xi. (4) 士師, criminal judge, A., XVIII. ii ; XIX. xix.

壯
ch'wang

Vigorous, in manhood, A., XVI. vii.

壹
yi

Once, D.M., xviii. 2. 壹是, one and all, G.L.T., 6.

壽
shâu

Longevity, long-lived, D.M., xvii. 2. A., VI. xxi.

THE 35TH RADICAL, 夂.

夏
hsiâ

(1) Name of an ancient dynasty, D.M., xxviii. 5. A., II. xxiii. 2, *et al.* 夏后氏, the founder of the Hsiâ dynasty, A., III. xxi. 1. (2) Great. 諸夏, a name of China, A., III. v. (3) Used in a man's name, A., XVIII. xi. (4) 子夏, the designation of one of Confucius's disciples, A., I. vii, *et al., saepe.*

THE 36TH RADICAL, 夕.

夕
hsi

The evening, A., IV. viii.

外
wâi

(1) Without, beyond, external, G.L.c., vi. 2. D.M., xiv. 1, xxv. 3. (2) As a verb. To make secondary, G.L.c., x. 8.

夙
sû

Early. ? = from day to day, D.M., xxix. 6.

多
to

Many, much, A., II. xviii. 2 ; IV. xii ; VII. xxvii, *et al.* ? XIX. xxiv. 1, where 多=祇, only ; and D.M., xxvi. 9, where it = a little.

夜
yê

(1) Night, A., IX. xvi ; XV. xxx. D.M., xxix. 6. (2) 叔夜, a man's designation, A., XVIII. xi.

夢
măng

To dream, A., VII. v.

THE 37TH RADICAL, 大.

大
tâ

Great ; greatly, *passim.* 大夫, see 夫.

大
t'âi

In 4th tone, with aspirate. Excessive, A., VI. i. 3. Used for 太, D.M., xviii.

天
t'ien

Heaven. (1) The material heaven, or firmament, D.M., xii. 3, xxvi. 5, *et al.* A., XIX. xxv. 3. (2) More commonly, the character stands for the supreme, governing Power, the author of man's nature, and orderer of his lot, G.L.c., i. 2. D.M., i. 1, xiv. 3, xvii. 3, 4, xx. 7, 18, xxxii. 1, 2, 3, xxxiii. 6. (上天), A., II. iv. 4 ; III. xiii. 2, xxiv ; V. xii ; VI. xxvi ; VII. xxii ; VIII. xix. 1 ; IX. v. 3, vi. 2, xi. 2 ; XI. viii ; XII. v. 3 ; XIV. xxxvii. 2 ; XVI. viii. 1, 2 ; XVII. xix. 3 ; XX. i. 1. (3) In the Doctrine of the Mean (not in the Analects), we find the phrase 天地 of very frequent occurrence, sometimes denoting the material heavens and earth, but more frequently as a dualisation of nature, producing, transforming, completing, i. 5, xii. 2, 4, xxii, *et al.* (4) 天子, a designation of the sovereign, G.L.T., 6. D.M., xvii. 1, *et al.* A., III. ii ; XVI. ii. (5) 天下, see 下.

太
t'âi

(1) 太王, one of the ancestors of the Châu dynasty, D.M., xviii. 2, 3. (2) 太宰, title of a high officer, A., IX. vi. 1, 3. (3) 太師, Grand music-master, A., III. xxiii ; VIII. xv ; XVIII. ix. (4) 太甲, the title of a Book of the Shû-ching, G.L.c., i. 2.

夫
fú

(1) An individual man. 匹夫, a common man, A., IX. xxv ; XIV. xviii. 3. With 鄙 = a fellow, A., IX. vii ; XVII. xv. 夫婦, husband and wife, D.M., xii. 2, 4, xx. 8. A., XIV. xviii. 3. (2) 大夫, a general name, applicable to all the ministers or great officers at a court, D.M., xviii. 3. A., V. xviii. 2 ; X. ii. 1, *et al., saepe.* (3) 夫人, title of the wife of the prince of a State, A., XVI. xiv. (4) 夫子, master, my, our, your master, applied often to Confucius, but not confined to him, A., I. x. 1, 2 ; III. xxiv ; IV. xv. 2, *et al., saepe.*

夫
fú

The 2nd tone. (1) An initial particle, which may generally be rendered by *now*, D.M., xix. 2, xxxii. 1. A., VI. xxviii. 2 ;

XI. x. 3, xiii. 3, *et al.*, *saepe*. (2) A final particle, with exclamatory force, D.M., v, xvi. 5. A., VI. viii, xxv ; VII. x. 1 ; VIII. iii. 1, *et al.*, *saepe*. (3) Neither at the beginning nor end of sentences and clauses, as a kind of demonstrative, D.M., xxvi. 9. A., XI. ix. 3, xxiv. 2, 4, *et al.* (4) After some verbs, as a preposition, between them and their regimen, G.L.c., x. 16. A., XVI. i. 9 ; XVII. ix. 1, xxi. 4.

夭
yâo

夭夭, exuberant in foliage, G.L.c., ix. 6. 夭夭如, looking pleased, A., VII. iv.

失
shih

To lose, to fail of or in, G.L.c., x. 5, 11, 18. D.M., viii, xiv. 5, xviii. 2. A., I. xiii ; IV. xxii, *et al.*, *saepe*.

夷
i

(1) To squat upon the heels, A., XIV. xlvi. (2) A name denoting rude and barbarous tribes, appropriate to those on the east of China, of whom there were nine tribes, A., IX. xiii. 1. It is generally associated with 狄, A., III. v ; XIII. xix. D.M., xiv. 2. 四夷, G.L.c., x. 15. (3) As a posthumous title, A., V. xxii, *et al.* (4) Part of a name, A., XVIII. viii. 1, 4.

奏
tsâu

To perform, as music, D.M., xix. 5. To present, approach (but the meaning is doubtful), D.M., xxxiii. 4.

奔
pân

To run away, flee, A., VI. xiii.

奚
hsi

Why, how, what, A., II. xxi. 1, 2 ; III. ii ; VII. xviii. 2 ; XI. xiv ; XIII. iii. 1, 3, v ; XIV. xx. 1, 2. 奚自, from whom, A., XIV. xli.

奪
t'o

Rapine ; to take away, carry off, G.L.c., x. 8. A., IX. xxv ; XIV. x. 3 ; XVII. xviii. 不可奪, cannot be carried from his principles, A., VIII. vi.

奢
ch'ê

Wasteful, extravagant, A., III. iv. 3 ; VII. xxxv.

奥
âo

The south-west corner of an apartment, A., III. xiii. 1.

臭
âo

A name, A., XIV. vi. The form in the text is incorrect.

THE 38TH RADICAL, 女.

女
nü

女子, girls, = concubines, A., XVII. xxv. 女樂, female musicians, A., XVIII. iv.

女
jû or zû

For 汝. You, both nominative and objective, A., II. xvii, *et al.*

奴
nü

A slave, A., XVIII. i.

好
hâo

Good, lovely, goodness, excellence, G.L.c., vi. 1. A., XIX. xxiii. 2.

好
hâo

The 3rd tone. To love, like, be fond of, *passim*. 兩君之好, the loving, i. e. the friendly meeting, of two princes, A., III. xxii. 3.

如
jû or zû

(1) As, and may often be rendered as when, as if, *passim*. We find 如此, such, so, with the synonyms 如斯 and 如是. 不如, not as, but sometimes meaning—there is nothing like, the best thing is to. We have also 辟如 and 譬如, may be compared to. (2) If. In this sense it is often followed by 有. (3) 如何 and 何如, see on 何. (4) After adjectives, it = like, or our termination *ly*. See many instances in the A., Bk. X. (5) 如 = or, A., XI.xxv. 10. (6) Observe 如其仁, A., XIV. xvii. 2.

妖
yâo

Prodigies, inauspicious appearances of plants, &c., D.M., xxiv.

妻
ts'i

A wife, D.M., xv. 2. A., XVI. xiv.

妻
ch'i

In 3rd tone. To give to one to wife, A., V. i. 1, 2 ; XI. v.

始
shih

The beginning ; at first ; to begin, G.L.T., 3. D.M., xxv. 2. A., I. xv. 3 ; III. viii. 3, xxiii ; V. ix. 2 ; VIII. xv ; XIII. viii ; XIX. xii. 2.

姓
hsing

A surname, the patronymic of a family or clan, A., VII. xxx. 2. 百姓, a designation for the mass of the people, D.M., xx. 13, 14. A., XII. ix. 4 ; XIV. xlv ; XX. i. 5.

威
wei

Majestic, A., VII. xxxvii ; XX. ii. 1, 2. To fear ; to be feared, D.M., xxxiii. 4. A., I. viii. 1. 威儀, see 儀, G.L.c., iii. 4. D.M., xxvii. 3.

婦
fû

夫婦, husband and wife, D.M., xii. 2, 4, xx. 8. A., XIV. xviii. 3. 婦人, a woman, A., VIII. xx. 3.

媚
mei

To flatter, pay court to, A., III. xiii. 1.

媢
mâo

To be jealous, G.L.c., x. 14.

嫁
chiâ

To marry, be married to. Spoken of the woman, G.L.c., ix. 2.

THE 39TH RADICAL, 子.

子
tsze

(1) A son, G.L.c., viii. 2, ix. 2, 8. D.M., xiii. 4, xv. 2, xviii. 1, 3, xx. 1. A., III. xv ; VI. iv (= a calf), *et al.*, *saepe*. But in some instances, it is as much *child* as *son*. (2) A daughter, a young woman, G.L.c., ix. 6. A., V. i. 1, 2 ; VII. xxx. 2 (a play on the term) ; XI. v. 女子,

A., XVII. xxv.   (3) As a verb, to treat as children, D.M., xx. 12, 13.   (4) Every-where applied to Confucius, = the Master. (5) It follows surnames and honorary epithets.   (6) It enters often into the designations of the disciples of Confucius, and others.   (7) In conversations = you, Sir, the gentlemen. 二三子, ye, my disciples, my friends.   (8) Chiefs, officers, A., XIV. xxii. 3, 4, 5.   (9) A title of nobility, count, viscount, A., XVIII. i. (10) 子孫, descendants, *saepe*.   (11) 君 子, *passim*.   Generally, the superior man, with a moral and intellectual significance of varying degree.   Often = a ruler.   Sometimes, the highest style of man, the Sage.   (12) 天子, the sove-reign; see on 天. 弟子, see 弟. 人子, see 人. 小子, see 小. 童 子, see 童.

孔
k'ung
(1) Very, D.M., xxxiii. 2.   (2) A sur-name.   That of Confucius. 孔子, *passim*. 孔氏, A., XIV. xli, xlii. 1. 孔文子, A., V. xiv.

存
s'un
To be preserved, to be alive, to con-tinue, to be, D.M., xix. 5, xxviii. 5.   A., VIII. iv. 3.

孝
hsiâo
Filial piety, to be filial, A., II. v. 1, 2, vi, vii, viii, xx, xxi. 2; VIII. xxi; XIII. xx. 2, *et al.*, *saepe*.

孟
măng
(1) The eldest, A., VII. xxx. 2.   (2) A surname, that of one of *the three great families* of Lû, A., II. v. 1, 2 (孟孫), vi ; V. vii; VI. xiii; XIV. xii; XVIII. iii ; XIX. xviii, xix.   G.L.c., x. 22.

孤
kû
(1) Fatherless, an orphan, G.L.c., x. 1. A., VIII. vi.   (2) Solitary, alone, A., IV. xxv.

季
chi
The youngest.   Used in designations, A., XVIII. xi.   A surname, that of one of the three families of Lû, A., III. i (季氏), *et al.*; XIV. xxxviii; XVI. i. 13 (季孫); XVIII. iii (季). 季 康子, A., II. xx; VI. vi. 1 ; XI. vi ; XII. xvii, xviii, xix. 季子然, A., XI. xxiii. 季桓子, A., XVIII. iv. The disciple Tsze-lû was a 季, A., V. xxv, *et al.*

孫
sun
(1) A grandson. 子孫, descendants, G.L.c., x. 14.   D.M., xvii. 1, xviii. 2. A., XVI. i. 8, iii.   (2) Used in double surnames, A., XIX. xxiii, xxiv.—XIV. xxxviii.—XVI. i. 13.—II. v. 2.—III. xiii ; XIV. xx. 2.—XIX. xxii.

孫
sun
The 3rd tone, used for 遜.   Com-plaisant, docile, obedient, A., VII. xxxv ; XIV. iv, *et al.*

孰
shû
Who? which? D.M., xxxii. 3.   A., III. xv, xxii. 3, *et al.*, *saepe*.   What? A., III. i.

學
hsio
To learn; learned; learning, G.L.T., 1. D.M., xx. 9, 10, 19, 20.   A., I. i. 1, vi, vii, viii, xiv, *et al.*, *saepe*.

孺
jü or zû
A surname, A., XVII. xx.

孽
nieh
Unlucky omens of prodigious animals, D.M., xxiv.

THE 40TH RADICAL, 宀.

守
shâu
To keep, to maintain, D.M., vii.   A., VIII. xiii. 1; XV. xxxii. 1, 2, 3 ; XVI. i. 12.

安
ân
(1) A condition of entire tranquillity, G.L.T., 2.   A., XVI. i. 10.   (2) Without any effort, D.M., xx. 9.   A., VII. xxxvii. (3) Comfort, at ease, A., I. xiv ; XVII. xxi. 4, 5.   (4) To rest in, A., II. x. 3; IV. ii.   (5) To give rest to, A., V. xxv. 4 ; XIV. xlv ; XVI. i. 11.   (6) An inter-rogative, = how? where? A., XI. xxv. 10.

宋
sung
The name of a State, D.M., xxviii. 5. A., III. ix ; VI. xiv.

完
wan
Complete, A., XIII. viii.

宏
hung
To enlarge, A., XV. xxviii.

宗
tsung
(1) Honourable, pertaining to one's ancestors. 宗廟, the ancestral temple, D.M., xvii. 1, *et al.*   A., X. i. 2, *et al.* 宗器, D.M., xix. 3. 宗族, kindred, A., XIII. xx. 2.   (2) To follow as master, A., I. xiii.   (3) 高宗, an ancient sove-reign, A., XIV. xliii.

官
kwan
An officer of government, generally, D.M., xx. 14.   A., III. xxii. 2 ; XIV. xliii. 2 ; XIX. xxiii. 3 ; XX. i. 6.

定
ting
Determined, settled, G.L.T., 2.   D.M., xx. 16.   A., XVI. vii.   To settle, G.L.c., ix. 3.

宜
î
(1) Right, what is right, D.M., xx. 5, xxv. 3.   (2) Reasonable, to be expected, A., XIX. xxi. 1, 4.   (3) As a verb, to regulate, discharge duty to, G.L.c., ix. 6, 7.   D.M., xv. 2, xvii. 4.

客
k'o
Strangers, guests. 賓客, A., V. vii. 4 ; XV. xx. 2.

宮
kung
A house, A., XIX. xxiii. 2. 宮室, VIII. xxi.

室
shih
(1) An apartment, the inner rooms of a house, D.M., xxxiii. 3.   A., IX. xxx ; XI. xiv. 2, xix.   So, 室家, A., XIX. xxiii. 2.   (2) A family, A., V. vii. 3 ; VI. xii ; XIII. viii.   So 室家, D.M., xv. 2. 公室, the ducal house, A., XVI. iii.   (3) 宮室, a house, A., VIII. xxi.

害
hài

Injury, to injure, G.L.c., x. 23. D.M., xxx. 3. A., II. xvi ; XV. viii.

宰
tsǎi

(1) Governor or commandant of a town, A., V. vii. 3 ; VI. iii. 3, vii, xii ; XI. xxiv ; XIII. xvii. (2) Head minister to a chief, A., XIII. ii. (3) 冢宰, a premier, A., XIV. xliii. (4) The surname of one of Confucius's disciples, A., V. ix, *et al.*

宴
yen

Feasting, A., XVI. v.

家
chiā

(1) The family, G.L.T., 4, 5. G.L.c., viii. 1, 3, ix. 1, 3, 5. 家人, the household, G.L.c., ix. 6. 室家, D.M., xv. 2. (2) A family, the name for the possessions of the chiefs in a State, G.L.c., x. 22, 23. D.M., ix, xx. 11, 12, 15, xxiv. A., III. ii ; V. vii. 3 ; XII. ii, xx. 3, 5, 6 ; XVI. i. 10 ; XVII. xviii ; XIX. xxv. 4. (3) 室家, apartments, A., XIX. xxiii. 2.

容
yung

(1) To bear, admit, A., X. iv. 1. (2) Forbearance, to forbear, G.L., x. 14. D.M., xxxi. 1. A., XX. iii. To command forbearance, D.M., xxvii. 7. (3) Deportment, A., VIII. iv. 3 ; X. vi. 1. 容色, a placid appearance, A., X. v. 2. (4) 從容, easy, unconstrained, D.M., xx. 18. (5) A name, A., V. i. 2 ; XI. v.

宿
sù

(1) To stop over night, A., XIV. xli ; XVIII. vii. 3. To keep over night, A., X. viii. 8 ; XII. xii. 2. (2) Asleep and perching, A., VII. xxvi.

寄
chì

To commit to one's charge, A., VIII. vi.

密
mì

Concentrative, D.M., xxxi. 1.

富
fù

Rich, riches, G.L.c., vi. 4. D.M., xvii. 1, xviii. 2. A., I. xv. 1, *et al.* Metaphorically, A., XII. xxii. 5. To enrich, A., XIII. ix. 3, 4 ; XX. i. 4. Often joined with 貴.

寒
han

Cold, wintry, A., IX. xxvii.

察
ch'ǎ

(1) To examine, to study ; studious, D.M., vi, xxxi. 1. A., II. x. 3, *et al.* To look after, G.L.c., x. 22. (2) To be displayed, D.M., xii. 3, 4.

寡
kwǎ

(1) Few, to make few, G.L.c., x. 19. D.M., xxix. 1. A., II. xviii. 2 ; VIII. v, *et al.* (2) 寡小君, a designation of the wife of the prince of a State, A., XVI. xiv.

寧
ning

After 與 with intervening words, than so and so, it is better to, G.L.c., x. 22. A., III. iv. 3, xiii. 1, *et al.*

寢
ch'in

To sleep, be in bed, A., V. ix ; X. viii. 9, xvi. 1 ; XI. xi. 3 ; XV. xxx. 寢衣, sleeping dress, A., X. vi. 6.

實
shih

(1) Full, A., VIII. v. (2) Fruit, A., IX. xxi. 1. (3) Really, G.L.c., x. 14.

寬
k'wan

Generous, magnanimous, D.M., x. 3, xxxi. 1. A., III. xxvi ; XVII. vi ; XX. i. 9.

審
shǎn

To examine accurately, discriminate, D.M., xx. 19. A., XX. i. 6.

寮
liáo

A name, A., XIV. xxxviii.

寶
páo

Precious ; precious things ; a jewel, G.L.c., x. 12, 13. D.M., xxvi. 9. A., XVII. i. 2.

THE 41ST RADICAL, 寸.

封
fǎng

A boundary or border. 封人, a border-warden, A., III. xxiv.

射
shě

Archery, D.M., xiv. 5. A., III. vii, xvi ; IX. ii. 2 ; XIV. vi. Read *shih*, A., VII. xxvi, to shoot with an arrow and string attached.

射
yì

To dislike, be disliked, D.M., xvi. 4, xxix. 6.

將
chiang

(1) Shall, will, to be going to, to be about to, D.M., xxiv. A., III. xxiv ; XVI. i. 1, 2, 6, *et al.* (2) 將聖, a Sage, or thereabouts, A., IX. vi. 2. (3) 將命, to act as *internuncius*, A., XIV. xlvii. 1 ; XVII. xx.

專
chwan

(1) Alone, unassisted, A., XIII. v. (2) Assuming, presuming. 自專, D.M., xxviii. 1.

尊
tsun

(1) Honourable in dignity, D.M., xvii. 1, xviii. 2. (2) To honour, D.M., xix. 5, xx. 5, 12, 13, 14, *et al.* A., XIX. iii ; XX. ii. 1, 2.

對
túi

To reply to, in reply. Spoken of an inferior answering a superior, *passim.* The only case where we can conceive of an equality between the parties is A., XVIII. vi. 3.

THE 42ND RADICAL, 小.

小
hsiáo

Small, smallness, in small matters, D.M., xii. 2, xxx. 3. A., I. xii. 1 ; II. xxii, *et al., saepe.* 小人, see on 人. 小子, my little children, my disciples, A., V. xxi ; VIII. iii ; XI. xvi. 2 ; XVII. ix. 小=we, the disciples, A., XVII. xix. 2. The disciples, A., XIX. xii. I, a little child, A., XX. i. 3. 小君, 小童, designations of the wife of the prince of a State, A., XVI. xiv.

少
sháo

(1) A little, A., XIII. viii. (2) 少師, the assistant music-master, A., XVIII. ix. 6. (3) 少連, a name, A., XVIII. viii. 1, 3.

少
sháo

In 4th tone. Young, youth, A., V. xxv. 4 ; IX. vi. 3, ix ; XVI. vii.

尚
shang

(1) To esteem, A., XIV. vi; XVII. xxiii. To add to, esteem above, A., IV. vi. 1. To place over, D.M., xxxiii. 1. (2) Still, likewise, G.L.c., x. 14. (3) Pray, let it be, D.M., xxxiii. 3.

THE 43RD RADICAL, 尢.

尤
yu

尤人, to blame men, D.M., xiv. 3. A., XIV. xxxvii. 2. Occasions for blame, A., II. xviii. 2.

就
chiû

(1) To approach to, A., I. xiv; XVI. i. 6. (2) To complete, for the good of, A., XII. xix.

THE 44TH RADICAL, 尸.

尸
shih

Corpse-like, A., X. xvi. 1.

尺
ch'ih

A cubit, A., VIII. vi.

尼
ni

仲尼, Confucius, D.M., ii. 1, xxx. 1. A., XIX. xxii, xxiii, xxiv, xxv.

尹
yin

(1) To correct. 令尹, good Corrector, designation of the chief minister of Ch'û, A., V. xviii. 1. (2) 伊尹, an ancient minister, A., XII. xxii. 6. (3) 師尹, an ancient minister, Grand-teacher, G.L.c., x. 4.

居
chü

(1) To dwell in, to reside, G.L.c., vi. 2. D.M., xxvi. 9. A., II. i, *et al., saepe.* With a reference to privacy, A., X. vi. 7, vii. 2, xvi. 1; XI. xxv. 3; XIII. viii, *et al.* (2) Metaphorically, applied to situations, virtues, D.M., x. 3, 4, xxvii. 7. A., III. xxvi, *et al., saepe.* (3) To keep, A., V. xvii. (4) To sit down, A., XVII. viii. 2. (5) Comfort, A., XIV. iii. 居室, the economy of a family, A., XIII. viii.

屋
wû

A house, G.L.c., vi. 4. D.M., xxxiii. 3.

屏
ping

In 3rd tone. To put away, A., XX. ii. 1. 屏氣, to keep in the breath, A., X. iv. 4.

屢
lü

Often, generally, A., V. iv. 2; XI. xviii. 1, 2.

履
li

(1) To tread on, A., VIII. iii; X. iv. 2. (2) The name of the sovereign T'ang, A., XX. i. 3.

THE 46TH RADICAL, 山.

山
shan

(1) A hill, mountain, mountains, G.L.c., x. 4. D.M., xxvi. 9. A., V. xvii; VI. iv, xxi; X. xviii. 2. A mound, A., IX. xviii. (2) 泰山, the name of a mountain, A., III. vi. (3) 公山, a double surname, A., XVII. v.

峻
tsun

Lofty, great, G.L.c., i. 3, x. 5. D.M., xxvii. 2.

崇
ts'ung

To exalt; to honour and obey, D.M., xxvii. 6. A., XII. x, xxi. 1, 3.

崩
păng

The fall of a mountain. Metaphorically, downfall, to be ruined, A., XVI. i. 12; XVII. xxi. 2.

崔
ts'ûi

崔子, an officer of Ch'i, A., V. xviii. 2.

嶽
yo

The name of a mountain, D.M., xxvi. 9.

巍
wei

巍巍乎, how majestic! A., VIII. xviii, xix. 1, 2.

嚴
yen

嚴嚴, precipitous, G.L.c., x. 4.

THE 47TH RADICAL, 巛.

川
ch'wan

A stream, streams, A., VI. iv; IX. xvi. 川流, flowing streams, river-currents, D.M., xxx. 3.

州
châu

2,500 families. 州里, a neighbourhood, A., XV. v. 2.

THE 48TH RADICAL, 工.

工
kung

A mechanic, an artisan, A., XV. ix. 百工, the various artisans, D.M., xx. 12, 13, 14. A., XIX. vii. 1.

左
tso

(1) The left, on the left, G.L.c., x. 2. D.M., xvi. 3. A., XIV. xviii. 2. 左右手, to move the left arm or the right, A., X. iii. 2. (2) 左丘, a surname, A., V. xxiv. Some make 左 alone to be the surname.

巧
ch'iáo

Fine, artful, specious, A., I. iii; III. viii. 1; V. xxiv; XV. xxvi; XVII. xvii.

巫
wû

(1) A wizard, a witch, A., XIII. xxii. (2) 巫馬, a double surname, A., VII. xxx. 2, 3.

THE 49TH RADICAL, 已.

己
chî

Self. Himself, yourself, and plural, *passim.* Observe 總己, A., XIV. xliii. 2. Used for 他, G.L.c., vi. 2.

已
i

(1) To stop, end, D.M., xi. 2, xxvi. 10. A., XVII. xxii; XVIII. v. 1. In the phrase 不得已, not to be able to stop, what is the result of necessity, A., XII. vii. 2, 3. (2) To retire from, resign, A., V. xviii. 1. (3) 已矣乎, and 已矣夫, it is all over, A., V. xxvi; IX. viii; XV. xii. (4) 而已, often followed by 矣, and stop, and nothing more, D.M., xxv. 3. A., VI. v; VIII. xx. 3; XII. vi, *et al.* (5) 也已, 已矣, and 已夫, all serve to give emphasis to the statement

or assertion which has preceded, A., I. xiv, xv. 3 ; II. xvi. 1 ; III. viii. 3, *et al.*, *saepe*. (6) Indicates the past or present-complete tense, A., VIII. x ; XVIII. vii. 5.

巷
hsiang

(1) A lane, A., VI. ix.   (2) 達巷, the name of a village, A., IX. ii.

巽
sun

Yielding, A., IX. xxiii.

THE 50TH RADICAL, 巾.

市
shih

A market, the market-place, A., X. viii. 5 ; XIV. xxxviii. 1.

布
pû

(1) Linen-cloth, A., X. vii. 1.   (2) To be displayed, D.M., xx. 2.

希
hsî

(1) Few, rarely, A., V. xxii ; XVI. ii. (2) To stop, pause, A., XI. xxv. 7.

帑
nû

Children, D.M., xv. 2.

帛
pâi

Silk, A., XVII. xi.

帝
tî

(1) God, A., XX. i. 3.   上帝, see 上. (2) A sovereign or ruler.   帝典, the Canon of the Tì Yâo, name of a portion of the Shû-ching, G.L.c., i. 3.

帥
shwâi

A commander, general, A., IX. xxv.

帥
sû

To lead on, A., XII. xvii. G.L.c., ix. 4.

師
shih

(1) The multitude, the people, G.L.c., x. 5.   (2) A host, properly of 2,500 men. 師旅, A., XI. xxv. 4.   (3) A teacher, A., II. xi ; VII. xxi ; XV. xxxv ; XIX. xxii. 2.   (4) 士師, the chief criminal judge, A., XVIII. ii ; XIX. xix.   (5) 太師樂, 太師, the Grand music-master, A., III. xxiii ; VIII. xv ; XVIII. ix. 1.   少師, the assistant ditto, A., XVIII. ix. 5.   師, alone, A., XV. xli. 1, 2.   (6) The grand teacher, one of the highest officers, G.L.c., x. 4.   (7) The name of one of Confucius's disciples, A., XI. xv, xvii. 3.

席
hsi

A mat, A., X. ix, xiii ; XV. xli. 1.

帶
tâi

A sash, A., V. vii. 4.

常
ch'ang

Constant, regular, G.L.c., x. 11. A., XIX. xxii. 2.

帷
wei

A curtain, curtain-shaped, A., X. vi. 9.

幬
tâo

To curtain, overspread, D.M., xxx. 2.

THE 51ST RADICAL, 干.

干
kan

(1) To seek for, with a view to, A., II. xviii. 1.   (2) A shield.   干戈, shields and spears, = war, A., XVI. i. 13.   (3) 比干, an uncle of the tyrant Châu, A., XVIII. 1.   (4) The name of a band-master of Lû, A., XVIII. ix. 2.

平
p'ing

(1) A state of perfect tranquillity ; to bring to, or be brought to, such a state, G.L.T., 5. G.L.c., x. 1. D.M., xxxiii. 5. (2) Level, A., IX. xviii.   平生, the whole life, A., XIV. xiii. 2.   (3) An honorary epithet, A., V. xvi.

年
nien

A year, years, the year, D.M., xviii. 3. A., I. xi, *et al.*, *saepe*.

幸
hsing

Luck, fortunate, fortunately, D.M., xiv. 4. A., VI. ii, xvii ; VII. xxx. 3 ; XI. vi.

THE 52ND RADICAL, 幺.

幼
yû

Young, A., XIV. xlvi ; XVIII. vii. 5.

幾
chî

(1) What is small, = mildly, A., IV. xviii.   (2) Influence, what may be expected from, A., XIII. xv. 1, 3, 4, 5.   (3) 庶幾, perhaps, peradventure, D.M., xxix. 6.

THE 53RD RADICAL, 广.

序
hsü

To arrange in order, D.M., xix. 4.

府
fû

A treasury, G.L.c., x. 21. A., XI. xiii. 1.

庭
t'ing

The court of a house, A., III. i ; XVI. xiii. 2, 3.

度
tû

Measures, D.M., xxviii. 2.   法度, the laws, A., XX. i. 6.

度
to

To surmise, conjecture, D.M., xvi. 4.

庫
k'û

An arsenal, G.L.c., x. 21.

庶
shû

(1) Numerous, A., XIII. ix. 2, 3.   庶民, the numerous, the masses of (= the common) people, D.M., xx. 12, 13, xxix. 3. (2) 庶幾, and 庶乎, perhaps, near to, D.M., xxix. 6. A., XI. xviii. 1.

庸
yung

(1) Ordinary, D.M., xii. 4.   (2) Use, course.   In the phrase—中庸, D.M., ii. 1, 2, iii, vii, viii, ix, xi. 3, xxvii. 6. A., VI. xxvii.

康
k'ang

(1) The honorary name of one of the chiefs of the Chî family, A., II. xx ; VI. vii ; X. xi. 2 ; XI. vi ; XII. xvii, xviii, xix ; XIV. xx.   (2) 康誥, title of a Book in the Shû-ching, G.L.c., i. 1, ii. 2, ix. 2, x. 11.

庾 *yü*
A measure for grain, containing about 120 English pints, A., VI. iii. 1.

廉 *lien*
Modesty, reserve, A., XVII. xvi. 2.

廋 *sâu*
To be concealed, A., II. x. 4, 5.

廐 *chiû*
A stable, A., X. xii.

廟 *miâo*
A temple. In the phrases—祖廟, D.M., xix. 3. 宗廟, D.M., xvii. 1, xviii. 2, xix. 4, 6. A., XI. xxv. 6, 12; XIV. xx. 2; XIX. xxiii. 3. 大廟, A., III. xv; X. xiv.

廢 *fei*
(1) To stop short, D.M., xi. 2. A., VI. x. (2) To fail, to cause to fail, put aside, D.M., xx. 16. A., XIV. xxxviii. 2; XV. xxii; XVIII. vii. 5. 廢國, fallen States, D.M., xx. 14. (3) To be out of office, A., V. i. 2; XVIII. viii. 4; XX. i. 6.

廣 *kwang*
Broad, expanded. Spoken of the earth, D.M., xxvi. 9. Of the mind, G.L.c., vi. 4. D.M., xxvii. 6.

THE 54TH RADICAL, 廴.

廷 *t'ing*
朝廷, the court (=courtyard) of a sovereign or ruler, A., X. i. 2.

建 *chien*
To set up, D.M., xxix. 3.

THE 55TH RADICAL, 廾.

弈 *yî*
To play at chess, A., XVII. xxii.

THE 56TH RADICAL, 弋.

弋 *yî*
To shoot with an arrow having a string attached to it, A., VII. xxvi.

式 *shih*
The cross-bar in front of a carriage; to bow forward to that bar, A., X. xvi. 3.

弒 *shih*
To commit parricide or regicide, A., V. xviii. 2; XI. xxiii. 6; XIV. xxii. 1, 2.

THE 57TH RADICAL, 弓.

弓 *kung*
仲弓, the designation of one of Confucius's disciples, A., VI. i. 2, 3, iv, et al.

弔 *tiâo*
To condole with mourners, A., X. vi. 10.

弗 *fú*
(1) Not, D.M., viii, xi. 1, 2, et al. A., III. vi; V. viii. 3; VI. xxv; XII. xv. (2) 弗擾, a man's name, A., XVII. v.

弘 *hwang*
Large in mind, A., VIII. vii. To enlarge, A., XV. xxviii; XIX. ii.

弟 *tî*
(1) A younger brother. 兄弟, elder and younger brothers, a brother; see on 兄. 昆弟, the same, D.M., xx. 8, 13. A., XI. iv. (2) Used for 悌, the duty of a younger brother, A., I. ii. 1; XIV. xlvi. G.L.c., ix. 1, x. 1. (3) 弟子, = a youth, A., I. vi; II. viii. A disciple, disciples, A., VI. ii; VII. xxxiii; VIII. iii; IX. ii. 2; XI. vi. 1.

弦 *hsien*
Stringed instruments; properly the strings of such, A., XVII. iv. 1. The same as 絃.

張 *chang*
(1) 張, and 子張, the designation of one of Confucius's disciples, A., II. xviii. 1, xxiii. 1; V. xviii. 1; XIX. xv, xvi, et al., saepe. (2) 朱張, a man's name, A., XVIII. viii. 1.

強 *ch'iang*
Energy, forcefulness, D.M., x. 1, 2, 3, 4, 5. Strong, energetic, D.M., xx. 21; xxxi. 1.

強 *chiang*
In 3rd tone. 勉強, using strenuous effort, D.M., xx. 9.

彌 *mi*
More, still more, A., IX. x. 1.

THE 59TH RADICAL, 彡.

形 *hsing*
To appear, be manifested, G.L.c., vi. 2. D.M., xxiii. 1.

彥 *yen*
Elegant, accomplished, G.L.c., x. 14.

彫 *tiâo*
To lose their leaves, A., IX. xxvii.

彬 *pin*
彬彬, equally blended, A., VI. xvi.

彭 *p'âng*
An ancient worthy, called 老彭 by Confucius, A., VII. i.

THE 60TH RADICAL, 彳.

彼 *pi*
That, that man, = he, him, A., XIV. x. 2; XVI. i. 6. G.L.c., iii. 4, x. 4, 22. 在彼, there, D.M., xxix. 6.

往 *wang*
(1) To go, going, A., IX. xviii; XVII. i. 1, v. 1, vii. 1, 2; XVIII. ii. 1. D.M., xx. 14. 而往, and onwards, A., III. x. (2) The gone, the past, A., I. xv. 3; III. xxi. 2; VII. xxviii. 2; XVIII. v.

征 *chăng*
征伐, punitive military expeditions, A., XVI. ii.

待 *tăi*
(1) To wait, wait for, A., IX. xii; XIII. iii. 1. D.M., xxvii. 4. (2) To treat, A., XVIII. iii.

律 *lü*
To imitate, follow as a model, D.M., xxx. 1.

後 *hâu*
(1) As a noun. That which is after, the back, saepe. 在後, A., IX. x. 1. Preceded by 之, A., XIV. xxii. 4, 5, et al. A successor, A., XIV. xv. (2) As an adjective, D.M., xi. 1, et al. 後死者,

A., IX. v. 3. 後生, A., IX. xxii. (3) As an adverb. Afterwards, *saepe*. Often follows 然 and 而. (4) As a verb. To come after, fall behind, make an after consideration, A., III. viii. 2 ; VI. xiii, xx ; XI. xxii, xxv. 8 ; XII. xxi. 3 ; XV. v. 3, xxxvii ; XVIII. vii. 1.

徑 *ching*

A short, cross, path, A., VI. xiii.

得 *tĕ*

(1) To attain to, to be found, G.L.T., 2. D.M., xx. 18, 20. (2) To get, with an objective following, *saepe*. Without an objective, getting, anything as gain to be got, A., XVI. vii, x. 1 ; XIX. i. (3) The auxiliary *can* often followed by 而, *saepe*. (4) Followed by an adjective, and often in the question 焉得... can be＝can be considered, A., IV. i ; V. x, xviii. 1, 2, *et al.* (5) 不得已, could not but, A., XII. vii. 2, 3. (6) 自得, to be one's self, D.M., xiv. 2.

徒 *t'ŭ*

(1) On foot, A., XI. vii. 2. (2) Vainly, without cause, A., XVII. v. 3. (3) Disciple, associate, A., XI. xvi. 2 ; XVIII. vi. 3, 4.

徙 *hsi*

To move towards, A., VII. iii ; XII. x. 1.

從 *ts'ung*

To follow ; to act according to, G.L.c., ix. 4, x. 2. D.M., xxviii. 5, xxix. 2. A., II. iv. 6, xiii, *et al.*, *saepe*. 從政, to be engaged in government. Generally, in a subordinate capacity, A., VI. vi ; XIII. xiii, xx. 4 ; XVIII. v. 1. But not necessarily subordinate in, A., XX. ii. 1. 從事, to be engaged in affairs, to act, A., VIII. v. 1 ; XVII. i. 2.

從 *tsung*

In 4th tone. Proceeding on, A., III. xxiii.

從 *tsung*

In 4th tone. To be in close attendance on. Always 從者 or 從我者, A., III. xxiv ; V. vi ; XI. ii. 1, ix. 1 ; XV. i. 2.

從 *sung*

從容, naturally and easily, D.M., xx. 18.

御 *yü*

To drive a carriage, A., II. v. 2 ; IX. ii. 2.

復 *fŭ*

(1) To make good, A., I. xiii. (2) To report a commission, A., X. iii. 4. (3) To return to, A., X. iv. 5 ; XII. i. 1. (4) To repeat, A., XI. v.

復 *fău*

Again, A., VI. vii ; VII. v. As a verb, A., VII. viii.

循 *hsün*

(1) 循循然, by orderly method, A., IX. x. 2. (2) Fastened to the ground, A., X. v. 1.

微 *wei*

(1) That which is minute, minute, D.M., i. 3, xvi. 5, xxvii. 6, xxxiii. 1. Reduced, A., XVI. iii. (2) A negative particle, if not, A., XIV. xviii. 2. (3) 微子, the viscount of the State Wei, A., XVIII. i. (4) 微生, a double surname, A., V. xxiii.—XIV. xxxiv.

徵 *chăng*

(1) To be evidenced, D.M., xxvi. 2, 3. (2) To attest, be attested, D.M., xxviii. 5, xxix. 2, 3. A., III. ix.

德 *tĕ*

Virtue, virtuous, *passim*. Energy, influence, D.M., xvi. 1. A., XII. xix.

徹 *ch'êh*

(1) To remove, A., III. ii. (2) Name for the Chău law of tithe, A., XII. ix. 2, 3.

微 *hsiăo*

(1) To seek, D.M., xix. 4. (2) To copy another's and pretend that it is one's own ; to pry out, A., XVII. xxiv. 2.

THE 61ST RADICAL, 心.

心 *shin*

The heart, the mind ;—denotes the mental constitution generally. Is not found in the Chung Yung, G.L.T., 4, 5. G.L.c., vi. 4, vii. 1, 2, 3, ix. 2, x. 14. A., II. iv. 6 ; VI. v ; XIV. xlii. 1 ; XVII. xxii ; XX. i. 3, 7.

必 *pi*

Must, used as an auxiliary ; often ＝ will certainly, would certainly. Sometimes also with no verb following, *passim*. 必也, what must＝what is necessary is... Sometimes conditionally, G.L.c., iv. 1. A., III. vii ; VI. vii, xxviii ; VII. x. 3 ; XIII. iii. 2, xxi. 毋必, no arbitrary predeterminations, A., IX. iv.

忍 *jên* or *zăn*

To bear, forbear, A., III. i ; XV. xxvi.

忒 *t'i*

To be wrong, in error, G.L.c., ix. 8.

志 *chih*

The will, aim, G.L.c., iv. 1. D.M., xix. 2, xxxiii. 2. A., I. xi, *et al.*, *saepe*. 志士, the determined scholar, A., XV. viii.

忌 *chi*

忌憚, dread, caution, D.M., ii. 2.

忘 *wang*

To forget, be forgotten, A., VII. xviii. 2 ; XII. xxi. 3 ; XIV. xiii. 2 ; XIX. v. G.L.c., iii. 4, 5.

忠 *chung*

(1) Self-devotion, generous sincerity. Often in combination with 信, G.L.c., x. 18. D.M., xiii. 3, xx. 14. A., iv, xv. 2 ; V. xxvii, *et al.* (2) Faithful, loyal, A., I. iv, viii. 2 ; II. xx ; III. xix ; V. xviii. 1 ; XII. xxiii ; XIV. viii ; XV. v. 2 ; XVI. x.

忿 *făn*

Anger, to be angry, A., XII. xxi. 3 ; XVI. x ; XVII. xvi. 2. G.L.c., vii. 1.

忮 *chih*

To dislike, A., IX. xxvi. 2.

念
nien

To think of, keep in mind, A., V. xxii.

忽
hŭ

(1) 忽焉 = 忽然, suddenly, A., IX. x. (2) In names. 召忽, A., XIV. xvii. 仲忽, A., XVIII. xi.

怍
tso

To be ashamed, modest, A., XIV. xxi.

怒
nŭ

Anger, to show anger, A., VI. ii. D.M., i. 4, xxxiii. 4.

思
sze

(1) To think, to think of; thought, thoughts, thinking, D.M., xx. 7, 18, 19, 20. A., II. ii, xv; IV. xvii, *et al., saepe.* (2) A final particle, D.M., xvi. 4. (3) 原思, a disciple of Confucius, A., VI. iii. 3.

怡
i

怡怡如, looking pleased, A., X. iv. 5; XIII. xxviii.

急
chi

The distressed, distress, A., VI. iii. 2.

性
hsing

Nature, the nature (of man), G.L.c., x. 17. D.M., i. 1, xxi, xxii, xxv. 3, xxvii. 6. A., V. xii; XVII. ii.

怨
yüan

(1) To murmur against, be murmured against. Resentment, in thought, word, or deed, D.M., xiv. 3, xx. 13. A., IV. xii; V. xxii, *et al., saepe.* (2) What provokes resentment, injury, A., XIV. xxxvi. 1, 3.

怪
kwâi

Extraordinary things, A., VII. xx. D.M., xi. 1.

恆
hăng

(1) Constantly; constancy, G.L.c., x. 19. A., VII. xxv. 2, 3; XIII. xxii. 1, 2. (2) 陳恆, an officer of Ch'i, A., XIV. xxii. 2.

恐
k'ung

To be afraid of, to be in danger of, A., V. xiii; VIII. xvii; XVI. i. 13; XIX. iv. 恐懼, G.L.c., vii. 1. D.M., i. 2.

恕
shŭ

The principle of reciprocity, making our own feelings the rule for our dealing with others, A., IV. xv. 2; XV. xxiii. G.L.c., ix. 4. D.M., xiii. 3.

恤
hsŭ

To commiserate, treat compassionately, G.L.c., x. 1.

恥
ch'ih

Shame, a sense of shame, what is shameful, to be ashamed of, D.M., xx. 10. A., I. xiii; II. iii. 1, 2; IV. ix, xxii; V. xiv, xxiv; VIII. xiii. 3; IX. xxvi. 1; XIII. xx; XIV. i, xxix. 1.

恂
hsün

Reverently careful, G.L.c., iii. 4. 恂如, simple and sincere-like, A., X. i. 1.

悔
hŭi

To regret, to repent, have occasion for repentance, D.M., xi. 3. A., II. xviii. 2; VII. x. 3.

息
hsi

(1) To breathe, A., X. iv. 4. (2) To stop, cease, D.M., xx. 2, xxvi. 1, 2.

恭
kung

To revere, be reverential, sedate, reverence, D.M., xxxiii. 5. A., I. xiii; V. xv, xxiv; VII. xxxvii; VIII. ii; XII. v. 4; XIII. xix; XVI. x. 恭 = too modest, A., XIX. xxv. 1. 恭己, he made himself reverent, A., XV. iv.

悖
pei

Contrary to right, contradictory, to collide, G.L.c., x. 10. D.M., xxix. 3, xxx. 3.

悠
yü

Reaching far, D.M., xxvi. 3, 4, 6, 8.

患
hwan

To be grieved, anxious about, A., I. xvi; III. xxiv; IV. xiv; XII. v. 4, xviii; XIV. xxxii; XVI. i. 10; XVII. xv. 2, 3. 憂患, G.L.c., vii. 1. 患難, distress and difficulty, D.M., xiv. 2.

悲
pei

A man's name, A., XVII. xx.

悱
fei

Unable to explain one's self, A., VII. viii.

情
ch'ing

Sincerity, the real state of a case, G.L.c., iv. A., XIII. iv. 3; XIX. xix.

惑
hwo

(1) To be deceived, deluded, delusion, D.M., xx. 13. A., XII. x. 1, 2, xxi. 1, 3; XIV. xxxviii. (2) To doubt, have misgivings, D.M., xxix. 3, 4. A., II. iv. 3; VII. xxviii; IX. xxviii; XI. xxi; XIV. xxx.

惜
hsi

惜乎, alas! A., IX. xx; XII. viii. 2.

惟
wei

A particle, generally initial, but sometimes *in* a clause. Sometimes it can hardly be translated, G.L.c., iii. 1, x. 11. A., II. xxi. 2. Often it = *only*, especially when medial, G.L.c., x. 12. D.M., xviii. 1, xxxiii. 5. A., IV. iii; VII. x. 1; XIX. xii. 2.

悾
k'ung

悾悾, simple, A., VIII. xvi.

惠
hŭi

Favours, A., IV. xi. Kind, beneficent; kindness, A., V. xv; XIV. x. 1; XVII. vi; XX. ii. 1, 2.

惡
o

(1) Wickedness, what is bad, G.L.c., viii. 1, 2. D.M., vi. A., IV. iv; V. xxii, *et al.* (2) Bad, disagreeable, spoiled, G.L.c., vi. 1. A., IV. ix; VIII. xxi; IX. viii. 2.

惡
wû

To dislike, to hate, G.L.c., vi. 1, viii. 1, x. 2, 3, 14, 17. D.M. and A., *saepe.*

惡
wû

The 1st tone. How, A., IV. v. 2.

惰
to

Indolent, A., IX. xix. Rude, G.L.c., viii. 1.

愆
ch'ien

Fault, error, A., XVI. vi.

愈
yü

To be superior to, A., V. viii. 1; XI. xv. 2.

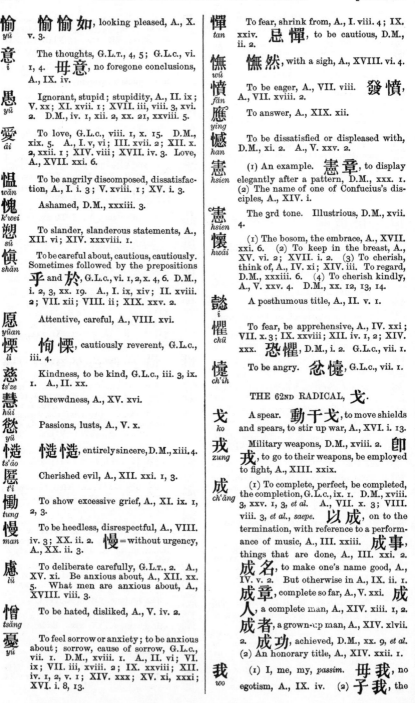

愉 *yü*

愉愉如, looking pleased, A., X. v. 3.

意 *i*

The thoughts, G.L.T., 4, 5; G.L.c., vi. 1, 4. 毋意, no foregone conclusions, A., IX. iv.

愚 *yü*

Ignorant, stupid; stupidity, A., II. ix; V. xx; XI. xvii. 1; XVII. iii, viii. 3, xvi. 2. D.M., iv. 1, xii. 2, xx. 21, xxviii. 5.

愛 *ái*

To love, G.L.c., viii. 1, x. 15. D.M., xix. 5. A., I. v, vi; III. xvii. 2; XII. x. 2, xxii. 1; XIV. viii; XVII. iv. 3. Love, A., XVII. xxi. 6.

惋 *wăn*

To be angrily discomposed, dissatisfaction, A., I. i. 3; V. xviii. 1; XV. i. 3.

愧 *k'wei*

Ashamed, D.M., xxxiii. 3.

愬 *sü*

To slander, slanderous statements, A., XII. vi; XIV. xxxviii. 1.

慎 *shăn*

To be careful about, cautious, cautiously. Sometimes followed by the prepositions 乎 and 於, G.L.c., vi. 1, 2, x. 4, 6. D.M., i. 2, 3, xx. 19. A., I. ix, xiv; II. xviii. 2; VII. xii; VIII. ii; XIX. xxv. 2.

愿 *yüan*

Attentive, careful, A., VIII. xvi.

慄 *li*

恂慄, cautiously reverent, G.L.c., iii. 4.

慈 *ts'ze*

Kindness, to be kind, G.L.c., iii. 3, ix. 1. A., II. xx.

慧 *hüi*

Shrewdness, A., XV. xvi.

慾 *yü*

Passions, lusts, A., V. x.

慥 *ts'áo*

慥慥, entirely sincere, D.M., xiii. 4.

慝 *t'i*

Cherished evil, A., XII. xxi. 1, 3.

慟 *tung*

To show excessive grief, A., XI. ix. 1, 2, 3.

慢 *man*

To be heedless, disrespectful, A., VIII. iv. 3; XX. ii. 2. 慢＝without urgency, A., XX. ii. 3.

慮 *lü*

To deliberate carefully, G.L.T., 2. A., XV. xi. Be anxious about, A., XII. xx. 5. What men are anxious about, A., XVIII. viii. 3.

憎 *tsăng*

To be hated, disliked, A., V. iv. 2.

憂 *yü*

To feel sorrow or anxiety; to be anxious about; sorrow, cause of sorrow, G.L.c., vii. 1. D.M., xviii. 1. A., II. vi; VI. ix; VII. iii, xviii. 2; IX. xxviii; XII. iv. 1, 2, v. 1; XIV. xxx; XV. xi, xxxi; XVI. i. 8, 13.

憚 *tan*

To fear, shrink from, A., I. viii. 4; IX. xxiv. 忌憚, to be cautious, D.M., ii. 2.

憮 *wü*

憮然, with a sigh, A., XVIII. vi. 4.

憤 *făn*

To be eager, A., VII. viii. 發憤, A., VII. xviii. 2.

應 *ying*

To answer, A., XIX. xii.

憾 *han*

To be dissatisfied or displeased with, D.M., xi. 2. A., V. xxv. 2.

憲 *hsien*

(1) An example. 憲章, to display elegantly after a pattern, D.M., xxx. 1. (2) The name of one of Confucius's disciples, A., XIV. i.

憲 *hsien*

The 3rd tone. Illustrious, D.M., xvii. 4.

懷 *hwái*

(1) The bosom, the embrace, A., XVII. xxi. 6. (2) To keep in the breast, A., XV. vi. 2; XVII. i. 2. (3) To cherish, think of, A., IV. xi; XIV. iii. To regard, D.M., xxxiii. 6. (4) To cherish kindly, A., V. xxv. 4. D.M., xx. 12, 13, 14.

懿 *i*

A posthumous title, A., II. v. 1.

懼 *chü*

To fear, be apprehensive, A., IV. xxi; VII. x. 3; IX. xxviii; XII. iv. 1, 2; XIV. xxx. 恐懼, D.M., i. 2. G.L.c., vii. 1.

懫 *ch'ih*

To be angry. 忿懫, G.L.c., vii. 1.

THE 62ND RADICAL, 戈.

戈 *ko*

A spear. 動干戈, to move shields and spears, to stir up war, A., XVI. i. 13.

戎 *zung*

Military weapons, D.M., xviii. 2. 即戎, to go to their weapons, be employed to fight, A., XIII. xxix.

成 *ch'ăng*

(1) To complete, perfect, be completed, the completion, G.L.c., ix. 1. D.M., xviii. 3, xxv. 1, 3, et al. A., VII. x. 3; VIII. viii. 3, et al., saepe. 以成, on to the termination, with reference to a performance of music, A., III. xxiii. 成事, things that are done, A., III. xxi. 2. 成名, to make one's name good, A., IV. v. 2. But otherwise in A., IX. ii. 1. 成章, complete so far, A., V. xxi. 成人, a complete man, A., XIV. xiii. 1, 2. 成者, a grown-up man, A., XIV. xlvii. 2. 成功, achieved, D.M., xx. 9, et al. (2) An honorary title, A., XIV. xxii. 1.

我 *wo*

(1) I, me, my, *passim*. 毋我, no egotism, A., IX. iv. (2) 子我, the

designation of one of Confucius's disciples, A., III. xxi. 1; VI. xxiv; XI. ii. 2; XVII. xxi. 1, 6.

戒
chieh
(1) To guard against, A., XVI. vii. To be careful. 戒愼, D.M., i. 2. (2) To notify, warn, A., XX. ii. 3.

或
ho
(1) Some one, some persons, D.M., xx. 9. A., II. xxi. 1; XIV. x. 1; *et al., saepe.* (2) Perhaps, A., II. xxiii. 2; XI. xxv. 3; XIII. xxii. 2; XVII. xvi. 1; XIX. xxiii. 4.

戚
ch'i
To grieve deeply, A., III. iv. 3. 戚戚, to be in great distress, A., VII. xxxvi.

戮
lû
Disgrace, A., V. i. 2.

戰
chan
(1) To fight, fighting, war, A., VII. xii; XIII. xxx. (2) To fear, dread. 戰栗, A., III. xxi. 1; 戰戰, VIII. iii; 戰色, X. v. 1.

戲
hsî
To be in sport, A., XVII. iv. 4.

戲
hû
An interjection. 於戲, G.L.c., iii. 5.

THE 63RD RADICAL, 戸.

戸
hû
A door, A., VI. xv; XVII. xx.

戻
li
(1) Perverse, perverseness. 貪戻, G.L.c., ix. 3. 忿戻, A., XVII. xvi. 2. (2) Reaching to, D.M., xii. 3.

所
so
(1) A place, A., II. i; IX. xiv. (2) What, that which, the case and gender depending on the rest of the sentence, *passim.* 無所, nothing, 無所不, everything; variously used, G.L.c., ii. 4, vi. 2, A., X. vi. 8; XVII. xv. 3. Used also in swearing, = if in anything, A., VI. xxvi. (3) 所以, whereby, *passim.* 所 alone, = 所以, A., XIII. iii. 6.

THE 64TH RADICAL, 手.

手
shâu
The hand, hands, G.L.c., vi. 3. A., VI. viii; VIII. iii; IX. xi. 3; XIII. iii. 6. The arm, A., X. iii. 2.

才
ts'âi
Talents, abilities, A., VIII. xi, xx. 3; IX. x. 3; XI. vii. 2; XIII. ii. 1, 2.

扶
fû
To support, A., XVI. i. 6.

承
chăng
(1) To assist, as at a sacrifice, D.M., xvi. 3. A., XII. ii. (2) To receive,—in sequence, A., XIII. xxii. 2.

折
chêh
To break off, to settle, A., XII. xii. 1.

抑
yi
(1) Or, D.M., x. 2. A., I. x. 1. (2) But, A., VII. xxxiii; XIX. xii. 1. Followed by 亦, A., XIII. xx. 3; XIV. xxxiii. 1.

技
chih
Ability, skill, G.L.c., x. 14.

拂
fû
To oppose, outrage, G.L.c., x. 17.

拒
chü
To oppose, put away, A., XIX. iii.

拖
t'o
To draw. 拖紳, to draw the girdle across, A., X. xiii. 3.

指
chih
To point to, G.L.c., vi. 3. A., III. xi; X. xvii. 2.

拳
ch'üan
拳拳, the appearance of holding firm, D.M., viii.

拜
pâi
To bow, pay one's respects, perform obeisance, A., IX. iii. 2; X. xi. 1, 2; XVII. i.

拱
kung
To fold the hands across the breast, A., XVIII. vii. 2.

持
ch'ih
To hold up, sustain, D.M., xx. 14, xxx. 2. A., XVI. i. 6.

振
chăn
To contain, D.M., xxvi. 9.

授
shâu
(1) To give to, entrust, A., X. v. 1; XIII. v. 1. (2) To give up. 授命, A., XIV. xiii. 3.

探
t'an
To try. 探湯, to try—i. e. to put the hand into—boiling water, A., XVI. xi. 1.

掌
chang
The palm, D.M., xix. 6. A., III. xi.

掃
sâo
To sweep, A., XIX. xii. 1.

措
ts'û
(1) To arrange, place, D.M., xxv. 3. A., XIII. iii. 6. (2) To put by, give over, D.M., xx. 20.

接
chieh
接輿, the name of a recluse, A., XVIII. v.

揚
yang
To display, publish, D.M., vi.

揖
yi
To bow to, A., III. vii; VII. xxx. 2; X. iii. 2, v. 1.

掩
yen
To cover over; be concealed, G.L.c., vi. 2. D.M., xvi. 5.

揭
ch'i
To hold up the clothes in crossing through water, A., XIV. xlii. 2.

援
yüan
To drag and hold, = to contemn, D.M., xiv. 3.

損
sun
To diminish, be injurious, A., II. xxiii. 2; XVI. iv, v.

摯
chih
The name of a music-master, A., VIII. xv; XVIII. ix.

撤
chêh

To remove, put away, A., X. viii. 6.

撰
chan

Cherished purposes, A., XI. xxv. 7.

播
po

To shake. 播鼗, master of the hand-drum, A., XVIII. ix. 4.

擇
chăi

To choose, D.M., vii, viii, xx. 18. A., IV. i ; VII. xxi, xxvii ; XX. ii. 2.

攫
hwŭ

A trap, D.M., vii.

撮
ts'o

A handful, D.M., xxvi. 9.

擊
chi

To strike. 擊磬, to play on the musical stone, A., XIV. xlii. 1.

據
chŭ

To grasp firmly, A., VII. vi. 2.

擯
pin

To receive visitors officially, A., X. iii. 1.

擾
zâo

弗擾, a man's name, A., XVII. v.

攘
zang

To steal,—on some temptation, A., XIII. xviii. 1.

攝
sheh

(1) To hold up, as the clothes, A., X. iv. 4. (2) To unite,—as several offices in one person, A., III. xxii. 2. (3) To be pressed, straitened, A., XI. xxv. 4.

THE 66TH RADICAL, 攴.

改
kâi

To alter, to change. Both active and neuter, D.M., xiii. 2. A., I. viii. 4, xi ; V. ix. 2; VI. ix ; VII. iii, xxi (here it simply = to avoid) ; IX. xxiii, xxiv ; XI. xiii. 2 ; XV. xxix ; XVII. xxi. 3 ; XIX. xviii.

攻
kung

To assail, = to reprove, A., XI. xvi. 2 ; XII. xxi. 3. 攻 = to study, A., II. xvi.

放
fang

(1) To drive, put away, G.L.c., x. 15 ; A., XV. x. 6. (2) To indulge, give license to, A., XVIII. viii. 4. (3) A name, A., III. iv, vi.

放
fang

In 3rd tone. To accord with ; having regard to, A., IV. xii.

政
chăng

Government ; the principles of government ; a government charge, *passim.*
政 = laws, A., II. iii. 1. 爲政, to administer government, as supreme or subordinate, A., II. i, xxi. 1 ; XII. xix. 從政, to be engaged in government, as subordinate, A., VI. vi ; XIII. xiii. 1, xx. 4 ; XVIII. v. 1. Excepting, perhaps, A., XX. ii. 1.

故
kù

(1) Therefore, *passim.* We have frequently 是故, with the same meaning, but perhaps a little more emphasis. Observe A., III. ix, where 故 is at the end

of the clause, = because, that is the cause. (2) Old, what is old, A., II. xi ; XVIII. x. D.M., xxvii. 6 (the second occurrence).

敏
min

To be earnest and active, earnest activity, A., I. xiv ; IV. xxiv ; V. xiv ; VII. xix ; XVII. vi ; XX. i. 9. Combining the idea of intelligence, A., XII. i. 2, ii. As a verb, to hasten, produce quickly, D.M., xx. 3.

教
chiǎo

To teach, instruct, G.L.c., ix. 1, 6, 7. D.M., x. 3. A., II. xx ; VII. xxiv ; XIII. ix. 4, xxix ; XV. xxxviii ; XX. ii. 3. 不教, uninstructed, A., XIII. xxx. Instruction, D.M., i. 1, xxi.

救
chiŭ

To stop, to save from, A., III. vi.

敖
âo

敖惰, arrogant and rude, G.L.c., viii. 1.

敗
pâi

(1) Gone, spoiled, as meat, A., X. viii. 2. (2) 司敗, minister of crime, A., VII. xxx.

敝
pî

To spoil ; spoiled,—spoken of clothes, A., V. xxv. 2 ; IX. xxvi.

敢
kan

To presume, to dare, D.M., xiii. 4, xxviii. 4. A., V. viii. 2 ; VI. xiii, *et al., saepe.* 豈敢, how dare I ?—an expression of humility, A., VII. xxxiii. 1. In the 1st person, often = our 'allow me.' A., XI. xi, xxi. 1 ; XIII. xx. 2, 3. Observe A., XX. i. 3. 果敢, presumptuous, A., XVII. xxiv. 1.

散
san

To scatter, disperse, G.L.c., x. 9. To be scattered, disorganised, A., XIX. xix.

敦
tun

Liberal, generous, great, D.M., xxvii. 6, xxx. 3.

敬
chăng

(1) To reverence, to respect ; to be reverential, cherish the feeling of reverence, *passim.* To be reverenced, D.M., xxxi. 1. In reference to business, A., I. v ; VI. i. 3 ; XIII. xix ; XV. xxxvii ; XVI. x. 畏敬, to be filled with awe and reverence, G.L.c., viii. 1. (2) An honorary epithet, A., VIII. iv. 1.

數
shǔ

(1) Some, several, A., VII. xvi ; XIX. xxiii. 3. (2) 歷數, the determined time (for the succession), A., XX. i. 1.

數
so

Frequently, A., IV. xxvi.

斂
lien

To ingather. Applied to imposts, G.L.c., x. 22. D.M., xx. 14. A., XI. xvi.

THE 67TH RADICAL, 文.

文
wăn

(1) The characters of the language, D.M., xxviii. 2, 3. A., XV. xxv. (2) Records, literary monuments, A., III. ix. (3) Literature, polite studies, A., I. vi ; VI. xxv ; VII. xxiv, xxxii ; IX. x. 2 ;

XI. ii. 2; XII. xv, xxiv; XVI. i. 11. (4) Accomplished, accomplishments, elegance, D.M., xxxi. 1, xxxiii. 1. A., III. xiv; V. xiv; VI. xvi; XII. viii. 1, 3; XIV. xiii. 1 (as an honorary designation, compare XIV. xix. 2). (5) 文 = the cause of truth, A., IX. v. 2, 3. (6) 文章, elegant manners and discourses; elegant institutions, A., V. xii; VIII. xix. 2. (7) Used as the honorary epithet, becoming in effect the name, D.M., xviii. 1, 2, 3, *et al.* G.L.c., iii. 3. A., IX. v. 2; XIX. xxii. 2.—A., XIV. xvi.—A., V. xiv.—A., V. xvii; XV. xiii.—A., V. xviii. 2.—A., V. xix.—A., XIV. xiv, xix. Used also in the name 子文, A., V. xviii.

文 *wăn*

In 4th tone. To gloss, A., XIX. viii.

斐 *fei*

Accomplished, G.L.c., iii. 4. 斐然, A., V. xxi.

THE 68TH RADICAL, 斗.

斗 *tău*

A peck-measure, A., XIII. xx. 4.

THE 69TH RADICAL, 斤.

斯 *sze*

(1) This, these, *passim*. Its antecedent is often a clause. (2) Forthwith, A., X. x. 1, xviii. 1; XIV. xlii. 2, and perhaps some other places.

新 *hsin*

To renovate, G.L.c., ii. 1. New, what is new, G.L.c., iii. 2, 3. D.M., xxvii. 6. A., II. xi; V. xviii; XVII. xxi. 3.

斷 *twan*

In 4th tone. 斷斷兮, plain and sincere, G.L.c., x. 14.

THE 70TH RADICAL, 方.

方 *fang*

(1) A region, regions, D.M., x. 2, 3, 4. A., I. i. 2; XX. i. 3. 四方, the four quarters, = all parts of the kingdom, or of a State, D.M., xx. 13. A., XIII. iv. 3; XX. i. 6. 方 = any quarter, A., XIII. v, xx. A settled definite place, A., IV. xix. (2) Tablets of wood, D.M., xx. 2. (3) An art, the way, A., VI. xxviii. 3. (4) Right rules, A., XI. xxv. 4. (5) Square, A., XI. xxv. 5, 11. (6) To compare, A., XIV. xxxi. (7) Then, A., XVI. vii. (8) Used in a designation, A., XVIII. ix. 3.

於 *yü*

Passim. Its proper meaning is *in, at, on*, in regard to place. But after many verbs and adjectives we must translate by other prepositions, as *from, to*, &c. After the possessive 之, it = *in relation to.* After adjectives it forms the comparative degree, and = *than*, D.M., xxxiii. 4. A., XI. xvi. 1; XIX. xxv. 1. Observe 於我, A., X. xv. 1, = on me, be it mine.

於 *wü*

An exclamation, G.L.c., iii. 3, 5. D.M., xxvi. 10.

施 *shih*

(1) To give, do, use, D.M., xiii. 3, 4. A., II. xxi. 2; XII. ii; XV. xxiii. G.L.c., x. 8. (2) To make a display of, A., V. xxv. 3.

施 *shih*

In 4th tone. To confer on, so as to reach to, D.M., xxxi. 5. A., VI. xxviii. 1. There is not much appreciable difference between the character in this tone and the last.

施 *ch'ih*

For 弛, to treat remissly, A., XVIII. x.

旅 *lü*

(1) A body of 500 soldiers. 師旅, 軍旅, forces, A., XI. xxv. 4; XIV. xx. 2; XV. i. 1. (2) All, general, D.M., xix. 4. (3) The name of a sacrifice, A., III. vi.

族 *tsŭ*

The circle of relatives, A., XIII. xx. 2.

THE 71ST RADICAL, 无.

旣 *chi*

(1) A particle of past time, = have, having, having been, D.M., xv. 2, xxvii. 7. A., III. x, xxi. 2; IX. v. 2, x. 3, *et al.*, *saepe*. (2) Used adverbially. That done, = then, by-and-by, A., XIV. xlii. 2. (3) Used for 餼, or 氣, *k'e*. Rations, D.M., xx. 14.

THE 72ND RADICAL, 日.

日 *zăh*

(1) The sun, D.M., xxvi. 9, xxx. 2, xxxi. 4. A., XIX. xxi, xxiv. (2) A day, days, G.L.c., ii. 1. A., II. ix; IV. vi. 2; VII. ix. 2, *et al.*, *saepe*. (3) Adverbially. Daily, D.M., xx. 14, xxxiii. 1. A., I. iv. On some days, A., VI. v. 日日, every day, G.L.c., ii. 1.

旨 *chih*

What is pleasant, spoken of food, A., XVII. xxi. 5.

昆 *kwăn*

An elder brother, D.M., xx. 8. 昆弟, brothers; the younger branches of one's relatives, generally, D.M., xx. 13. A., XI. iv.

明 *ming*

(1) Clear, illustrious, brilliant; clearly, G.L.T., 1, 4. G.L.c., i. 2. D.M., xx. 19, 20, xxiii, xxvi. 3, 4, 5, 8, xxvii. 6, xxx. 2, xxxiii. 6. A., XVI. x. (2) To illustrate, G.L.T., 1, 4. G.L.c., i. 1, 3, 4. (3) Intelligence, intelligent, D.M., xx. 21, xxi, xxvi. 8, xxxi. 1, xxxii. 3. A., II. ix. (4) To understand, D.M., iv. 1, xix. 6. (5) To purify, purification; clean, D.M., xvi. 3, xx. 14. A., X. vii. 1. (6) 明日, next day, A., XV. i. 1; XVIII. vii. 4. (7) 公明, as a double surname, A., XIV. xiv. In names, A., V. xxiv.—A., VI. xii.

易 *yi*

(1) To change, A., I. vii; XVIII. vi. 3, 4. (2) The name of the Yǐ classic, A., VII. xvi.

易
i

In 4th tone. (1) Easy, easily, A., VIII. xii; XIII. xv. 2, xxv; XIV. xi, xliv; XVII. iv. 3. Easily preserved, G.L.c., x. 5. Ease, = calmness, tranquillity, D.M., xiv. 4. (3) Minute attention to observances, A., III. iv. 3.

昔
hsi

Formerly. 昔者, A., VIII. v; XVI. i. 4; XVII. iv. 3, vii. 2.

星
hsing

A star, stars, A., II. i. D.M., xxvi. 9.

春
ch'un

The spring, A., XI. xxv. 7. D.M., xix. 3.

昭
châo

(1) Bright; to be clearly seen; clearly, A., XX. i. 3. D.M., xxvi. 4, xxxiii. 2. (2) 昭穆, the tablets in the ancestral temple, according to the order of precedence, D.M., xix. 4. (3) Honorary epithet of a duke of Lû, A., VII. xxx.

是
shih

(1) This, these, *passim*. It often resumes a previous clause, and often contains the copula, = this is. 如是, 若是, thus, such. 是故, 是以, therefore. Also 是用, A., V. xxii. (2) To be, A., IX. xxx. 1; XI. xx; XVI. i. 3, 4, 7, *et al.* (3) Right, A., XVII. iv. 4. (4) 壹是, = all, G.L.T., 6.

時
shih

(1) Time, times, A., XVI. vii. D.M., xxx. 1. Opportunity, A., XVII. i. 2. (2) The seasons, D.M., xxx. 2. Seasonal, D.M., xix. 3. A., X. viii. 2. (3) Seasonably, at proper times, D.M., xx. 14, xxxi. 2. A., XIV. xxx. 2. 以時, A., I. v. (4) Always, D.M., ii. 2, xxv. 3. A., I. i. 1. (5) To time, watch, A., XVII. i. 1.

晉
tsin

The name of a State, A., XIV. xvi.

晏
yen

(1) Late, A., XIII. xiv. (2) A surname, A., V. xvi.

晝
châu

The daytime; adverbially, A., V. ix. 1; IX. xvi.

晨
ch'ăn

The morning. 晨門, style of a gate-keeper, A., XIV. xli.

晢
hsi

Designation of one of Confucius's disciples, A., XI. xxv. 1.

暇
hsiâ

Leisure, A., XIV. xxxi.

暑
shû

Warm weather, A., X. vi. 3.

景
ching

An honorary epithet, A., XII. xi; XVI. xii; XVIII. iii. 景伯, an honorary designation, A., XIV. xxxviii; XIX. xxiii. 2.

暴
pâo

(1) Violence, oppression, G.L.c., ix. 4. A., VIII. iv. 3; XX. ii. 3. (2) To attack, or strike, unarmed, A., VII. x. 3.

曆
lî

Calculated and represented, A., XX. i. 1.

THE 73RD RADICAL, 曰.

曰
yüeh

To speak, to say, saying, *passim*. Generally the nominative is expressed, but sometimes has to be supplied from the connexion. Or 曰 = it is said, D.M., xxvii. 5, *et al.* Sometimes it = namely, D.M., xx. 8, 12, *et al.* 蓋曰, meaning, for it says, or we may assume that it says, D.M., xxvi. 10.

曲
ch'ü

(1) Bent, A., VII. xv. (2) Shoots, what is small, D.M., xxiii.

更
kăng

To change, A., XIX. xxi.

書
shû

(1) To write, A., XV. v. 4. Writing, writings, books, D.M., xxviii. 3. A., XI. xxiv. 3. (2) The Shû-ching, or Classic of History, A., II. xxi. 2; VII. xvii; XIV. xliii. 1. (3) 楚書, the name of a Book, G.L.c., x. 12.

曾
tsăng

The surname of one of Confucius's principal disciples, and of his father, G.L.c., vi. 3. A., I. iv, *et al., saepe.* A., XI. xxv. 1, 8.

曾
ts'ăng

In 2nd tone. A conjunction, = then, but, A., II. viii; III. vi; XI. xxiii. 2.

會
hûi

(1) To associate with, A., XII. xxiv. (2) Interviews of the princes with the sovereign, A., XI. xxv. 6, 12.

THE 74TH RADICAL, 月.

月
yüeh

(1) The moon, D.M., xxvi. 9, xxx. 2, xxxi. 4. A., XIX. xxi, xxiv. (2) A month, months, D.M., vii. A., VI. v; VII. xiii; X. vi. 11; XIII. x; XVII. i. 2. Monthly, from month to month, D.M., xx. 14. A., XIX. 5.

有
yü

(1) To have, possess, *passim*. Followed by 者, = he who possesses, they who have. But sometimes the 者 is omitted, as in A., I. xiv; VIII. iv; XX. i. 1, *et al.* In this sense it not only governs nouns, but is used as an auxiliary to verbs, both active and passive. (2) The impersonal substantive verb, there is, there was, *passim*. In very many instances, it is difficult to say whether the character is used thus, or as in 1. 有之, and the negative 未之有 at the end of sentences, are to be observed, G.L.T., 7. A., I. ii. 1; IV. vi. 3, *et al.* 何有 = there is no difficulty, A., IV. xiii, *et al.* But this not always, A., VII. ii, *et al.* Observe A., XIX. ii. (3) The surname of one of Confucius's disciples, A., I. ii. 1, xii, xiii; XII. ix. 1, 2. The name of another, A., III. vi; VII. xiv, *et al., saepe.*

有 *yŭ*
In 4th tone. And, A., II. iv. 1 ; X. vi. 6.

朋 *p'ăng*
A fellow-student; a friend, friends, A., I. i. 2. 朋友, see under 友.

服 *fŭ*
(1) To wear, A., XV. x. 4. Metaphorically, D.M., viii. Clothes, D.M., xvi. 3, xx. 14. A., VIII. xxi ; X. vi. 2, 11, *et al.* (2) To submit, A., XIII. iv. 3 ; XVI. i. 11, 12. 服事, to serve, A., VIII. xx. 4. 服勞, to undergo the labour, A., II. viii. (3) 子服, a branch, surname, A., XIV. xxxviii ; XIX. xxiii. 2.

胡 *hŭ*
How, D.M., xiii. 4.

朕 *chăn*
I ; now used for the imperial *We*, A., XX. i. 3.

朔 *so*
The first day of the moon, A., III. xvii, 1.

望 *wang*
To look towards, admiring and expecting, D.M., xxix. 5. A., XIX. ix ; XX. ii. 2. 望＝to compare one's self to, A., V. viii. 2.

朝 *chăo*
(1) Morning, in the morning, A., IV. viii ; XII. xxi. 3. (2) A name, A., VI. xiv.

朝 *ch'áo*
(1) The court, A., V. vii. 4 ; XIV. xxxviii ; XIX. xxiii. 1. (2) To be in court, appear in court, A., X. ii. 1, vi. 11 ; XIV. xxii. 2. 退朝, to return from court, A., X. xii ; XIII. xiv. (3) To hold a court, give audience, D.M., xx. 14. A., XVIII. iv. (4) Court, as an adjective, A., X. x. 11, xiii. 3. (5) A name, A., XIX. xxii.

期 *ch'i*
(1) A fixed time, A., XX. ii. 3. (2) A name, A., VII. xxx. 2, 3.

期 *chi*
A round year, D.M., xviii. 3. A., XVII. xxi. 1, 2. 期月, a round month, D.M., vii.

朞 *chi*
朞月, a round year, A., XIII. x ; meaning the months of a round year.

THE 75TH RADICAL, 木.

木 *mú*
(1) Trees, D.M., xxvi. 9. A., XVII. ix. 7 ; XIX. xii. 2. (2) Wood, A., V. ix. 1. (3) Wooden, A., III. xxiv. (4) Simple, plain, A., XIII. xxvii.

未 *wei*
Not yet, *passim*. We may sometimes translate by *not*, but the force of the *yet* is always to be detected. It is joined with 嘗, A., III. xxiv ; VI. xii ; VII. vii, ix ; IX. xxx. 2. Its power, in common with other negatives, to attract 之 to itself, and make it precede the verb which governs it, is to be noted, G.L.T., 7. G.L.C., ix. 4. A., I. ii. 2 ; V. v, x, xiii ; *et al.*

末 *mo*
(1) The end, the product, result, in opposition to 本, the root, G.L.T., 3, 7. G.L.C., x. 7. (2) Small, trivial, D.M., xxxiii. 6. A., XIX. xii. 1. (3) In old age, D.M., xviii. 3. (4) Not, do not, A., IX. x. 3, xxiii ; XIV. xlii. 3 ; XV. xv ; XVII. v. 2.

本 *păn*
The root ; what is radical, essential, G.L.T., 3, 6, 7. G.L.c., iv, v, x. 7, 8. D.M., i. 4, xxxii. 1. A., I. ii. 2 ; XIX. xii. 1. What is first to be attended to, A., III. iv. 1. To be rooted, D.M., xxix. 3.

朱 *chú*
(1) Vermilion colour, A., XVII. xviii. (2) A surname, A., XVIII. viii.

朽 *hsiŭ*
Rotten, A., V. ix. 1.

杇 *wû*
To plaster, A., V. ix. 1.

杞 *ch'i*
The name of a State, A., III. ix. D.M., xxviii. 5.

杖 *chang*
A staff, A., XIV. xlvi ; XVIII. vii. 1. 杖者, those who carried staffs, A., X. x. 1.

束 *shú*
(1) To bind, gird, A., V. vii. 4. (2) A bundle of strips of dried flesh, A., VII. vii.

林 *lin*
A surname, A., III. iv. 1, vi.

東 *tung*
(1) The east, eastern, A., XVII. v. 3. To turn to the east, A., X. xiii. 3. (2) 東蒙, a mountain, A., XVI. i. 4. 東里, a place in Tsin, A., XIV. ix. 1.

某 *mău*
So-and-so, A., XV. xli. 1.

松 *sung*
The pine-tree, A., III. xxi. 1 ; IX. xxvii.

枉 *wang*
Crooked, used metaphorically, A., II. ix ; XII. xxii. 3, 4. With verbal force, A., XVIII. ii.

枕 *chăn*
To use as a pillow, A., VII. xv.

材 *ts'âi*
Qualities, D.M., xvii. 3. In A., V. vi, the meaning is uncertain.

果 *kwo*
(1) Determined, decided, A., VI. vi ; XIV. xlii. 3. 果敢, A., XVII. xxiv. (2) To carry into effect, A., XIII. xx. 3. (3) Really, D.M., xx. 21.

柏 *păi*
The cypress-tree, A., III. xxi. 1 ; IX. xxvii.

柙 *hsiâ*
A cage for wild beasts, A., XVI. i. 7.

柔 *zăn*
(1) Gentle, mild, D.M., x. 3, xxxi. 1. To treat gently, D.M., xx. 12, 13, 14. (2) Weak, D.M., xx. 21. (3) Mild, soft, in a bad sense, A., XVI. iv.

析 *hsî*
To be split ; divisions, A., XVI. i. 12.

柯
ko

An axe-handle, D.M., xiii. 2.

柳
liŭ

柳下, the name of a place or house, A., XV. xiii ; XVIII. ii, viii. 1, 3.

栖
hsî

栖栖者, one who keeps roosting, or hanging, about, A., XIV. xxxiv. 1.

栗
lî

戰栗, the appearance of being frightened, A., III. xxi. 1.

校
chiáo

To enter into altercation, A., VIII. v.

柴
ch'ái

Name of one of Confucius's disciples, A., XI. xvii. 1.

格
ko

(1) ? To investigate, G.L.T., 4, 5. (2) To come to, approach, D.M., xvi. 4. (3) To become correct, A., II. iii. 2.

桃
t'áo

The peach-tree, G.L.c., ix. 6.

桀
chieh

The last sovereign of the Hsiâ dynasty, a tyrant, G.L.c., ix. 4. 桀溺, a recluse, A., XVIII. vi. 1, 3.

栽
tsái

To flourish, as a tree, D.M., xvii. 3.

桓
hwan

(1) 桓公, a famous duke of Ch'î, A., XIV. xvi, xvii, xviii. (2) A surname, A., VII. xii. (3) 三桓, the three principal families in Lû, A., XVI. xxii.

桑
sang

子桑, apparently a double surname, A., VI. i. 2.

桴
fú

A raft, A., V. vi.

梁
liang

A bridge, A., X. xviii. 2.

梲
chŭeh

Small pillars, supporting the rafters of a house, A., V. xvii.

棄
ch'i

To abandon, throw away, neglect, A., V. xviii. 2 ; XIII. xix, xxx ; XVII. xiv ; XVIII. x.

棺
kwan

An inner coffin, A., XI. vii. 2.

椁
ko

An outer coffin, A., XI. vii. 1, 2.

棣
tì

唐棣, the aspen plum, A., IX. xxxi. 1.

棘
chi

A surname, A., XII. viii.

根
ch'ang

A name, A., V. x.

植
chih

To stick in the ground, A., XVIII. vii. 1.

極
chí

The very utmost, as a noun and adverb, G.L.c., ii. 4. D.M., xxvii. 2, 6.

楚
ch'ŭ

The name of a State, G.L.c., x. 12. A., XVIII. ix. 2.

榮
jung

Glorious, A., XIX. xxv. 4.

樂
yo

(1) Music, *saepe*. 女樂, female musicians, A., XVIII. iv. (2) 大師樂, Grand music-master, A., III. xxiii.

樂
lê

Pleasure, joy ; to rejoice in, feel joy, *saepe*.

樊
fan

A surname, A., II. v ; VI. xx ; XII. xxi, xxii ; XIII. iv, xix.

樂
áo

To find pleasure in, A., VI. xxi ; XVI. v. 好樂, G.L.c., vii. 1.

樹
shu

(1) Trees, = vegetation, D.M., xx. 3. (2) A screen, A., III. xxii. 3.

機
chi

A spring, source of influence, G.L.c., ix. 3.

權
ch'üan

A weight, weights, A., XX. i. 6. To weigh, A., IX. xxix. The exigency of the times, as if determined by weighing, A., XVIII. viii. 4.

櫝
tú

A coffer, a repository, A., XVI. i. 7.

THE 76TH RADICAL, 欠.

次
ts'ze

(1) Next in order or degree, D.M., xxiii. 1. A., VII. xxvii ; XIII. xx. 2, 3 ; XVI. ix. In A., XIV. xxxix. 2, 3, 4, 其次 only = some. (2) 造次, in moments of haste, A., IV. v. 3.

欲
yŭ

(1) To desire, to wish, G.L.T., 4. A., II. iv. 6 ; III. x, xvii. 1, *et al., saepe.* (2) To be covetous, = 貪, A., XII. xviii ; XIV. ii, xiii. 1. In A., XX. ii. 1, 2, 欲 is distinguished from 貪.

欺
ch'i

To deceive, impose upon ; to be deceived, G.L.c., vi. 1. A., VI. xxiv ; IX. xi. 2 ; XIV. xxiii.

歌
ko

To sing, A., VII. ix. 2, xxxi ; XVII. iv, xx ; XVIII. v.

歎
t'an

To sigh, with the idea of admiration, A., IX. x. 1 ; XI. xxv. 7.

THE 77TH RADICAL, 止.

止
chih

(1) To rest ; where to rest, G.L.T., 1, 2. G.L.c., iii. 1, 2, 3. (2) To stop, desist, D.M., xiii. 2. A., IX. xviii, xx ; XI. xxiii. 3 ; XII. xxiii ; XVI. i. 6 ; XIX. xiv. (3) To detain, A., XVIII. vii. 1.

正
chăng

(1) To rectify, to adjust ; be rectified, G.L.T., 4, 5. G.L.c., vii. 1, 3, ix. 8. D.M., xiv. 3. A., I. xiv ; VIII. iv. 3 ; *et al., saepe.* (2) Correct, correctness, correctly, G.L.c., vii. 1. D.M., xxxi. 1. A., X. viii. 3, ix. (In some of these examples, correct = square, straight), A., XIII. 3, 5, vi ; XIV. xvi. (3) Just, exactly, A., VII. xxxiii. Observe A., XVII. x.

正
_{chang}

In 1st tone. The bull's eye in a target, D.M., xiv. 5.

此
_{ts'ze}

This, *saepe*. 如此, thus, G.L.c., ix. 3. D.M., xvi. 5, xxvi. 6, xxviii. 1. 在此, here, D.M., xxix. 6. The character does not occur in the Analects.

武
_{wŭ}

(1) The honorary epithet of the first sovereign of the Châu dynasty, D.M., xviii. 1, 2, 3, *et al.*, *saepe*. The name of his music, A., III. xxv. (2) The honorary epithet of others, A., XIV. xiii, xv.—A., V. xx.—A., II. vi; V. vii.—A., XIX. xxiii, xxiv. (3) A name, A., XVIII. ix. 4. (4) 武城, name of a place, A., VI. xii; XVII. iv.

歲
_{sùi}

The year, years, A., IX. xxvii; XVII. i. 2.

歸
_{kwei}

(1) To return, A., V. xxi; XI. xxv. 7. (2) To revert to, A., I. ix; XII. i. 1. (3) To turn to, D.M., xx. 13. To flow to, A., XIX. xx. 歸心, to turn to in heart, A., XX. i. 7. (4) To turn to, depend on, A., X. xv. 1. (5) To present, A., XVII. i. 1; XVIII. iv. (6) 歸=to be married, G.L.c., ix. 6. (7) 三歸, see on 三.

THE 78TH RADICAL, 歹.

死
_{sze}

To die; death; the dead, D.M., x. 4, 5, xix. 5. A., II. v. 3; IV. viii; XI. vi, vii. 1, 2, viii, ix, x, xi, xii. 2, xxii, *et al.*, *saepe*. 後死者, a future mortal, A., IX. v. 3; said by Confucius of himself.

殆
_{t'ai}

Dangerous;—both what is perilous, and being in peril, G.L.c., x. 14. A., II. xv; XV. x. 6; XVIII. v. 1.

殖
_{chih}

To be largely produced; to be amassed, D.M., xxvi. 9. A., XI. xviii. 2.

殘
_{ts'an}

Vicious, violently bad, A., XIII. xi.

殯
_{pin}

To coffin, = to bury, A., X. xv. 1.

THE 79TH RADICAL, 殳.

殺
_{shâ}

To kill, A., XII. xix; XIV. xvii. 1, xviii. 1; XV. viii; XVIII. vii. 3; XX. ii. 3. 殺=Capital punishments, A., XIII. xi.

殺
_{shâi}

Gradually decreasing, D.M., xx. 5. A., X. iv. 9.

殷
_{yin}

The name of a dynasty, G.L.c., x. 5. D.M., xxviii. 5. A., II. xxiii. 2, *et al.*

殿
_{tien}

In 4th tone. To bring up the rear, A., VI. xiii.

毀
_{hûi}

(1) To blame excessively, revile, A., XV. xxiv; XIX. xxiv. (2) To be broken, A., XVI. i. 7.

毅
_i

Determined and enduring, D.M., xxxi. 1. A., VIII. vii. 1; XIII. xxvii.

THE 80TH RADICAL, 毋.

毋
_{wû}

Do not, = do not do, do not have, &c., G.L.c., vi. 1, x. 2. A., VI. iii. 4; IX. xxiv; XI. xxv. 2; XII. xxiii. In A., IX. iv, it is taken as = 無, the simple negative, but its ordinary meaning may be retained.

母
_{mŭ}

A mother, A., VI. iii. 1. 父母, a parent, parents, G.L.c., x. 3. D.M., xv. 3, xviii. 3. A., I. vii; II. vi; IV. xviii, xix, xxi; XI. iv; XVII. xxi. 6; XVIII. ii.

每
_{mei}

Every, A., III. xv; X. xiv.

THE 81ST RADICAL, 比.

比
_{pi}

To compare, be compared, A., VII. i.

比
_{pi}

In 4th tone. (1) To follow, A., IV. x. (2) Partisanly, A., II. xiv. (3) Joined with 及, within, by the time of, A., XI. xxv. 4, 5.

THE 82ND RADICAL, 毛.

毛
_{mâo}

The hair, a hair, D.M., xix. 4, xxxiii. 6.

THE 83RD RADICAL, 氏.

氏
_{shih}

A family, i.e. a branch family. Follows surnames, and denotes particular individuals, A., III. i, *et al.*—A., III. xxi.—XIV. x. 3.—III. xxii.—XIV. xli, xlii.—XIX. xix.

民
_{min}

(1) The people, the multitude, *passim*. (2) = 人, man, men, A., VI. xx; XV. xxxiv. And perhaps in some other places, as D.M., iii. A., VI. xxvii; XVI. ix; XVII. xvi.

THE 84TH RADICAL, 气.

氣
_{ch'i}

Breath, A., X. iv. 4. 血氣, blood and breath, = the physical powers, A., XVI. vii. 有血氣者, mankind, D.M., xxxi. 4. Observe 辭氣, A., VIII. iv. 3, and 食氣, A., X. viii. 4.

THE 85TH RADICAL, 水.

水
_{shŭi}

Water, D.M., xxvi. 9, xxx. 1. A., VI. xxi; VII. xv; XV. xxxiv.

永
_{yung}

To perpetuate, perpetual, D.M., xxix. 6. A., XX. i. 1.

汎
_{fan}

Universally, A., I. vi.

求
_{ch'iû}

(1) To seek for; also to ask, request, G.L.c., ix. 2, 4. D.M., xiii. 4, xiv. 3, 5. A., I. x. 1, 2, xiv; IV. xiv, *et al.*, *saepe*. (2) The name of one of Confucius's disciples, A., V. vii. 3; VI. vi, x, *et al.*, *saepe*.

汝
_{wăn}

The name of a stream, A., VI. vii.

沂
i
The name of a stream, A., XI. xxv. 7.

沐
mŭ
沐浴, to bathe, A., XIV. xxii. 2. See note there.

沒
mŭ
and
mei
(1) To die, be dead, A., I. xi; IX. v. 2. 沒世, after death, G.L.c., iii. 5. A., XV. xix. Others understand the phrase as = 'till death.' (2) To exhaust, be exhausted, A., XVII. xxi. 3. 沒階, to the last step, A., X. iv. 5. 沒齒, toothless, A., XIV. x. 3.

沛
p'ei
顚沛, in danger, in confusion, A., IV. v. 3.

河
ho
Rivers, a river, D.M., xxvi. 9. A., VII. x. 3. *The* river, i. e. the Yellow river, A., IX. viii; XVIII. ix. 3.

治
ch'ih
To regulate, manage, govern, G.L.T., 4. G.L.c., ix. 1, 5, x. 1. D.M., xiii. 2, xx. 6, 11, 14, 17. A., V. vii. 2; XIV. xxvi.

治
chih
To be regulated; to be well governed, G.L.T., 5, 7. A., VIII. xx. 1; XV. iv.

沮
chŭ
長沮, the designation of a recluse, A., XVIII. vi. 1, 2.

沽
kŭ
To sell, A., IX. xii. Retailed, A., X. viii. 5.

泥
ni
In 4th tone. To be obstructed, inapplicable, A., XIX. iv.

泉
ch'üan
A fountain, a spring, D.M., xxxi. 2, 3.

法
fă
(1) A model; to imitate, G.L.c., ix. 8. D.M., xxix. 5. (2) Law-like = strict; laws, A., IX. xxiii; XX. i. 6.

泰
t'ai
(1) A dignified ease, A., VII. xxv. 3. Opposed to 驕, A., XIII. xxvi; XX. ii. 1, 2. (2) Arrogant, A., IX. iii. 2. Coupled with 驕, G.L.c., x. 18. (3) 泰山, the name of a mountain, A., III. vi. 泰伯, honorary designation of an ancient worthy, A., VIII. i.

洋
yang
洋溢, to overflow, D.M., xxxi. 4. 洋洋乎, the appearance of vast swelling waters, grandly, D.M., xvi. 3, xxvii. 2. A., VIII. xv.

洒
shăi
To sprinkle, A., XIX. xii. 1.

洫
hsüeh
A water-channel, a ditch. 溝洫, A., VIII. xxi.

津
chin
A ford, A., XVIII. vi. 1, 2.

洩
hsiĕh
To leak, D.M., xxvi. 9.

流
liŭ
(1) Flowing, a current, D.M., xxx. 3. (2) Weak, unstable, D.M., x. 5. (3) To banish, G.L.c., x. 15. (4) 下流, a low-lying situation, A., XVII. xxiv. 1; XIX. xx.

浩
hâo
浩浩, vast, D.M., xxxii. 2.

浮
fâu
To float, floating, A., V. vi; VII. xv.

浴
yŭ
To wash, A., XI. xxv. 7. 沐浴, to bathe, A., XIV. xxii. 2.

海
hâi
The sea, seas, D.M., xxvi. 9. A., V. vi; XVIII. ix. 5. 四海, a name for the kingdom, the world, D.M., xvii. 1, xviii. 2. A., XII. v. 4; XX. i. 1.

浸
chin
To soak, A., XII. vi.

涖
lì
The approach of a superior; to govern, preside over, A., XV. xxxii. 2, 3.

湼
nieh
To steep in muddy water, A., XVII. vii. 3.

淇
ch'i
The name of a stream, G.L.c., iii. 4.

淡
tan
Insipid, D.M., xxxiii. 1.

淫
yĕn
Licentious, A., III. xx; XV. x. 6.

深
shăn
Deep, A., VIII. iii; XIV. xlii. 2.

清
ch'ing
Pure, purity, A., V. xviii. 2; XVIII. viii. 4.

淵
yüan
(1) A gulf, an abyss; deep, the deep, D.M., xii. 3, xxxi. 2, 3, xxxii. 2. A., VIII. iii. (2) The name of Confucius's favourite disciple, A., V. xxv; VII. x. 1, *et al.*, *saepe.*

淺
ch'ien
Shallow, A., XIV. xlii. 2.

溫
wăn
(1) Benign, unpretending, A., II. xi; VII. xxxvii; XVI. x; XIX. ix. D.M., xxxi. 1, xxxiii. 1. (2) To cherish, know thoroughly, A., II. xi. D.M., xxvii. 6.

游
yŭ
(1) To ramble, to seek recreation, A., VII. vi. 4. (2) 子游, the designation of one of Confucius's disciples, A., II. vii; IV. xxvi, *et al.*, *saepe.*

測
ts'ĕ
To fathom. 不測, unfathomable, D.M., xxvi. 7, 9.

湯
t'ang
(1) Boiling water, A., XVI. xi. (2) Name of the first sovereign of the Shang dynasty, G.L.c., ii. 1. A., XII. xxii. 6.

縢
t'ăng
The name of a State, A., XIV. xii.

滔
t'âo
滔滔, the appearance of an inundation, A., XVIII. vi. 3.

漆
ch'i

漆雕, a double surname, A., V. v.

溺
ni

桀溺, the name of a recluse, A., XVIII. vi.

溢
yi

洋溢, to overflow, D.M., xxxi. 4.

溥
p'ü

Great, all-embracing, D.M., xxxi. 2, 3.

漏
lâu

To leak. 屋漏, the part of a house open to the light of heaven, D.M., xxxiii. 3.

溝
kâu

A ditch. 溝洫, A., VIII. xxi. 溝瀆, A., XIV. xviii. 3.

漢
han

The name of a river, A., XVIII. ix. 4.

潔
chieh

To purify, pure, A., VII. xxviii. 2 ; XVIII. vii. 5.

潤
zun

To soak, moisten, enrich, adorn, G.L.c., vi. 4. A., XII. vi ; XIV. ix.

滅
mieh

(1) To extinguish ; be extinguished, A., XX. i. 7. (2) 滅明, a name, A., VI. xii.

潛
ch'ien

To dive, sink, D.M., xxxiii. 2.

澹
t'an

澹臺, a double surname, A., VI. xii.

濟
chi

To help, benefit, A., VI. xxviii. 1.

瀆
tû

A ditch. 溝瀆, A., XIV. xviii. 3.

澳
yü

A bank, the winding and curving of a river's banks, G.L.c., iii. 4.

濫
lan

To overflow, exceed due bounds, A., XV. i. 3.

灌
kwan

To pour out a libation, A., III. x.

THE 86TH RADICAL, 火.

火
hwo

Fire, A., XV. xxxiv. 改火, 'to change the fire,' i. e. to get fire from all the different kinds of wood, A., XVII. xxi. 3.

烈
lieh

Violent, A., X. xvi. 5.

裁
tsâi

I. q. 災, calamity, D.M., xxviii. 1.

焉
yen

A final particle, *passim.* (1) It is found at the end of clauses, when the mind expects the sequel, G.L.c., vii. 2. D.M., xi. 1, xiii. 4. A., V. xxiii ; VI. vii ; *et al., saepe.* (2) It is found at the end of sentences, and gives a liveliness to the style, D.M., x. 5, xiv. 2. A., I. xiv ; IV. xvii ; *et al., saepe.* (3) It is found often at the end of correlative clauses and sentences, G.L.c., viii. 1, x. 14. D.M., i. 5, xii. 2, xxvi. 9.

A., VIII. xiii. 3 ; XI. xxiv. 3 ; XIII. xx. 2, *et al.* (4) Observe D.M., xxix. 2. A., V. xv.

焉
yen

In 1st tone. An interrogative particle, generally best translated by 'how.' It is placed at the beginning of the clause to which it belongs, unless where another particle, or the nominative, immediately precedes, D.M., xxxii. 1. A., II. x. 4 ; III. xxii. 3 ; IV. i ; V. ii, iv. 2, x, xviii. 1, 2 ; *et al., saepe.*

無
wû

No, not, to be without, not to have, *passim.* Joined to verbs, adjectives, and nouns. It is often followed by 所, A., III. vii ; IX. ii. 1, *et al.* The 所 must sometimes be understood, A., XX. iii. 1, 2, 3, *et al.* 無...不, a strong affirmation, often with 所 between, G.L.c., ii. 4, vi. 2, *et al.* So 未一無, A., VII. vii. 1. 無乃...乎, 無害...乎, forms of interrogation, A., IX. xi. 3 ; VI. i. 3, *et al.* Opposed to 有, standing absolutely, = the state of being without, A., IX. xi. 2 ; VIII. v. 1. So 無之, there is not it, opposed to 有之, G.L.c., ix. 1. Observe 無以爲, it is of no use doing so, A., XIX. xxiv.

焚
fân

To be burned, A., X. xii.

然
zan

(1) So, A., III. xiii. 2 ; VI. xxiv ; VIII. xx. 3 ; XIV. xiii. 2. 然=yes, A., XV. ii. 2, xli. 3 ; XVII. vii. 3 ; XVIII. vi. 3. 然則, so then, well then. 然而, so but, A., XI. xv. 2, xviii. 5 ; XIX. xv. (2) To be right, A., VI. i. 4. (3) 然後, and afterwards, A., VI. xvi ; IX. xiv, xxvii ; *et al.* (4) Added to adjectives, forming adverbs, G.L.c., vi. 2. D.M., xxxiii. 1. A., V. xxi ; IX. x. 1, 2 ; XIX. ix ; XX. ii. 2, *et al.*—Observe A., VIII. xxi ; XI. xii. 2 ; XIV. vi. 1. (5) 子然, name of a member of the 季 family, A., XI. xxiii.

煥
hwan

煥乎, how glorious, A., VIII. xix. 2.

照
châo

To enlighten, to shine on, D.M., xxxi. 4.

熙
hsi

Bright, G.L.c., iii. 3.

熟
shû

Cooked, to cook, A., X. xiii. 1.

燕
yen

(1) A feast, D.M., xix. 4. (2) Easy and unoccupied, A., VII. iv.

燧 *sui* 鑽燧, to obtain fire by boring, or friction, A., XVII. xxi. 3.

THE 87TH RADICAL, 爪.

爭 *tsăng* To wrangle, to strive, G.L.c., x. 8. D.M., xxxiii. 4. A., III. vii ; XV. xxi.

爲 *wei* (1) To do, to make, G.L.c., vi. 2, x. 18. D.M., xi. 1, xiii. 1, xvi. 1. A., III. xxvi ; XIV. xv, xviii ; XIX. iv, xv, xvi ; *et al.*, *saepe.* 爲 = to be in charge of, to administer, to govern, D.M., xx. 12, 15. A., II. i ; IV. xiii ; XI. xxv. 4, 5 ; XIII. iii. 1, xi, *et al.* 何爲 = why, A., XIV. xxxiv, xxxvii. 2. (2) To be, G.L.c., x. 15. D.M., vi, xvii. 1. A., I. ii. 2, xii ; VI. ii, iii. 3, vii, xi, xii ; *et al.*, *saepe.* At the beginning of clauses, it may be often translated by who is, D.M., xxii, xxiii, *et al.* (3) Before nouns of relation, and others, it = to play, to show one's self to be, G.L.c., iii. 3, ix. 8. D.M., viii. 8. A., I. ii. 1 ; XIII. xv. 2, 3, 4, *et al.* (4) 以爲, with or without intermediate words. To take to be = to regard as, to consider, to have to be ; to use to make, G.L.T., 6, x. 12, 13, 22. D.M., xviii. 1. A., II. viii ; III. viii, xviii, xxiv ; XIV. ii. 1, 2, iii, iii. 1, 2, xix. 2, *et al.*, *saepe.* Sometimes 爲 is found alone, without the 以, A., IX. xi. 2 ; XIX. ii ; XI. xxiv. 3, *et al.* Observe A., XII. viii ; XIII. v ; XIX. xxiv. Observe also 爲之奴, A., XVIII. i, and the same idiom in other places.

爲 *wei* In 4th tone. For, because of, in behalf of, with a view to, because ; to be for, D.M., xix. 4 (?). A., I. iv ; III. xvi, xxii. 5 ; VI. iii. 1, vii ; VII. xiv. 1, 2 ; XI. ix. 3, xvi. 1 ; XIII. xviii. 2 ; XIV. xxv ; XV. xxxix.

爵 *chio* Rank, dignity, D.M., ix, xix. 4.

THE 88TH RADICAL, 父.

父 *fù* A father, *saepe.* 諸父昆弟, uncles and cousins, D.M., xx. 13. So 父兄, A., IX. xv. 父母, parents, a parent, *saepe.* 父父, the other being the father, A., XII. xi. 1, 2. 人父, see 人.

父 *fù* In 3rd tone. 莒父, name of a place, A., XIII. xvii.

THE 89TH RADICAL, 爻.

爾 *r* (1) You, your, G.L.c., x. 4. D.M., xv. 2, xxxiii. 3. A., III. xxiv. 2 ; V. xi, xxv. 1, *et al.*, *saepe.* (2) After adjectives, making adverbs, A., IX. x. 3 ; XI. xxv. 4 ; XVII. iv. 2. (3) A final particle, synonymous with

耳, simply, just, D.M., xiii. 4. A., X. i. 2. 云爾, so, just, used at the end of a sentence, A., VII. xviii. 2, xxxiii.

THE 90TH RADICAL, 爿.

牆 *ch'iang* A wall, A., V. ix. 1 ; XVII. x ; XIX. xxiii. 2, 3. 蕭牆, a screen in a prince's court, A., XVI. i. 13.

THE 91ST RADICAL, 片.

片 *p'ien* A splinter, a half, A., XII. xii.

版 *pan* Tables of population, A., X. xvi. 3.

牖 *yù* A window, A., VI. viii.

THE 93RD RADICAL, 牛.

牛 *niû* (1) A cow, an ox, the cow kind, A., VI. iv ; XVII. iv. 2. G.L.c., x. 22. (2) 伯牛, the designation of one of the disciples, A., VI. viii ; XI. ii. 2. 司馬牛, a disciple of Confucius, A., XII. iii, iv, v. 中牟, the name of a place, A., XVII. vii. 2.

牟 *mâu* Surname of one of Confucius's disciples, A., IX. vi. 4.

牢 *lâo* The male of animals, translated *victim*, A., XX. i. 3.

牡 *mâu* A thing, things. 萬物, all things, D.M., xxvi. 5. 物 = animals and things, D.M., xxii. 物 = men and things, D.M., xxv. 2, 3.

物 *wù*

犂 *li* 犂牛, a brindled cow, A., VI. iv.

THE 94TH RADICAL, 犬.

犬 *ch'ŭan* A dog, A., II. vii ; XII. viii. 3.

犯 *fan* (1) To offend, be offended, against, A., ii. 1 ; VIII. v. To withstand to the face, A., XIV. xxiii. (2) 舊犯, uncle Fan, G.L.c., x. 13.

狂 *k'wang* Ardent, ambitious, extravagant, extravagance, A., V. xxi ; VIII. xvi ; XIII. xxi. 1 ; XVII. viii. 3, xvi. 2. A madman, A., XVIII. v. 1.

狄 *tî* The name of the northern barbarians, 夷狄, barbarous tribes, D.M., xiv. 2. A., III. v ; XIII. xix.

狎 *hsiâ* (1) To be familiar with, A., X. xvi. 2. (2) To be disrespectful to, A., XVI. viii. 2.

狐 *hù* A fox, A., IX. xxvi. 1 ; X. vi. 4, 7.

狷 *chûan* Cautious and decided, A., XIII. xxi.

猗 *î* 猗猗, the appearance of luxuriance, G.L.c., iii. 4.

猛 *mâng* Fierce, A., VII. xxxvii; XX. ii. 1, 2.

猶 *yû* (1) As, G.L.c., iv. A., V. xviii. 2; VII. xxxii; XI. x, xv; XII. viii. 3, xiii; XVII. x, xii; XIX. xxv. 3. (2) Still, yet, D.M., xii. 2, xiii. 2, xxxiii. 6. A., VI. xxviii. 1; VIII. xvii; XII. ix. 3; XIV. xxxviii. 1, xlv; XV. xxv. 1; XVII. xxii; XVIII. v. 1; XIX. xxv. 3.

獄 *yü* Litigations, A., XII. xii.

獨 *tû* (1) Only, A., XII. v. (2) Alone, A., XVI. xiii. 2, 3. 其獨, the being alone, G.L.c., vi. 1, 2. D.M., i. 3.

獲 *hwo* To obtain; acquisition, A., VI. xx. To obtain the confidence of, to gain, D.M., xx. 6, 17. 獲罪, to sin, offend, against, A., III. xiii. 2.

獻 *hsien* (1) Used for 賢, wise men, A., III. ix. (2) An honorary epithet, G.L.c., x. 22.

獸 *shâu* Wild animals, D.M., xxvi. 9. A., XVII. ix. 7; XVIII. vi. 4.

THE 95TH RADICAL, 玄.

玄 *hsüan* Dark-coloured, A., X. vi. 10; XX. i. 3.

率 *hsü* (1) To follow, accord with, D.M., i. 1. (2) 率爾, hastily, A., XI. xxv. 4.

THE 96TH RADICAL, 玉.

玉 *yü* (1) Jade; used generally for precious stones; a gem, gems, A., IX. xii; XVI. i. 7; XVII. xi. (2) 伯玉, a designation, A., XIV. xxvi; XV. xi. 2.

王 *wang* (1) A king, kings, A., XIII. xii. 先王, the former kings, G.L.c., iii. 5. A., I. xii. 2. A former king, A., XVI. i. 4. (2) 王孫, a double surname, A., III. xiii; XIV. xx. 2.

王° *wang* The 4th tone. To exercise true, kingly authority, D.M., xviii. 3, xxix. 1. 追王°, to carry up the title of king to, D.M., xviii. 3.

理 *lî* Distinctive, discriminating, D.M., xxxi. 1, xxxiii. 1.

琢 *cho* To cut, as jewels or gems, G.L.c., iii. 4. A., I. xv. 2.

琴 *ch'in* A harpsichord or lute, D.M., xv. 2.

瑟 *shê* (1) Stern, majestic, G.L.c., iii. 4. (2) The harpsichord, A., XI. xiv. 1, xxv. 7; XVII. xx. 1. 琴瑟, D.M., xv. 2.

璉 *lien* A gemmed vessel, used in sacrifice. 瑚璉, A., V. iii.

瑚 *hû* Same as the above.

THE 97TH RADICAL, 瓜.

瓜 *kwâ* A gourd. 匏瓜, A., XVII. vii. 4. Supposed to be instead of 必, A., X. viii. 10.

瓢 *p'iâo* A calabash, A., VI. ix.

THE 99TH RADICAL, 甘.

甘 *kan* Sweet, to enjoy as sweet or pleasant, A., XVII. xxi. 5.

甚 *shăn* Excessive, to an exceeding degree, A., VII. v, xxviii. 2; VIII. x. 甚於…, more important than, A., XV. xxxiv.

THE 100TH RADICAL, 生.

生 *shêng* (1) To produce, to be produced, G.L.c., x. 19. D.M., xvii. 3, xx. 5, xxvi. 7, 9. A., I. ii. 2; VII. xxii; XVII. xix. 3. (2) To be born, D.M., xx. 9, xxviii. 1. A., VII. xix. 生而知之, born with knowledge, A., XVI. ix; VI. xvii. (3) To live, A., VI. xvii; XII. x. 2; XVII. xxi. 6. The living, when living, D.M., xix. 5. A., II. v. 3; X. xiii. 1. Life, A., XI. xi; XII. v. 3; XV. viii; XIX. xxv. 4. 先生, elders, A., II. viii; XIV. xlvii. 2. 後生, a youth, A., IX. xxii. 平生, the life-time, A., XIV. xiii. 2. (4) 微生, a double surname, A., XIV. xxxiv.—V. xxiii.

產 *ch'ân* 子產, the designation of a statesman of Confucius's time, A., V. xv; XIV. ix, x.

THE 101ST RADICAL, 用.

用 *yung* (1) To use, to employ (in office); to expend, G.L.c., ii. 4, x. 19. D.M., vi, xxviii. 5. 自用, D.M., xxviii. 5. A., I. v, xii. 1; VII. x; XIII. iv. 3, *et al.* 焉用, why use? = of what use is? A., V. iv. 2; XII. xix; XVI. i. 6; XVII. iv. 2. (2) 是用=是以, thereby, A., V. xxii.

甫 *fû* 章甫, a certain cap of ceremony, A., XI. xxv. 6.

甯 *ning* A surname, A., V. xx.

THE 102ND RADICAL, 田.

由 *yû* (1) From, proceeding from, A., XII. i. 1. 所由, motives, A., II. x. 2. 由

= by, to proceed by, to follow, A., I. xii. 1 ; VI. xii, xv ; VIII. ix ; IX. x. 3. (2) name of Tsze-lû, one of Confucius's disciples, A., II. xvii ; V. vi, vii ; *et al., saepe.* 仲由, A., VI. vi ; XI. xxiii ; XVIII. vi. 3.

申 *shăn* (1) To repeat, D.M., xvii. 4. (2) 申如, easy-like, A., VII. iv. (3) A surname, A., V. x.

甲 *chiă* 太甲, the name of a Book in the Shû-ching, G.L.c., i. 2.

畏 *wei* To respect, A., IX. xxii. 畏敬, G.L.c., viii. 1. To reverence, D.M., xx. 13. To stand in awe of, A., XVI. viii. 1, 2 ; XX. ii. 2. To be put in fear, A., IX. v ; XI. xxii.

畔 *pan* To transgress what is right, A., VI. xxv; XII. xv. To rebel, A., XVII. v, vii. 2.

畜 *ch'ŭ* To breed, nourish, G.L.c., x. 22. A., X. xiii. 1.

畝 *mău* A name, A., XIV. xxxiv.

畫 *hwă* To mark off by a line, to limit one's self, A., VI. x.

異 *i* (1) Different (followed by 乎 and 於), A., I. x. 2 ; XI. xxv. 7 ; XII. x. 3 ; *et al.* 異 = other, A., XVI. xiv. (2) Strange, extraordinary, A., II. xvi ; XI. xxiii. 2.

當 *tang* (1) To undertake, sustain, A., XV. xxxv. (2) As a preposition, in, in regard to, A., X. vi. 3 ; XIX. xii. 1.

畿 *chi* The imperial domain, G.L.c., iii. 1.

疆 *chiang* A boundary, a limit. 無疆, boundless, D.M., xxvi. 5.

THE 103RD RADICAL, 疋.

疏 *shû* (1) Distance—in feeling, A., IV. xxvi. (2) Coarse, A., VII. xv ; X. viii. 10 ; XIV. x. 3.

疑 *i* To doubt, doubtful points, D.M., xxix. 3, 4. A., II. xviii. 2 ; XII. xx. 6 ; XVI. x.

THE 104TH RADICAL, 疒.

疚 *chiû* A chronic illness ; spoken of the mind, dolorous, dissatisfied, D.M., xx. 16, xxxiii. 2. A., XII. iv. 2.

疾 *chî* (1) Sickness, to be sick, ill, A., II. vi ; VI. viii ; VIII. iii, iv ; X. xiii. 3 ; XVII. xx. Spoken of conduct, A., XVII. xvi. 疾病, A., VII. xxxiv, *et al.* (2) To dislike, A., VIII. x ; XIV. xxxiv. 2 ; XV. xix ; XVI. i. 9. 媢疾, to be jealous, G.L.c., x. 14. (3) Actively, hastily, G.L.c., x. 19. A., X. xvii. 2.

病 *ping* (1) Severe sickness. To become sick, A., IX. xi. 2 ; XV. i. 2. 疾病, A., VII. xxxiv ; IX. xi. 1. (2) To be solicitous about, distressed about, A., VI. xxviii. 1 ; XIV. xlv ; XV. xviii.

THE 105TH RADICAL, 癶.

登 *tăng* To ascend, D.M., xv. 1.

發 *fă* To send forth, = to produce, D.M., xxvii. 2. Passive, to be put, to go, forth, D.M., i. 4. Impulsive, D.M., xxxi. 1. So, 發憤, A., VII. xviii. 2. 發 = to help out, A., VII. viii. 發 = to set forth, to illustrate, A., II. ix. To make illustrious, G.L.c., x. 20. To increase, G.L.c., x. 20.

THE 106TH RADICAL, 白.

白 *păi* White, A., XI. v ; XVII. vii. 3. 白 = naked, applied to weapons, D.M., ix.

百 *păi* A hundred, D.M., xxvii. 3, xxix. 3, 4. A., II. ii, *et al.* 百 = all, used as a round number for the whole of a class. 百工, D.M., xx. 12, 13. A., XIX. vii. 百辟, D.M., xxxiii. 5. 百世, A., II. xxiii. 2. 百官, A., XIV. xliii. 2 ; XIX. xxiii. 3. 百物, A., XVII. xix. 3. 百姓, the people, D.M., xx. 13, 14. A., XII. ix. 4, *et al.* 百乘之家, a house of 100 chariots, the highest officer in a State, G.L.c., x. 22. A., V. vii. 3. 百里之命, authority over 100 *li*, a large State, A., VIII. vi.

的 *ti* 的然, seeking display, D.M., xxxiii. 1.

皆 *chieh* All. At the commencement of clauses, with reference to preceding statements. If it have a noun with it, the noun always precedes. G.L.t., 6. G.L.c., 1, 4. D.M., i. 4, vii. A., II. vii. 1 ; VII. xvii ; XI. ii. 1 ; *et al., saepe.*

皇 *hwang* Great, august. 皇皇后帝, most great and sovereign God, A., XX. i. 3.

皦 *chiăo* Clear, distinct, A., III. xxiii.

THE 107TH RADICAL, 皮.

皮 *p'i* The hides of animals. A piece of skin or leather, A., III. xvi.

THE 108TH RADICAL, 皿.

盈 *ying* Full, A., VII. xxv. 3. To fill, A., VIII. xv.

益 *yi* (1) To add to ; more, A., II. xxiii. 2 ; VI. iii. 1 ; XI. xvi. 1 ; XIII. i. 2. 益者,

one who has made progress, A., XIV. xlvii. i, 2. (2) Of advantage, profitable, G.L.c., vi. 2. A., XV. xxx ; XVI. iv, v.

盍
ho

Why not ? A., V. xxv. 1 ; XII. ix. 2.

盛
shăng

Complete, abundant, rich, G.L.c., iii.4. D.M., XVI. i. 3. 盛服, D.M., xx. 14. A., VIII. xx. 3 ; X. xvi. 4.

盜
tăo

Robbing ; a thief, G.L.c., x. 22. A., XII. xviii ; XVII. xii, xxiii.

盡
chin

To carry out, give full development to ; completely. G.L.c., iv. D.M., xiii. 4, xxii, xxvi. 7, xxvii. 6. A., III. xviii, xxv ; VIII. xxi.

監
chien

To inspect, to view, G.L.c., x. 5. A., III. xiv.

盪
tang

盪舟, to push a boat on the dry land, A., XIV. vi.

盤
p'an

A bathing-tub, G.L.c., i. 1.

盧
lú

Used for 蘆, a kind of rush, D.M., xx. 3.

THE 109TH RADICAL, 目.

目
mŭ

(1) The eye, G.L.c., vi. 3. A., III. viii. 1. (2) An index, steps, processes, A., XII. i. 2.

盼
p'an

The black and white of the eye well defined, A., III. viii. 1.

直
chih

Upright, straightforward, A., II. xix ; VI. xvii ; VIII. ii, xvi ; *et al.*, *saepe.* 直道, to pursue the straight path, A., XV. xxiv. 2 ; XVIII. ii. 直=justice, A., XIV. xxxvi. 3.

相
hsiang

Mutually, one another, D.M., xxx. 3. A., XV. xxxix ; XVII. ii.

相
hsiang

In 4th tone. (1) To be observed, D.M., xxxiii. 3. (2) To assist, A., III. ii. To act as minister to, A., XIV. xviii. 1, 2 ; XVI. i. 12. (3) An assistant at interviews of ceremony, XI. xxv. 6. (4) To lead, guide, as the blind, A., XV. xli. 3.

省
hsing

To examine, inspect, D.M., xx. 14, xxxiii. 2. A., I.iv ; II. ix ; IV. xvii ; XII. iv. 2.

眩
hsüan

To be deceived, D.M., xx. 13.

衆
chung

All, used absolutely, G.L.c., ix. 1, x. 5. A., I. vi ; VI. xxviii. 1, *et al.*, *saepe.* Followed by a noun, A., II. i. Many, in opposition to 寡, G.L.c., x. 19. A., XX. ii. 2.

睨
i

To look askance, D.M., xiii. 2.

睹
tŭ

To see, D.M., i. 2.

睿
zŭi

Intelligent, perspicacious, D.M., xxxi. 1.

瞻
chan

To look to, G.L.c., iii.4. With reverence, G.L.c., x. 4. A., IX. x. 1. 瞻視, A., XX. ii. 2.

瞽
kŭ

Blind, A., IX. ix ; X. xvi. 2. 瞽=blindness, A., XVI. vi.

THE 110TH RADICAL, 矛.

矜
ching

(1) To show compassion to, D.M., xx. 14. A., XIX. iii. 哀矜, G.L.c., viii. 1. A., XIX. xix. (2) Dignified, stern dignity, A., XV. xxi ; XVII. xvi. 2.

THE 111TH RADICAL, 矢.

矢
shih

(1) An arrow, A., XV. vi. (2) 矢之, to swear, protest, A., VI. xxvi.

矣
i

A final particle, found *passim*. It gives definiteness and decision to statements, and is peculiarly appropriate to a terse, conversational style. Where the last clause of a sentence or paragraph commences with 則, 斯, or 亦, the final character is nearly always 矣. It is used also after 已 and 而已, and before the particles of exclamation,— 夫, 乎, and 哉.

知
chih

To know, to understand, *passim*. Sometimes = to acknowledge, i. e. to know and approve or employ, A., I. i. 3 ; IV. xiv ; VIII. xvi ; XI. xxv. 3 ; *et al.*, *saepe.* 知=knowledge, G.L.T., 4, 5.

知°
chih

In 4th tone, used for 智, wisdom, wise, to be wise, D.M., iv, vi, vii, xx. 8, 10, xxv. 3, xxxi. 1, xxxii. 3. A., IV. i, ii ; V. xvii, xx ; XVII. i. 2, iii, viii. 3, xxiv. 2 ; *et al.*

矩
chŭ

The instrument the square ; used metaphorically, G.L.c., x. 1, 2. A., II. iv. 6.

短
twan

Short, A., VI. ii ; X. vi. 5 ; XI. vi.

矧
chăn

How much more (or less), D.M., xvi. 4.

矯
chiáo

Bold, firm, D.M., x. 5.

THE 112TH RADICAL, 石.

石
shih

(1) A stone, a rock, D.M., xxvi. G.L.c., x. 4. (2) 石門, the name of a place, A., XIV. xli.

破
p'o

To split open, D.M., xii. 2.

硜
k'ăng

硜硜, the appearance of a worthless man ; with 然, stupid-like, A., XIII. xx. 3 ; XIV. xlii. 2.

磋
ts'o — To file or plane; to polish, G.L.c., iii. 4. A., I. xv. 2.

碩
shih — Great,—in size, G.L.c., viii. 2.

磨
mo — To grind, G.L.c., iii. 4. A., I. xv. 2; XVII. vii. 3.

磷
lin — A thin stone, to become thin, A., XVII. vii. 3.

磬
ch'ing — An instrument of music, a ringing stone. 擊磬, A., XIV. xlii. 1.

THE 113TH RADICAL, 示.

示
shih — Used synonymously with 視, to see, look at, D.M., xix. 6. A., III. xi.

祀
sze — To sacrifice to, D.M., xviii. 3, xix. 6. 祭祀, sacrifices, D.M., xvi. 9.

社
shê — The altars of the spirits of the land, A., III. xxi; XI. xxiv. 3. 社稷之臣, a minister in direct connexion with the sovereign, A., XVI. i. 4. In D.M., xix. 6, 社 is said to be the place of sacrifice to the Earth.

祇
ch'i — The spirit, or spirits of the earth, A., VII. xxxiv. Read *chih*, just, only, A., XII. x. 3.

祖
tsŭ — 祖述, to hand down as if from his ancestors, D.M., xxx. 1.

神
shan — A spirit, spirits, D.M., xvi. 4, xxiv. 1. A., III. xii. 1. 鬼神, spiritual beings, spirits, D.M., xvi. 1, xxix. 3, 4. A., VI. xx; VIII. xxi; XI. xi. 上下神祇, the spirits of the upper and lower worlds, A., VII. xxxiv.

祥
hs'iang — 禎祥, happy omens, D.M., xxiv.

祝
chú — 祝鮀, = the litanist T'o, A., VI. xiv; XIV. xx. 2.

祭
chi — To sacrifice, to sacrifice to, offered in sacrifice, D.M., xviii. 3. A., II. v. 3; xxiv. 1; III. xii. 1; X. viii. 8, 10, xiii. 2, xv. 3; XII; XIX. 1. A sacrifice, sacrifices, A., III. xii. 1; XX. i. 8. 祭祀 D.M., xvi. 3.

祿
lú — Emolument, revenue, D.M., ix, xvii. 2, 4, xx. 14. A., II. xviii. 1, 2; XV. xxxi; XVI. iii; XX. i. 1.

禍
hwo — Calamity, unhappiness, D.M., xxiv.

禆
p'i — A surname, A., XIV. ix.

禎
ching — See 祥.

福
fú — Happiness, D.M., xxiv.

禦
yü — To oppose, to meet, A., V. iv. 2.

禘
ti — The great, royal, sacrifice, D.M., xix. 6. A., III. x, xi.

禮
li — The fitness or propriety of things; rules of propriety; ceremonies, *passim*.

禱
táo — To pray, A., III. xiii. 2; VII. xxxiv.

THE 114TH RADICAL, 禸.

禹
yü — The founder of the Hsiâ dynasty, A., VIII. xviii, xxi; XIV. vi; XX. i. 2.

禽
ch'in — (1) Birds, D.M., xxvi. 9. (2) 子禽, the designation of one of Confucius's disciples, A., I. x; XIX. xxv.

THE 115TH RADICAL, 禾.

私
szû — Private, A., X. v. 3. 其私, his privacy, i.e. his conduct in private, A., II. ix.

秀
hsiû — The flowering of plants, A., IX. xxi.

秉
ping — The name of a measure of grain, A., IV. iii. 1.

秋
ch'iû — The season of autumn, D.M., xix. 3.

科
k'o — A class, degree, A., III. xvi.

秦
ch'in — The name of a State, A., XVIII. ix. 2. 秦誓, name of a Book in the Shû-ching, G.L.c., x. 14.

移
i — To remove, be changed, A., XVII. iii.

稟
lin — Rations, D.M., xx. 14.

稱
ch'äng — To call, designate, A., XVI. xiv. To speak of, A., XVII. xxiv. 1. To speak of with approbation, to praise, A., VIII. i; XIII. xx. 2; XIV. xxxv; XV. xix; XVI. xii.

稱
ch'äng — In 4th tone. According to, equivalent to, D.M., xx. 14.

稷
chi — (1) The altars of the spirits of the grain, A., XI. xxiv. 3. 社稷之臣, A., XVI. i. 4, see 社. (2) A minister of Yâo and Shun, A., XIV. vi.

稻
táo — Paddy; good rice, A., XVII. xxi. 4.

稼
chiá — To sow seed; husbandry, A., XIII. iv. 1, 3; XIV. vi.

穀
kú — (1) Grain, A., XVII. xxi. 3. 五穀, the five kinds of grain, A., XVIII. v. 1,

vii. (2) 穀 =emolument, A., XIV. i.
(3) Good, A., VIII. xii.

穆
mú

(1) Grave; profound, D.M., xxvi. 10.
穆穆, G.L.c., iii. 3. A., III. ii. (2)
昭穆, the order in which the tablets
of ancestors, and their descendants,
were arranged in the ancestral temple, D.M.,
xix. 4.

THE 116TH RADICAL, 穴.

空
k'ung

Empty. 空空如, empty- or ig-
norant-like, A., IX. vii.

空
k'ung

In 4th tone. To be reduced to extremity, in want, A., XI. xviii. 1.

穿
ch'wan

To perforate; dig through, A., XVII.
xii.

突
t'ǔ

仲突, a designation, A., XVIII. xi.

窒
chi

Stopped up, =unobservant of propriety,
A., XVII. xxiv.

窬
yǔ

To climb over a wall. So, Chû Hsî,
A., XVII. xii. 1.

窮
ch'iung

To exhaust. 不窮, 無窮, D.M.,
xx. 16, xxvi. 9, inexhaustible. To be exhausted, reduced to extremity, A., XV. i. 2;
XX. i. 1.

窺
k'wei

To peep. 窺見, to take a view, A.,
XIX. xxiii. 2.

竊
ch'ieh

(1) To steal, A., XII. xviii; XV. xiii.
(2) To usurp; an expression of humility,
= to venture, A., VII. i.

竈
tsâo

The fireplace; the furnace, A., III.
xiii. 1.

THE 117TH RADICAL, 立.

立
li

(1) To stand, D.M., x. 5. A., V. vii. 4;
X. iii. 2, iv. 2, x. 2, xvii. 1; *et al.* (2) To
establish; to be established, D.M., xx. 13,
16, xxxii. 1. A., I. ii. 2; II. iv. 2; IV.
xiv; VI. xxviii. 2; XIX. xxv. 4; *et al.*

章
chang

(1) To display, be displayed, D.M., xxvi.
6, xxx. 1, xxxiii. 1. (2) 文章, elegant
ways and manifestations, A., V. xii;
VIII. xix. 成章, complete and
accomplished, A., V. xxi. (3) 章甫,
name of a cap of ceremony, A., XI. xxv. 6.

童
t'ung

童子, a youth, a lad, A., VII. xxviii.
1; XI. xxv. 7; XIV. xlvii. 1.

竭
chieh

To exert to the utmost, A., I. vii; IX.
x. 3. To exhaust, A., IX. vii.

端
twan

(1) A beginning or end, extremities,
D.M., vi. A., IX. vii. 造端, to make
a beginning, D.M., xii. 4. (2) Doctrines,
A., II. xvi. (3) The name of a robe of
ceremony, A., XI. xxv. 6.

THE 118TH RADICAL, 竹.

笑
hsiāo

To smile, to laugh, A., III. viii. 1; XIV.
xiv. 1, 2; XVII. xvii.

等
tǎng

(1) A class; degree, D.M., xx. 5. (2)
A step of a stair, A., X. iv. 5.

答
tǎ

To reply, A., XIV. vi.

策
ts'ê

(1) A tablet of bamboo, D.M., xx. 2.
(2) To whip, A., VI. xiii.

筲
shâo

A bamboo vessel. 斗筲之人,
men who are mere utensils, A., XIII.
xx. 4.

算
hsüan

To reckon, take into account, A., XIII.
xx. 4.

節
chieh

(1) A division, what is regularly defined, D.M., i. 4. A., XVIII. vii. 5. (2)
An emergency, a decisive time, A., VIII.
vi. (3) To regulate, A., I. xii. 2. 節
= to economise, A., I. v. To discriminate,
A., XVI. v. (4) The capitals of pillars,
A., V. xvii.

管
kwan

A surname. 管氏, A., III. xxii. 2, 3.
管仲, A., III. xxii. 1, 2, 3; XIV. x. 3,
xvii. 1, 2, xviii. 1, 2.

箕
chi

The name of a State, A., XVIII. i. 1.

篤
tú

Liberal, D.M., xvii. 3. Firm and sincere; firmly and sincerely, D.M., xx. 19,
20, xxxiii. 6. A., VIII. xiii. 1; XI. xx;
XV. v. 2; XIX. ii, vi.

簞
tan

A small round bamboo basket, A., VI.
ix.

簣
kwei

A basket for carrying earth, A., IX.
xviii.

簡
chien

(1) Hasty, A., V. xxi. (2) An easy
negligence, A., VI. i. 2, 3. D.M., xxxiii. 1.
(3) To examine, A., XX. i. 3.

籩
pien

A sacrificial vessel, for holding fruits
and seeds, A., VIII. iv. 2.

THE 119TH RADICAL, 米.

粟
hsü

Rice in the husk, used for grain generally, A., VI. iii. 1, 3. 粟 =revenue, A.,
XII. xi. 3.

精
ching

(1) Rice finely cleaned, A., X. viii. 1.
(2) Minute, exact, D.M., xxvii. 6.

糞
fǎn

Excrement, =dirty, A., V. ix. 1.

糧
liang

Provisions, A., XV. i. 2.

THE 120TH RADICAL, 糸.

糾
chiǔ

A name, A., XIV. xvii. 1, xviii. 1.

約
yo

(1) To bind, to restrain, A., VI. xxv; IX. x. 2; XII. xv. 以約, to use restraint, be cautious, A., IV. xxiii. (2) Straitened, A., VII. xxv. 3. 約 = poverty, straitened circumstances, A., IV. ii.

紅
hung

Red (intermediate colour), A., X. vi. 2.

紂
châu

Epithet of the last emperor of the Shang dynasty, A., XIV. xx. 桀紂, G.L.c., ix. 4.

純
ch'un

(1) Silken, made of silk, A., IX. iii. 1. (2) Harmonious, A., III. xxiii. (3) Singleness, D.M., xxvi. 10.

納
nâ

To make to enter, D.M., vii. To present, A., XX. ii. 3.

素
sù

White, A., X. vi. 4. The plain ground, before colours are laid on, A., III. viii. 1, 2. In D.M., xiv. 1, 2, it seems to mean— the present condition.

素
hsi

For 索, to inquire into, D.M., xi. 1.

紫
tsze

Reddish, purple, A., X. vi. 2; XVII. xviii.

細
hsi

Small, minute, A., X. viii. 1.

紳
shăn

A sash or girdle, with the ends hanging down, A., X. xiii. 3; XV. v. 4.

紺
kan

Of a deep purple colour, A., X. vi. 1.

終
chung

(1) An end. 終始, G.L.T., 3. D.M. xxv. 1. (2) To be brought to a conclusion, to succeed, G.L.c., x. 21. To come to an end, to terminate, A., XX. i. 1. (3) Death, the dead. 愼終, to attend carefully to the funeral rites to parents, A., I. ix. (4) Perpetual, D.M., xxix. 6. Perpetually, A., XVII. xxvi. 終不, never, G.L.c., iii. 4. 終日, the whole day, A., II. ix; XV. xvi, xxx; XVII. xxxii. 終身, all one's life, continually, A., IX. xxvi. 3; XV. xxiii. 終食之間, the space of a meal, A., IV. v. 3.

絕
chüeh

To be broken off, D.M., xx. 14. A., XX. i. 7. 絕 = to be without, A., IX. iv. To be exhausted, A., XV. i. 2. 自絕, to cut one's self off from, A., XIX. xxiv.

給
chieh

口給, smartnesses of speech, A., V. iv. 2.

緤
hsieh

縲緤 = bonds, fetters, A., V. i. 1.

絞
chiáo

Rude, rudeness, A., VIII. ii; XVII. viii. 3.

絢
hsüan

The colouring—ornamental portion— of a picture, A., III. viii. 1.

稀
ch'i

Made of a fine texture, A., X. vi. 3.

綌
chi

Of a coarser texture, A., X. vi. 3.

綱
kang

To use a net, A., VII. xxvi.

綏
sùi

(1) A string or strap, attached to a carriage, A., X. xvii. 1. (2) To make happy, A., XIX. xxv. 4.

絜
hsieh

To measure. 絜矩之道, the principle of reciprocity, G.L.c., x. 1, 2.

經
ching

(1) Standard, invariable rules, D.M., xx. 12, 15, xxxii. 1. As a verb, see 綸. (2) To strangle, A., XIV. xvii. 3.

維
wei

A particle, initial, = but, only, and used as the copula, G.L.c., ii. 3, x. 4. D.M., xxvi. 10. A., III. ii.

綽
ch'o

公綽, a member of the Măng family, A., XIV. xii, xiii.

綸
lun

經綸, to adjust, D.M., xxxii. 1.

緒
hsü

The end of the silk on a cocoon; a beginning; an enterprise, D.M., xviii. 2.

緝
ch'i

緝熙, bright and unceasing, G.L.c., iii. 3.

緡
mien

緡蠻, the twittering of a bird, G.L.c., iii. 2.

縱
tsung

(1) To let go, not to restrict, A., IX. vi. 2. (2) Although, A., IX. xi. 3.

總
tsung

總己, attended to their several duties, A., XIV. xliii. 2.

緅
tsău

Of a puce colour, A., X. vi. 1.

縲
lûi

A black rope. 縲絏, bonds, A., V. i. 1.

緇
tsze

Of a black colour, A., X. vi. 4; XVII. vii. 3.

繆
miù

Error, mistake, D.M., xxix. 3. In the 4th tone.

繫
hsi

To be hung up, suspended, D.M., xxvi. 9. A., XVII. vii. 4.

繚
liâo

A name, A., XVIII. ix. 2.

繪
hui

To paint, lay on various colours, A., III. viii. 2.

繹
yi

To draw out, unfold, A., IX. xxiii. 繹如, flowing on, drawn out, spoken of music, A., III. xxiii.

縕
wăn

In 3rd tone. Quilted with hemp, A., IX. xxvi. 1.

繼
chi

To connect, continue, D.M., xix. 2, xx. 14. A., II. xxiii. 2; XX. i. 7. 繼富, to make the rich more rich, A., VI. iii. 2.

纘
tswan

To continue, D.M., xviii. 2.

THE 121st RADICAL, 缶·

缺
chüeh

A name, A., XVIII. ix. 2.

THE 122nd RADICAL, 网·

罔
wang

Labour lost, A., II. xv. To lose, be without, A., VI. xvii. To be entrapped, befooled, A., VI. xxiv.

罕
han

Seldom, A., IX. i.

罟
kŭ

A net, for catching fish, D.M., vii.

罪
tsui

A crime; offence, A., V. i. 1; XX. i. 3. 獲罪, to offend against, A., III. xiii. 2.

罰
fă

To punish. 刑罰, punishments; but when distinguished, 罰 is a fine, A., XIII. iii. 6.

罷
pă

To cease; to give over, A., IX. x. 3.

THE 123rd RADICAL, 羊·

羊
yang

A sheep, or goat, G.L.c., x. 22. A., III. xvii. 1, 2; XII. viii. 3; XIII. xviii.

美
mei

Goodness, excellence, beauty, excellent quality, G.L.c., viii. 1. A., I. xii. 1; IV. i; VI. xiv; VIII. xi, xxi; XII. xvi; XIII. viii; XIX. xxiii. 3. 五美, the five excellent qualities of government, A., XX. ii. 1. Beautiful, elegant, A., III. viii, xxv; IX. xii.

羔
kăo

(1) A lamb, or kid, A., X. vi. 4, 10. (2) 子羔, the designation of one of Confucius's disciples, A., XI. xxiv.

羞
sâu

Shame, disgrace, A., XIII. xxii. 2.

羣
ch'ün

(1) A flock, = a class; all of a class, D.M., xx. 12, 13. A., XV. xvi; XVIII. vi. 4. (2) Sociable, to be sociable, A., XV. xxi; XVII. ix. 4.

義
i

(1) What is right, righteousness, G.L.c., x. 22, 23. D.M., xx. 5. A., I. xiii; II. xxiv. 2, et passim. (2) Meaning, D.M., xix. 6.

羹
kăng

Soup, A., X. viii. 10.

THE 124TH RADICAL, 羽·

羽
yü

子羽, the designation of a minister of Chăng, the Kung-sun Hûi. See the Tso-chwan, under the 29th year of duke Hsiang (B.C. 544), A., XIV. ix.

翌
i

A famous archer of antiquity, A., XIV. vi.

習
hsi

To practise, A., I. i. 1, iv. By practice, A., XVII. ii.

翔
hsiang

To fly round, or backwards and forwards, A., X. xviii. 1.

翕
hsi

翕如, applied to music, A., III. xxiii.

翼
yi

Wings. 翼如, wing-like, A., X. iii. 3, iv. 5.

THE 125TH RADICAL, 老·

老
lăo

(1) Old, to be old; the old, G.L.c., x. 1. A., V. xxv. 4; XIII. iv. 1; XIV. xlvi; XVI. vii; XVIII. iii. Old age, A., VII. xviii. 2. To treat as old, G.L.c., x. 1. (2) A chief officer, A., XIV. xii.

考
k'ăo

To examine, D.M., xxix. 3. To examine and determine, D.M., xxviii. 2.

者
chê

(1) He (or they) who; this (or that), these (or those), who (or which). It is put after the words (verbs, adjectives, nouns) and clauses to which it belongs, G.L.T., 4. G.L.c., x. 4, 9, 19, 21, 23. A., XIX. iii, iv, xii. 2, xxii. 2; et passim. (2) It stands at the end of the first member of a clause or sentence, when the next gives a description or explanation of the subject of the other, terminated generally by the particle 也, but not always, G.L.c., vi. 1, ix. 1, x. 7. D.M., xix. 2, xxv. 1, 2, 3. A., XII. xvii; et al., saepe. (3) 也者 together, at the end of the first member of a sentence, resume a previous word, and lead on to an explanation or account of it, D.M., i. 2, 4, xx. 3. A., XII. xx. 5, 6. The case in A., XI. xxv. 11, is different. (4) 者也 often occurs at the end of sentences, preceded, though sometimes not, by 者, G.L.c., ix. 2, x. 21. D.M., xxix. 6. A., XVIII. vii. 4; XIX. xvii; et al., saepe.—In all these cases the proper meaning of 者, as in case 1, is apparent. But (5) we find it where that can hardly be traced, and where sometimes we might translate it by one or that, and at other times by so, such a thing, with a dash, but there are cases where it cannot be translated, G.L.T., 7. G.L.c., ix. 4. A., VI. ii, xii; XI. vi; XII. vi. 2, 3; XVI. i. 5, xiii. 4; XVII. vi; XIX. xxv. 4. (6) It forms adverbs with 昔 and 古, A., XVII. vii. 2, xvi; et al. Observe A., IX. xvi; III. x.

THE 126TH RADICAL, 而·

而
r

Passim. A conjunction. (1) And, G.L.T., 2, 5. G.L.c., ix. 2, 4, 6, 7, 8. D.M., i. 4, ii. 2, xx. 6, 9, 14, 17. A., I. i. 1, ii. 2, iv, v, vi, vii, xi. 2; et al., saepissime. (2) And yet, G.L.T., 7. G.L.c., iii. 2, vii. 2, x. 14, 15. D.M., xxxiii. 1, 3, 4, et al., saepissime. The 'and yet' is often nearly, or altogether, = but, A., II. xiv; VII. xxvi; XIII. xxv, xxvi; et al., saepe. It may often be translated by 'if,' A., III. xxii. 3; VII. xi, xxv. 3, xxx. 2, xxxi; et al. (3) It is used idiomatically, or for the rhythm, after adverbs, A., XI. xxv. 4 ; XIV. xx. 1, xlii. 2; XVII. iv. 2 ; *et al.* Observe 然 而, A., XIX. xx. 1. (4) After 得 (and sometimes 可), and before a verb, it forms the passive of that verb, A., XIX. xxiv,xxv. 3; *et al.* (5) 而 = or, A., XII. i. 1. (6) 而今而後, henceforth, both now and hereafter, A., VIII. iii. (7) It is often followed by 已, 已也, 已矣, D.M., xxv. 3. A., VI. v. 3 ; XIV. xlv, *et al.* (8) Used for 汝, you, D.M., x. 2. (9) A., IX. xxx. 1, a mere expletive. 已 而已而, A., XVIII. v. 1.

THE 127TH RADICAL, 耒.

耕 *kăng*　To plough ; to do field-work, A., XV. xxxi ; XVIII. vi. 1.

耦 *ǎu*　Two together, A., XVIII. vi. 1.

耰 *yǔ*　To cover the seed, A., XVIII. vi. 3.

THE 128TH RADICAL, 耳.

耳 *r*　(1) The ear, A., II. iv. 5 ; VIII. xv. (2) A final particle, = simply, A., XVII. iv. 4. (3) An expletive, A., VI. xii. See note *in loc.*

耽 *tan*　Yielding pleasure, D.M., xv. 2.

聘 *p'ing*　The sending of envoys to one another, or to court, by the princes of the States, D.M., xx. 14.

聖 *shang*　Intelligent, perspicacious, G.L.c., x. 11. D.M., xxxii. 3. Sage, possessing the highest knowledge and excellence. 聖 者, a sage, D.M., xi. 3, xxxi. 1. A., VI. xxviii. 1 ; VII. xxxiii ; IX. vi. 1, 2.

聚 *chü*　To collect, be collected, G.L.c., x. 9. 聚歛, to collect imposts, G.L.c., x. 22. A., XI. xvi. 1.

聞 *wăn*　To hear ; to become acquainted with by report, *passim.* 聽而不聞, to hear and not understand, G.L.c., vii. 2. D.M., xvi. 2.

聞 *wăn*　In 4th tone. To be heard of, notoriety, A., XII. xx. 3, 4, 6.

聰 *ts'ung*　Quick in apprehension, D.M., xxxi. 1, xxxii. 3. To hear distinctly, A., XVI. x.

聲 *shěng*　A sound, D.M., xxxiii. 6. A., XVII. iv. 1. 聲 = songs, A., XV. x. 6; XVII. xviii. 聲名, fame, D.M., xxxi. 4.

聽 *t'ing*　To hear, to listen to, G.L.c., iv, vii. 2. D.M., xvi. 2. A., V. ix. 2 ; XII. i. 2, xiii; XVI. x ; XVII. xiv. 聽於, to receive instructions from, A., XIV. xliii. 2.

THE 129TH RADICAL, 聿.

肆 *sze*　(1) To expose a criminal's corpse, A., XIV. xxxviii. 1. (2) Unrestrained, a disregard of smaller matters, A., XVII. xvi. 2. (3) A shop, a stall for goods, A., XIX. vii.

THE 130TH RADICAL, 肉.

肉 *zâu*　Flesh, meat, A., VII. xiii ; X. viii. 2, 4, 8, xv. 2.

肖 *hsiâo*　不肖, not equal to, degenerate, worthless, D.M., iv, xii. 2.

肝 *kan*　The liver. 其肺肝, his lungs and liver, = his inward thoughts, G.L.c., vi. 2.

胏 *hsǐ*　A name, A., XVII. vii. 1, 2.

肺 *fei*　The lungs. See *kan* above.

育 *yǔ*　To be nourished, D.M., i. 5, xxx. 3. To nourish, D.M., xvii. 2. 天地之 化育, the transforming and nourishing of Heaven and Earth. Also D.M., xxii. 2, xxxii. 1.

肫 *chun*　肫肫其仁, earnestly sincere was his perfect humanity, D.M., xxxii. 2.

肥 *fei*　Fat, A., VI. iii. 2.

肩 *chien*　The shoulder, A., XIX. xxiii. 2.

胖 *pan*　At ease. Some say, corpulent, G.L.c., vi. 4.

肱 *kwang*　The arm, A., VII. xv.

脛 *hsing*　The leg below the knee, the shank, A., XIV. xlvi.

能 *năng*　To be able ; can. As the auxiliary, *passim.* It is often used absolutely ;— to can, D.M., iii, ix, xi. 3, xiii. 4. A., XI. xxv. 6 ; XIV. xxx, *et al.* The able, competent, D.M., xx. 14. A., II. xx ; *et al.* 能 = the having power, ability, A., VIII. v ; IX. vi. 1, 2, 3, *et al.*

脩 *hsiŭ*　(1) Dried slices of flesh, A., VII. vii. (2) To cultivate. In G.L.c. and D.M., *passim.* 脩身, 自脩, to cultivate one's self. To repair, D.M., xix. 3. To reform, A., XII. xxi. 1, 2. To restore, A., XX. i. 6. 脩飾, A., XIV. ix. 脩 often appears as 修.

脯 *fu* Dried meat, A., X. viii. 5.

膚 *fu* (1) The skin, A., XII. vi. (2) A name, A., XIX. xix.

膺 *ying* The breast. 服膺, to wear on the breast, D.M., viii.

腥 *hsing* Raw, undressed meat, A., X. xiii. 1.

膾 *kwái* Minced, cut small, A., X. viii. 1.

THE 131st RADICAL, 臣.

臣 *ch'ăn* A minister; the correlate of 君, G.L.c., x. 14, 22. D.M., xiii. 4, xx. 8, 12, 13, 14. A., III. xix, *et saepe.* 大臣, D.M., xx. 12, 13. A., XI. xxiii. 1; XVIII. x. 羣臣, D.M., xx. 12, 13. 具臣, A., XI. xxiii. 3. 陪臣, A., XVI. ii. To play—be—the minister. 臣臣, A., XII. xi. 2, 3. 人臣, G.L.c., iii. 3.

臧 *tsang* (1) Good, thoroughly good, A., IX. xxvi. 2, 3. (2) A surname, A., V. xvii; XV. xiii.

臨 *lin* To oversee; to draw near to, on the part of a superior. Spoken of government, D.M., xxxi. 1. A., II. xx; VI. i. 3. 臨喪, A., III. xxvi. 臨事, A., VII. x. 3. 臨冰, A., VIII. iii. 臨大節, A., VIII. vi.

THE 132nd RADICAL, 自.

自 *tsze* (1) From, as a preposition, G.L.T., 6. G.L.c., x. 14, 23. D.M., xv. 1, xvii. 4, xxi. 1. A., I. i. 2 ; IV. xvii, *et al., saepe.* As a noun, the origin, source, D.M., xxxiii. 1. (2) Self, of all persons. Generally joined with verbs, 自用, 自脩, &c., self-use, self-cultivation, &c., G.L.c., i. 4, iii. 4, vi. 1. D.M., xiv. 2, xxv. 1, 3, xxviii. 1. A., XII. xxiii. 1; XIV. xviii. 3, xxx. 2.

臭 *ch'au* Smell, a smell, G.L.c., vi. 1. D.M., xxxiii. 6. A., X. viii. 2.

皐 *kǎo* 皐陶, an ancient statesman, A., XII. xxii. 6.

THE 133rd RADICAL, 至.

至 *chih* (1) To come, to arrive at ; sometimes = to, till, G.L.c., x. 22. D.M., xxxi. 4. A., VII. xviii. 2, xxix ; IX. viii ; XVIII. vii. 4. 無所不至, a man will do anything bad, G.L.c., vi. 2. A., XVII. xv. 3. 至於, down to ; to come to, as to, G.L.T., 6. A., II. vii ; III. xxiv ; V. xviii. 2 ; VI. xii, xxii ; VII. xiii ; VIII.

xii. 1. (2) Most, making the superlative degree, G.L.T., 1. G.L.c., iii. 4. D.M., xxii, xxiii, xxiv, xxvi. 1, xxvii. 5, xxxi. 1, xxxii. 1. A., VIII. i, xx. 4 ; XIII. iv. 3. (3) The highest degree ; to exist in the highest degree, G.L.c., v. D.M., iii, xii. 2, 4, xix. 5, xxxiii. 6. A., VI. xxvii. To become complete, G.L.T., 5.

致 *chih* (1) To carry to the utmost, to perfection, G.L.T., 4. D.M., i. 5, xxiii, xxvii. 6. A., VIII. xxi ; XIX. iv, vii. 自致, to exert one's self to the utmost, A., XIX. xvii. To be carried to perfection, A., XIX. xiv. Observe 致期 A., XX. ii. 3. (2) 致身, 致命, to devote one's person, life, A., I. vii ; XIX. i.

臺 *t'ái* 澹臺, a surname, A., VI. xii.

THE 134th RADICAL, 臼.

臾 *yü* (1) 須臾, an instant, D.M., i. 2. (2) 顓臾, the name of a small State, A., XVI. i.

與 *yü* In 3rd tone. (1) With, along with ; to be with, to associate with, G.L.c., iii. 3, x. 15. D.M., xxiii. 1, xxxiii. 1. A., I. iv, vii, xv. 3, *et passim.* (2) And, A., IX. i, ix ; XI. xxiii. 2, 4, 6, *et al.* Sometimes it must be translated by 'or,' A., XI. xv, *et al.* (3) Followed by 寧, and by 豈若, than, G.L.c., x. 22. A., III. iv. 3, xiii. 1 ; VII. xxxv ; IX. xi. 3 ; XVIII. vi. 3. (4) To give to, A., I. x. 1 ; V. xxiii ; VI. iii. 1, 3, 4 ; XX. ii. 3. (5) To grant, concede to, allow, A., V. viii. 3 ; VII. xxviii. 2 ; XI. xxv. 7. (6) To wait for, A., XVII. i. 2. 歲不我與. (7) Observe 與比, A., IV. x ; 異與之言, A., IX. xxiii ; 丘不與易, A., XVIII. vi. 4.

與 *yü* (1) In 2nd tone. A final particle, sometimes interrogative, sometimes of admiration, and sometimes of doubt or hesitancy. As interrogative, it generally implies that the answer will be in the affirmative. As indicating doubt or hesitancy, we find it preceded by other final particles. It is followed also by other particles of exclamation, D.M., vi, x. 2, xvii. 1, xxvii. 7. A., I. ii. 2, x. 1, 2, xv. 2, *et al., passim.* Observe A., V. ix. 1, 2 ; XIV. xxxviii. 2. (2) 與與, the appearance of dignity and satisfaction, A., X. ii. 2.

與 *yü* In 4th tone. Sharing in ; concerned with, D.M., xii. 2. A., III. xii. 2 ; VIII. xviii ; IX. v. 3 ; XIII. xiv.

興 *hsing* (1) To rise, A., XV. i. 2. 興 = to become, G.L.c., ix. 3, x. 1. So, followed by 於, A., VIII. ii. 2. To be produced, D.M., xxvi. 9. To be aroused, stimulated, A., VIII. viii. 1; XVII. ix. 2. (2) To flourish, D.M., xxiv. A., XIII. iii. 6. To make to flourish; to raise, D.M., xxvii. 7. A., XIII. xv. 1, 3; XX. i. 7.

舉
chŭ

(1) To raise; employ, promote, G.L.c., x. 16. D.M., xx. 14. A., II. xix, xx; XII. xxii. 3, 4, 6; XIII. ii. 1, 2; XV. xxii; XX. i. 7. To present; set forth (in discourse), A., VII. viii. Passive, to be established, D.M., xx. 2. (2) To rise, A., X. xviii. 1.

舊
chiŭ

Old, of former times, G.L.c., ii. 3. A., V., xviii. 1, xxii; XI. xiii. 2; XVII. xxi. 3. 故舊, = old friends or ministers, A., VIII. ii. 2; XVIII. x. 舊犯, see 犯.

THE 135TH RADICAL, 舌.

舌
shĕ

The tongue, A., XII. viii. 2.

舍
shĕ

The 3rd tone, for 捨. (1) To reject, A., VI. iv. To neglect, A., XIII. ii. 2. To leave unemployed, A., VII. x. To lay aside, A., XI. xxv. 7. To omit; decline, A., XVI. i. 9. (2) To cease; give over, A., IX. xvi.

舒
shŭ

舒, = economy, G.L.c., x. 19.

THE 136TH RADICAL, 舛.

舜
shun

The ancient sovereign, D.M., vi, xvii. 1. A., VIII. xviii, *et al.* 堯舜, G.L.c., ix. 4. D.M., xxxi. 1. A., VII. xxviii; XIV. xlv.

舞
wŭ

(1) Pantomimes, A., III. i; XV. x. 5. (2) 舞雩, = the rain-altars, A., XI. xxv. 7; XII. xx. 1.

THE 137TH RADICAL, 舟.

舟
chău

A ship, a boat, D.M., xxxi. 4. A., XIV. vi.

THE 138TH RADICAL, 艮.

艮
liang

Good, upright, A., I. x.

THE 139TH RADICAL, 色.

色
shĕ

(1) Colour, appearance, especially as variously seen in the countenance; the countenance, G.L.c., vi. 1. D.M., xxxiii. 6. A., I. iii; II. viii; V. xviii; *et al.*, *saepe*. 顏色, A., VIII. iv. 3; X. v. 2; XVI. vi. 潤色, to give the proper finish, A., XIV. ix. (2) Beauty, and the desire for its enjoyment, D.M., xx. 14. A., I. vii; IX. xvii; XV. xii; XVI. vii.

THE 140TH RADICAL, 艸.

芸
yün

In some copies for 耘. To weed, A., XVIII. vii. 1.

苗
miăo

Grain springing, or growing up, G.L.c., viii. 2. A., IX. xxi.

苟
kău

(1) If, if indeed, G.L.c., ii. 1. D.M., xxvii. 5, xxviii. 4, xxxii. 3. A., IV. iv; VII. xxx. 3, *et al.* (2) Improper, irregular, A., XIII. iii. 7. (3) Indicating indifference, A., XIII. viii.

若
jo or zo

(1) As, as if, G.L.c., x. 14. A., VIII. v. (2) As, like, equal to, A., I. xv. 1; XIII. xv. 1, 4; XIV. xiii; XVIII. iii, vi. 3. (3) Such as, = this, A., V. ii; XI. xii. 2; XIV. vi. Observe A., VII. xxxiii. (4) The name of one of Confucius's disciples, A., XII. ix.

萑
zăn

Weak, soft, A., XVII. xii.

茲
tsze

This, A., IX. v. 2. Found also under Classifier 95. But, as the K'ang-hsî dictionary explains, the two characters originally differed both in form and meaning.

草
ts'âo

(1) Grass, A., XII. xix. 草木, grasses and trees, = plants, D.M., xxvi. 9. A., XVII. ix. 7; XIX. xii. 2. (2) A rough copy. 草創, to make the first copy, A., XIV. ix.

荊
ching

A cadet of the ruling family of Wei, A., XIII. viii.

荷
ho

In 4th tone. To bear, carry, A., XIV. xlii. 1; XVIII. vii. 1.

莊
chwang

(1) Grave; gravity, dignity, D.M., xxxi. 1. A., II. xx; XI. xx; XV. xxxii. 2, 3. (2) An honorary epithet, A., XIV. xiii.— A., XIX. xviii.

莞
kwan

莞爾, smilingly, A., XVII. iv. 2.

莒
chŭ

莒父, the name of a small city of Lû, A., XIII. xvii.

莫
mo

(1) Not, G.L.c., viii. 2. D.M., xii. 2. A., VI. xv, *et al.*, *saepe*. 莫不 occurs as a strong affirmative, D.M., iv. 2, xxxi. 3, 4. The power of 莫, like other negatives, to attract immediately to itself the object of the verb following, is to be noted, D.M., vii. A., IV. xiv; XIII. xv. 4, 5; XIV. xviii. 3. It stands sometimes without a preceding noun, and = no one, A., XIV. xxxvii. 1, *et al.* So, in the passive, D.M., i. 3. (2) 無莫, has no predetermined objection, A., IX. iv. (3) ? perhaps, A., VII. xxxii.

莫
mŭ

Used for 暮. 莫春, the last month of spring, A., XI. xxv. 7.

菑
tsăi

I. q. 災, calamities, G.L.c., x. 17, 23.

菜 *ts'ài* Vegetables, edible herbs, A., X. viii. 10.

華 *hwâ* (1) *I. q.* 花. Flowers, A., IX. xxx. 1.
(2) 公西華, and 子華, one of Confucius's disciples, A., VI. iii ; VII. xxxiii ; XI. xxi, xxv.

華 *hwâ* In 4th tone. Name of the most western of the five mountains, D.M., xxvi. 9.

菲 *fei* Poor, sparing, A., VIII. xxi.

萬 *wan* Ten thousand. 萬物, all things, D.M., i. 5, xxvi. 9, xxvii. 2, xxx. 3. 萬方, the myriad regions, i. e. throughout the kingdom, A., XX. i. 3.

著 *chù* To display, G.L.c., vi. 2. To become manifest, the being displayed, D.M., xxiii, xxxiii. 1.

葬 *tsang* To bury ; to be buried ; a burial, D.M., xviii. 3. A., II. v. 3 ; IX. xi. 3 ; XI. x. 1, 2.

葸 *hsì* Timid, timidity, A., VIII. ii.

菉 *lù* *I. q.* 綠. Green, G.L.c., iii. 4.

蓋 *kài* (1) The conjunction 'for,' D.M., xxvi. 10. A., XVI. i. 10. (2) An introductory hypothetical particle, A., IV. vi. 3 ; VII. xxvii. (3) 蓋=as a rule, A., XIII. iii. 4 ; XVI. ii. 1.

葉 *yeh* Leaves, foliage, G.L.c., ix. 6.

葉 *sheh* The name of a State, A., VII. xviii ; XIII. xvi, xviii.

蒲 *p'û* A kind of rush, D.M., xx. 3.

蓁 *chăn* 蓁蓁, luxuriant, G.L.c., ix. 6.

蓍 *shih* The milfoil (*Ptarmica Sibirica*), D.M., xxiv.

蕟 *t'iáo* A bamboo basket, A., XVIII. vii. 1.

蒙 *măng* The name of a mountain, A., XVI. i. 4.

蔡 *ts'ài* (1) The name of a State, A., XI. ii. 1 ; XVIII. ix. 2. (2) The name of a large tortoise, A., V. xvii.

蔽 *pi* (1) To cover, to comprehend, A., II. ii. (2) To cover, to becloud ; to hide, keep in obscurity, A., XVII. viii. 1, 2 ; XX. i. 3.

蕢 *kwei* A straw basket, A., XIV. xlii. 1.

蕩 *tang* (1) Large. 蕩蕩乎, how vast ! A., VIII. xix. 1. (2) Dissipation of mind, A., XVII. viii. 3. Wild license,

A., XVII. xvi. 2. (3) 蕩蕩, easy and composed, A., VII. xxxv. ? should here be read *t'ang*.
The name of a State, A., XIV. xii.

薛 *hsieh*

薄 *po* Thin, A., VIII. iii. 薄=neglected, G.L.T., 7. 薄來, coming with small contributions, D.M., xx. 14. 薄責, requiring little from, A., XVI. xiv.

蕭 *hsiáo* 蕭牆, a screen, A., XVI. i. 13.

薦 *chien* To present an offering in sacrifice, D.M., xix. 3. A., X. xiii. 1.

薨 *hung* To decease ;—used of a prince, A., XIV. xliii. 2.

藏 *ts'ang* To store away, to keep, G.L.c., ix. 4. A., IX. xii. To keep retired, A., VII. x. 1.

藏 *tsang* In 4th tone. Things to be treasured, D.M., xxvi. 9.

藝 *i* (1) The polite arts, A., VII. vi. 4. (2) Having various ability and arts, A., VI. vi ; IX. vi. 4 ; XIV. xiii. 1.

藥 *yo* Physic, A., X. xi. 2.

藻 *tsáo* Duckweed, A., V. xvii.

薑 *chiang* Ginger, A., X. viii. 6.

蘧 *chü* A surname, A., XIV. xxvi ; XV. vi. 2.

THE 141ST RADICAL, 虍.

虎 *hû* A tiger, A., VII. x. 3 ; XII. viii. 3 ; XVI. i. 7.

虐 *nio* Cruelty, oppression, A., XX. ii. 3.

處 *ch'û* In 3rd tone, a verb. To dwell in ; to occupy, A., IV. i, ii, v. 居處, to dwell in retirement, A., XIII. xix ; XVII. xxi. 5.

虛 *hsü* Empty, A., VII. xxv. 3 ; VIII. v.

虞 *yü* (1) The accepted surname or dynastic name of Shun, A., VIII. xx. 3. (2) 虞仲, for 吳仲, A., XVIII. viii. 1, 4.

THE 142ND RADICAL, 虫.

The iguanodon, D.M., xxvi. 9.

蚤 *tsáo* *I. q.* 早, early, D.M., xxix. 6.

蚊 *chiáo*

蠻 *man* (1) The barbarians of the south. 蠻貊, barbarians, generally, D.M., xxxi. 4. A., XV. v. 2. (2) 緡蠻, the twittering of a bird, G.L.c., iii. 2.

THE 143RD RADICAL, 血.

血 *hsieh* Blood. 凡有血氣者, = all men, D.M., xxxi. 4. 血氣未定, = the animal passions, physical powers, A., XVI. vii.

THE 144TH RADICAL, 行.

行 *hsing* (1) To go ; walk, D.M., xv. 1. A., VI. xii ; X. iv. 2, xiii. 4, *et al.* Applied to the movements of the sun and moon, D.M., xxx. 2, 3, *et al.* 行 = to depart ; take one's leave, A., XV. i. 1 ; XVIII. iii, *et al.* (2) To do, practise ; to be practised, D.M., iv. 1, xi. 1, xii. 2, *et al., saepe.* A., II. xiii, xviii. 2, xxii, *et al., saepe.* To act, absolutely, as a neuter verb, D.M., xi. 2, xiv. 1, 2, xx. 10, xxix. 5, xxxi. 3. A., I. vi, xii. 2, *et al., saepe.* 行 = to command, A., VII. x. 2. To undertake the duties of office, A., VII. x. 1. 行己, the conduct of one's self, A., V. xix ; XIII. xx. 躬行君子, A., VII. xxxii. 行 = to succeed, A., XII. vi ; XX. i. 6, *et al.*

行 *hsing* In 4th tone. Conduct, actions ;—a noun, D.M., xiii. 4, xx. 16. A., I. xi ; II. xviii. 2 ; IV. xxv ; *et al., saepe.*

行 *hang* In 4th tone. 行行, bold-looking, A., XI. xii. 1.

衡 *hăng* A yoke, A., XV. v. 3.

衞 *wei* The name of a State, A., VII. xiv ; IX. xiv ; *et al.*

THE 145TH RADICAL, 衣.

衣 *i* Clothes, a garment, D.M., xviii. 2. A., IV. ix ; X. iii. 2, vi. 4, 6, vii. 1 ; XX. ii. 2. 衣服, A., VIII. xxi. 裳衣, where 裳 denotes the clothes for the lower part of the body, D.M., xix. 3. A., IX. ix.

衣 *i* In 4th tone. To wear, A., V. xxv. 2 ; VI. iii. 2 ; IX. xxvi ; XVII. xxi. 4.

哀 *āi* Honorary epithet of a duke of Lû, D.M., xx. 1. A., II. xix, *et al.*

衽 *zăn* Also written 袵. (1) The lapel in front of a coat, buttoning on the right breast, A., XIV. xviii. 2. (2) To sleep on, make a mat of, A., x. 4.

表 *piáo* To wear outside, A., X. vi. 3.

衰 *shwāi* To decay, decline, A., VII. v ; XVI. vii ; XVIII. v.

縗 *ts'āi* Mourning clothes, with the edges either unhemmed (齊衰), or frayed (斬衰), A., IX. ix ; X. xvi. 2.

袂 *mi* Sleeves, A., X. vi. 5.

被 *p'ei* 被髮, dishevelled hair, A., XIV. xviii. 2.

袍 *p'áo* A robe, A., IX. xxvi.

裁 *ts'ái* To cut and shape clothes ;—used metaphorically, A., V. xxi.

裕 *yǔ* Generous, D.M., xxxi. 1.

裘 *ch'iú* Fur garments, A., V. xxv. 2 ; VI. iii. 2 ; X. vi. 4, 5, 10.

裳 *shang* The lower garment. 裳衣, A., IX. ix ; X. vi. 9.

襁 *chiang* A cloth in which infants are strapped to the back. 襁負, to carry on the back, A., XIII. iv. 3.

褻 *hsieh* Undress, A., X. vi. 2, 5, xvi. 2.

襄 *hsiang* A name, A., XVIII. ix. 5.

襜 *chan* 襜如, evenly adjusted, A., X. iii. 2.

襲 *hsi* To follow, accord with, D.M., xxx. 1.

THE 146TH RADICAL, 西.

西 *hsi* 公西, a double surname, A., VII. xxxiii ; XI. xxi, xxv.

要 *yáo* (1) An agreement, A., XIV. xiii. 2. (2) To force, A., XIV. xv.

覆 *fú* To overthrow, D.M., xvii. 3. A., XVII. xviii. To throw down, as earth on the ground, A., IX. xviii.

覆 *fáu* In 4th tone. To overspread, cover, D.M., xxvi. 4, 9, xxx. 2, xxxi. 4.

THE 147TH RADICAL, 見.

見 *chien* To see, *passim.* 視而不見, to see and not perceive, G.L.c., vii. 2. D.M., xvi. 1. Before other verbs, forming the passive voice, D.M., xi. 3. A., XVII. xxvi.

見 *hsien* (1) To be manifest, D.M., i. 3, xxiv. xxvi. 6, xxxi. 3. A., VIII. xiii. 2 ; XV. i. 3. (2) To have an interview ; to introduce, A., III. xxiv ; VII. xxviii. 1 ; XV. xli ; XVI. i. 2 ; XVIII. vii. 3.

視 *shih* To observe, to look at, G.L.c., vi. 2, 3. D.M., xiii. 2. A., II. x ; XII. i. 2 ; XVI. x. 視而不見, G.L.c., vii. 2. D.M., xvi. 2. 尊其瞻視, to throw a dignity into his looks, A., XX. ii. 2. To visit, to see, A., X. xiii. 3. To regard, look upon, A., XI. x. 3. To require, look for, A., XX. ii. 3.

親
ch'in

(1) To love, show affection to, G.L.c., iii. 5. D.M., xix. 5, xx. 5, 13, 14, xxxi. 4. (2) To approach to, seek to be intimate with, A., I. vi, xiii, 其親 = proper persons to be intimate with. (3) Personal, one's self, A., XVII. vii. 不親指, did not use his fingers, A., X. xvii. 2. (4) Relatives, D.M., xx. 5, 13, 14. A., VIII. ii. 2; XVIII. x; XX. i. 5. (5) Parents, a parent, G.L.c., x. 13. D.M., xx. 7, 17. A., XII. xxi. 3; XIX. xvii. (6) Said to be used for 新, G.L.T., i.

覿
ti

An envoy's private interview and audience, A., X. v. 3.

觀
kwan

To look at; to mark, A., I. xi; II. x. 2; III. x, xxvi; IV. vii; V. ix. 2; VIII. xi; XII. xx. 5; XIX. iv. 詩可以觀, the odes may be used for purposes of self-contemplation, A., XVII. ix. 3.

覺
chio

To apprehend. 先覺者, one who is of quick apprehension, A., XIV. xiii.

THE 148TH RADICAL, 角.

角
chio

A horn; horned, A., VI. iv.

觚
kû

A drinking-vessel, made with corners, A., VI. xxiii.

THE 149TH RADICAL, 言.

言
yen

(1) A word, words; a saying, a sentence, G.L.c., ix. 3, x. 9. D.M., vi, xiii. 4, xx. 16, xxvi. 7, xxvii. 7, xxxiii. 4. A., I. iii, xiii, xiv; II. ii, xiii; et al., passim. To speak; to speak of; to tell. D.M., xxix. 5, xxxi. 3, xxxiii. 3. A., I. vii, xv. 3; II. ix, xviii. 2, et al., passim. 言 = meaning, D.M., xii. 3. (2) The surname of 子遊, one of Confucius's disciples, A., XIV. xii. 2.

訐
chieh

To expose people's secrets, A., XVII. xxiv. 2.

討
t'áo

(1) To punish, A., XIV. xxii. 2. (2) 討論, to examine and discuss, A., XIV. ix.

訒
zan

Words spoken slowly and cautiously, A., XII. iii. 2, 3.

訕
shan

To rail at, slander, A., XVII. xxiv.

託
t'o

To entrust, be entrusted, with, A., VIII. vi.

訟
sung

Litigations, G.L.c., iv. A., XII. xiii. 訟 = to accuse, A., V. xxvi.

訥
no

Slow in speaking, A., IV. xxiv. Modest, A., XIII. xxvii.

設
shê

To set forth, display, D.M., xix. 3.

詐
chá

Deceitful, A., IX. xi. 2. Deceit, A., XVII. xvi. 2. Deception, attempts to deceive, A., XIV. xxxiii.

詠
yung

To sing, A., XI. xxv. 7.

試
shih

(1) To try, examine, D.M., xx. 14. A., XV. xxiv. (2) To be used, have official employment, A., IX. vi. 4.

誄
lêi

A collection of Prayers of Eulogy, A., VII. xxxiv.

誅
chû

To reprove, A., V. ix. 1.

詩
shih

The Book of Poetry; the pieces in the Book of Poetry, A., I. xv. 3; II. ii; III. viii. 3; VII. xvii; VIII. viii. 1; XIII. v; XVI. xiii. 2, 5; XVII. ix. 1, 2. 詩曰, 詩云, saepe.

語
yü

To speak; to speak of, D.M., xii. 2. A., VII. xx; X. viii. 9. Words, sayings, A., IX. xxiii; XII. i. 2, ii; XVI. xi. 1, 2.

語
yü

In 4th tone. To speak to; to tell, A., III. xxiii; VI. xix; IX. xix; XIII. xviii. 1; XVII. viii. 2; XIX. xxiii.

誠
ch'ǎng

To make, be made, sincere; sincerely, G.L.T., 4, 5. G.L.c., vi. 1, 2, 4. In the Doctrine of the Mean, the term has a mystical significance, D.M., xvi. 5, xx. 17, 18, xxi, xxii, xxiii, xxiv, xxv. 1, 2, 3, xxvi. 1, xxxii. 1. Really, sincerely, G.L.c., ix. 2. A., XII. x. 3. True, A., XIII. xi.

誦
sung

To repeat; hum over, A., IX. xxvi. 3; XIII. v.

說
shwo

(1) To speak of; the speaking (what is said), D.M., xxviii. 5. A., III. xxi. 2; XII. viii. 2; XVII. xiv. (2) Meaning, A., III. xi.

說
yüeh

For 悅. To be pleased; pleased with; a matter of pleasure, D.M., xxxi. 3. A., I. i. 1; V. v; VI. x, xxvi; IX. xxiii; XI. iii; XIII. xvi. 2, xxv; XVII. v. 2.

誥
kào

To enjoin upon; instructions. 康誥, the name of a Book in the Shû-ching, G.L.c., i. 1, ii. 2, ix. 2, x. 11.

誨
hûi

To instruct; teach, A., II. xvii; VII. ii, vii, xxxiii; XIV. viii.

誓
shih

To declare solemnly; an oath. 秦誓, the name of a Book in the Shû-ching, G.L.c., x. 14.

誰
shûi

Who, whom, A., VI. xv; VII. x. 2; IX. xi. 2; XI. ix. 3; XV. xxiv; XVI. i. 7; XVIII. vi. 2, 3, 4; XX. ii. 2.

誾
yin

The appearance of being bland, yet precise, A., X. ii. 2; XI. xii.

諂
chan

To flatter; flattering, A., I. xv. 1; II. xxiv; III. xviii.

諟 *shih* This, or to examine, G.L.c., i. 2.

諼 *hsüan* To forget, G.L.c., iii. 4.

諶 *shăn* A name, A., XIV. ix.

諺 *yen* A common saying, a proverb, G.L.c., viii. 2.

請 *ch'ing* To request; to beg. In the first person, sometimes merely a polite way of expressing a purpose, A., III. xxiv; VI. iii; VII. xxxiv; XI. vii. 1; XII. i. 2, ii; XIII. i. 2, iv. 1; XIV. xxii. 2; XVII. vi.

諛 *wû* To delude; impose on, A., XIX. xxi. 2.

誘 *yû* To lead on, A., IX. x. 2.

諒 *liang* Sincere, A., XVI. iv. Simple and sincere, A., XIV. xviii. 3; XV. xxxvi.

諒 *liang* In 1st tone. In the phrase 諒陰, A., XIV. xliii. 1.

謂 *wei* (1) To say to, A., II. xxi. 1; III. vi; V. viii. 1, *et al., saepe.* (2) To say of, A., III. i, xv, xxv; XVIII. viii. 3, 4, *et al., saepe.* (3) To call; to be called, G.L.c., iv, v, vi. 1, 2, vii. 1, 3, viii. 1, 3, ix. 1, 3, x. 1, 15, 17, 22, 23. D.M., i. 4, xxi. A., I. vii, xi, xiv, *et al., saepe.* Observe the idiom, 之謂, G.L.c., x. 2, 3. D.M., i. 1, xxvii. 7. A., I. xv. 2; XVI. xii. 2. 謂之 is different. 何謂 = what is meant? A., III. viii. 1, xiii. 1; IV. xv. 2; XX. ii. 1, 2, 3, *et al., saepe.*

論 *lun* To discourse, discuss, A., XI. xx; XIV. ix.

諾 *no* (1) Oh! yes, A., VII. xiv. 1; XVII. i. 2. (2) A promise, A., XII. xii. 2.

諸 *chû* (1) As a preposition,—in, to, from, &c., and sometimes cannot be translated, G.L.c., ix. 4, x. 15. D.M., vii, xiii. 3, *et al.* A., I. xv. 3; III. xi; V. xi, xxiii; XVII. i. 1, iv. 3, vii. 2, *et al.* (2) As an interrogative, = 之乎, A., VI. iv; VII. xxxiv; IX. xii; XI. xxi; XII. xi. 3, *et al.* (3) Apparently = 此, this, A., VI. xxviii. 1; XIV. xlv. (4) Not merely one, all, D.M., xx. 13. A., II. xix; XII. xxii. 3, 4. (5) Observe 其諸, A., I. x. 2, and 譬諸, A., XVII. xii; XIX. xii. 2. (6) 諸夏, a name of China, A., III. v. (7) 諸侯, the princes of the empire, a prince, D.M., xviii. 3, xx. 12, 13, 14. A., XI. xxv. 12; XIV. xvii. 2, xviii. 2; XVI. ii.

諫 *chien* To remonstrate with, reprove, A., III. xxi. 2; IV. xviii; XVIII. i, v. 1; XIX. x.

謀 *mâu* To plan; plan about; plans, A., I. iv; VII. x. 3; VIII. xiv; XIV. xxvii; XV. xxvi, xxxi, xxxix; XVI. i. 13.

謹 *chin* Earnestly careful, D.M., xiii. 4. A., I. vi; X. i. 2. To give attention to, A., XX. i. 6.

識 *shih* To know, become acquainted with, A., XVII. ix. 7.

識 *chih* In 4th tone. To remember, A., VII. ii, xxvii; XV. ii. 1; XIX. xxii. 2.

講 *chiang* To discourse about, A., VII. iii.

謗 *pang* To vilify, A., XIX. x.

譎 *chüeh* Crafty, A., XIV. xvi.

謙 *ch'ieh* 自謙, self-enjoyment, G.L.c., vi. 1.

讒 *chan* Slander, A., XII. vi.

證 *chăng* To testify, bear witness to, A., XIII. xviii. 1.

譬 *p'i* To compare; a comparison, A., VI. xxviii. 3. 譬如, may be compared to, A., II. i; IX. xviii. 譬諸, is like to, A., XVII. xii; XIX. xii. 2. 譬之, let me compare it, A., XIX. xxiii. 2.

譽 *yû* Renown; to praise, D.M., xxix. 6. Read in the 2nd tone, with the same meaning, A., XV. xxiv.

議 *i* To discourse with, to discuss, A., IV. ix; XVI. ii. 3. To discuss and settle, to arrange, D.M., xxviii. 2.

讀 *tû* To read, study, A., XI. xxiv. 3.

變 *pien* To change; changes, D.M., x. 5, xxiii, xxvi. 6. A., VI. xxii; X. vii. 2, xvi. 2, 4, 5; XIX. ix.

讓 *zang* Courteous, humble, G.L.c., ix. 3. A., XI. xxv. 10. To decline, yield, A., VIII. i; XV. xxxv. 禮讓, the complaisance of propriety, A., IV. xiii.

讒 *ch'an* Slander, = slanderers, D.M., xx. 14.

THE 151st RADICAL, 豆.

豆 *tâu* A wooden vessel used at sacrifices, 籩豆, A., VIII. iv. 3. 俎豆, A., XV. i. 1.

豈 *ch'i* How, A., VII. xxxiii; IX. xxx; XIV. xiv. 2, xviii. 3. Followed by 哉, 也 哉, and 乎, A., XVII. v. 3, vii. 4; XVIII. vi. 3; XIX. xxv.

THE 152ND RADICAL, 豕.

豚 *t'un*
A small pig, G.L.c., x. 22.　A., XVII. i. 1.

豫 *yü*
Preparation beforehand, D.M., xx. 16.

THE 153RD RADICAL, 豸.

豹 *p'áo*
A leopard, A., XII. viii. 3.

貊 *mâi*
The barbarous tribes of the north.　蠻貊, D.M., xxxi. 4.　A., XV. v. 2.

貌 *mâo*
Aspect, demeanour, A., VIII. iv. 3; XVI. x.　以貌, to use a ceremonious manner, A., X. xvi. 2.

貉 *hsio*
The badger, = badger's fur, A., IX. xxvi ; X. vi. 7.

THE 154TH RADICAL, 貝.

貞 *chǎn*
Correct and firm, A., XV. xxxvi.

負 *fù*
To carry on the back, A., X. xvi. 3; XIII. iv. 3.

財 *ts'âi*
Wealth, G.L.c., x. 6, 7, 9, 20, 21, 23.　財用, means of expenditure, D.M., xx. 13.　財 = sources of wealth, D.M., xxvi. 9.

貢 *kung*
子貢, one of Confucius's disciples, A., I. x. 1, 2, xv. 1, 2 ; II. xiii ; *et al., saepe.*

貧 *p'in*
Poor, being in a poor condition; poverty, D.M., xiv. 2.　A., I. xv. 1 ; IV. v. 1 ; VIII. x, xiii. 3 ; XIV. xi ; XV. xxxi ; XVI. i. 10.

貨 *hwo*
Goods, G.L.c., x. 10.　A., XI. xviii. 2. Riches, D.M., xx. 14.　Articles of value, D.M., xxvi. 9.

貪 *t'an*
To covet, desire, A., XX. ii. 1, 2.　To be ambitious, G.L.c., ix. 3.

貫 *kwan*
To go through, pervade, A., IV. xv. 1 ; XV. ii. 3.　It is difficult to assign its meaning in XI. xiii. 2.

貳 *r*
To repeat ; repeated, A., VI. ii. 2.　不貳, without doubleness, D.M., xxvi. 7.

責 *tsê*
To require from, A., XV. xiv.

貴 *kwei*
(1) Noble, being in an honourable condition.　Associated with 富, D.M., xiv. 2.　A., IV. v. 1 ; VII. xv ; VIII. xiii. 3 ; XII. v. 3.　Contrasted with 賤, D.M., xviii. 3, xix. 4.　Excellent, valuable, A., I. xii. 1 ; IX. xxiii.　(2) To esteem noble, D.M., xx. 14.　A., VIII. iv. 3.

費 *fei*
(1) Extended, reaching far and wide, D.M., xii. 1.　(2) To expend largely, A., XX. ii. 1, 2.

費 *pi*
The name of a city, A., VI. vii ; XI. xxiv ; XVI. i. 8 ; XVII. v.

賊 *tsêi*
To injure ; injury, A., XI. xxiv. 2 ; XX. ii. 3.　An injurious disregard of consequences, A., XVII. viii. 3.　A pest, A., XIV. xlvi.　Thieves or injurers, A., XVII. xiii.

賞 *shang*
To reward, D.M., xxxiii. 4.　A., XII. xviii.

賈 *chiǎ*
A price, A., IX. xii.　In the 2nd tone. A name, A., III. xiii ; XIV. xx.—A., XIV. xiv.

賢 *hsien*
(1) As an adjective, admirable, virtuous and talented, A., VI. ix ; XIII. ii. 1, 2, *et al.*　As a noun, 賢 and 賢者, worthies, men of talents and virtue, G.L.c., x. 16.　D.M., ɪv, xix. 4, xx. 5, 12, 13, 14. A., I. vii ; IV. xvii ; XV. ix, *et al., saepe.* As a verb, to treat as a *hsien*, G.L.c., iii. 5. A., I. vii.　(2) To surpass, be better than, A., XI. xv. 1 ; XVII. xxii ; XIX. xxiii. 1, xxv. 1.

賓 *pin*
A guest, a visitor, A., X. iii. 4 ; XII. ii. 賓客, A., V. vii. 4 ; XIV. xx. 2.

賜 *ts'ze*
(1) To give ; bestow, A., X. xiii. 1. Gifts, A., XIV. xviii. 2.　(2) The name of 子貢, one of Confucius's disciples, A., I. xv. 3 ; III. xvii. 2 ; *et al., saepe.*

賤 *chien*
(1) Mean, in a mean condition, D.M., xix. 4, xxviii. 1.　A., IX. vi. 3.　Associated with 貧, D.M., xiv. 2.　A., IV. v ; VIII. xiii. 3.　Contrasted with 貴, D.M., xviii. 3, xix. 4.　As a verb, to consider mean, G.L.c., viii. 1.　D.M., xx. 14.　(2) 子賤, one of Confucius's disciples, A., V. ii.

賚 *lái*
To bestow ; gifts, A., XX. i. 4.

賦 *fù*
= military levies, A., V. vii. 2.

質 *chih*
(1) Substantial, solid ; substantial qualities, A., VI. xvi ; XII. viii. 1, 3, xx. 5. 質 = essential, A., XV. xvii.　(2) To appear, present one's self, before, D.M., xxix. 3, 4.

贊 *chan*
To assist, D.M., xxii.

THE 155TH RADICAL, 赤.

赤 *ch'ih*
(1) 赤子, an infant, G.L.c., ix. 2. (2) The name of Tsze-hwâ, one of Confucius's disciples, A., V. vii. 4 ; VI. iii. 2 ; XI. xxi, xxv. 6, 12.

赦 *shê*
To pardon ; forgive, A., XIII. ii. 1 ; XX. i. 3.

赫 *hê*
赫兮, how distinguished ! G.L.c., iii. 4.　赫赫, greatly distinguished, G.L.c., x. 4.

THE 156TH RADICAL, 走.

起
ch'i
   To assist, bring out one's meaning, A., III. viii. 3.

趙
châo
   A great family of the State of Tsin, A., XIV. xii.

趨
ch'ü
   To walk quickly, A., IX. ix ; X. iii. 3, iv. 5. A., XVI. xiii. 2, 3 ; XVIII. v. 2.

THE 157TH RADICAL, 足.

足
tsû
   (1) The feet, A., VIII. iii ; X. iii. 1, iv. 3, v. 1 ; XIII. iii. 6. (2) Sufficient, to be sufficient ; fit, G.L.c., ix. 8, x. 19. D.M., xiii. 4, xx. 13, xxvii. 7, xxviii. 5, xxxi. 1. A., II. ix ; III. ix ; IV. vi. 2, ix, *et al.*, *saepe.* 使足民, to secure sufficient for the people, A., XI. xxv. 5.

足
chü
   In 4th tone. Excessive, A.,V. xxiv.

跲
chieh
   To stumble, D.M., xx. 16.

踐
chien
   To tread on, A.,XI.xix. 踐=to occupy, D.M., xix. 5.

踖
chi
   踧踖, to move reverently, A., X. ii. 2, iv. 5.

踧
tsû
   踧踖, see 踖.

踰
yü
   To step over ; transgress, A., II. iv. 6 ; XIX. xi, xxiv.

路
lû
   (1) 道路, the road, A., IX. xi. 3. (2) 子路, one of Confucius's disciples, D.M., x. 1. A., V. vi, vii, xiii, xxv. 2, 4, *et al.*, *saepe.* 季路, *idem*, A., V. xxv ; XI. ii. 1, 2, xi ; XVI. i. 2. (3) 顏路, the father of Yen Hûi, A., XI. vii. 1.

蹈
tâo
   To trample on, D.M., ix. To tread (the path of virtue), A., XV. xxxiv.

躍
yo
   To leap, D.M., xii. 3.

踽
hsü
   踽踽, the feet dragging along, A., X. v. 1.

躁
tsâo
   Hurried ; rashness, A., XVI. vi.

躄
ch'io
   The legs bending under, A., X. iii. 1, iv. 3.

THE 158TH RADICAL, 身.

身
shên
   (1) The body, A., X. vi. 6 ; XV. viii. (2) One's own person, the person, G.L.T., 4, 5, 6. G.L.c., vi. 4, *et al.* D.M., xiv. 5, xx. 4, 7, 11, 12, 13, 14, 17, *et al.* A., I. iv, vii, *et al.* In some cases, we might translate by *body.* (3) 終身, all one's life, continually, A., IX. xxvi. 3 ; XV. xxiii.

躬
kung
   (1) The body, A., X. iv. 1, 4, v. 1 ; XX. i. 1. (2) In one's own person, A., IV. xxii ; VII. xxxii ; XIII. xviii ; XIV. vi ; XV. xiv ; XX. i. 3.

THE 159TH RADICAL, 車.

車
chü
   A carriage, D.M., xxviii. 3, xxxi. 4. A., II. xxii ; V. xxv. 2 ; X. xv. 2, xvii. 1, 2 ; XI. vii. 1 ; XIV. xvii. 2.

軍
chün
   An army. 三軍, the forces of a great State, A., VII. x. 2 ; IX. xxv. 軍旅, A., XIV. xx. 2 ; XV. i. 1.

軌
kwei
   The rut of a wheel. 軌=size, standard, D.M., xxviii. 3.

軏
yüeh
   An arrangement for yoking the horses in a light carriage, A., II. xxii.

輅
lû
   A State carriage, A., XV. x. 3.

輶
yû
   Light, not heavy, D.M., xxxiii. 6.

載
tsâi
   (1) To contain, D.M., xii. 2, xxvi. 4, 9, xxx. 2, xxxi. 4. (2) Business, doings, D.M., xxxiii. 6.

輔
fû
   To assist, A., XII. xxiv.

輕
ch'ing
   Light, not heavy, A., V. xxv. 2 ; VI. iii. 2.

輗
i
   The cross-bar for yoking the oxen in a large carriage, A., II. xxii.

輿
yü
   (1) A carriage, A., XV. v. 3 ; XVIII. vi. 2. (2) 接輿, a name, A., XVIII. v.

輟
chüeh
   To desist, stop, A., XVIII. vi. 3.

THE 160TH RADICAL, 辛.

辟
p'i
   (1) Partial, perverse, G.L.c., viii. 1, x. 4. (2) Specious, A., XI. xvii. 3 ; XVI. iv.

辟
pi
   A sovereign ; applicable to the sovereign as well as the princes. In the Analects only of the princes, D.M., xxxiii. 5. A., III. ii.

辟
pi
   I. q. 避. To escape ; withdraw from, D.M., vii. A., XIV. xxxix. 1, 2, 3, 4 ; XVIII. v. 2, vi. 3.

辟
p'i
   I. q. 譬. 辟如, may be compared to, D.M., xv. 1, xxx. 2.

辨
pien
   To discriminate ; to discover, D.M., xix. 4, xx. 19, 20. A., XII. x. 1, xxi. 1.

辭
ts'ze
   (1) Language ; speech, G.L.c., iv. A., XV. xl. 辭氣, =words and tones, A., VIII. iv. 3. 爲之辭, to frame excuses for, A., XVI. i. 9. (2) To refuse, decline, D.M., ix. A., VI. iii. 3, vii ; XVII. xx.

THE 161st RADICAL, 辰.

辰 *ch'ăn*
The constellations of the zodiac, D.M., xxvi. 9. 北辰, the north pole star, A., II. i.

農 *năng*
A husbandman, A., XIII. iv. 1.

辱 *zŭ*
Disgrace ; to disgrace, A., I. xiii ; IV. xxvi ; XII. xxiii ; XIII. xx ; XVIII. viii. 2, 3.

THE 162nd RADICAL, 辶.

迅 *hsin*
Sudden, A., X. xvi. 5.

迂 *yü*
Wide of the mark, A., XIII. iii. 3.

近 *chin*
To be near to, G.L.T., 3. D.M., xx. 10, xxix. 5. A., I. xiii, *et al.* Nearness, D.M., xxxiii. 1. (In what is near, i. e. one's self), A., VI. xxviii. 3 ; XIX. vi.

迎 *ying*
To meet, D.M., xx. 14.

述 *shŭ*
To transmit; carry forward, D.M., xviii. 1, xix. 2, xxx. 1. A., VII. i ; XVII. xix. 2. To be handed down to posterity, D.M., xi. 1. A., XIV. xlvi.

迷 *mi*
To leave to error, A., XVII. i. 2.

适 *kwo*
A name, A., XIV. vi.—伯适, A., XVIII. xi.

追 *chŭi*
To go back in thought, and act according to what may be required, D.M., xviii. 3. A., I. ix. To go forward in the same way, A., XVIII. v.

進 *chin*
To advance, go forward, A., VI. xiii ; VII. xxviii. 2 ; IX. xviii, xx ; X. iii. 3, iv. 5 ; XIII. xxi ; XIX. xii. Actively, to call, to urge, forward, A., III. xxx. 2 ; XI. xxi. 先進, 後進=先輩, 後輩, A., XI. i. 1, 2.

迹 *chi*
Footsteps, A., XI. xix.

逆 *ni*
To anticipate, A., XIV. xxxiii.

送 *sung*
To escort, send away in a complimentary manner, D.M., xx. 14. A., X. xi. 1.

逬 *păng* or *ping*
I. q. 屏. To drive out, G.L.c., x. 15.

逞 *ch'ěng*
To unloose, = to relax, A., X. iv. 5.

造 *tsâo*
To make. 造端, to make a beginning, D.M., xii. 4.

造 *ts'âo*
造次, in urgency and haste, A., IV. v. 3.

通 *t'ung*
To reach to, D.M., xxxi. 4. Reaching everywhere, = universal, A., XVII. xxi. 6. 不通, not to get through, or forward, G.L.c., x. 14.

速 *sù*
Quick ; rapidly, quickly, A., XIII. xvii. 1 ; XIV. xlvii. 2.

逮 *tâi*
To come to, to reach to, G.L.c., x. 17. D.M., xix. 4. A., IV. xxii ; XVI. iii.

逝 *shih*
To pass—be passing—on, A., IX. xvi ; XVII. i. 2. 可逝也, may be made to go to, A., VI. xxiv.

退 *t'ŭi*
(1) To retire, withdraw, A., II. ix ; VII. xxviii. 2, xxx. 2 ; X. iii. 4 ; XII. xxiii. 4 ; XVII. xiii. 2, 3, 5 ; XIX. xii. 1. To return from, A., X. xii ; XIII. xiv. 1. (2) To remove, G.L.c., x. 16. To repress, A., XI. xxi.

逸 *yi*
(1) To retire from the world into obscurity, A., XVIII. viii. 1 ; XX. i. 7. (2) 夷逸, a man's name, A., XVIII. viii.

遂 *sŭi*
(1) Accomplished, having had its, or their, course, A., III. xxi. 2. (2) Then, accordingly, A., XV. i. 1.

遇 *yü*
To meet, A., XVII. i. 1 ; XVIII. vii. 1.

遊 *yü*
To ramble, A., XII. xxi. 1. With a bad meaning in 佚遊, idleness and sauntering, A., XVI. v. To go abroad, A., IV. xix.

過 *kwo*
To go beyond, transgress ; to be wrong, D.M., iv. A., V. vi ; XI. xv. 1, 3 ; XIV. xiv. 2 ; XIX. viii. A transgression, error, fault, G.L.c., x. 16. D.M., xxix. 1. A., I. viii. 4 ; IV. vii ; V. xxvi ; *et al.*, *saepe.*

過 *kwo*
In 1st tone. To go, or pass by, A., IX. ix ; X. iv. 3 ; XIV. xlii. 1 ; XVI. xiii. 2, 3 ; XVIII. v. 1, vi. 1.

道 *tâo*
Anciently, in 3rd tone. (1) A road, a path, A., IX. xi. 3 ; XVII, xiv. 中道, midway, A., VI. x. Very often with a moral application, the path as of the Mean, in the Doctrine of the Mean, *et al.;* the course or courses, the ways proper to. Sometimes it = the right way, what is right and true, A., IV. v. 1, viii, ix ; *et al.* (2) Doctrine, principles, teachings, A., IV. xv. 1 ; V. vi ; VI. xv ; XIV. xxxviii ; XV. xxviii ; *et al.*, *saepe.* 有道, principled ; 無道, unprincipled :— sometimes spoken of individuals, A., I. xiv ; but generally descriptive of the state of a country, as well or ill-governed, D.M., xxvii. 7. A., III. xxiv ; XVI. ii. 1, 2, 3 ; *et al.*, *saepe.*

道 *tâo*
Anciently (as now), in 4th tone. (1) To proceed by, D.M., xxvii. 6. (2) To say, to mean, G.L.c., iii. 4, x. 5, 11. To say, to speak to, A., XII. xxiii. 1. A., XIV. xxx. 2 ; XVI. 5. (3) To govern, administer, i. q. 導, A., I. v ; II. iii. 1, 2.

達 *tâ*
(1) To reach to, D.M., xviii. 3. A., XIV. xxiv, xxxviii. 2. To carry out, A., VI. xxviii. 2; XIII. xvii; XVI. xi. 2. (2) Intelligent; to know what to think or do, A., VI. vi; X. xi. 2; XII. xxii. 2; XIII. v; XV. xl. (3) Universal, reaching everywhere, D.M., i. 4, xix. 1, xxviii. (4) Distinguished, notorious, A., XII. xx. 1, 2, 4, 5. (5) 伯達, a man's name, A., XVIII. xi. 達巷, the name of a village, A., IX. ii.

違 *wei*
(1) To oppose, G.L.c., x. 14. A., II. v. 1, 2, ix; IX. iii. 2; XIII. xv. 4, 5. To act contrary to, A., IV. v. 3; VI. v; XII. xx. 6. (2) To be distant from, D.M., xiii. 3. To leave, A., V. xviii. 2. (3) To abandon a purpose, A., IV. xviii.

遠 *yüan*
To be at a distance, to become distant, G.L.c., ix. 2. D.M., xiii. 1, 2, 3, xv. 1. A., XII. xiii. 6; XVII. ii. Distant, to a distance; from a distance, D.M., xx. 12, 13, 14, xxvi. 3. A., I. i. 2, ix; IV. xix; VII. xxix; VIII. vii. 1, 2; IX. xxx. 1, 2; XIII. xvi. 2; XV. xi; XVI. i. 11, 12; XIX. iv. What is remote, D.M., xxiii. 1. 遠=far-seeing, A., XII. vi. Observe 遠之, D.M., xxix. 5. A., XVII. ix. 6.

遠 *yüan*
In 4th tone. To put away to a distance; to keep one's self at a distance from, G.L.c., x. 16. D.M., xx. 14. A., I. xiii; VI. xx; VIII. iv. 3; XV. x. 6, xiv; XVI. xiii. 5; XVII. xxv.

適 *shih*
To go, proceed, to, A., VI. iii. 2; IX. xxix; XIII. ix. 1; XVIII. ix. 1, 2.

適 *ti*
To have the mind set on anything, A., IV. x.

遯 *tun*
I. q. 遁. To withdraw, lie hid, from, D.M., xi. 3.

遷 *ch'ien*
To transfer, remove, A., VI. ii; X. vii. 2.

遲 *ch'ih*
樊遲, the name of one of Confucius's disciples; i. q. 樊須, A., II. v. 2, 3; VI. xx; XII. xxi, xxii; XIII. iv, xix.

遺 *wei*
To neglect, be neglected, A., VIII. ii. 2. Observe D.M., xvi. 2.

選 *hsüan*
To choose, select, A., XII. xxii. 6.

遵 *tsun*
To follow, to observe, D.M., xi. 2.

邇 *r*
Near. What is near, D.M., xv. 1. Observe A., XVII. ix. 6. 邇=shallow, D.M., vi.

THE 163RD RADICAL, 邑.

邑 *yi*
A city or town, A., V. vii. 3; XIV. x. 3. A hamlet, A., V. xxvii. 駢邑, the city or town of P'ien, A., XIV. x. 3.

邦 *pang*
A country, a State, G.L.c., ii. 3. A., I. x. 1; III. xxii. 3; *et saepe.* 邦家, a State embracing the families of its high officers, A., XIX. xxv. 4, *et al.* 邦畿, the royal domain, G.L.c., iii. 1.

郊 *chiâo*
The royal sacrifice to Heaven, D.M., xix. 6.

邪 *hsieh*
Depraved, A., II. ii.

郁 *yü*
郁郁乎, how complete and elegant! A., III. xiv.

鄉 *hsiang*
(1) A village, A., XVII. xiii. Joined with 黨, A., VI. iii. 4; X. i. 1; XIII. xx. 2. 鄉人, villagers, A., X. x. 1, 2; XIII. xxiv. (2) 互鄉, the name of a place, A., VII. xxviii.

鄉 *hsiang*
In 4th tone. Formerly, A., XII. xxii. 4.

鄙 *p'i*
Mean; lowness, A., VIII. iv. 3; IX. vi. 3; XIV. xlii. 2. 鄙夫, A., IX. vii; XVII. xv.

鄰 *lin*
A neighbour, neighbours, A., IV. xxv; V. xxiii. A neighbourhood, A., VI. iii. 4.

邱 *ch'iü*
I. q. 丘. In some editions, G.L.c., iii. 2.

鄭 *chǎng*
The name of a State, A., XV. x. 6; XVII. xviii.

鄹 *tsâu*
The native city of Confucius, A., III. xv.

THE 164TH RADICAL, 酉.

配 *p'ei*
To appear before, G.L.c., x. 5. To be the co-equal of, D.M., xxvi. 5, xxxi. 4.

酒 *chiü*
Wine; spirits, A., II. viii; IX. xv; X. viii. 4, 5, x. 1.

酬 *ch'âu*
To pledge,—in drinking, D.M., xix. 4.

醬 *chiang*
Sauce, pickle, A., X. viii. 3.

醫 *i*
作醫, to be a doctor, A., XIII. xxii.

醯 *hsi*
Vinegar, A., V. xxiii.

THE 166TH RADICAL, 里.

里 *li*
(1) A village, or neighbourhood, A., IV. i. 隣里, A., VI. iii. 4. A., XV. v. 2. (2) A measure of length, of 360 paces:—anciently=1897½ English feet; now=1826 feet, G.L.c., iii. 1. A., VIII. vi. (3) 東里, the name of a place in Ch'ing, A., XIV. ix.

重
chung
Heavy, what is heavy, A., VIII. vii. 1, 2. To feel; to be heavy, D.M., xxvi. 9. Grave, A., I. viii. 1. Earnest, great, D.M., xx. 13. To make large, D.M., xx. 14. To attach importance to, A., XX. i. 8.

野
yeh
Rude, uncultivated, A., VI. xvi; XIII. iii. 4. 野人, A., XI. i. 1.

量
liang
Measures of capacity, A., XX. i. 6. A measure, limit, A., X. viii. 4. 不知量, not to know one's own capacity, A., XIX. xxiv.

THE 167TH RADICAL, 金.

金
chin
Metal. 金 = arms, D.M., x. 4.

鈇
fú
An axe, a hatchet. 鈇鉞, D.M., xxxiii. 4.

鉞
yüeh
A battle-axe, see above.

釜
fú
A measure containing 64 *shǎng*, A., VI. iii. 1.

釣
tiáo
To angle, A., VII. xxvi.

錦
chin
Embroidered clóthes, D.M., xxxiii. 1. A., XVII. xxi. 4.

銘
ming
To engrave; be engraved, G.L.c., ii. 1.

錯
ts'o
Alternatingly, D.M., xxx. 2.

錯
ts'ú
To set aside, A., II. xix; XII. xxii. 3, 4.

鏗
k'ǎng
鏗爾, while it was yet twanging; spoken of the sound of a harpsichord, A., XI. xxv. 7.

鐸
to
木鐸, a bell with a wooden clapper, A., III. xxiv.

鑽
tswan
To bore; to penetrate, A., IX. x. 1. 鑽燧, to bore wood to procure fire, A., XVII. xxi. 3.

鐘
chung
A bell, A., XVII. xi.

THE 168TH RADICAL, 長.

長
ch'ang
(1) Long, A., X. vi. 5. 長府, the Long Treasury, A., XI. xiii. 1. (2) Said of time, A. iv. ii. 長 = always, A., VII. xxxvi. (3) 長沮, a recluse, A., XVIII. vi. 公冶長, a disciple, and son-in-law of Confucius, A., V. i.

長
chang
(1) In 3rd tone. Old, A., XI. xxv. 2. Grown up, A., XIV. xlvi; XVII. vii. 5. (長幼). Elders, G.L.c., ix. 1, x. 2. To treat as elders should be treated,

G.L.c., x. 1. (2) To preside over, high in station, G.L.c., x. 23.

長
chang
In 4th tone. More than, A., X. vi. 6.

THE 169TH RADICAL, 門.

門
mun
(1) A door, a gate, A., II. xxii. 3; VI. xiii; XII. ii; XIV. xlii. Spoken by Confucius of his door, i. e. his school, A., XI. ii. 1, xiv. 中門, to stand in the middle of the gateway, A., X. iv. 2. 門人, disciples, A., IV. xv. 2; VII. xxviii; IX. xi; XI. x. 1, 2, xiv. 2; XIX. iii, xii. So, 門弟子, A., VIII. iii; IX. ii. 2. (2) 石門, the name of a place, or barrier-pass, A., XIV. xli.

閑
hsien
A boundary, or fending line, A., XIX. xi.

閒
hsien
At leisure, retired, G.L.c., vi. 2.

閒
chien
An interval. Used as a preposition, following its regimen, with 之 before it, = between, A., IV. v. 3; XI. xxv. 4; XVIII. iii. 病閒, during an intermission of sickness, A., IX. xi. 2.

間
chien
In 4th tone. To find a crevice or flaw, A., VIII. xxi; XI. iv.

閾
yi
The threshold, A., X. iv. 2.

闇
ǎn
闇然, secret, concealed, D.M., xxxiii. 1.

闕
ch'üeh
(1) To put aside, exercise reserve, A., II. xviii. 2. 闕如, A., XIII. iii. 4. (2) 闕文, a blank left in the writing, A., XV. xxv. (3) The name of a village, A., XIV. xlvii.

關
kwan
關雎, the first ode in the Shih-ching, A., III. xx; VIII. xv.

開
k'ǎi
The name of one of Confucius's disciples, A., V. v.

閔
min
The surname of one of Confucius's disciples, A., VI. vii; XI. ii, iv, xii, xiii.

THE 170TH RADICAL, 阜.

防
fang
The name of a city in Lû, A., XIV. xv.

阼
tsû
The steps, or staircase, on the east. 阼階, A., X. x. 2.

附
fú
附益, to increase one's wealth, A., XI. xvi. 1.

阱
ching
A pitfall, D.M., vii.

陋
lâu
(1) Narrow, A., VI. ix.   (2) Rude, un-cultivated; rudeness, A., IX. xiii. 2.

降
chiang
(1) To descend, A., X. iv. 5.   (2) To surrender (act.), A., XVIII. viii. 2, 3.

陵
ling
(1) A mound, A., XIX. xxiv.   (2) To insult, D.M., xiv. 3.

陰
ăn
諒陰, the shed where the sovereign spent his three years of mourning, A., XIV. xliii. 1.

陳
ch'ăn
(1) To arrange; display; exert, D.M., xix. 3.   A., XVI. i. 6.   (2) The name of a State, A., V. xxi; VII. xxx; XI. ii; XV. 2. (3) 陳恆 (honorary epithet 成), an officer of Ch'í, A., XIV. xxii.   陳文 (honorary epithet), another officer of Ch'í, A., V. xviii. 2.   陳亢, a disciple of Confucius, *i. q.* 子禽, A., XVI. xiii.

陳
chăn
The arrangement of the ranks of an army, = tactics, A., XV. i. 1.

陷
hsien
(1) 陷阱, to be taken in a pitfall, D.M., vii.   (2) To be made to fall into, A., VI. xxiv.

陪
p'ei
陪臣, the family ministers belonging to the officers of a State, A., XVI. ii.

隅
yü
A corner, G.L.c., iii. 2.   A., VII. viii.

陽
yang
(1) 陽膚, a disciple of Tsăng Shăn, who was made criminal judge of Lû, A., XIX. xix.   (2) 首陽, the name of a mountain, A., XVI. xii.   (3) 陽貨, the name of an usurping officer of Lû, A., XVII. i.   (4) Name of an assistant music-master of Lû, A., XVIII. ix. 5.

隊
chûi
To fall, D.M., xxxi. 4.

陶
yâo
皐陶, a minister of Shun, A., XII. xxii. 6.

階
chieh
Steps of a stair, A., X. iv. 5, x. 2; XV. xli. 1; XIX. xxv. 3.

險
hsien
Dangerous, difficult, places.   行險, to walk in dangerous paths, D.M., xiv. 4.

隨
sûi
季隨, an officer of Châu, A., XVIII. xi.

際
chi
A conjunction, or meeting, A., VIII. xx. 3.

隱
yin
Secret; what is secret, D.M., i. 3, xii. 1. To keep secret, conceal, D.M., vi.   A., VII. xxiii; XIII. xviii. 2.   To live in obscurity, D.M., xi. 1.   A., VIII. xiii. 2; XVI. vi, xi. 2; XVIII. vii. 4, viii. 4.

THE 172ND RADICAL, 隹·

雉
chih
A pheasant, A., X. xviii. 2.

雌
ts'ze
The female of birds.   雌雉, a hen-pheasant, A., X. xviii. 2.

雅
yă
(1) Frequently, A., VII. xvii.   (2) The name of the odes in the second and third parts of the Shih-ching, A., IX. xiv; XVII. xviii.

睢
chü
關睢, the name of the first ode in the Shih-ching, A., III. xx; VIII. xv.

雍
yung
(1) The name of an ode in the Shih-ching, A., III. ii.   (2) The name of one of Confucius's disciples, Nan Yung, styled Chung-kung, A., V. iv; VI. i; XII. ii.

雖
sûi
Although, G.L.c., ii. 3, ix. 2, *et al.* D.M., xxviii. 4, xxxiii. 2.   A., I. vii; VI. ix; IX. iii. 2, *et al.*, *saepe.*   It is often followed by an adjective, without a verb, and may be translated *even, even in the case of.*   Observe A., VI. xxiv, and IX. xviii.

集
chi
To settle, A., X. xviii. 1.

雞
chī
Fowls, a fowl, G.L.c., x. 22.   A., XVII. iv. 2; XVIII. vii. 3.

離
li
To be scattered; dispersions, A., XVI. i. 12.

離
li
In 4th tone.   To go away from; to be left, D.M., i. 2.

難
nan
Difficult; to be difficult; difficulty, A., II. viii; VI. xiv; VII. xxv. 3, xxviii. 1; VIII. xx. 3; XII. iii. 3; XIII. xv. 2, 3, *et al.*   What is difficult, A., VI. xx; XIV. ii. 2; XIX. xv.

難
nan
In 4th tone.   Trouble, calamity, A., XVI. x.   患難, D.M., xiv. 2.

雕
tiâo
(1) To carve, A., V. ix. 1.   (2) Part of a double surname, A., V. v.

THE 173RD RADICAL, 雨·

雩
yü
The name of a sacrifice to pray for rain. They danced about the altars.   Hence 舞雩 = rain-altars, A., XI. xxv. 7; XII. xxi.

雲
yün
Clouds, a cloud, A., VII. xv.

雷
lêi
Thunder, A., X. xvi. 5.

霜
shwang
Hoar-frost, D.M., xxxi. 4.

露
lû
Dew, D.M., xxxi. 4.

霸
pá
To exercise authority over men by strength; to make to have such authority, A., XIV. xviii. 2.

靈
ling　靈 (honorary epithet) 公, a duke of Wei, A., XIV. xx ; XV. i.

THE 174TH RADICAL, 青.

靜
chǎng　Calm and unperturbed ; tranquil, G.L.T., 2. A., VI. xxi.

THE 175TH RADICAL, 非.

非
fei　Not, *saepe*. It very often stands at the beginning of the clause, or member to which it belongs, and = it is not that . . . ; if not, &c. 非 = what is contrary to, D.M., xx. 14. A., XVIII. vi. 4, i. 2. 非 不, not but, = an affirmation, A., VI. x.

靡
mi　Not, D.M., xxxiii. 4.

THE 176TH RADICAL, 面.

面
mien　The face. 南面, the face to the south ; the position of a sovereign, A., VI. i. 1 ; XV. iv. 牆面, the face towards a wall, A., XVII. x.

THE 177TH RADICAL, 革.

革
ko　The portions of armour, made of leather, D.M., x. 4.

鞠
chü　To bend. 鞠躬, A., X. iv. 1, 4, v. 1.

鞭
pien　A whip, A., VII. xi.

鞹
kwo　*I. q.* 鞹, a bare hide, a hide with the hair taken off, A., XII. viii. 3.

THE 178TH RADICAL, 韋.

韞
wǎn　To store up, to keep, A., IX. xii.

THE 180TH RADICAL, 音.

韶
sháo　The music of Shun, A., III. xxv ; VII. xiii ; XV. x. 5.

THE 181ST RADICAL, 頁.

順
shun　To be obedient to, in accordance with, D.M., xx. 17. A., II. iv. 5 ; XIII. iii. 5. To have complacence, D.M., xv. 3.

須
hsü　(1) 須臾, a short time, an instant, D.M., i. 2. (2) 樊須, one of Confucius's disciples, *i. q.* 樊遲, A., XIII. iv. 2.

頌
sung　Praise-songs. The name of the last part of the Shih-ching, A., IX. xiv.

願
yüan　To desire ; to wish ; to like, D.M., xiii. 3, xiv. 1. A., V. xxv. 2, 3, 4 ; XI. xxv. 6.

顏
yen　(1) 顏色, the countenance, A., VIII. iv. 3 ; X. iv. 5 ; XVI. vi. (2) The surname of Confucius's favourite disciple. See 回 and 淵 顏路, Hûi's father, A., XI. vii.

顓
chwan　顓臾, the name of a small State, A., XVI. i.

類
lêi　Sorts, classes, A., XV. xxxviii.

顚
tien　To fall ; fallen, A., XVI. i. 6. 顚沛, in peril, A., IV. v. 3.

顧
kû　To contemplate, G.L.c., i. 2. To have regard to, D.M., xiii. 4. To turn the head round to look, A., X. iii. 4, xvii. 2.

顯
hsien　To be manifest ; illustrious, D.M., i. 3, xvi. 5, xviii. 2, xxvi. 10, xxxiii. 1. Observe xxxiii. 5.

THE 182ND RADICAL, 風.

風
fêng　The wind, D.M., xxxiii. 1. A., X. xvi. 5 ; XII. xix. To enjoy the breeze ; to take the air, A., XI. xxv. 7.

THE 183RD RADICAL, 飛.

飛
fei　To fly, D.M., xii. 3.

THE 184TH RADICAL, 食.

食
shih　(1) To eat, G.L.c., vii. 2. D.M., iv. 2. A., I. xiv, *et al., saepe*. 食 = to consume, G.L.c., x. 19. 食 = to enjoy, A., XI. xi. 3. To be eaten, A., XVII. vii. 4. 終食之間, a meal's time, A., IV. v. 3. 食 = food, D.M., xix. 3. A., IV. ix ; VIII. xxi ; X. vii. 2, *et al.* (2) 月之食, an eclipse, A., XIX. xxi.

食
tsze　(1) Rice ; food generally, A., II. viii ; VI. ix ; VII. xv ; X. viii. 1, 2, 4, 10 ; XIV. x. 3. (2) To give food to ; to feast, A., XVIII. vii. 3.

飲
yin　To drink, D.M., iv. 2. A., X. x. 1. As a noun, (?) A., VI. ix ; VIII. xxxi.

飲
yin　In 4th tone. To give to drink, A., III. vii.

飪
zǎn　Meat overdone. 失飪不食, he did not eat anything that was not well done, A., X. viii. 2.

飯
fǎn　(1) To eat. 飯疏食, A., VII. xv ; XIV. x. 3. In those instances, perhaps 飯 = for food. To taste, A., X. xiii. 2. (2) 亞飯, 三飯, 四飯, see 亞, 三, 四, A., XVIII. ix.

飾
shih　To ornament, A., X. vi. 1. Observe 修飾之, A., XIV. ix. 1.

飽
pâo

To eat to the full; satiety, A., I. xiv; VII. ix; XVII. xxii.

養
yang

To nourish; to bring up, G.L.c., ix. 2. A., V. xv. 養 = to have about one; to manage, A., XVII. xxv.

養
yang

In 4th tone. To nourish, to support a superior, A., II. vii.

餘
yü

That which is over. 其餘, the others, A., II. xviii. 2; VI. v; VIII. xi. Superabundant, A., I. vi. 有餘, having excess, D.M., xiii. 4.

餒
nëi

(1) Hunger, want, A., XV. xxxi. (2) Rotten, gone, A., X. viii. 2; spoken of fish.

餲
o

Hungry, = to die of famine, A., XVI. xii. 1.

餲
i

Rice sour, or with a bad odour, A., X. viii. 2.

餼
ch'i

餼羊, the sheep offered at the inauguration of the new moon, A., III. xvii. 1.

饌
chwan

Provisions, A., X. xvi. 4. 先生饌, to set before one's elders, A., II. viii.

餲
i

食餲, rice injured by damp, A., X. viii. 2.

饑
chi

A famine;—specifically of the grain crop, A., XII. ix. 1. 饑饉, a famine, A., XI. xxv. 4.

饉
chin

A famine;—specifically of vegetables. See 饑.

饋
kwei

To present; anything presented, A., X. xi. 2, xv. 2.

饗
hsiang

To enjoy; to accept a sacrifice, D.M., xvii. 1, xviii. 2.

THE 185TH RADICAL, 首.

首
shâu

首陽, the name of a mountain, A., XVI. xii. 1.

首
shâu

In 4th tone. The direction of the head, A., X. xiii. 3.

THE 187TH RADICAL, 馬.

馬
mâ

(1) A horse, horses, G.L.c., x. 22. A., II. vii; V. xviii. 2, xxv. 2; VI. iii. 2, xiii; X. xii, xv. 2; XV. xxv; XVI. xii. 1. (2) 司馬, a double surname, A., XII. iii, iv, v. 巫馬, also a double surname, A., VII. xxx.

馮
p'ăng

馮河, to attempt to cross a river without using a boat, A., VII. x. 3.

駟
sze

A team of four horses, A., XII. viii. 2; XVI. xii.

駕
chiâ

The yoking of a carriage, A., X. xiii. 4.

騂
hsing

Red. Spoken of a calf to be sacrificed, A., VI. iv.

驕
chiâo

To be proud; pride, G.L.c., x. 18. D.M., xxvii. 7. A., I. xv. 1; VIII. xi; XIII. xxvi; XIV. xi; XVI. v; XX. ii. 1, 2.

驅
ch'ü

To drive, D.M., vii.

驥
ch'i

A horse that could go 1000 *li* in a day, = a good horse, A., XIV. xxxv.

騫
ch'ien

子騫, the designation of one of Confucius's disciples, A., VI. vii; XI. ii, iv, xiii.

驪
kwâ

季驪, the name of an officer of the Châu dynasty, A., XVIII. xi.

騈
p'ien

The name of a town, A., XIV. x. 3.

THE 188TH RADICAL, 骨.

體
t'i

(1) The body, G.L.c., vi. 4. 四體, the four limbs, D.M., xxiv. vii. 1. (2) As a verb. To treat with consideration, D.M., xx. 12, 13. To enter into, be incorporate with, D.M., xvi. 2.

THE 189TH RADICAL, 高.

高
kâo

(1) High, D.M., xv. 1, xxvi. 3, 4, 5, 8, xxvii. 6. A., IX. x. 1. (2) 高宗, the honorary epithet of the sovereign 武丁, A., XIV. xliii. (3) A name, 微生高, A., V. xxiii.

THE 190TH RADICAL, 髟.

髮
fâ

The hair, A., XIV. xviii. 2.

THE 191ST RADICAL, 鬥.

鬪
tâu

To contend; quarrelsomeness, A., XVI. vii.

THE 194TH RADICAL, 鬼.

鬼
kwei

Manes, the spirit or spirits of the departed, A., II. xxiv; XI. xi. 鬼神, spiritual beings;—sometimes exclusively manes, D.M., xvi, xxix. 3, 4. A., VI. xx; VIII. xxi.

魏
wei

The name of a great family of Tsin, A., XIV. xii.

魋
t'ûi

桓魋 a bad officer of Sung, for whom Confucius was once mistaken, A., VII. xxii.

THE 195TH RADICAL, 魚.

魚
yü

(1) A fish, fishes, fish, D.M., xii. 3, xxvi. 9. A., X. viii. 2. (2) 魚子, an historiographer, A., XV. vi. (3) 伯魚, the designation of Confucius's son, A., XVI. xiii. 1; XVII. x.

魯
lû

(1) Dull, blunt, A., XI. xvii. 2. (2) The name of a State, A., III. xxiii; V. ii; VI. xxii, *et al.* 魯公, A., XVIII. x.

鮮 _hsien_ (superscript c)

In 3rd tone. Few, rare; seldom, G.L.c., viii. 1. D.M., iii, iv. 2. A., I. ii. 1, iii; IV. xxiii; VI. xxvii; XV. iii; XVII. xvii.

鮀 _t'o_

An officer of Wei, A., VI. xiv; XIV. xxii. 2.

鯉 _li_

The name of Confucius's son, A., XI. vii. 2; XVI. xiii. 2, 3.

THE 196TH RADICAL, 鳥.

鳥 _niǎo_

A bird, birds, G.L.c., iii. 2. A., VIII. iv. 2; IX. viii; XVII. ix. 7; XVIII. vi. 4.

鳳 _fâng_

A fabulous bird, the phœnix, A., IX. viii. Applied to Confucius, A., XVIII. v. 1.

鳴 _ming_

(1) The cry of a bird, A., VIII. iv. 2. (2) To sound, to beat, A., XI. xvi. 2.

鳶 _yüan_

A kind of hawk, D.M., xii. 3.

鵠 _kŭ_

Used as = the bull's eye in a target, D.M., xiv. 5.

THE 198TH RADICAL, 鹿.

麑 _ni_

A fawn, A., X. vi. 4.

THE 200TH RADICAL, 麻.

麻 _mâ_

Hemp = linen, A., IX. iii. 1.

THE 201ST RADICAL, 黃.

黃 _hwang_

Yellow, G.L.c., iii. 2. A., X. vi. 4.

THE 202ND RADICAL, 黍.

黎 _li_

Black. 黎民, the black-haired people, = the people, G.L.c., x. 14.

THE 203RD RADICAL, 黑.

默 _mo_

To be silent, silence, D.M., xxvii. 7. A., VII. ii.

黜 _ch'ŭ_

To be dismissed from office, A., XVIII. ii.

點 _tien_

The name of 曾晳, one of Confucius's disciples, A., XI. xxv. 7.

黨 _tang_

(1) A village, A., IX. ii; XIV. xlvii. 1. 鄉黨, A., VI. iii. 4; X. i. 1. (2) A class, A., IV. vii. 黨 = school, pupils, A., V. xxi. 吾黨, we, among us, A., XIII. xviii. 1, 2. (3) A partisan, partisanly, A., VII. xxx. 2; XV. xxi.

THE 204TH RADICAL, 黹.

黼 _fû_

An apron, belonging to the sovereign's dress at sacrifices, A., VIII. xxi.

THE 205TH RADICAL, 黽.

黿 _yüan_

A large sea-turtle, D.M., xxvi. 9.

鼈 _pieh_

A turtle, D.M., xxvi. 9.

鼉 _t'o_

An iguana, D.M., xxvi. 9.

THE 207TH RADICAL, 鼓.

鼓 _kŭ_

(1) A drum, drums, A., XI. xvi. 2; XVII. xi. (2) Drum-master, A., XVIII. ix. 3. (3) To strike, to play on, D.M., xv. 2. A., XI. xxv. 7. Anciently, for the third of these senses the character 鼓 was used.

鼗 _t'âo_

A kind of hand-drum. 播鼗, to shake the hand-drum, A., XVIII. ix. 4.

THE 210TH RADICAL, 齊.

齊 _ch'i_

(1) To regulate, G.L.t., 4, 5. G.L.c., viii. 1, 3; ix. 1, 5. To give uniformity to, A., II. iii. 1, 2. To equal; be equal with, A., IV. xvii. (2) The name of a State, A., V. xviii. 2; VI. iii. 1, 2, xxii; VII. xiii; XII. xi; XVI. xii; XVIII. iii, iv, ix.— XIV. xvi. (3) In 叔齊, it is the honorary epithet, A., V. xxii; XVI. xii; XVIII. viii. 1, 2.

齊 _châi_

To fast; religious adjustment, D.M., xvi. 3; xx. 14; xxxi. 1. A., VII. xii; X. vii. 1, 2; xiii. 10.

齊 _tsze_

The lower edge of a garment, A., X. iv. 4. 齊衰, in mourning, A., IX. ix; X. xvi. 2.

THE 211TH RADICAL, 齒.

齒 _ch'ih_

The teeth, A., XIV. x. 3. Used for years, age, D.M., xix. 4.

THE 212TH RADICAL, 龍.

龍 _lung_

A dragon, dragons, D.M., xxvi. 9.

THE 213TH RADICAL, 龜.

龜 _kwei_

A tortoise, D.M., xxiv. A., XVI. i. 7.

OMISSION.

To 博, the last character in col. 1, p. 457, add '(2) A certain game, A., XVII. xxii.'

A CATALOGUE OF
SELECTED DOVER BOOKS
IN ALL FIELDS OF INTEREST

A CATALOGUE OF SELECTED DOVER
BOOKS IN ALL FIELDS OF INTEREST

CELESTIAL OBJECTS FOR COMMON TELESCOPES, T. W. Webb. The most used book in amateur astronomy: inestimable aid for locating and identifying nearly 4,000 celestial objects. Edited, updated by Margaret W. Mayall. 77 illustrations. Total of 645pp. 5⅜ x 8½.
20917-2, 20918-0 Pa., Two-vol. set $10.00

HISTORICAL STUDIES IN THE LANGUAGE OF CHEMISTRY, M. P. Crosland. The important part language has played in the development of chemistry from the symbolism of alchemy to the adoption of systematic nomenclature in 1892. ". . . wholeheartedly recommended,"—Science. 15 illustrations. 416pp. of text. 5⅝ x 8¼.   63702-6 Pa. $7.50

BURNHAM'S CELESTIAL HANDBOOK, Robert Burnham, Jr. Thorough, readable guide to the stars beyond our solar system. Exhaustive treatment, fully illustrated. Breakdown is alphabetical by constellation: Andromeda to Cetus in Vol. 1; Chamaeleon to Orion in Vol. 2; and Pavo to Vulpecula in Vol. 3. Hundreds of illustrations. Total of about 2000pp. 6⅛ x 9¼.
23567-X, 23568-8, 23673-0 Pa., Three-vol. set $32.85

THEORY OF WING SECTIONS: INCLUDING A SUMMARY OF AIR-FOIL DATA, Ira H. Abbott and A. E. von Doenhoff. Concise compilation of subatomic aerodynamic characteristics of modern NASA wing sections, plus description of theory. 350pp. of tables. 693pp. 5⅜ x 8½.
60586-8 Pa. $9.95

DE RE METALLICA, Georgius Agricola. Translated by Herbert C. Hoover and Lou H. Hoover. The famous Hoover translation of greatest treatise on technological chemistry, engineering, geology, mining of early modern times (1556). All 289 original woodcuts. 638pp. 6¾ x 11.
60006-8 Clothbd. $19.95

THE ORIGIN OF CONTINENTS AND OCEANS, Alfred Wegener. One of the most influential, most controversial books in science, the classic statement for continental drift. Full 1966 translation of Wegener's final (1929) version. 64 illustrations. 246pp. 5⅜ x 8½.(EBE)61708-4 Pa. $5.00

THE PRINCIPLES OF PSYCHOLOGY, William James. Famous long course complete, unabridged. Stream of thought, time perception, memory, experimental methods; great work decades ahead of its time. Still valid, useful; read in many classes. 94 figures. Total of 1391pp. 5⅜ x 8½.
20381-6, 20382-4 Pa., Two-vol. set $17.90

YUCATAN BEFORE AND AFTER THE CONQUEST, Diego de Landa. First English translation of basic book in Maya studies, the only significant account of Yucatan written in the early post-Conquest era. Translated by distinguished Maya scholar William Gates. Appendices, introduction, 4 maps and over 120 illustrations added by translator. 162pp. 5⅜ x 8½.
23622-6 Pa. $3.00

THE MALAY ARCHIPELAGO, Alfred R. Wallace. Spirited travel account by one of founders of modern biology. Touches on zoology, botany, ethnography, geography, and geology. 62 illustrations, maps. 515pp. 5⅜ x 8½.
20187-2 Pa. $6.95

THE DISCOVERY OF THE TOMB OF TUTANKHAMEN, Howard Carter, A. C. Mace. Accompany Carter in the thrill of discovery, as ruined passage suddenly reveals unique, untouched, fabulously rich tomb. Fascinating account, with 106 illustrations. New introduction by J. M. White. Total of 382pp. 5⅜ x 8½. (Available in U.S. only) 23500-9 Pa. $5.50

THE WORLD'S GREATEST SPEECHES, edited by Lewis Copeland and Lawrence W. Lamm. Vast collection of 278 speeches from Greeks up to present. Powerful and effective models; unique look at history. Revised to 1970. Indices. 842pp. 5⅜ x 8½. 20468-5 Pa. $9.95

THE 100 GREATEST ADVERTISEMENTS, Julian Watkins. The priceless ingredient; His master's voice; 99 44/100% pure; over 100 others. How they were written, their impact, etc. Remarkable record. 130 illustrations. 233pp. 7⅞ x 10 3/5. 20540-1 Pa. $6.95

CRUICKSHANK PRINTS FOR HAND COLORING, George Cruickshank. 18 illustrations, one side of a page, on fine-quality paper suitable for watercolors. Caricatures of people in society (c. 1820) full of trenchant wit. Very large format. 32pp. 11 x 16. 23684-6 Pa. $6.00

THIRTY-TWO COLOR POSTCARDS OF TWENTIETH-CENTURY AMERICAN ART, Whitney Museum of American Art. Reproduced in full color in postcard form are 31 art works and one shot of the museum. Calder, Hopper, Rauschenberg, others. Detachable. 16pp. 8¼ x 11.
23629-3 Pa. $3.50

MUSIC OF THE SPHERES: THE MATERIAL UNIVERSE FROM ATOM TO QUASAR SIMPLY EXPLAINED, Guy Murchie. Planets, stars, geology, atoms, radiation, relativity, quantum theory, light, antimatter, similar topics. 319 figures. 664pp. 5⅜ x 8½.
21809-0, 21810-4 Pa., Two-vol. set $11.00

EINSTEIN'S THEORY OF RELATIVITY, Max Born. Finest semi-technical account; covers Einstein, Lorentz, Minkowski, and others, with much detail, much explanation of ideas and math not readily available elsewhere on this level. For student, non-specialist. 376pp. 5⅜ x 8½.
60769-0 Pa. $5.00

THE SENSE OF BEAUTY, George Santayana. Masterfully written discussion of nature of beauty, materials of beauty, form, expression; art, literature, social sciences all involved. 168pp. 5⅜ x 8½. 20238-0 Pa. $3.50

ON THE IMPROVEMENT OF THE UNDERSTANDING, Benedict Spinoza. Also contains *Ethics, Correspondence,* all in excellent R. Elwes translation. Basic works on entry to philosophy, pantheism, exchange of ideas with great contemporaries. 402pp. 5⅜ x 8½. 20250-X Pa. $5.95

THE TRAGIC SENSE OF LIFE, Miguel de Unamuno. Acknowledged masterpiece of existential literature, one of most important books of 20th century. Introduction by Madariaga. 367pp. 5⅜ x 8½.

20257-7 Pa. $6.00

THE GUIDE FOR THE PERPLEXED, Moses Maimonides. Great classic of medieval Judaism attempts to reconcile revealed religion (Pentateuch, commentaries) with Aristotelian philosophy. Important historically, still relevant in problems. Unabridged Friedlander translation. Total of 473pp. 5⅜ x 8½. 20351-4 Pa. $6.95

THE I CHING (THE BOOK OF CHANGES), translated by James Legge. Complete translation of basic text plus appendices by Confucius, and Chinese commentary of most penetrating divination manual ever prepared. Indispensable to study of early Oriental civilizations, to modern inquiring reader. 448pp. 5⅜ x 8½. 21062-6 Pa. $6.00

THE EGYPTIAN BOOK OF THE DEAD, E. A. Wallis Budge. Complete reproduction of Ani's papyrus, finest ever found. Full hieroglyphic text, interlinear transliteration, word for word translation, smooth translation. Basic work, for Egyptology, for modern study of psychic matters. Total of 533pp. 6½ x 9¼. (USCO) 21866-X Pa. $8.50

THE GODS OF THE EGYPTIANS, E. A. Wallis Budge. Never excelled for richness, fullness: all gods, goddesses, demons, mythical figures of Ancient Egypt; their legends, rites, incarnations, variations, powers, etc. Many hieroglyphic texts cited. Over 225 illustrations, plus 6 color plates. Total of 988pp. 6⅛ x 9¼. (EBE)

22055-9, 22056-7 Pa., Two-vol. set $20.00

THE STANDARD BOOK OF QUILT MAKING AND COLLECTING, Marguerite Ickis. Full information, full-sized patterns for making 46 traditional quilts, also 150 other patterns. Quilted cloths, lame, satin quilts, etc. 483 illustrations. 273pp. 6⅞ x 9⅝. 20582-7 Pa. $5.95

CORAL GARDENS AND THEIR MAGIC, Bronsilaw Malinowski. Classic study of the methods of tilling the soil and of agricultural rites in the Trobriand Islands of Melanesia. Author is one of the most important figures in the field of modern social anthropology. 143 illustrations. Indexes. Total of 911pp. of text. 5⅝ x 8¼. (Available in U.S. only)

23597-1 Pa. $12.95

THE PHILOSOPHY OF HISTORY, Georg W. Hegel. Great classic of Western thought develops concept that history is not chance but a rational process, the evolution of freedom. 457pp. 5⅜ x 8½.   20112-0 Pa. $6.00

LANGUAGE, TRUTH AND LOGIC, Alfred J. Ayer. Famous, clear introduction to Vienna, Cambridge schools of Logical Positivism. Role of philosophy, elimination of metaphysics, nature of analysis, etc. 160pp. 5⅜ x 8½. (USCO)   20010-8 Pa. $2.50

A PREFACE TO LOGIC, Morris R. Cohen. Great City College teacher in renowned, easily followed exposition of formal logic, probability, values, logic and world order and similar topics; no previous background needed. 209pp. 5⅜ x 8½.   23517-3 Pa. $4.95

REASON AND NATURE, Morris R. Cohen. Brilliant analysis of reason and its multitudinous ramifications by charismatic teacher. Interdisciplinary, synthesizing work widely praised when it first appeared in 1931. Second (1953) edition. Indexes. 496pp. 5⅜ x 8½.   23633-1 Pa. $7.50

AN ESSAY CONCERNING HUMAN UNDERSTANDING, John Locke. The only complete edition of enormously important classic, with authoritative editorial material by A. C. Fraser. Total of 1176pp. 5⅜ x 8½.
20530-4, 20531-2 Pa., Two-vol. set $16.00

HANDBOOK OF MATHEMATICAL FUNCTIONS WITH FORMULAS, GRAPHS, AND MATHEMATICAL TABLES, edited by Milton Abramowitz and Irene A. Stegun. Vast compendium: 29 sets of tables, some to as high as 20 places. 1,046pp. 8 x 10½.   61272-4 Pa. $17.95

MATHEMATICS FOR THE PHYSICAL SCIENCES, Herbert S. Wilf. Highly acclaimed work offers clear presentations of vector spaces and matrices, orthogonal functions, roots of polynomial equations, conformal mapping, calculus of variations, etc. Knowledge of theory of. functions of real and complex variables is assumed. Exercises and solutions. Index. 284pp. 5⅝ x 8¼.   63635-6 Pa. $5.00

THE PRINCIPLE OF RELATIVITY, Albert Einstein et al. Eleven most important original papers on special and general theories. Seven by Einstein, two by Lorentz, one each by Minkowski and Weyl. All translated, unabridged. 216pp. 5⅜ x 8½.   60081-5 Pa. $3.50

THERMODYNAMICS, Enrico Fermi. A classic of modern science. Clear, organized treatment of systems, first and second laws, entropy, thermodynamic potentials, gaseous reactions, dilute solutions, entropy constant. No math beyond calculus required. Problems. 160pp. 5⅜ x 8½.
60361-X Pa. $4.00

ELEMENTARY MECHANICS OF FLUIDS, Hunter Rouse. Classic undergraduate text widely considered to be far better than many later books. Ranges from fluid velocity and acceleration to role of compressibility in fluid motion. Numerous examples, questions, problems. 224 illustrations. 376pp. 5⅝ x 8¼.   63699-2 Pa. $7..00

THE AMERICAN SENATOR, Anthony Trollope. Little known, long unavailable Trollope novel on a grand scale. Here are humorous comment on American vs. English culture, and stunning portrayal of a heroine/villainess. Superb evocation of Victorian village life. 561pp. 5⅜ x 8½.
23801-6 Pa. **$7.95**

WAS IT MURDER? James Hilton. The author of *Lost Horizon* and *Goodbye, Mr. Chips* wrote one detective novel (under a pen-name) which was quickly forgotten and virtually lost, even at the height of Hilton's fame. This edition brings it back—a finely crafted public school puzzle resplendent with Hilton's stylish atmosphere. A thoroughly English thriller by the creator of Shangri-la. 252pp. 5⅜ x 8. (Available in U.S. only)
23774-5 Pa. $3.00

CENTRAL PARK: A PHOTOGRAPHIC GUIDE, Victor Laredo and Henry Hope Reed. 121 superb photographs show dramatic views of Central Park: Bethesda Fountain, Cleopatra's Needle, Sheep Meadow, the Blockhouse, plus people engaged in many park activities: ice skating, bike riding, etc. Captions by former Curator of Central Park, Henry Hope Reed, provide historical view, changes, etc. Also photos of N.Y. landmarks on park's periphery. 96pp. 8½ x 11. 23750-8 Pa. $4.50

NANTUCKET IN THE NINETEENTH CENTURY, Clay Lancaster. 180 rare photographs, stereographs, maps, drawings and floor plans recreate unique American island society. Authentic scenes of shipwreck, lighthouses, streets, homes are arranged in geographic sequence to provide walking-tour guide to old Nantucket existing today. Introduction, captions. 160pp. 8⅞ x 11¾. 23747-8 Pa. $7.95

STONE AND MAN: A PHOTOGRAPHIC EXPLORATION, Andreas Feininger. 106 photographs by *Life* photographer Feininger portray man's deep passion for stone through the ages. Stonehenge-like megaliths, fortified towns, sculpted marble and crumbling tenements show textures, beauties, fascination. 128pp. 9¼ x 10¾. 23756-7 Pa. $5.95

CIRCLES, A MATHEMATICAL VIEW, D. Pedoe. Fundamental aspects of college geometry, non-Euclidean geometry, and other branches of mathematics: representing circle by point. Poincare model, isoperimetric property, etc. Stimulating recreational reading. 66 figures. 96pp. 5⅝ x 8¼.
63698-4 Pa. $3.50

THE DISCOVERY OF NEPTUNE, Morton Grosser. Dramatic scientific history of the investigations leading up to the actual discovery of the eighth planet of our solar system. Lucid, well-researched book by well-known historian of science. 172pp. 5⅜ x 8½. 23726-5 Pa. $3.50

THE DEVIL'S DICTIONARY. Ambrose Bierce. Barbed, bitter, brilliant witticisms in the form of a dictionary. Best, most ferocious satire America has produced. 145pp. 5⅜ x 8½. 20487-1 Pa. $2.50

HISTORY OF BACTERIOLOGY, William Bulloch. The only comprehensive history of bacteriology from the beginnings through the 19th century. Special emphasis is given to biography-Leeuwenhoek, etc. Brief accounts of 350 bacteriologists form a separate section. No clearer, fuller study, suitable to scientists and general readers, has yet been written. 52 illustrations. 448pp. 5⅝ x 8¼. 23761-3 Pa. $6.50

THE COMPLETE NONSENSE OF EDWARD LEAR, Edward Lear. All nonsense limericks, zany alphabets, Owl and Pussycat, songs, nonsense botany, etc., illustrated by Lear. Total of 321pp. 5⅜ x 8½. (Available in U.S. only) 20167-8 Pa. $4.50

INGENIOUS MATHEMATICAL PROBLEMS AND METHODS, Louis A. Graham. Sophisticated material from Graham *Dial*, applied and pure; stresses solution methods. Logic, number theory, networks, inversions, etc. 237pp. 5⅜ x 8½. 20545-2 Pa. $4.50

BEST MATHEMATICAL PUZZLES OF SAM LOYD, edited by Martin Gardner. Bizarre, original, whimsical puzzles by America's greatest puzzler. From fabulously rare *Cyclopedia*, including famous 14-15 puzzles, the Horse of a Different Color, 115 more. Elementary math. 150 illustrations. 167pp. 5⅜ x 8½. 20498-7 Pa. $3.50

THE BASIS OF COMBINATION IN CHESS, J. du Mont. Easy-to-follow, instructive book on elements of combination play, with chapters on each piece and every powerful combination team—two knights, bishop and knight, rook and bishop, etc. 250 diagrams. 218pp. 5⅜ x 8½. (Available in U.S. only) 23644-7 Pa. $4.50

MODERN CHESS STRATEGY, Ludek Pachman. The use of the queen, the active king, exchanges, pawn play, the center, weak squares, etc. Section on rook alone worth price of the book. Stress on the moderns. Often considered the most important book on strategy. 314pp. 5⅜ x 8½. 20290-9 Pa. $5.00

LASKER'S MANUAL OF CHESS, Dr. Emanuel Lasker. Great world champion offers very thorough coverage of all aspects of chess. Combinations, position play, openings, end game, aesthetics of chess, philosophy of struggle, much more. Filled with analyzed games. 390pp. 5⅜ x 8½. 20640-8 Pa. $5.95

500 MASTER GAMES OF CHESS, S. Tartakower, J. du Mont. Vast collection of great chess games from 1798-1938, with much material nowhere else readily available. Fully annotated, arranged by opening for easier study. 664pp. 5⅜ x 8½. 23208-5 Pa. $8.50

A GUIDE TO CHESS ENDINGS, Dr. Max Euwe, David Hooper. One of the finest modern works on chess endings. Thorough analysis of the most frequently encountered endings by former world champion. 331 examples, each with diagram. 248pp. 5⅜ x 8½. 23332-4 Pa. $3.95

THE COMPLETE BOOK OF DOLL MAKING AND COLLECTING, Catherine Christopher. Instructions, patterns for dozens of dolls, from rag doll on up to elaborate, historically accurate figures. Mould faces, sew clothing, make doll houses, etc. Also collecting information. Many illustrations. 288pp. 6 x 9. 22066-4 Pa. $4.95

THE DAGUERREOTYPE IN AMERICA, Beaumont Newhall. Wonderful portraits, 1850's townscapes, landscapes; full text plus 104 photographs. The basic book. Enlarged 1976 edition. 272pp. 8¼ x 11¼. 23322-7 Pa. $7.95

CRAFTSMAN HOMES, Gustav Stickley. 296 architectural drawings, floor plans, and photographs illustrate 40 different kinds of "Mission-style" homes from *The Craftsman* (1901-16), voice of American style of simplicity and organic harmony. Thorough coverage of Craftsman idea in text and picture, now collector's item. 224pp. 8⅛ x 11. 23791-5 Pa. $6.50

PEWTER-WORKING: INSTRUCTIONS AND PROJECTS, Burl N. Osborn. & Gordon O. Wilber. Introduction to pewter-working for amateur craftsman. History and characteristics of pewter; tools, materials, step-by-step instructions. Photos, line drawings, diagrams. Total of 160pp. 7⅞ x 10¾. 23786-9 Pa. $3.50

THE GREAT CHICAGO FIRE, edited by David Lowe. 10 dramatic, eyewitness accounts of the 1871 disaster, including one of the aftermath and rebuilding, plus 70 contemporary photographs and illustrations of the ruins—courthouse, Palmer House, Great Central Depot, etc. Introduction by David Lowe. 87pp. 8¼ x 11. 23771-0 Pa. $4.00

SILHOUETTES: A PICTORIAL ARCHIVE OF VARIED ILLUSTRATIONS, edited by Carol Belanger Grafton. Over 600 silhouettes from the 18th to 20th centuries include profiles and full figures of men and women, children, birds and animals, groups and scenes, nature, ships, an alphabet. Dozens of uses for commercial artists and craftspeople. 144pp. 8⅜ x 11¼. 23781-8 Pa. $4.50

ANIMALS: 1,419 COPYRIGHT-FREE ILLUSTRATIONS OF MAMMALS, BIRDS, FISH, INSECTS, ETC., edited by Jim Harter. Clear wood engravings present, in extremely lifelike poses, over 1,000 species of animals. One of the most extensive copyright-free pictorial sourcebooks of its kind. Captions. Index. 284pp. 9 x 12. 23766-4 Pa. $8.95

INDIAN DESIGNS FROM ANCIENT ECUADOR, Frederick W. Shaffer. 282 original designs by pre-Columbian Indians of Ecuador (500-1500 A.D.). Designs include people, mammals, birds, reptiles, fish, plants, heads, geometric designs. Use as is or alter for advertising, textiles, leathercraft, etc. Introduction. 95pp. 8¾ x 11¼. 23764-8 Pa. $4.50

SZIGETI ON THE VIOLIN, Joseph Szigeti. Genial, loosely structured tour by premier violinist, featuring a pleasant mixture of reminiscenes, insights into great music and musicians, innumerable tips for practicing violinists. 385 musical passages. 256pp. 5⅝ x 8¼. 23763-X Pa. $4.00

TONE POEMS, SERIES II: TILL EULENSPIEGELS LUSTIGE STREICHE, ALSO SPRACH ZARATHUSTRA, AND EIN HELDEN-LEBEN, Richard Strauss. Three important orchestral works, including very popular *Till Eulenspiegel's Marry Pranks,* reproduced in full score from original editions. Study score. 315pp. 9⅜ x 12¼. (Available in U.S. only)
23755-9 Pa. $8.95

TONE POEMS, SERIES I: DON JUAN, TOD UND VERKLARUNG AND DON QUIXOTE, Richard Strauss. Three of the most often performed and recorded works in entire orchestral repertoire, reproduced in full score from original editions. Study score. 286pp. 9⅜ x 12¼. (Available in U.S. only)
23754-0 Pa. $8.95

11 LATE STRING QUARTETS, Franz Joseph Haydn. The form which Haydn defined and "brought to perfection." *(Grove's).* 11 string quartets in complete score, his last and his best. The first in a projected series of the complete Haydn string quartets. Reliable modern Eulenberg edition, otherwise difficult to obtain. 320pp. 8⅜ x 11¼. (Available in U.S. only)
23753-2 Pa. $8.95

FOURTH, FIFTH AND SIXTH SYMPHONIES IN FULL SCORE, Peter Ilyitch Tchaikovsky. Complete orchestral scores of Symphony No. 4 in F Minor, Op. 36; Symphony No. 5 in E Minor, Op. 64; Symphony No. 6 in B Minor, "Pathetique," Op. 74. Bretikopf & Hartel eds. Study score. 480pp. 9⅜ x 12¼. 23861-X Pa. $10.95

THE MARRIAGE OF FIGARO: COMPLETE SCORE, Wolfgang A. Mozart. Finest comic opera ever written. Full score, not to be confused with piano renderings. Peters edition. Study score. 448pp. 9⅜ x 12¼. (Available in U.S. only) 23751-6 Pa. $12.95

"IMAGE" ON THE ART AND EVOLUTION OF THE FILM, edited by Marshall Deutelbaum. Pioneering book brings together for first time 38 groundbreaking articles on early silent films from *Image* and 263 illustrations newly shot from rare prints in the collection of the International Museum of Photography. A landmark work. Index. 256pp. 8¼ x 11.
23777-X Pa. $8.95

AROUND-THE-WORLD COOKY BOOK, Lois Lintner Sumption and Marguerite Lintner Ashbrook. 373 cooky and frosting recipes from 28 countries (America, Austria, China, Russia, Italy, etc.) include Viennese kisses, rice wafers, London strips, lady fingers, hony, sugar spice, maple cookies, etc. Clear instructions. All tested. 38 drawings. 182pp. 5⅜ x 8.
23802-4 Pa. $2.75

THE ART NOUVEAU STYLE, edited by Roberta Waddell. 579 rare photographs, not available elsewhere, of works in jewelry, metalwork, glass, ceramics, textiles, architecture and furniture by 175 artists—Mucha, Seguy, Lalique, Tiffany, Gaudin, Hohlwein, Saarinen, and many others. 288pp. 8⅜ x 11¼. 23515-7 Pa. $8.95

THE CURVES OF LIFE, Theodore A. Cook. Examination of shells, leaves, horns, human body, art, etc., in *"the* classic reference on how the golden ratio applies to spirals and helices in nature . . . . "—Martin Gardner. 426 illustrations. Total of 512pp. 5⅜ x 8½.   23701-X Pa. **$6.95**

AN ILLUSTRATED FLORA OF THE NORTHERN UNITED STATES AND CANADA, Nathaniel L. Britton, Addison Brown. Encyclopedic work covers 4666 species, ferns on up. Everything. Full botanical information, illustration for each. This earlier edition is preferred by many to more recent revisions. 1913 edition. Over 4000 illustrations, total of 2087pp. 6⅛ x 9¼.   22642-5, 22643-3, 22644-1 Pa., Three-vol. set **$28.50**

MANUAL OF THE GRASSES OF THE UNITED STATES, A. S. Hitchcock, U.S. Dept. of Agriculture. The basic study of American grasses, both indigenous and escapes, cultivated and wild. Over 1400 species. Full descriptions, information. Over 1100 maps, illustrations. Total of 1051pp. 5⅜ x 8½.   22717-0, 22718-9 Pa., Two-vol. set **$17.00**

THE CACTACEAE,, Nathaniel L. Britton, John N. Rose. Exhaustive, definitive. Every cactus in the world. Full botanical descriptions. Thorough statement of nomenclatures, habitat, detailed finding keys. The one book needed by every cactus enthusiast. Over 1275 illustrations. Total of 1080pp. 8 x 10¼.   21191-6, 21192-4 Clothbd., Two-vol. set **$50.00**

AMERICAN MEDICINAL PLANTS, Charles F. Millspaugh. Full descriptions, 180 plants covered: history; physical description; methods of preparation with all chemical constituents extracted; all claimed curative or adverse effects. 180 full-page plates. Classification table. 804pp. 6½ x 9¼.
23034-1 Pa. **$13.95**

A MODERN HERBAL, Margaret Grieve. Much the fullest, most exact, most useful compilation of herbal material. Gigantic alphabetical encyclopedia, from aconite to zedoary, gives botanical information, medical properties, folklore, economic uses, and much else. Indispensable to serious reader. 161 illustrations. 888pp. 6½ x 9¼. (Available in U.S. only)
22798-7, 22799-5 Pa., Two-vol. set **$15.00**

THE HERBAL or GENERAL HISTORY OF PLANTS, John Gerard. The 1633 edition revised and enlarged by Thomas Johnson. Containing almost 2850 plant descriptions and 2705 superb illustrations, Gerard's *Herbal* is a monumental work, the book all modern English herbals are derived from, the one herbal every serious enthusiast should have in its entirety. Original editions are worth perhaps $750. 1678pp. 8½ x 12¼.
23147-X Clothbd. **$75.00**

MANUAL OF THE TREES OF NORTH AMERICA, Charles S. Sargent. The basic survey of every native tree and tree-like shrub, 717 species in all. Extremely full descriptions, information on habitat, growth, locales, economics, etc. Necessary to every serious tree lover. Over 100 finding keys. 783 illustrations. Total of 986pp. 5⅜ x 8½.
20277-1, 20278-X Pa., Two-vol. set **$12.00**

GREAT NEWS PHOTOS AND THE STORIES BEHIND THEM, John Faber. Dramatic volume of 140 great news photos, 1855 through 1976, and revealing stories behind them, with both historical and technical information. Hindenburg disaster, shooting of Oswald, nomination of Jimmy Carter, etc. 160pp. 8¼ x 11. 23667-6 Pa. $6.00

CRUICKSHANK'S PHOTOGRAPHS OF BIRDS OF AMERICA, Allan D. Cruickshank. Great ornithologist, photographer presents 177 closeups, groupings, panoramas, flightings, etc., of about 150 different birds. Expanded *Wings in the Wilderness.* Introduction by Helen G. Crujckshank. 191pp. 8¼ x 11. 23497-5 Pa. $7.95

AMERICAN WILDLIFE AND PLANTS, A. C. Martin, et al. Describes food habits of more than 1000 species of mammals, birds, fish. Special treatment of important food plants. Over 300 illustrations. 500pp. 5⅜ x 8½. 20793-5 Pa. $6.50

THE PEOPLE CALLED SHAKERS, Edward D. Andrews. Lifetime of research, definitive study of Shakers: origins, beliefs, practices, dances, social organization, furniture and crafts, impact on 19th-century USA, present heritage. Indispensable to student of American history, collector. 33 illustrations. 351pp. 5⅜ x 8½. 21081-2 Pa. $4.50

OLD NEW YORK IN EARLY PHOTOGRAPHS, Mary Black. New York City as it was in 1853-1901, through 196 wonderful photographs from N.-Y. Historical Society. Great Blizzard, Lincoln's funeral procession, great buildings. 228pp. 9 x 12. 22907-6 Pa. $8.95

MR. LINCOLN'S CAMERA MAN: MATHEW BRADY, Roy Meredith. Over 300 Brady photos reproduced directly from original negatives, photos. Jackson, Webster, Grant, Lee, Carnegie, Barnum; Lincoln; Battle Smoke, Death of Rebel Sniper, Atlanta Just After Capture. Lively commentary. 368pp. 8⅜ x 11¼. 23021-X Pa. $11.95

TRAVELS OF WILLIAM BARTRAM, William Bartram. From 1773-8, Bartram explored Northern Florida, Georgia, Carolinas, and reported on wild life, plants, Indians, early settlers. Basic account for period, entertaining reading. Edited by Mark Van Doren. 13 illustrations. 141pp. 5⅜ x 8½. 20013-2 Pa. $6.00

THE GENTLEMAN AND CABINET MAKER'S DIRECTOR, Thomas Chippendale. Full reprint, 1762 style book, most influential of all time; chairs, tables, sofas, mirrors, cabinets, etc. 200 plates, plus 24 photographs of surviving pieces. 249pp. 9⅞ x 12¾. 21601-2 Pa. $8.95

AMERICAN CARRIAGES, SLEIGHS, SULKIES AND CARTS, edited by Don H. Berkebile. 168 Victorian illustrations from catalogues, trade journals, fully captioned. Useful for artists. Author is Assoc. Curator, Div. of Transportation of Smithsonian Institution. 168pp. 8½ x 9½. 23328-6 Pa. $5.00

SECOND PIATIGORSKY CUP, edited by Isaac Kashdan. One of the greatest tournament books ever produced in the English language. All 90 games of the 1966 tournament, annotated by players, most annotated by both players. Features Petrosian, Spassky, Fischer, Larsen, six others. 228pp. 5⅜ x 8½.   23572-6 Pa. $3.50

ENCYCLOPEDIA OF CARD TRICKS, revised and edited by Jean Hugard. How to perform over 600 card tricks, devised by the world's greatest magicians: impromptus, spelling tricks, key cards, using special packs, much, much more. Additional chapter on card technique. 66 illustrations. 402pp. 5⅜ x 8½. (Available in U.S. only)   21252-1 Pa. $5.95

MAGIC: STAGE ILLUSIONS, SPECIAL EFFECTS AND TRICK PHOTOGRAPHY, Albert A. Hopkins, Henry R. Evans. One of the great classics; fullest, most authorative explanation of vanishing lady, levitations, scores of other great stage effects. Also small magic, automata, stunts. 446 illustrations. 556pp. 5⅜ x 8½.   23344-8 Pa. $6.95

THE SECRETS OF HOUDINI, J. C. Cannell. Classic study of Houdini's incredible magic, exposing closely-kept professional secrets and revealing, in general terms, the whole art of stage magic. 67 illustrations. 279pp. 5⅜ x 8½.   22913-0 Pa. $4.00

HOFFMANN'S MODERN MAGIC, Professor Hoffmann. One of the best, and best-known, magicians' manuals of the past century. Hundreds of tricks from card tricks and simple sleight of hand to elaborate illusions involving construction of complicated machinery. 332 illustrations. 563pp. 5⅜ x 8½.   23623-4 Pa. $6.95

THOMAS NAST'S CHRISTMAS DRAWINGS, Thomas Nast. Almost all Christmas drawings by creator of image of Santa Claus as we know it, and one of America's foremost illustrators and political cartoonists. 66 illustrations. 3 illustrations in color on covers. 96pp. 8⅜ x 11¼.
                                                        23660-9 Pa. $3.50

FRENCH COUNTRY COOKING FOR AMERICANS, Louis Diat. 500 easy-to-make, authentic provincial recipes compiled by former head chef at New York's Fitz-Carlton Hotel: onion soup, lamb stew, potato pie, more. 309pp. 5⅜ x 8½.   23665-X Pa. $3.95

SAUCES, FRENCH AND FAMOUS, Louis Diat. Complete book gives over 200 specific recipes: bechamel, Bordelaise, hollandaise, Cumberland, apricot, etc. Author was one of this century's finest chefs, originator of vichyssoise and many other dishes. Index. 156pp. 5⅜ x 8.
                                                        23663-3 Pa. $2.75

TOLL HOUSE TRIED AND TRUE RECIPES, Ruth Graves Wakefield. Authentic recipes from the famous Mass. restaurant: popovers, veal and ham loaf, Toll House baked beans, chocolate cake crumb pudding, much more. Many helpful hints. Nearly 700 recipes. Index. 376pp. 5⅜ x 8½.
                                                        23560-2 Pa. $4.95

ILLUSTRATED GUIDE TO SHAKER FURNITURE, Robert Meader. Director, Shaker Museum, Old Chatham, presents up-to-date coverage of all furniture and appurtenances, with much on local styles not available elsewhere. 235 photos. 146pp. 9 x 12. 22819-3 Pa. $6.95

COOKING WITH BEER, Carole Fahy. Beer has as superb an effect on food as wine, and at fraction of cost. Over 250 recipes for appetizers, soups, main dishes, desserts, breads, etc. Index. 144pp. 5⅜ x 8½. (Available in U.S. only) 23661-7 Pa. $3.00

STEWS AND RAGOUTS, Kay Shaw Nelson. This international cookbook offers wide range of 108 recipes perfect for everyday, special occasions, meals-in-themselves, main dishes. Economical, nutritious, easy-to-prepare: goulash, Irish stew, boeuf bourguignon, etc. Index. 134pp. 5⅜ x 8½.
23662-5 Pa. $3.95

DELICIOUS MAIN COURSE DISHES, Marian Tracy. Main courses are the most important part of any meal. These 200 nutritious, economical recipes from around the world make every meal a delight. "I . . . have found it so useful in my own household,"—N.Y. Times. Index. 219pp. 5⅜ x 8½. 23664-1 Pa. $3.95

FIVE ACRES AND INDEPENDENCE, Maurice G. Kains. Great back-to-the-land classic explains basics of self-sufficient farming: economics, plants, crops, animals, orchards, soils, land selection, host of other necessary things. Do not confuse with skimpy faddist literature; Kains was one of America's greatest agriculturalists. 95 illustrations. 397pp. 5⅜ x 8½.
20974-1 Pa. $4.95

A PRACTICAL GUIDE FOR THE BEGINNING FARMER, Herbert Jacobs. Basic, extremely useful first book for anyone thinking about moving to the country and starting a farm. Simpler than Kains, with greater emphasis on country living in general. 246pp. 5⅜ x 8½.
23675-7 Pa. $3.95

PAPERMAKING, Dard Hunter. Definitive book on the subject by the foremost authority in the field. Chapters dealing with every aspect of history of craft in every part of the world. Over 320 illustrations. 2nd, revised and enlarged (1947) edition. 672pp. 5⅜ x 8½. 23619-6 Pa. $8.95

THE ART DECO STYLE, edited by Theodore Menten. Furniture, jewelry, metalwork, ceramics, fabrics, lighting fixtures, interior decors, exteriors, graphics from pure French sources. Best sampling around. Over 400 photographs. 183pp. 8⅜ x 11¼. 22824-X Pa. $6.95

ACKERMANN'S COSTUME PLATES, Rudolph Ackermann. Selection of 96 plates from the Repository of Arts, best published source of costume for English fashion during the early 19th century. 12 plates also in color. Captions, glossary and introduction by editor Stella Blum. Total of 120pp. 8⅜ x 11¼. 23690-0 Pa. $5.00

THE ANATOMY OF THE HORSE, George Stubbs. Often considered the great masterpiece of animal anatomy. Full reproduction of 1766 edition, plus prospectus; original text and modernized text. 36 plates. Introduction by Eleanor Garvey. 121pp. 11 x 14¾. 23402-9 Pa. **$8.95**

BRIDGMAN'S LIFE DRAWING, George B. Bridgman. More than 500 illustrative drawings and text teach you to abstract the body into its major masses, use light and shade, proportion; as well as specific areas of anatomy, of which Bridgman is master. 192pp. 6½ x 9¼. (Available in U.S. only) 22710-3 Pa. **$4.50**

ART NOUVEAU DESIGNS IN COLOR, Alphonse Mucha, Maurice Verneuil, Georges Auriol. Full-color reproduction of *Combinaisons ornementales* (c. 1900) by Art Nouveau masters. Floral, animal, geometric, interlacings, swashes—borders, frames, spots—all incredibly beautiful. 60 plates, hundreds of designs. 9⅜ x 8-1/16. 22885-1 Pa. **$4.50**

FULL-COLOR FLORAL DESIGNS IN THE ART NOUVEAU STYLE, E. A. Seguy. 166 motifs, on 40 plates, from *Les fleurs et leurs applications decoratives* (1902): borders, circular designs, repeats, allovers, "spots." All in authentic Art Nouveau colors. 48pp. 9⅜ x 12¼. 23439-8 Pa. **$6.00**

A DIDEROT PICTORIAL ENCYCLOPEDIA OF TRADES AND INDUSTRY, edited by Charles C. Gillispie. 485 most interesting plates from the great French Encyclopedia of the 18th century show hundreds of working figures, artifacts, process, land and cityscapes; glassmaking, papermaking, metal extraction, construction, weaving, making furniture, clothing, wigs, dozens of other activities. Plates fully explained. 920pp. 9 x 12. 22284-5, 22285-3 Clothbd., Two-vol. set **$50.00**

HANDBOOK OF EARLY ADVERTISING ART, Clarence P. Hornung. Largest collection of copyright-free early and antique advertising art ever compiled. Over 6,000 illustrations, from Franklin's time to the 1890's for special effects, novelty. Valuable source, almost inexhaustible.
Pictorial Volume. Agriculture, the zodiac, animals, autos, birds, Christmas, fire engines, flowers, trees, musical instruments, ships, games and sports, much more. Arranged by subject matter and use. 237 plates. 288pp. 9 x 12. 20122-8 Clothbd. **$15.00**

Typographical Volume. Roman and Gothic faces ranging from 10 point to 300 point, "Barnum," German and Old English faces, script, logotypes, scrolls and flourishes, 1115 ornamental initials, 67 complete alphabets, more. 310 plates. 320pp. 9 x 12. 20123-6 Clothbd. $15.00

CALLIGRAPHY (CALLIGRAPHIA LATINA), J. G. Schwandner. High point of 18th-century ornamental calligraphy. Very ornate initials, scrolls, borders, cherubs, birds, lettered examples. 172pp. 9 x 13. 20475-8 Pa. $7.95

GEOMETRY, RELATIVITY AND THE FOURTH DIMENSION, Rudolf Rucker. Exposition of fourth dimension, means of visualization, concepts of relativity as Flatland characters continue adventures. Popular, easily followed yet accurate, profound. 141 illustrations. 133pp. 5⅜ x 8½.
23400-2 Pa. $2.75

THE ORIGIN OF LIFE, A. I. Oparin. Modern classic in biochemistry, the first rigorous examination of possible evolution of life from nitrocarbon compounds. Non-technical, easily followed. Total of 295pp. 5⅜ x 8½.
60213-3 Pa. $5.95

PLANETS, STARS AND GALAXIES, A. E. Fanning. Comprehensive introductory survey: the sun, solar system, stars, galaxies, universe, cosmology; quasars, radio stars, etc. 24pp. of photographs. 189pp. 5⅜ x 8½. (Available in U.S. only)
21680-2 Pa. $3.75

THE THIRTEEN BOOKS OF EUCLID'S ELEMENTS, translated with introduction and commentary by Sir Thomas L. Heath. Definitive edition. Textual and linguistic. notes, mathematical analysis, 2500 years of critical commentary. Do not confuse with abridged school editions. Total of 1414pp. 5⅜ x 8½. 60088-2, 60089-0, 60090-4 Pa., Three-vol. set $19.50

Prices subject to change without notice.

Available at your book dealer or write for free catalogue to Dept. GI, Dover Publications, Inc., 31 East 2nd St. Mineola., N.Y. 11501. Dover publishes more than 175 books each year on science, elementary and advanced mathematics, biology, music, art, literary history, social sciences and other areas.